ABANDONED
Ireland

ABANDONED
Ireland

DOMINIC CONNOLLY

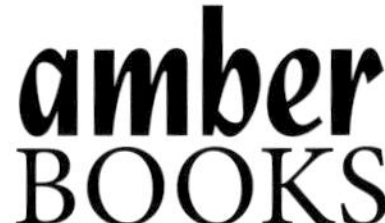

Published by Amber Books Ltd
United House
North Road
London
N7 9DP
United Kingdom
www.amberbooks.co.uk
Instagram: amberbooksltd
Facebook: amberbooks
Twitter: @amberbooks
Pinterest: amberbooksltd

ISBN: 978-1-83886-315-9

Project Editor: Michael Spilling
Designers: Rick Fawcett & Mark Batley
Picture Research: Terry Forshaw

Printed in China

Contents

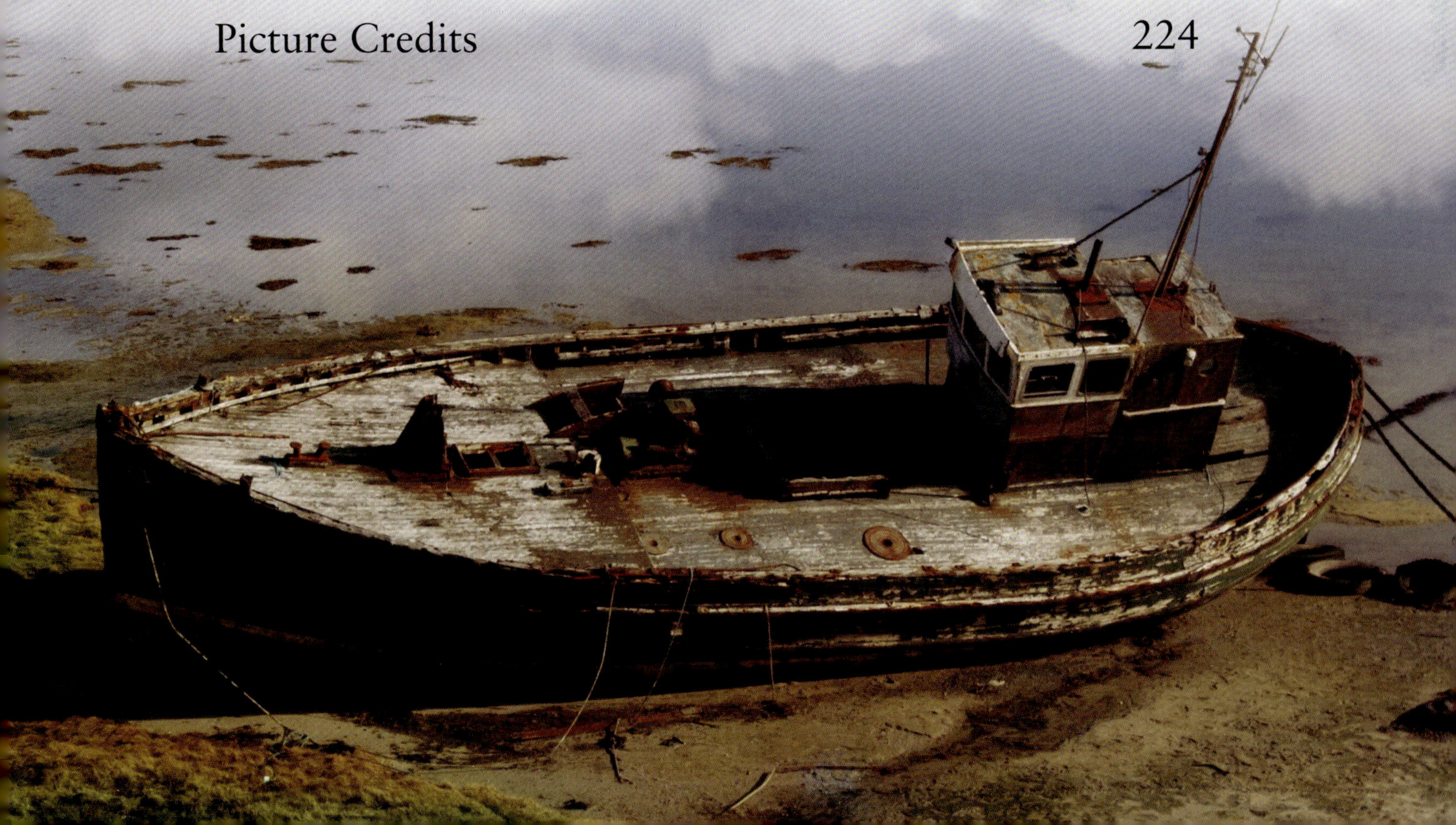

Introduction

THE ROMANS CALLED IT HIBERNIA – the land of winter – as if it were of no note. But in fact, Ireland is a land settled and fought over again and again by various peoples over many hundreds of years, all of whom have left their imprint on its soil.

The sheer determination with which the British and Irish, the Protestants and the Catholics, have fought for control of Ireland for centuries has of course had a major impact on what has been built – and abandoned – there across its counties, from castles to cathedrals, from public buildings to private estates. But this is only in addition to what Normans, Vikings and original settlers had brought to Ireland, along with those who spread early Christianity there and created its first institutions. The last two centuries in particular have seen the urbanisation of Ireland and, sparked by the Great Famine of the mid-19th century, the depopulation of much of the rural areas, leaving many abandoned houses, schools and villages. But similar fates have struck towns, cities and industrial sites, as different economic sectors' ups and downs over time have made some buildings redundant, with the rich as well as the poor suffering. However, Ireland always has the capacity to reinvent itself, with parts of the countryside being rediscovered for their heritage and stunning scenery, and built-up areas getting surprising new leases of life.

The Wonderful Barn, County Kildare
If anywhere symbolizes Ireland's rich and poor in one building, it is the Wonderful Barn. It was paid for by the wealthy landowners on whose estate it sits, but the various stories about why it was built range from concern for the poor to storing delicacies for the rich to eat, and from keeping grain to alleviate famine to being no more than a rich man's folly.

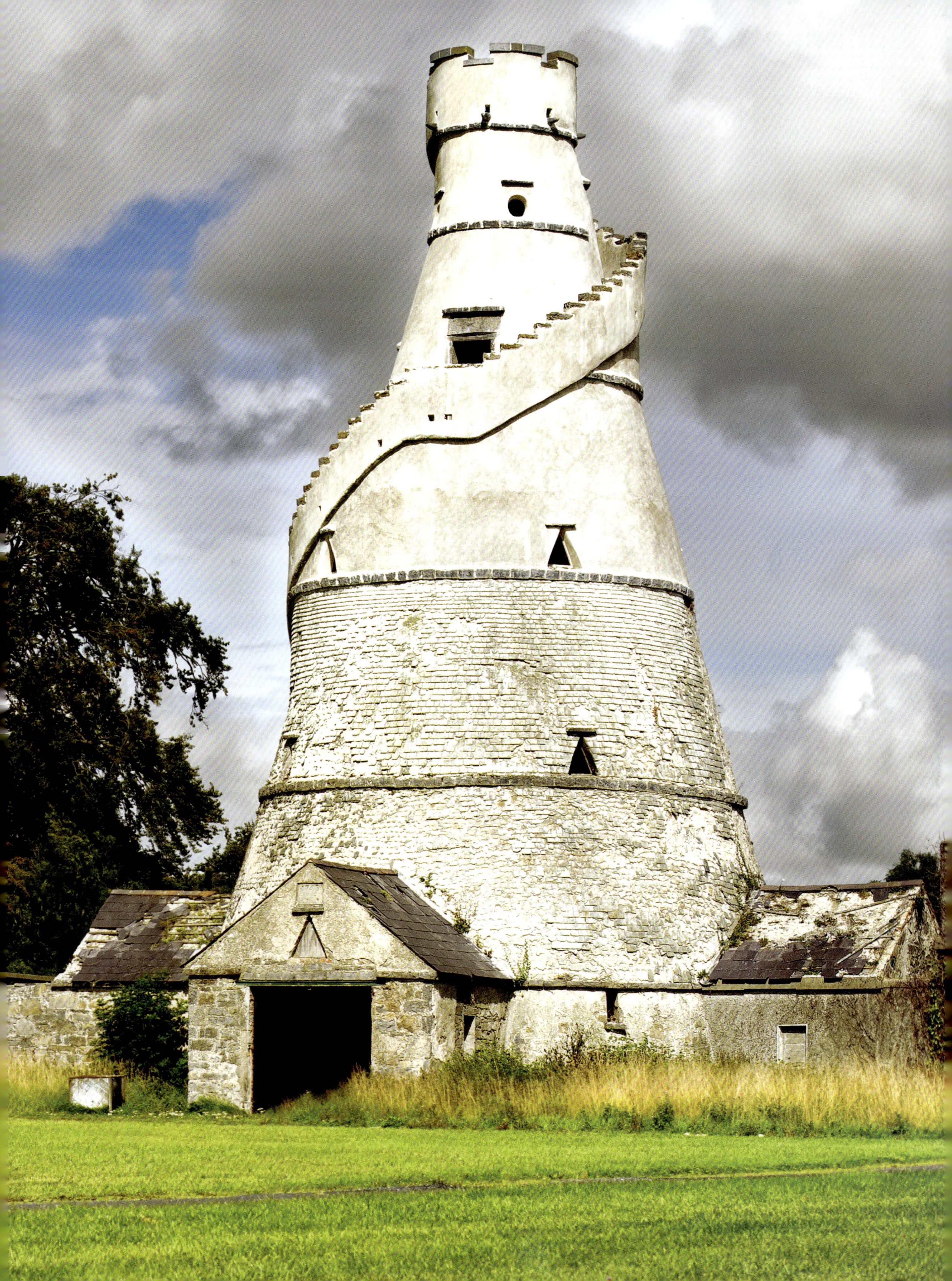

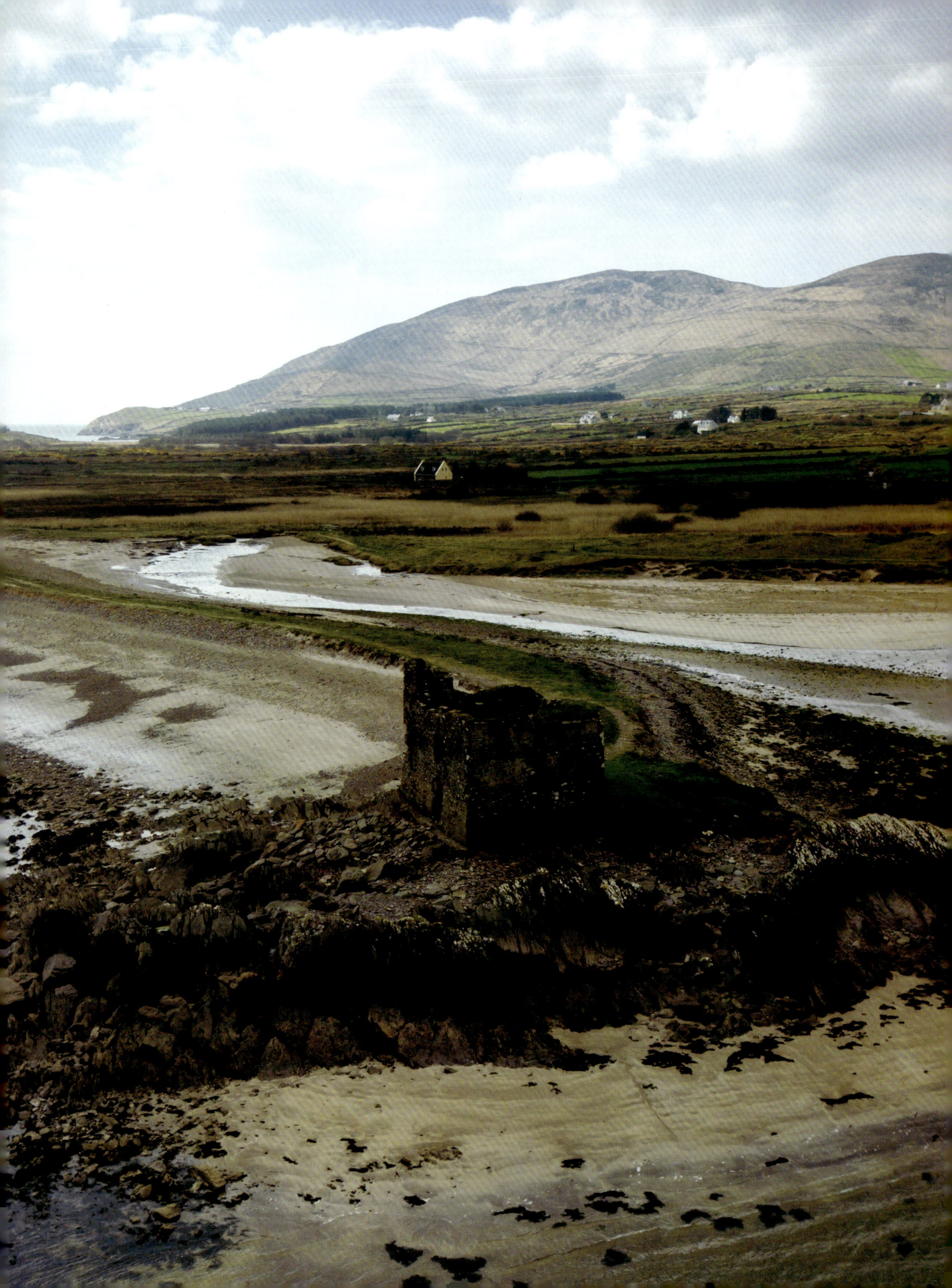

Castles & Houses

The castles and houses of Ireland tell of the clans that once ruled, and how their power was diminished by various waves of invasion and colonization from Britain. With these waves came new styles of buildings – the Irish chieftains' tower houses and the Norman strongholds being supplemented by more fortified castles in the 16th and 17th centuries, and then by grand Georgian and Victorian residences. As well as reflecting the changing political landscape of Ireland, the fortunes of these castles and houses also shed light on the Great Famine (1845–49) and show that the effects of the potato blight cut right through society, all the way to the top. As the stories of these Irish castles and houses are explored, naturally myths and legends emerge. There are also some surprising links to the likes of Winston Churchill, the Forum in Rome and even the rock band Led Zeppelin. The reasons for the abandonment of these buildings vary, but one of the main causes has been that they were never able to recover from being attacked. Also, of course, there is that perennial cause of devastation – fire. Nonetheless, some of the castles and houses are now back in use in other forms, hopefully leading the way for some of the less fortunate ones.

Ballinskelligs Castle, County Kerry
This ruin is also known as McCarthy Mor Tower, as it is reputed to have been a stronghold of the McCarthy clan. It stands on a strip of land stretching out into Ballinskelligs Bay. Built in the 16th century, it contains a concealed area called a murder hole, from which occupants could attack invaders passing below.

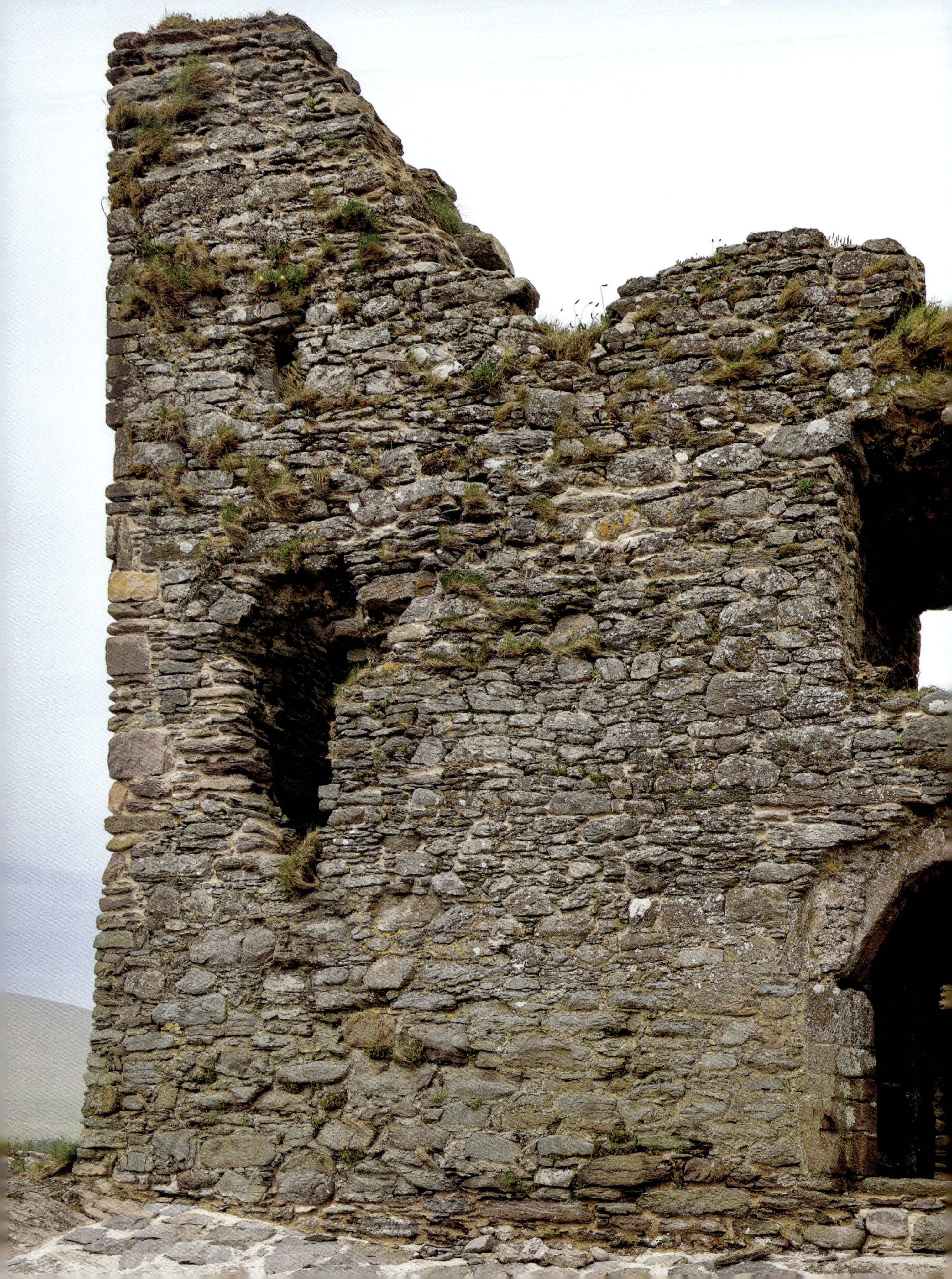

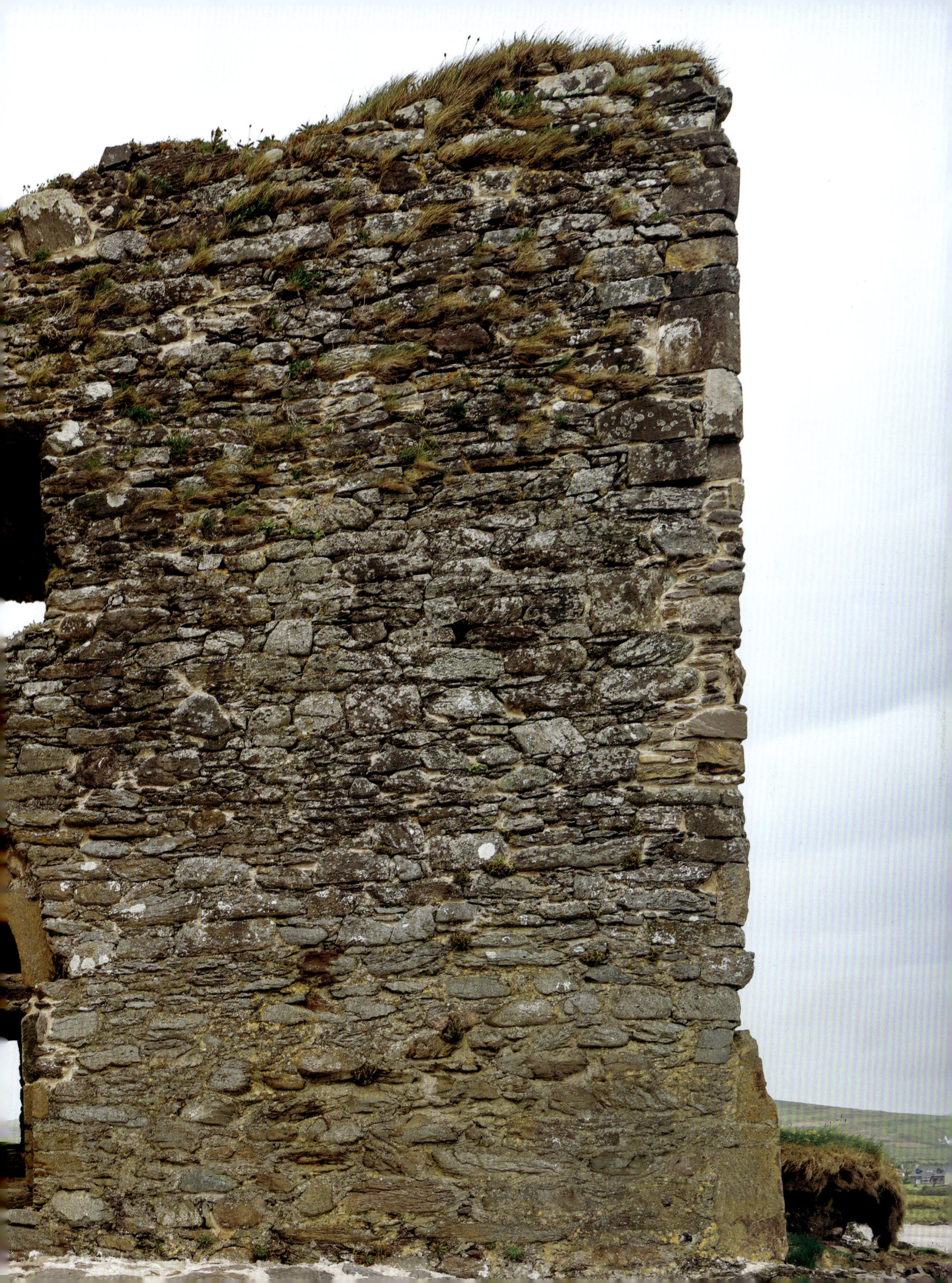

ALL PHOTOGRAPHS:
**Aughnanure Castle,
County Galway**
Built in the 16th century,
Aughnanure Castle is an example
of the tower houses that were
built in Scotland and Ireland
from the Middle Ages to act
as well-defended homes for
wealthy families. The castle was
built as a stronghold for the
O'Flaherty clan, whose motto
was 'Fortune favours the strong'.
Its banqueting hall is still intact.

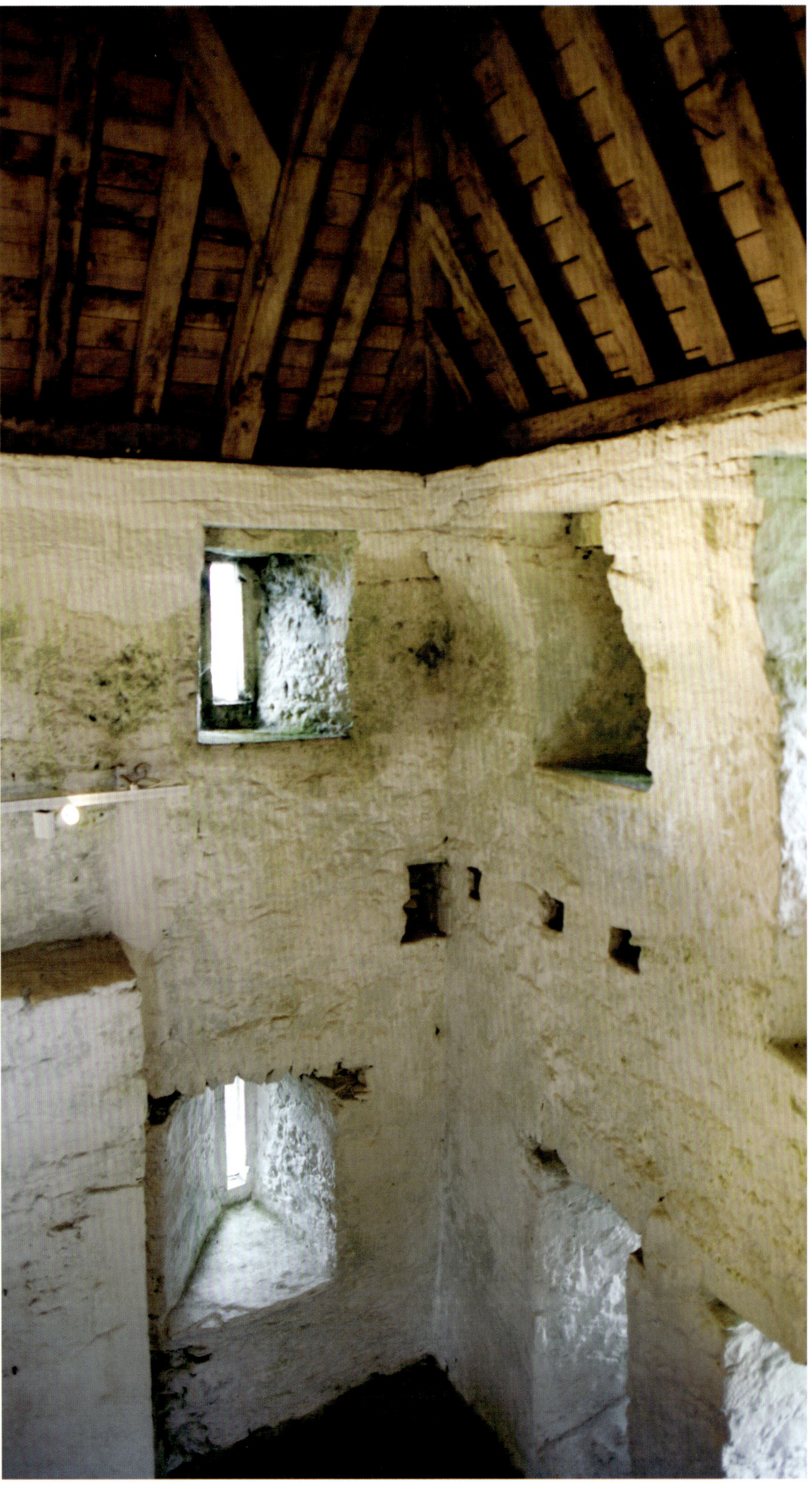

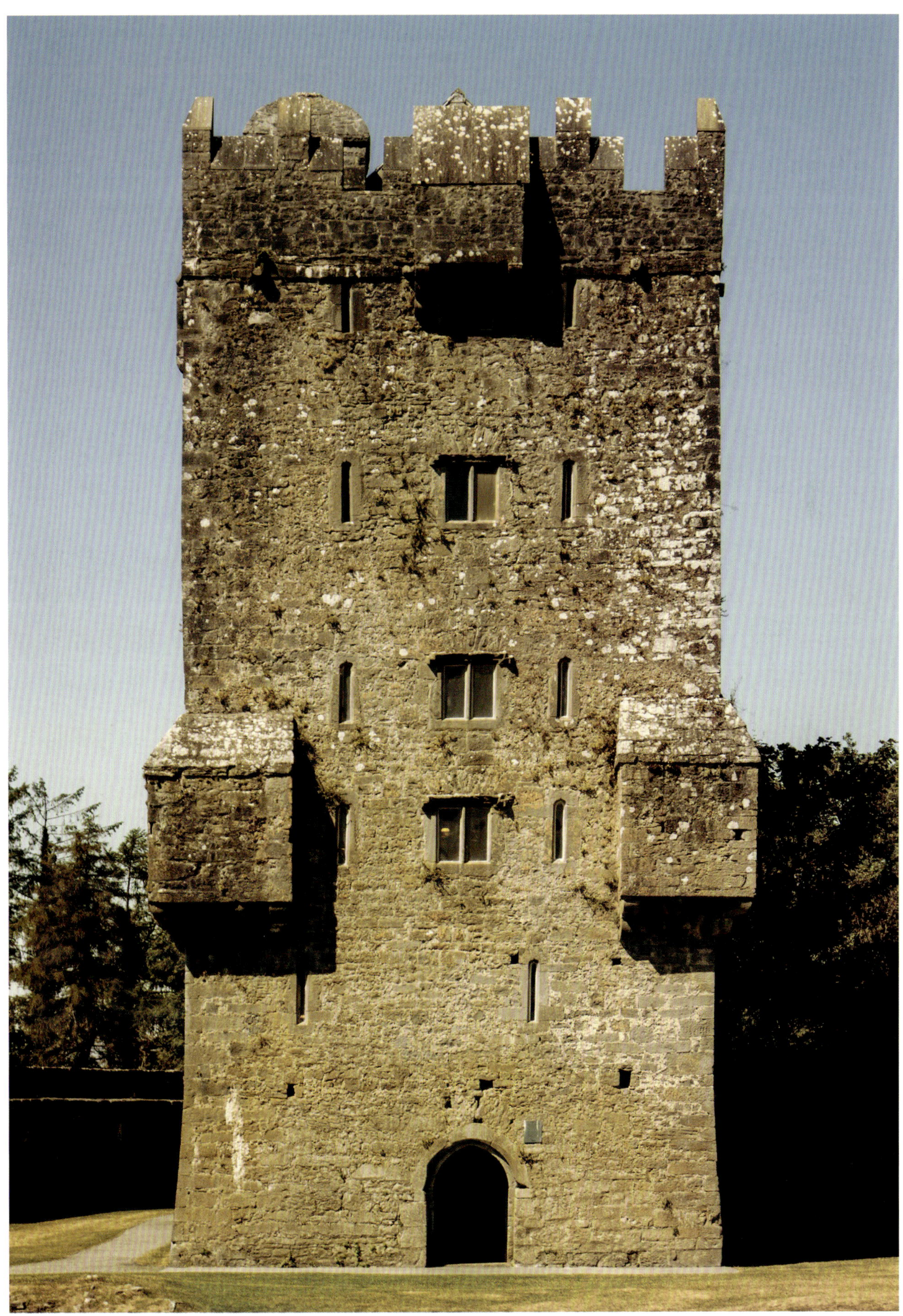

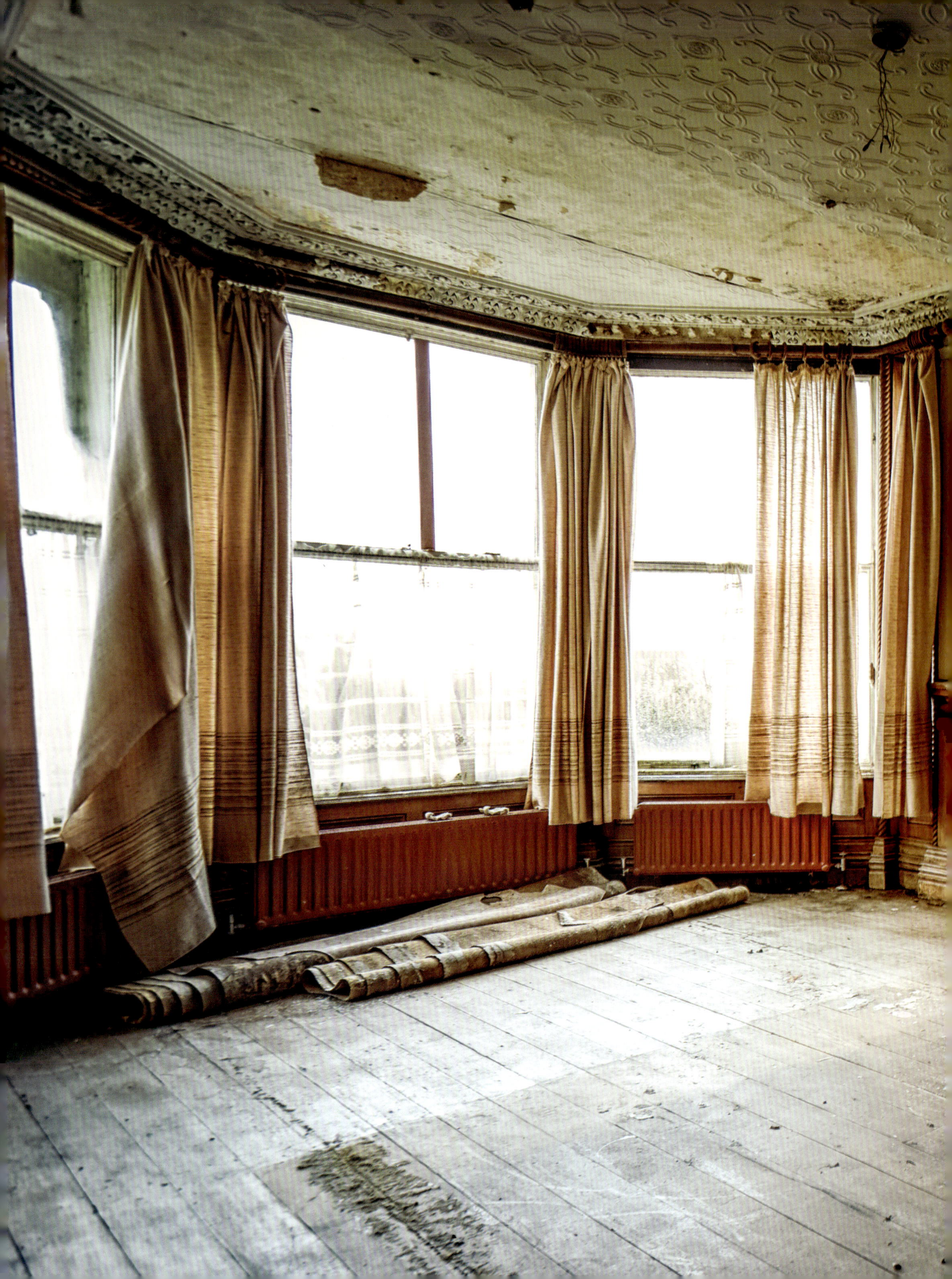

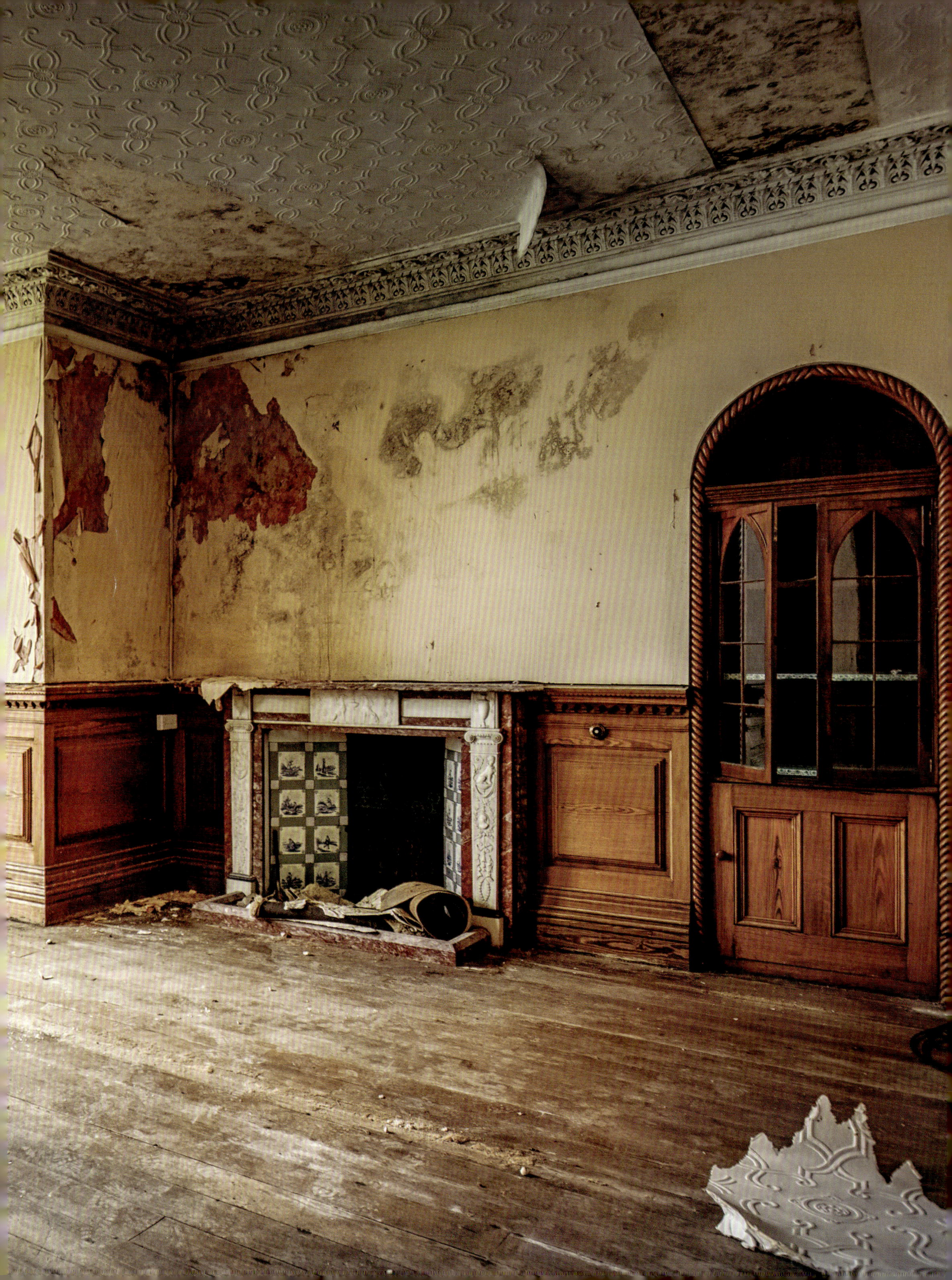

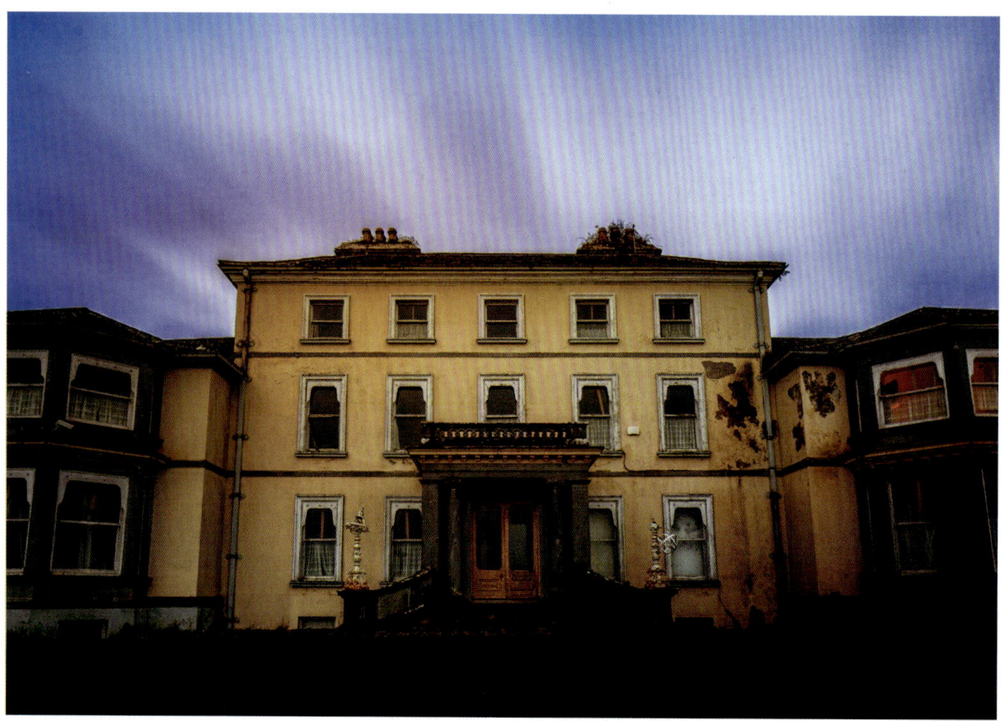

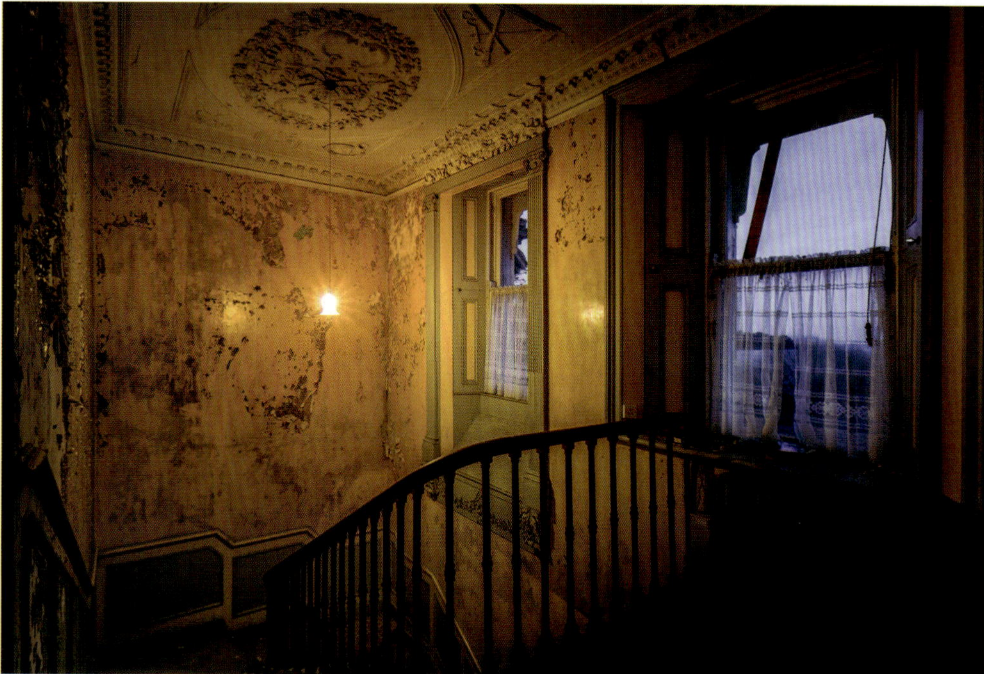

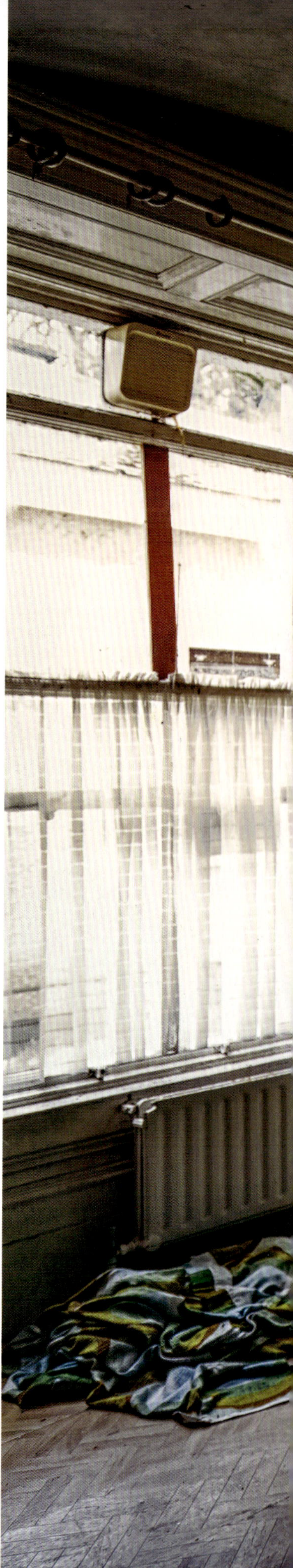

**Cahercon House,
Kildysart, County Clare**

This 60-room Georgian mansion house has had many lives. It has been a seminary for missionaries, a boarding school and a family home. Built around 1790 by the Scott family, it had wings added in the mid-19th century. The Scotts are said to have been good landlords to the tenants on their land, assisting them during the Great Famine, but this was to their detriment, as Cahercon was sold under the Encumbered Estates Act in 1854. It was later bought by the Vandeleur family, who had evicted 1000 of their own tenants in the late 1840s. In the 1920s, the Maynooth Mission to China purchased the estate and established a mission in Nancheng, where one of its priests was hacked to death, another died in captivity and a third was stoned and then banished from China, as Communism told hold of the country. In the late 20th century, the house was used as a boarding school and then as a community college, which closed in 2002.

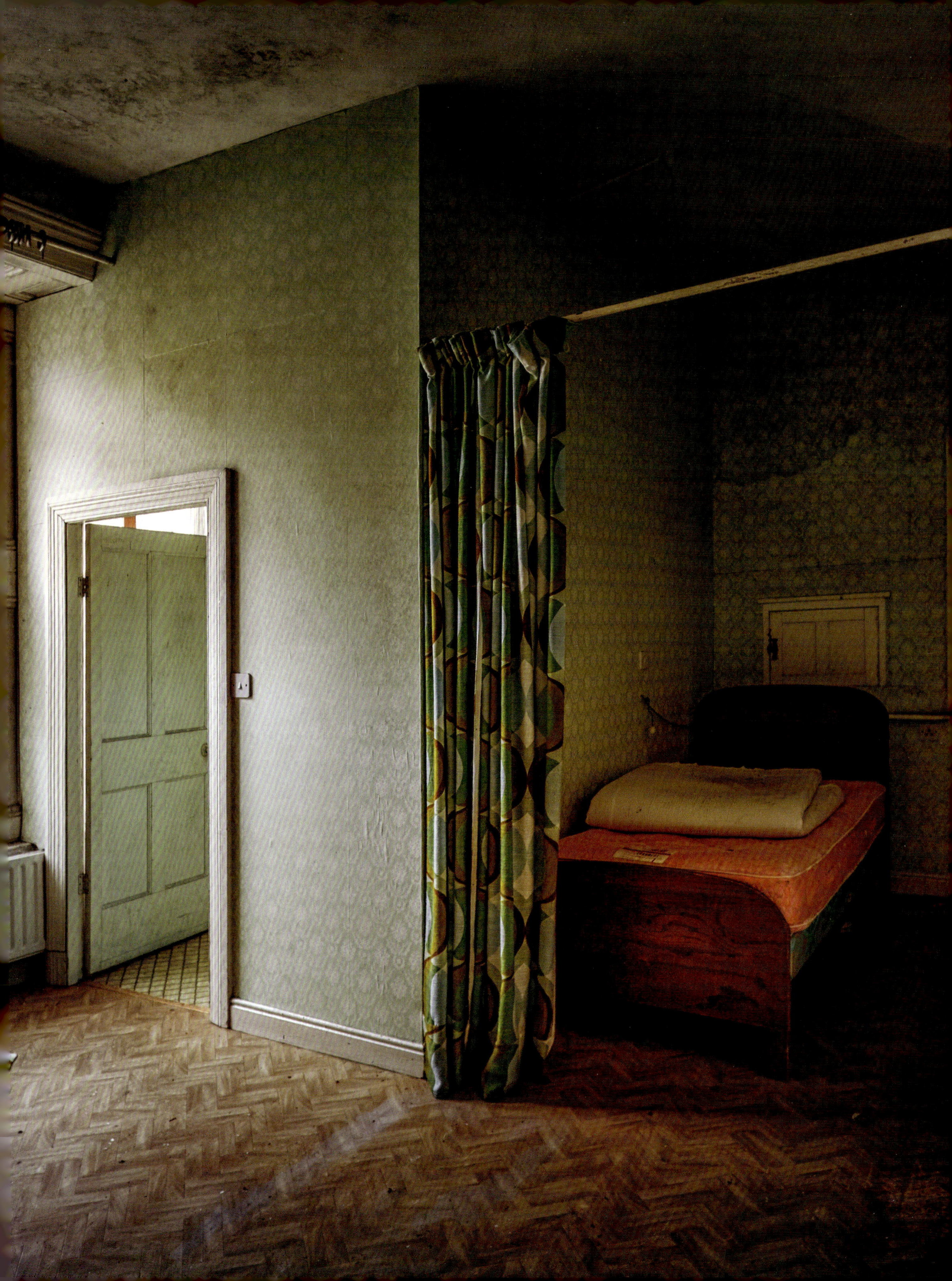

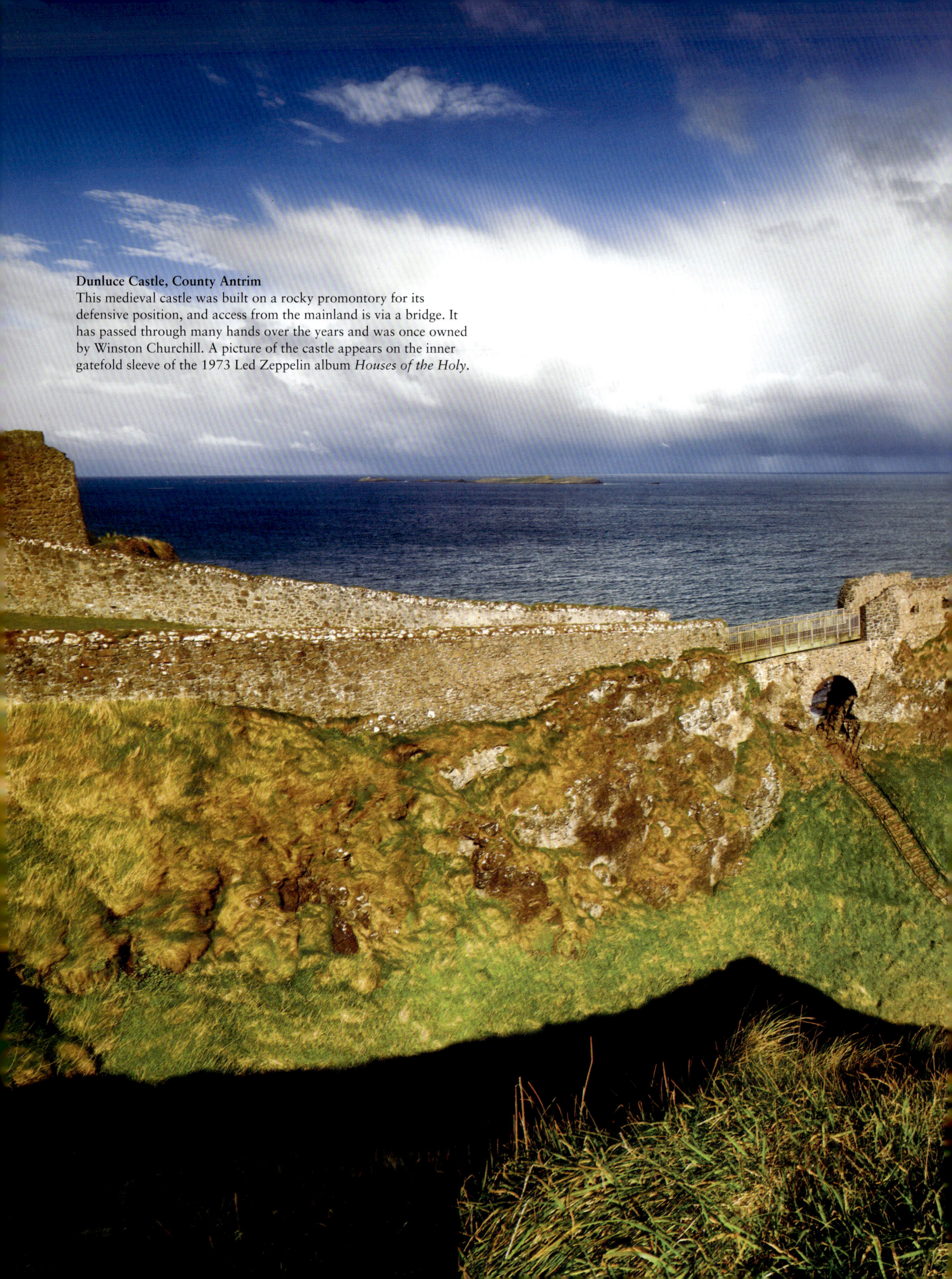

Dunluce Castle, County Antrim
This medieval castle was built on a rocky promontory for its defensive position, and access from the mainland is via a bridge. It has passed through many hands over the years and was once owned by Winston Churchill. A picture of the castle appears on the inner gatefold sleeve of the 1973 Led Zeppelin album *Houses of the Holy*.

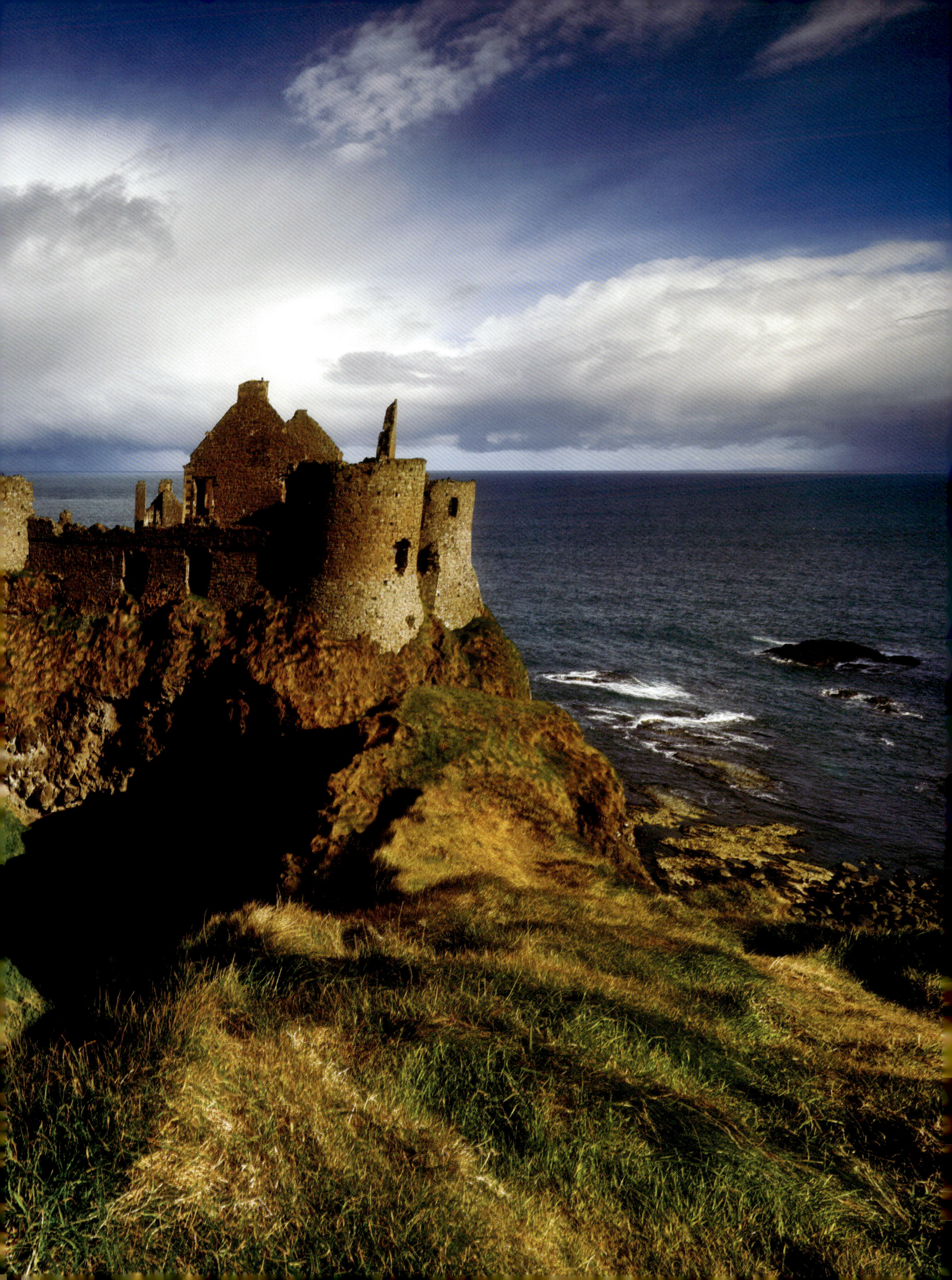

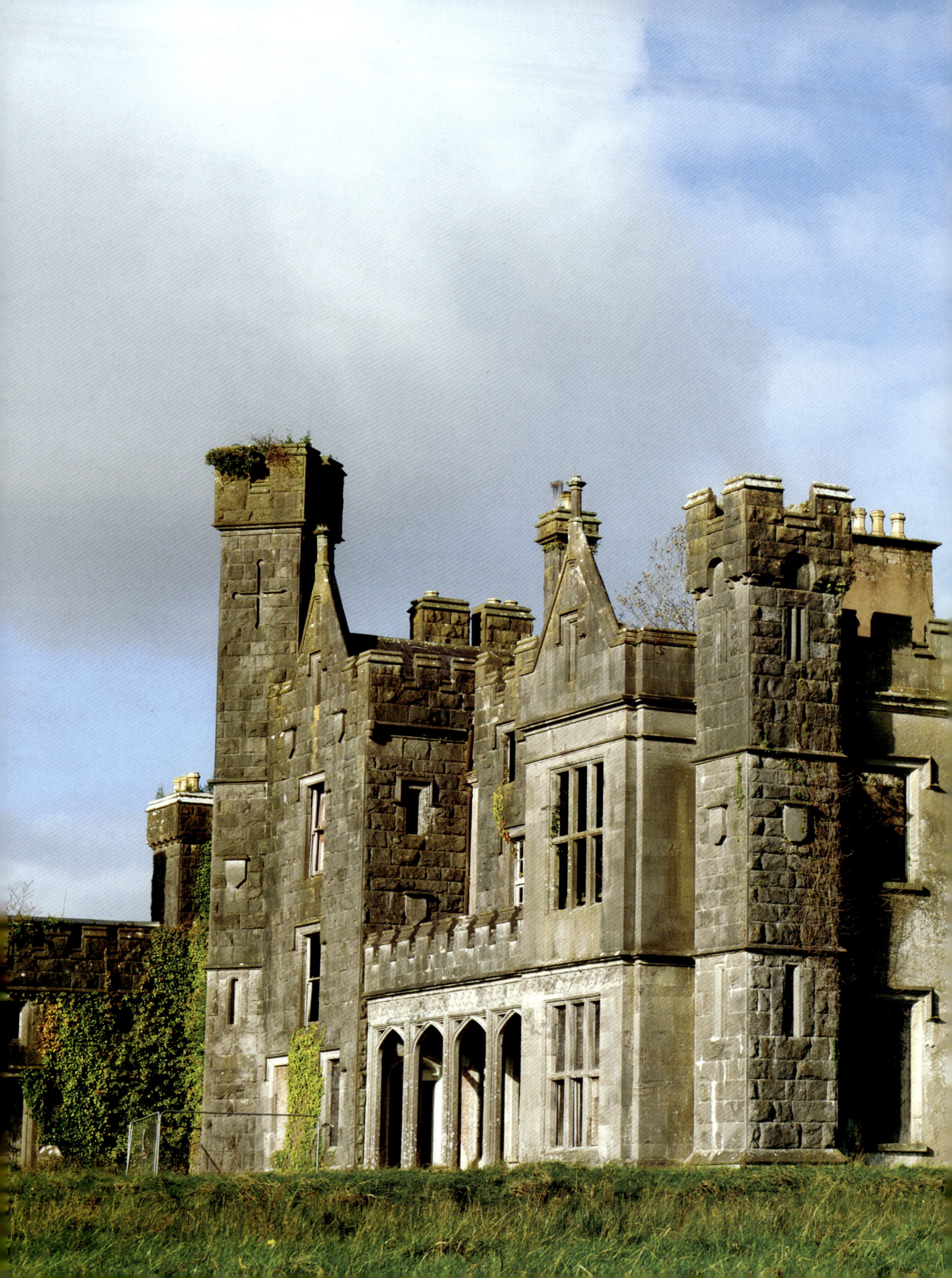

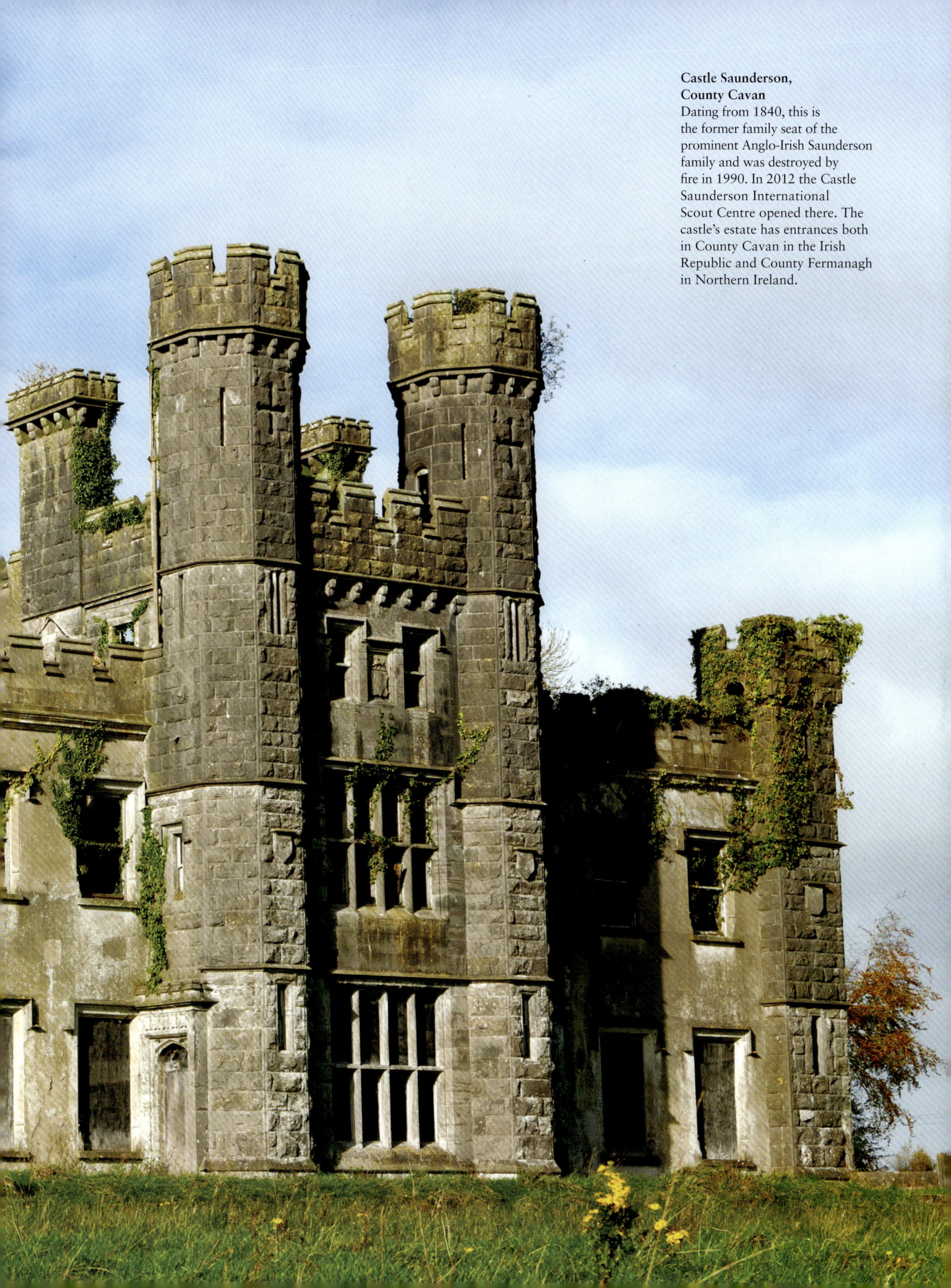

**Castle Saunderson,
County Cavan**
Dating from 1840, this is
the former family seat of the
prominent Anglo-Irish Saunderson
family and was destroyed by
fire in 1990. In 2012 the Castle
Saunderson International
Scout Centre opened there. The
castle's estate has entrances both
in County Cavan in the Irish
Republic and County Fermanagh
in Northern Ireland.

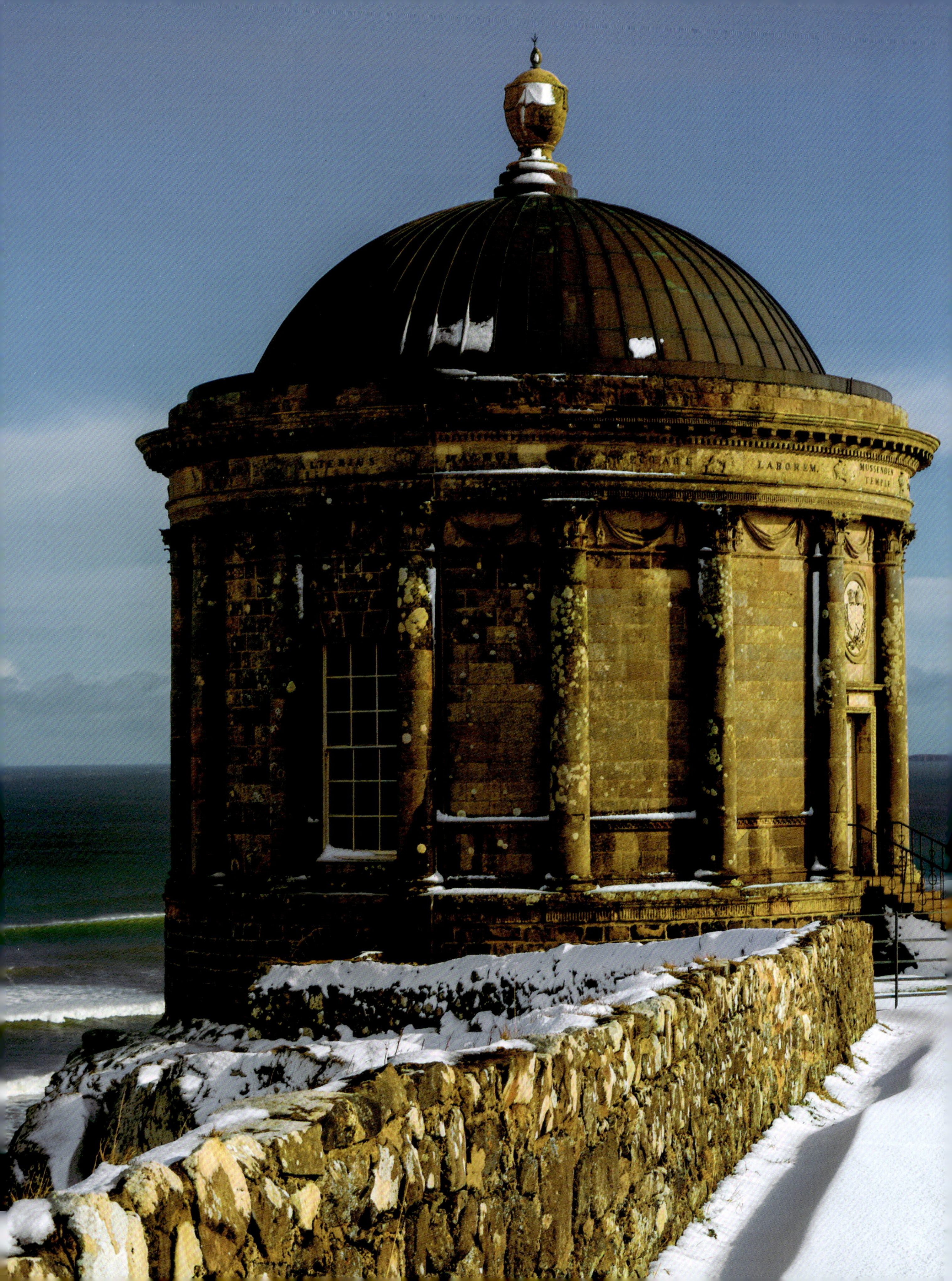

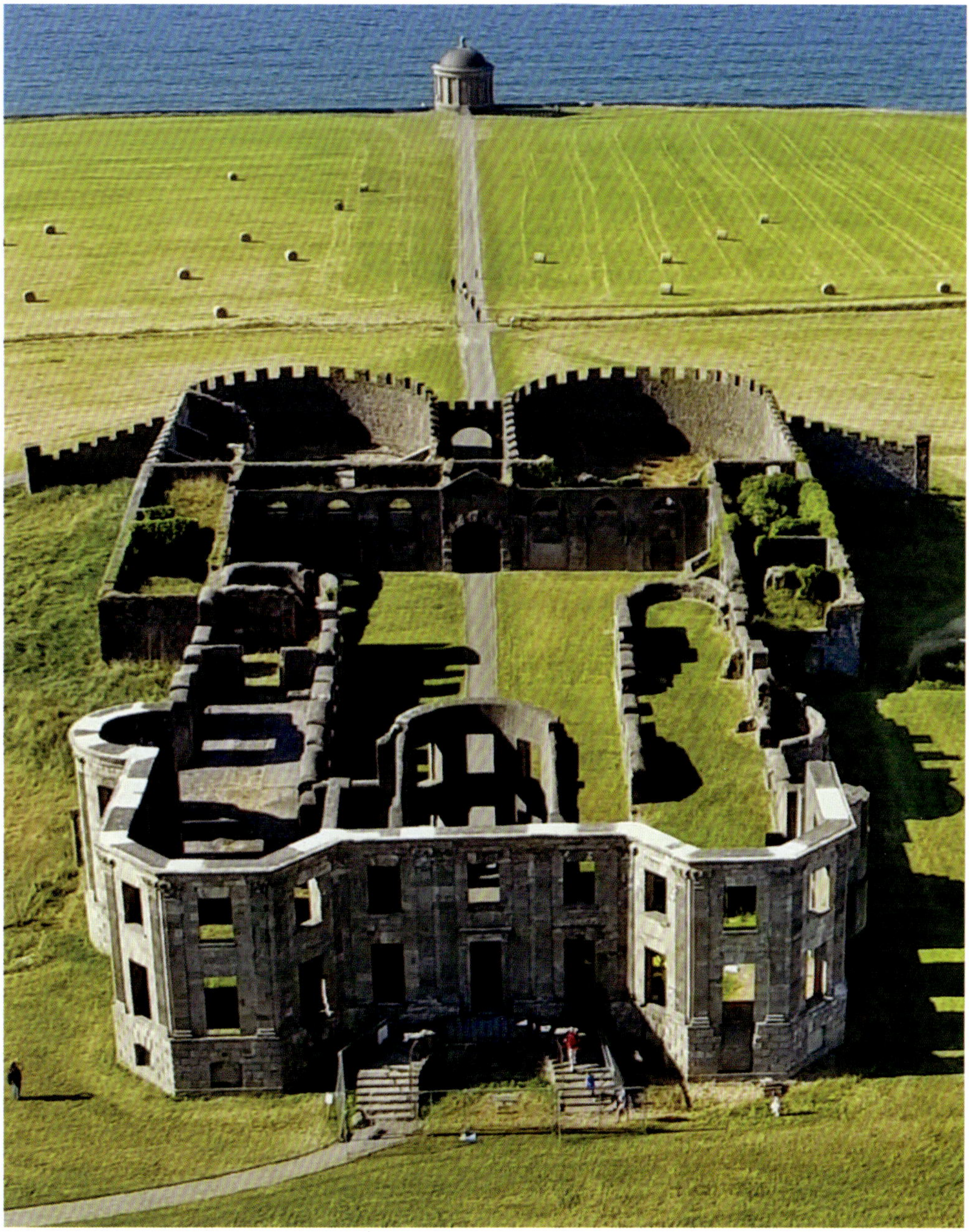

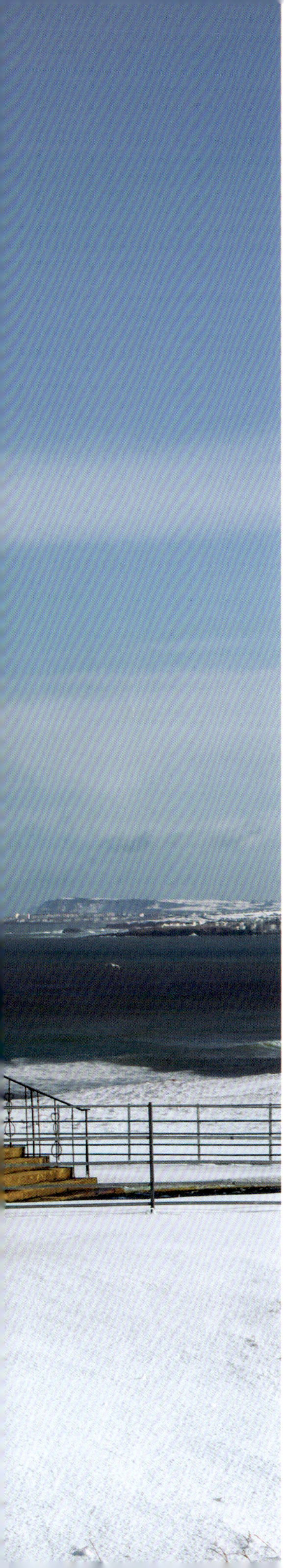

**Mussenden Temple and
Downhill Demesne,
County Derry**
Part of the Downhill estate,
Mussenden Temple was built
by Frederick, 4th Earl of Bristol
who served as the Church of
Ireland Lord Bishop of Derry
from 1768 to 1803. It is based
on the Temple of Vesta in Rome's
Forum and named after his
niece, Frideswide Mussenden.
The earl's Downhill Castle was
destroyed by fire in 1851.

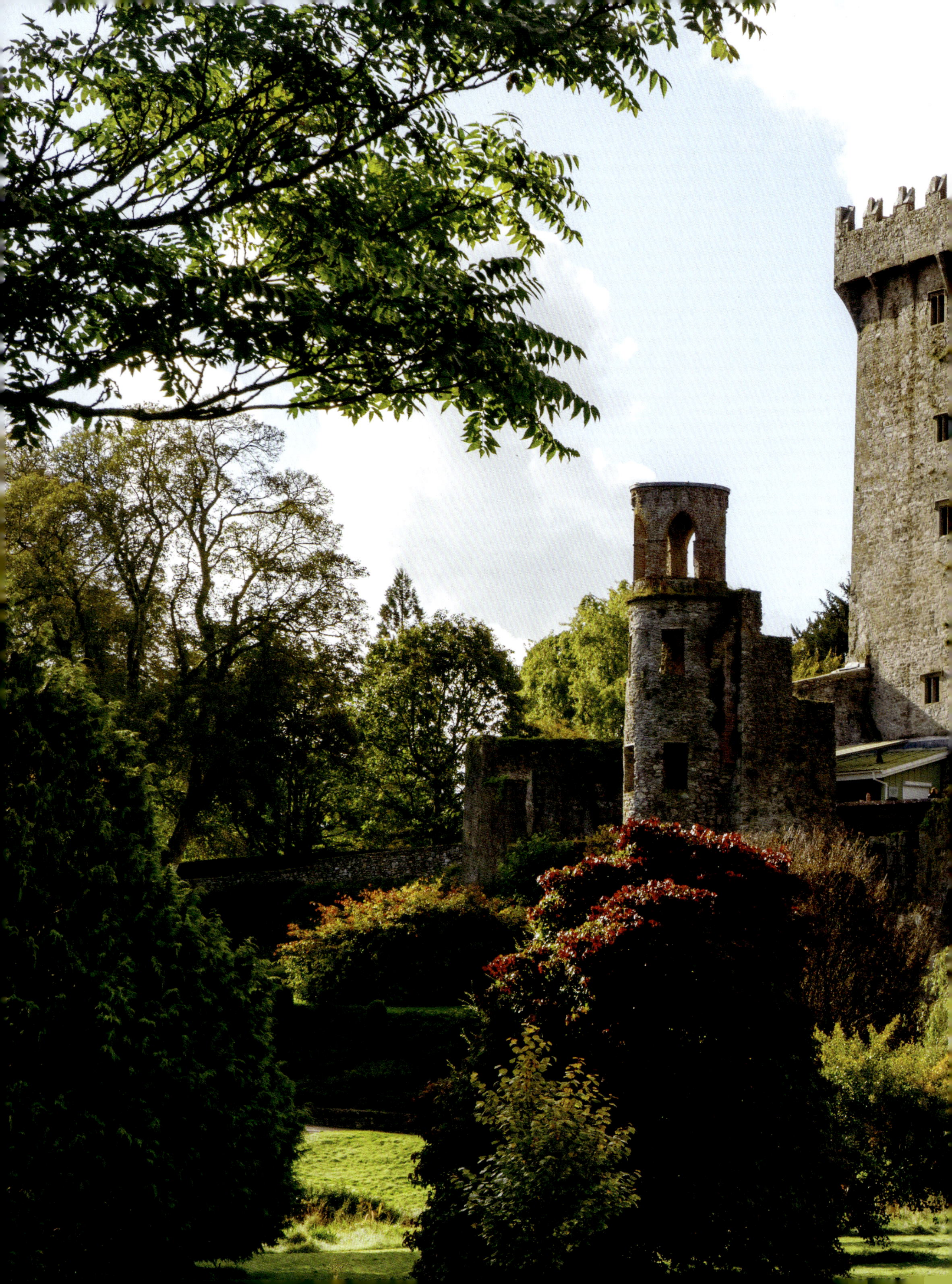

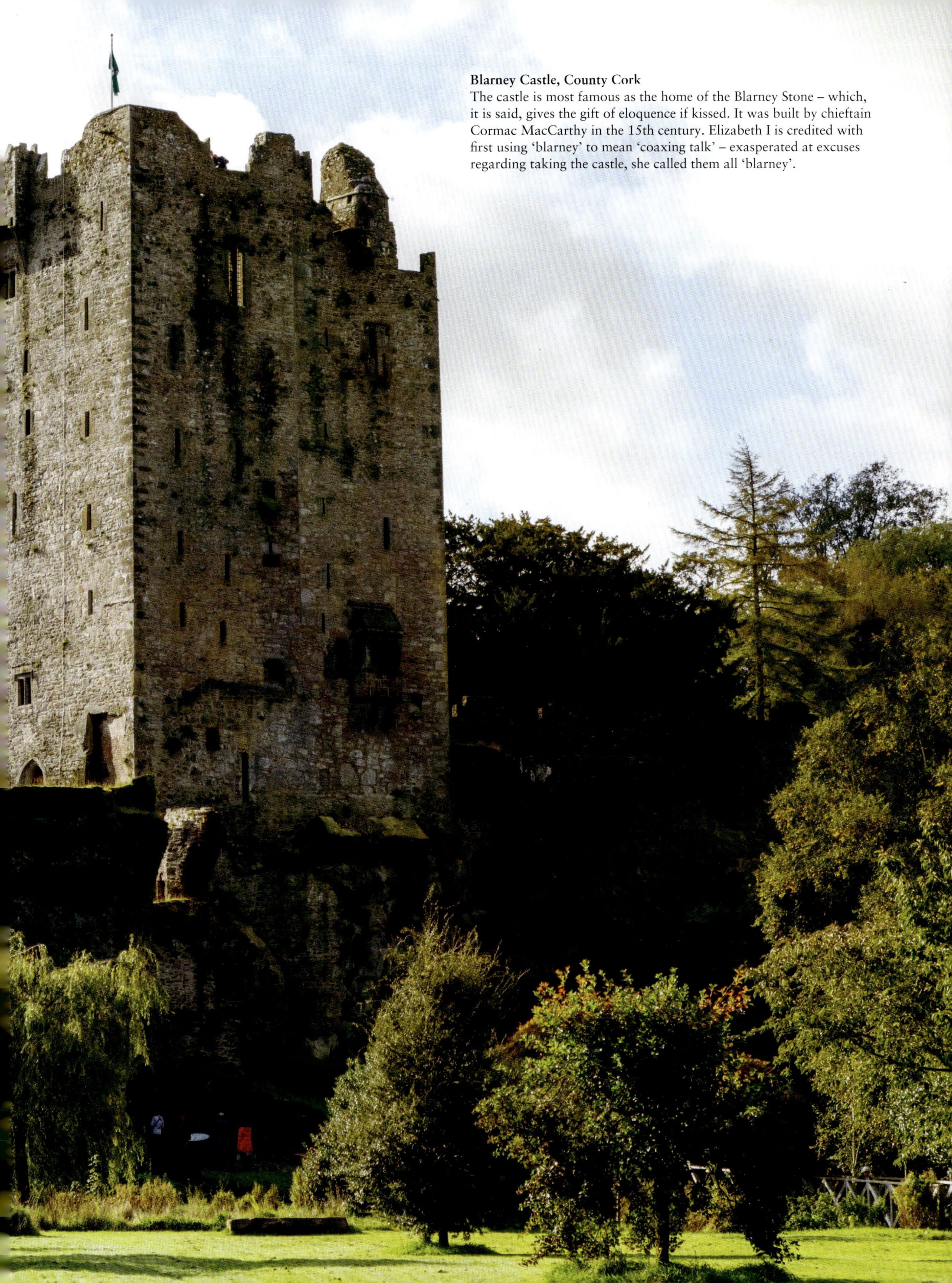

Blarney Castle, County Cork
The castle is most famous as the home of the Blarney Stone – which, it is said, gives the gift of eloquence if kissed. It was built by chieftain Cormac MacCarthy in the 15th century. Elizabeth I is credited with first using 'blarney' to mean 'coaxing talk' – exasperated at excuses regarding taking the castle, she called them all 'blarney'.

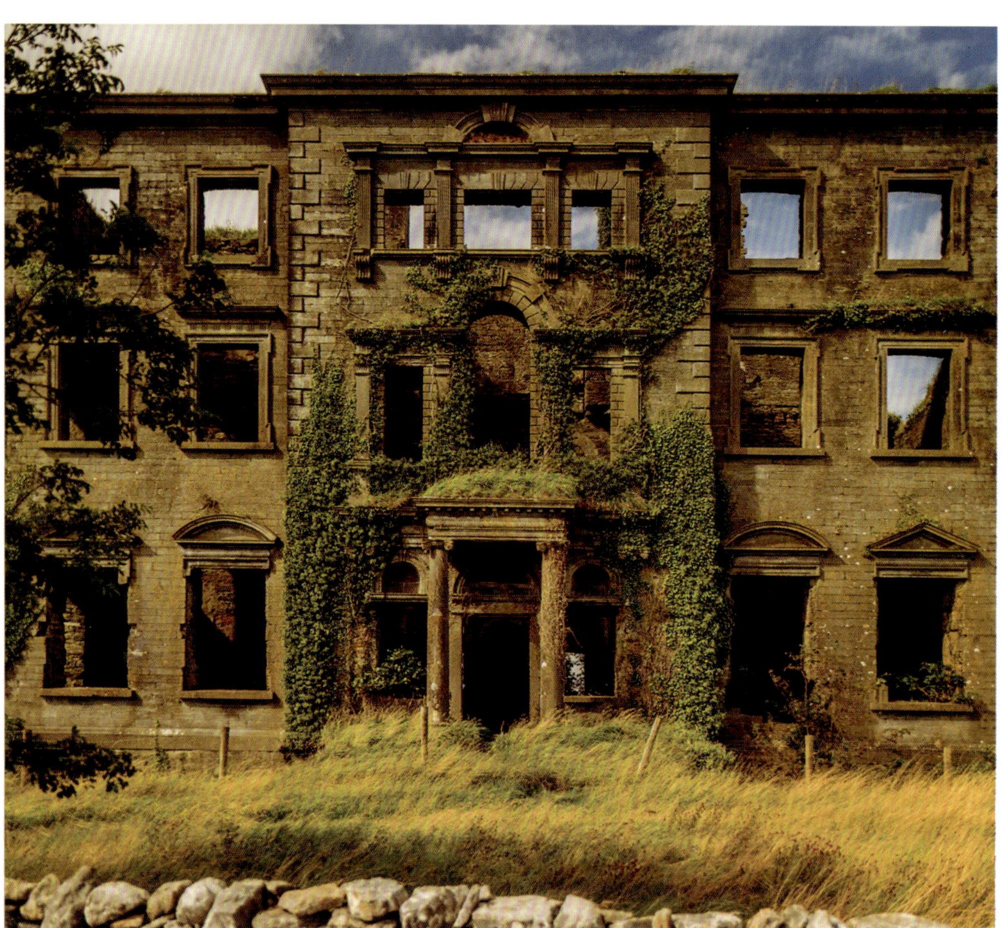

LEFT:
Tyrone House, County Galway
Built in 1779, Tyrone House was destroyed by the Irish Republican Army in 1920 amid rumours it was to be used as an infirmary by the Royal Irish Constabulary.

BELOW:
Ballyloughan Castle, County Carlow
Thought to have been built around 1300, Ballyloughan Castle is a remnant of the Anglo-Norman settlement of Ireland.

OPPOSITE ABOVE:
Granagh Castle, County Kilkenny
This 13th-century castle stands on the River Suir and local folklore has it that there is a tunnel from the castle under the river to the opposite bank.

OPPOSITE BELOW:
Tudenham Park House, County Westmeath
So impressive in its day was this 18th century house built for George Rochfort that his brother Robert had a folly built between it and his own house so that he would not have to look at the grander specimen.

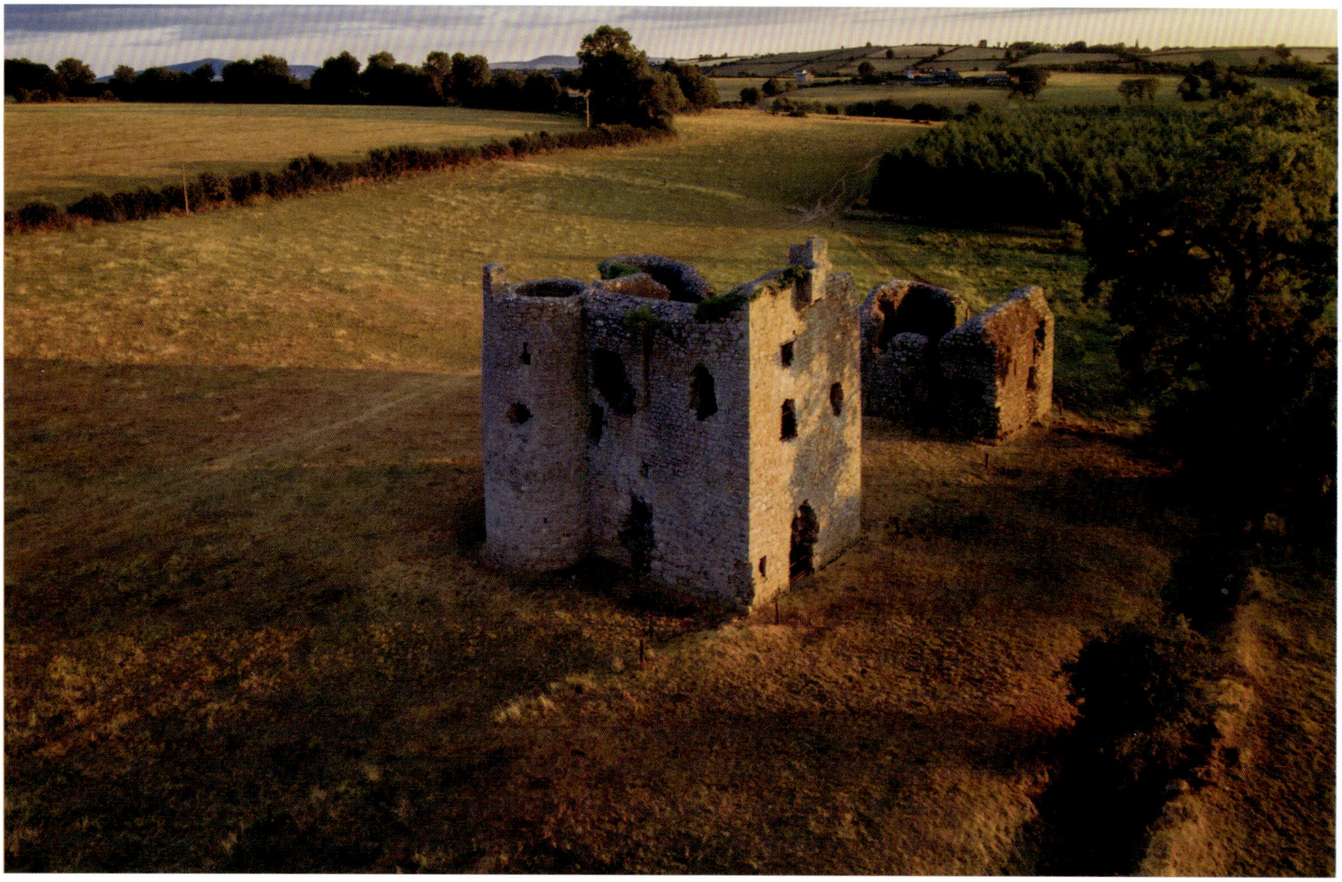

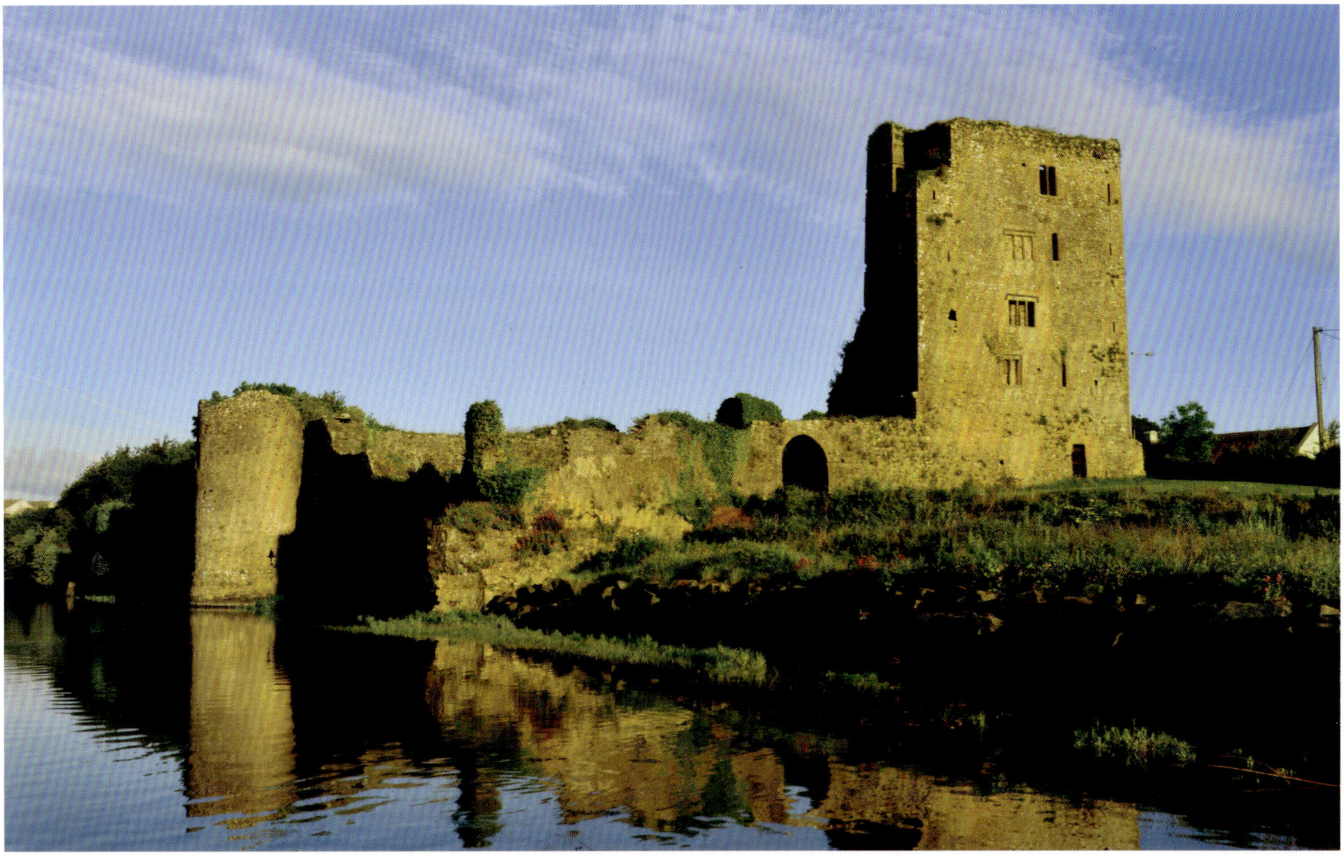

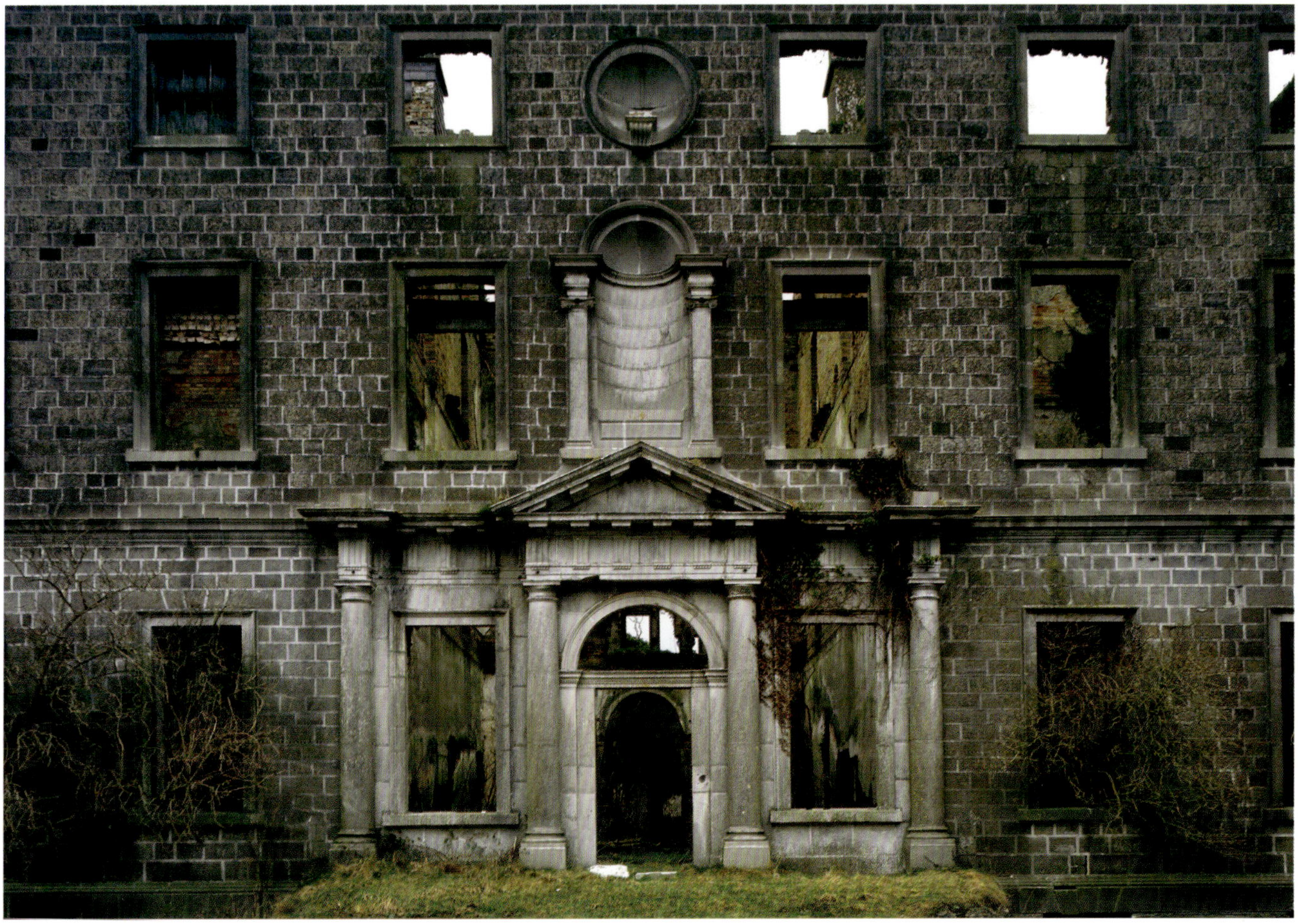

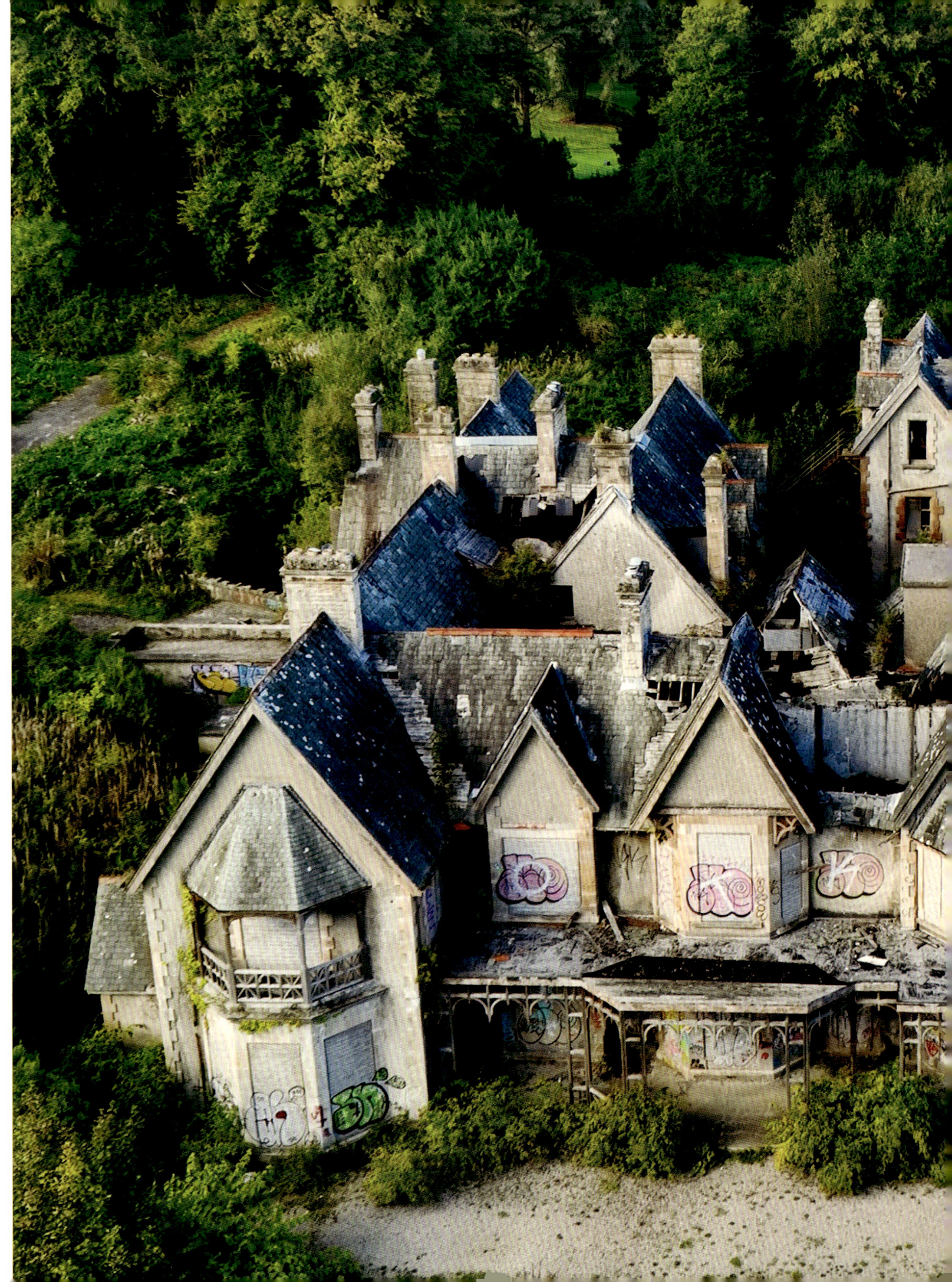

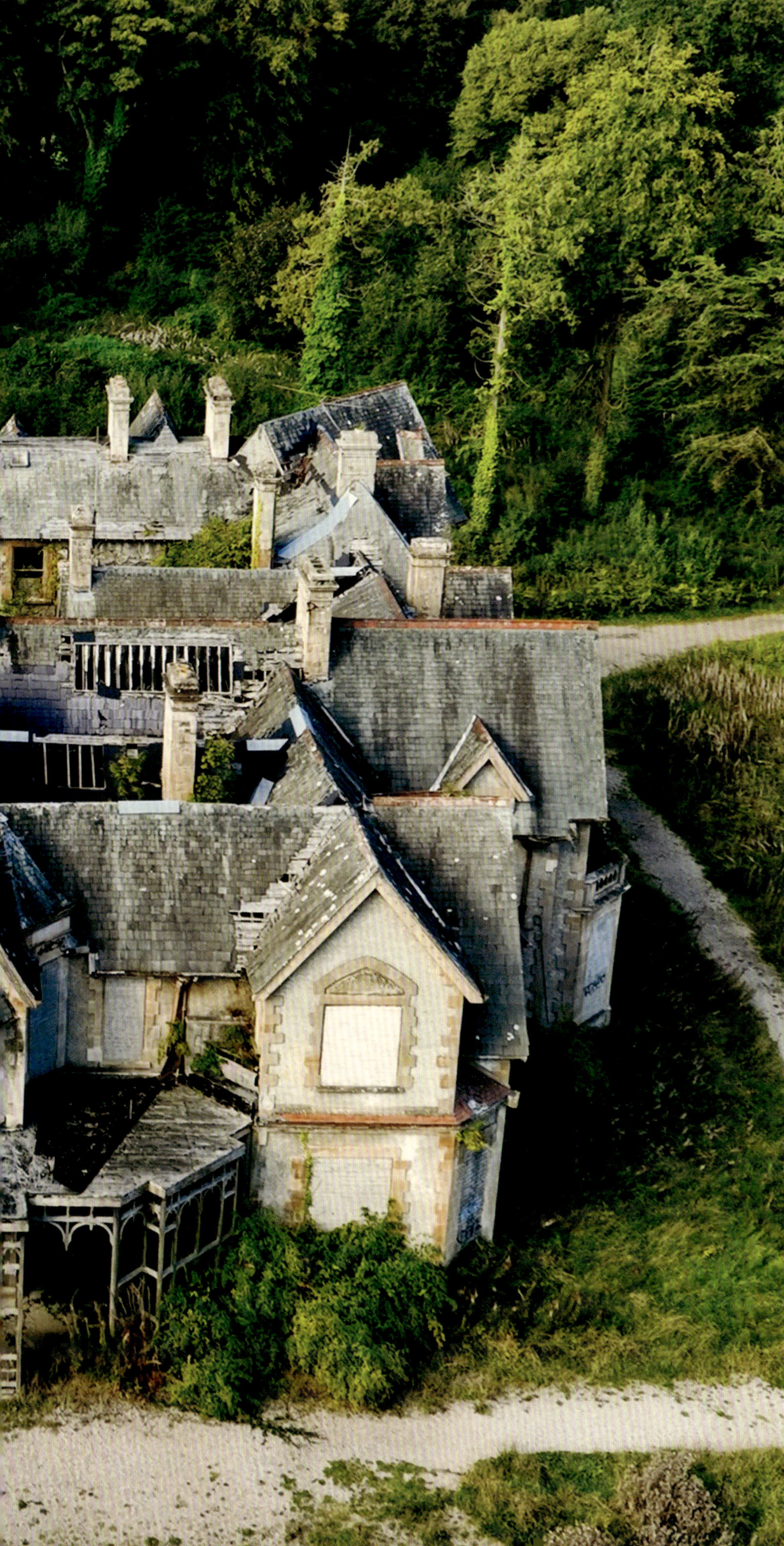

**Cairndhu House,
County Antrim**
Built as a summer residence in
1875 for a Scottish industrialist,
this sprawling house has also
been a convalescent home, a
military hospital and a film
location. Due to a number of
unexplained sightings, it is
probably best known in recent
times as 'the most haunted house
in Northern Ireland'.

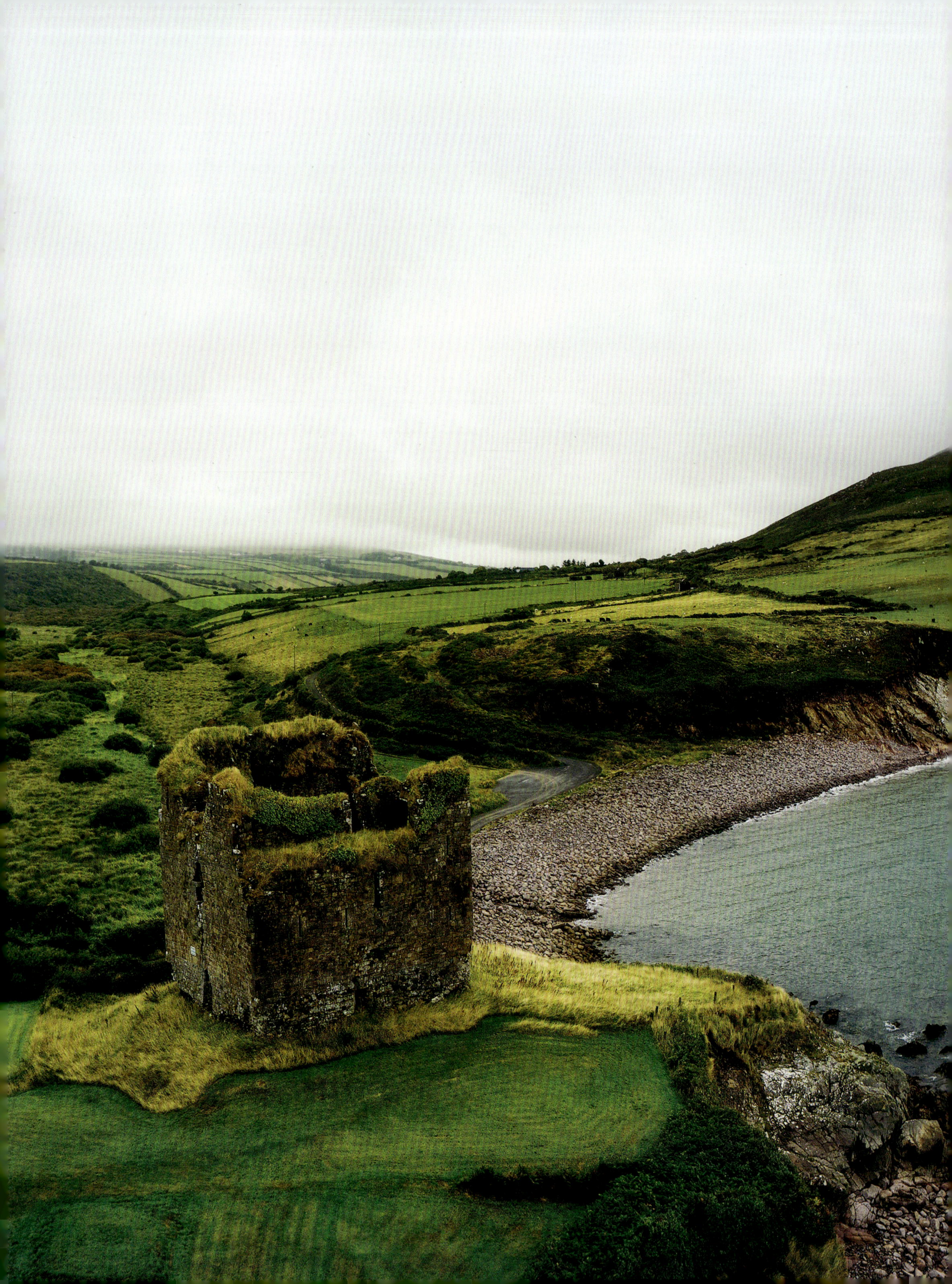

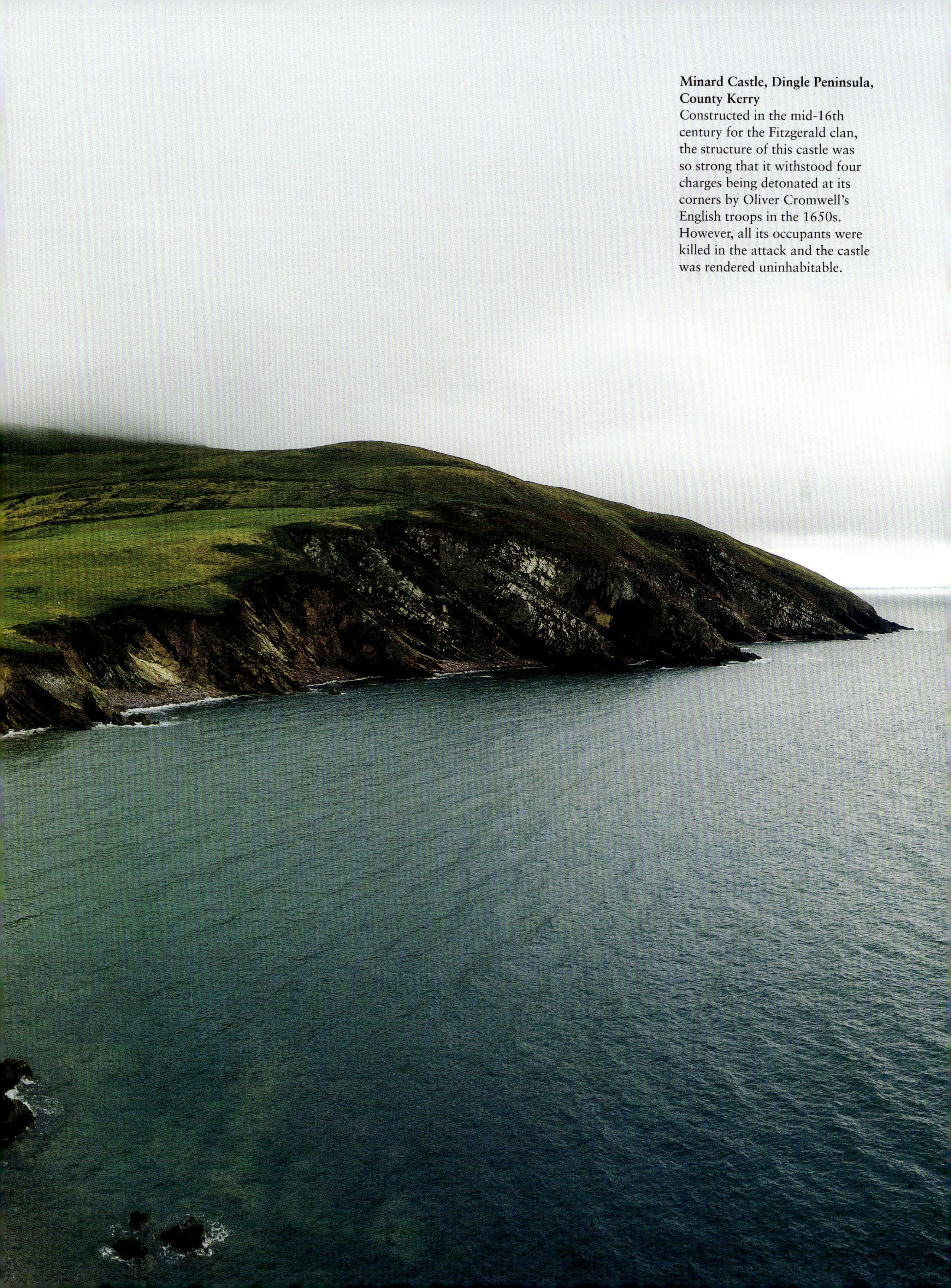

Minard Castle, Dingle Peninsula, County Kerry
Constructed in the mid-16th century for the Fitzgerald clan, the structure of this castle was so strong that it withstood four charges being detonated at its corners by Oliver Cromwell's English troops in the 1650s. However, all its occupants were killed in the attack and the castle was rendered uninhabitable.

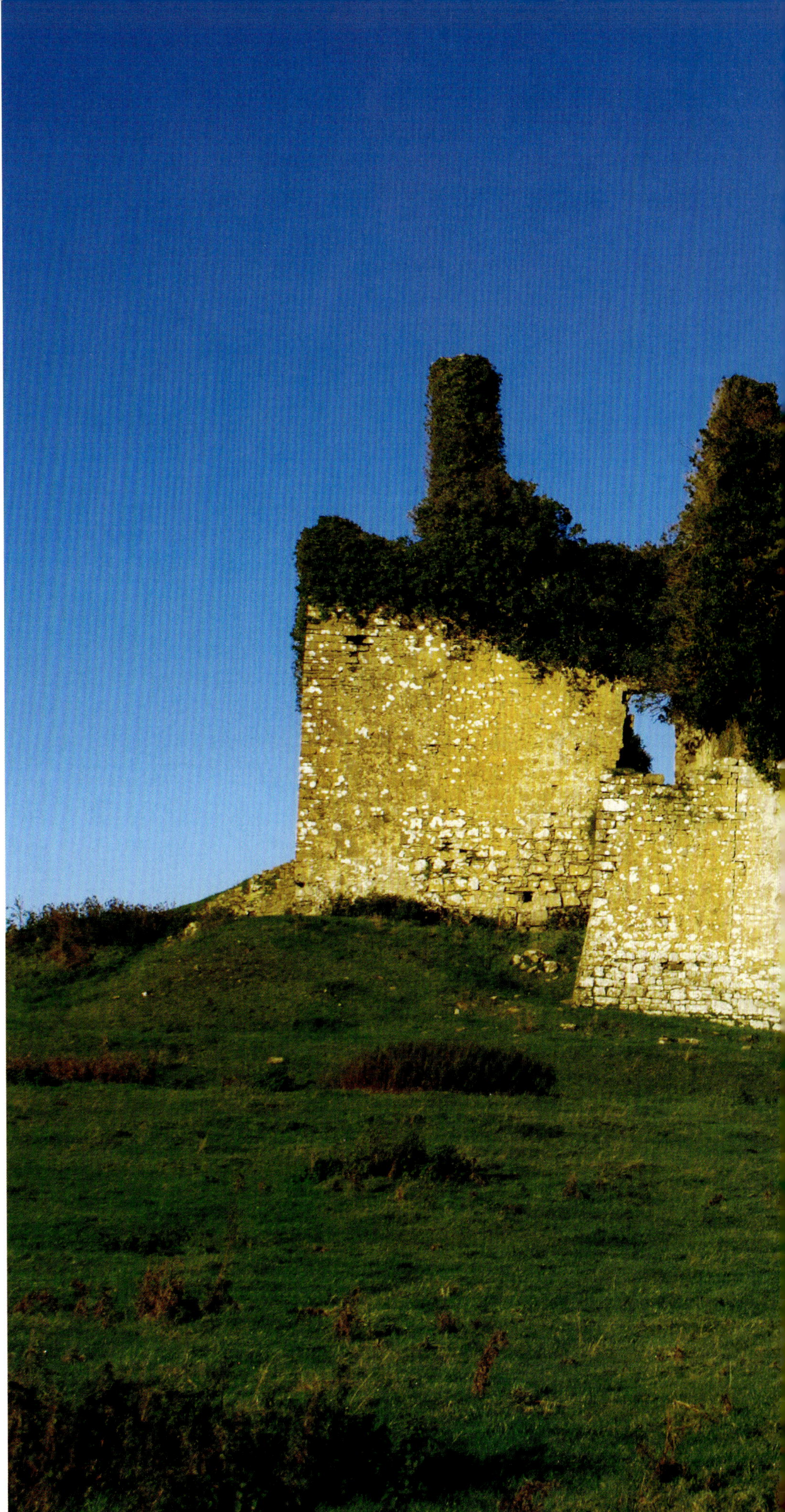

Carbury Castle, County Kildare
This Norman castle was much extended during the 16th and 17th centuries. Folklore has it that when St Patrick visited the site in pre-Norman days, he was served a greyhound on a dish out of disrespect. When he blessed the food, the dog sprang back to life and walked off.

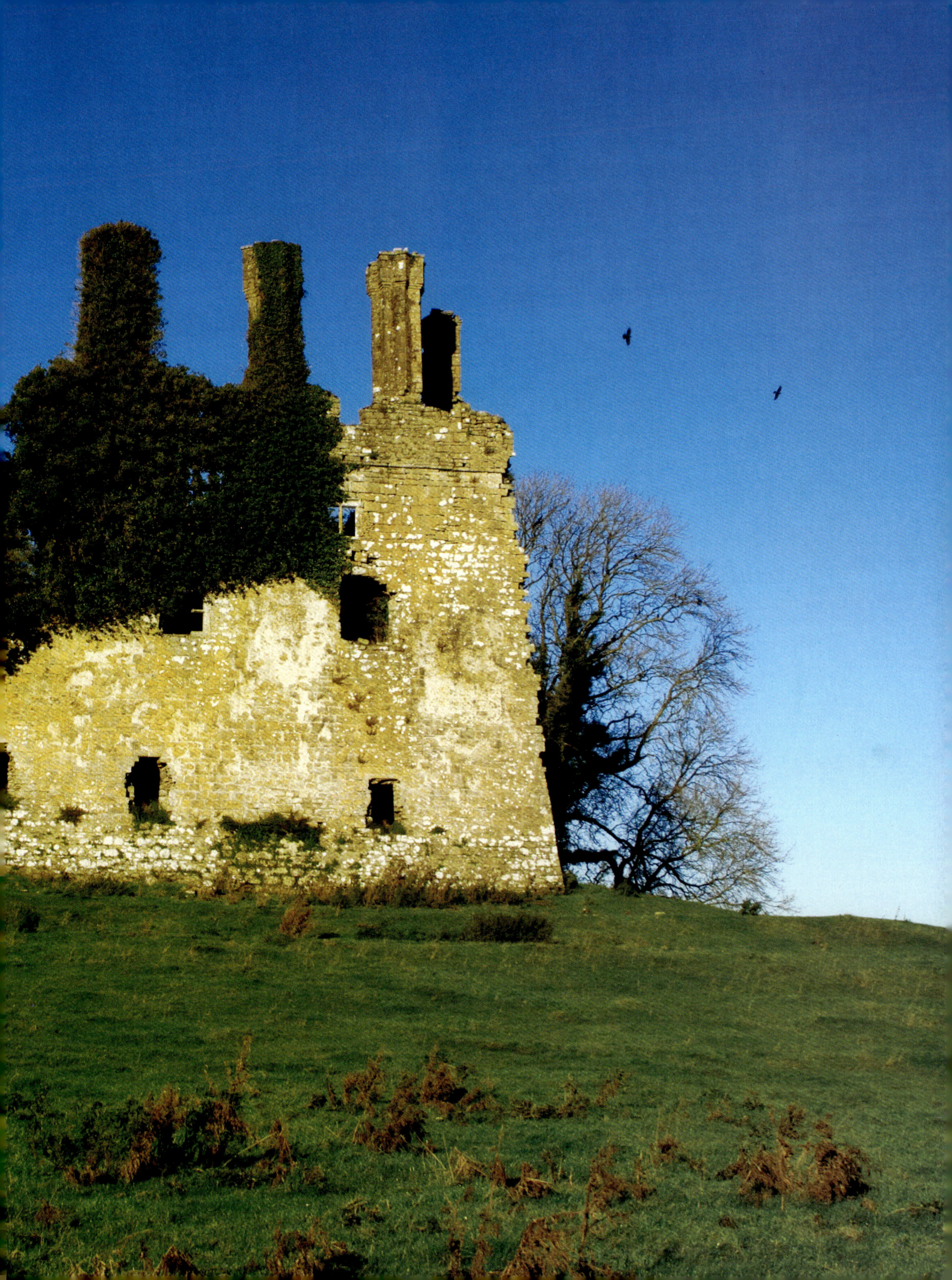

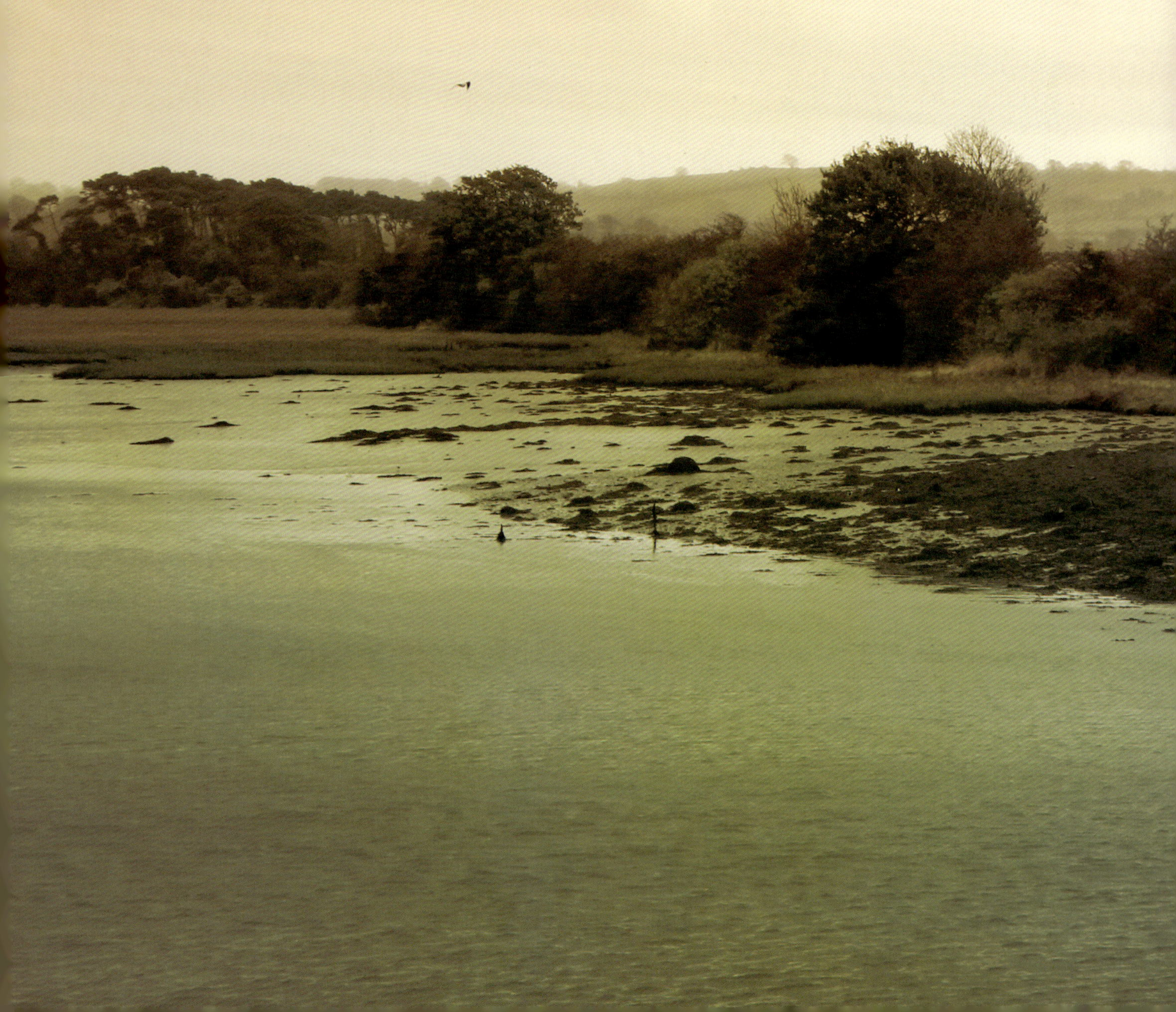

Belvelly Castle, County Cork
The tower house was built by the Anglo-Norman Hodnett family
and in the 16th century was owned by the English adventurer Walter
Raleigh, who at the time was trying to suppress feudal lords in
Ireland. In later centuries it fell into disrepair but was occupied by the
Irish Army during World War II. Previously, it had been used in the
17th century to garrison troops under the Anglo-Irish Roger Boyle,
the 1st Earl of Orrery, during the Irish Confederate Wars. It has a
strategic position on Great Island in Cork Harbour overlooking
a ford that was a link to the mainland.

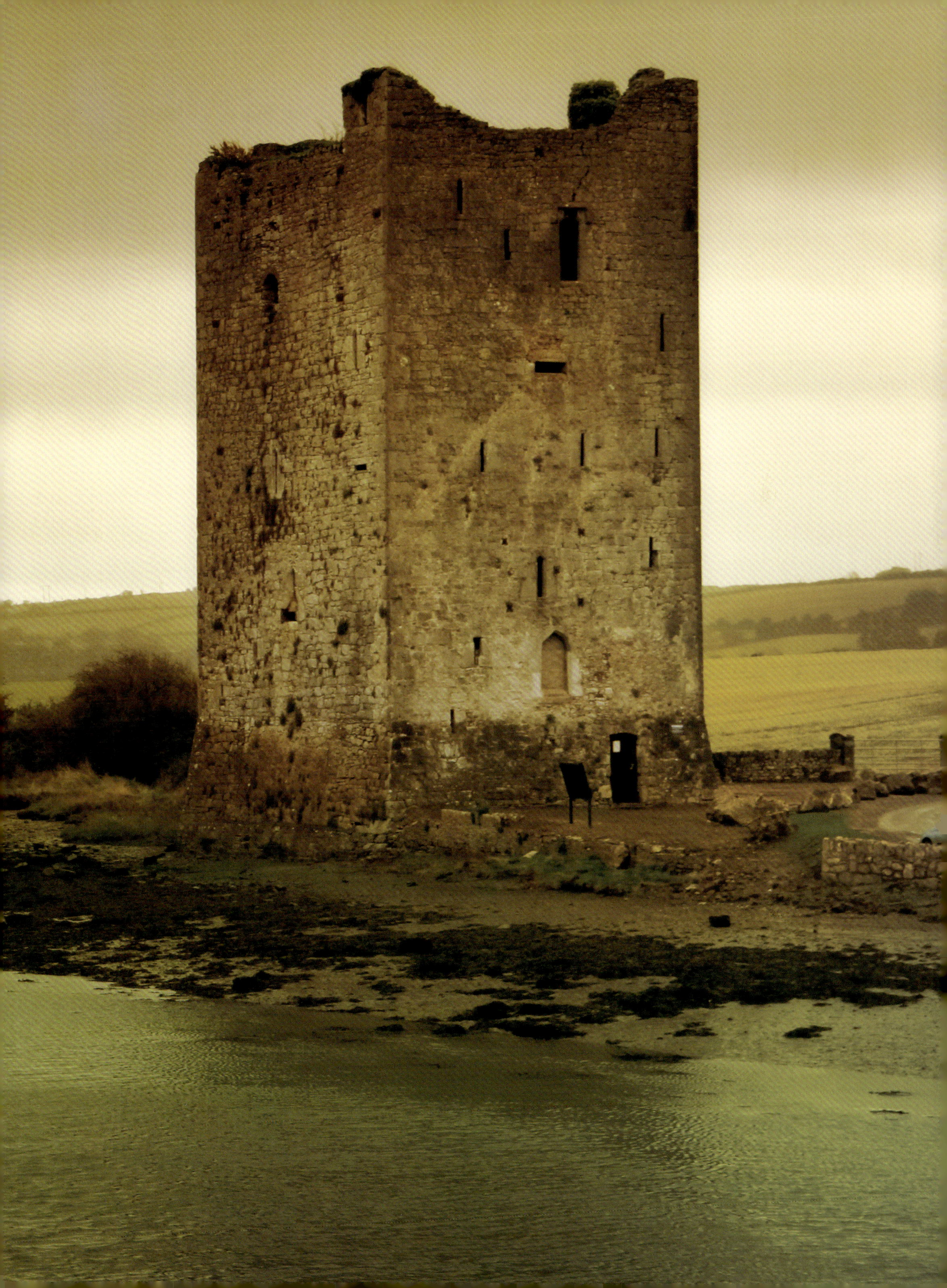

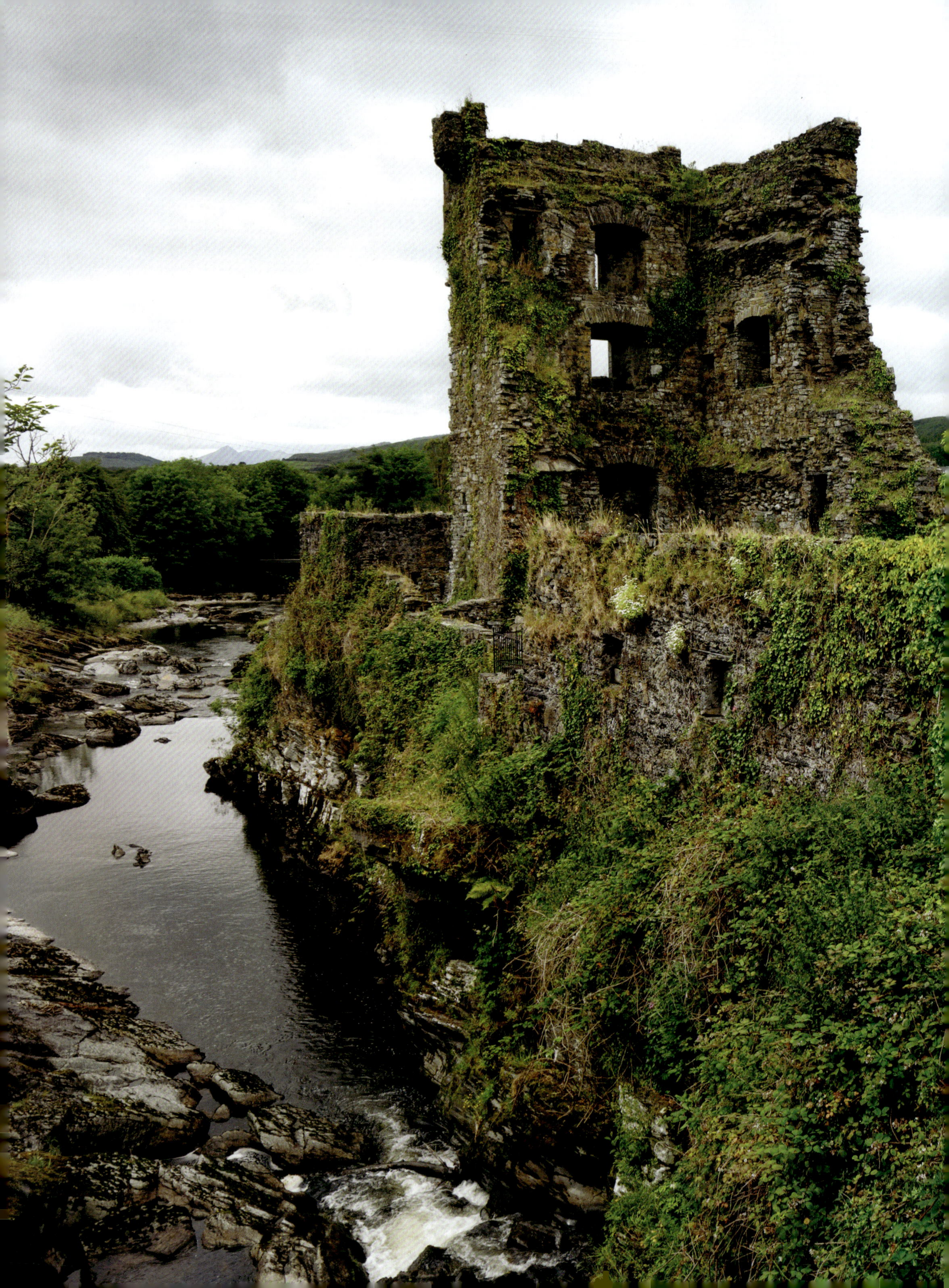

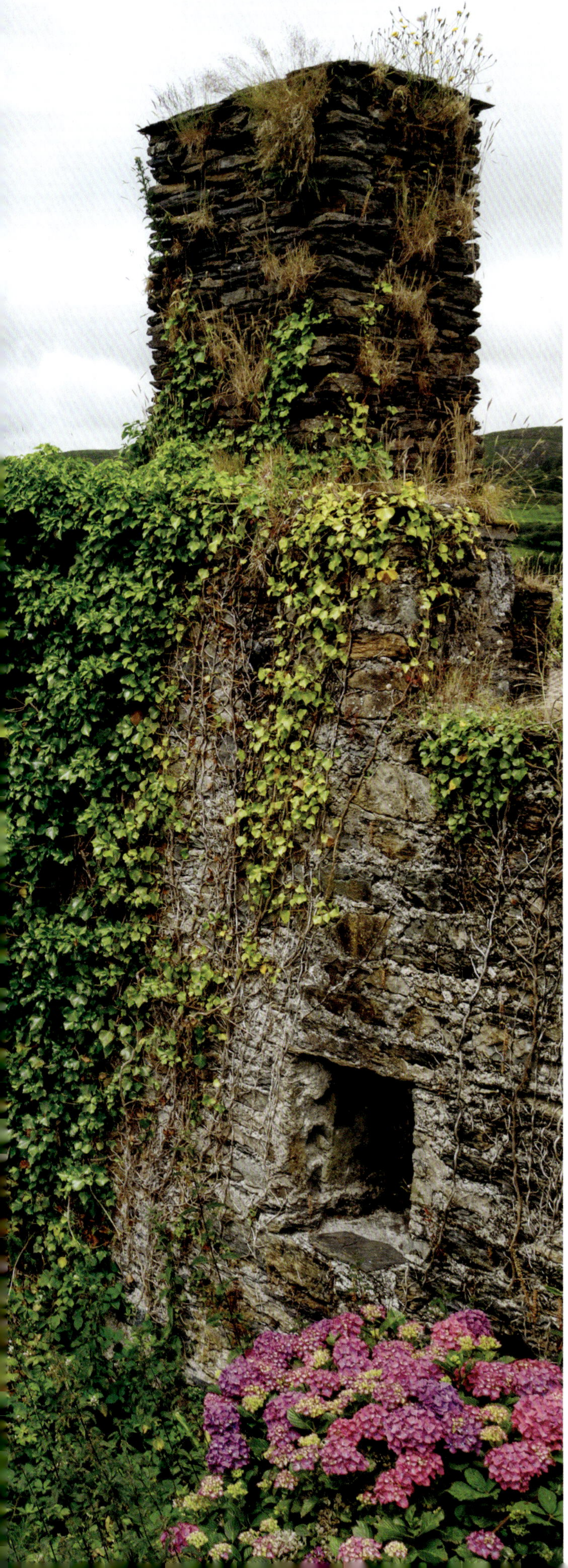

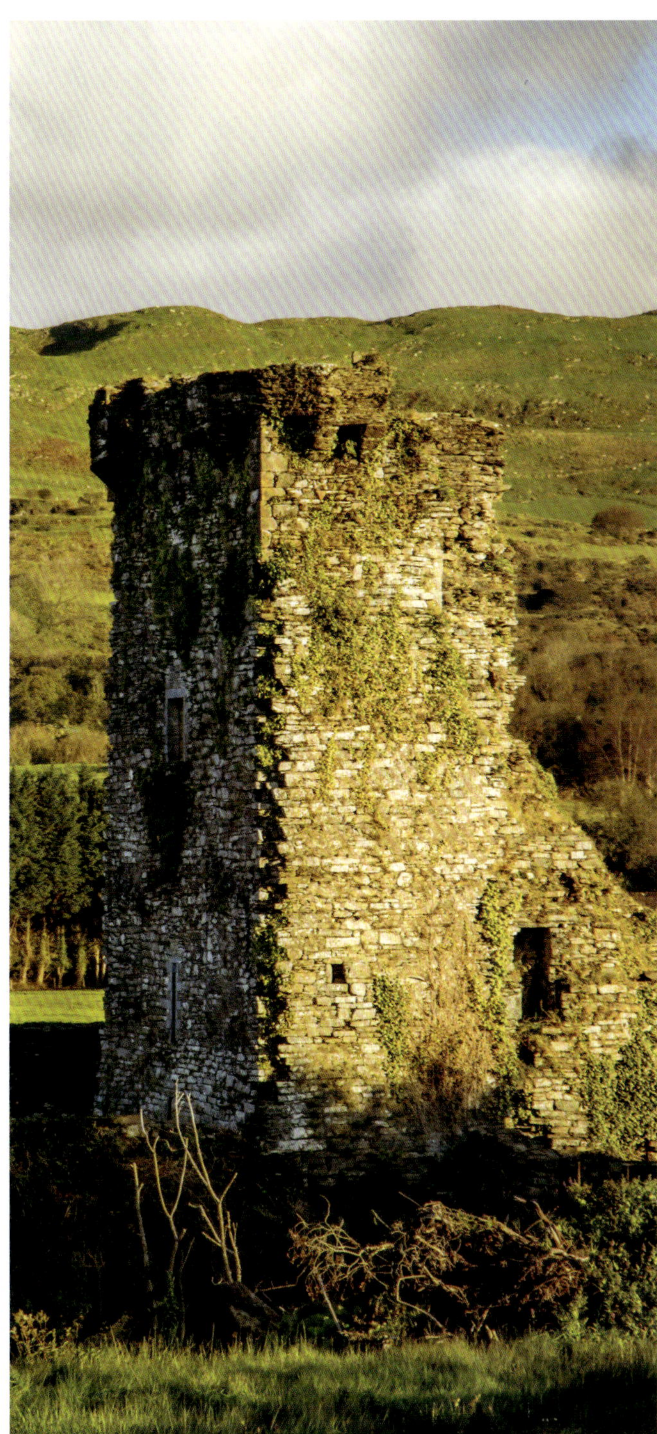

ALL PHOTOGRAPHS:
Carriganass Castle, County Cork
This circa-1540 tower house that overlooks the River Ouvane was built by the O'Sullivan Beare clan, who held on to it until they were driven out by the English in the early 17th century. A new house was built next to the castle, which led to the castle deteriorating into a ruin.

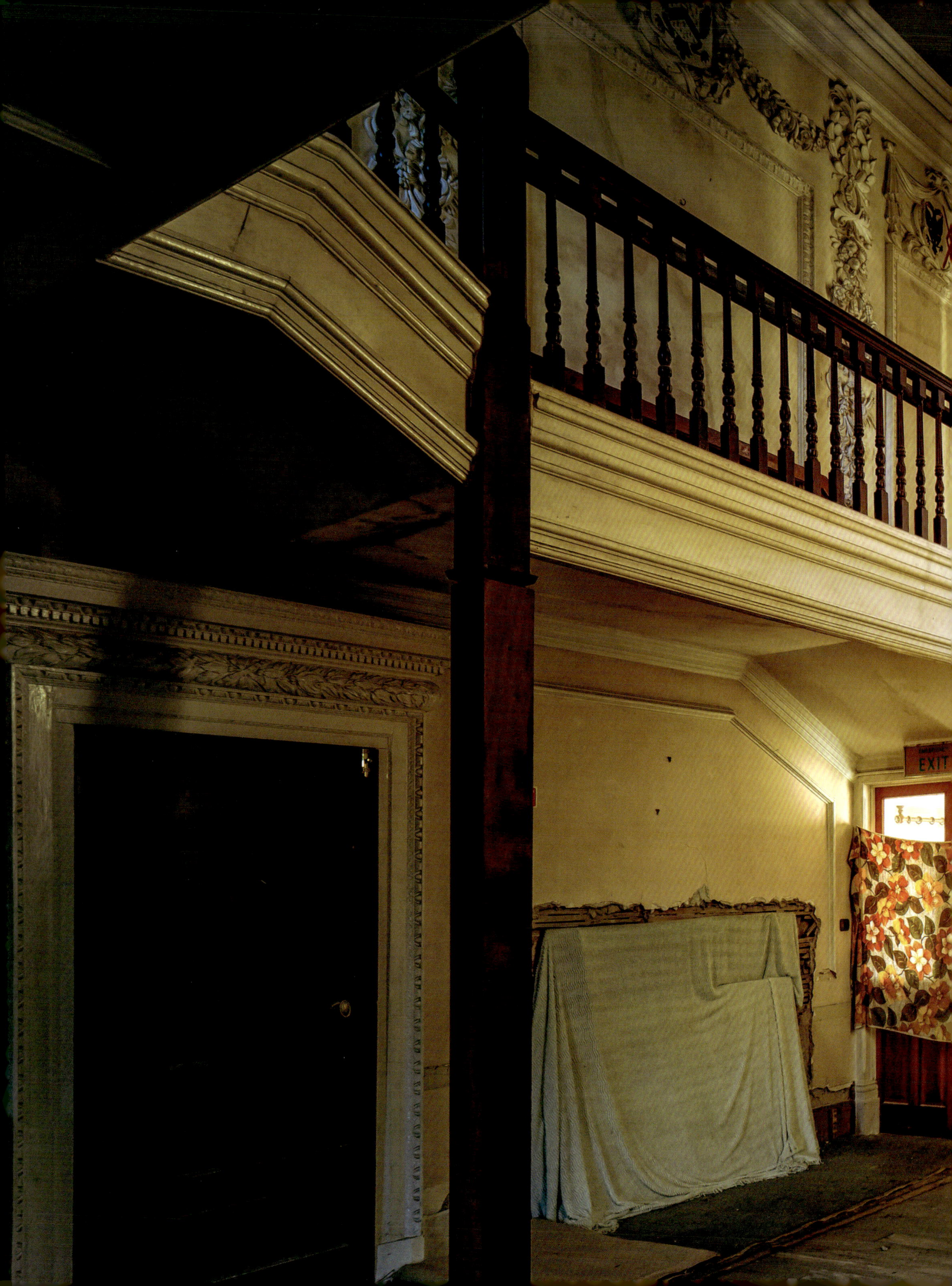

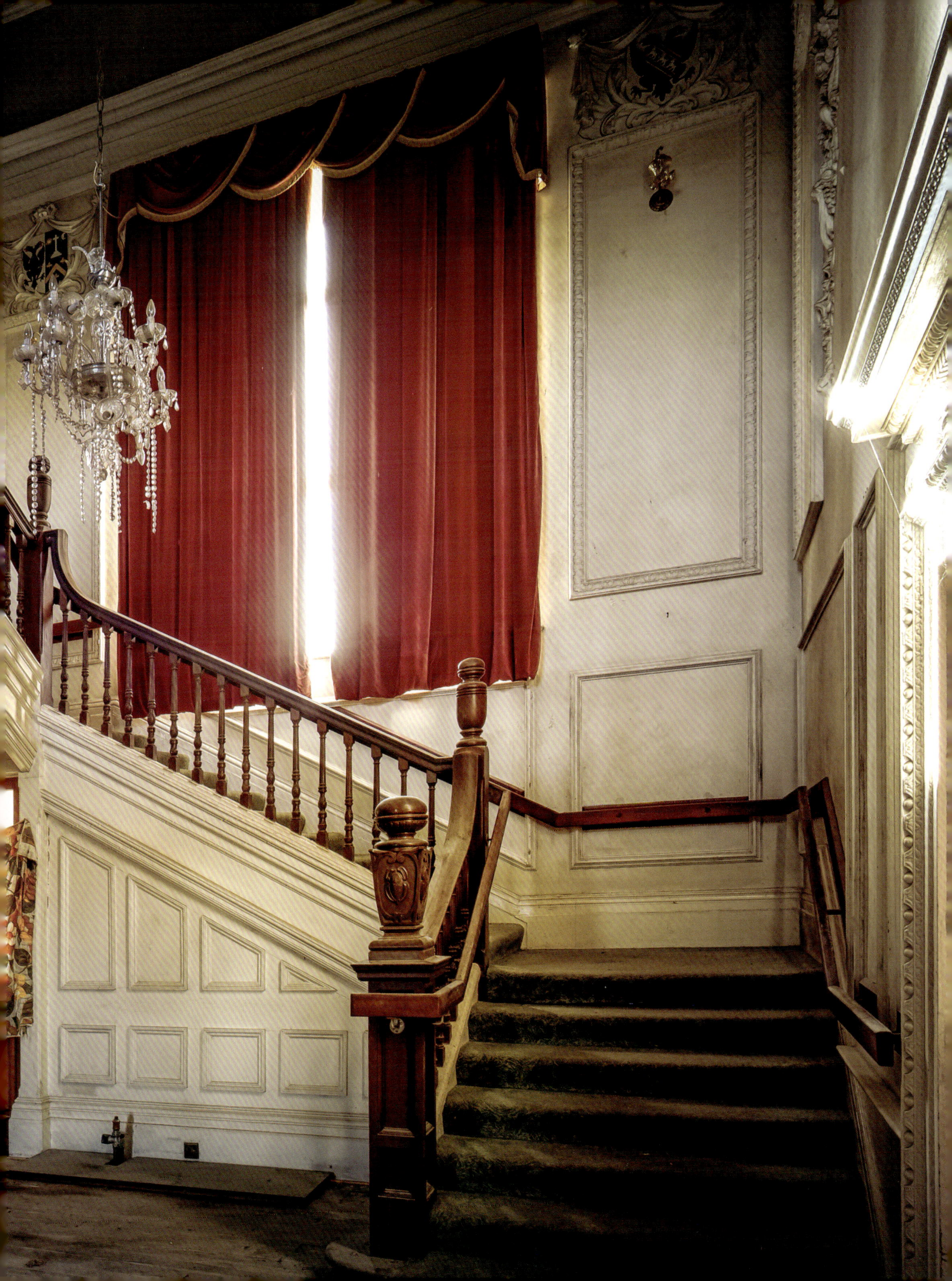

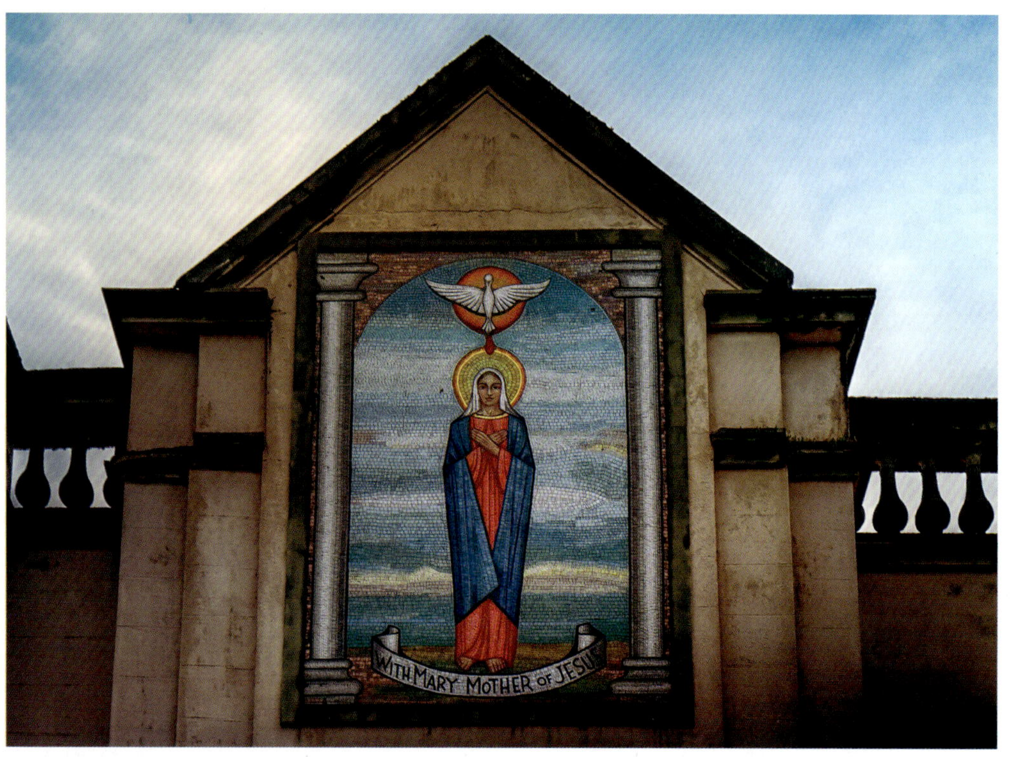

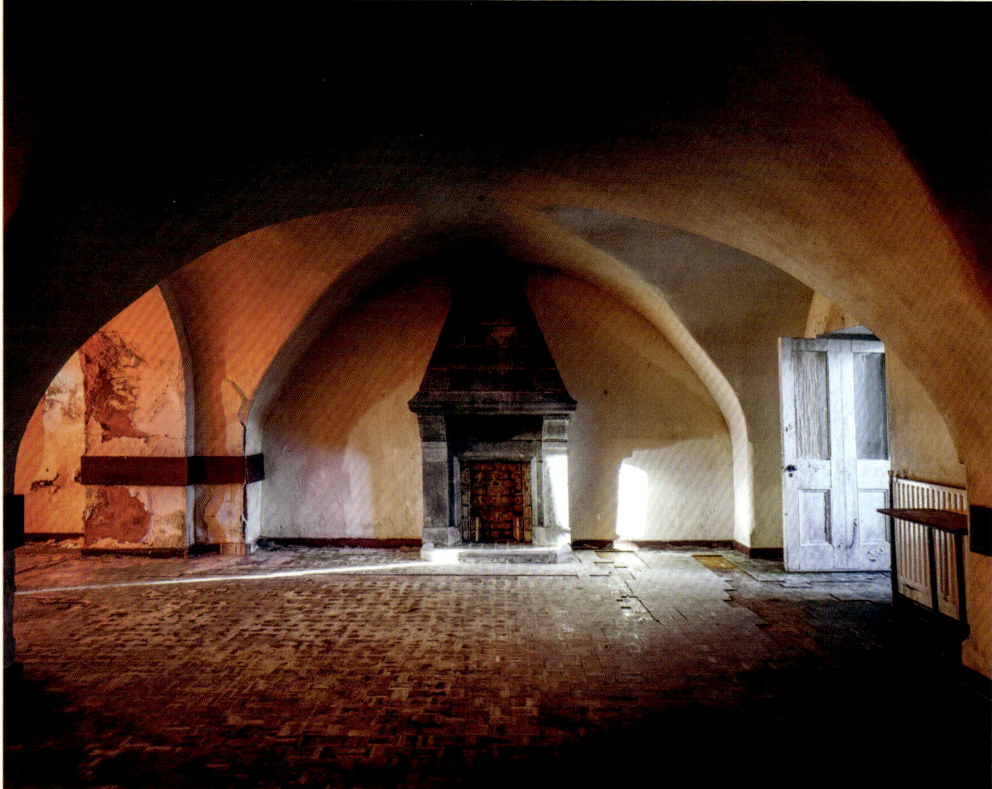

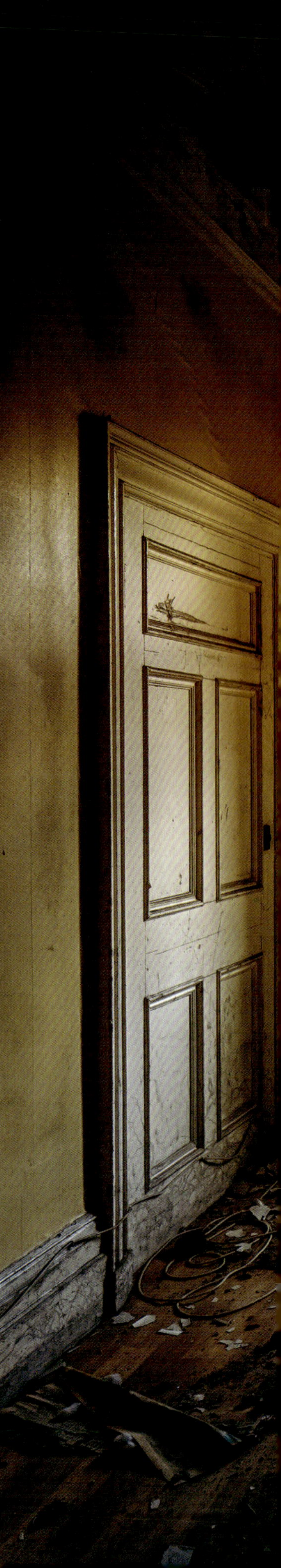

Castle MacGarrett, Claremorris, County Mayo
Built in 1811 after its 1694 predecessor was destroyed by fire, this grand house was the seat of the Browne family, until they sold it in the 1960s and it was bought by the Irish Land Commission. It was then used as a nursing home run by nuns but was sold again in 2005, and is yet to be redeveloped. The expansive residence had been extended in the early 20th century but one part of the first Castle MacGarrett that the 1811 version recycled from its previous incarnation was a vaulted room (above bottom) dating from 1700.

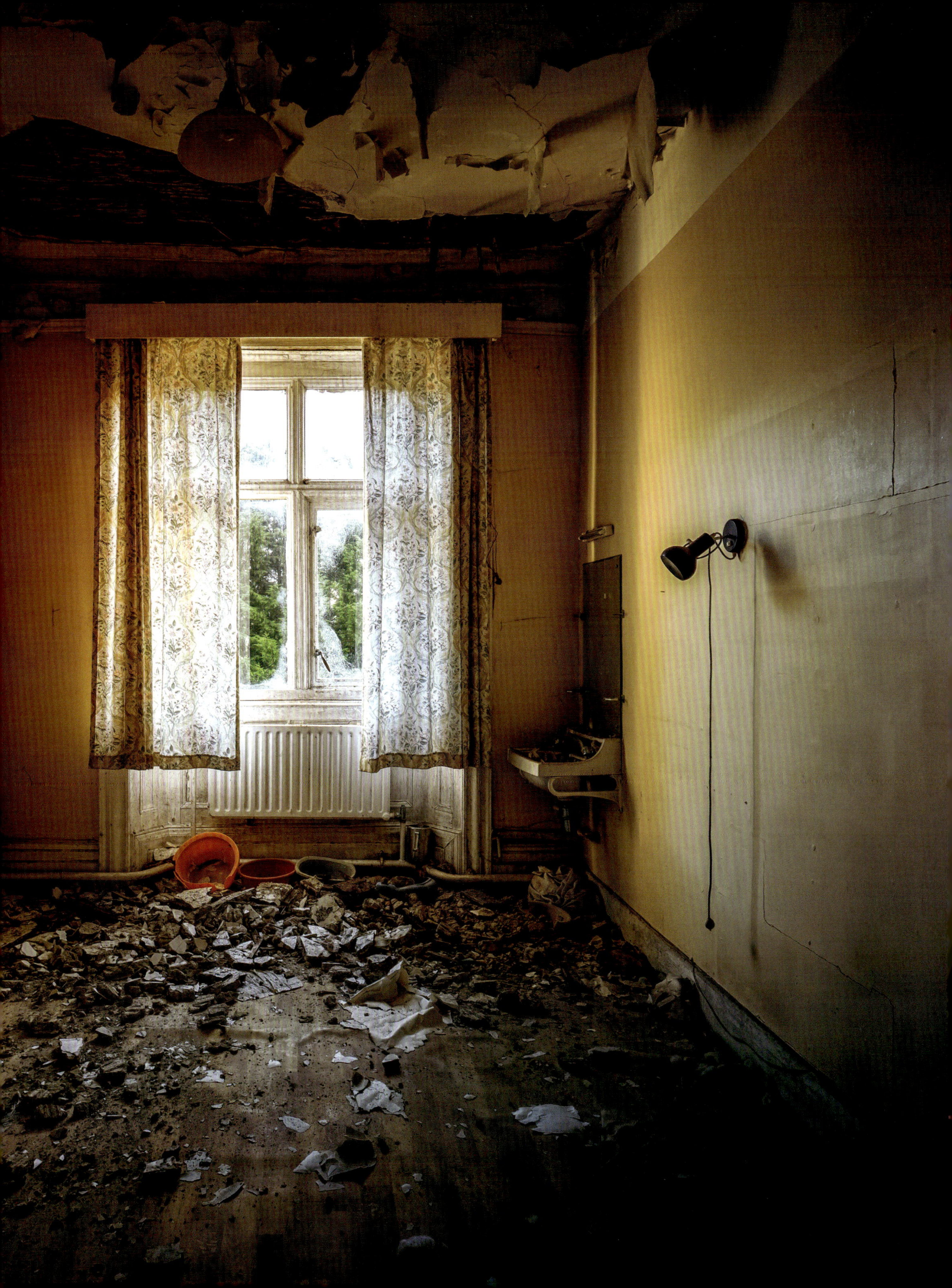

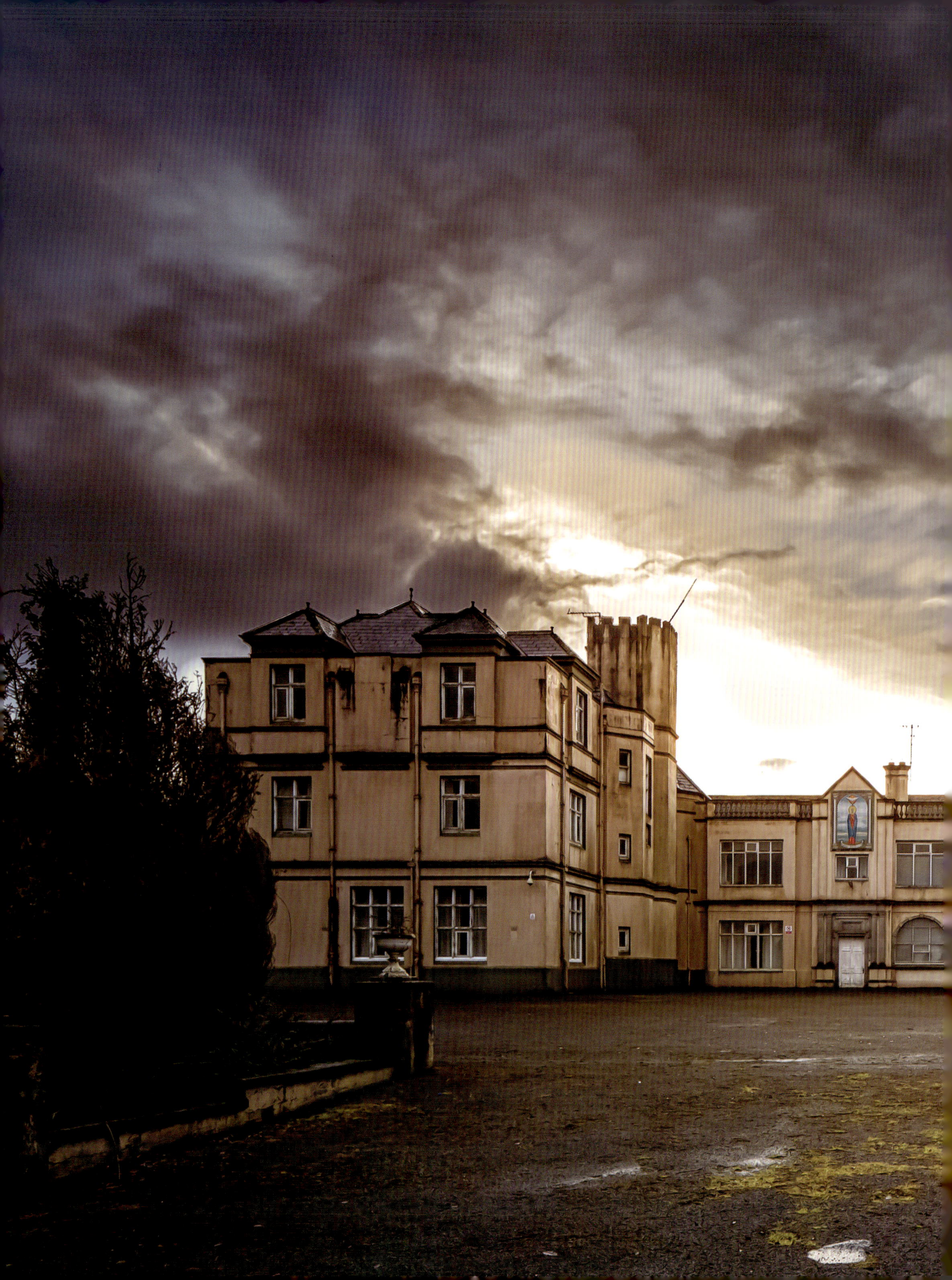

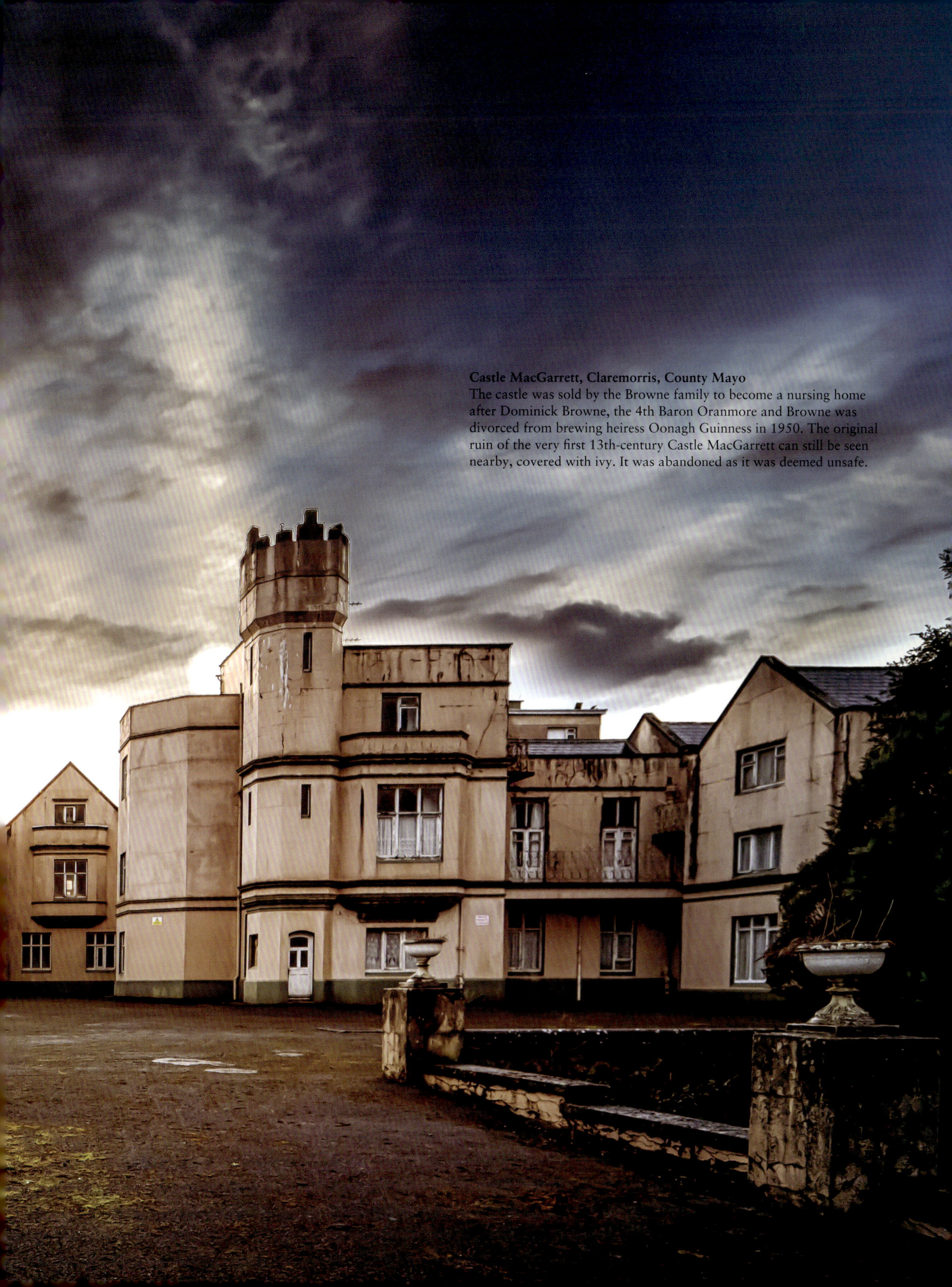

Castle MacGarrett, Claremorris, County Mayo
The castle was sold by the Browne family to become a nursing home after Dominick Browne, the 4th Baron Oranmore and Browne was divorced from brewing heiress Oonagh Guinness in 1950. The original ruin of the very first 13th-century Castle MacGarrett can still be seen nearby, covered with ivy. It was abandoned as it was deemed unsafe.

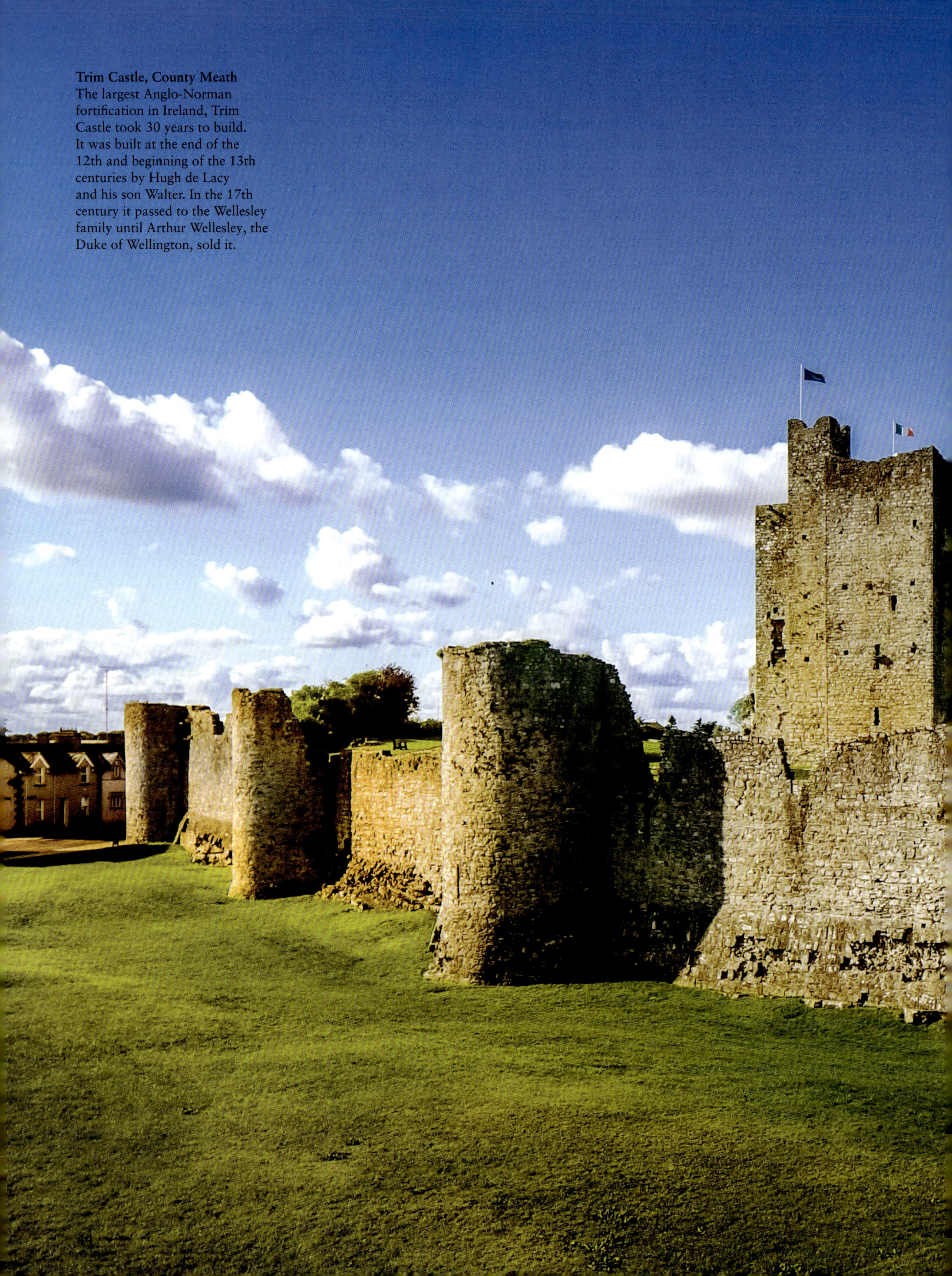

Trim Castle, County Meath
The largest Anglo-Norman fortification in Ireland, Trim Castle took 30 years to build. It was built at the end of the 12th and beginning of the 13th centuries by Hugh de Lacy and his son Walter. In the 17th century it passed to the Wellesley family until Arthur Wellesley, the Duke of Wellington, sold it.

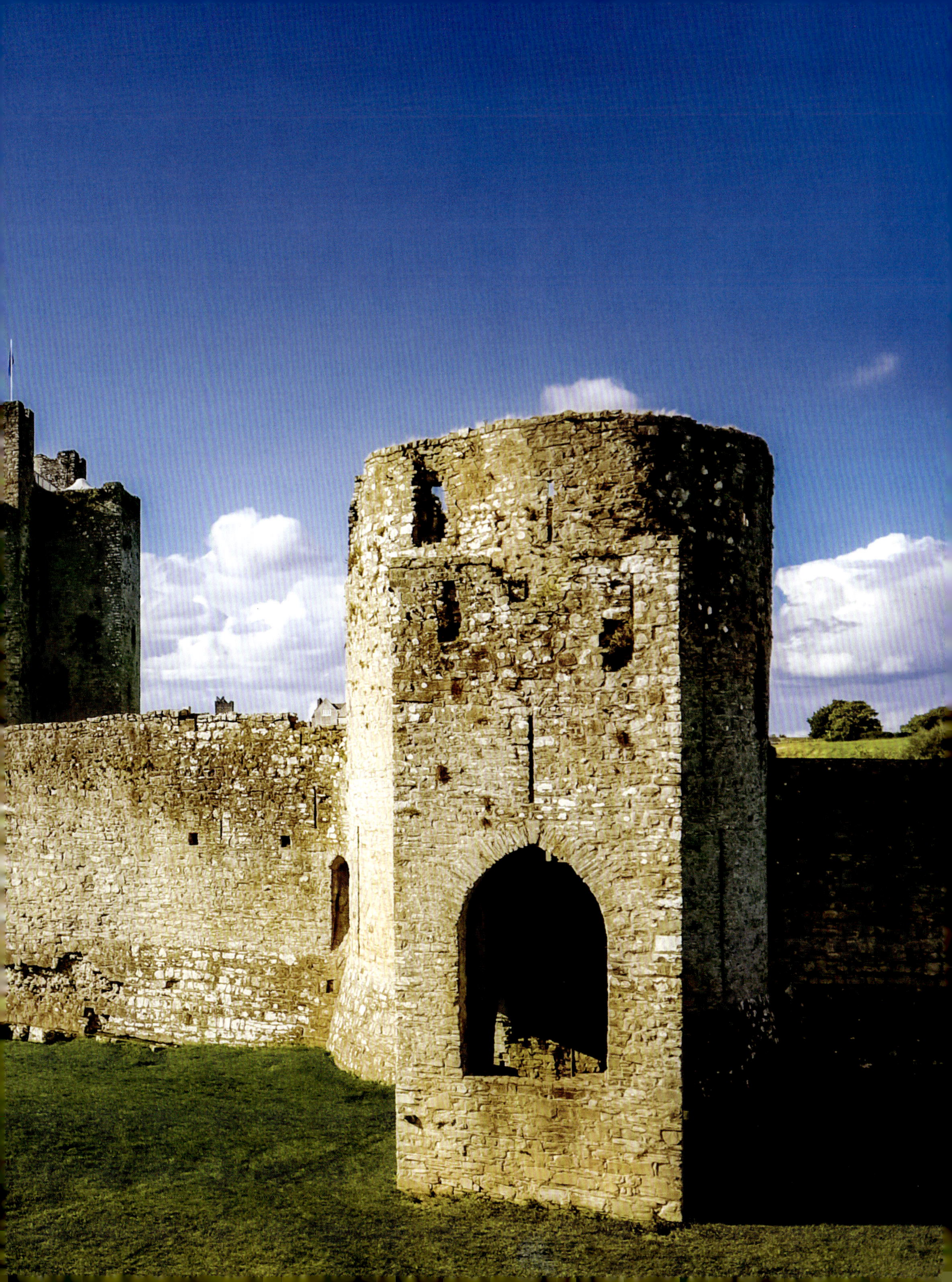

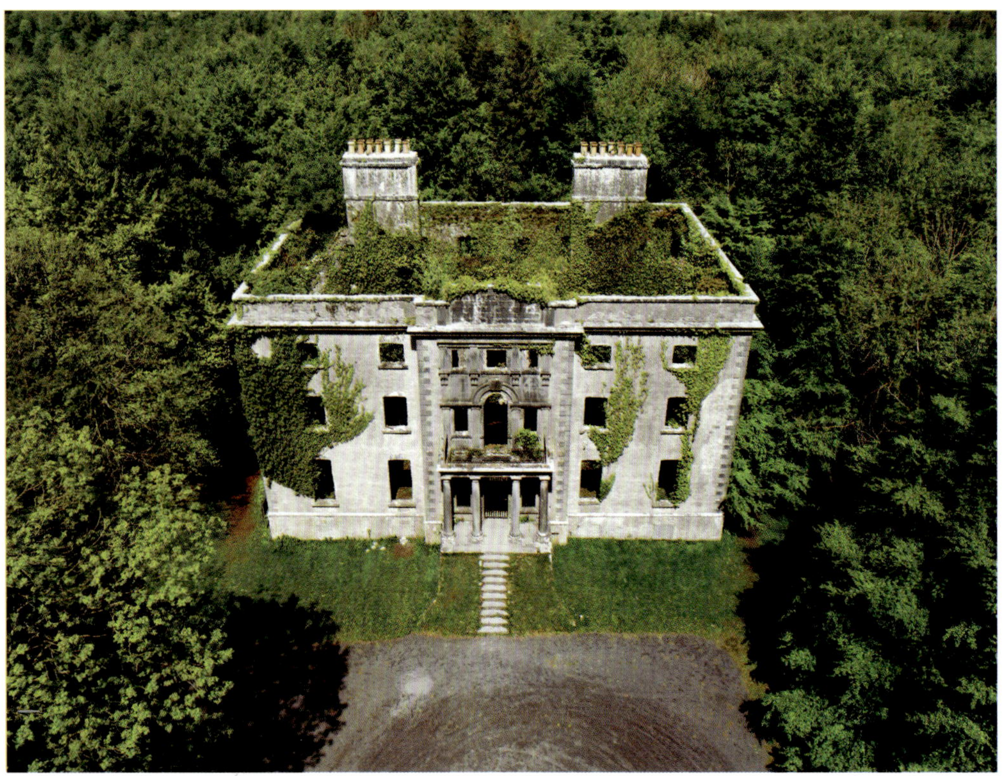

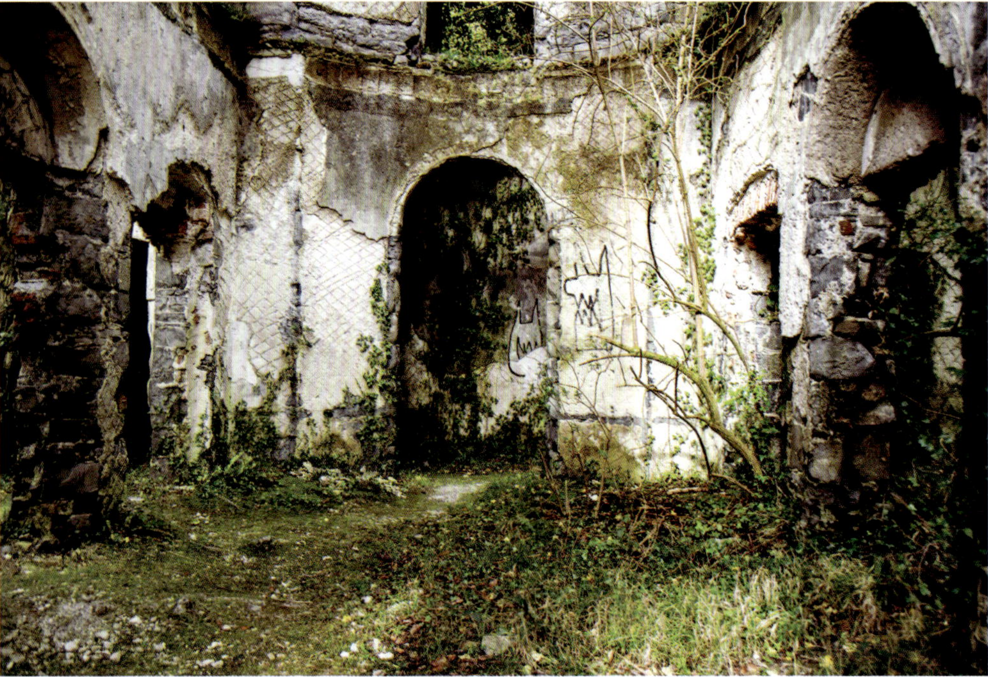

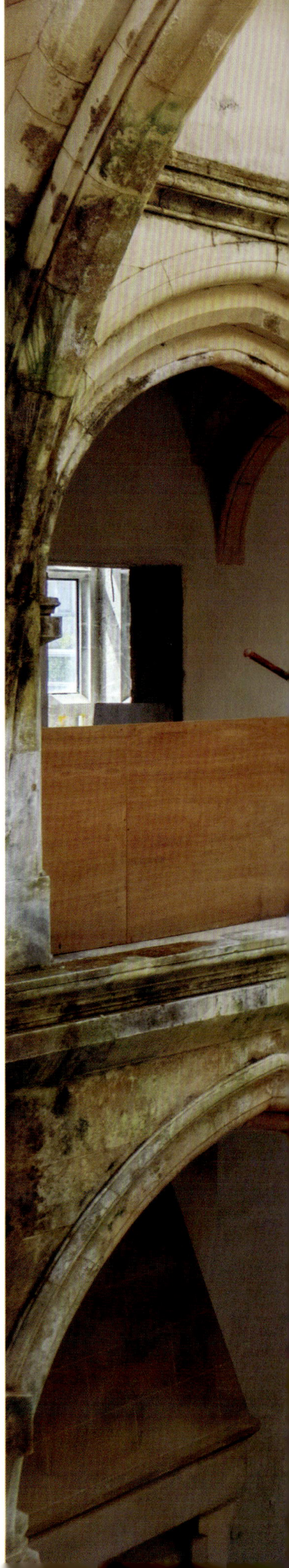

BOTH PHOTOGRAPHS ABOVE:

Moore Hall, County Mayo
This house was built at the end of the 18th century by George Moore, who had made a fortune in Spain in the wine and brandy trade. His descendants continued to live there until it was burned down in 1923 by opponents of the Anglo-Irish Treaty, as the-then owner, Maurice Moore, was pro-Treaty. It was designed by John Roberts, who was also the architect for Tyrone House in County Galway, as well as Waterford Cathedral. It stands in the limestone karst landscape of County Mayo, which provides the conditions for various exotic plants to grow.

RIGHT:

Puxley Manor, County Cork
Sitting next to the 15th-century ruins of Dunboy Castle, Puxley Manor was itself set alight by the IRA in the 1920s. It had been built in the 19th century as the home of the Puxley family, whose success came from local copper mines. However, when Henry Puxley's wife died in childbirth, he left, never to return.

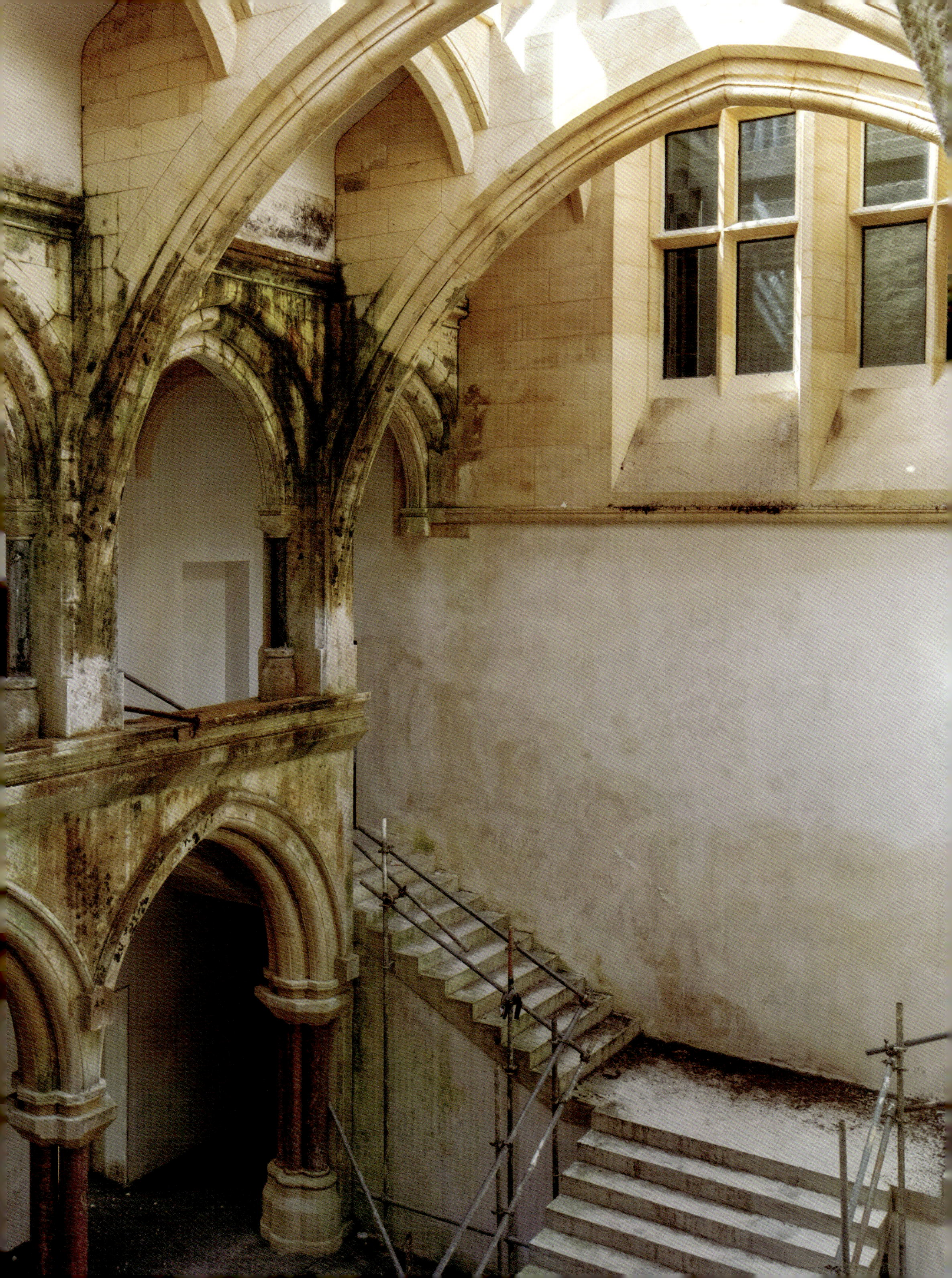

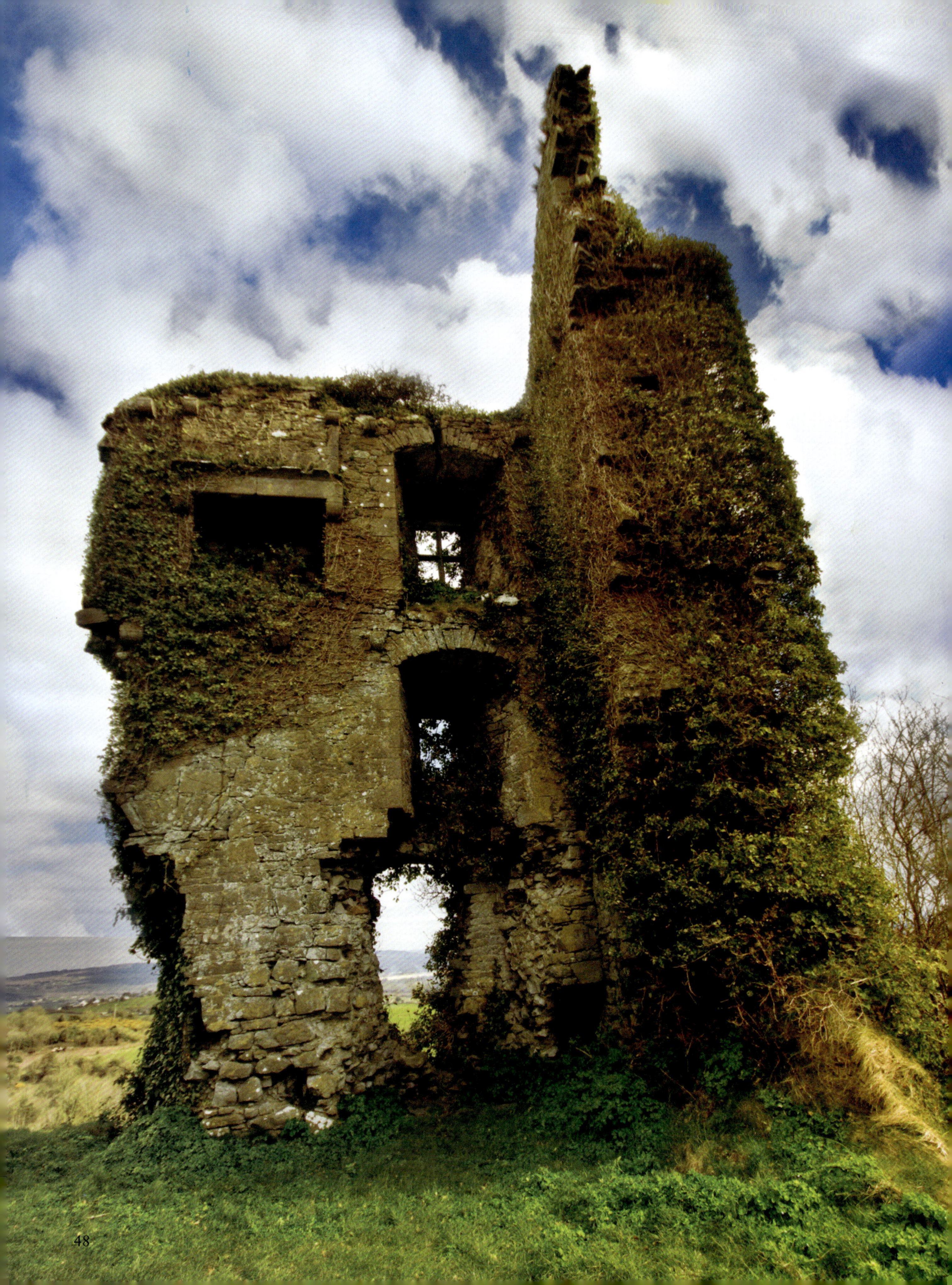

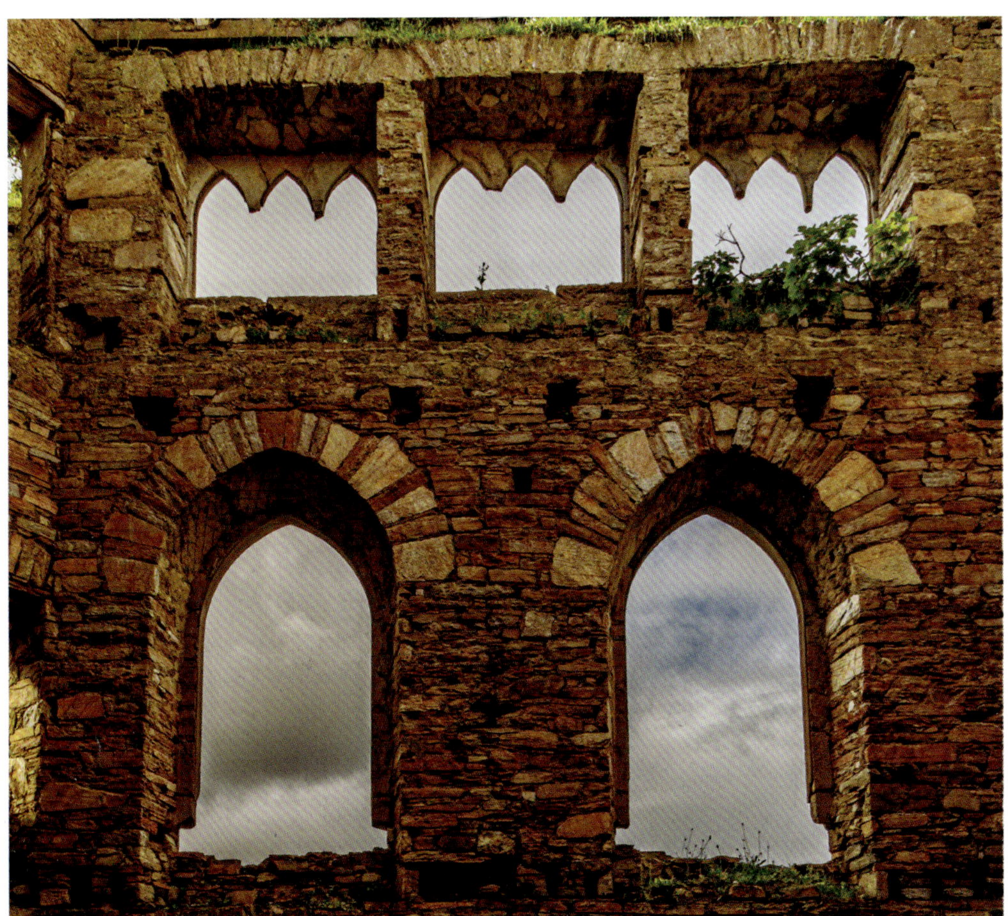

Carrigogunnell Castle, County Limerick
This 15th-century castle is on an outcrop overlooking the River Shannon. It was destroyed in 1691 when supporters of William III were attempting to take Limerick from those loyal to James II. According to pre-castle legend, a hag would light a candle on the rock every night, and, by morning, anyone who looked at it would be dead.

LEFT & BELOW:
Clifden Castle, County Galway
Built for landowner John D'Arcy in 1818, this Gothic Revival-style house suffered when the Great Famine struck, and many tenants could not pay their rent or emigrated. The D'Arcys went bankrupt. In the 20th century, the house was leased to joint tenants who stripped it of its remaining valuable assets.

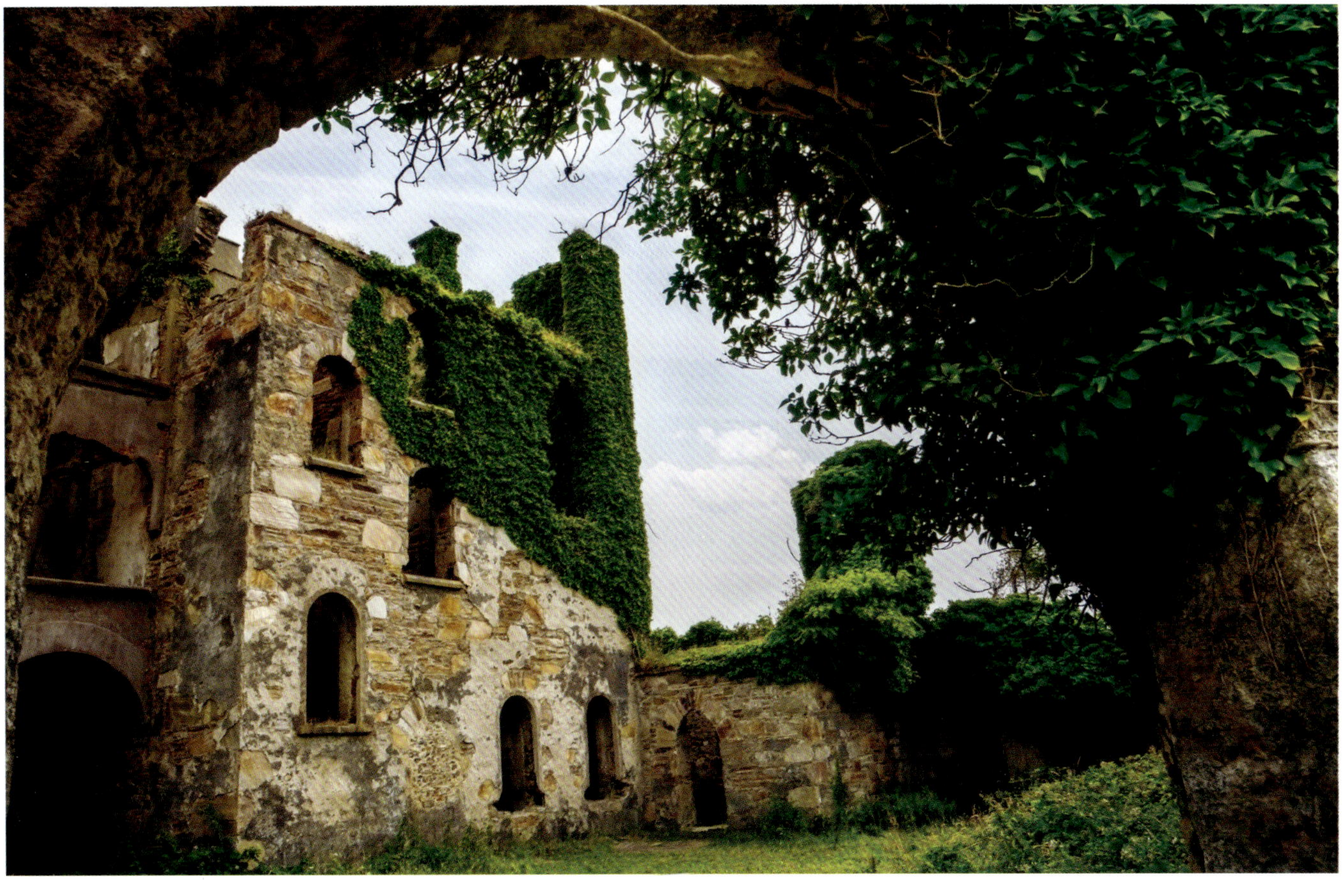

Monea Castle,
County Fermanagh
Completed in 1619, Monea
Castle is a plantation castle, built
as Britain colonized Ireland.
It was taken by the Irish in a
battle in 1641 but its demise is
connected to a fire that swept
through it in the 18th century.
A working farm now surrounds
the remains of the castle and
livestock graze around it.

Dunguaire Castle,
County Galway
A 16th-century tower house
overlooking Galway Bay, the
castle was built by the O'Hynes
clan and later passed to the
Martyns. In 1924 it was bought
by literary figure and surgeon
Oliver St John Gogarty, who
hosted the likes of W.B. Yeats
and George Bernard Shaw at
Dunguaire. It is said to be the most
photographed castle in Ireland.

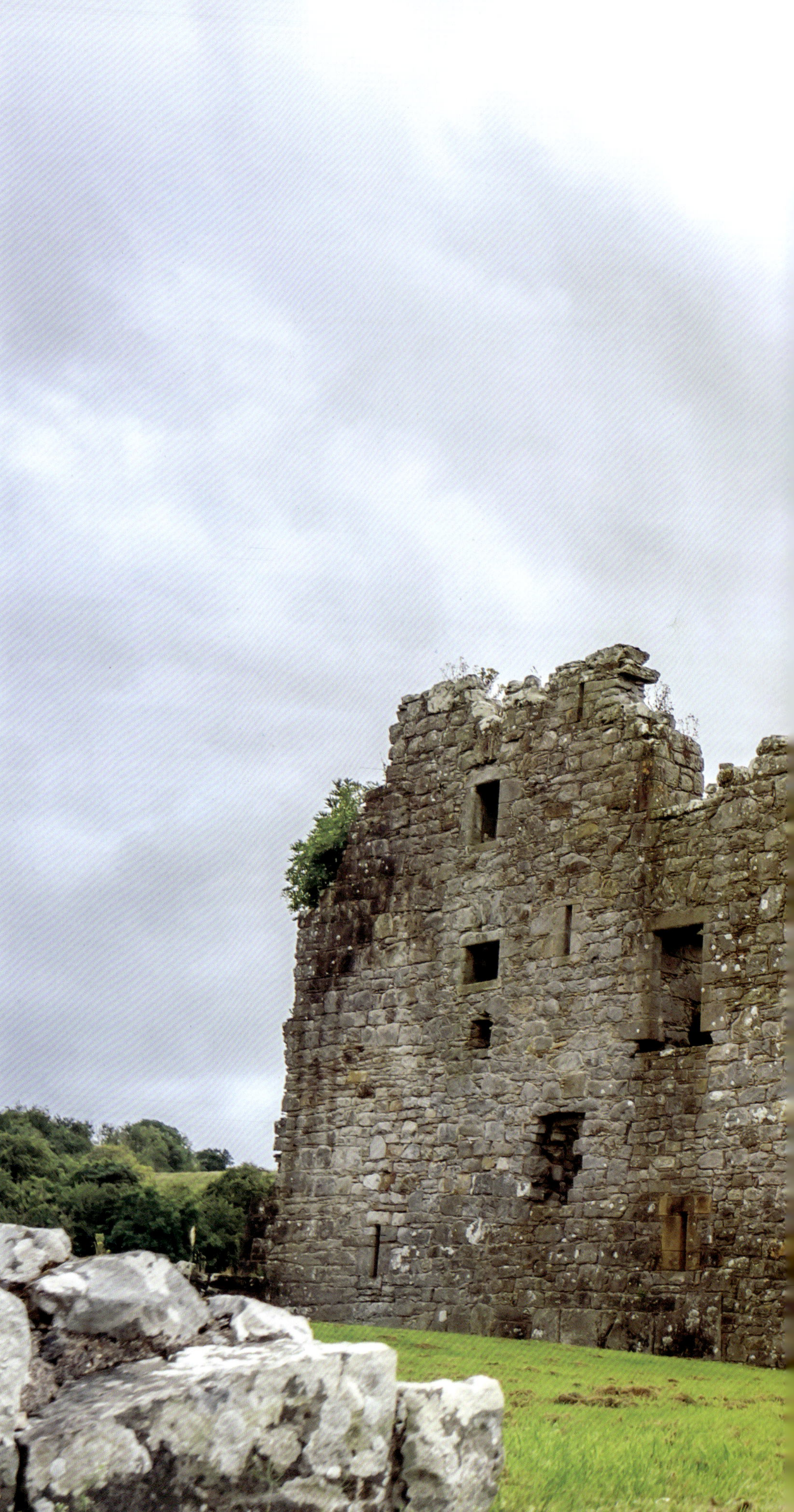

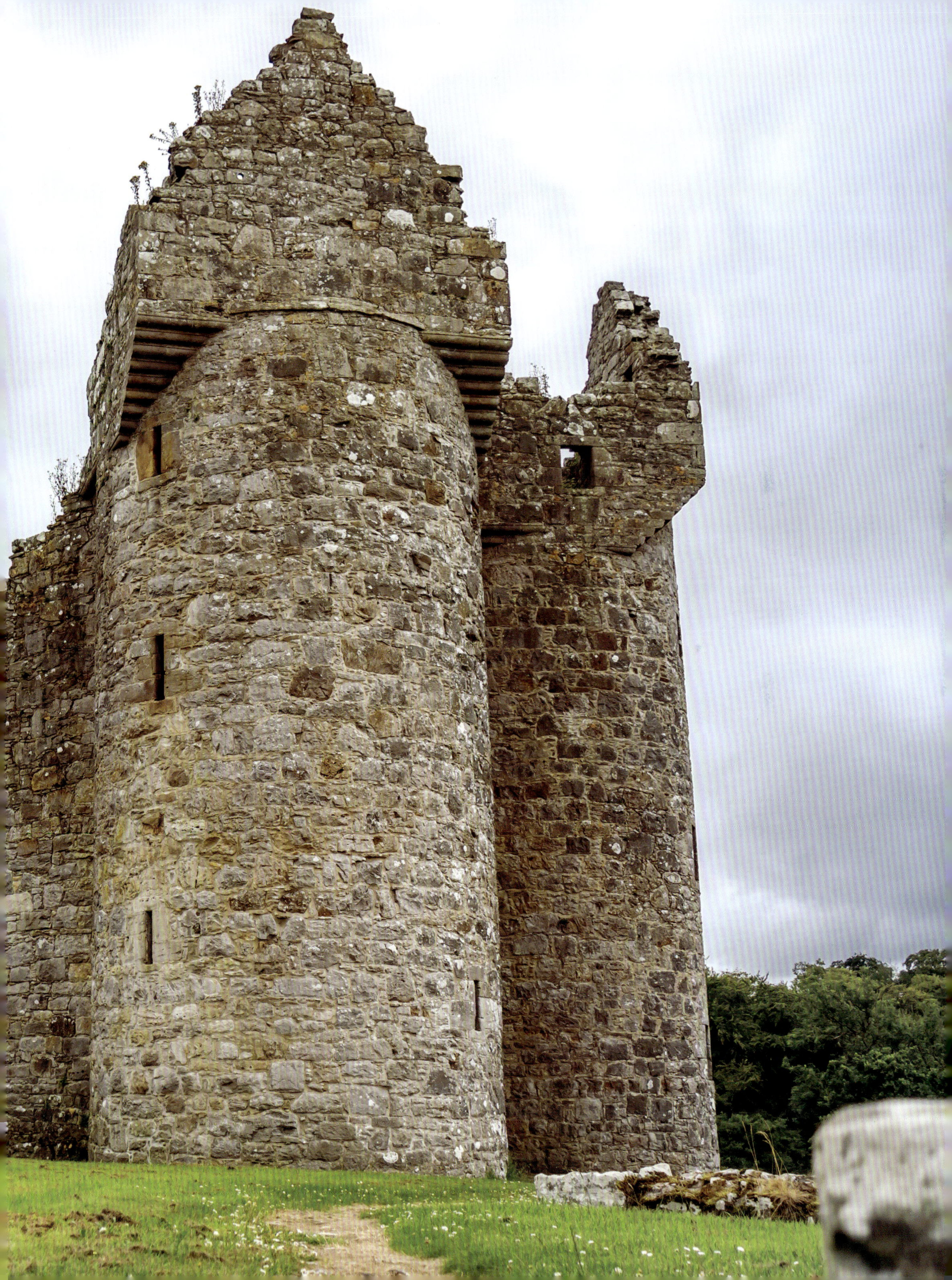

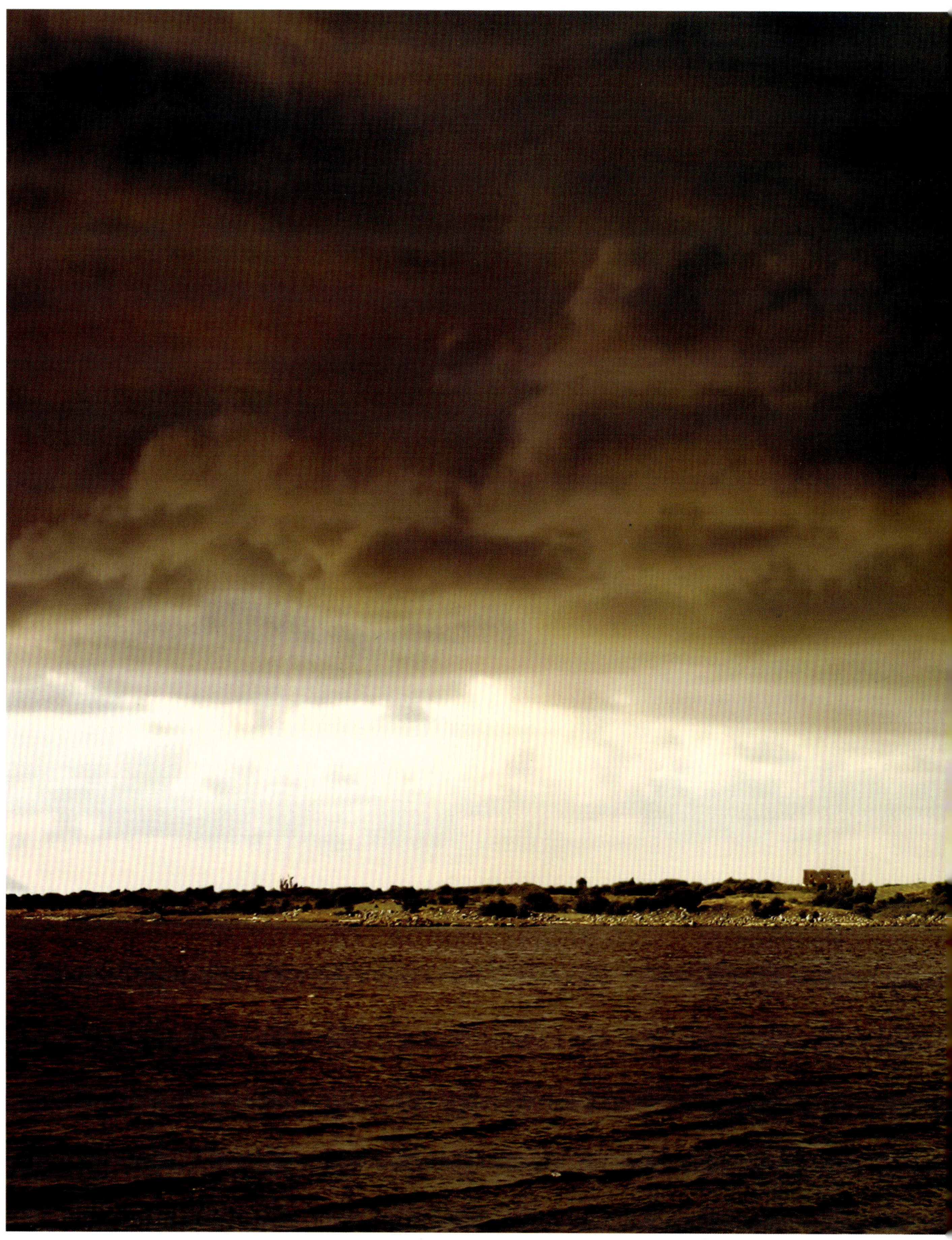

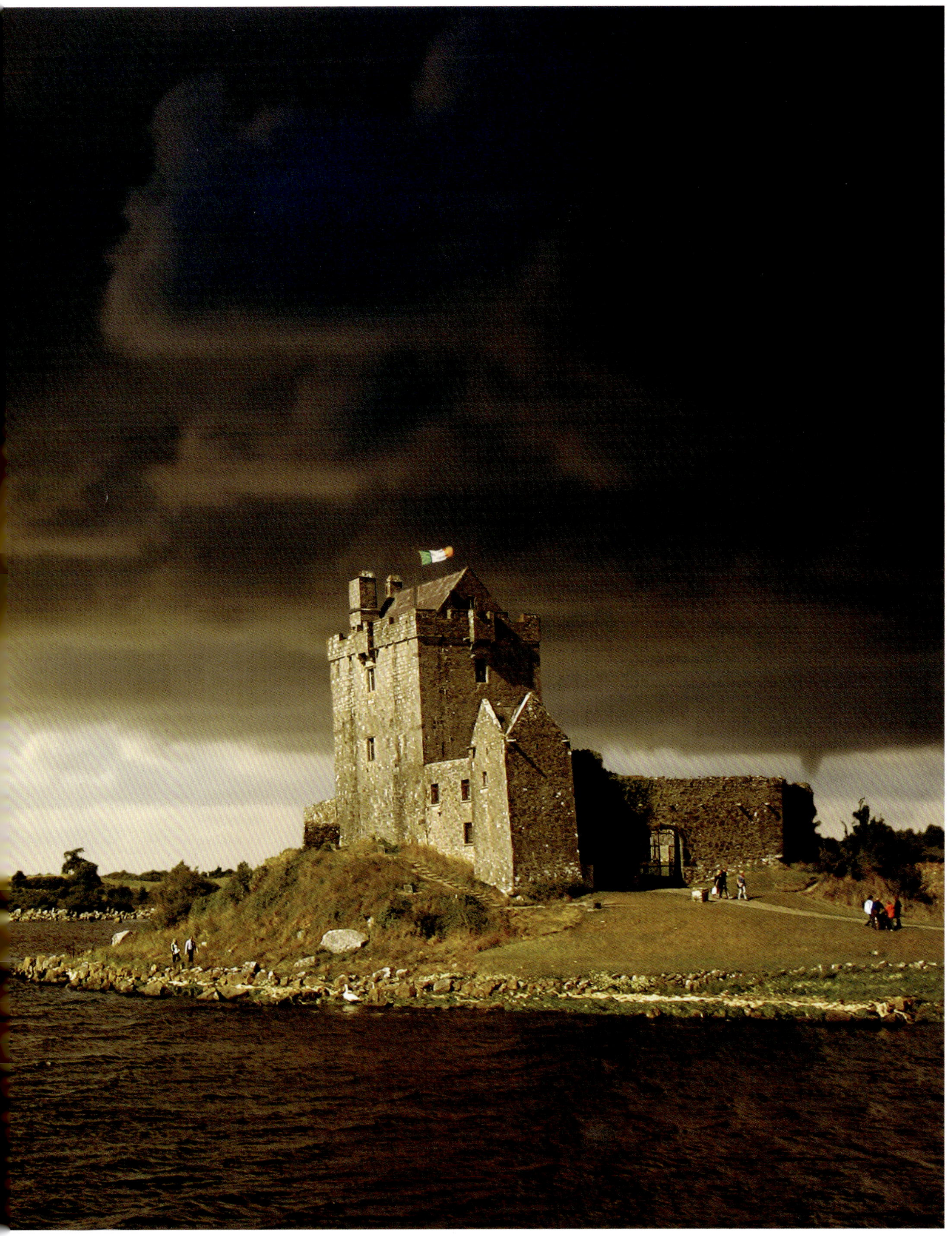

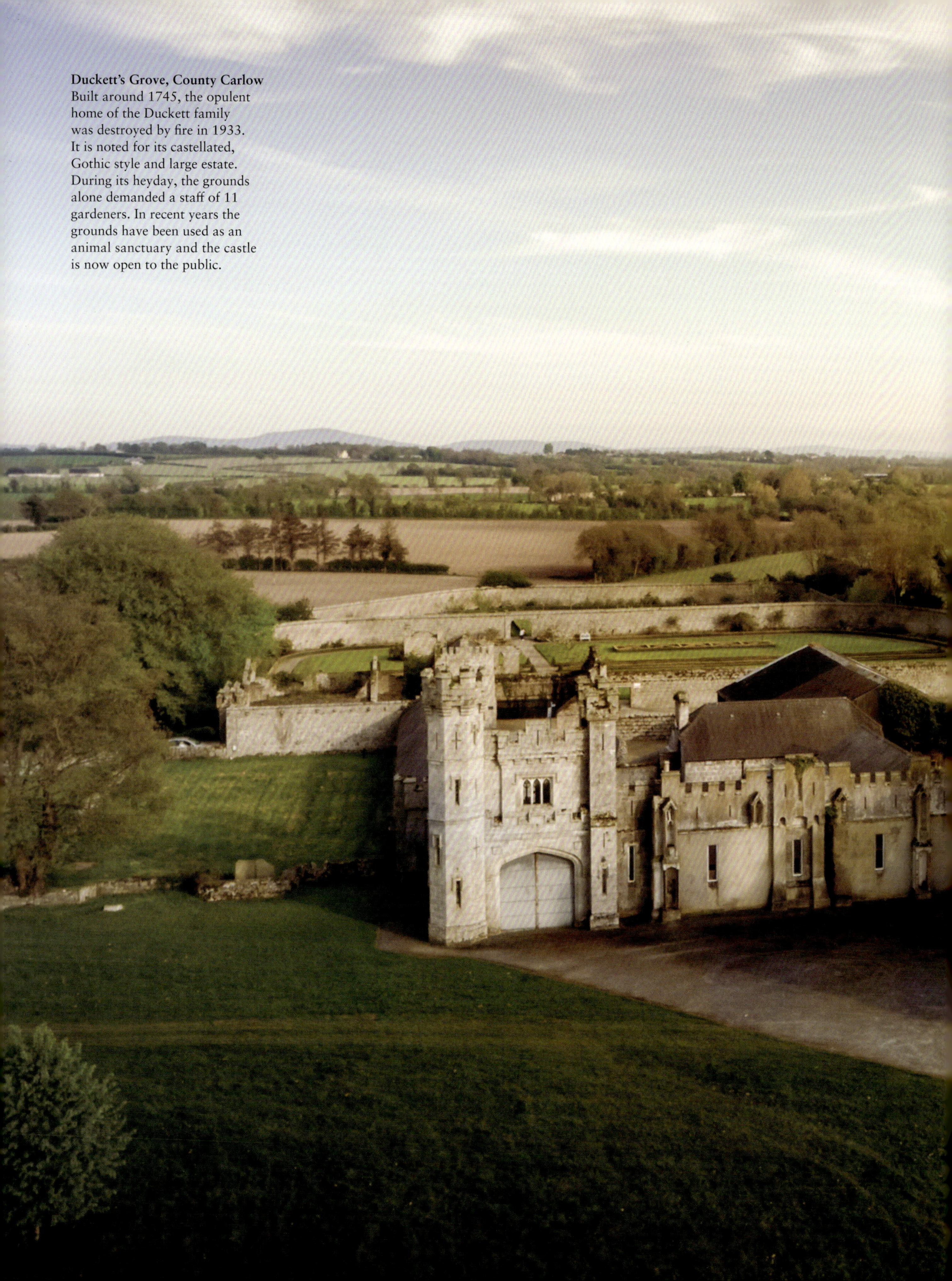

Duckett's Grove, County Carlow
Built around 1745, the opulent
home of the Duckett family
was destroyed by fire in 1933.
It is noted for its castellated,
Gothic style and large estate.
During its heyday, the grounds
alone demanded a staff of 11
gardeners. In recent years the
grounds have been used as an
animal sanctuary and the castle
is now open to the public.

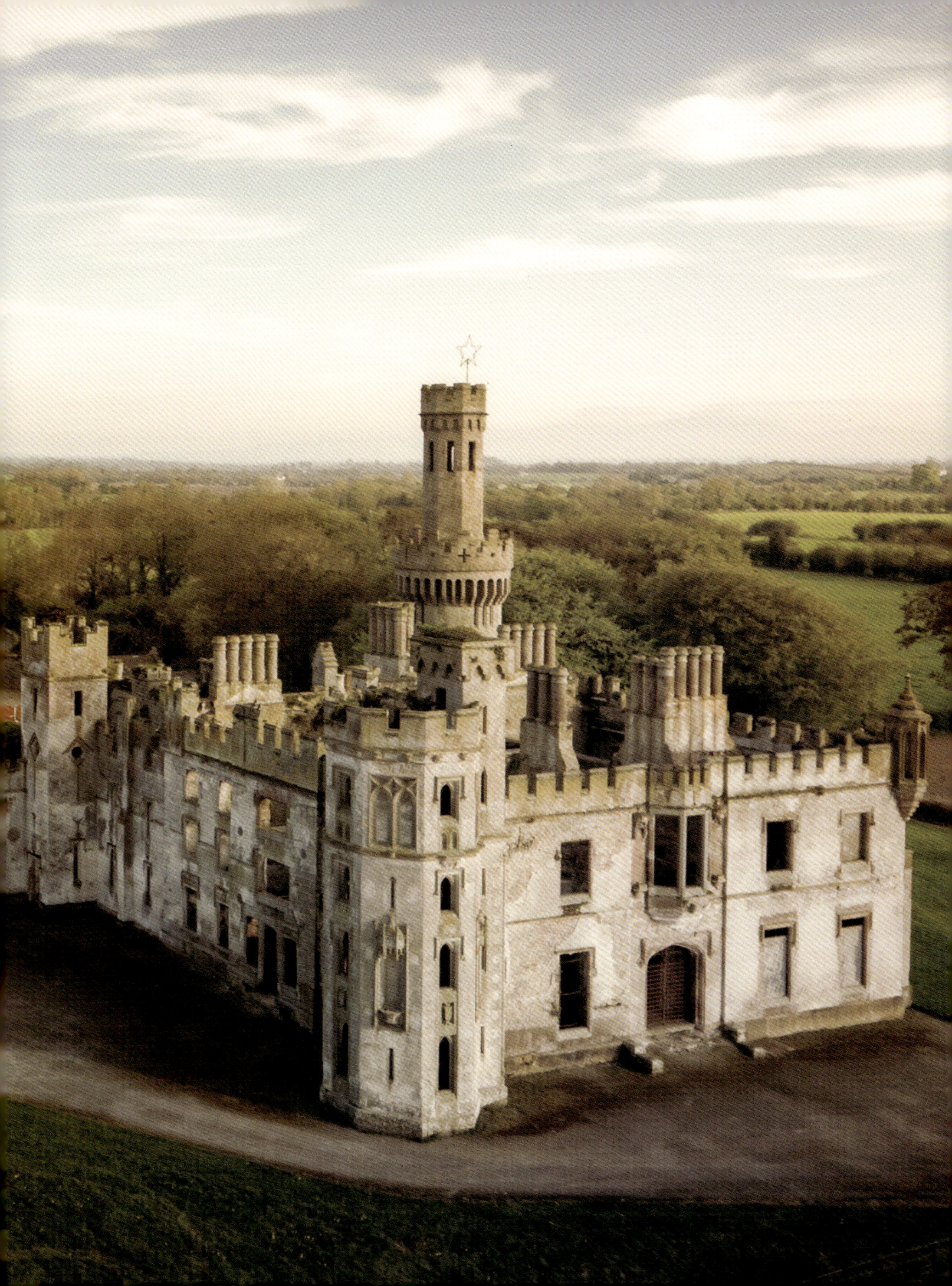

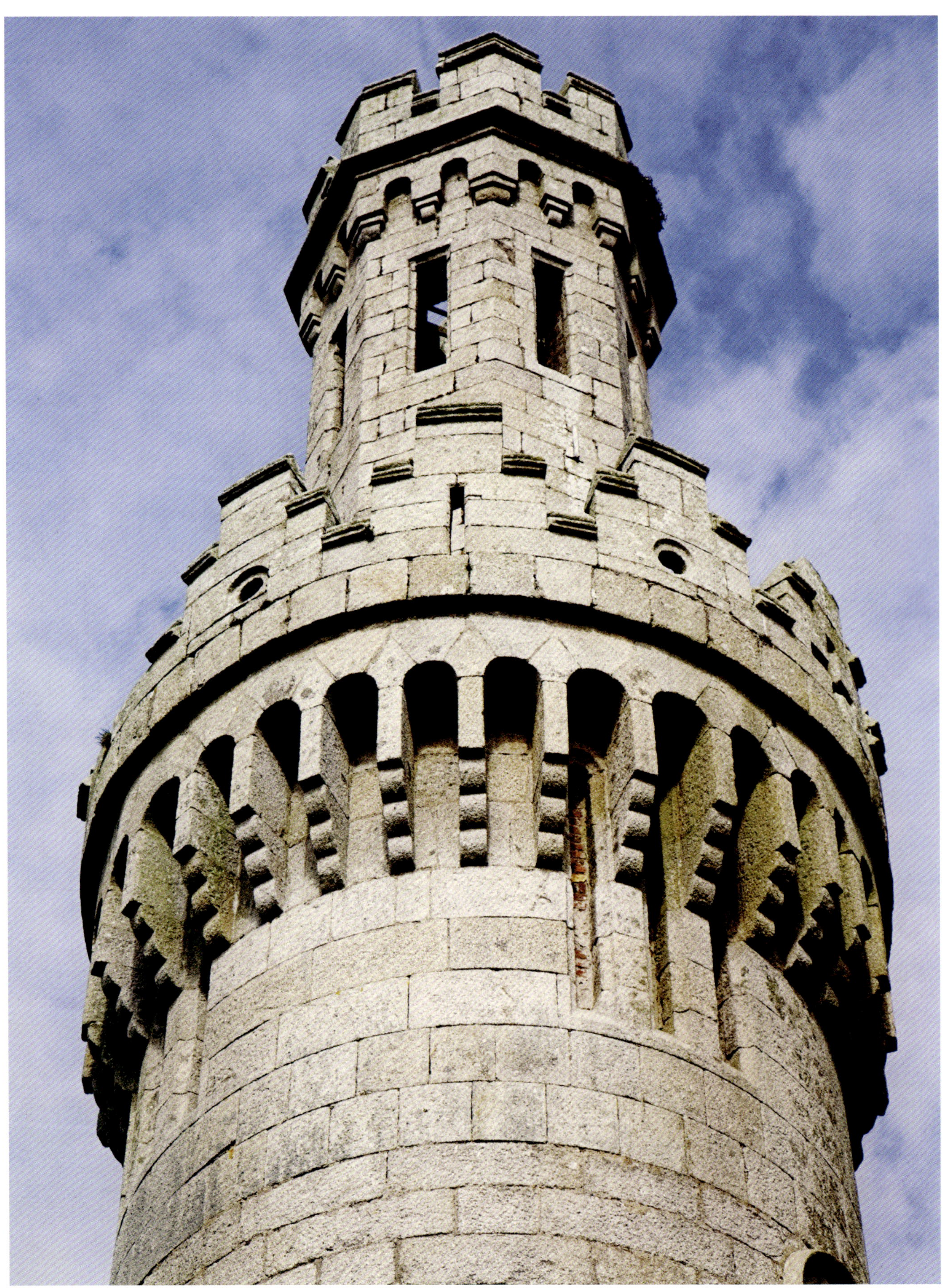

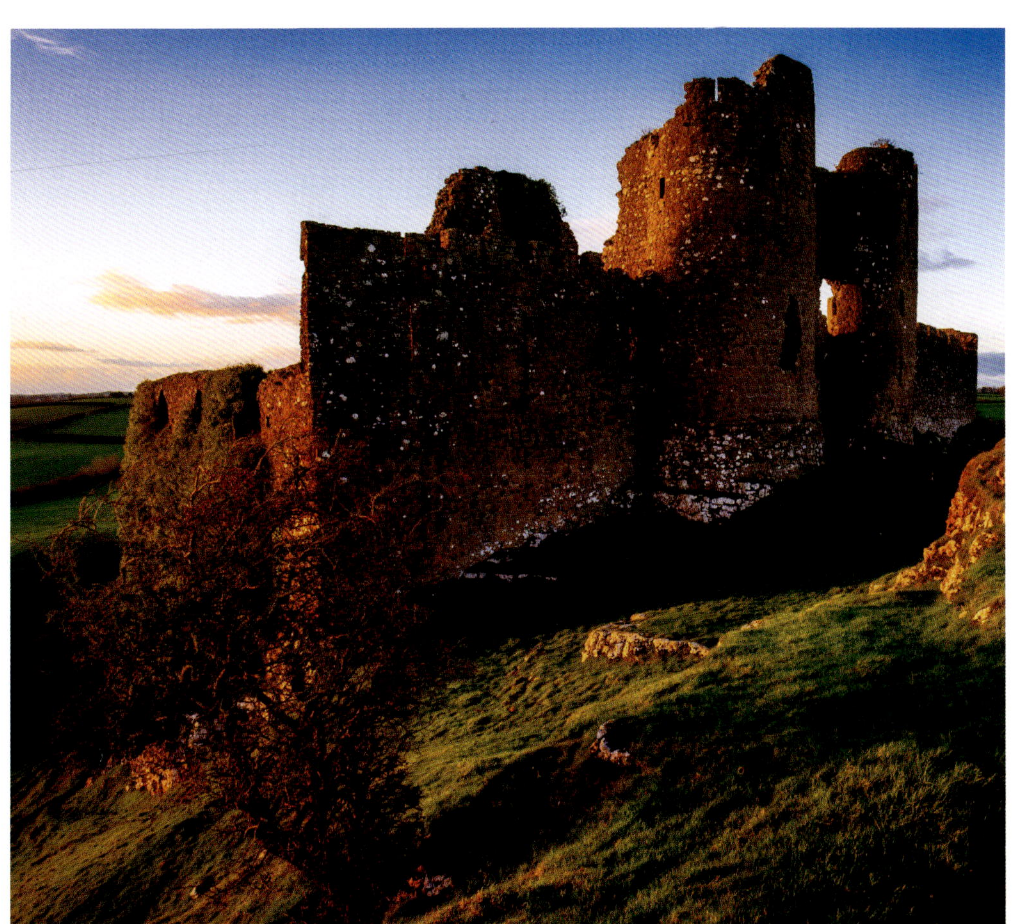

Duckett's Grove, County Carlow
The octagonal, granite viewing tower is the most recognizable feature of Duckett's Grove, and the house's first owner, John Duckett, would often spend time at the top of it, from where he could survey his walled gardens and the thousands of acres in the estate. Some of the original staircase to it still exists.

LEFT:

Roche Castle, County Louth
Standing on a rocky hilltop, this 13th-century Anglo-Norman castle can be viewed for miles around. It was built by Lady Rohesia de Verdun and it is said she promised to marry the architect but that when he went to claim her hand, she had him thrown out of one of the windows, known today as the 'murder window'.

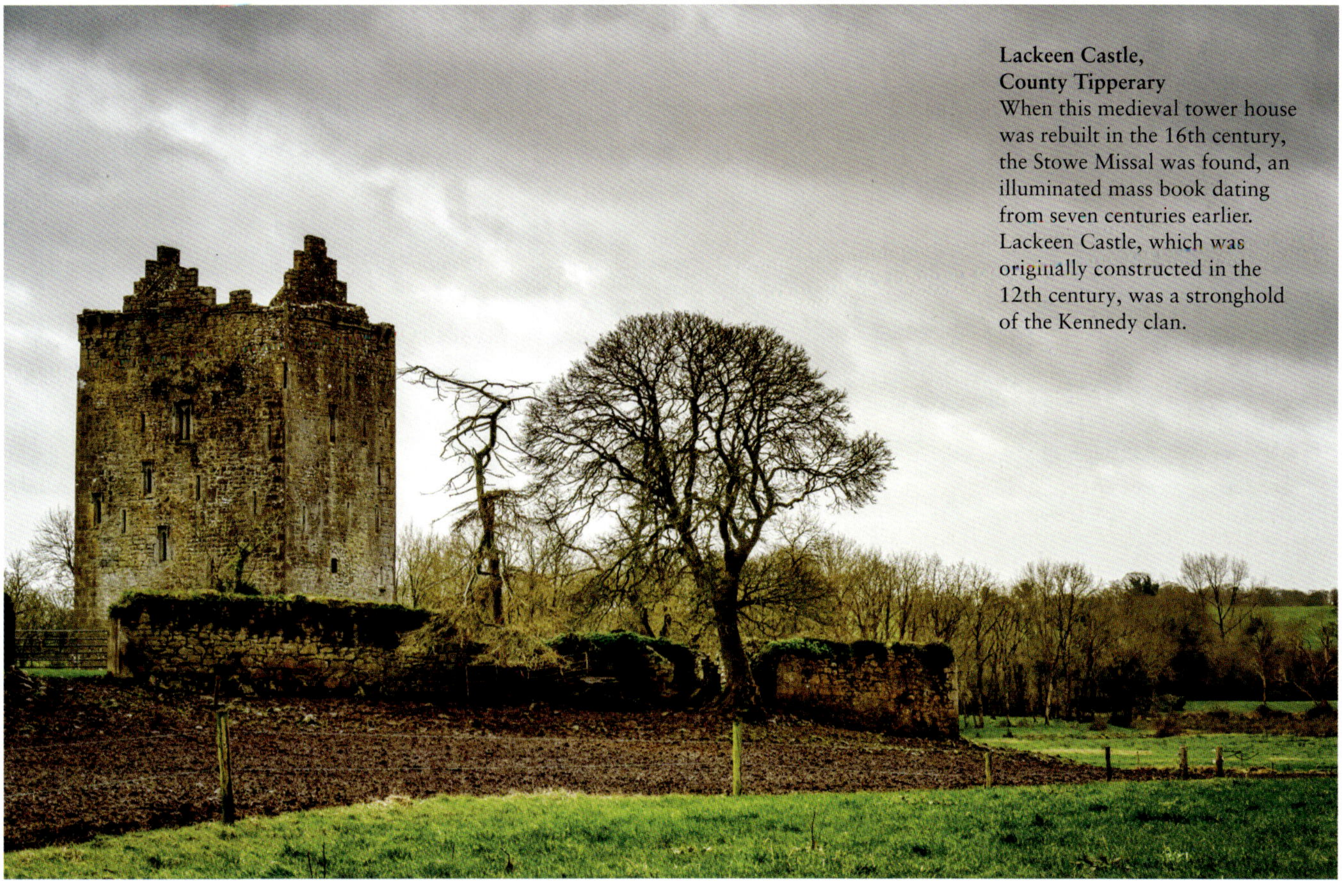

Lackeen Castle, County Tipperary
When this medieval tower house was rebuilt in the 16th century, the Stowe Missal was found, an illuminated mass book dating from seven centuries earlier. Lackeen Castle, which was originally constructed in the 12th century, was a stronghold of the Kennedy clan.

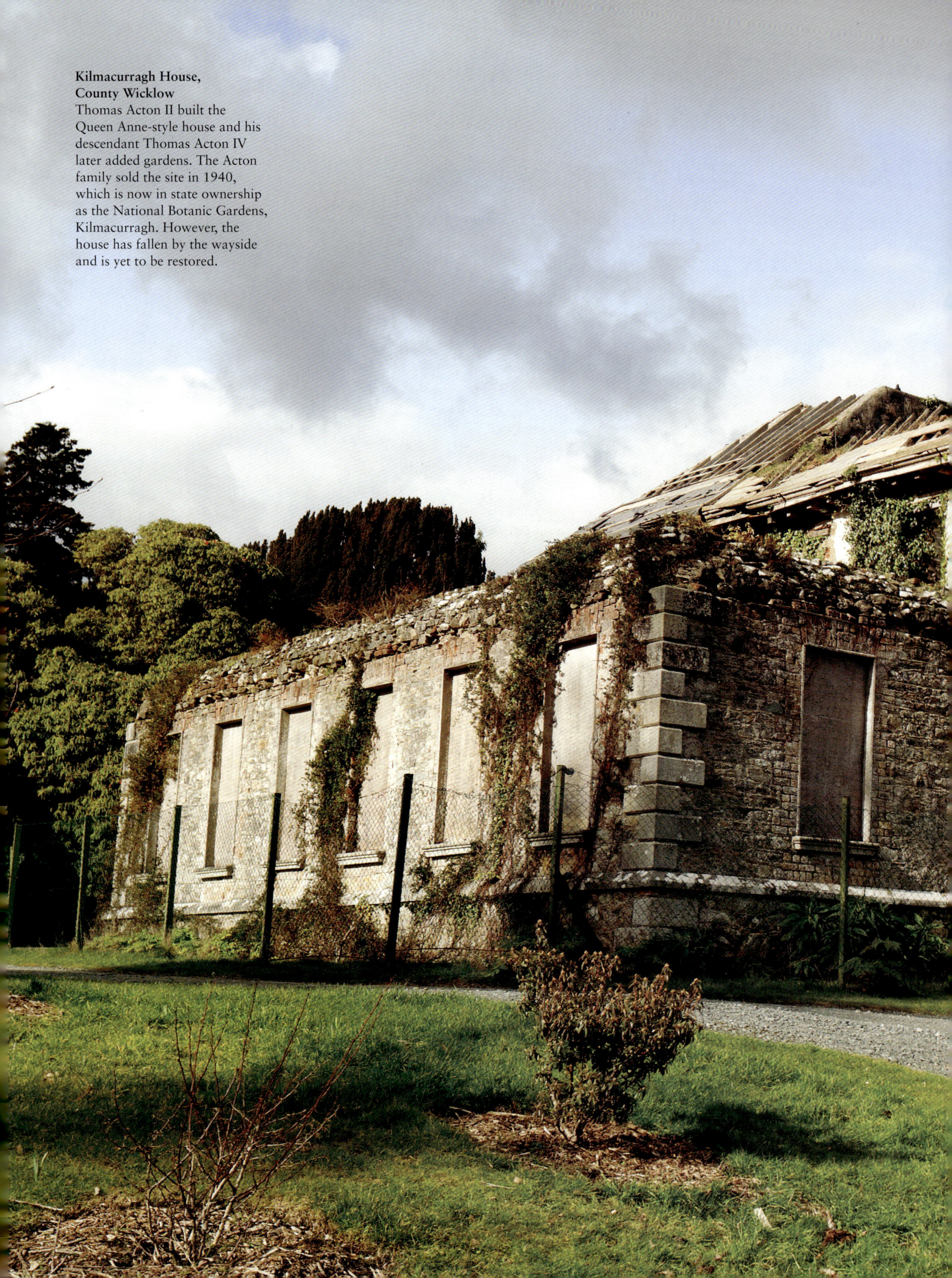

**Kilmacurragh House,
County Wicklow**
Thomas Acton II built the
Queen Anne-style house and his
descendant Thomas Acton IV
later added gardens. The Acton
family sold the site in 1940,
which is now in state ownership
as the National Botanic Gardens,
Kilmacurragh. However, the
house has fallen by the wayside
and is yet to be restored.

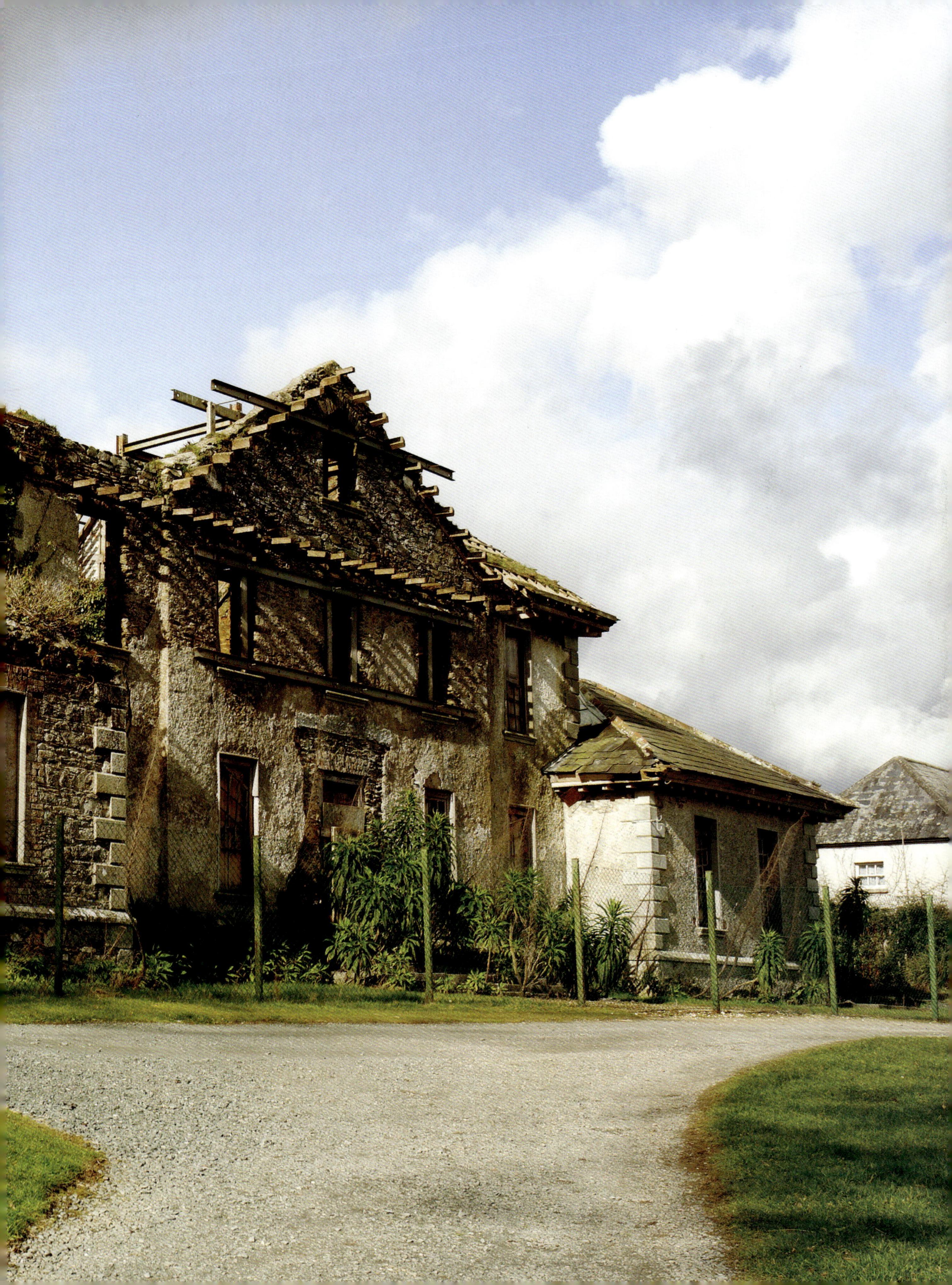

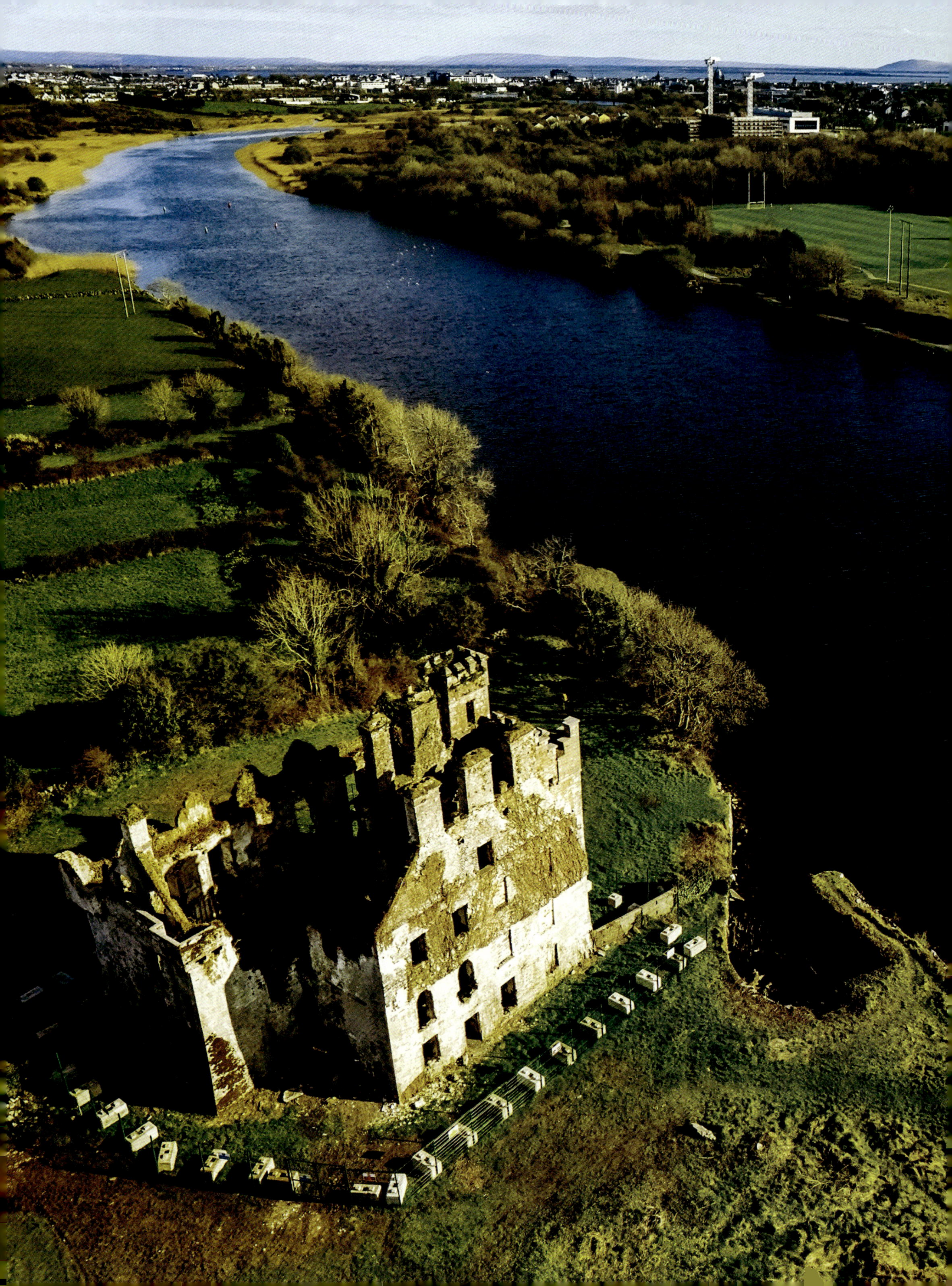

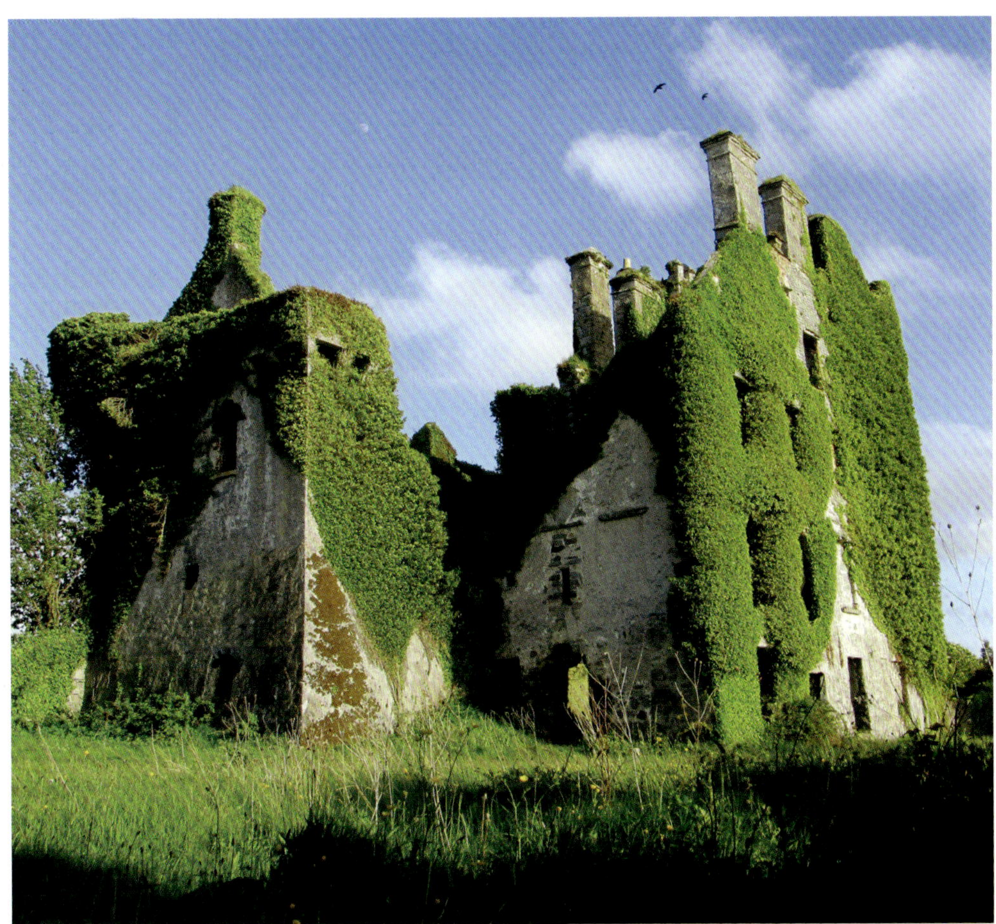

ALL PHOTOGRAPHS:
Menlo Castle, County Galway
Built by the Blake Family in the
16th century, Menlo Castle sits
on the banks of the River Corrib
just outside the city of Galway.
The family lived there until 1910,
when fire ripped through the
castle while Lord and Lady Blake
were away in Dublin. Their
daughter was in the castle at the
time; her body was never found
and she was presumed to have
perished in the fire. The castle
was a ruin after the fire and in
1923 the Land Commission
divided the Blake estate. In 1592
the Blakes had been described as
the richest family in Galway.

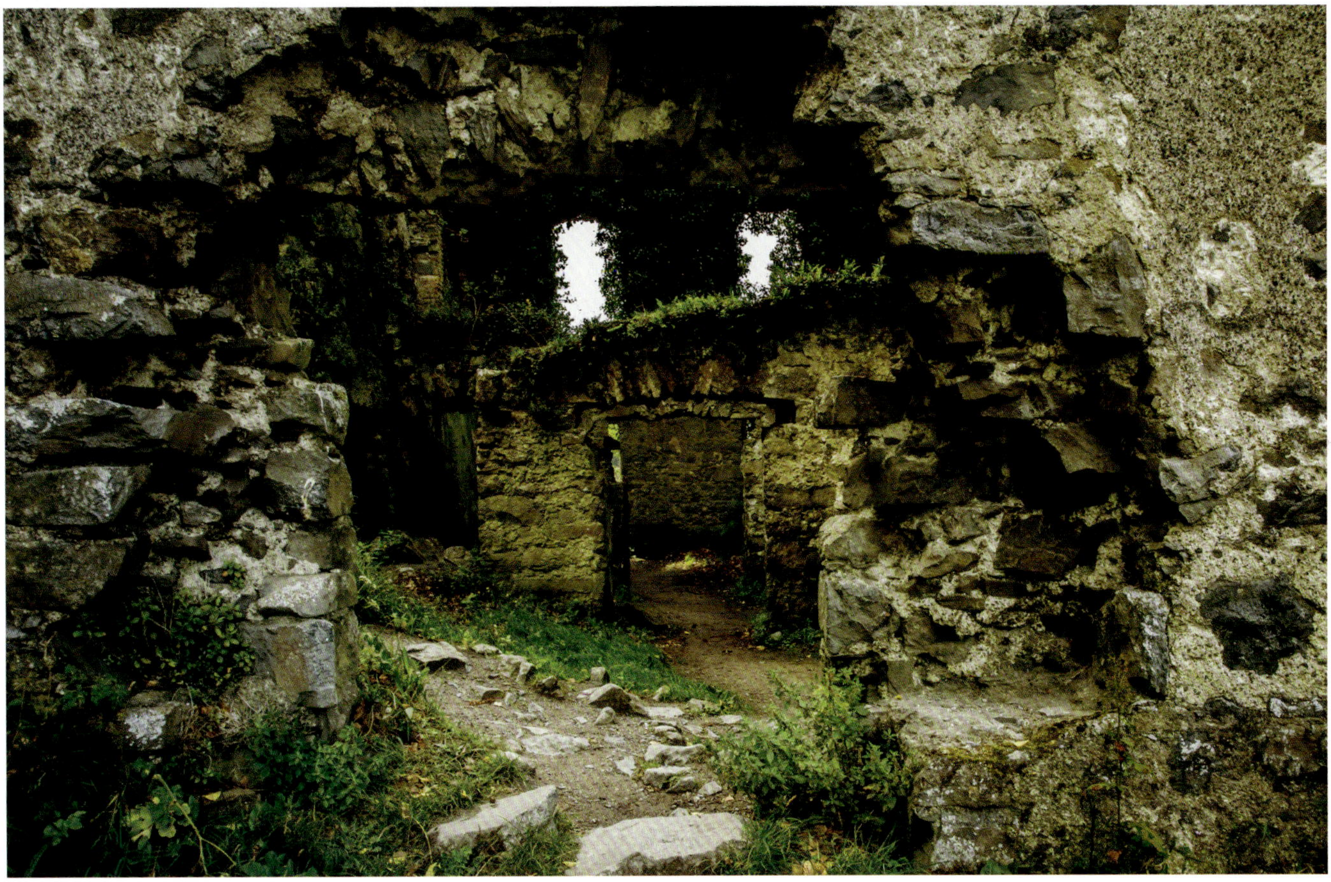

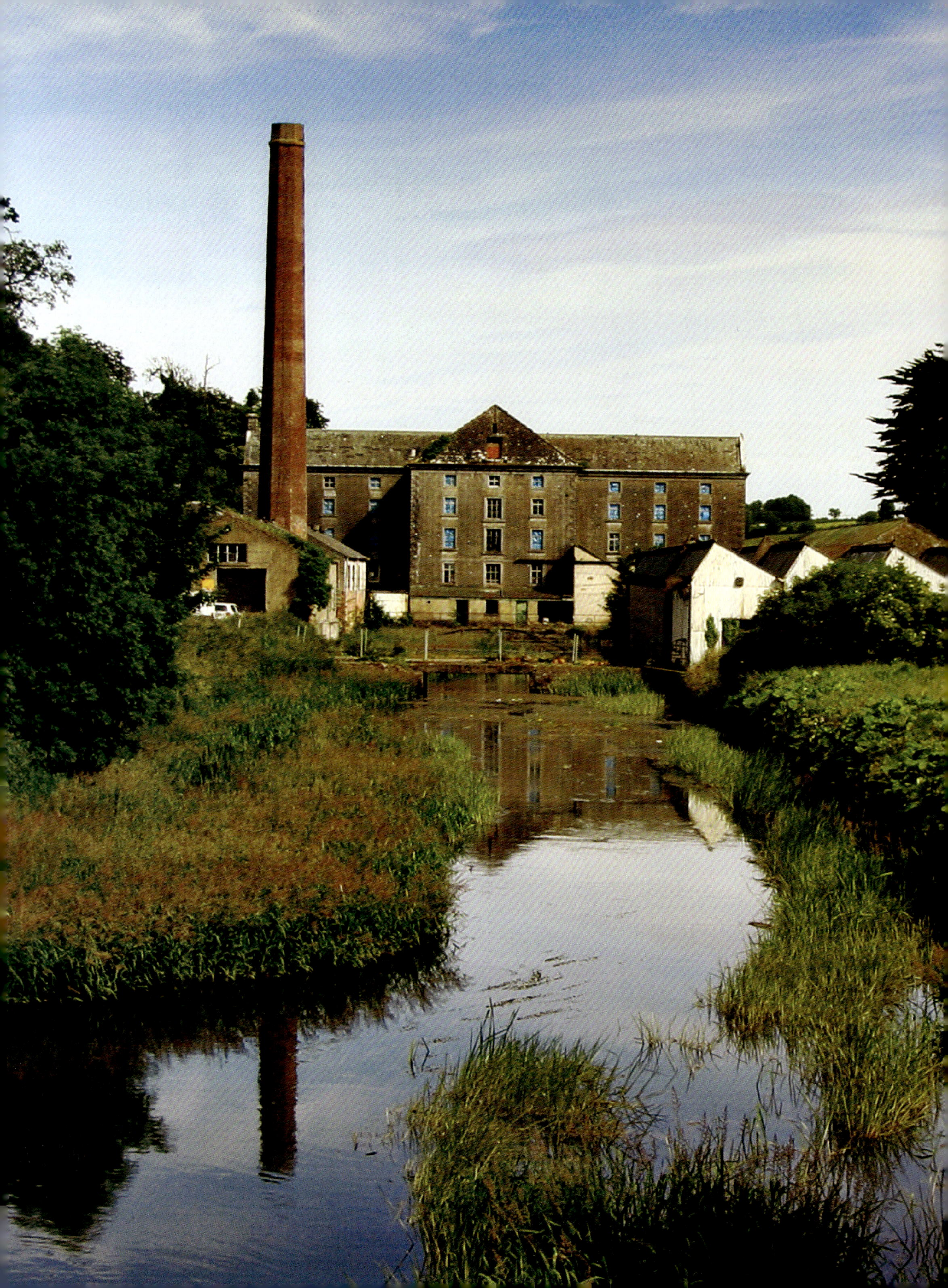

Transport & Industrial

For an island that is often thought of as green and rural, Ireland has a surprising industrial heritage, dating from the earliest mining and milling operations up to its large electricity-generating power plants of the 20th century. Many of the structures that are no longer used have been left to tell of a bygone age, but the adaptability of the Irish people is often also visible, as buildings – frequently mills – have been remodelled for more economically viable operations.

The industrialization of many parts of Ireland during the 19th century is evidenced by the expansion of the rail network – often to the remotest corners – in that golden age of steam. Yet, as elsewhere, changing economic fortunes – and the rise of vehicle ownership – in the 20th century caused many lines and stations to close. Surrounded by water, Ireland still has a thriving maritime industry, but it borders the vast Atlantic Ocean and winds and currents pound its shores, leaving a trail of shipwrecks along the coasts, particularly on the western side.

Whether it be an industrial plant, part of the railway network or a stranded ship, all tell a story of how Ireland has shifted with – and often effected – changing times.

OPPOSITE:
Old Mill, Slane, County Meath
Built in 1766, this was a corn mill powered by two large water wheels. Later it was converted into a textile mill. In the early 1900s, it briefly served as a hotel stop for passengers on pleasure steamers. Standing on the River Boyne, when first built it was the largest flour mill in Ireland.

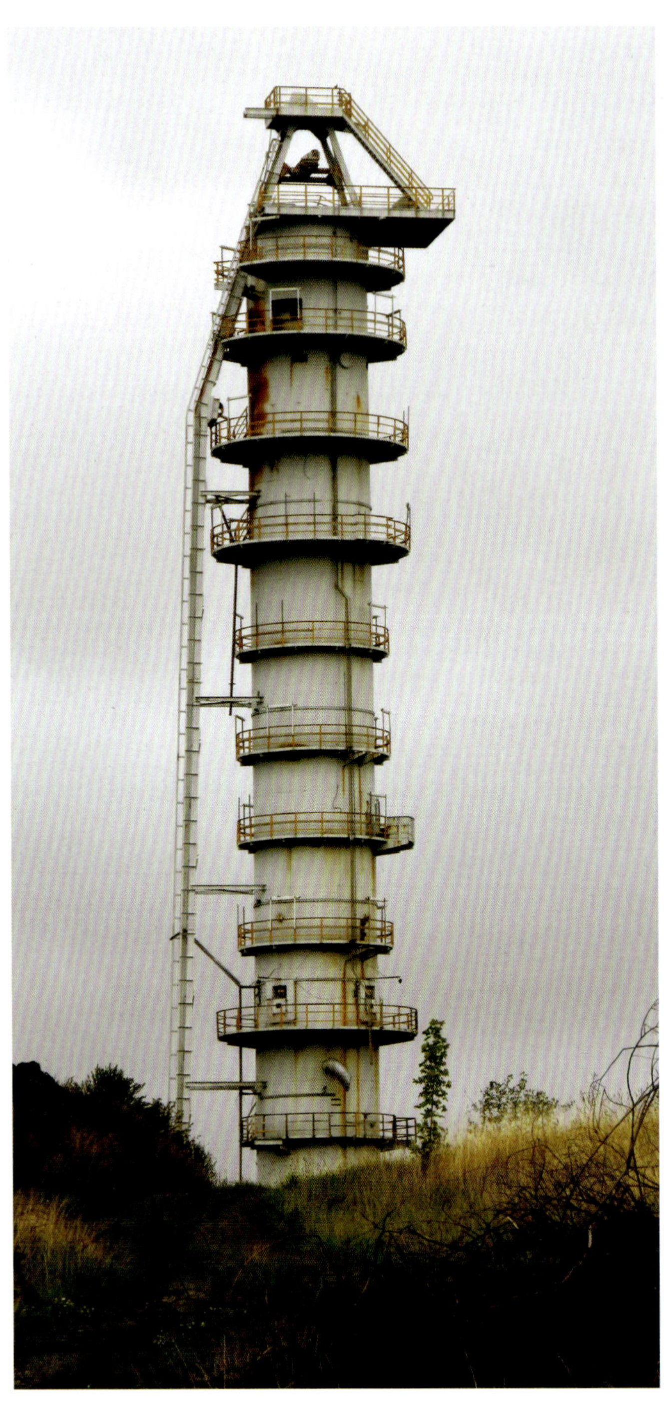

Carlow Sugar Factory, County Carlow
This tower was part of the Carlow Sugar Factory, which closed in 2005 after operating for 79 years. The factory processed local sugar beet and was the first sugar factory in the new Irish Free State. Such was the factory's dominance in Carlow that the sugar industry employed up to 1000 people there at one point.

Allihies Copper Mine, County Cork
In 1812 a rich copper deposit was found on the remote Beara Peninsula, resulting in the biggest copper mining enterprise in Ireland, established by the Puxley family. The miners would dig so deep they tunnelled below sea level, and the ore was shipped to Swansea for smelting. Mining ceased in 1884 and further attempts in the 20th century proved unviable.

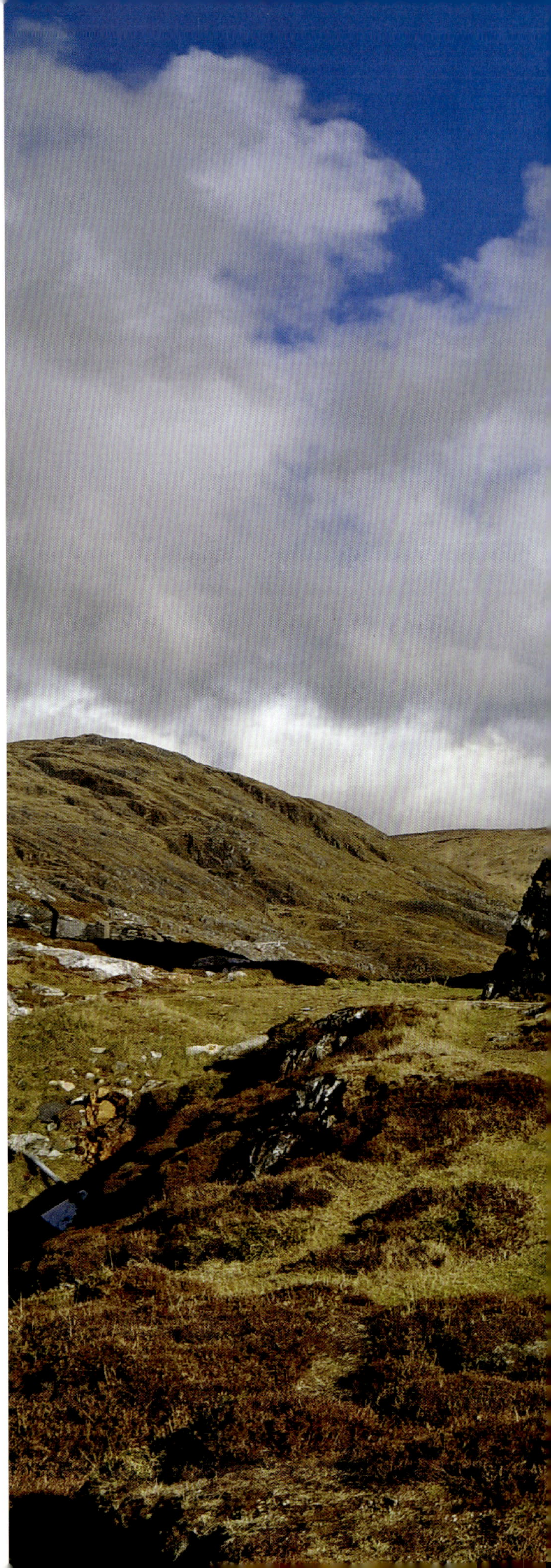

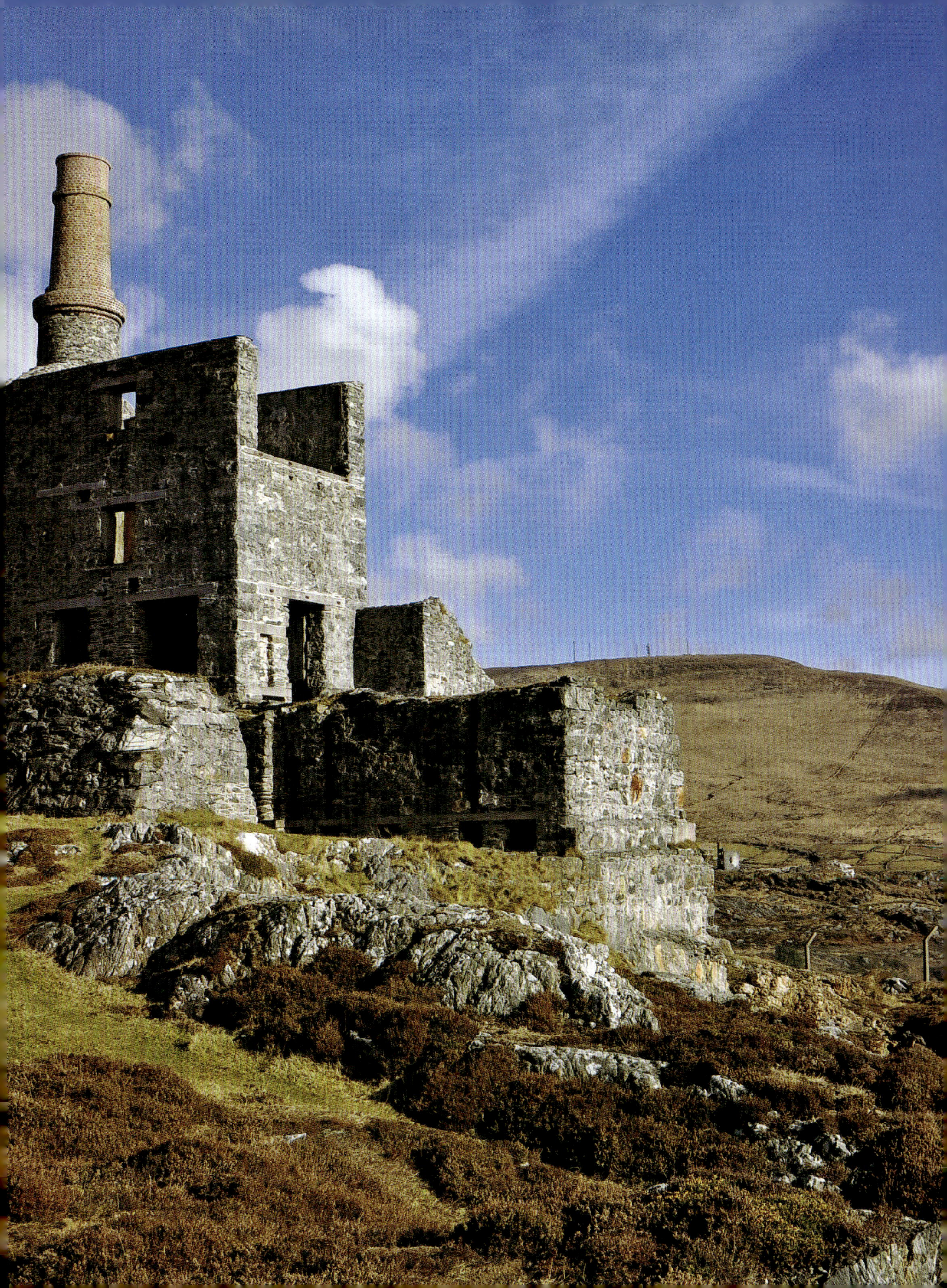

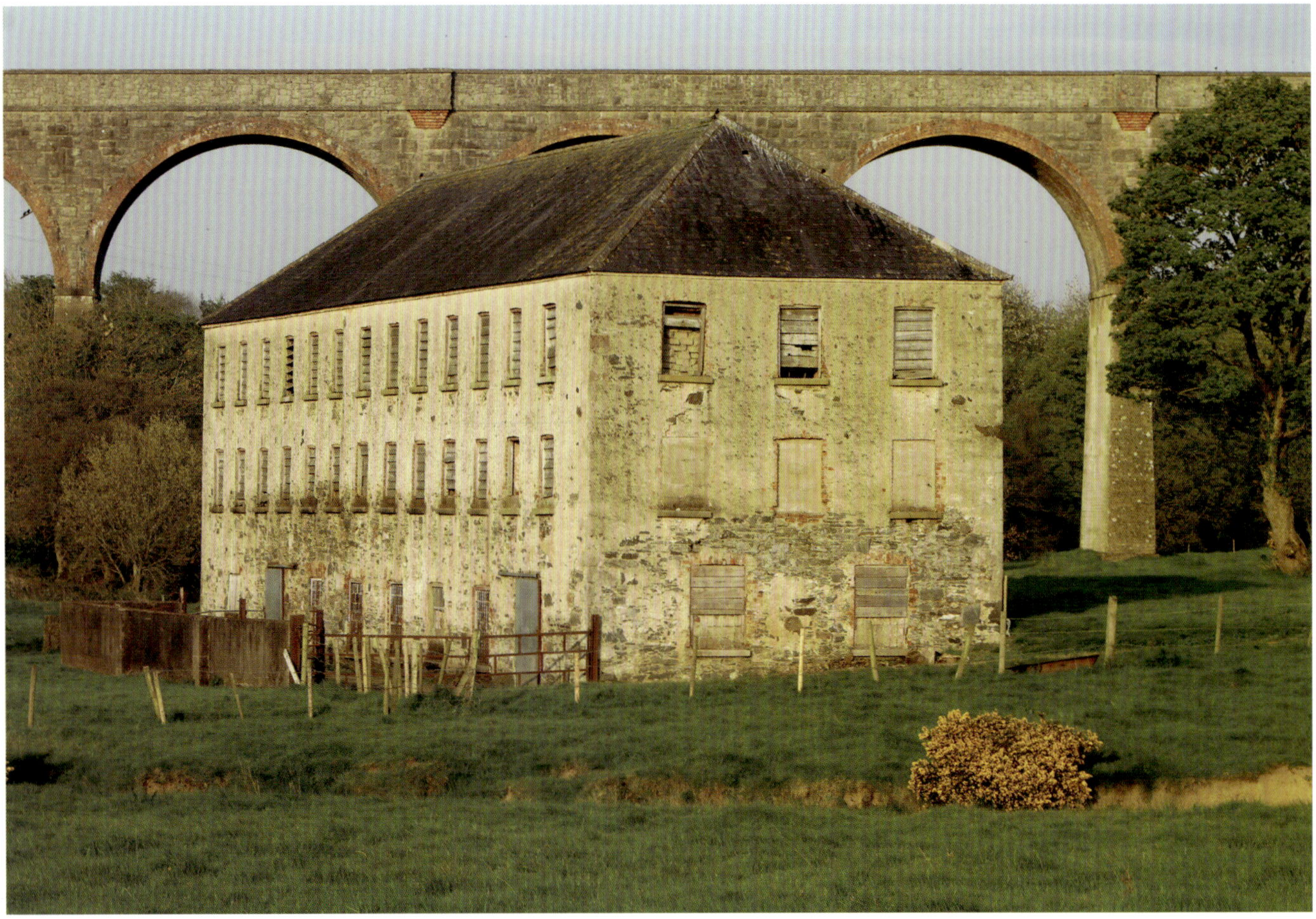

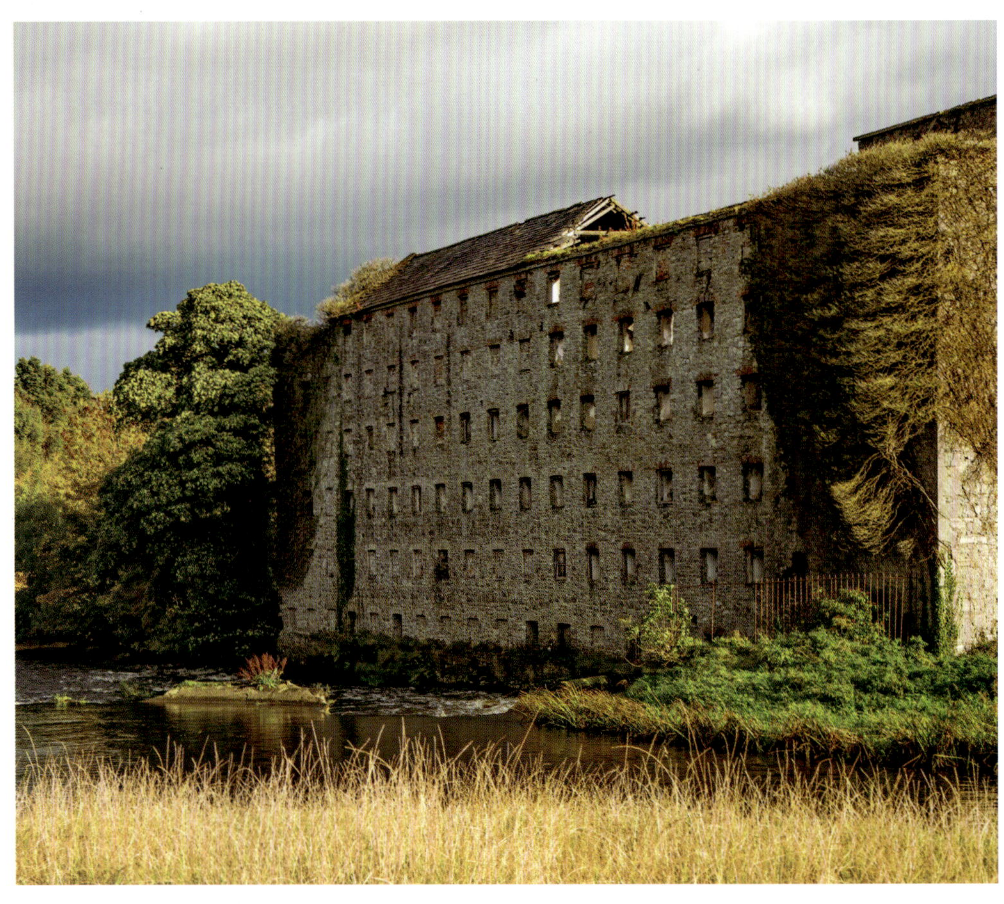

Tassagh Beetling Mill and Viaduct, County Armagh
The River Callan powered the machinery in this beetling mill, which completed the final stages of the linen-making process before steam power and electricity. The railway viaduct over the river was built in 1910.

RIGHT:

Blackwater Mill, Navan, County Meath
This 18th-century, six-storey corn mill was powered by a large water wheel, driven by the River Blackwater, a tributary of the Boyne. A failed attempt was made to frame one of the mill's early owners, John Fay, for the murder of a magistrate.

OPPOSITE:

Bolands Flour Mills, Dublin
The 19th-century Bolands buildings overlook Dublin's Grand Canal Dock. During the 1916 Easter Rising, rebel forces occupied them. Google bought them in 2018, with plans to develop a residential, business and retail complex.

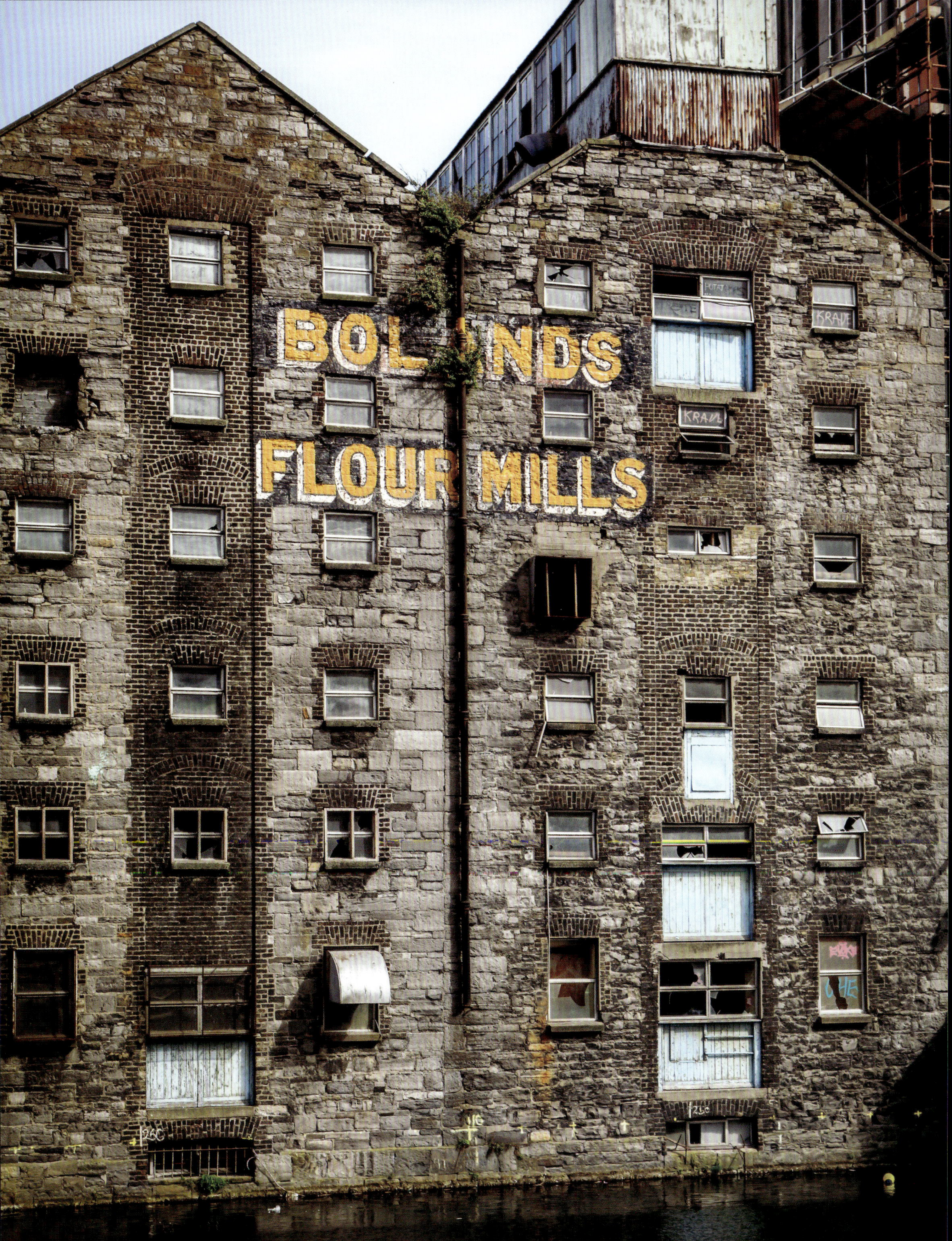

BOLANDS
FLOUR MILLS

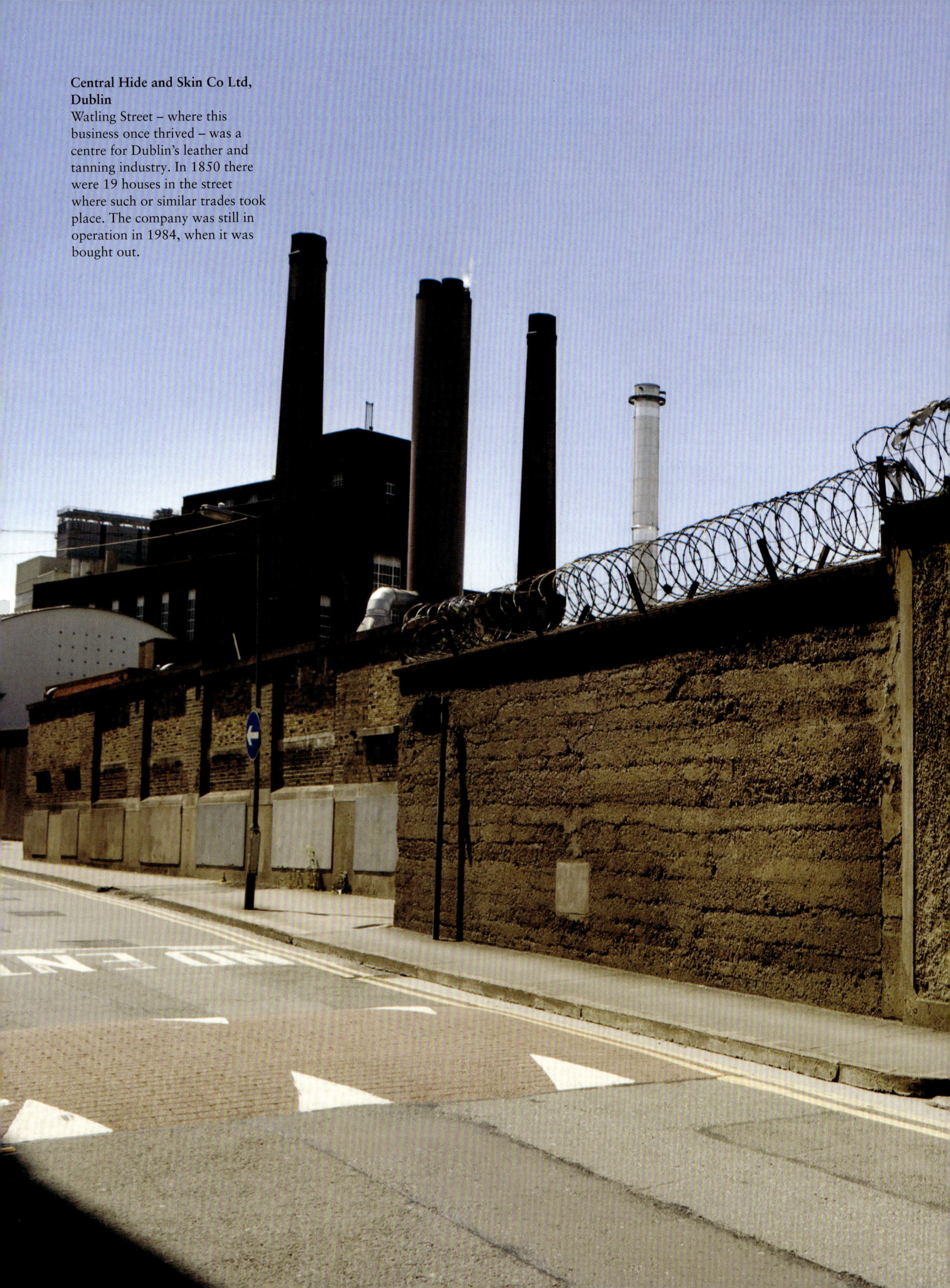

Central Hide and Skin Co Ltd, Dublin
Watling Street – where this business once thrived – was a centre for Dublin's leather and tanning industry. In 1850 there were 19 houses in the street where such or similar trades took place. The company was still in operation in 1984, when it was bought out.

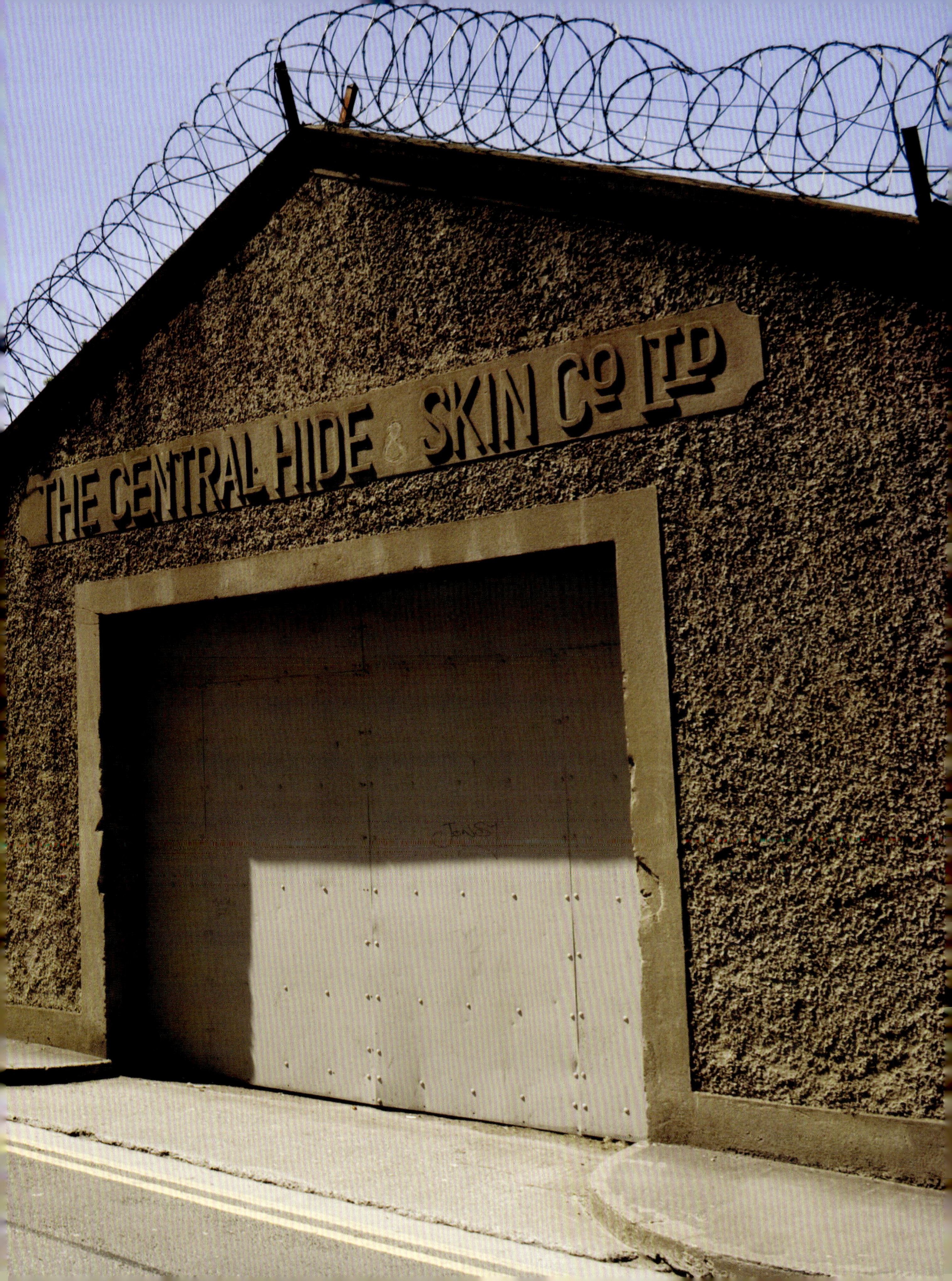

THE CENTRAL HIDE & SKIN Cº LTD

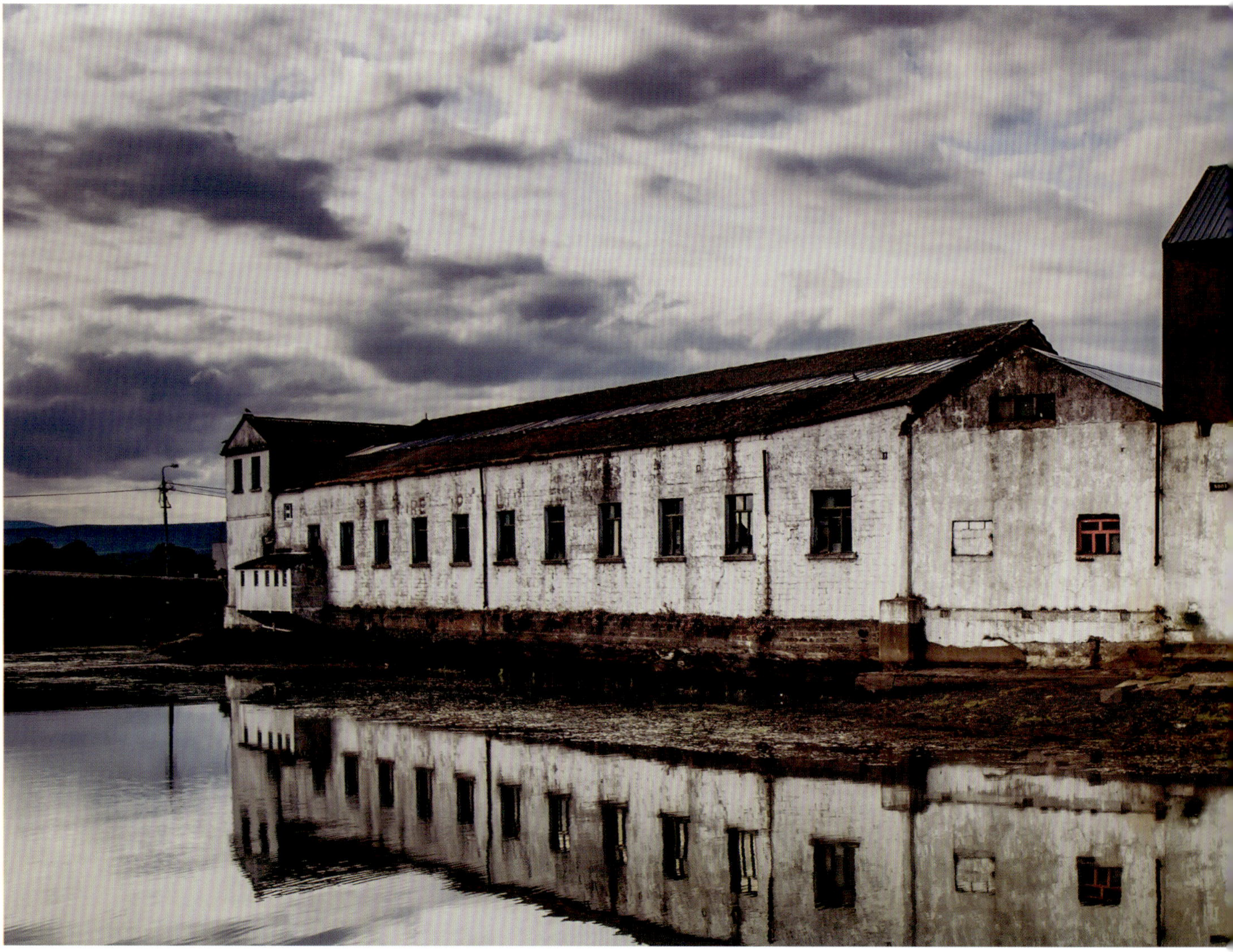

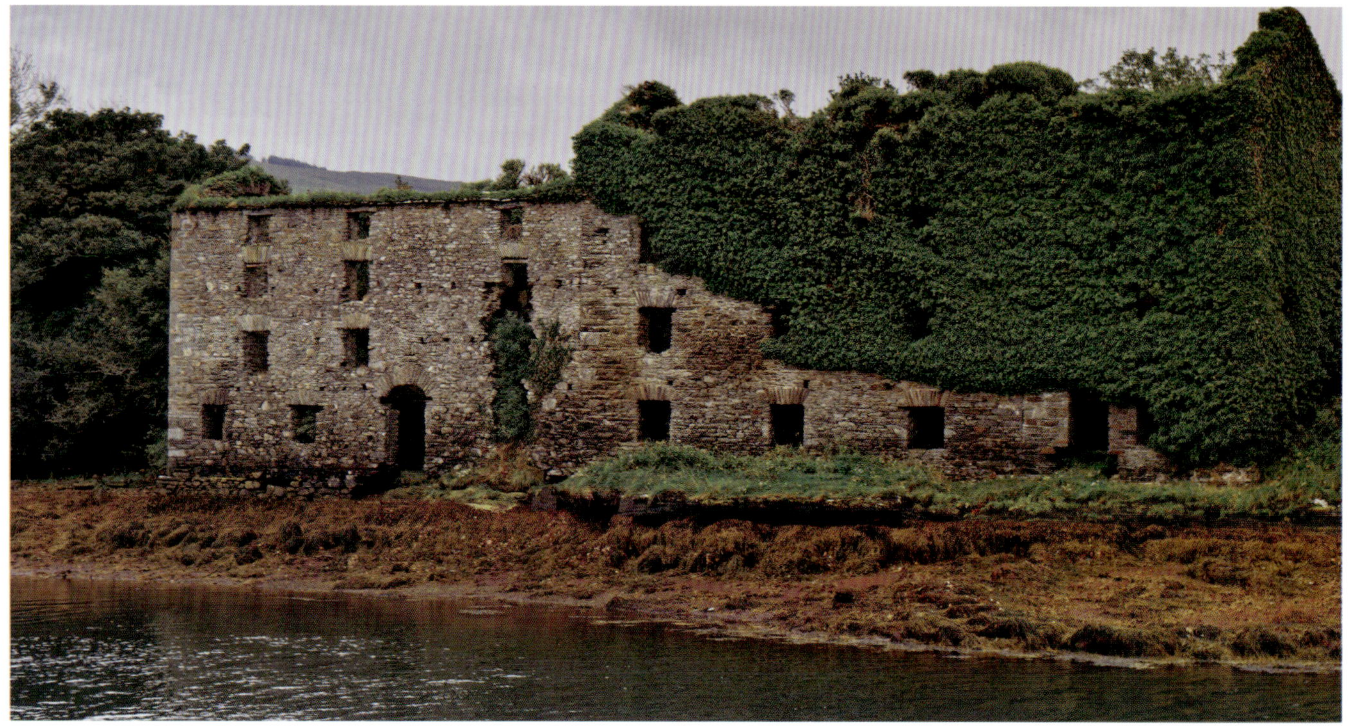

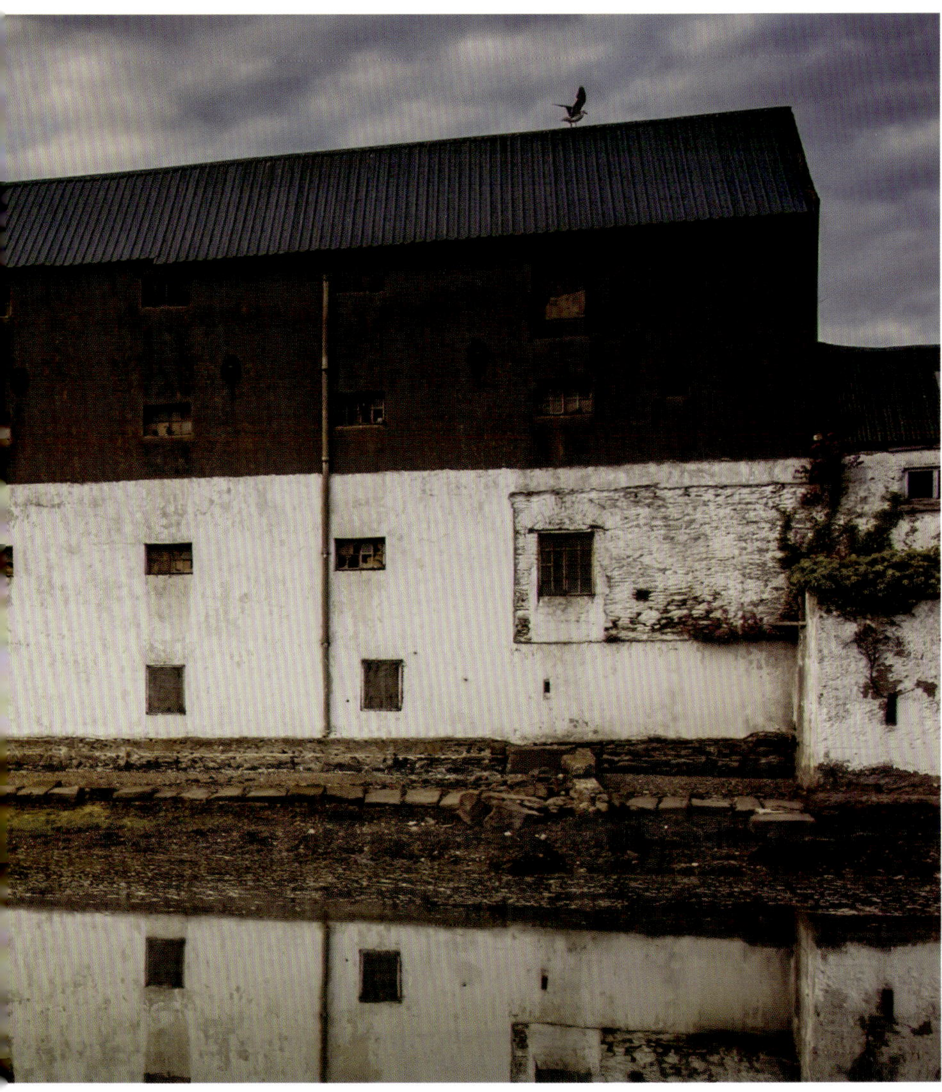

River Vartry, County Wicklow
The River Vartry flows from the Wicklow Mountains to the Irish Sea at the town of Wicklow itself, where these disused industrial buildings stand. On the way it is held by the Vartry Reservoir, an important water source for Dublin. This stretch of the river flowing into Wicklow harbour is also called the Leitrim.

OPPOSITE BELOW:
Old grain warehouse, Durrus, County Cork
This late 18th-century store in the village of Durrus was used to hold grain. At the time, such warehouses were increasingly important, as Ireland had been struck by famine in the 1740s when harvests failed.

BELOW:
Donaghy's Mill, Drogheda, County Louth
This mill, on the banks of the River Boyne, was converted into a shoe factory, and later used as offices and a gymnasium. After laying idle for a number of years, it was gutted by fire in 2019. It was first known as Westgate Mill and was a flax mill, crucial for the linen industry, and began operating in the mid-19th century.

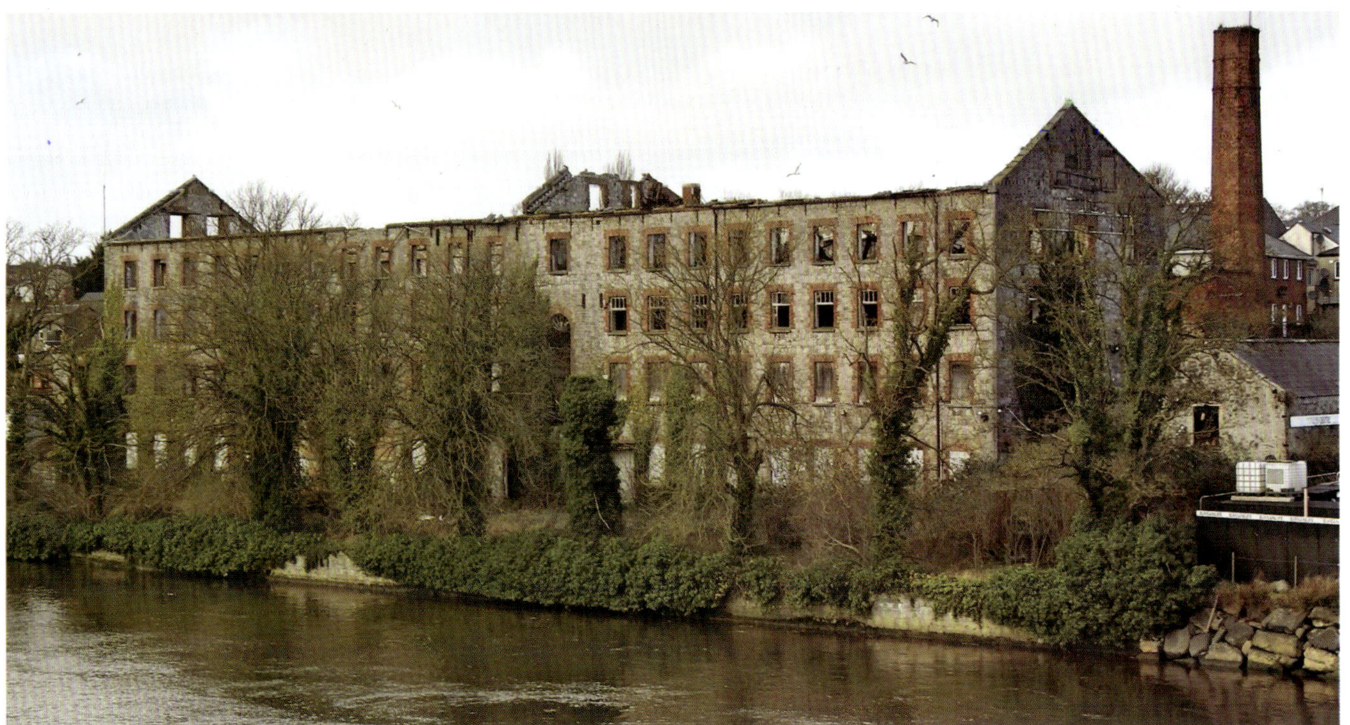

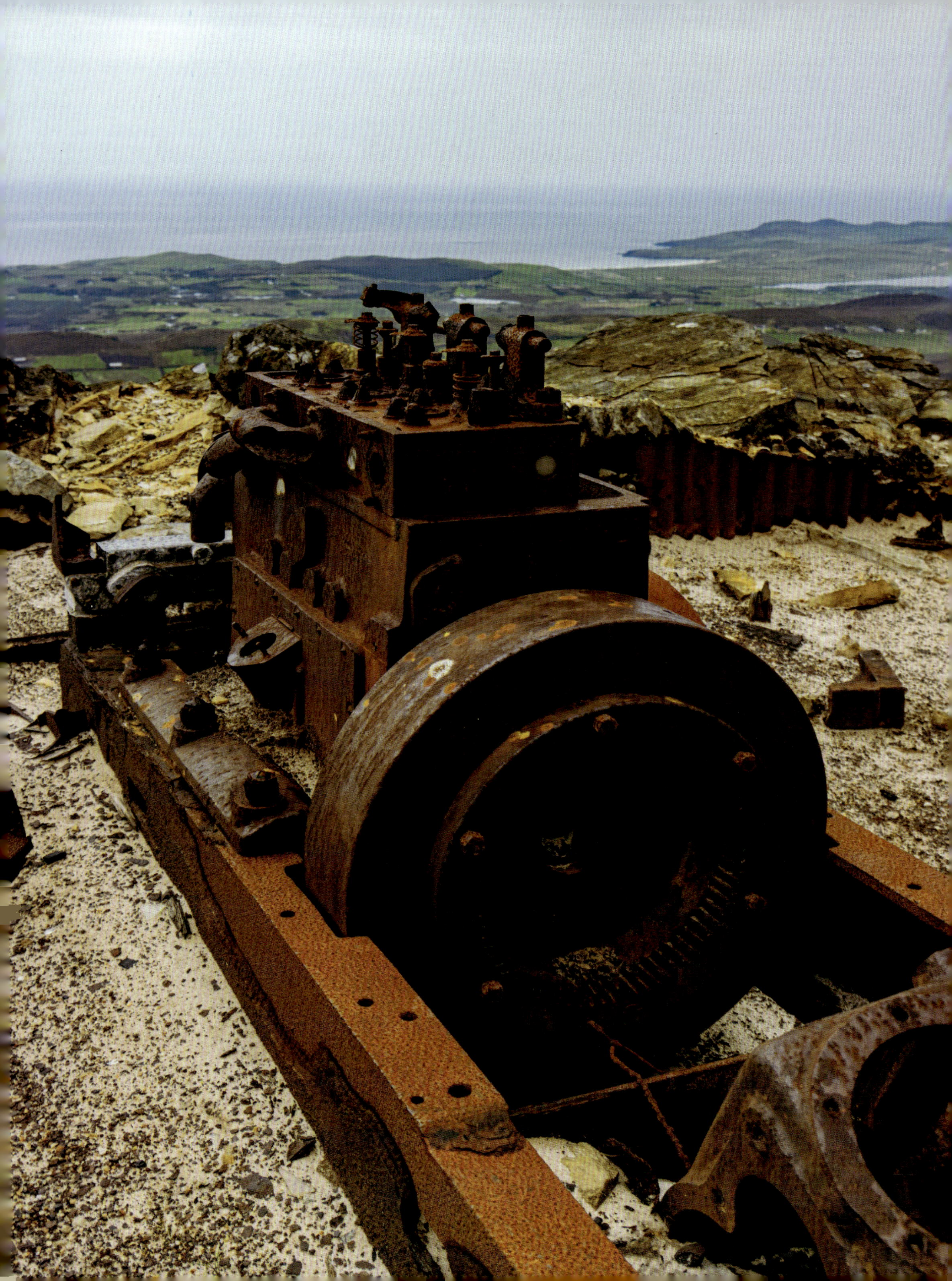

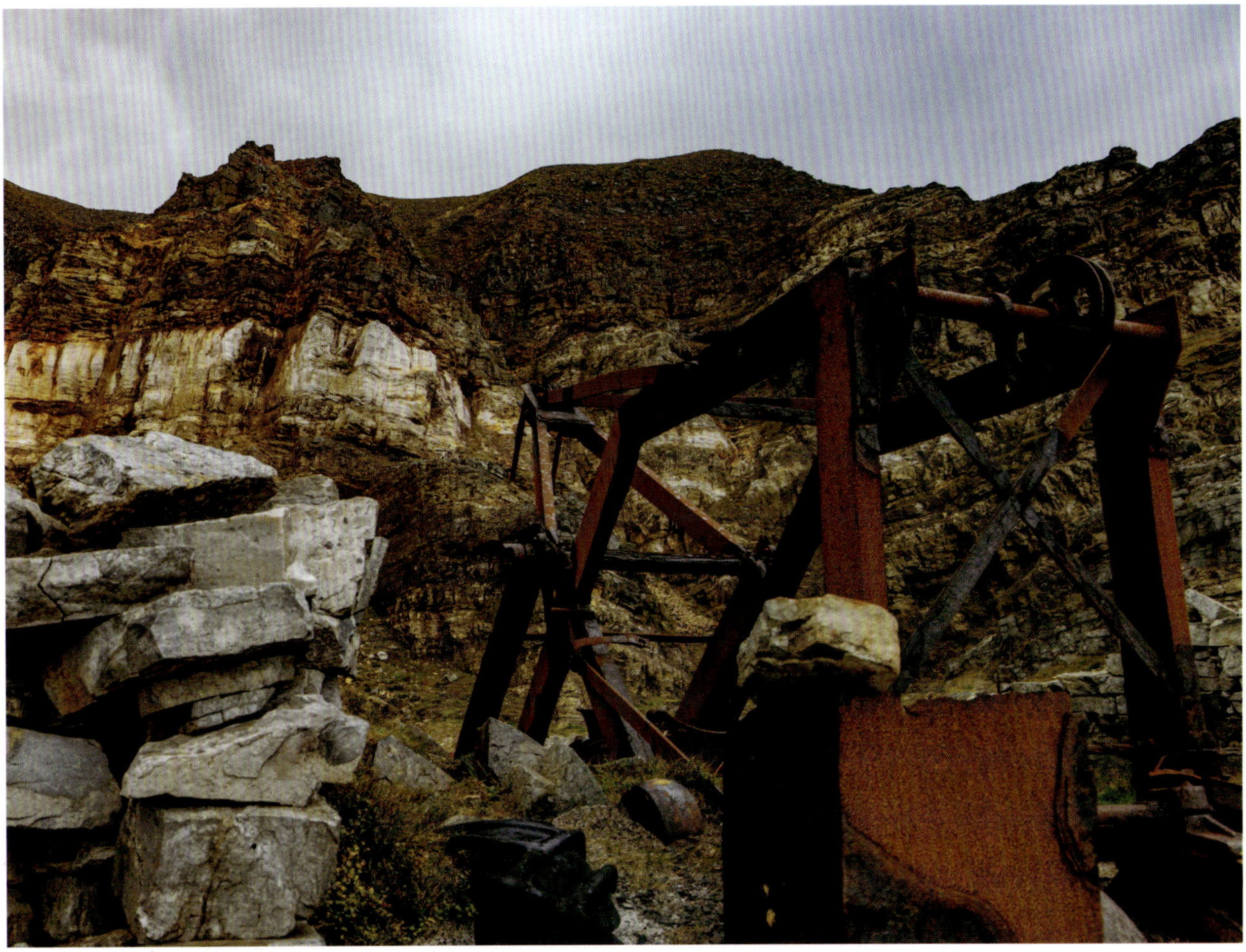

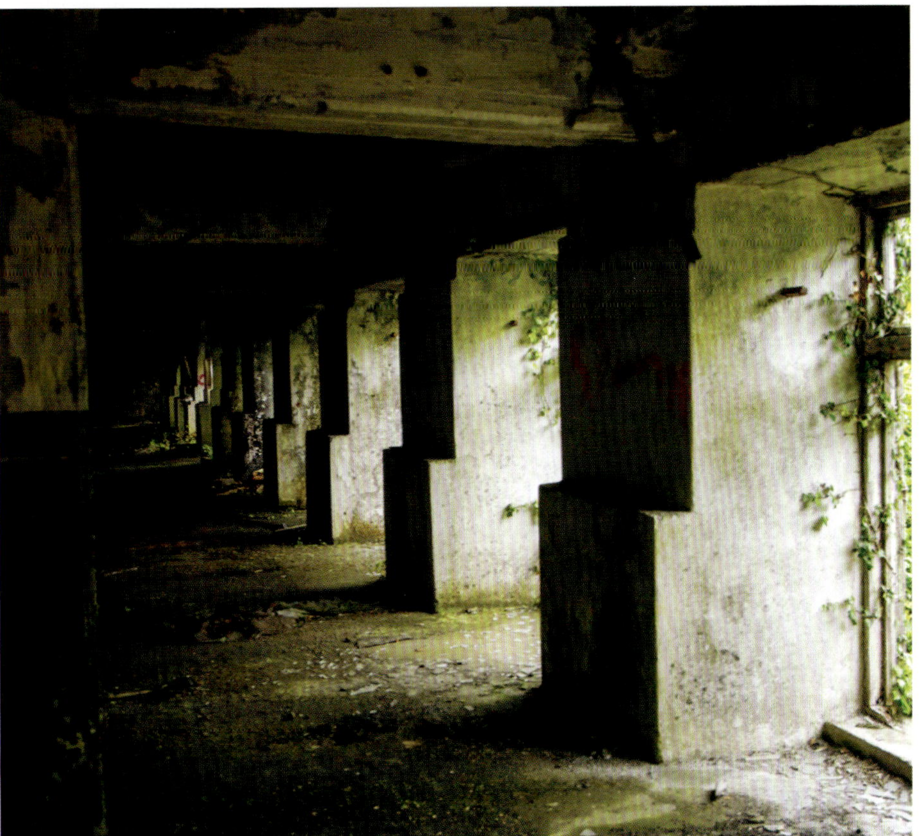

OPPOSITE & ABOVE:
**Muckish Mountain,
County Donegal**
High-grade sand was mined on Muckish Mountain, which sits in the Derryveagh Mountains, and was used mainly in the creation of glass. On the flat-topped mountain there are many remains of old mining equipment, rusting in the elements.

LEFT:
**Portlaw Tannery,
County Waterford**
At one stage, Portlaw Tannery was the largest in Europe, employing 600 people. It opened in 1935 on the ruins of a cotton mill, which had been built in the 19th century as part of one of the few 'industrial villages' in southern Ireland.

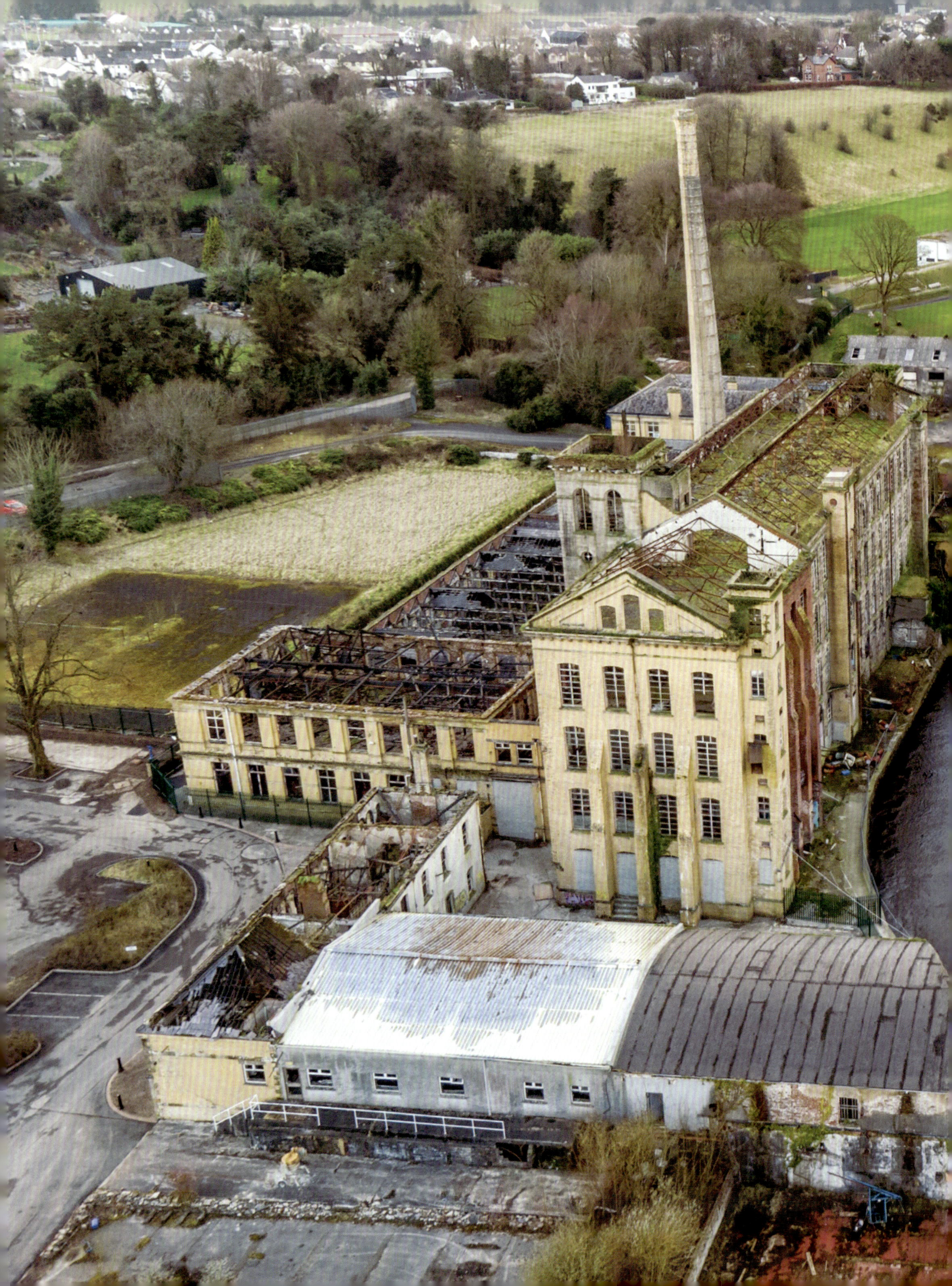

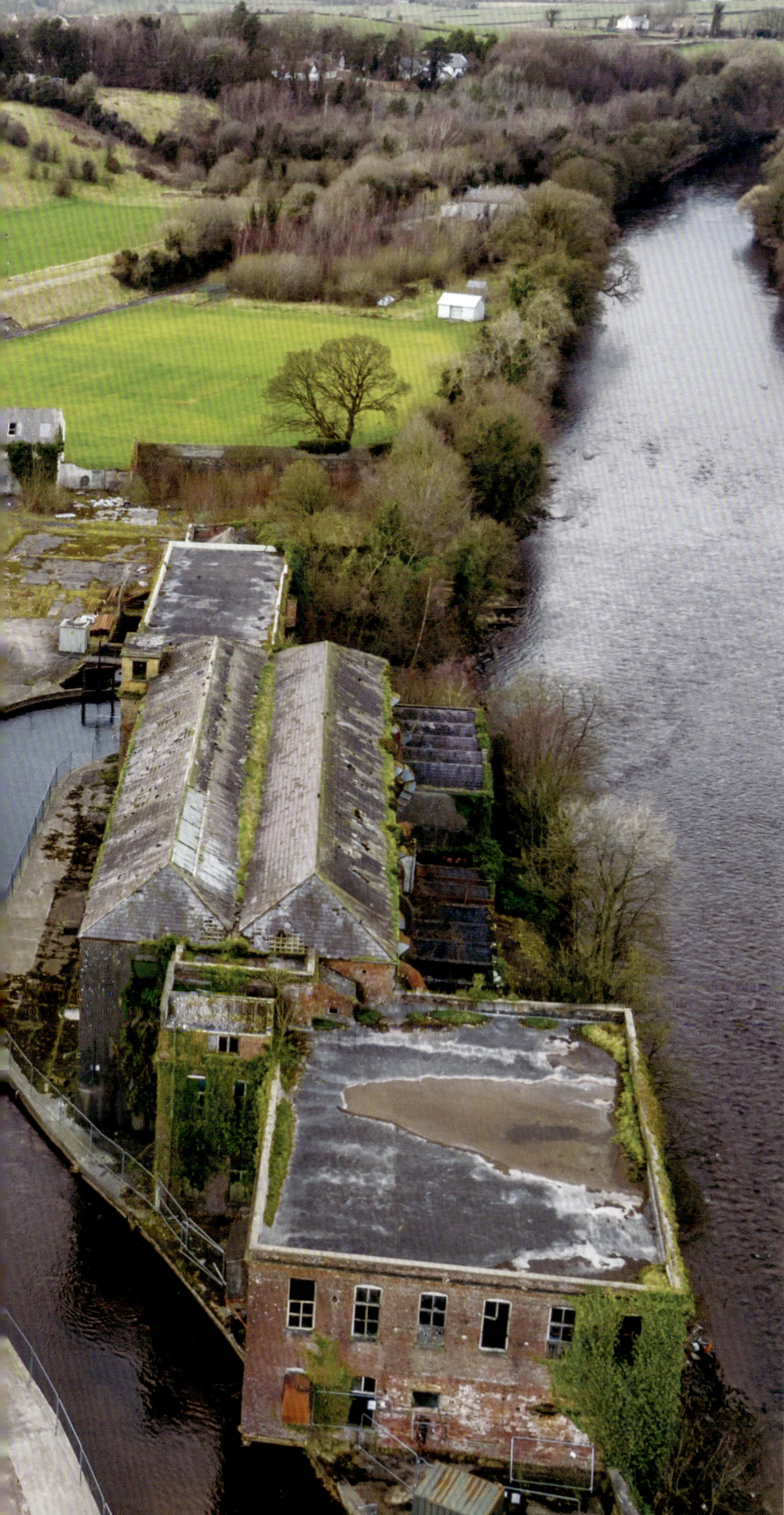

Sion Mills, County Tyrone
Standing on the wide, fast-flowing River Mourne, this 'industrial village' benefited from the immense power of the rushing waters to turn its wheels. It is claimed that the Mourne is the 'river running by' in the hymn 'All Things Bright and Beautiful', as the writer of the words, Cecil Frances Alexander, lived for a time in a rectory overlooking a weir on the Mourne at Sion Mills.

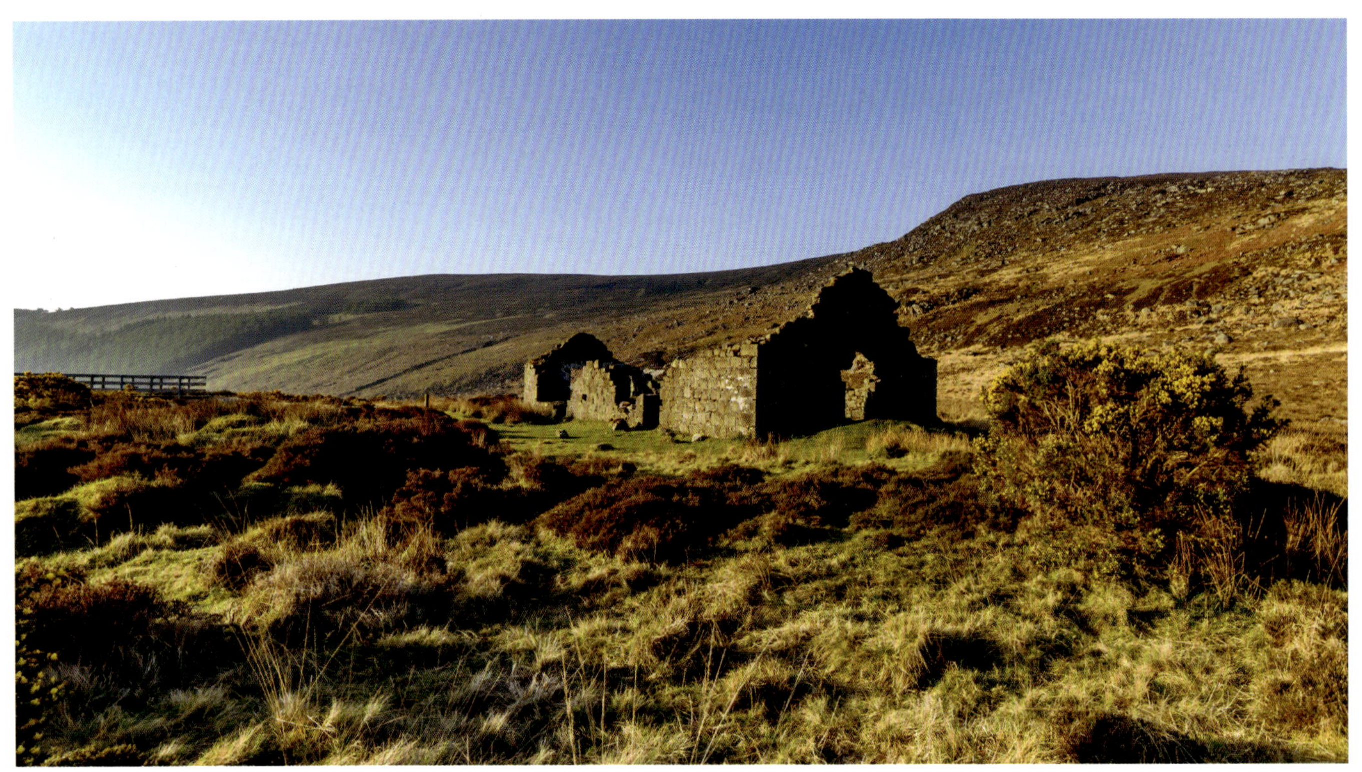

Disused granite quarry, County Wicklow

Granite has been quarried in the Wicklow Mountains for hundreds of years. It has been used in many of the buildings in Wicklow and Dublin, including the capital's General Post Office.

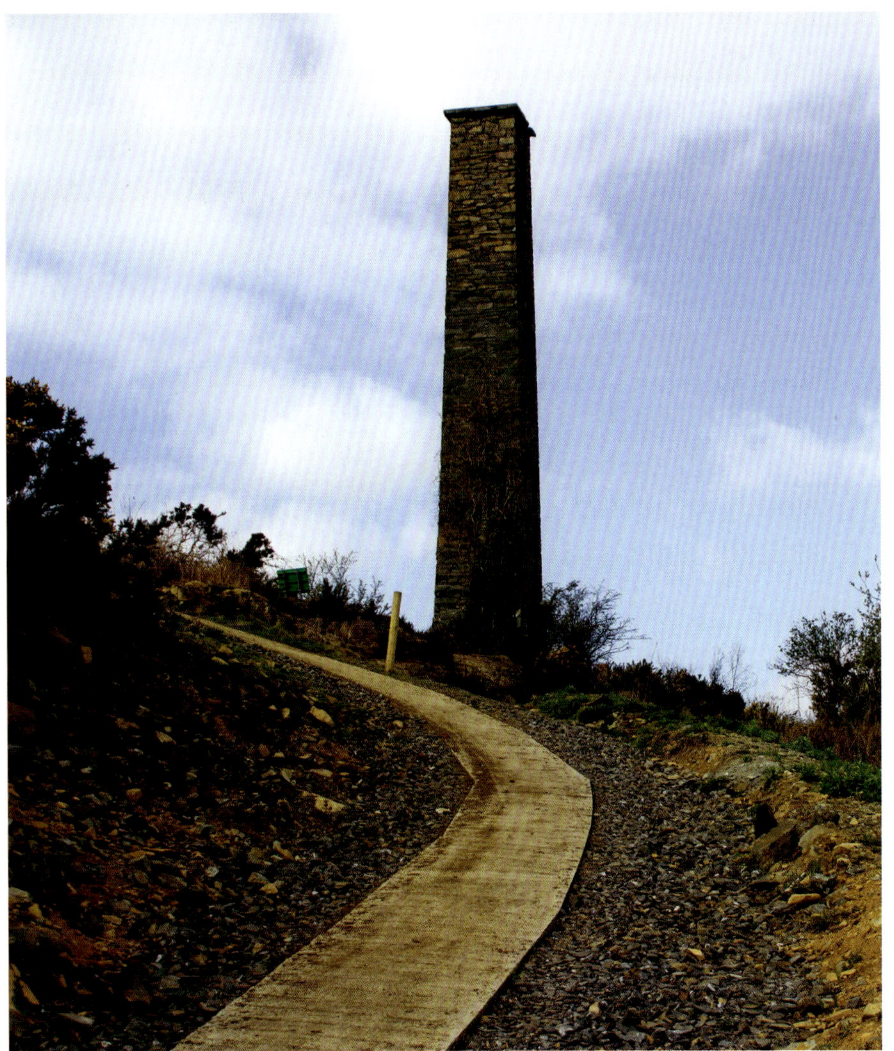

Conlig lead mines, County Down

Around 13,500 tonnes of lead were produced by the mines in this area between the late 17th century and the end of the 19th century. This picture shows a chimney from the South Engine House, built in the 19th century. Copper has also been mined extensively in the area.

OPPOSITE:

Tankardstown, Copper Coast Drive, County Waterford

The Tankardstown mine dates back to 1824 and was decommissioned in 1877. It is one of a series of former copper mines in the area, which have given rise to the area being called the Copper Coast and designated a UNESCO Geopark.

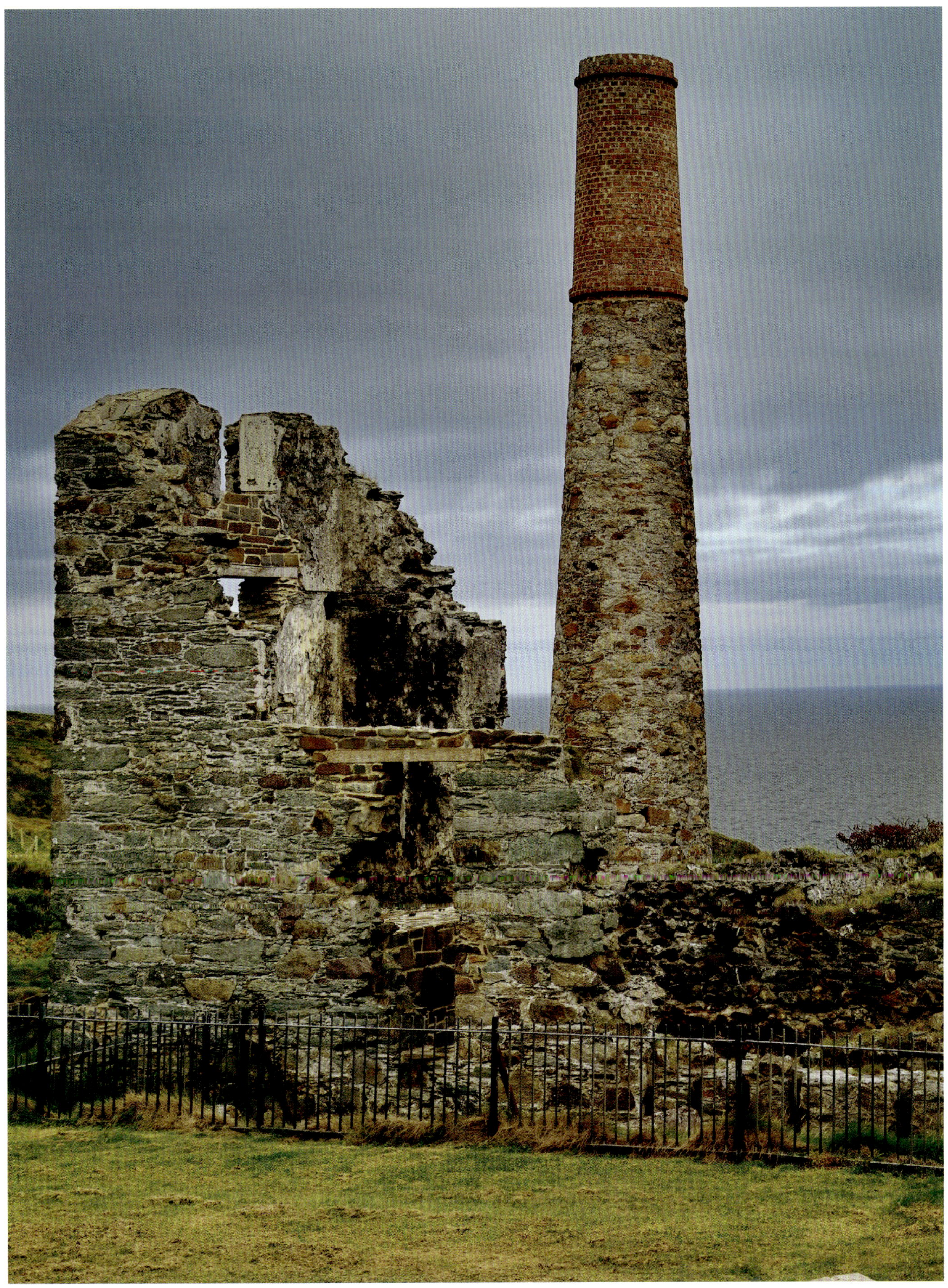

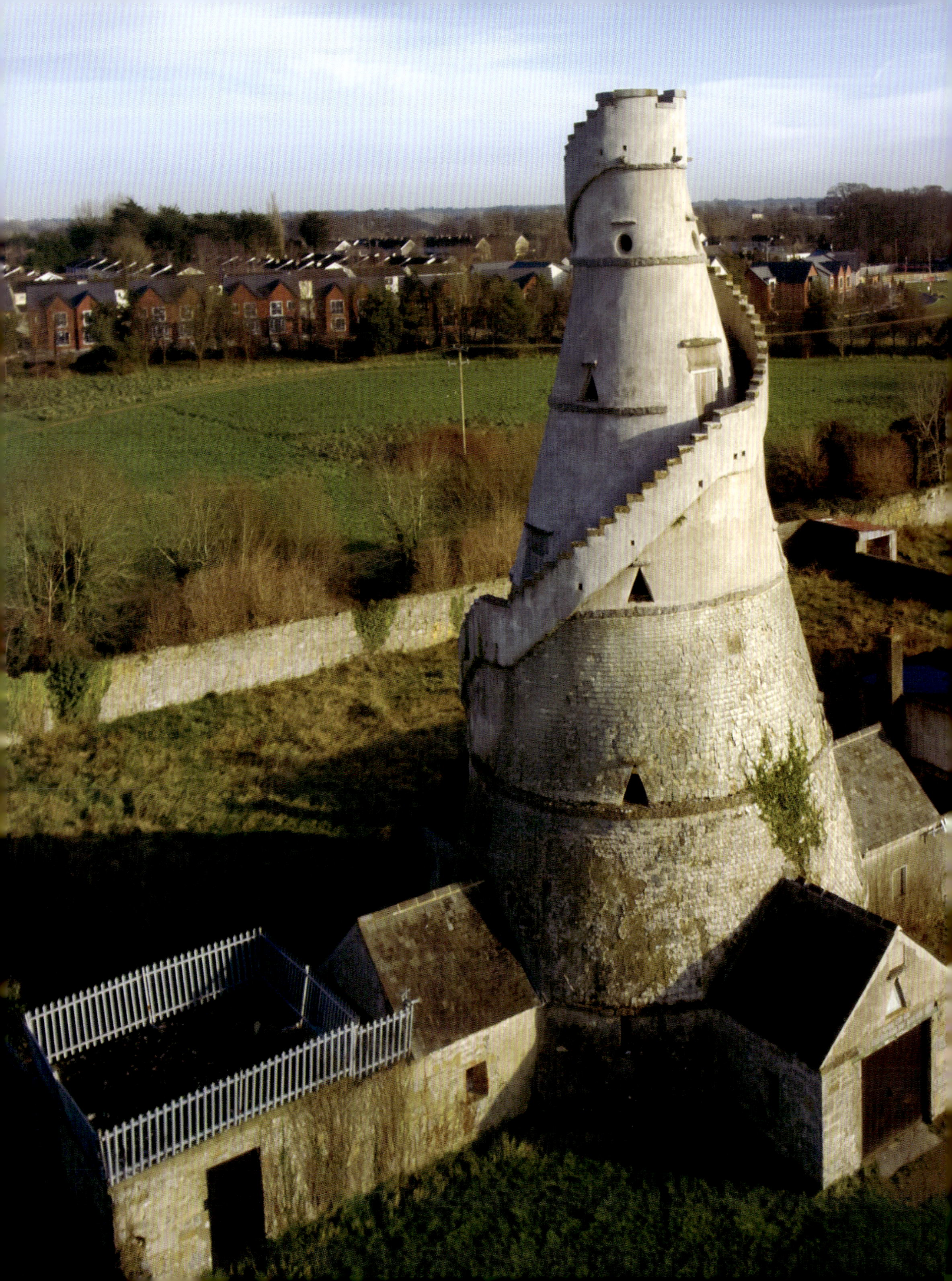

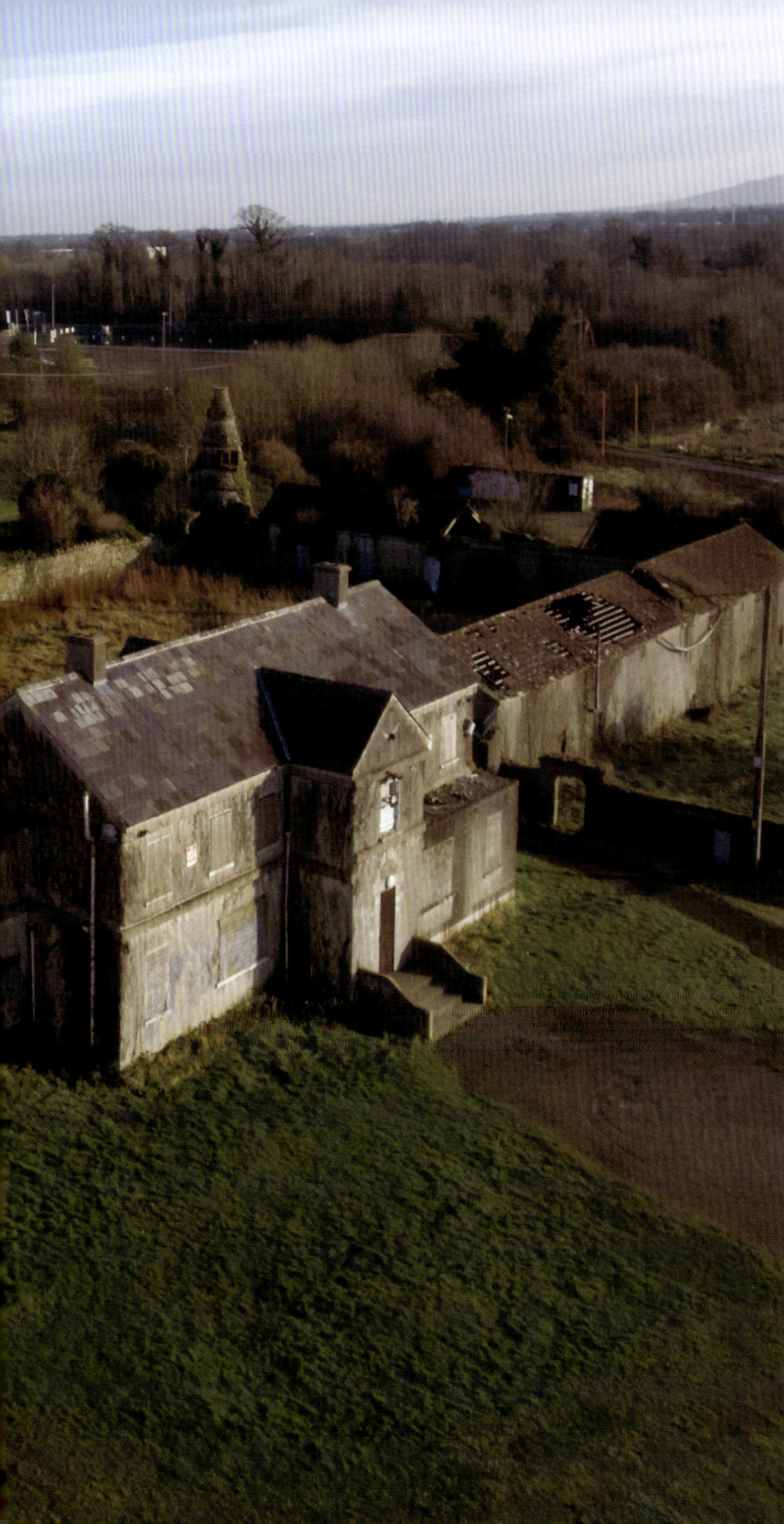

**The Wonderful Barn, Cellbridge,
County Kildare**
This corkscrew-shaped building
from 1743 sits on the edge of
the Castleton House Estate,
formerly of the Conolly family.
Several theories abound as to its
purpose: it was possibly to house
doves, which were a delicacy at
the time; it was a 'famine relief'
project to store grain and keep
locals employed; or it was purely
a folly, similar to the nearby
Conolly's Folly.

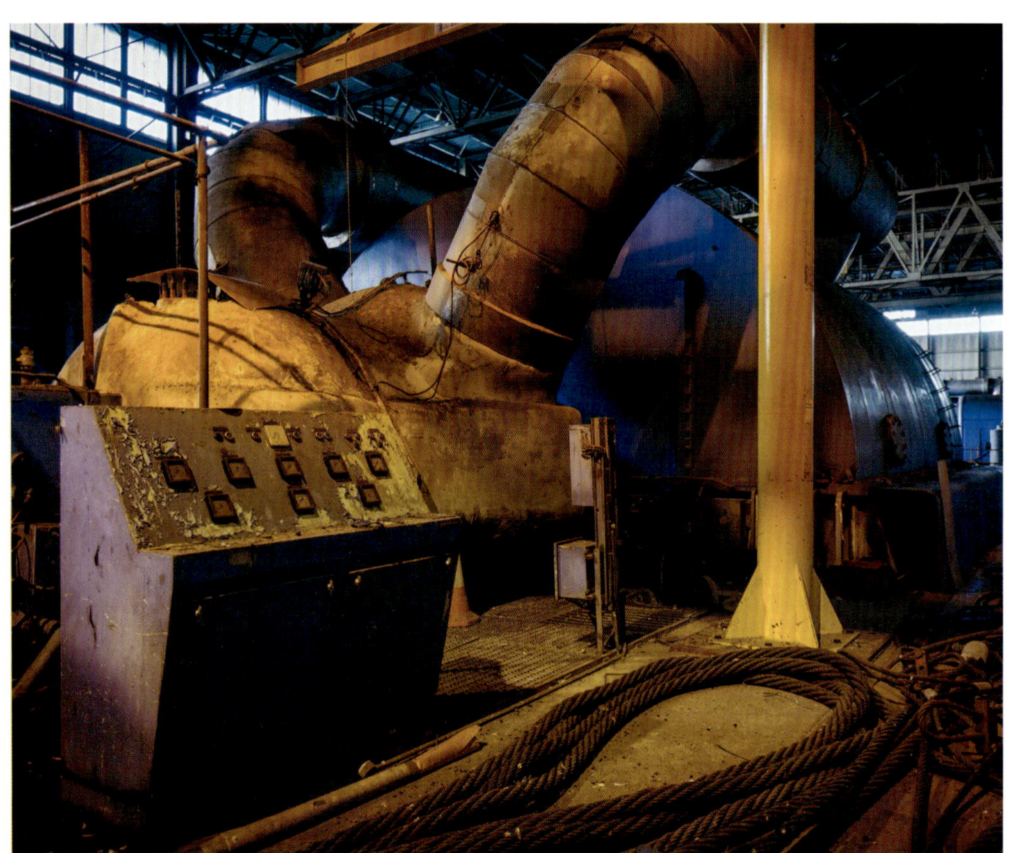

LEFT:
Poolbeg Generating Station, Dublin
Poolbeg sits on reclaimed land on the south bank of Dublin Port and boasts two towers more than 200m (650ft) high that dominate the skyline for miles around. In 2006 a decision was made that part of the oil and gas power plant would close. Construction had begun in 1965.

BELOW & OPPOSITE:
Marina Generating Station, County Cork
Operating from 1954, Marina Generating Station is in Cork city's docklands. The station was closed in September 2018 but plans for redevelopment have been drawn up, and it may be used for housing because it is close to Cork city centre. It has been described as Ireland's Battersea Power Station because of its chimney and red-brick structure. It is available as a filming location.

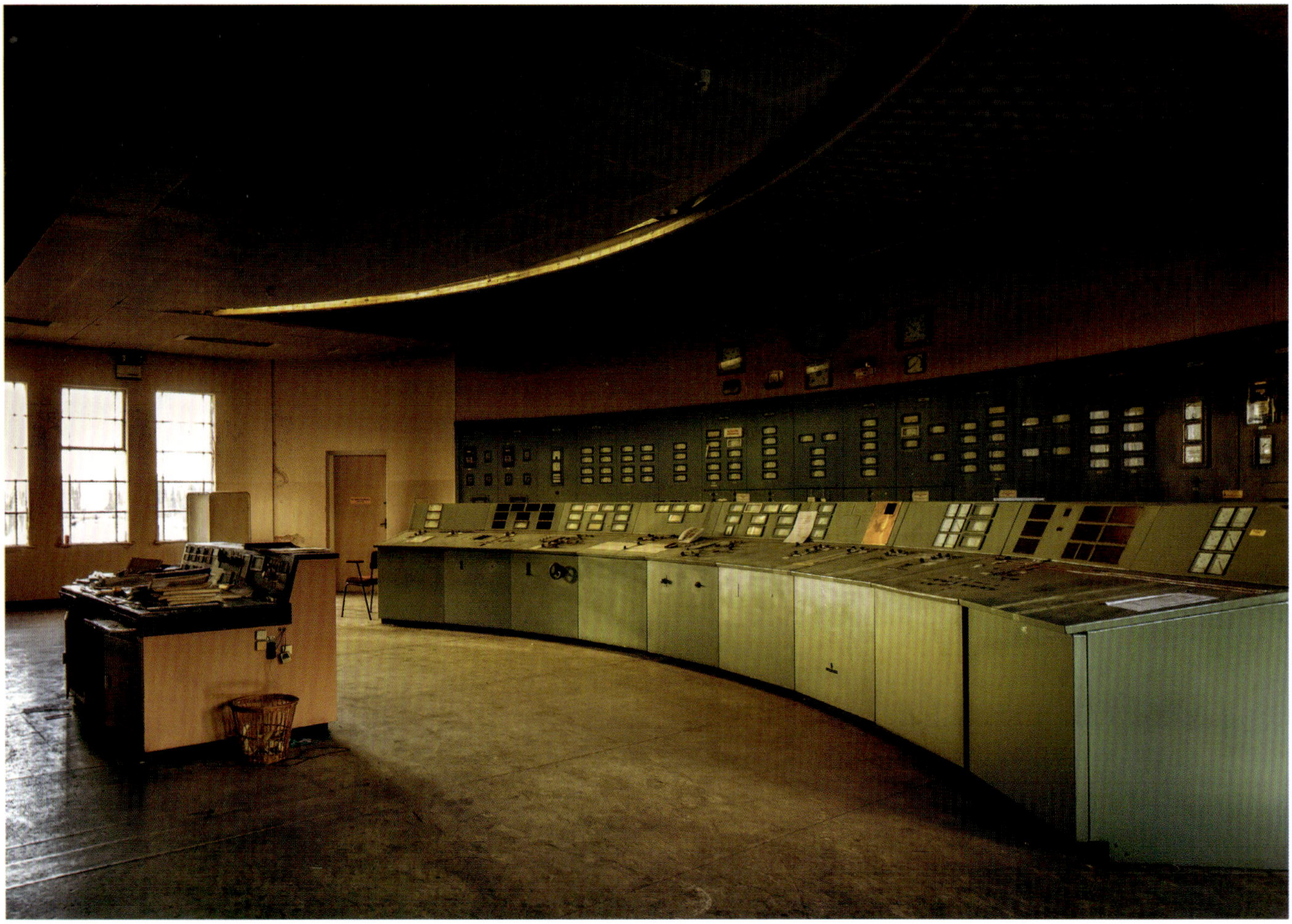

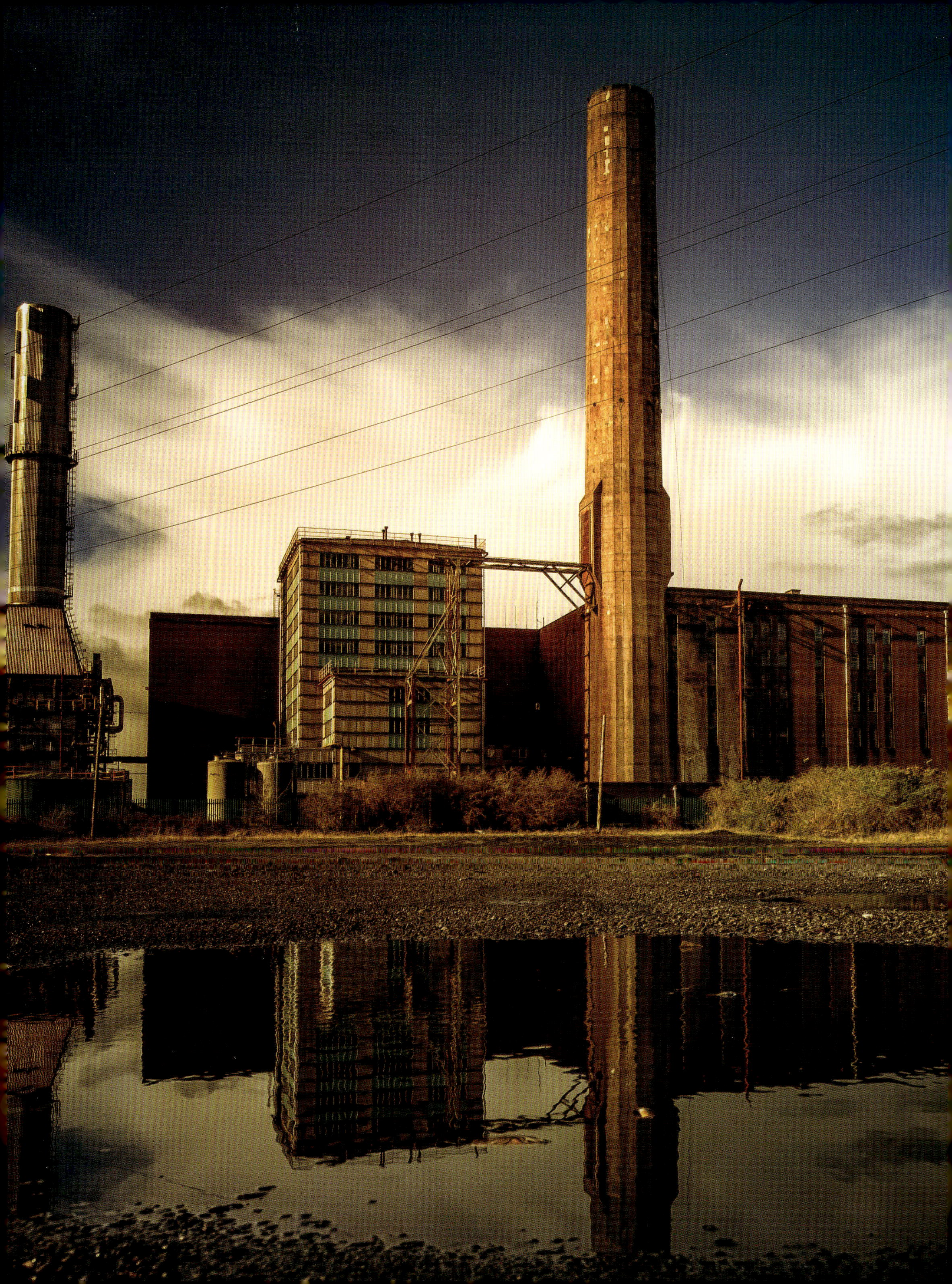

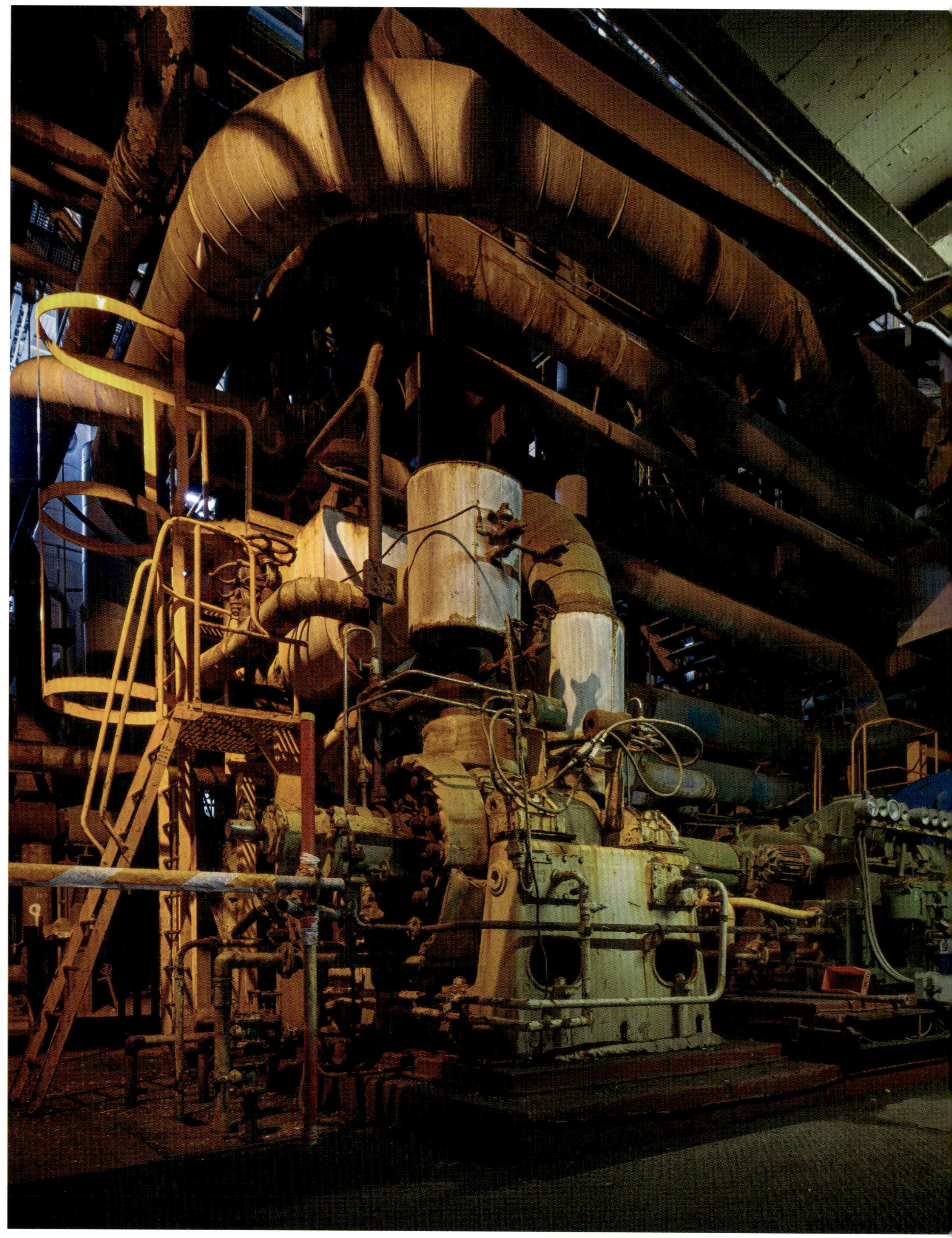

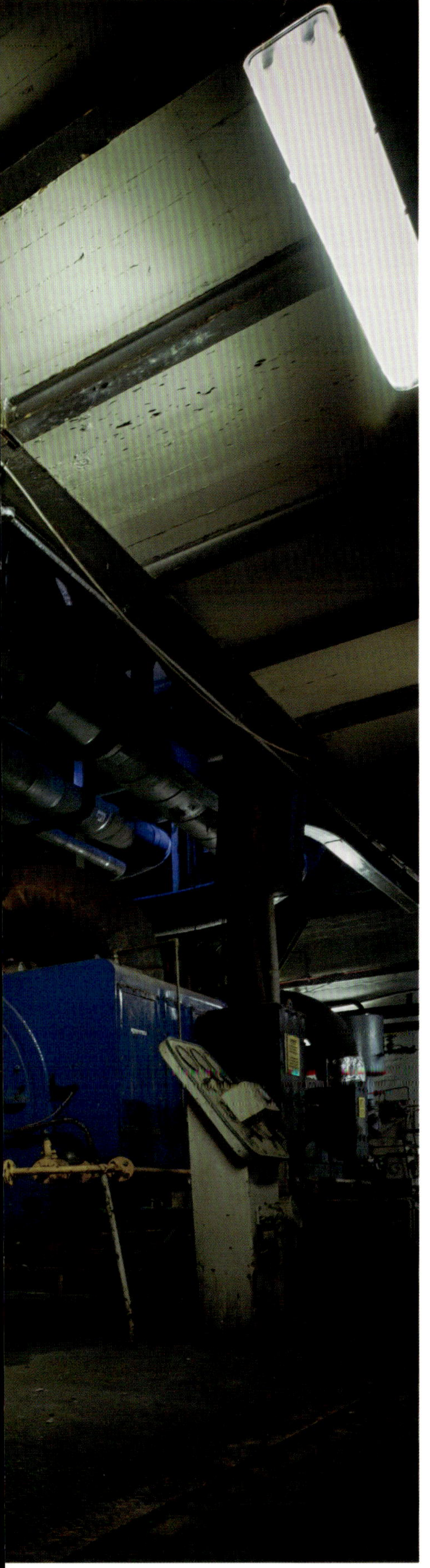

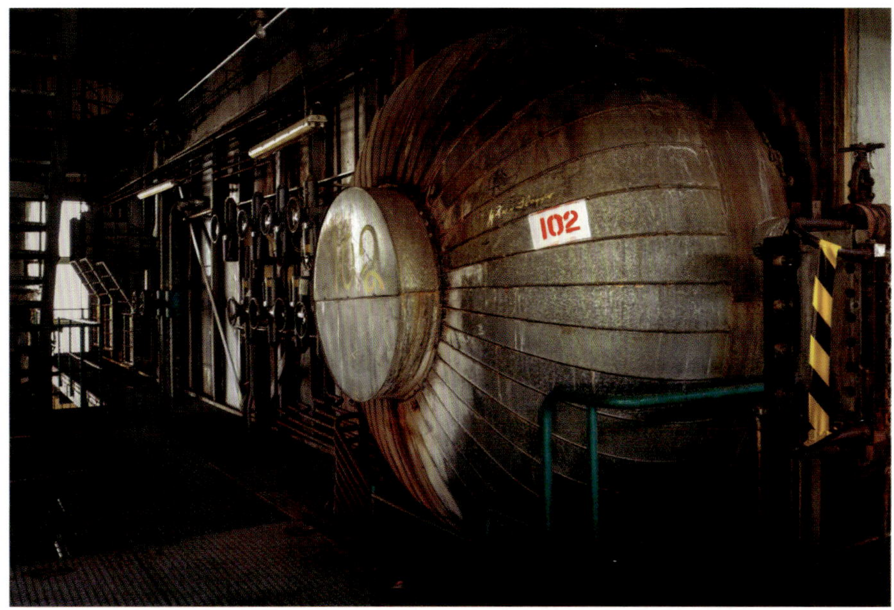

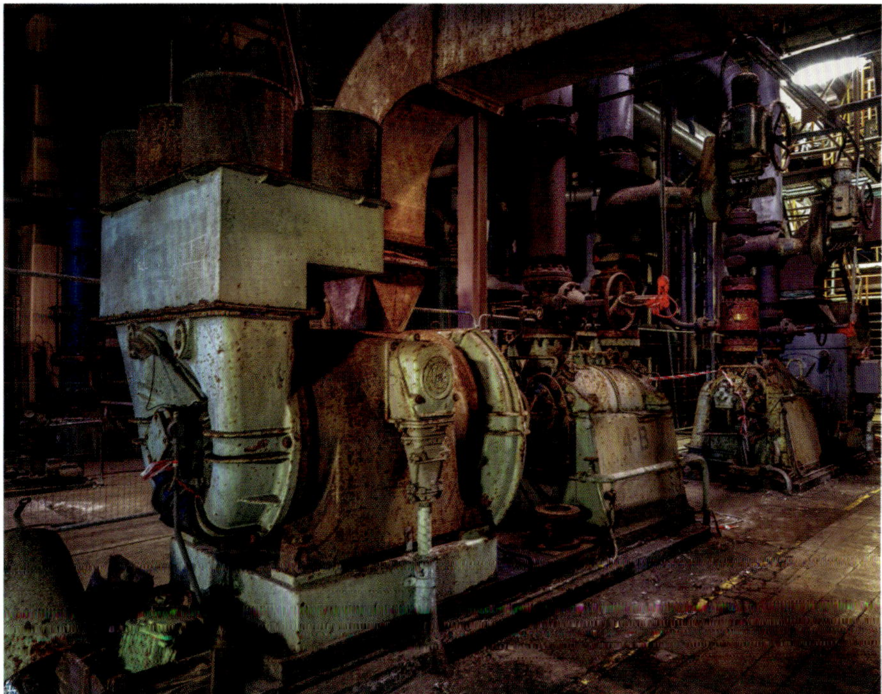

LEFT:
Poolbeg Generating Station, Dublin
In total, Poolbeg took 11 years to complete, the first phase ending in 1971 and the second in 1976. The station replaced an older electricity-generating plant on the site called Pigeon House, which started producing power in 1903. Poolbeg is named after the nearby Poolbeg lighthouse, which, like the power station's towers, is painted red.

ABOVE TOP:
Great Island Power Station, County Wexford
On the shores of Waterford Harbour, this power station was opened in 1967 and ran on oil and gas. In 2014 the oil operations were shut down although the station continues to power more than half a million homes throughout Ireland. Great Island is said to be where the first inhabitants of Ireland landed from Spain around 5000 years ago.

ABOVE BOTTOM:
Marina Generating Station, County Cork
This station was originally designed to run on oil and coal but, after the discovery of natural gas off the Cork coast, it was adapted to produce electricity from that too. It is run by the ESB (Electricity Supply Board), which was set up in 1927 by the fledgling Irish Free State.

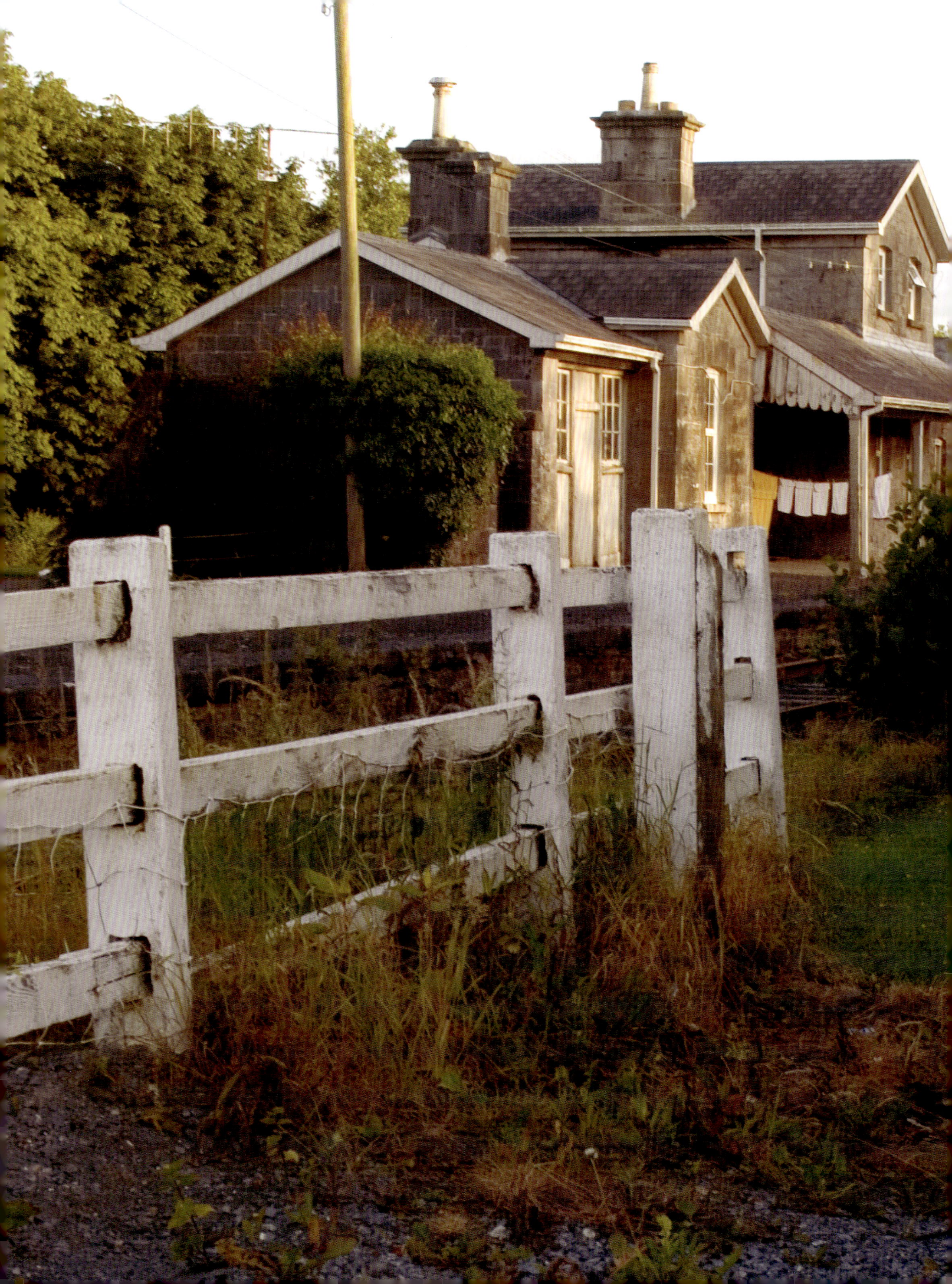

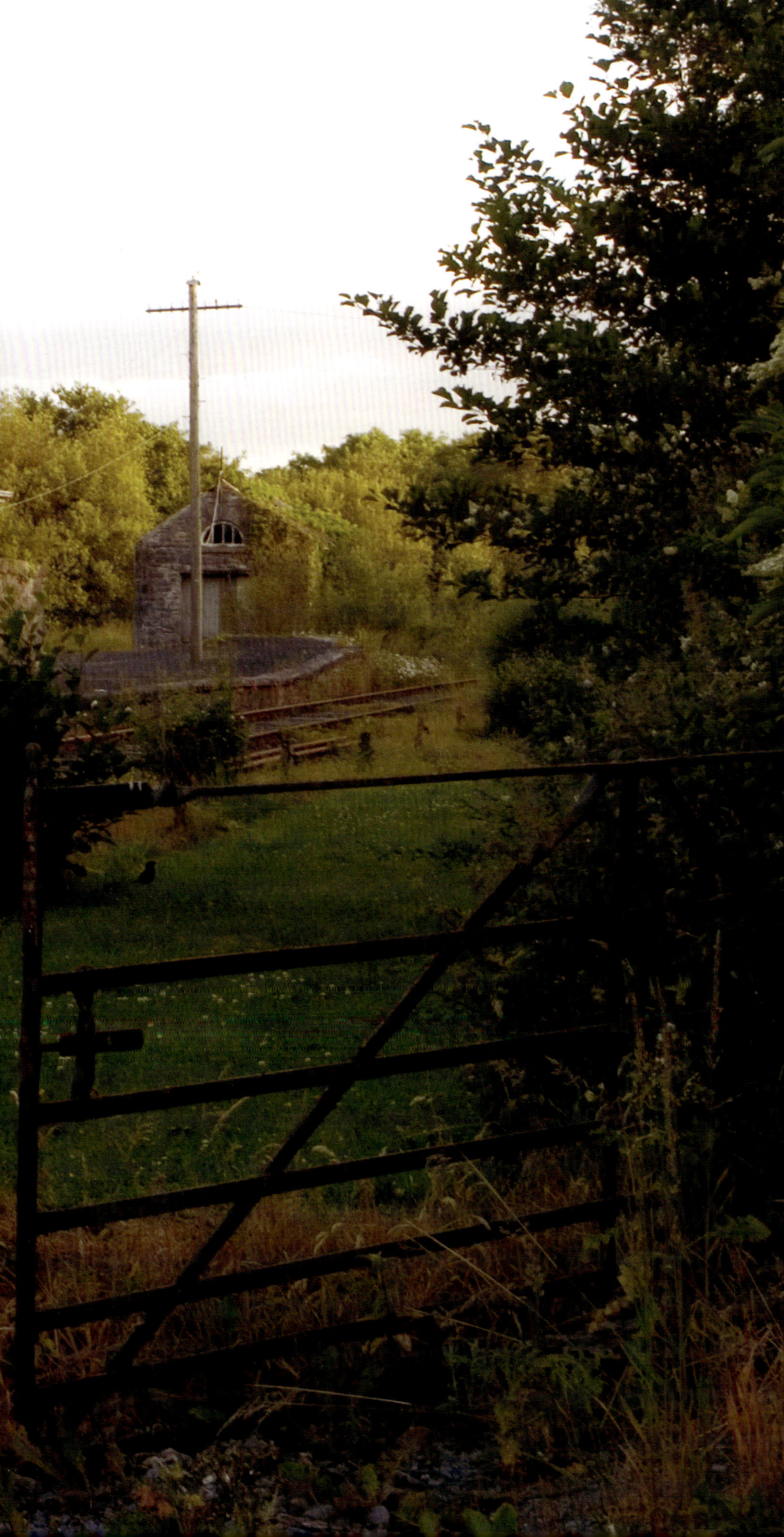

Adare Railway Station, County Limerick
From 1856, when it was opened by the Waterford and Limerick and Limerick and Foynes railways, this station served the village of Adare until 1963 for passengers. Freight services lasted for some years more. In 2022 steps were taken to reintroduce services that would take in Adare.

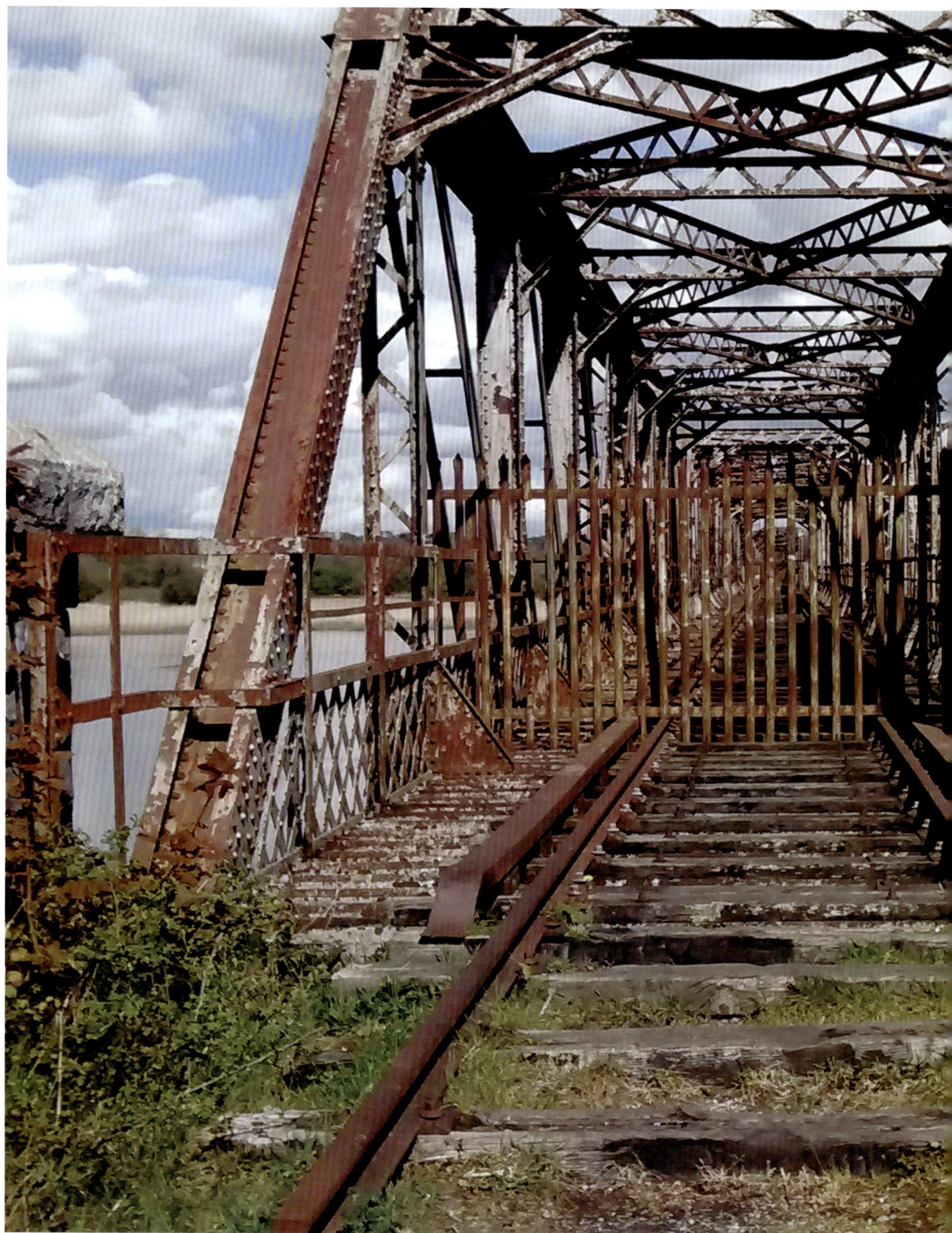

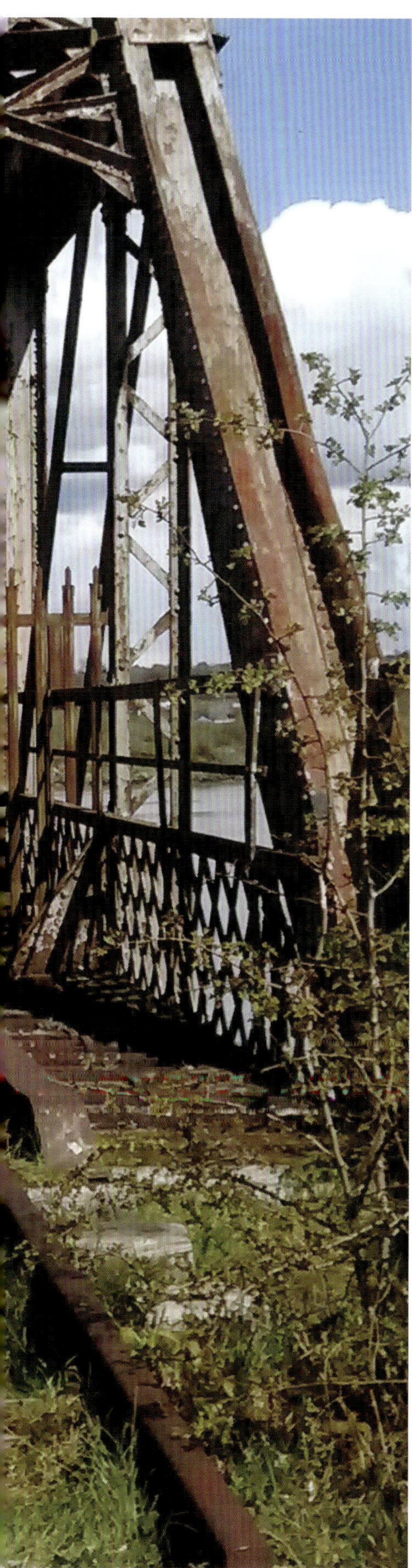

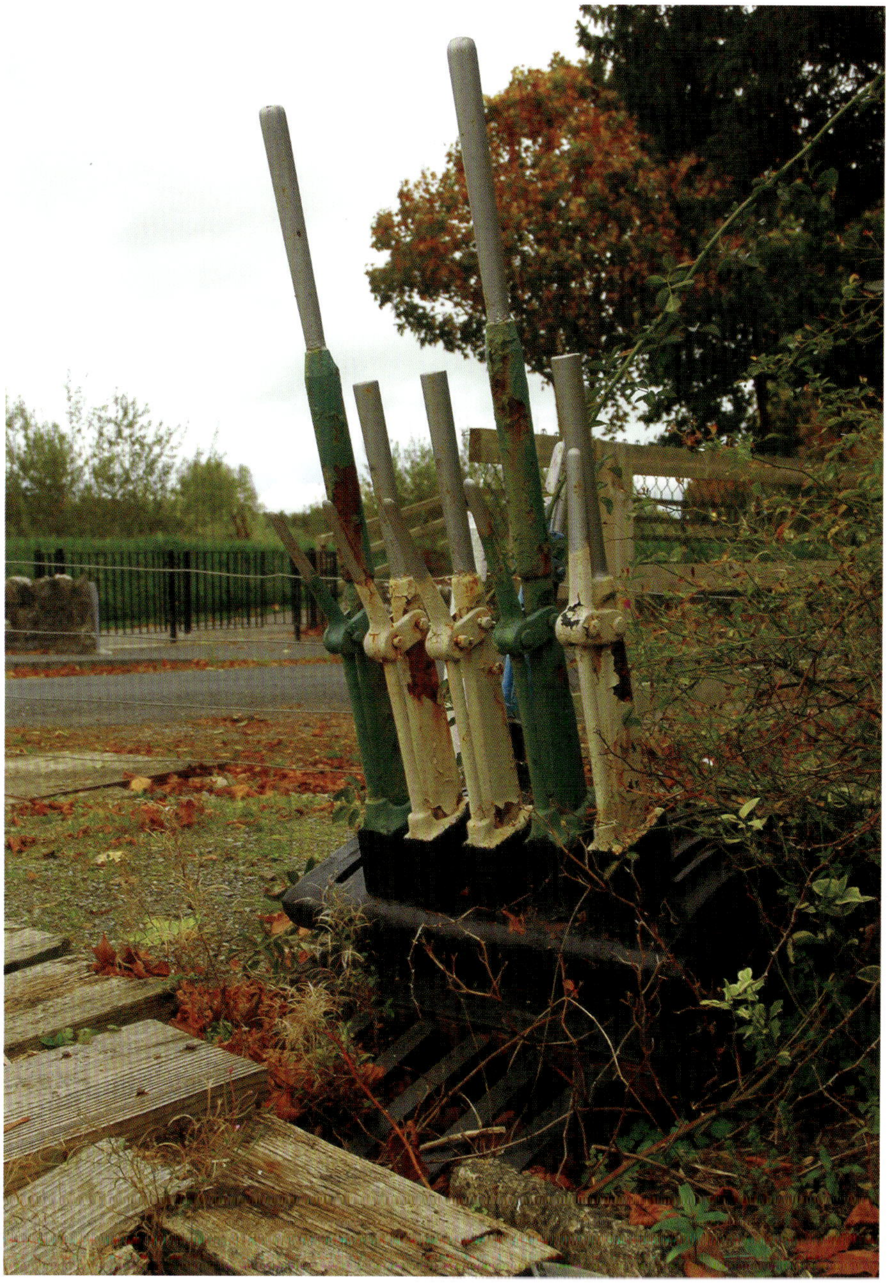

**Old Red Iron Bridge,
County Kilkenny/Waterford**
Once Ireland's longest bridge,
which first opened in 1906, this
links the counties of Kilkenny
and Waterford over the River
Suir. The railway bridge has
nine spans and 'Old Red' was
originally painted silver, but the
paint has peeled to reveal the
weathered metal beneath.

**Old railway switch, Adare,
County Limerick**
The old switch at Adare station
is unlikely to be used again.
Although there are plans for the
line to be operational, the track
has to be replaced. Visitors will
have plenty to see, as Adare is
designated a 'heritage town' by
the Irish government. It is the
home of Desmond Castle, two
former abbeys and an ex-priory.

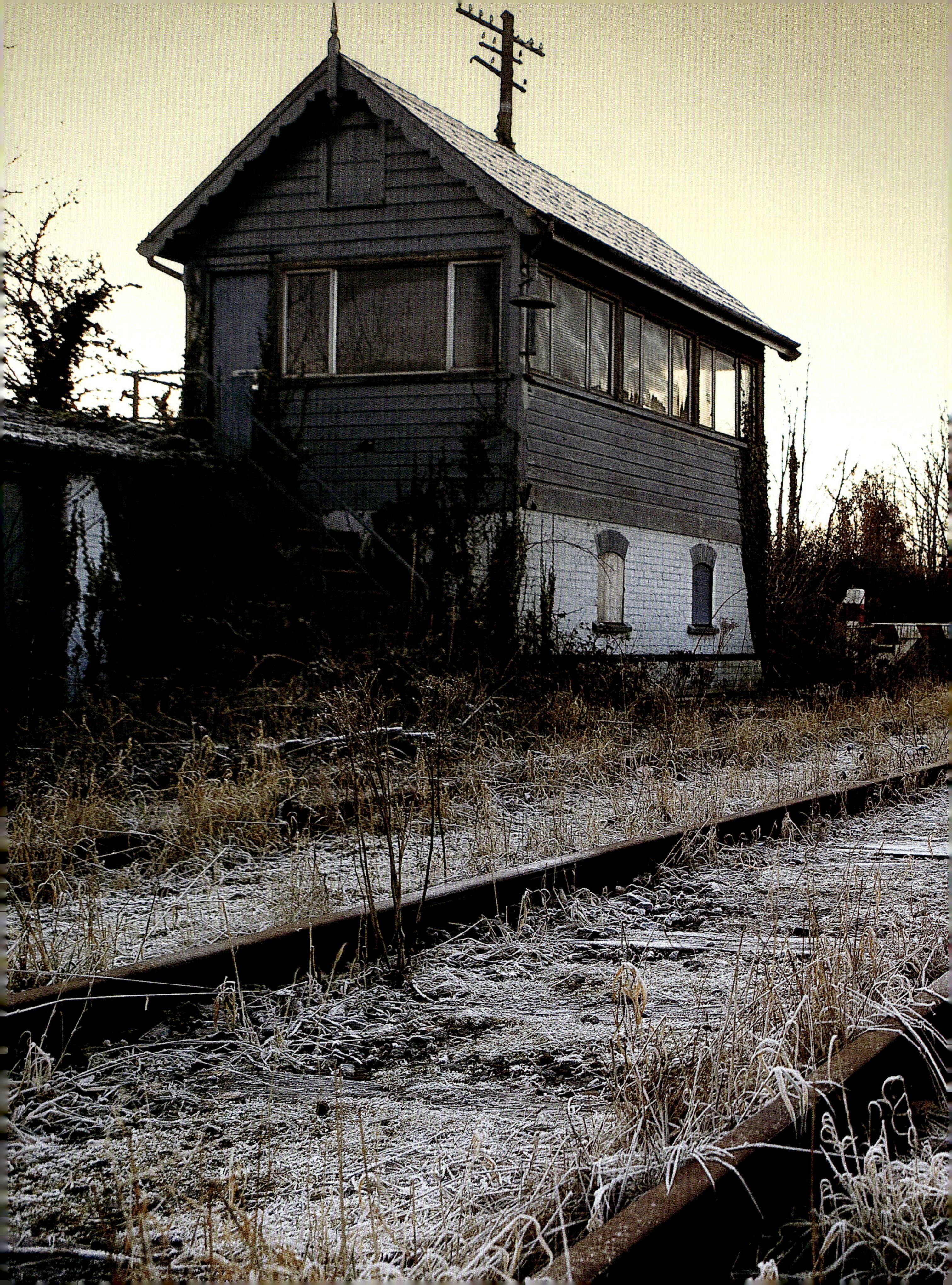

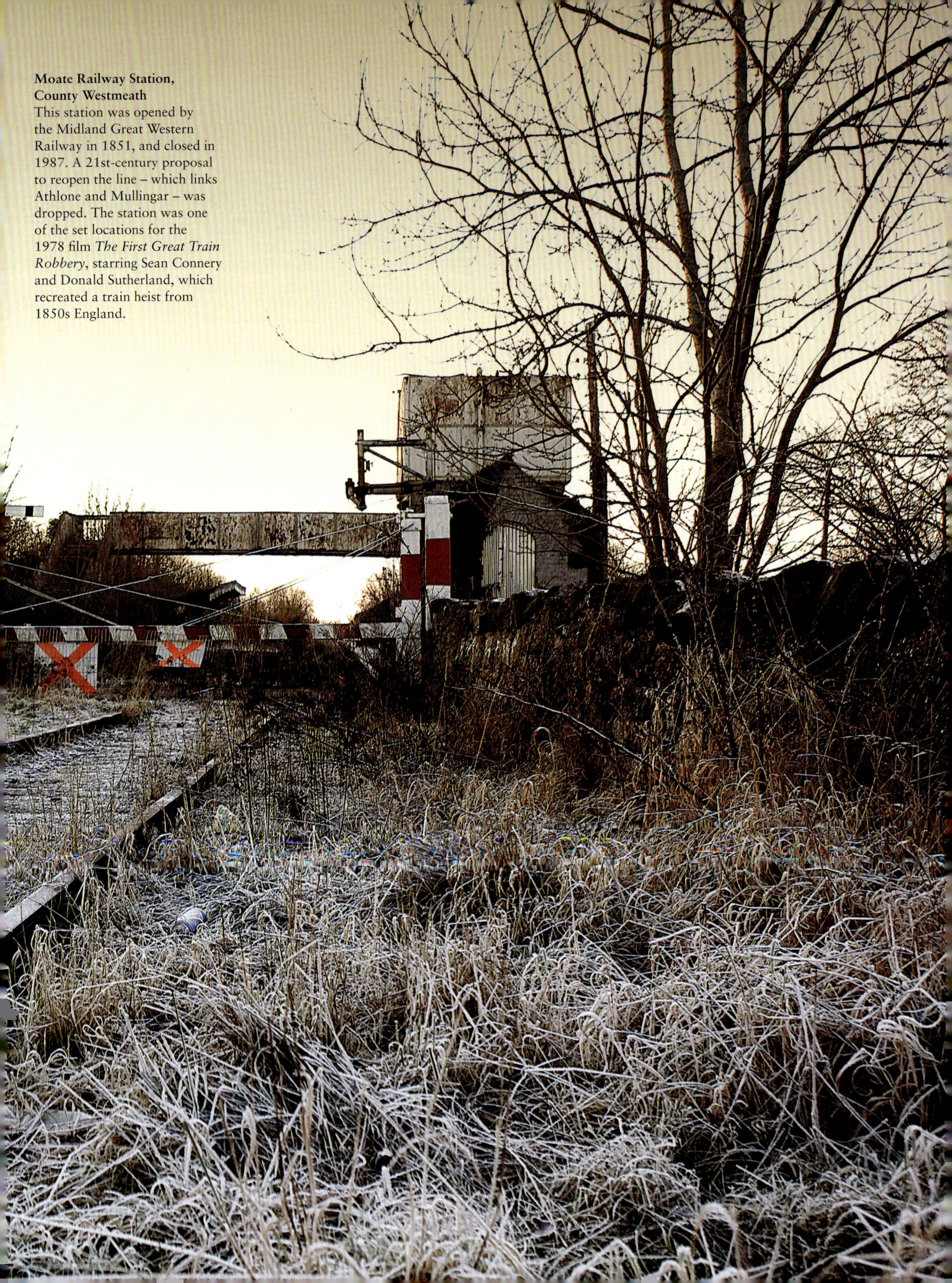

Moate Railway Station,
County Westmeath
This station was opened by
the Midland Great Western
Railway in 1851, and closed in
1987. A 21st-century proposal
to reopen the line – which links
Athlone and Mullingar – was
dropped. The station was one
of the set locations for the
1978 film *The First Great Train
Robbery*, starring Sean Connery
and Donald Sutherland, which
recreated a train heist from
1850s England.

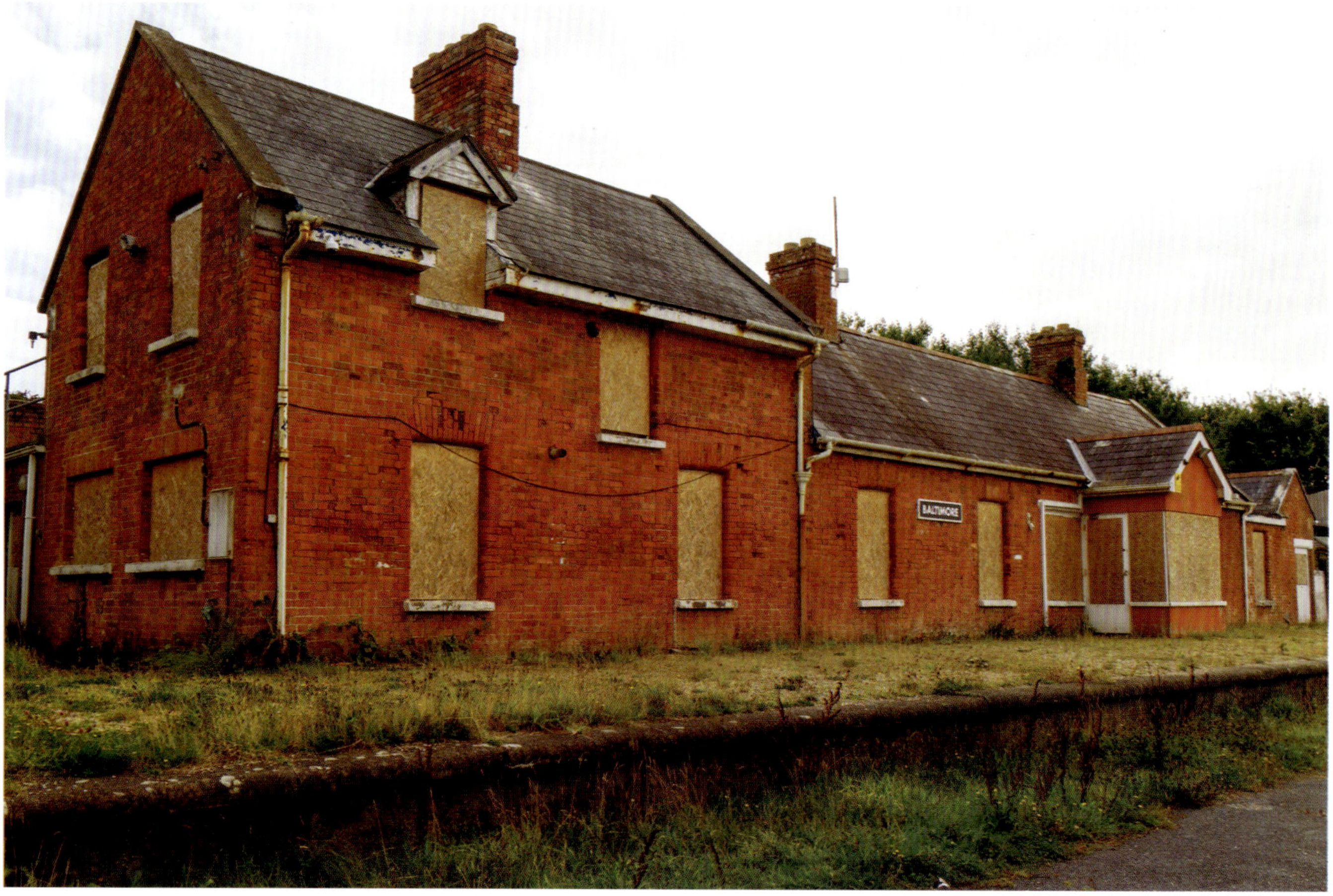

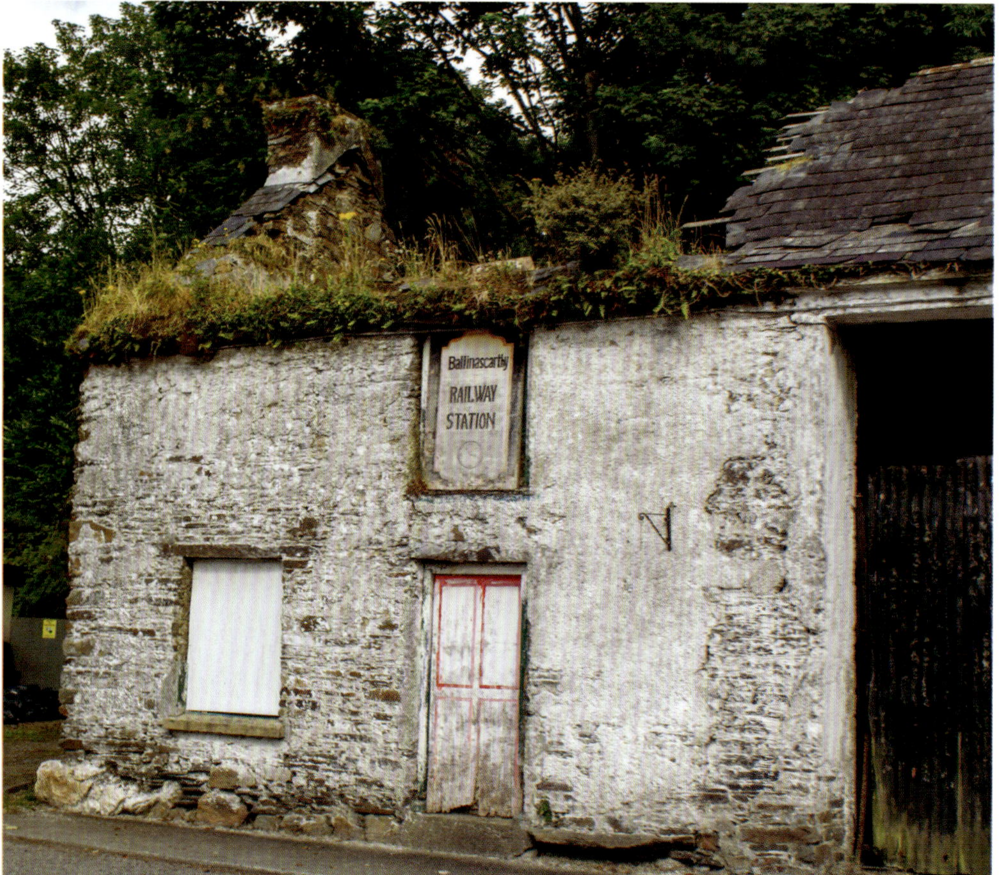

ABOVE:

Baltimore Railway Station, County Cork

Opened in 1893, this station – the terminus of a branch from Skibbereen, and the most southerly station in Ireland – operated until 1961. Between 1969 and 2013, the red-brick building was used as a sailing school.

LEFT:

Ballinascarthy Railway Station, County Cork

Like Baltimore station, this also closed on 1 April 1961, having first opened in 1886. The father of car manufacturer Henry Ford was born in the village of Ballinascarthy before his emigration to America, and there is a memorial to Henry Ford in the village.

OPPOSITE:

Parkmore Railway Station, County Antrim

This closed to passengers in 1930 and to freight in 1940. It was on the Ballymena, Cushendall and Red Bay Railway, which was opened to serve iron ore mines in the area and cut through the picturesque Glens of Antrim.

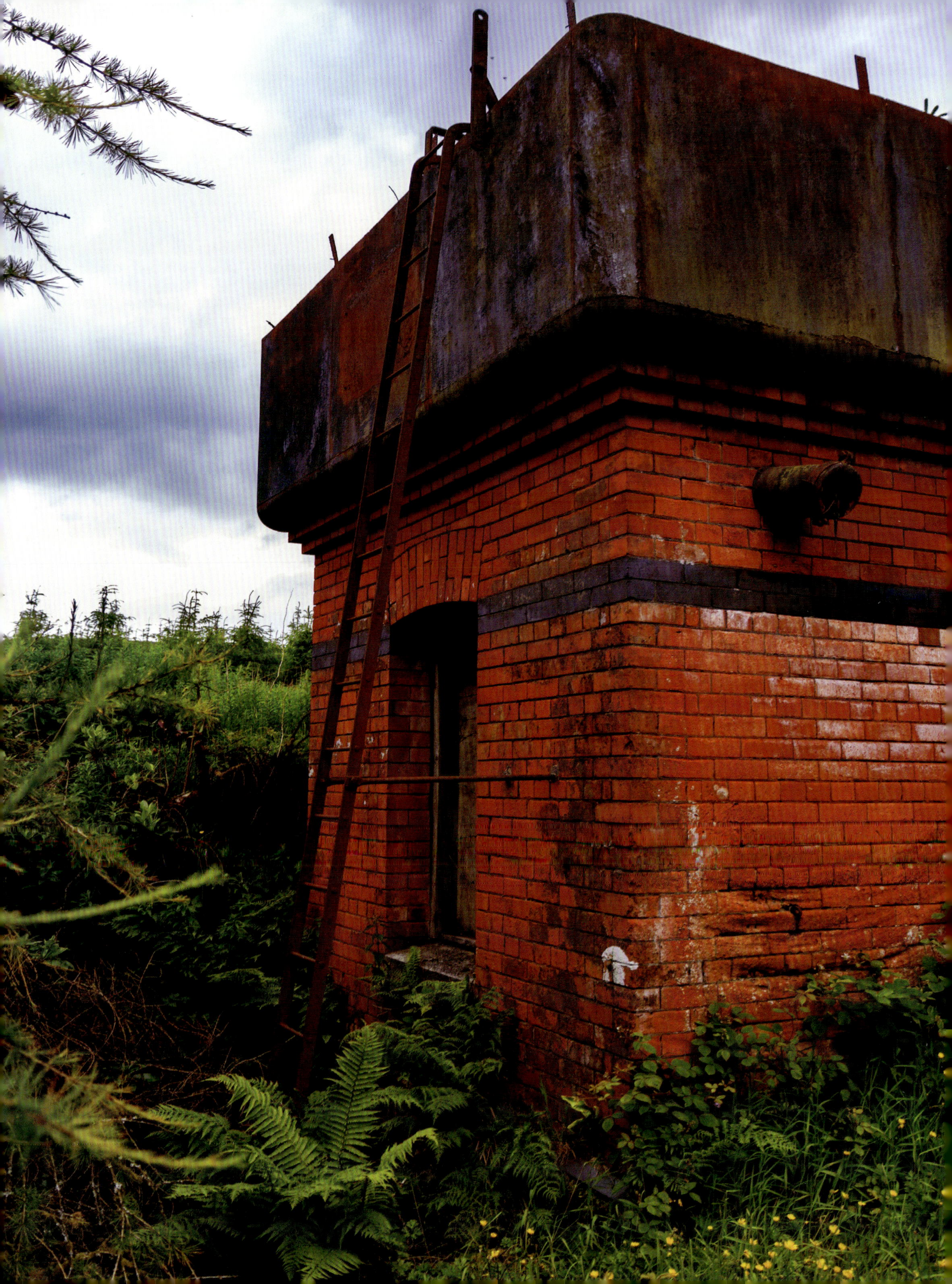

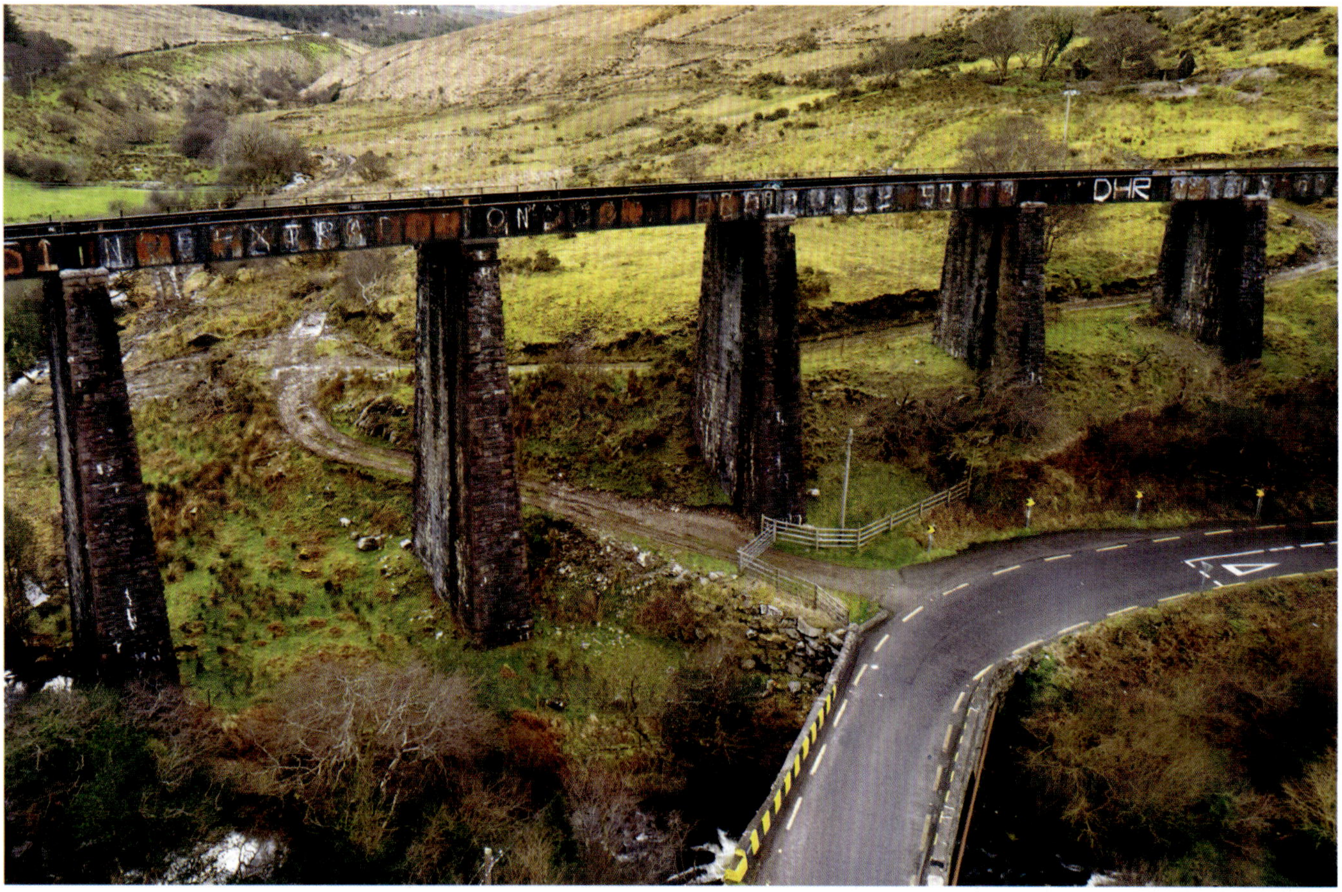

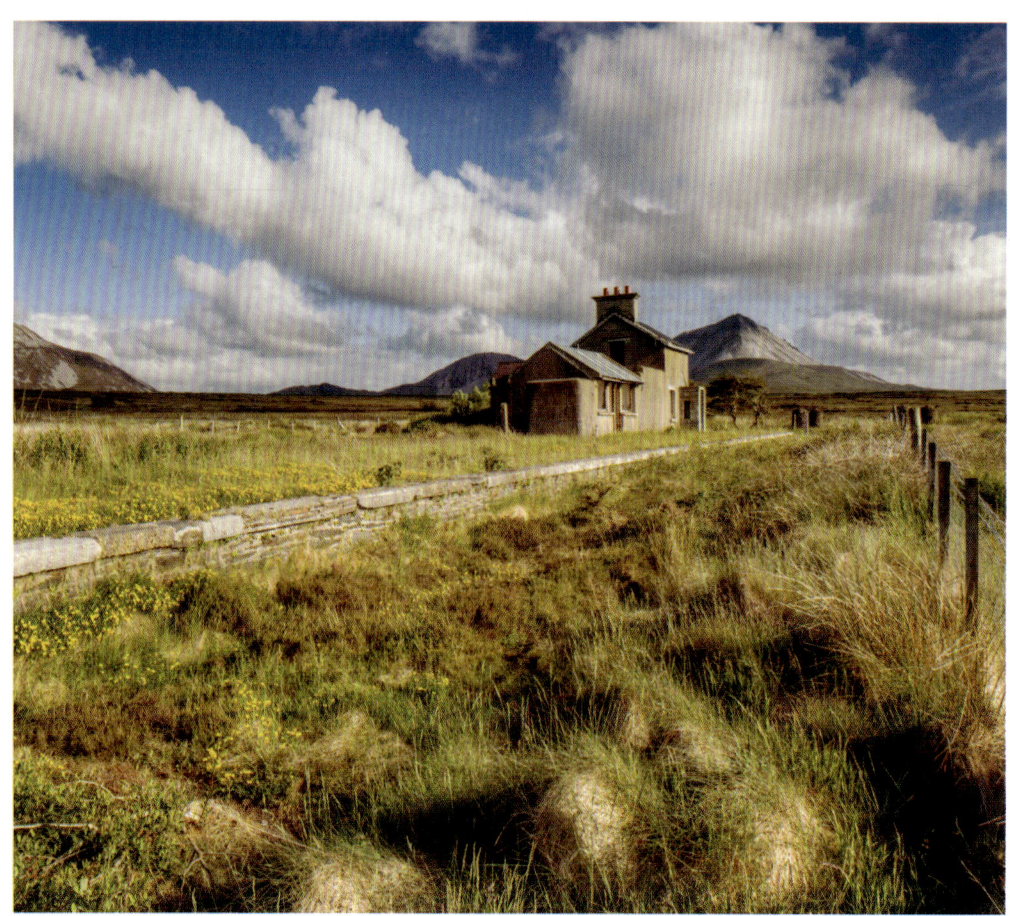

ABOVE:
Gleensk Railway Viaduct, County Kerry
There are 11 spans in this steel railway viaduct from 1893. It was used until 1960. It crosses the Gleensk River valley.

RIGHT:
Cashelnagore Railway Station, County Donegal
Cashelnagore station – sometimes spelled Cashelnagor – opened in 1903 and closed in 1940, on a line between Letterkenny and Burtonport.

OPPOSITE ABOVE:
Lispole Viaduct, County Kerry
This viaduct was first used in 1891, as part of the Tralee & Dingle Railway, and crosses the Owenalondrig River. The viaduct was constructed of stone and iron.

OPPOSITE BELOW:
Mullingar Railway Station, County Westmeath
The town of Mullingar, the county town of Westmeath, still has a working railway station, but also two disused ones – one that served the line to Athlone and the other on the Sligo line.

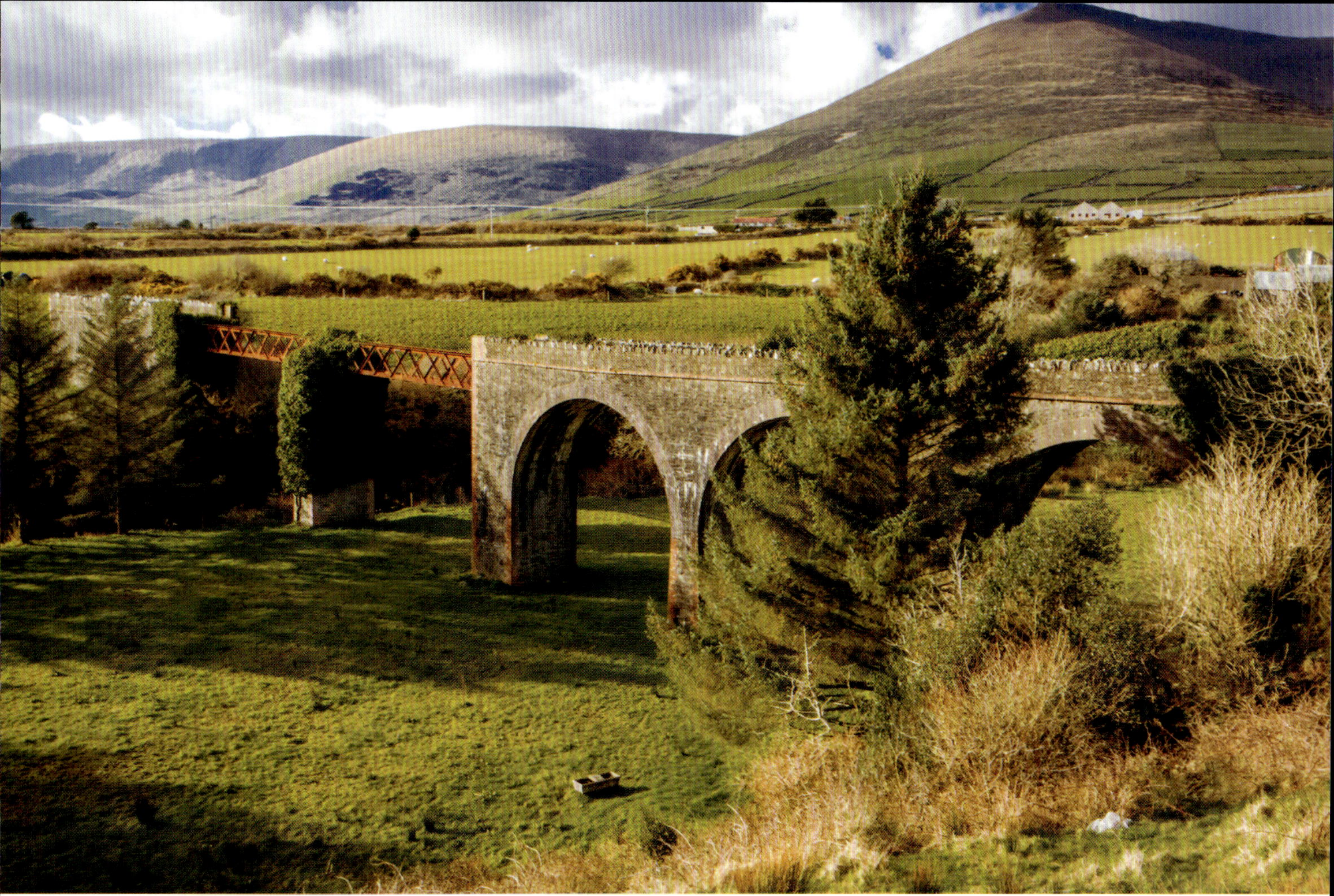

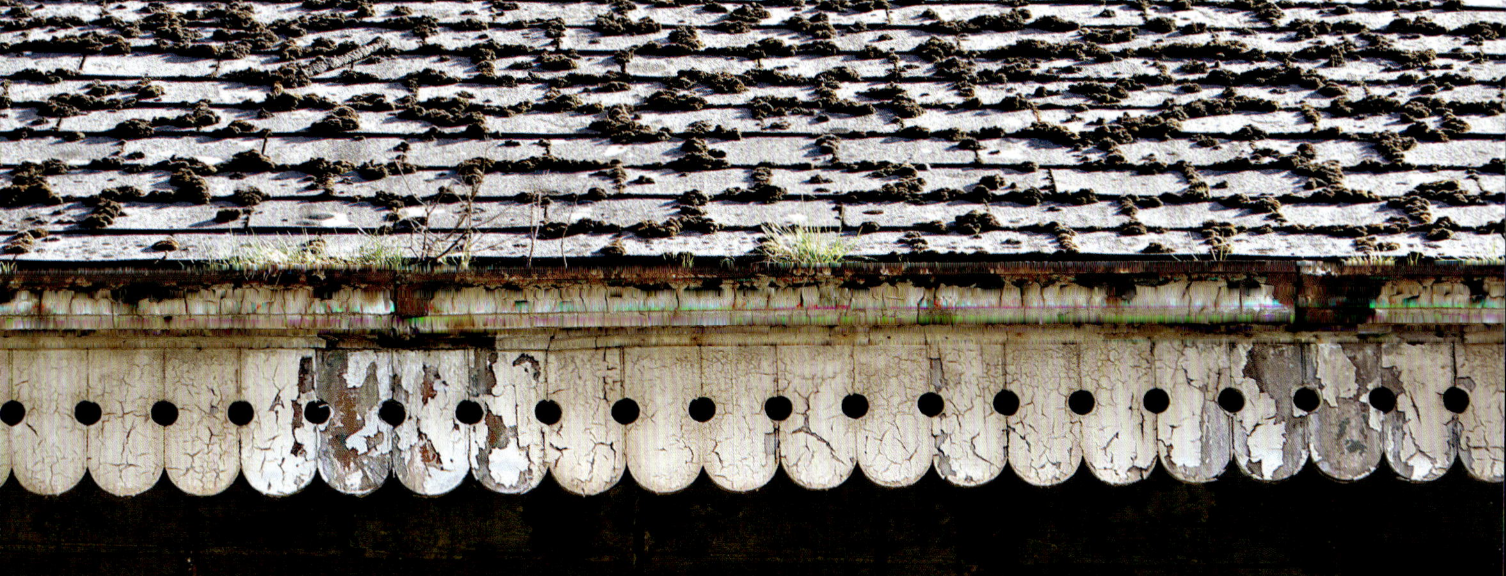

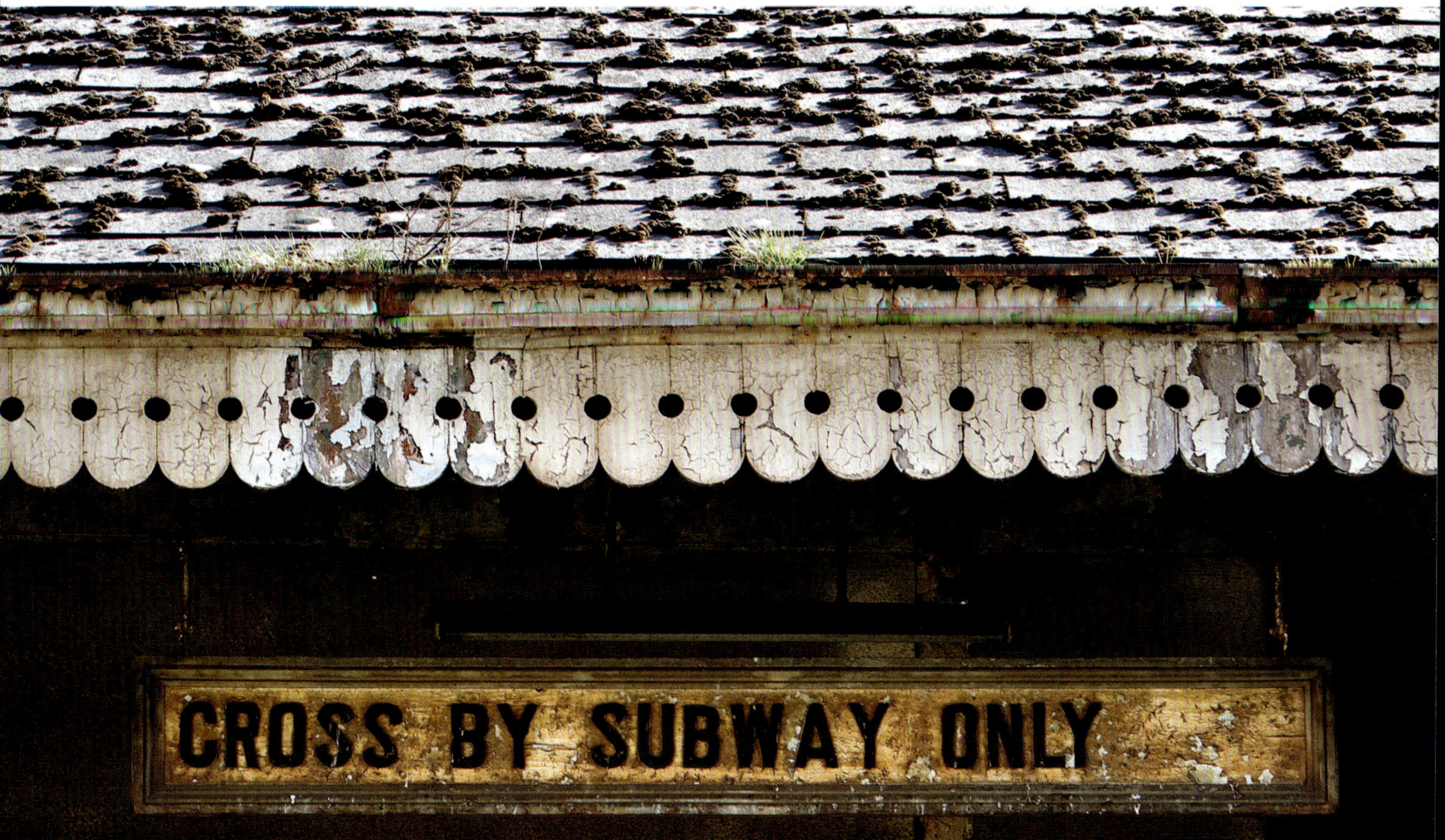

CROSS BY SUBWAY ONLY

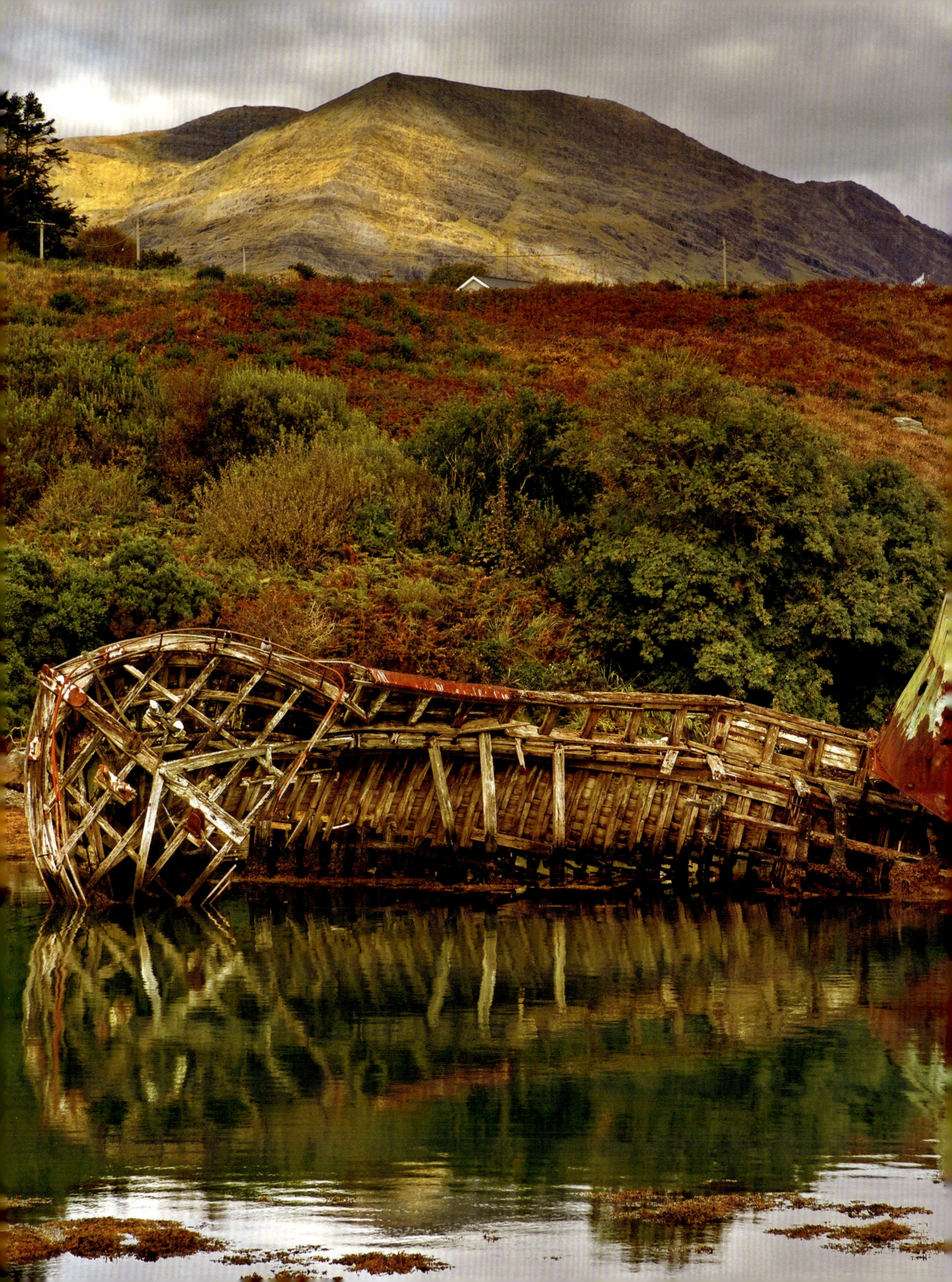

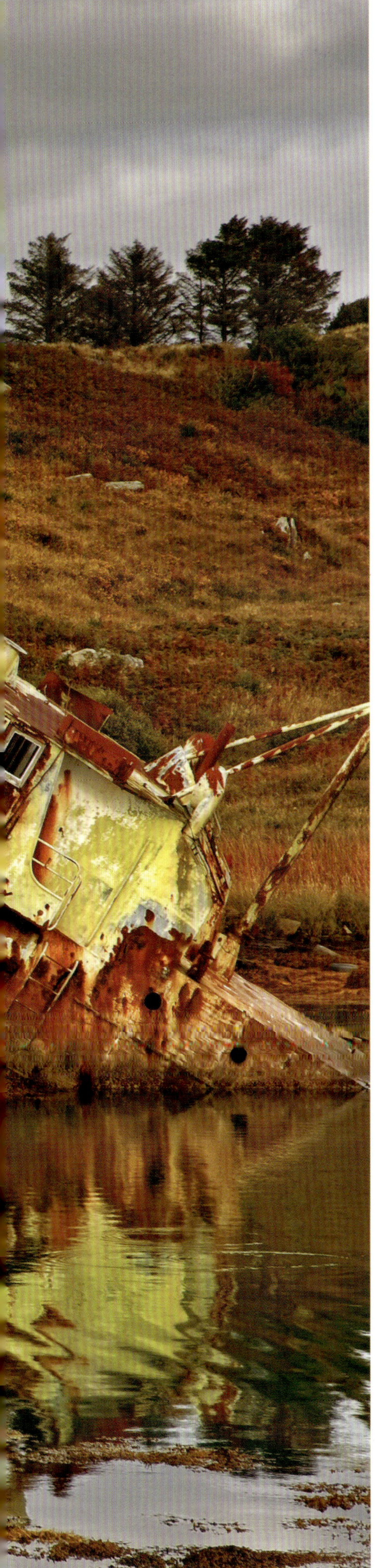

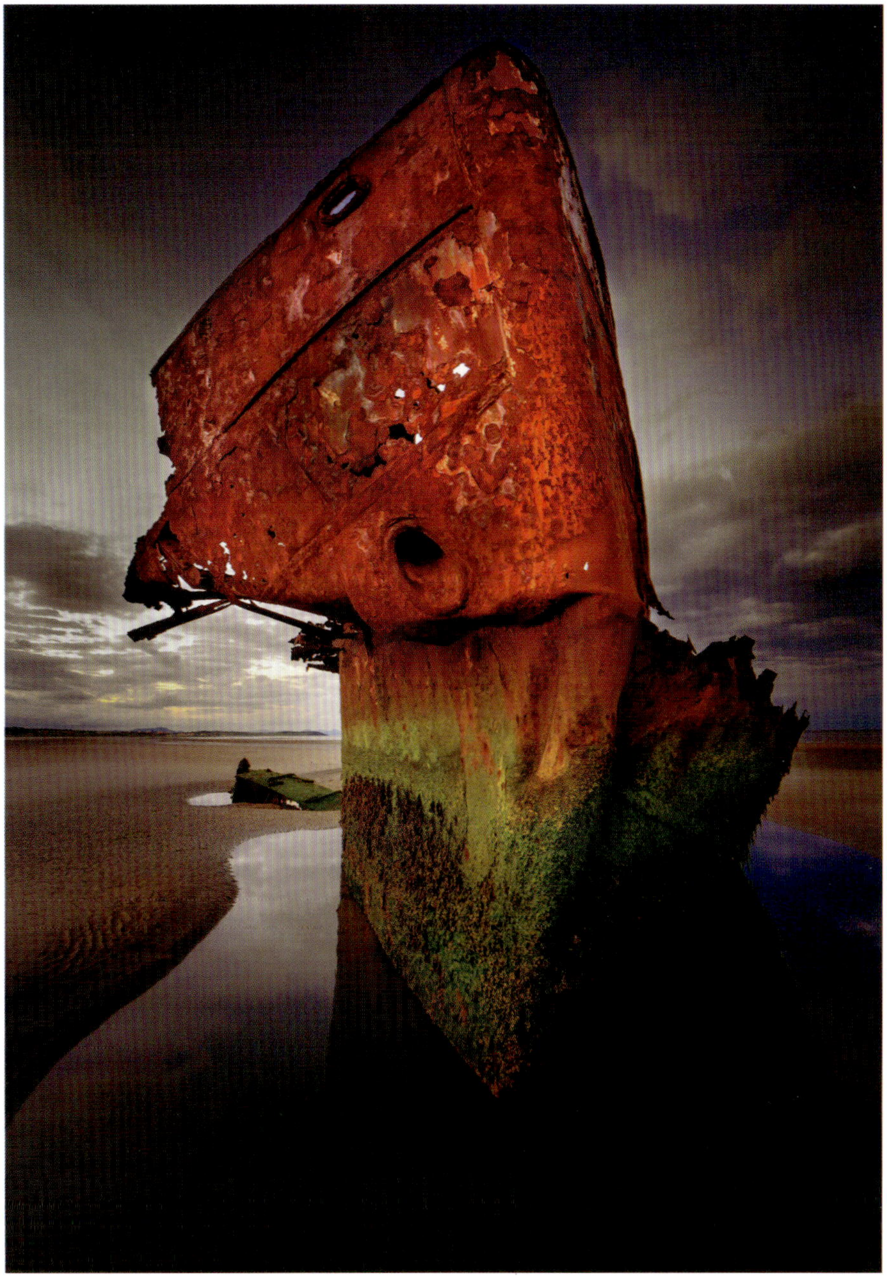

Castletownbere shipwreck, County Cork
The waters off Castletownbere, on the Beara Peninsula, are awash with shipwrecks, as it is a fishing port and a major commercial hub for the area. Not unexpectedly, it is part of western Ireland's storm-battered coastal route, the Wild Atlantic Way.

MV *Irish Trader*, Baltray, County Louth
This ship ran aground off Baltray in 1974 in stormy Irish Sea waters and has remained there on the flat, sandy beach ever since. Built in 1949, she was carrying fertilizer to Drogheda, having left Sharpness on the Bristol Channel.

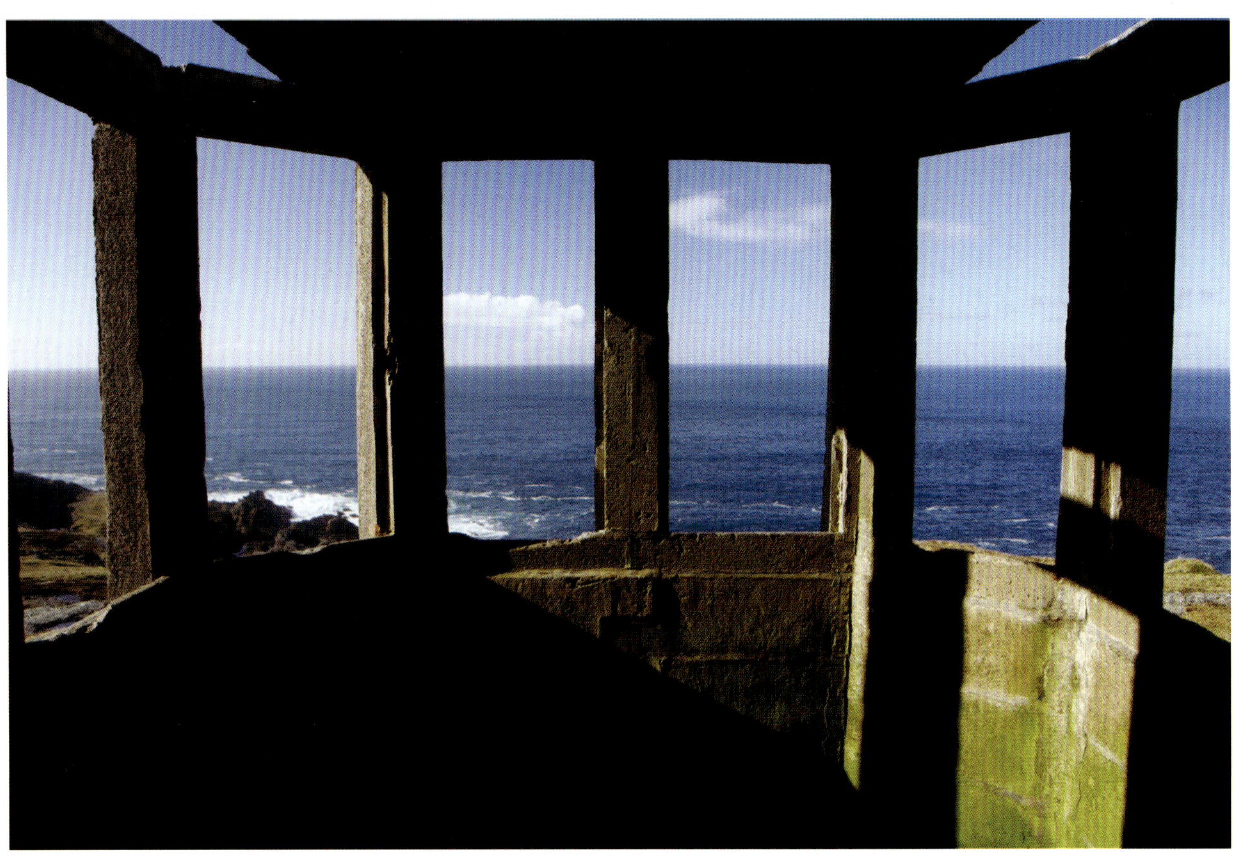

ABOVE:

Malin Head coastguard lookout station, County Donegal
Malin Head is the most northerly point of the Irish land mass, giving the coastguard lookout station there excellent views. There is a weather station and, as it gives its name to the sea area Malin, it is a regular feature of the BBC Shipping Forecast.

RIGHT:

Carrickfergus Radar Tower, Country Antrim
This installation is located on Carrickfergus Pier, which is next to the town's castle. It was used to monitor sea traffic coming in and out of Belfast Lough. It is scheduled to be refurbished.

OPPOSITE:

***Bád Eddie*, Bunbeg, County Donegal**
This fishing boat, the remains of which can be seen from the derelict Ostan Gweedore hotel that overlooks the waters here, was abandoned after running aground on the beach in the 1970s. Known as 'Bad Eddie's boat', she has become a local tourist attraction.

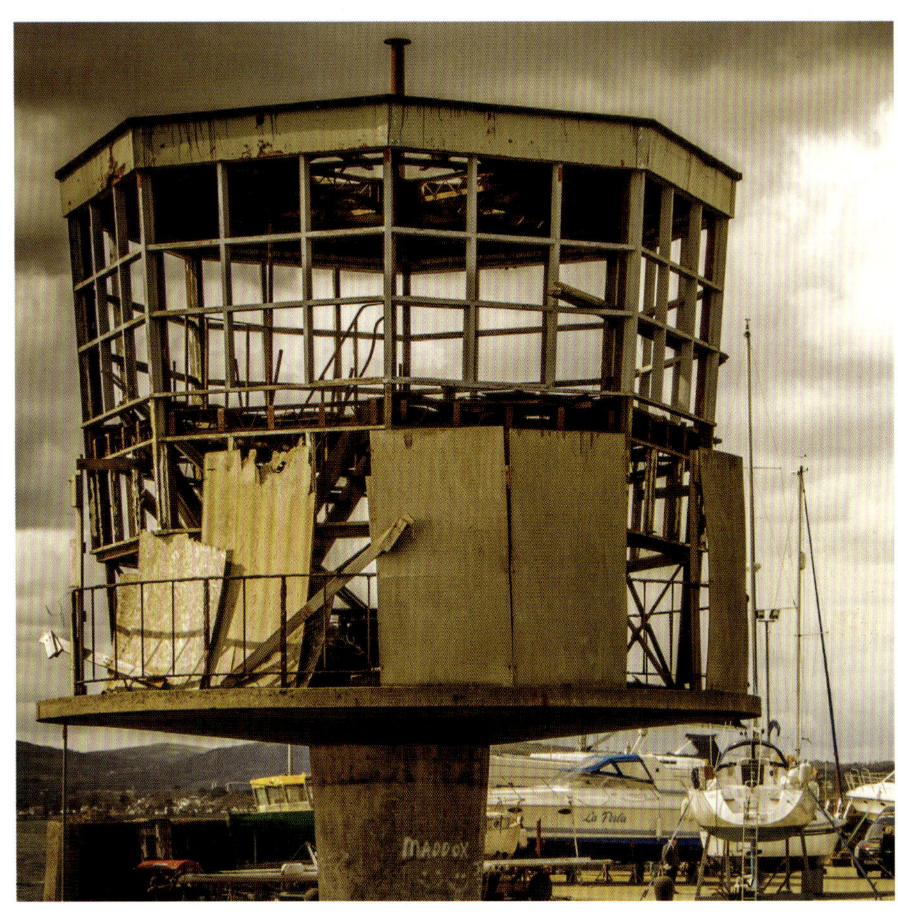

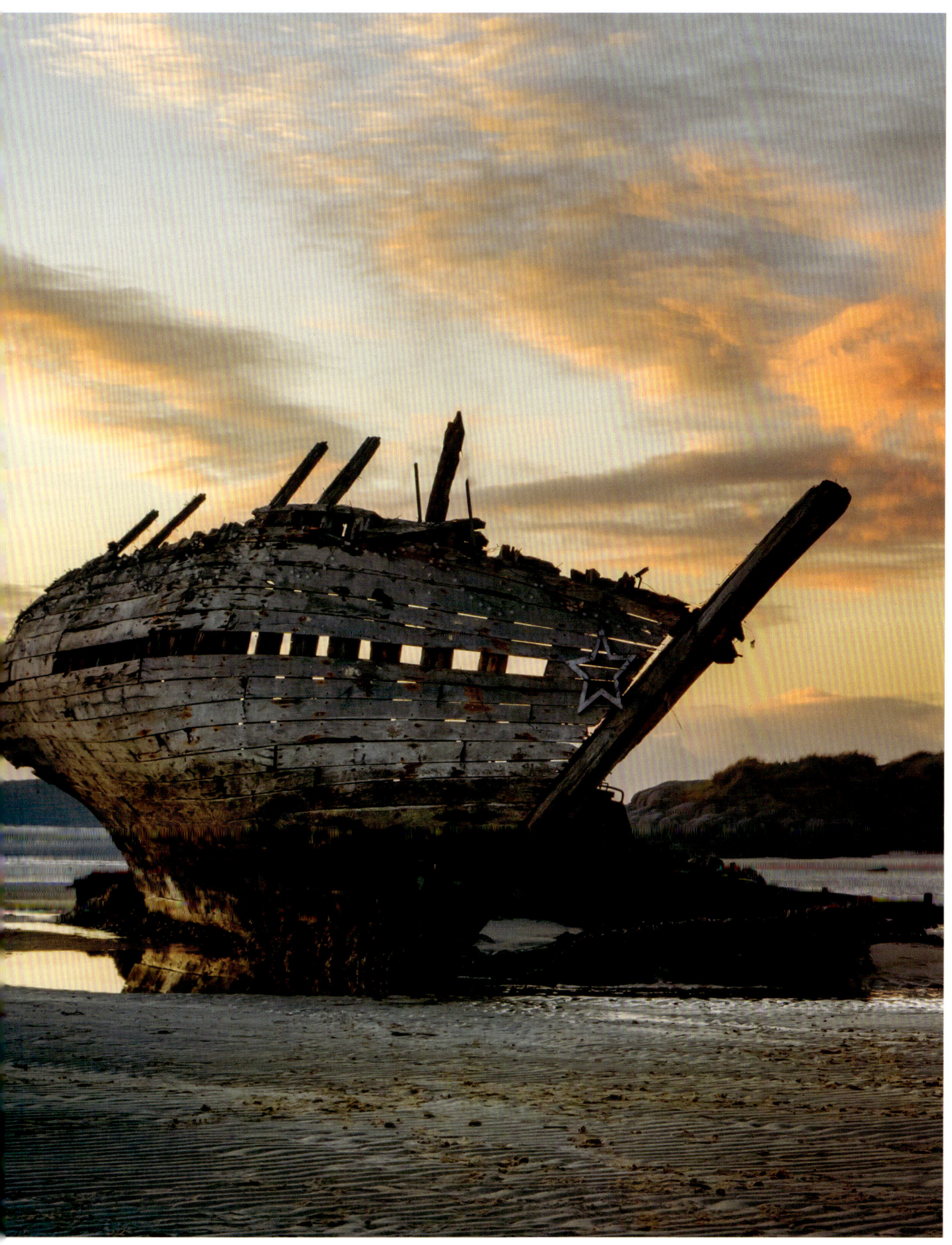

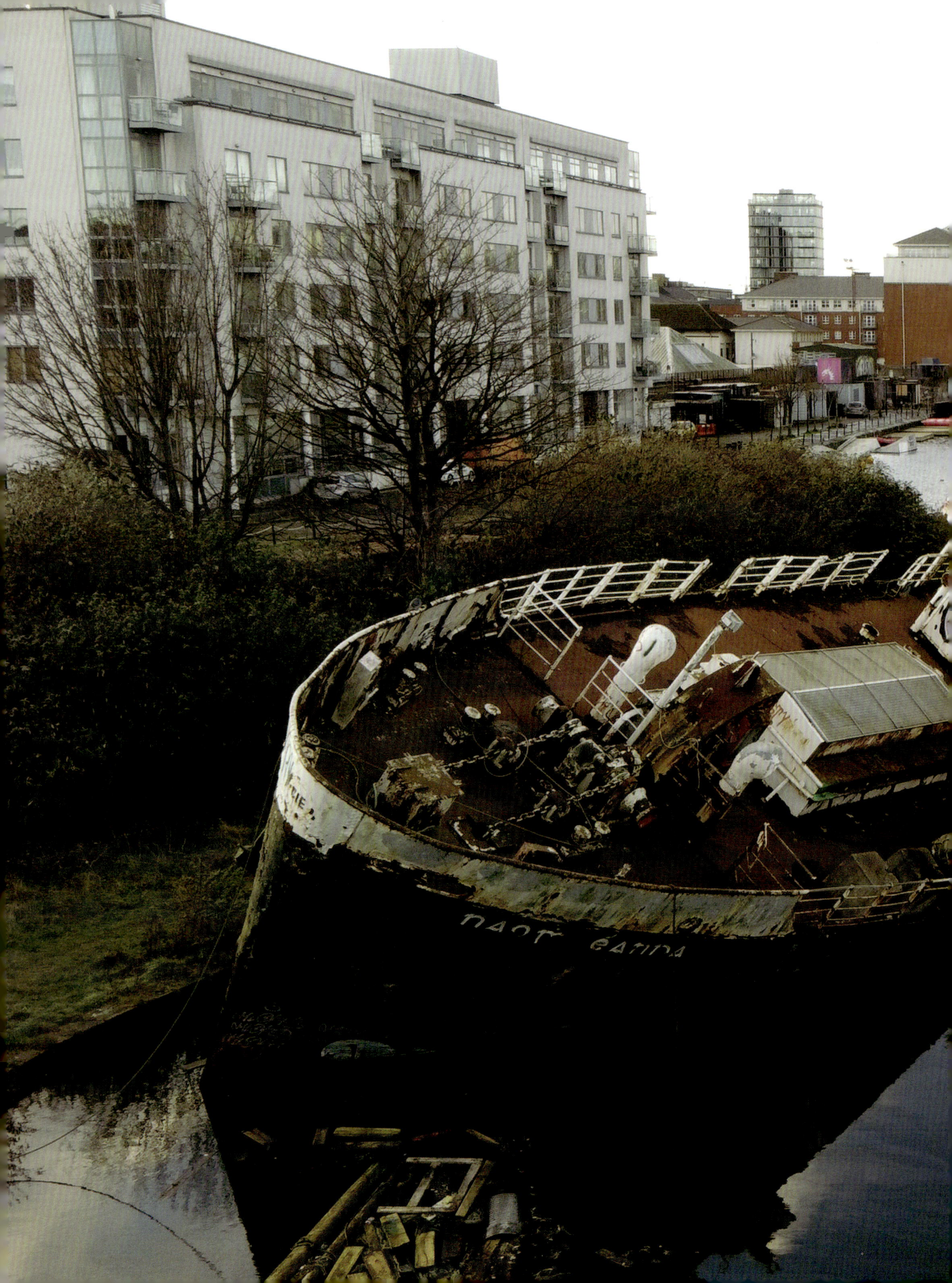
naoṁ éaṅna

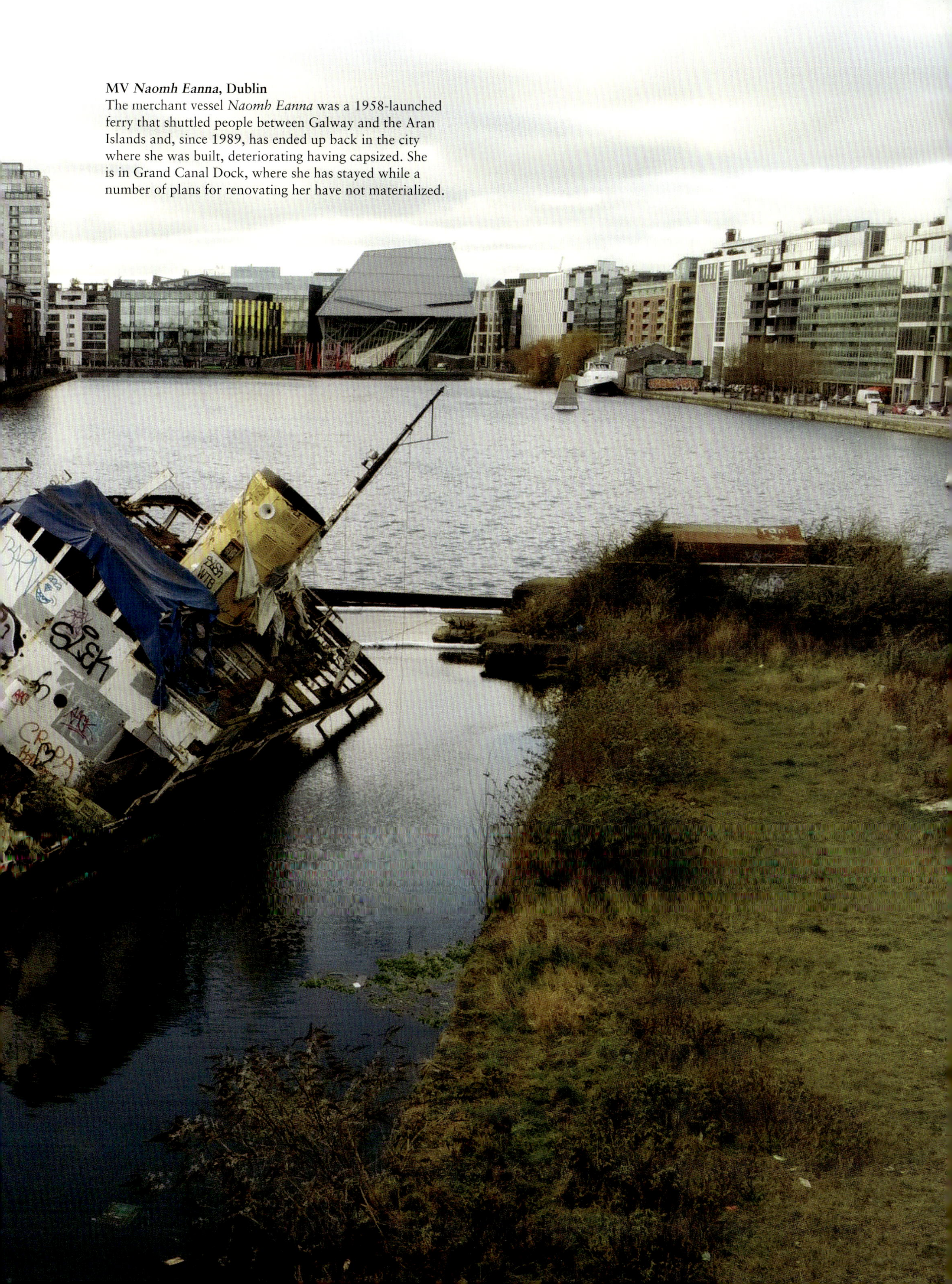

MV *Naomh Eanna*, Dublin
The merchant vessel *Naomh Eanna* was a 1958-launched ferry that shuttled people between Galway and the Aran Islands and, since 1989, has ended up back in the city where she was built, deteriorating having capsized. She is in Grand Canal Dock, where she has stayed while a number of plans for renovating her have not materialized.

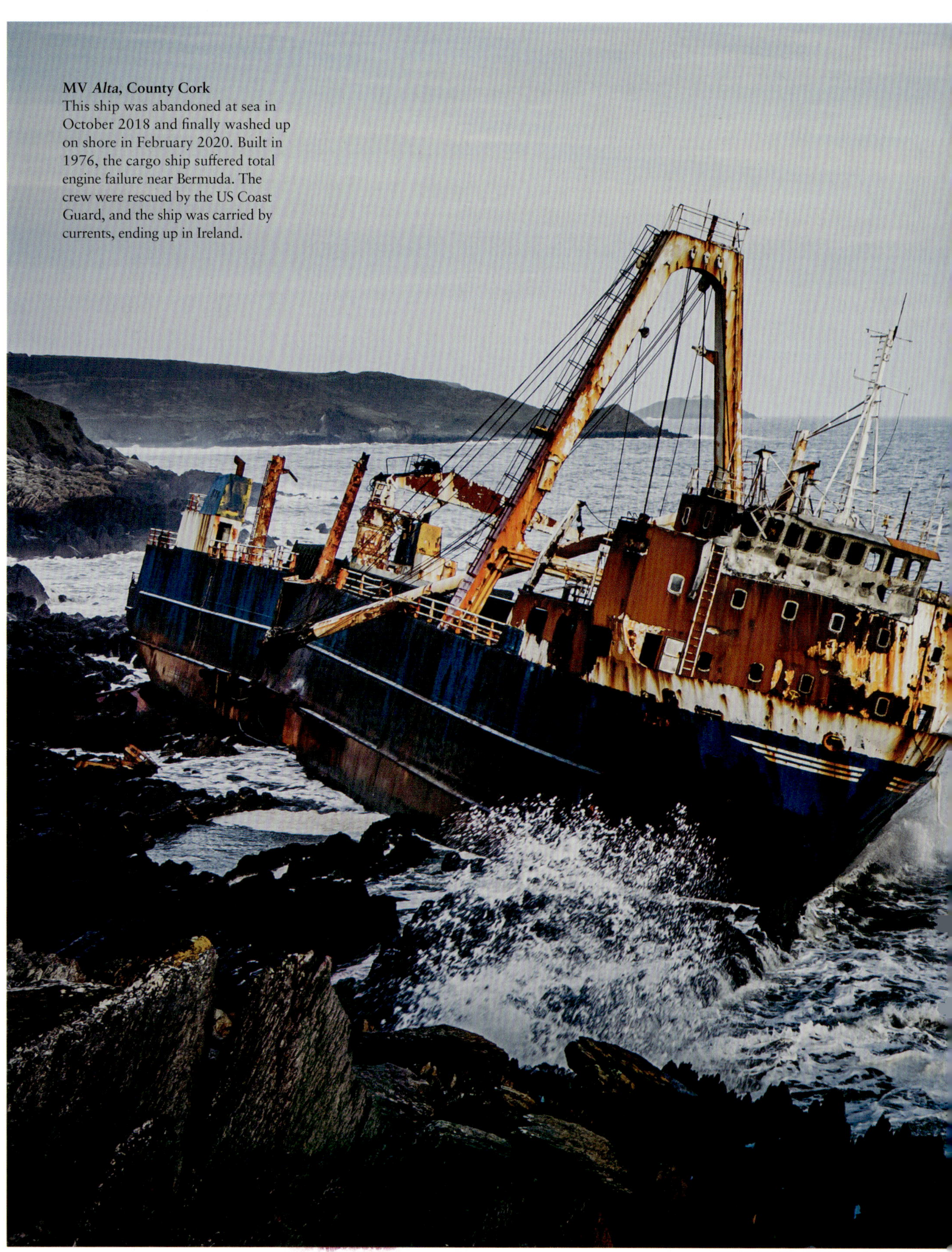

MV *Alta*, County Cork
This ship was abandoned at sea in October 2018 and finally washed up on shore in February 2020. Built in 1976, the cargo ship suffered total engine failure near Bermuda. The crew were rescued by the US Coast Guard, and the ship was carried by currents, ending up in Ireland.

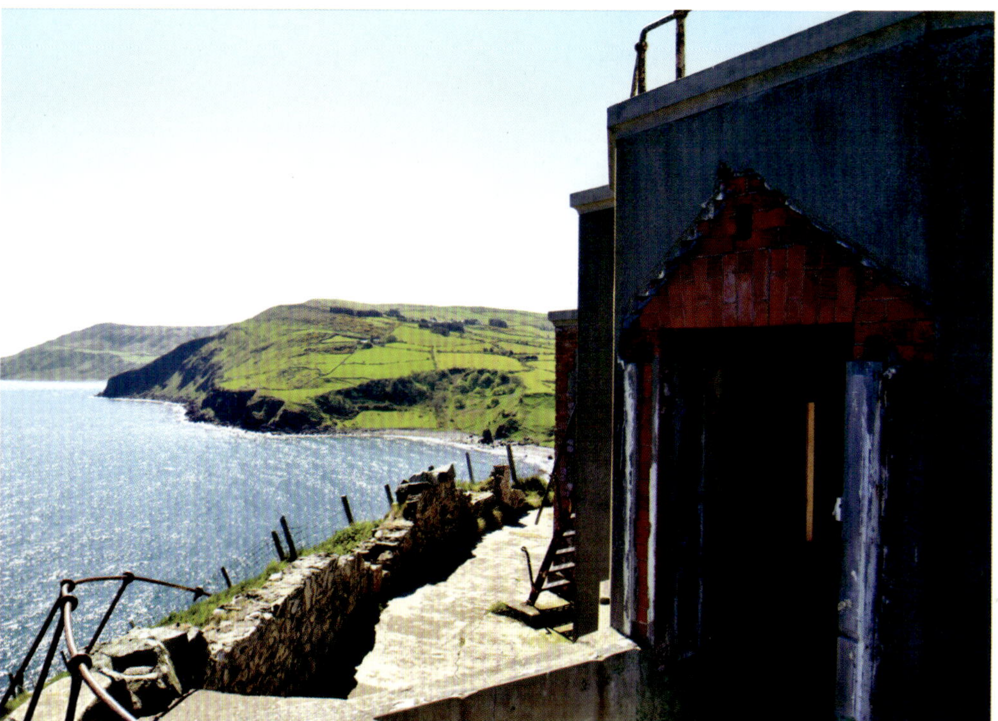

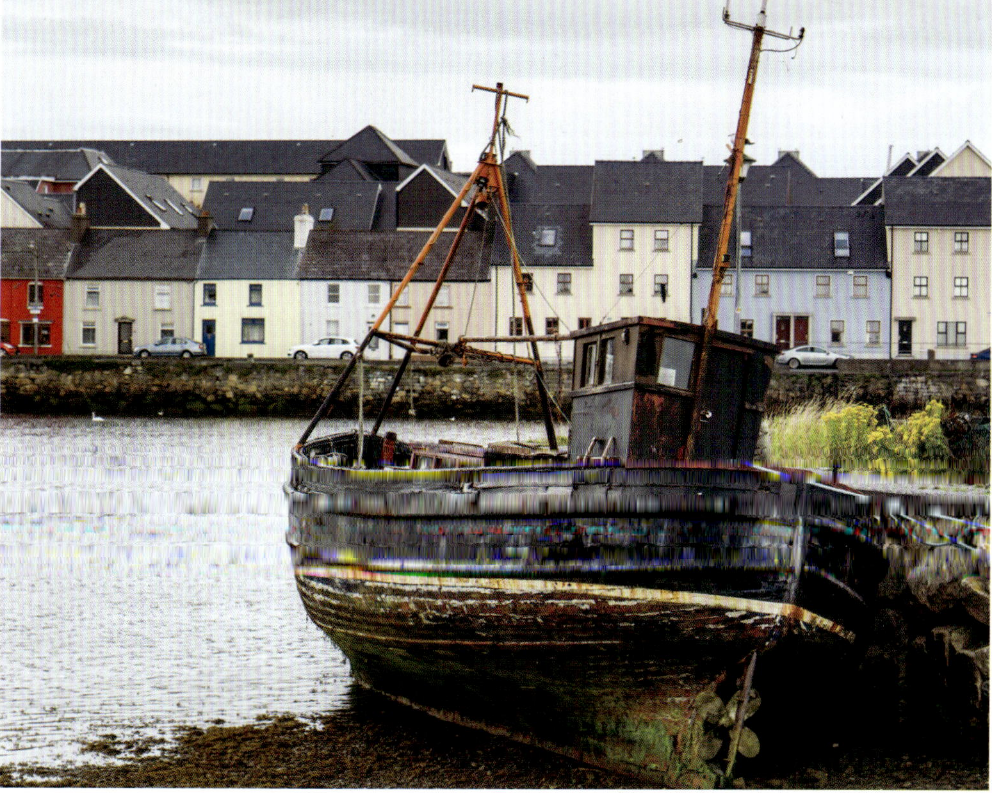

Torr Head Coastguard Station, County Antrim
Built in 1822 on the site of the ancient Barrach's
Fort, this coastguard station was ransacked a
century after its creation during a sectarian attack.
Torr Head is Ireland's closest point to Scotland and
you can see the Mull of Kintyre from it.

Wrecked fishing boat, Claddagh, Galway
'Claddagh' means 'shore' in Irish and the name has
been given to this area near the centre of Galway
city where the River Corrib meets Galway Bay.
This wreck of a fishing boat is apt, as the area was
home to a fishing village for hundreds of years.

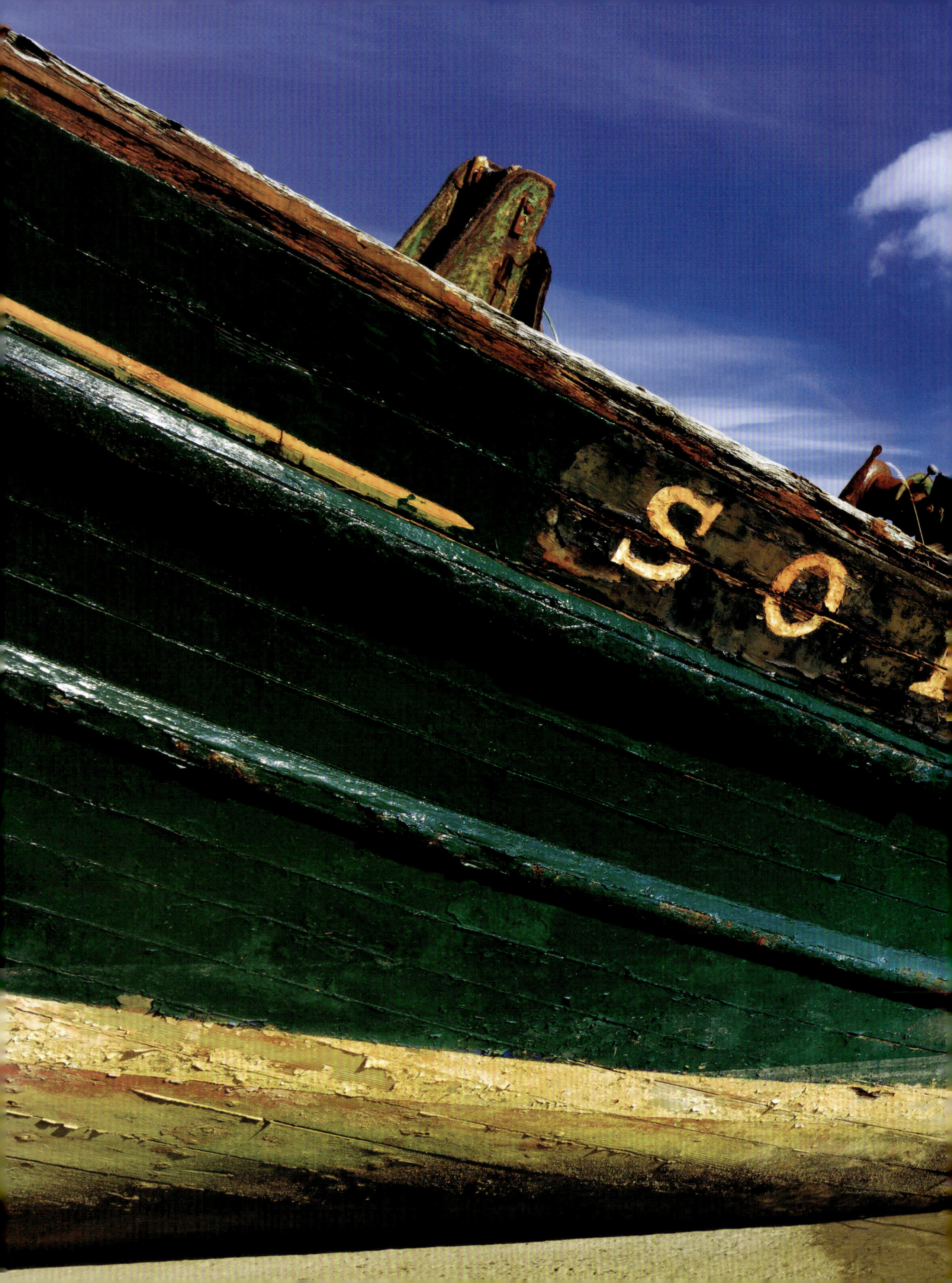

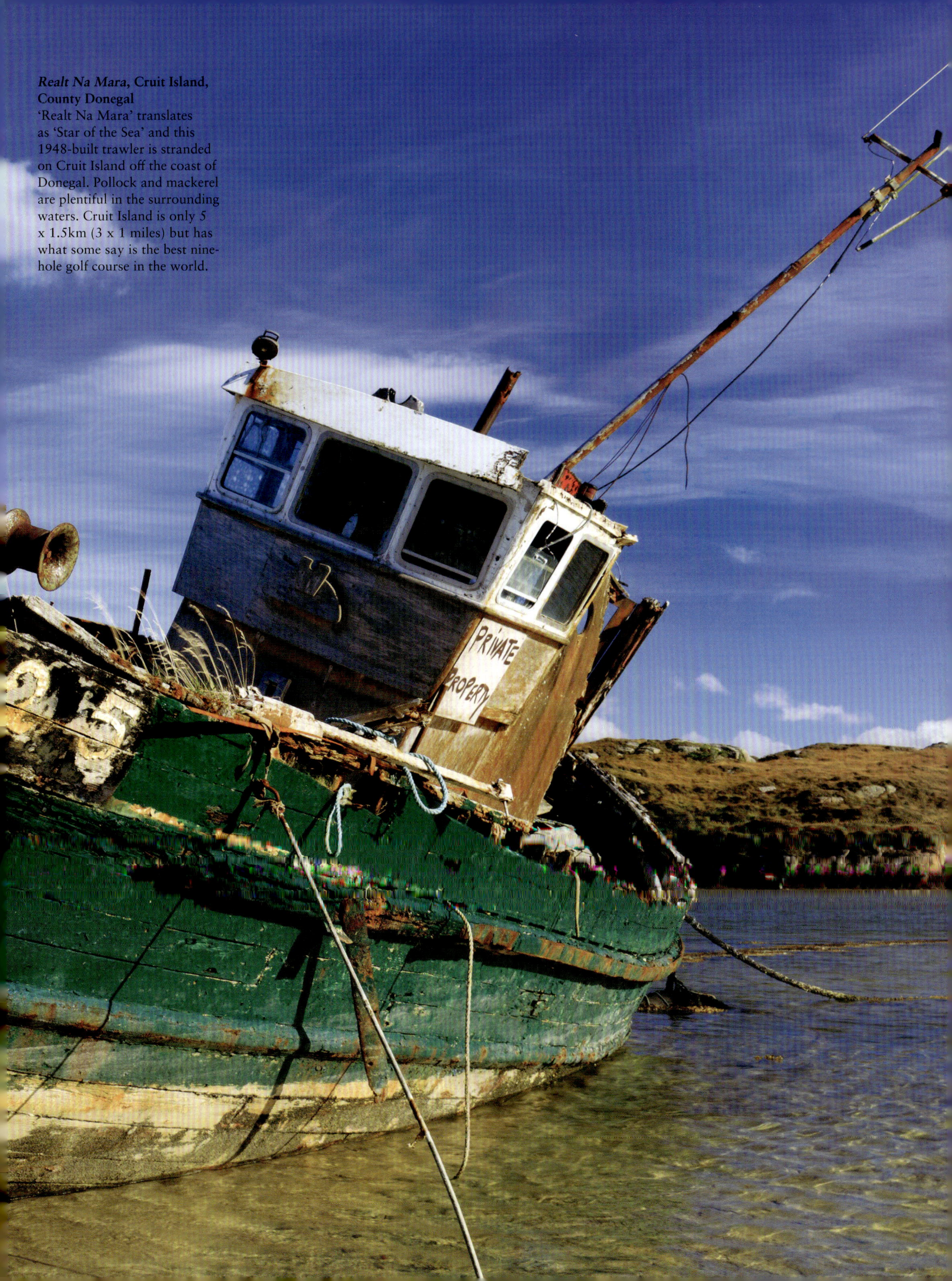

***Realt Na Mara*, Cruit Island, County Donegal**
'Realt Na Mara' translates as 'Star of the Sea' and this 1948-built trawler is stranded on Cruit Island off the coast of Donegal. Pollock and mackerel are plentiful in the surrounding waters. Cruit Island is only 5 x 1.5km (3 x 1 miles) but has what some say is the best nine-hole golf course in the world.

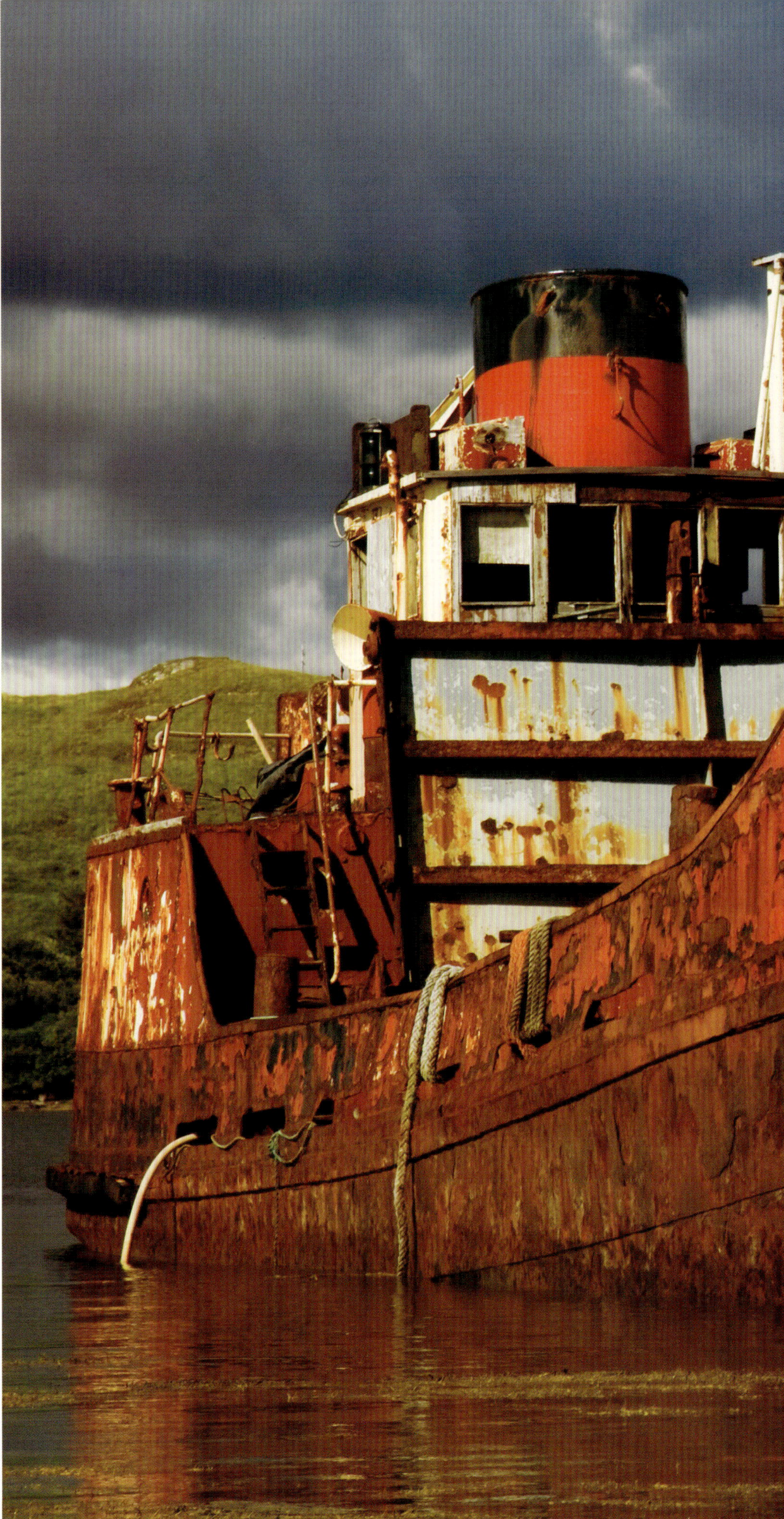

Abandoned ship, Letterfrack Pier, County Galway
This vessel has been tied up by a pier and left to rust away, her hull containing holes and water. Conversely, the village of Letterfrack, where she sits, is regarded as one of the most attractive in the west of Ireland and houses the visitor centre for Connemara National Park.

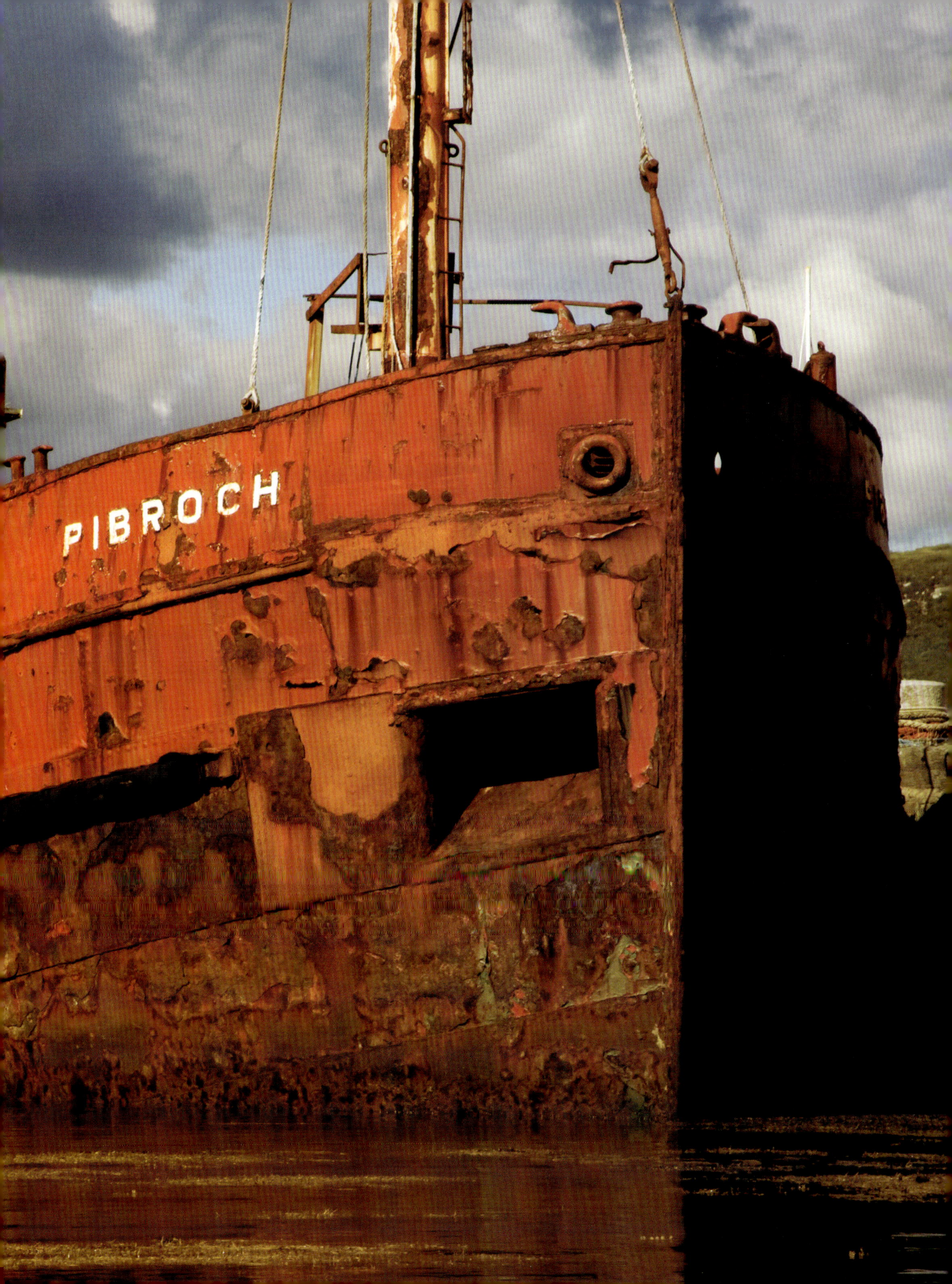
PIBROCH

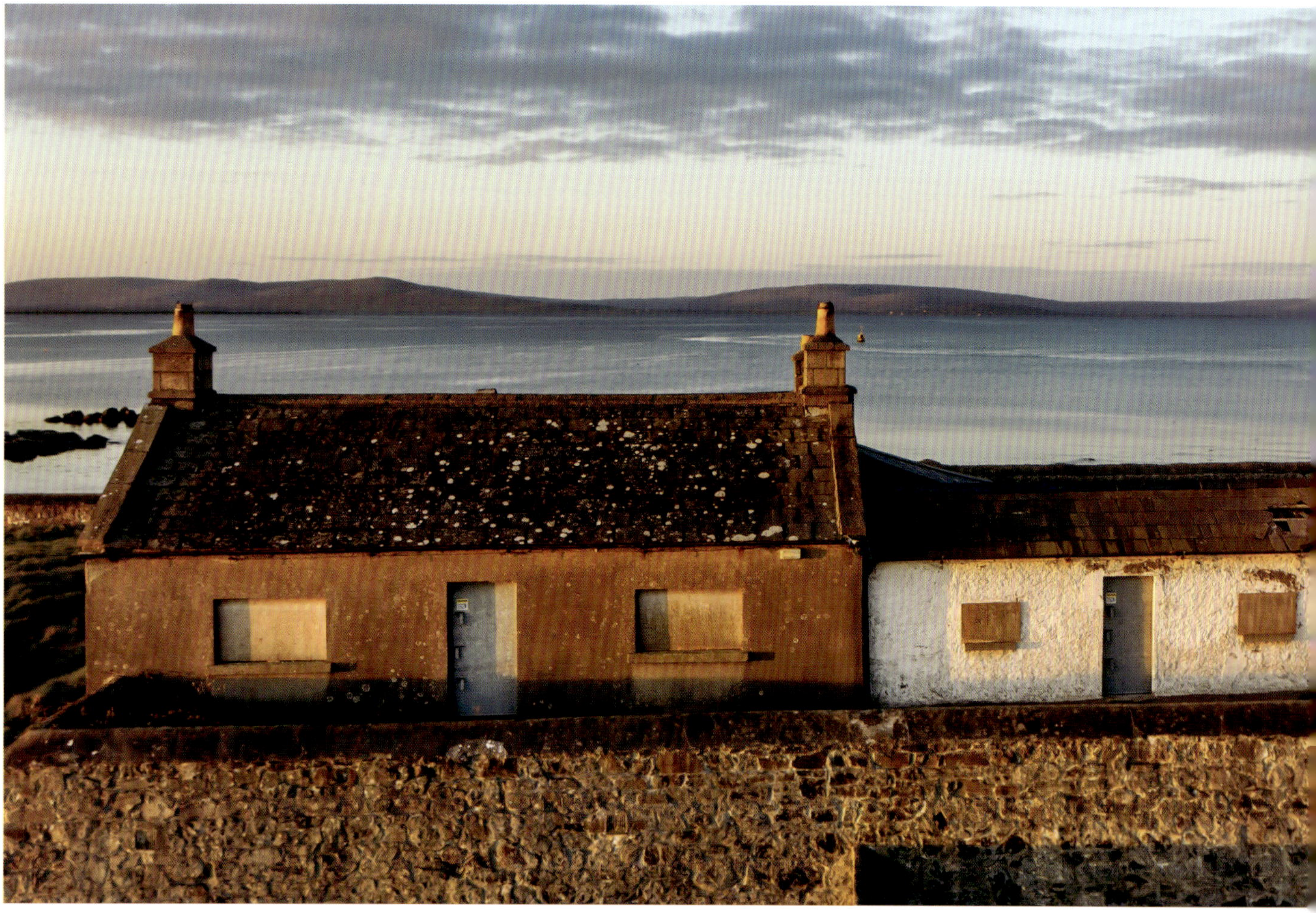

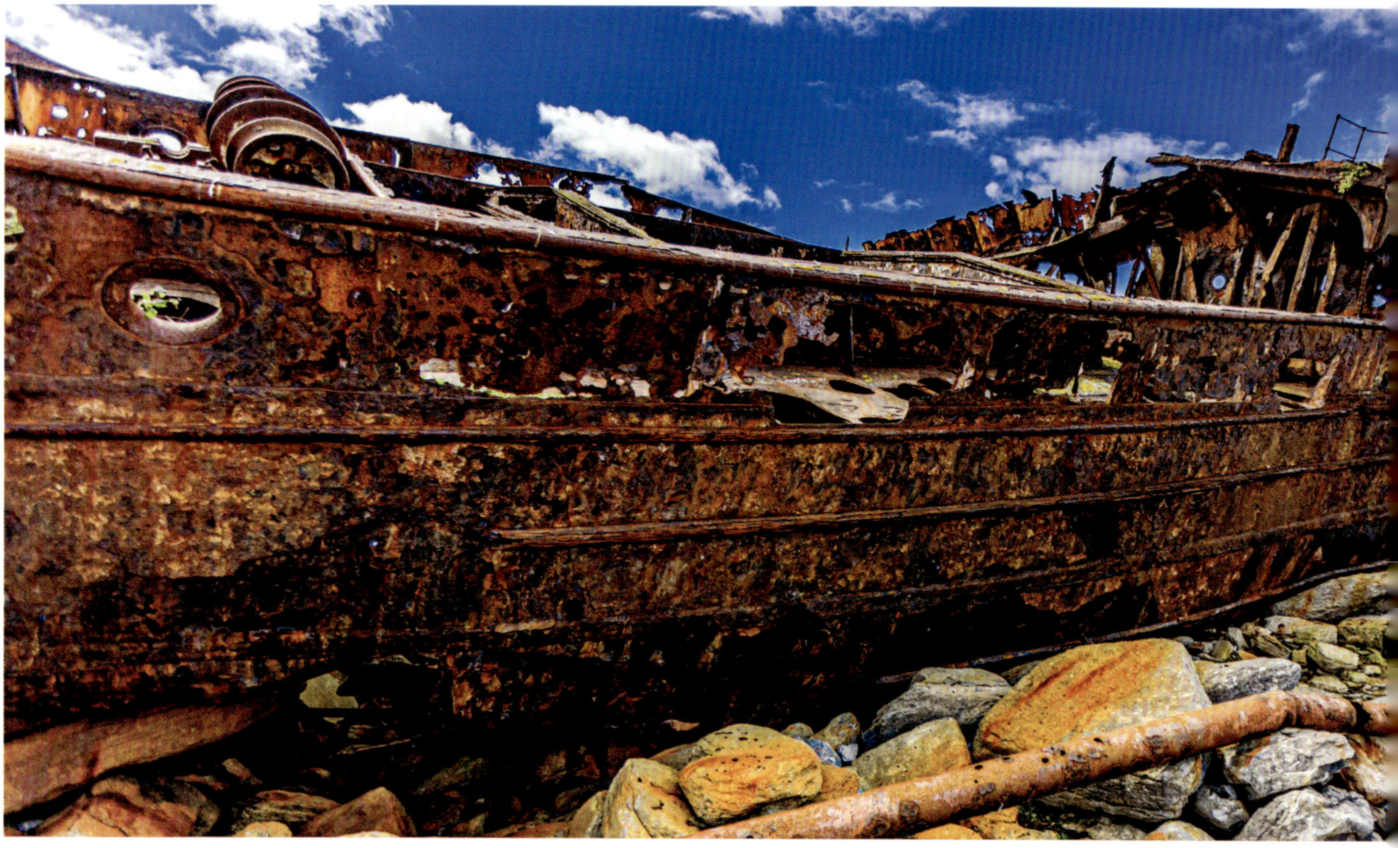

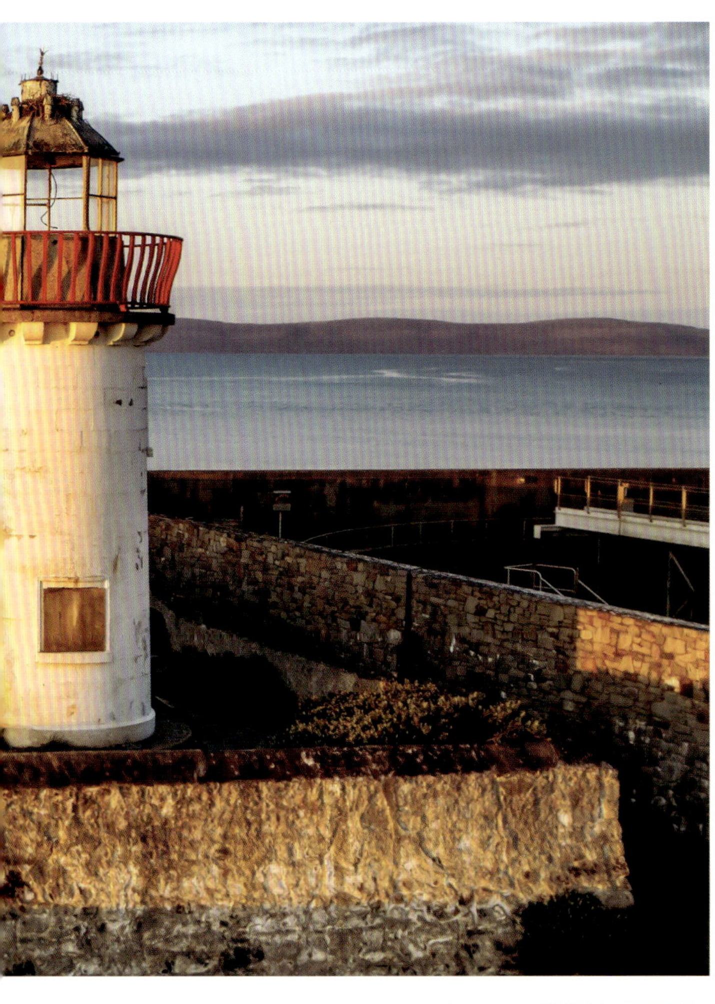

LEFT:

Mutton Island Lighthouse, Galway Harbour
Mutton Island Lighthouse was built in the early 19th century and was one of the few lighthouses in Ireland where the lighthouse keeper could also live. The island itself is located just off the coast at Galway city but is connected to the mainland by a causeway. As well as the lighthouse, the island contains a sewage works.

LEFT BOTTOM & BELOW:

MV *Plassey* shipwreck, Inisheer, Aran Islands, County Galway
This freighter, which had been built as the Royal Navy trawler HMS *Juliet*, was washed up in 1960 after a storm. The *Plassey* was carrying whiskey, stained glass and yarn. All the crew were rescued by locals from the island of Inisheer, where the freighter washed up. The wreck features in the opening credits of the 1990s television series *Father Ted*.

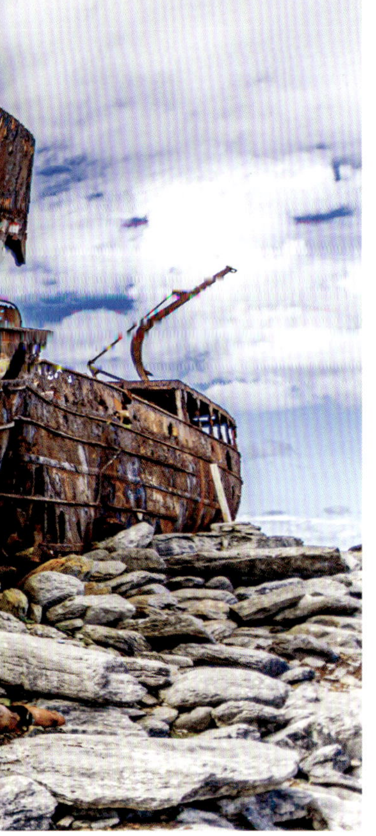

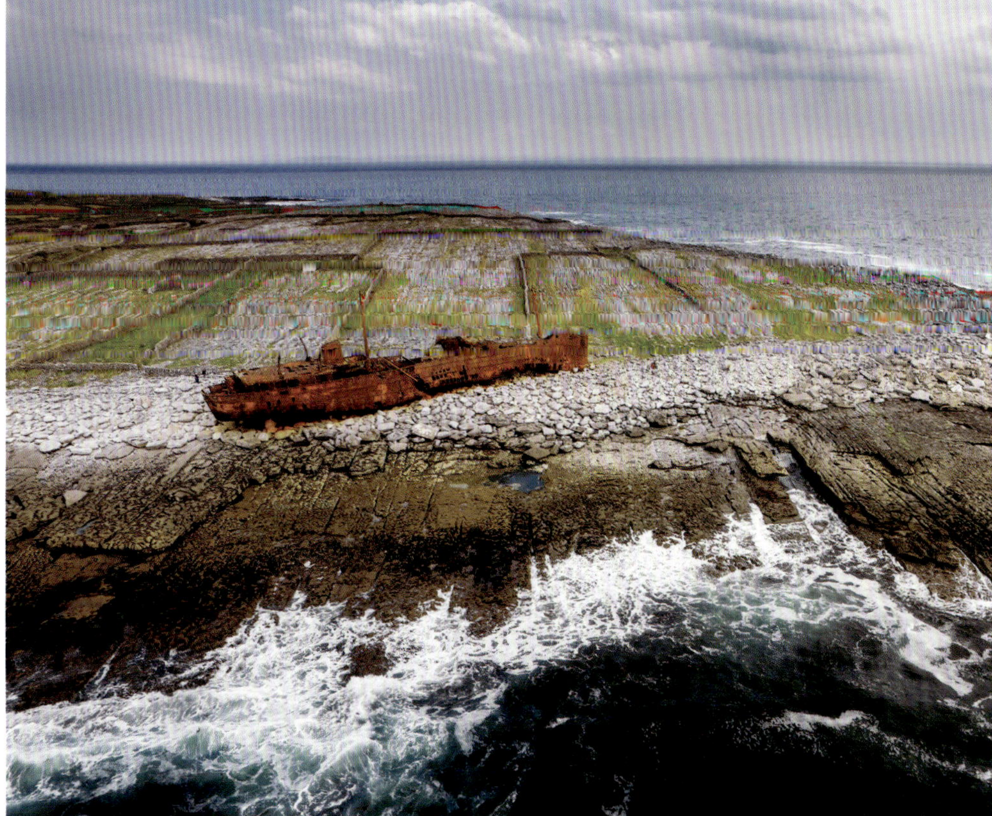

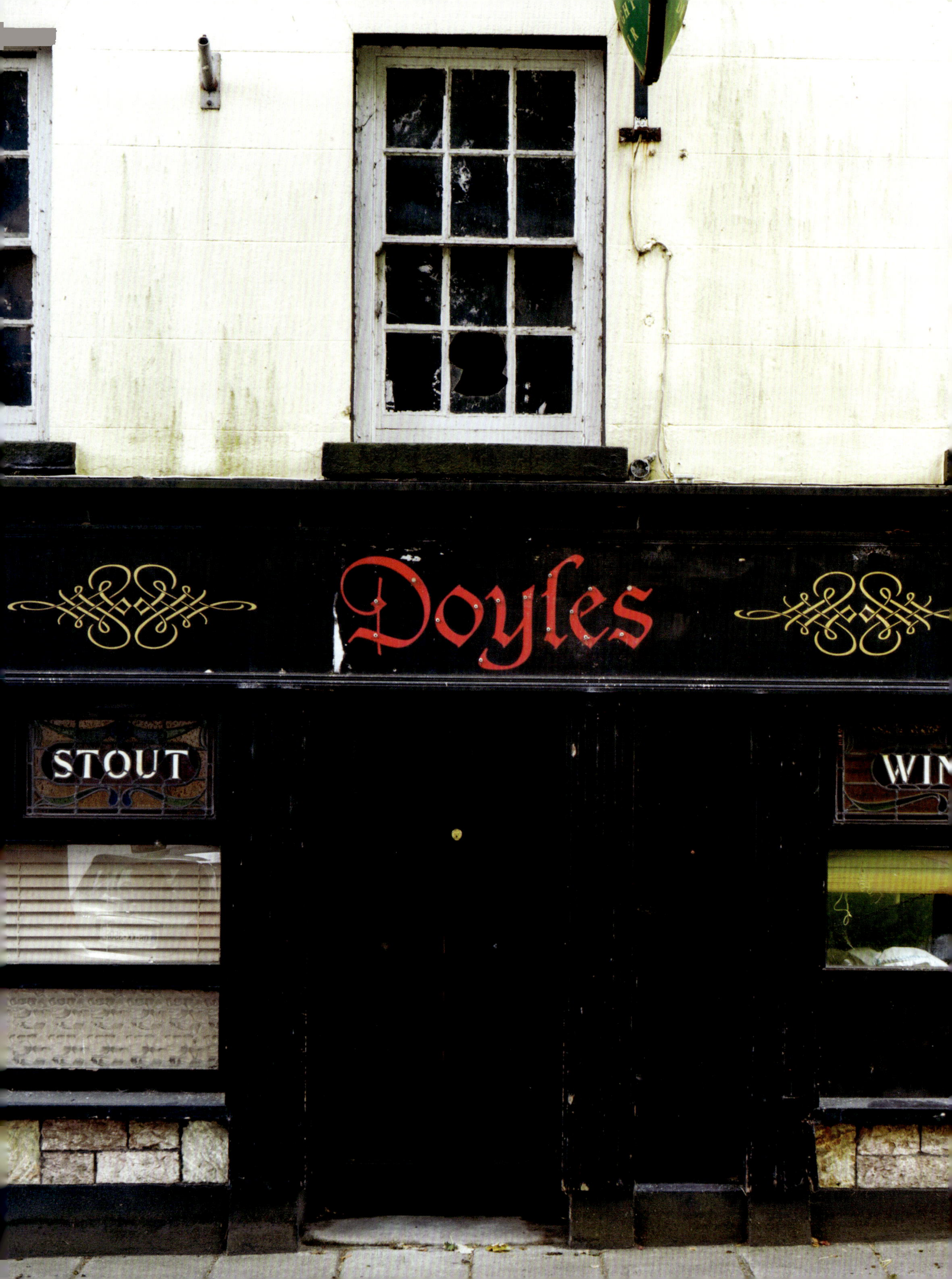

Doyles
STOUT
WIN

Town & City

The abandoned buildings of Ireland's towns and cities shine a spotlight particularly on the 20th and 21st centuries, and on the social, economic and political changes that have taken place. In recent years, bars and pubs have closed in large numbers, as the ban on smoking, lifestyle and population changes, as well as the Covid pandemic, have taken their toll. Also, the mass buying of products online has led to many retail outlets becoming unsustainable. However, such changes are not specific to Ireland, and have been happening in many countries.

Peculiar to the Irish Republic are the physical effects of the economic 'Celtic Tiger' boom of the late 1990s and early 2000s – and subsequent bust – that have left many new housing estates uninhabited. In Northern Ireland, the effects of the Troubles can be seen in buildings that have been targeted in atrocities.

Looking back further, the abandoned Guinness residences of Knockmaroon Lodge and Glenmaroon House in Dublin tell of the shift in power in Ireland during the early 20th century and, later, of death duties eroding the wealth of the rich. Nonetheless, whatever the reasons for these buildings being abandoned, what remains in so many cases is their distinctive nature – from the grandest to the tiniest.

OPPOSITE:

Doyle's, Inistioge, County Kilkenny
Inistioge's chocolate-box looks have led to the village being chosen as a film location. However, Doyle's pub, on the village square, has not endured, despite the early 19th-century building being listed in the National Inventory of Architectural Heritage. In its pomp, Doyle's would fly the Irish national flag on its frontage.

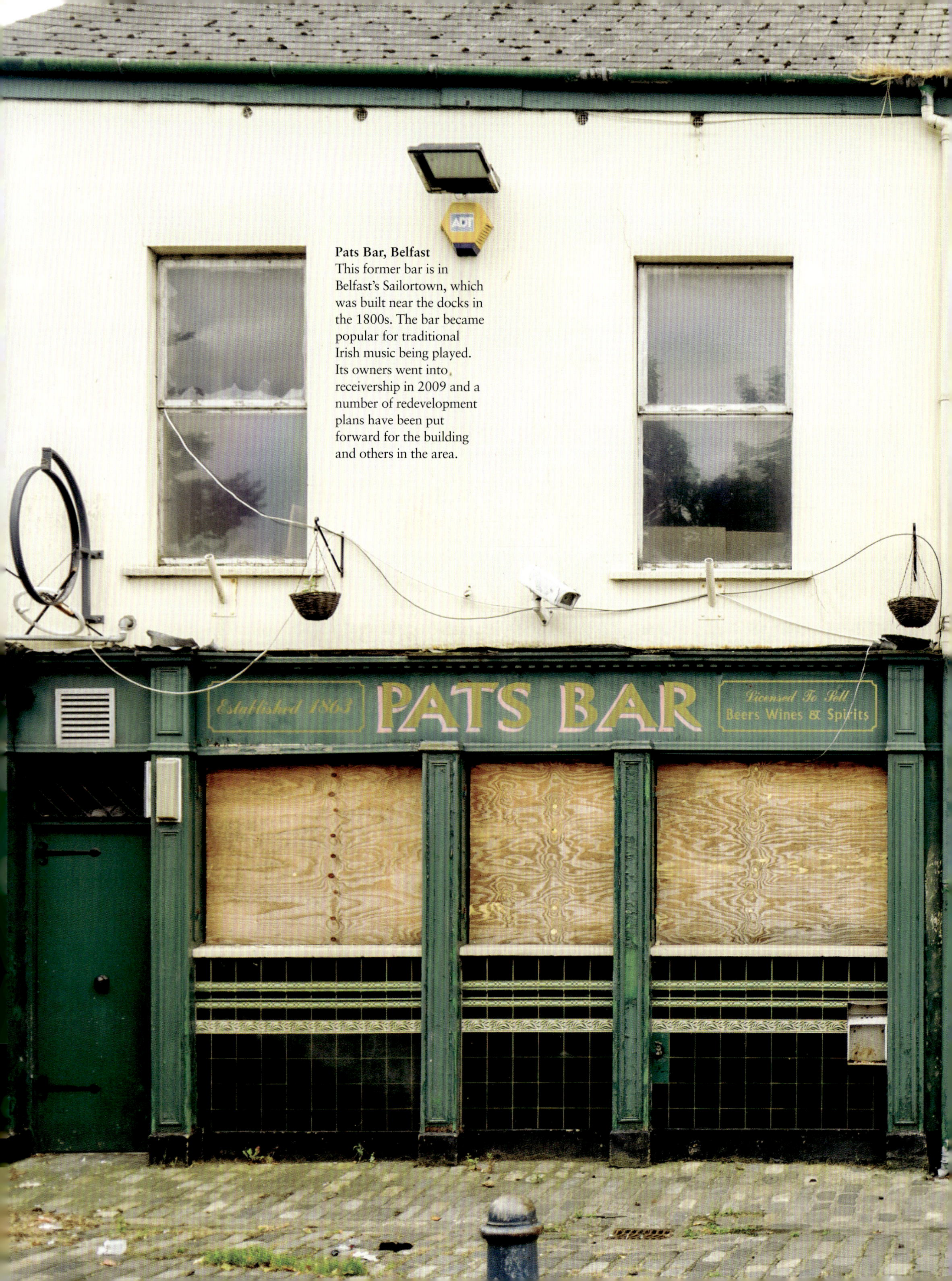

Pats Bar, Belfast
This former bar is in Belfast's Sailortown, which was built near the docks in the 1800s. The bar became popular for traditional Irish music being played. Its owners went into receivership in 2009 and a number of redevelopment plans have been put forward for the building and others in the area.

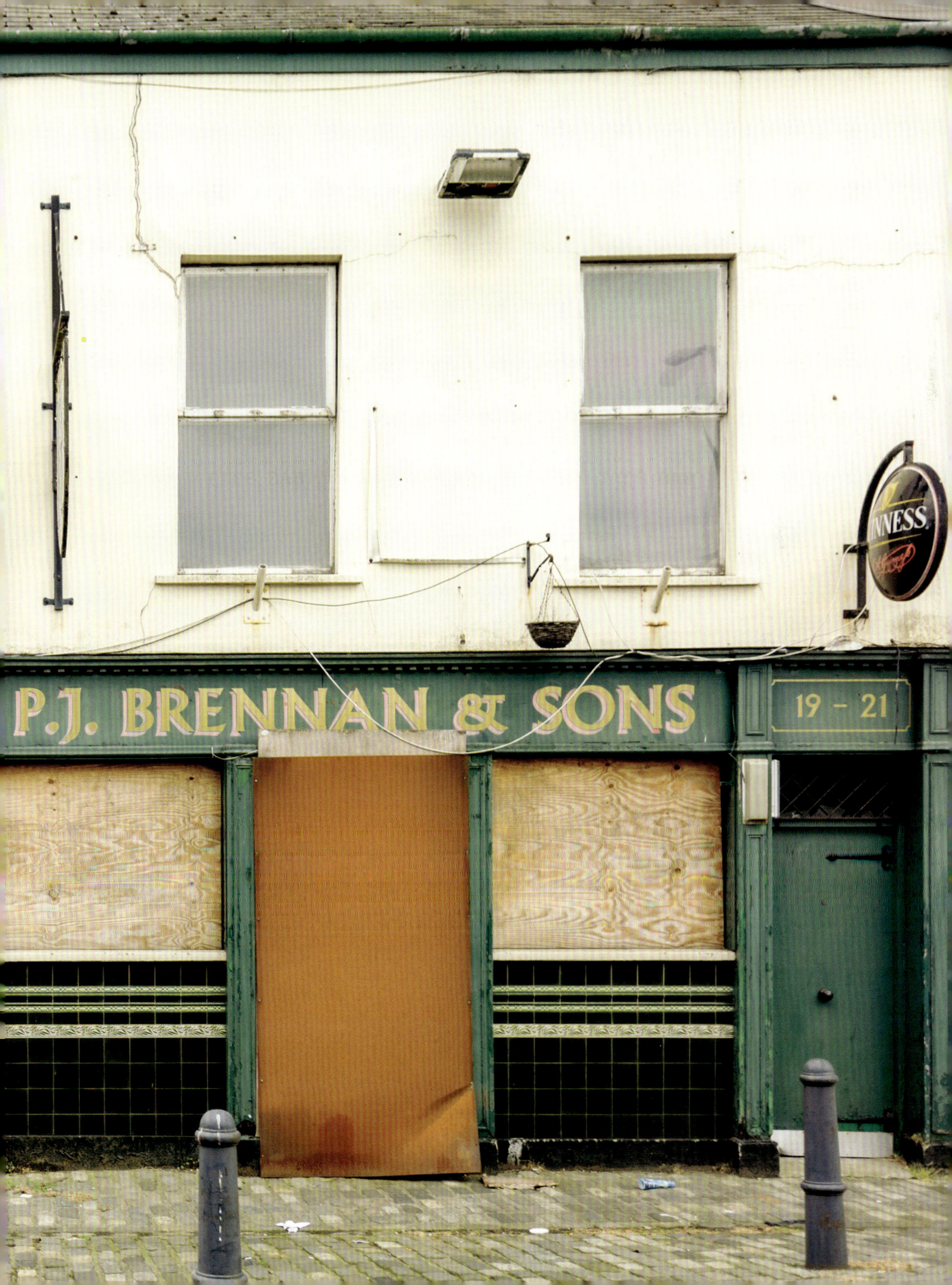
P.J. BRENNAN & SONS
19 - 21
GUINNESS

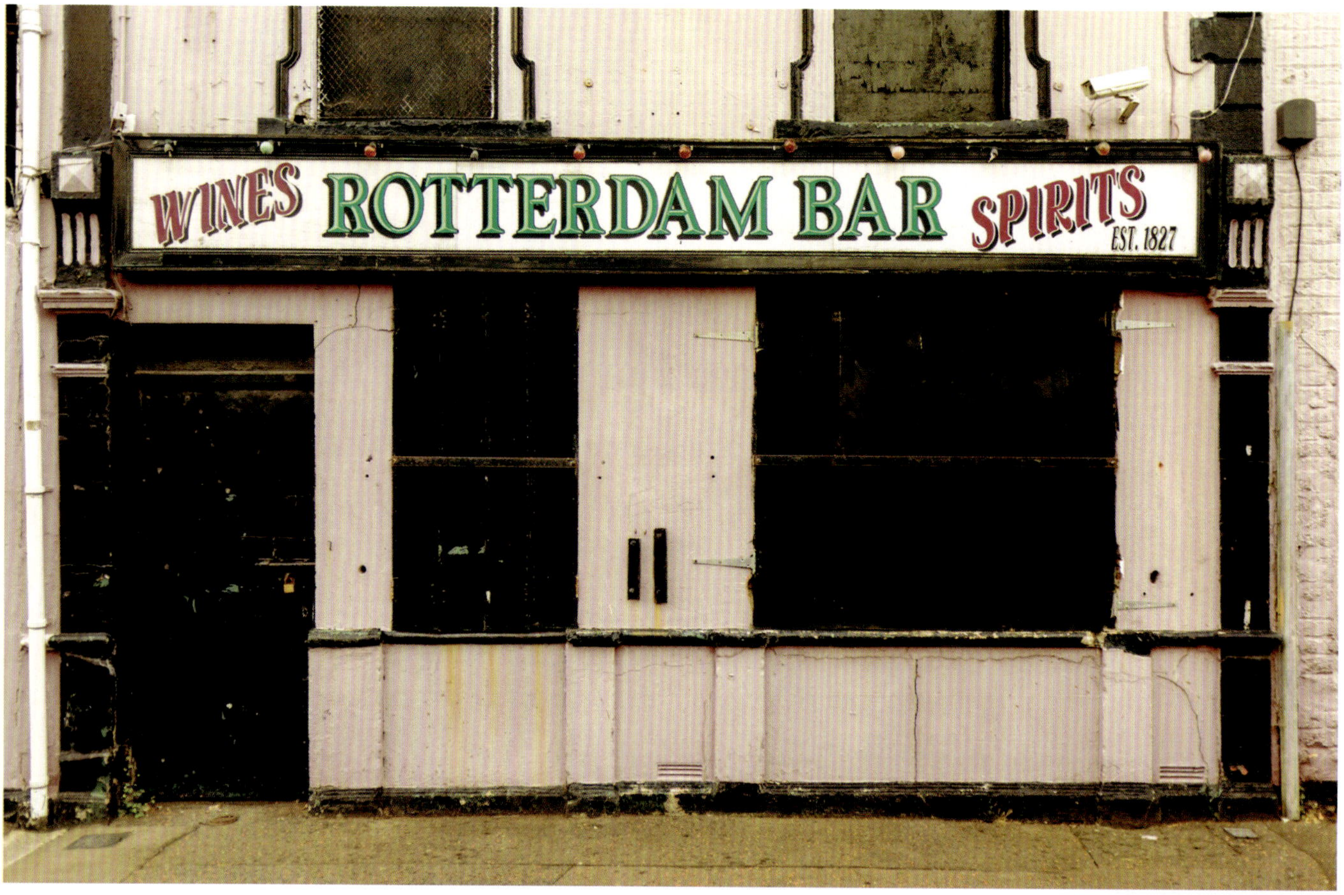

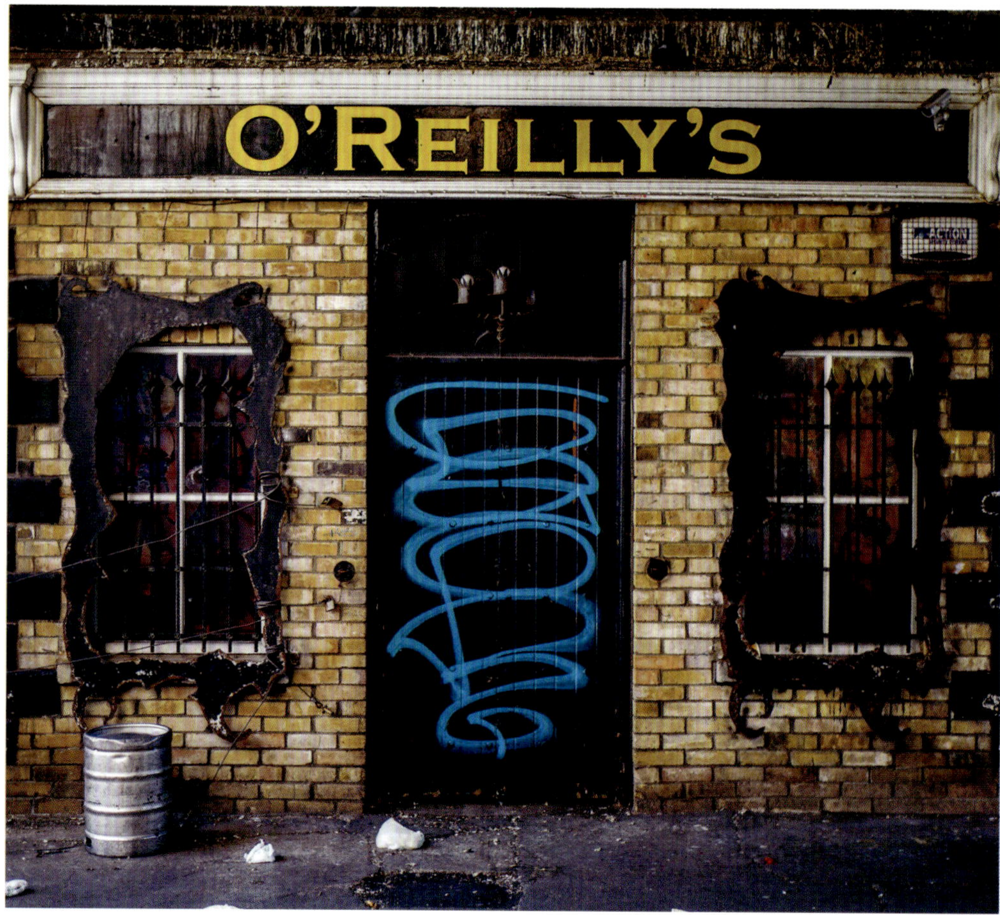

Rotterdam Bar, Belfast
This pub backed onto Pat's Bar (previous pages), and both were under the same ownership when they closed. Despite being bombed twice and suffering a fire, in the 1980s and 1990s the bar gained a reputation as a live music venue, where people from all sides of Belfast mixed.

O'Reilly's, Dublin
This pub sits beneath three arches under the Dublin Area Rapid Transit system's Tara Street station. Its gothic interior is in keeping with the rock music played there. It closed during the Covid pandemic.

D.W. Parke Chemist, Clonmel, County Tipperary
In 2016, a painting by John Doherty of this ornate shopfront – called *Prescriptions Accurately Prepared* – was sold at Sotheby's in London. The shop's founder, D.W. Parke, was a Protestant who emigrated to America as the creation of the Irish Free State saw customers shun him.

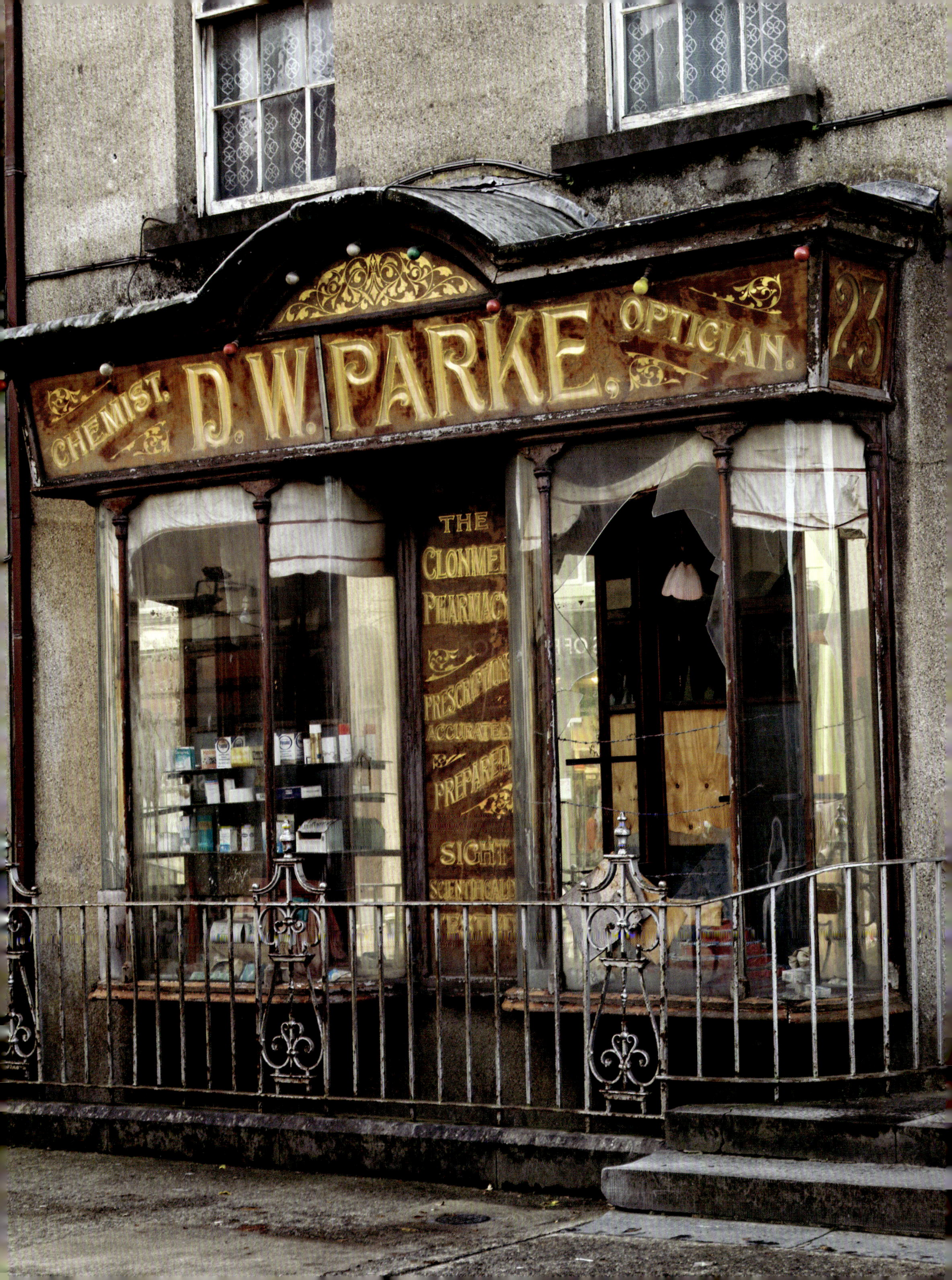

CHEMIST. D. W. PARKE, OPTICIAN. 23
THE
CLONMEL
PHARMACY
PRESCRIPTIONS
ACCURATELY
PREPARED
SIGHT
SCIENTIFICALLY
TESTED

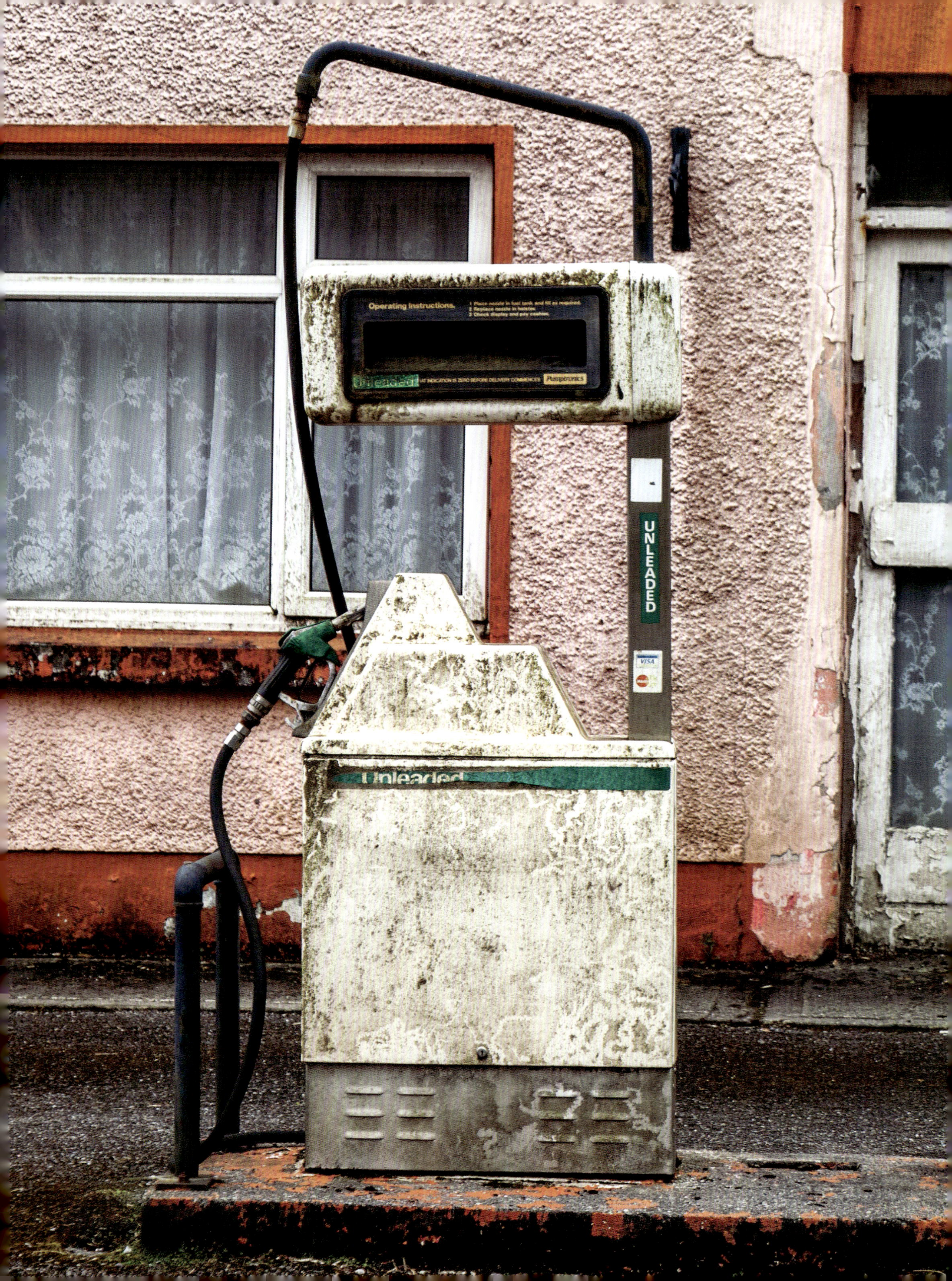

Operating Instructions.
1 Place nozzle in fuel tank and fill as required.
2 Replace nozzle in holster.
3 Check display and pay cashier.
Unleaded
AT INDICATION IS ZERO BEFORE DELIVERY COMMENCES
Pumptronics
UNLEADED
VISA
Unleaded

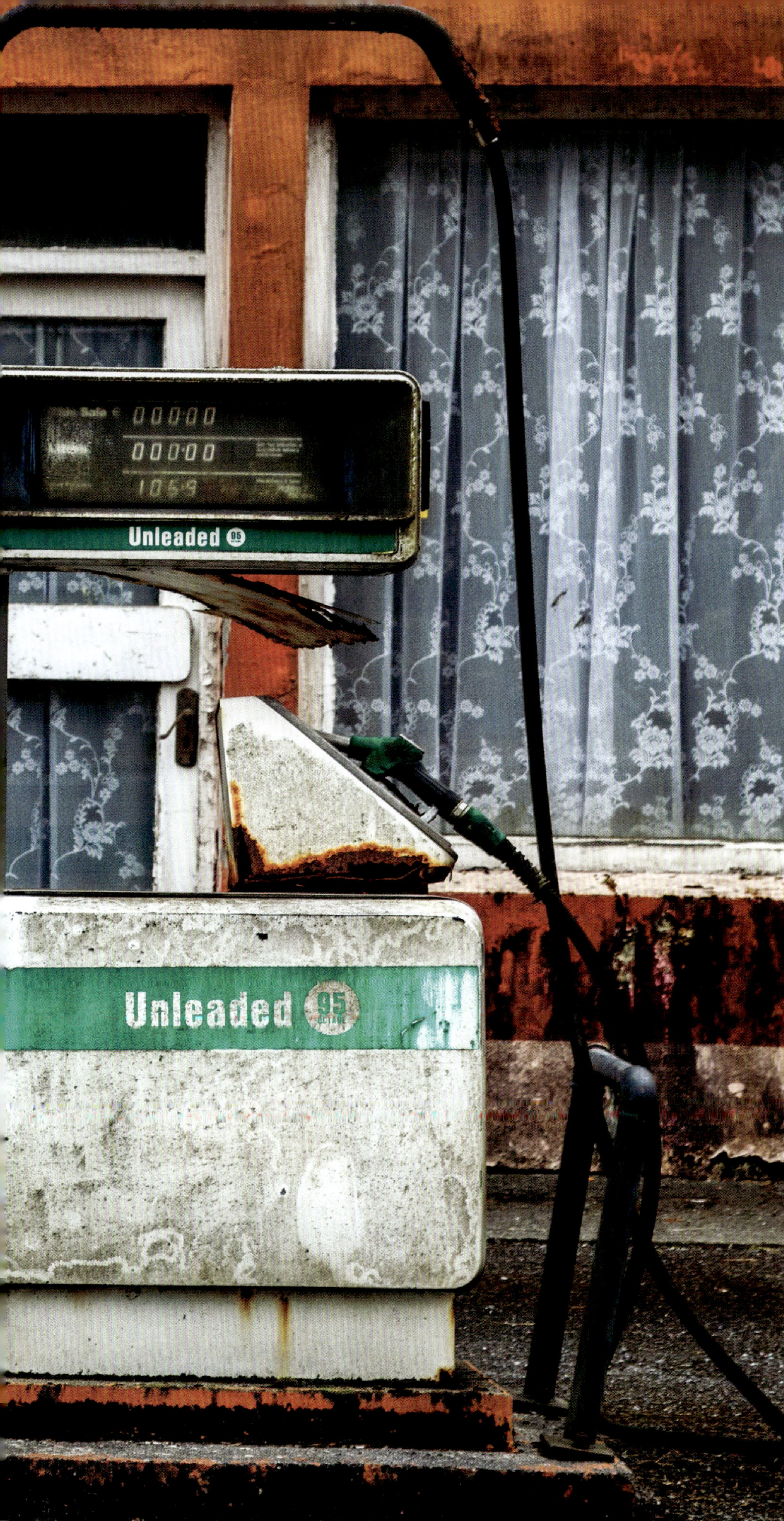

**Ballingeary foodmarket,
County Cork**
The remote Ballingeary
foodmarket with its old petrol
pumps stands in the Shehy
Mountains near the border
with County Kerry. According
to the 2016 census, more than
42 per cent of the population
speak Irish there on a daily basis,
and Ballingeary is part of the
Muskerry Gaeltacht, in which
Irish is spoken.

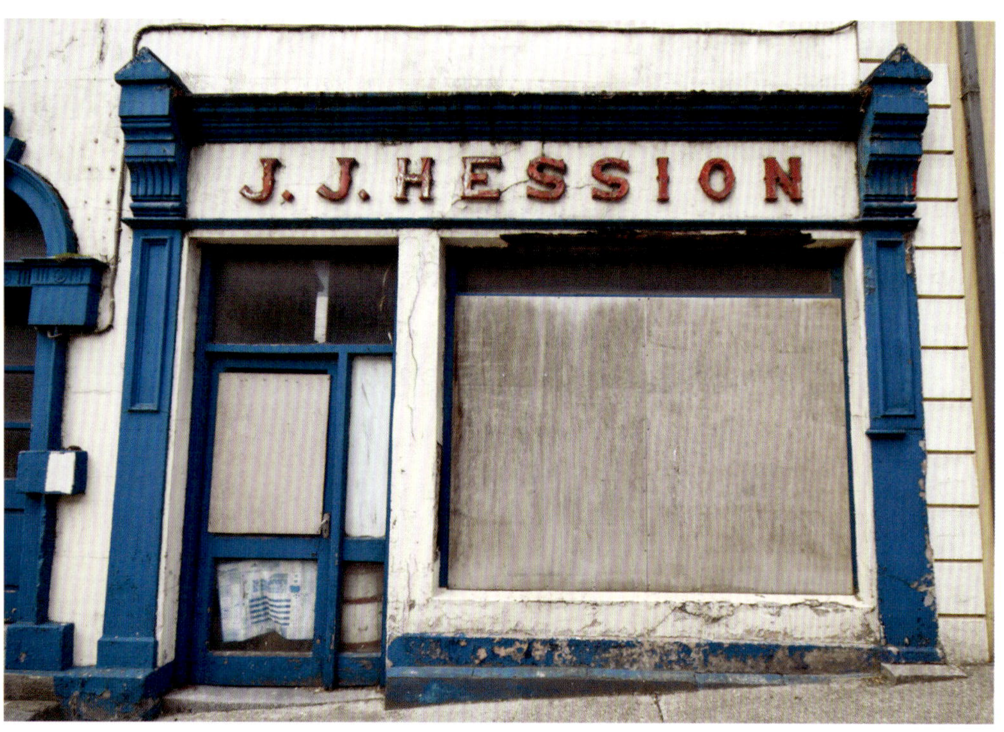

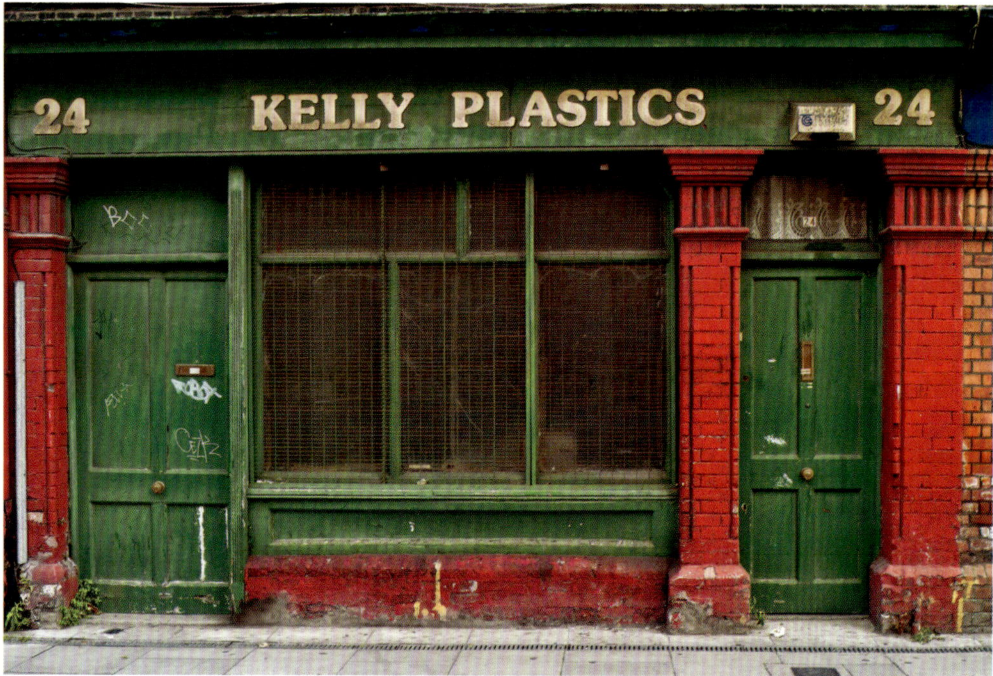

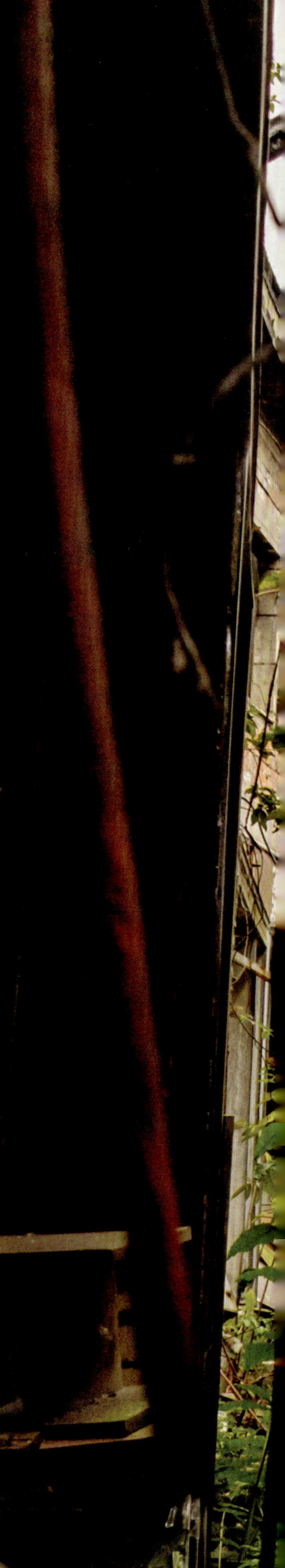

ABOVE TOP:

J.J. Hession, Ballinrobe, County Mayo
This was a grocery shop in the town of Ballinrobe, where Hession is a popular name. Michael Hession took over the shop from his parents and ran it in the post-war years, where it was often the first establishment in the town to stock exotic coffees and fruits.

ABOVE BOTTOM:

Kelly Plastics, Benburb Street, Dublin
Benburb Street (originally Barrack Street) has a long history as a red-light district, with much of the trade coming from the adjoining Collins Barracks, previously the Royal Barracks, now a museum. Many shops on the street have suffered a similar fate to Kelly Plastics.

RIGHT:

North Street Arcade, Belfast
This abandoned art deco-style shopping arcade in Belfast's Cathedral Quarter was constructed in the 1930s. A listed building, it has been derelict since suffering an arson attack in 2004. It had previously survived a bomb attack in 1976 in which two civilians and the two bombers died.

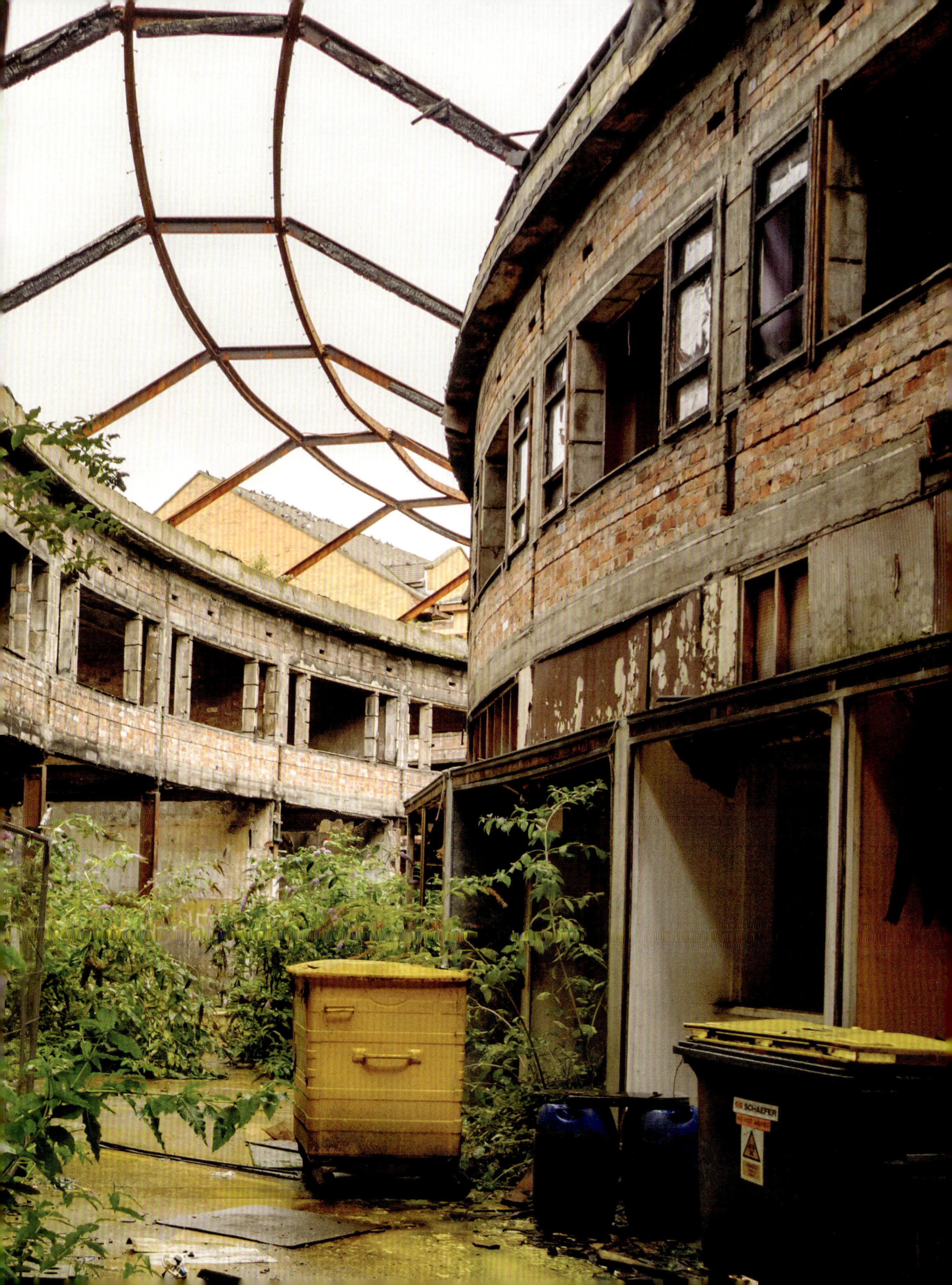

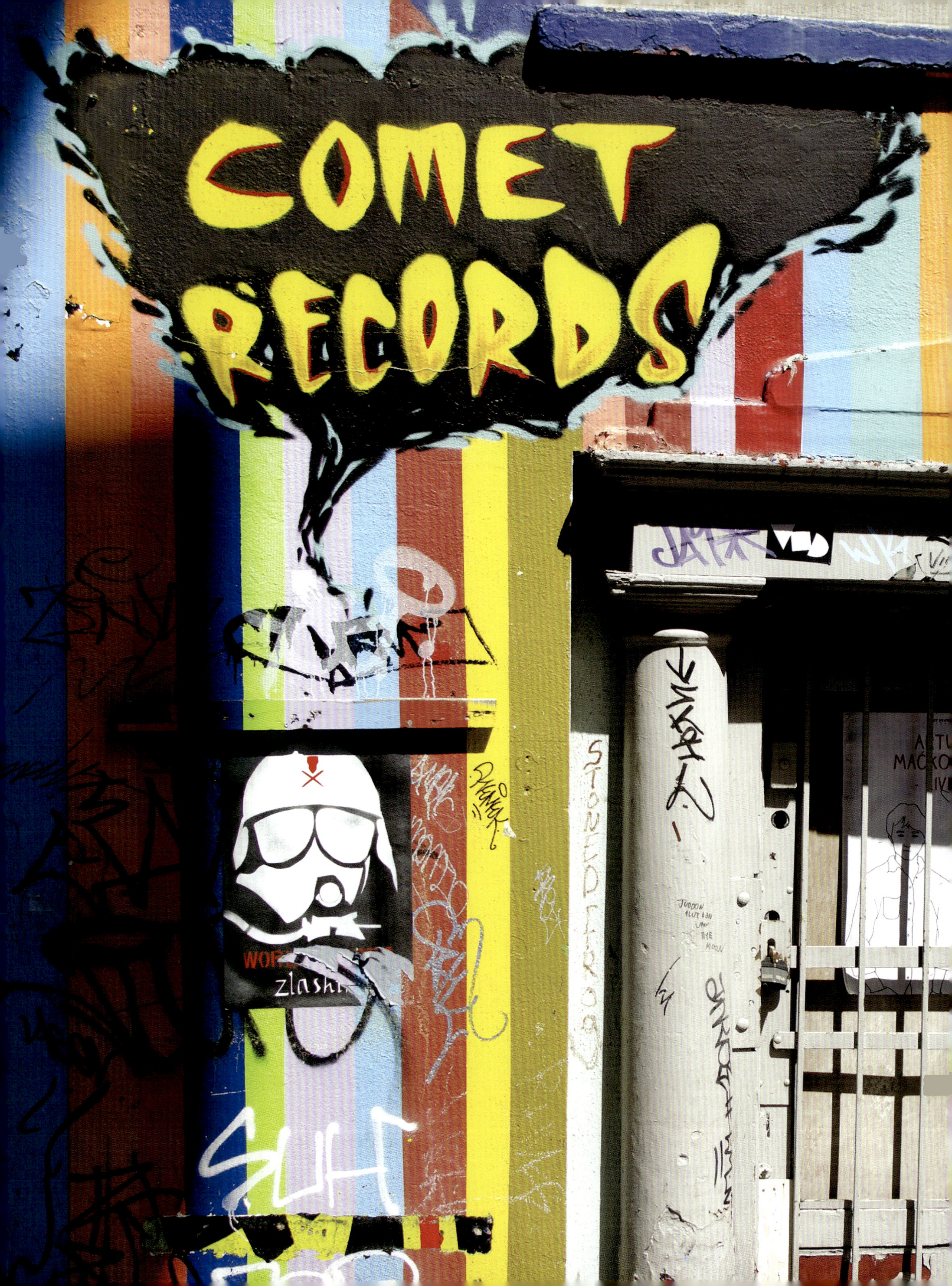

COMET
RECORDS

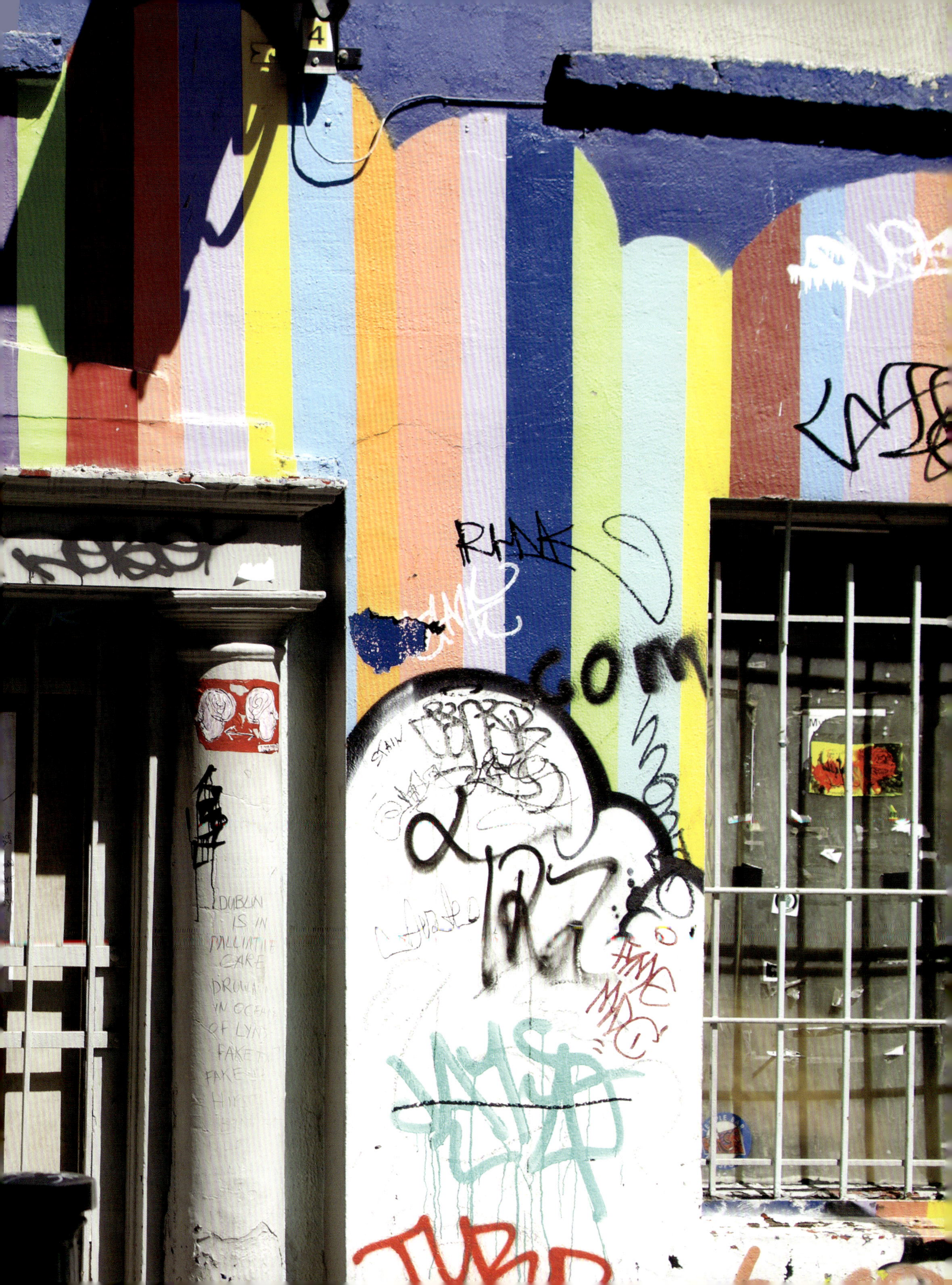

PREVIOUS PAGES:
Comet Records, Dublin
There have been a number of
premises for the Comet record
store in Dublin (and Cork) since
its foundation in 1984, with this
Temple Bar outlet being the last.
It closed in 2011 and Comet now
sells records online.

RIGHT:
**Feargal Quinn's Retail Therapy,
Drogheda, County Louth**
In 2011, retail expert Feargal
Quinn descended upon Drogheda
for an RTE series about
rejuvenating the town. Many
premises had become derelict
since the Celtic Tiger economic
boom of the late 1990s and mid-
2000s. The Feargal Quinn Retail
Therapy frontage on a disused
building – on a street of many
others – seems highly ironic.

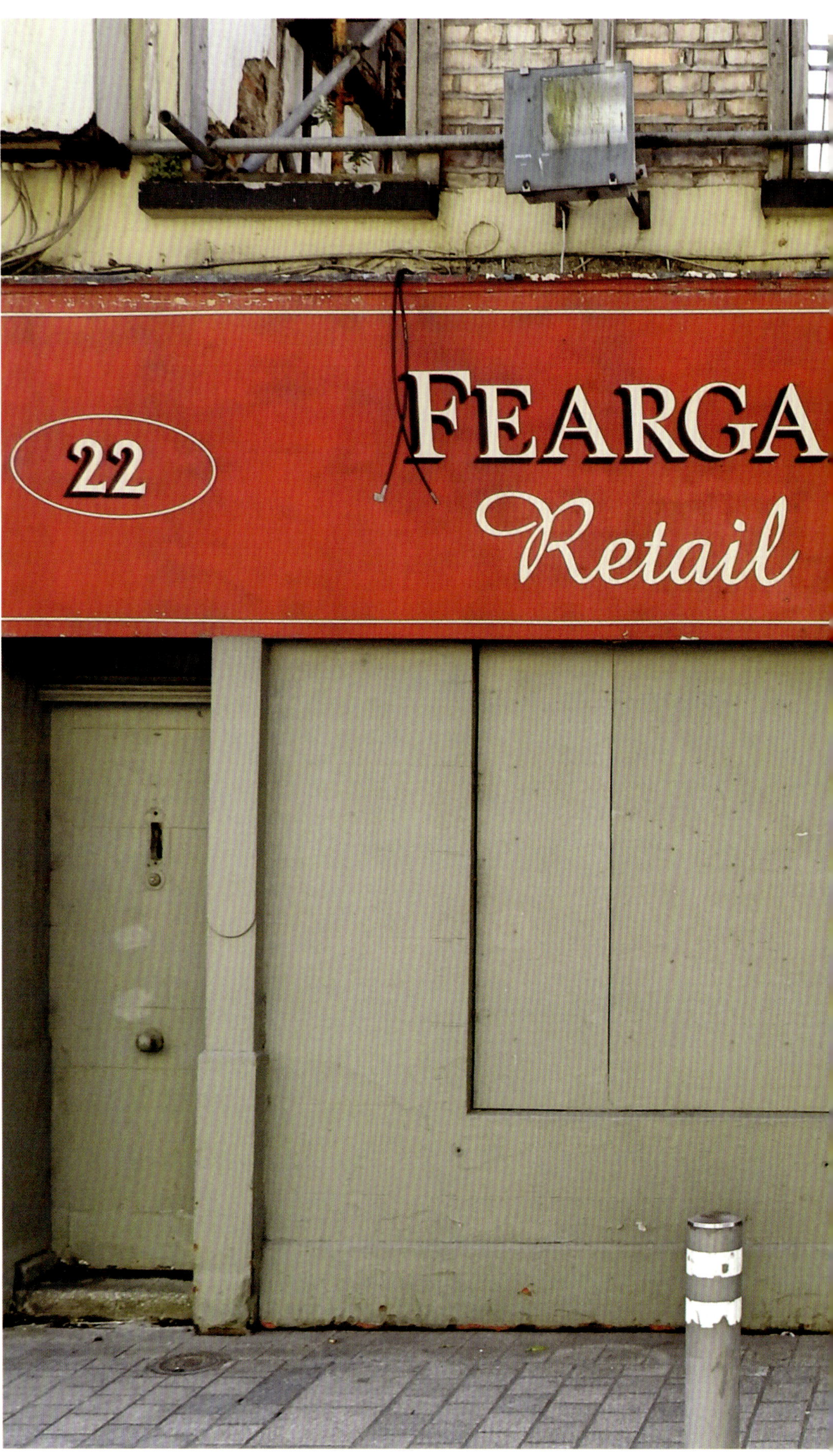
22
FEARGA
Retail

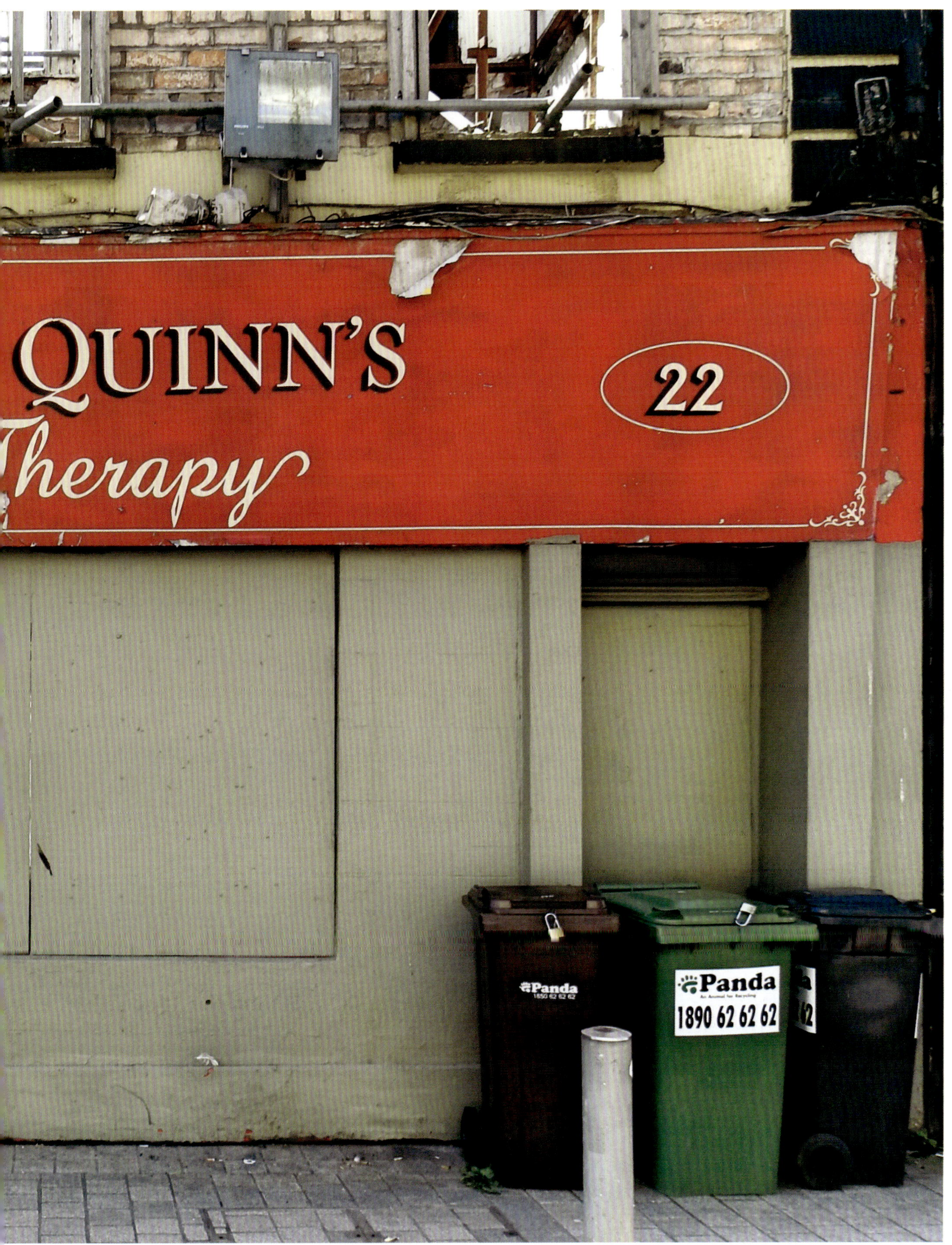

QUINN'S
Therapy
22
Panda
1850 62 62 62
Panda
An Animal for Recycling
1890 62 62 62

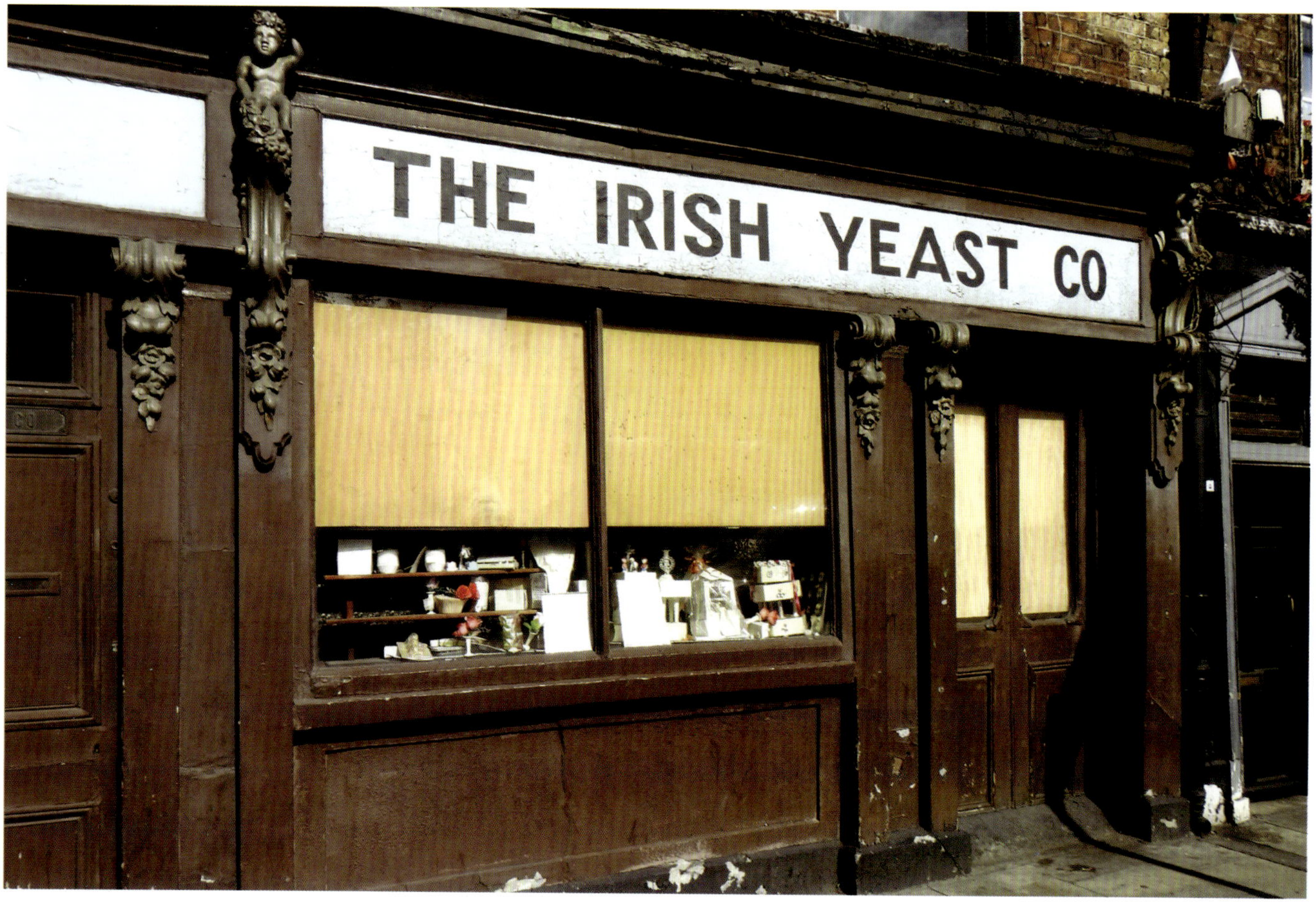

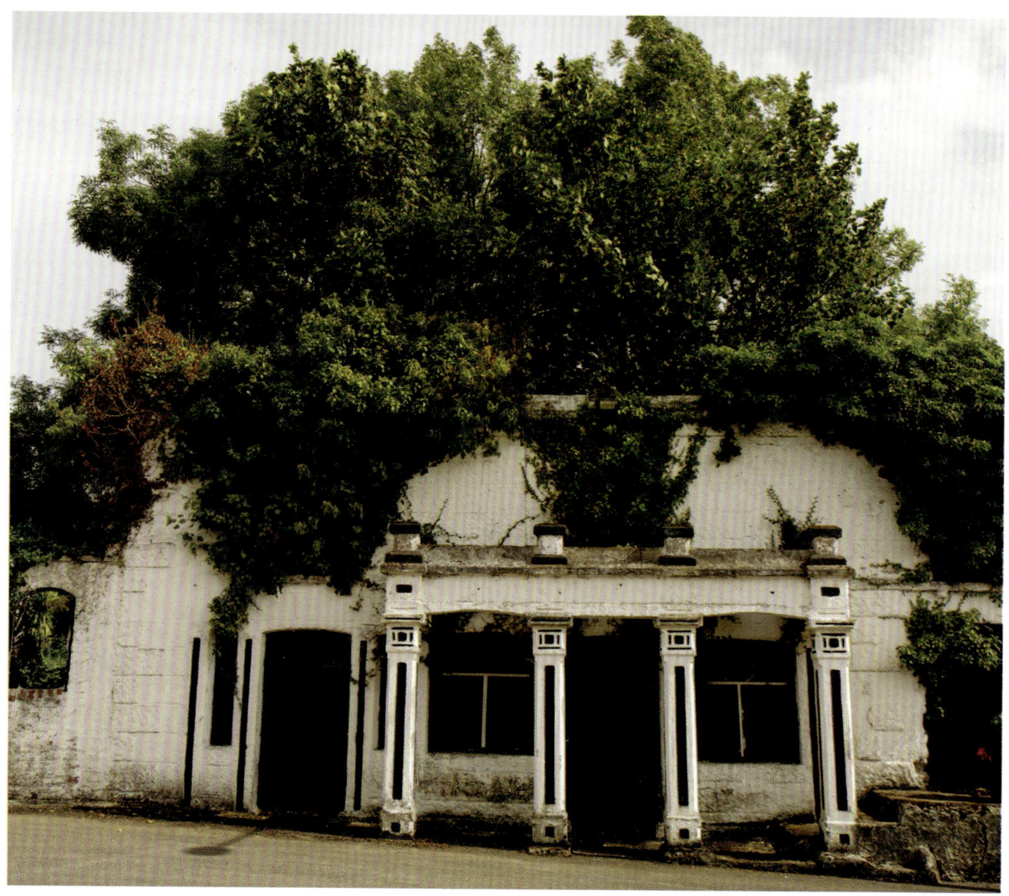

ABOVE:

**The Irish Yeast Co,
College Street, Dublin**
This shop began life in 1894 and was manned for many years by John Moreland, who was born – and lived for a long time – above it. The business provided yeast and baking supplies wholesale and retail. In 2021, the site was sold to the owner of a pub.

RIGHT:

Black Horse Inn, Tyrconnell Road, Inchicore, Dublin
The Black Horse Inn closed in 2018 and has been subject to a number of planning applications in recent years that would necessitate the demolition of the former pub, which has a nearby tram stop named after it. In 2011, a man died after being shot at the pub.

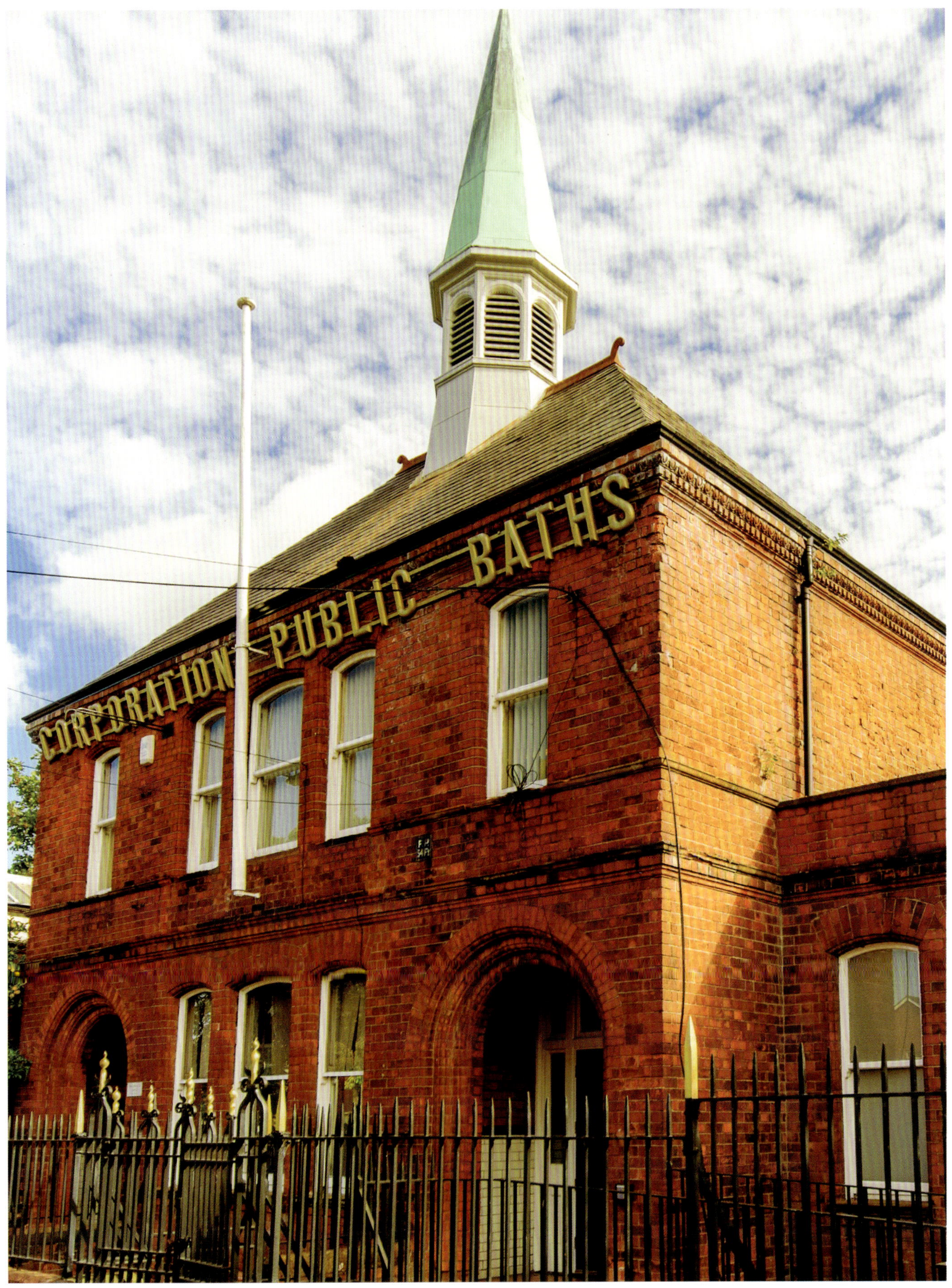
CORPORATION PUBLIC BATHS

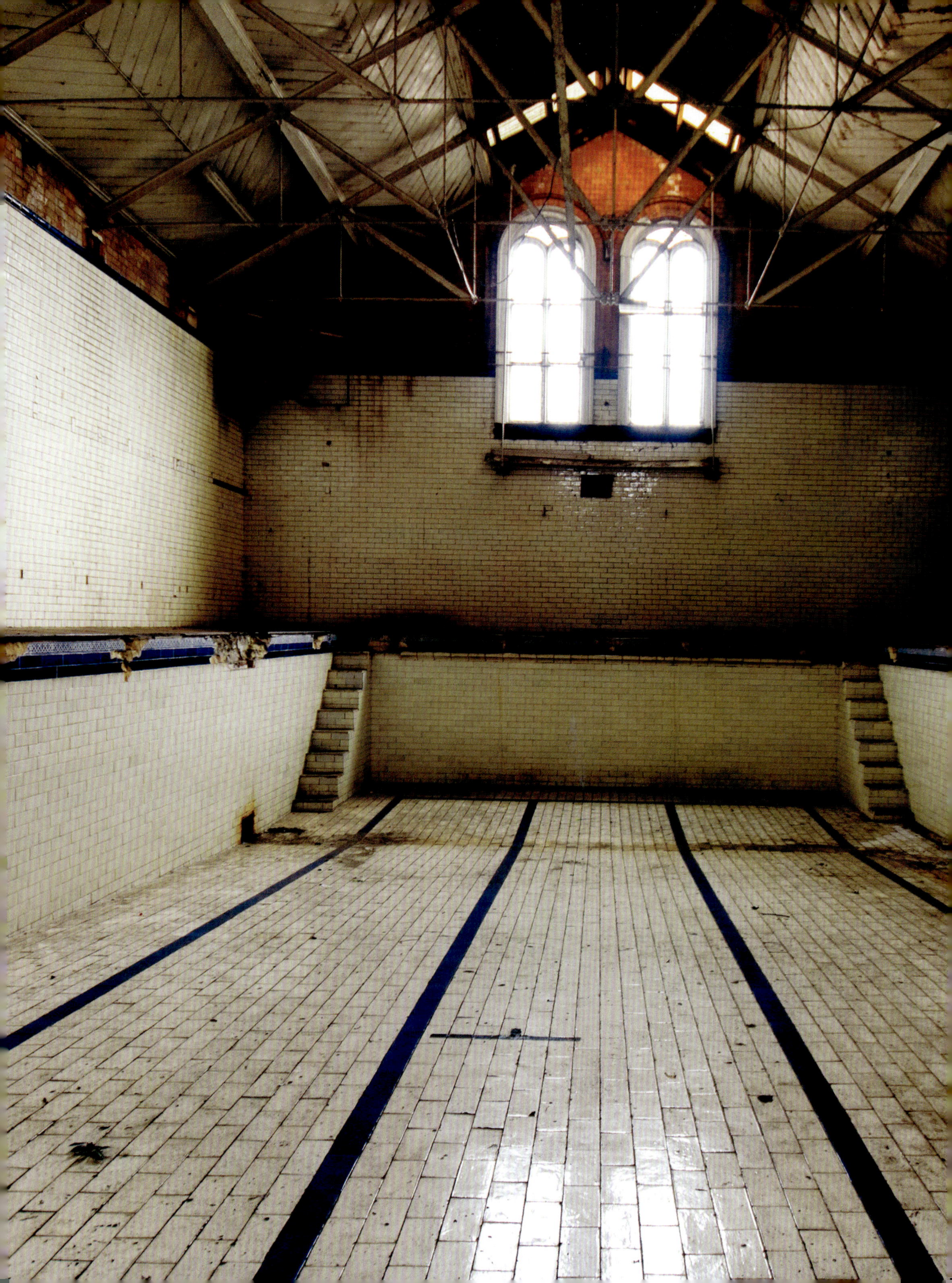

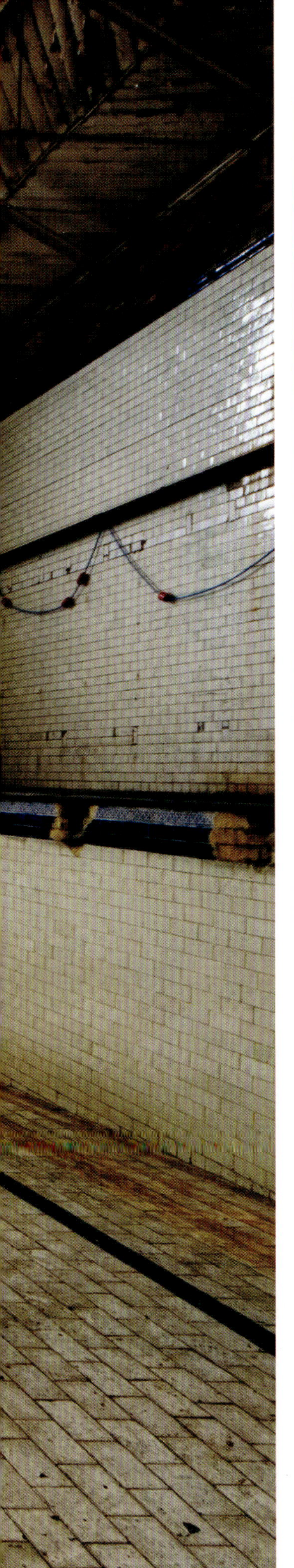

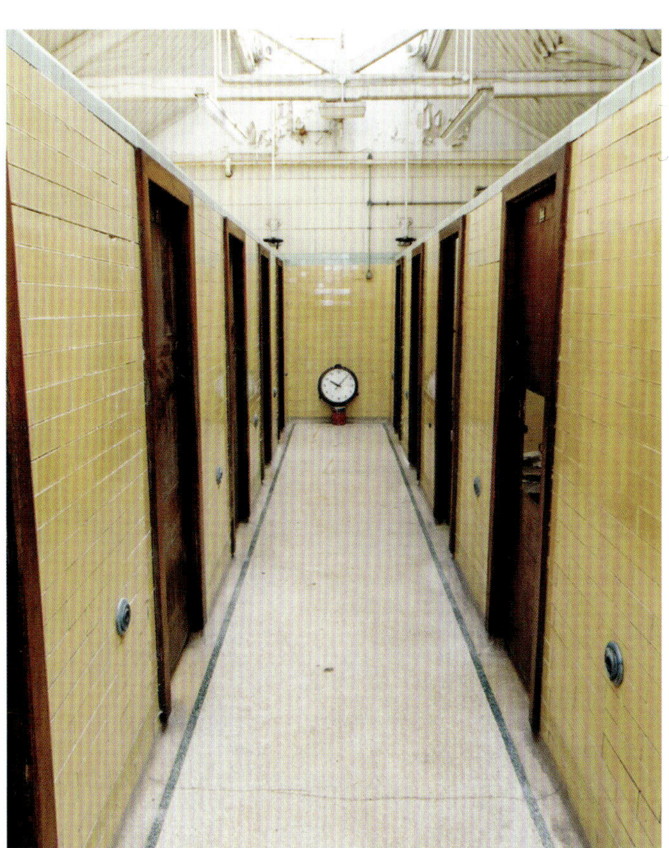

Templemore Baths, Belfast
Having opened at the end of the 19th century, Templemore Baths were often used by Harland & Wolff shipbuilders' employees living in East Belfast who did not have running water. During World War II the baths were repurposed to become a makeshift morgue and they have also served as a children's hospital. When they closed in 2020 for a £17 million redevelopment, they were the last functioning Victorian baths in Ireland.

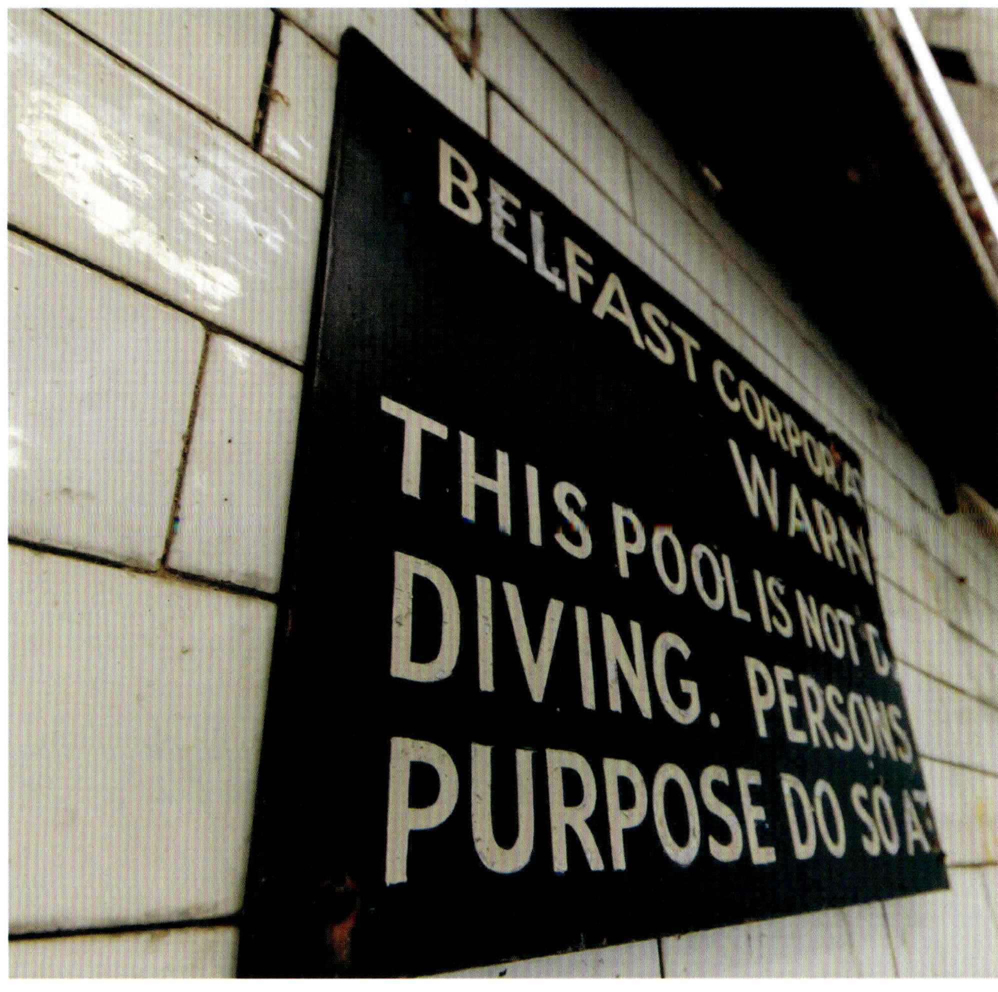

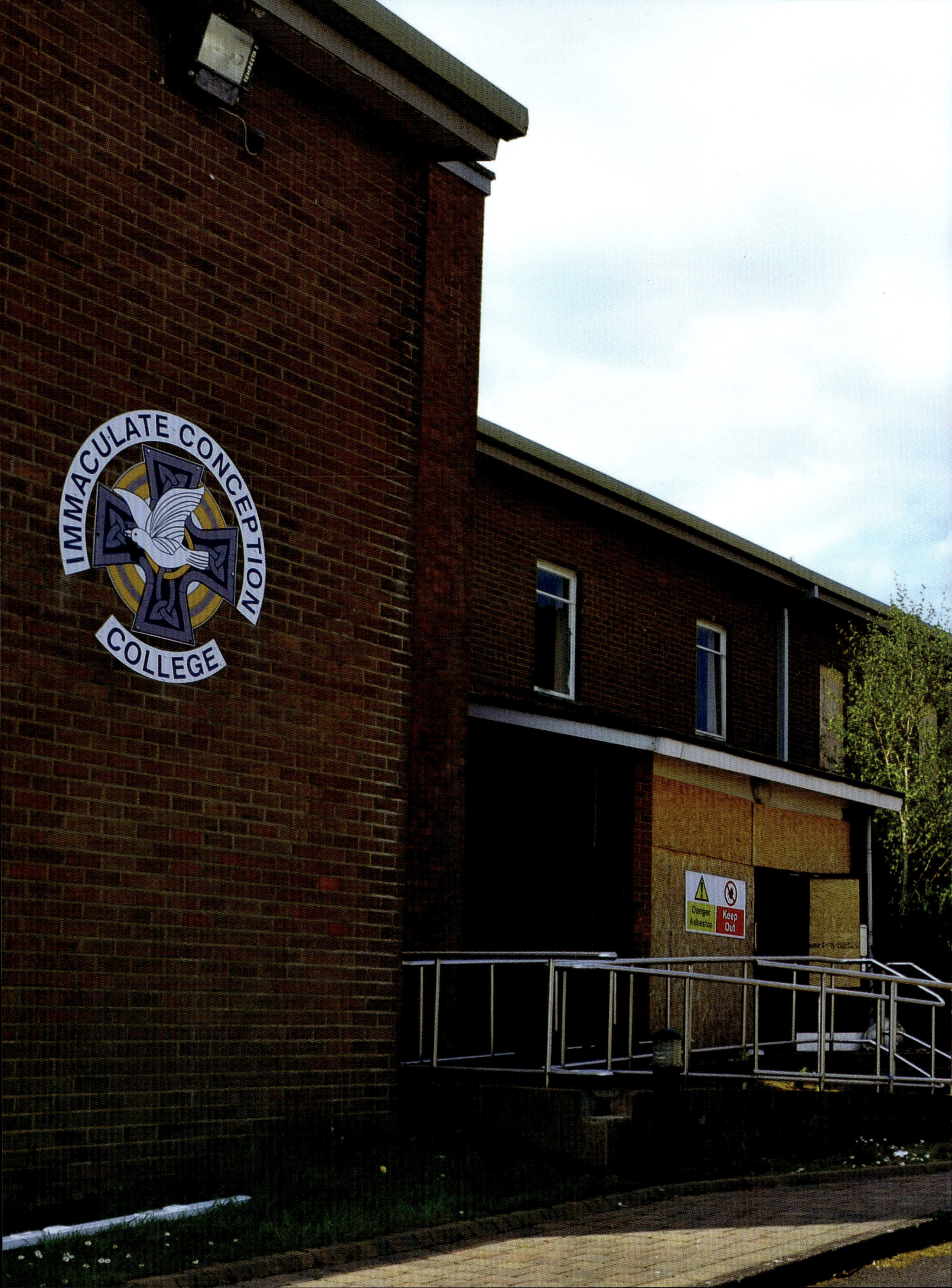

IMMACULATE CONCEPTION
COLLEGE
Danger
Asbestos
Keep
Out

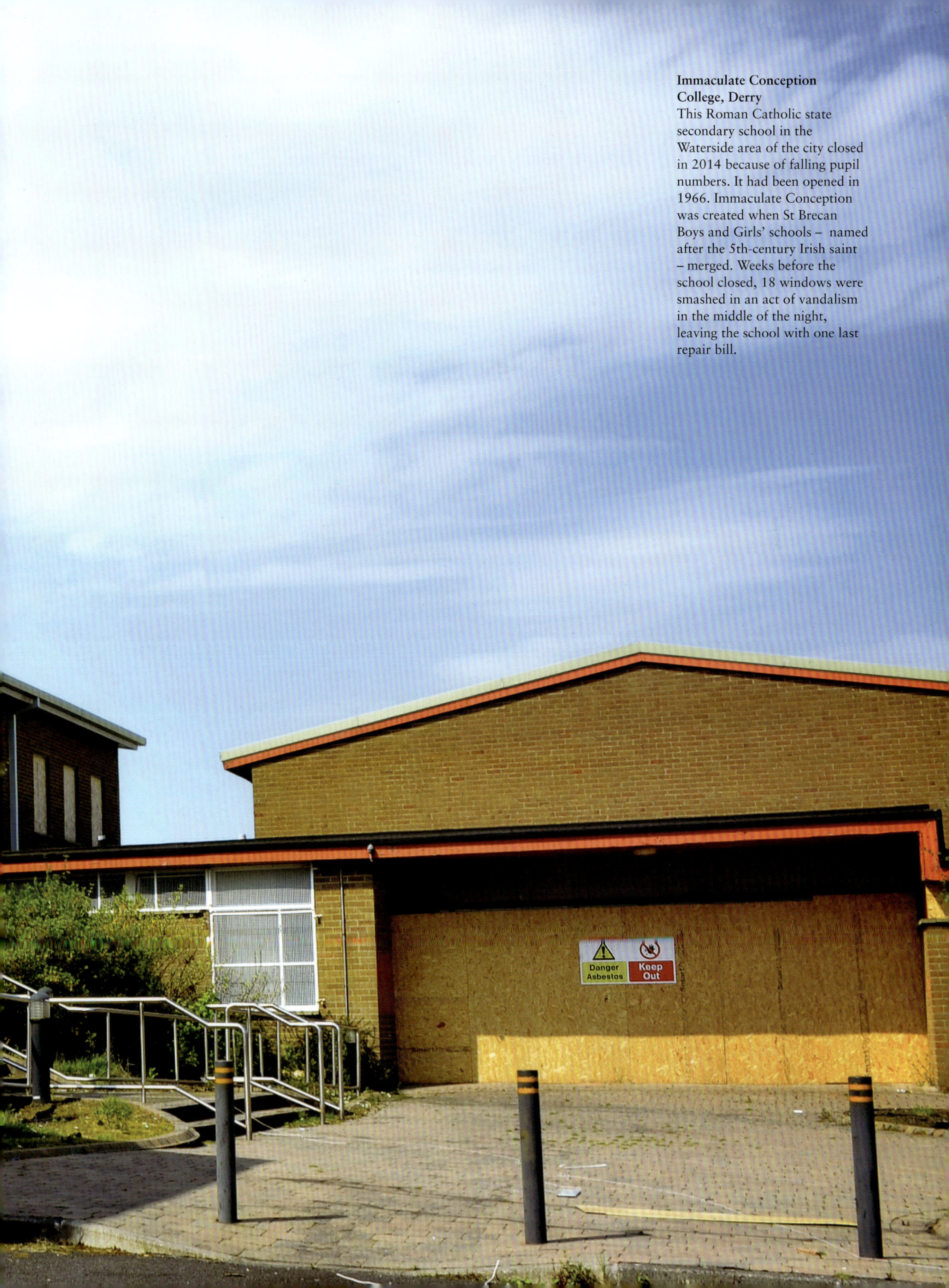

**Immaculate Conception
College, Derry**
This Roman Catholic state
secondary school in the
Waterside area of the city closed
in 2014 because of falling pupil
numbers. It had been opened in
1966. Immaculate Conception
was created when St Brecan
Boys and Girls' schools – named
after the 5th-century Irish saint
– merged. Weeks before the
school closed, 18 windows were
smashed in an act of vandalism
in the middle of the night,
leaving the school with one last
repair bill.

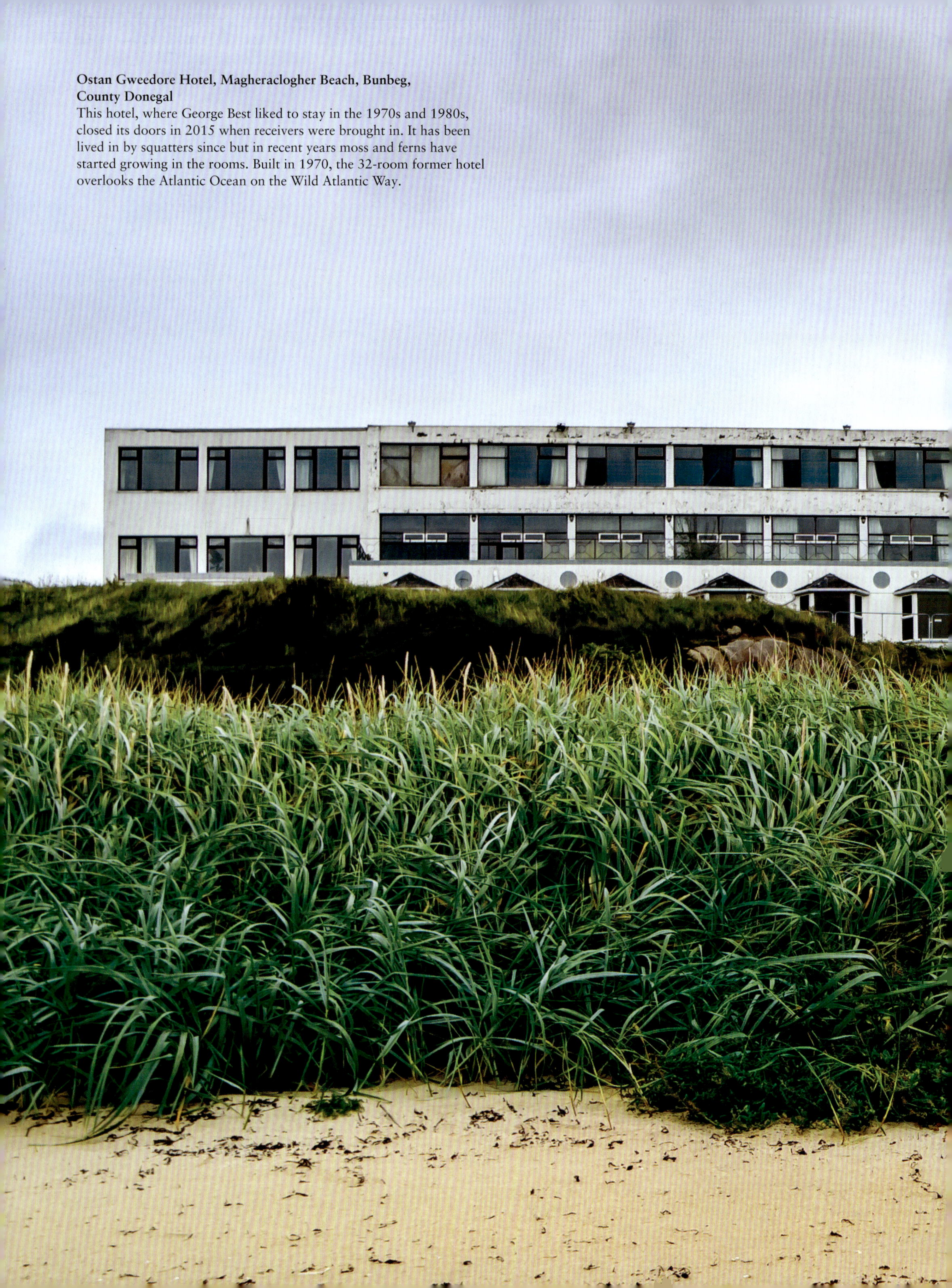

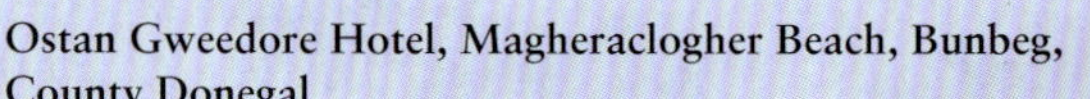

Ostan Gweedore Hotel, Magheraclogher Beach, Bunbeg, County Donegal
This hotel, where George Best liked to stay in the 1970s and 1980s, closed its doors in 2015 when receivers were brought in. It has been lived in by squatters since but in recent years moss and ferns have started growing in the rooms. Built in 1970, the 32-room former hotel overlooks the Atlantic Ocean on the Wild Atlantic Way.

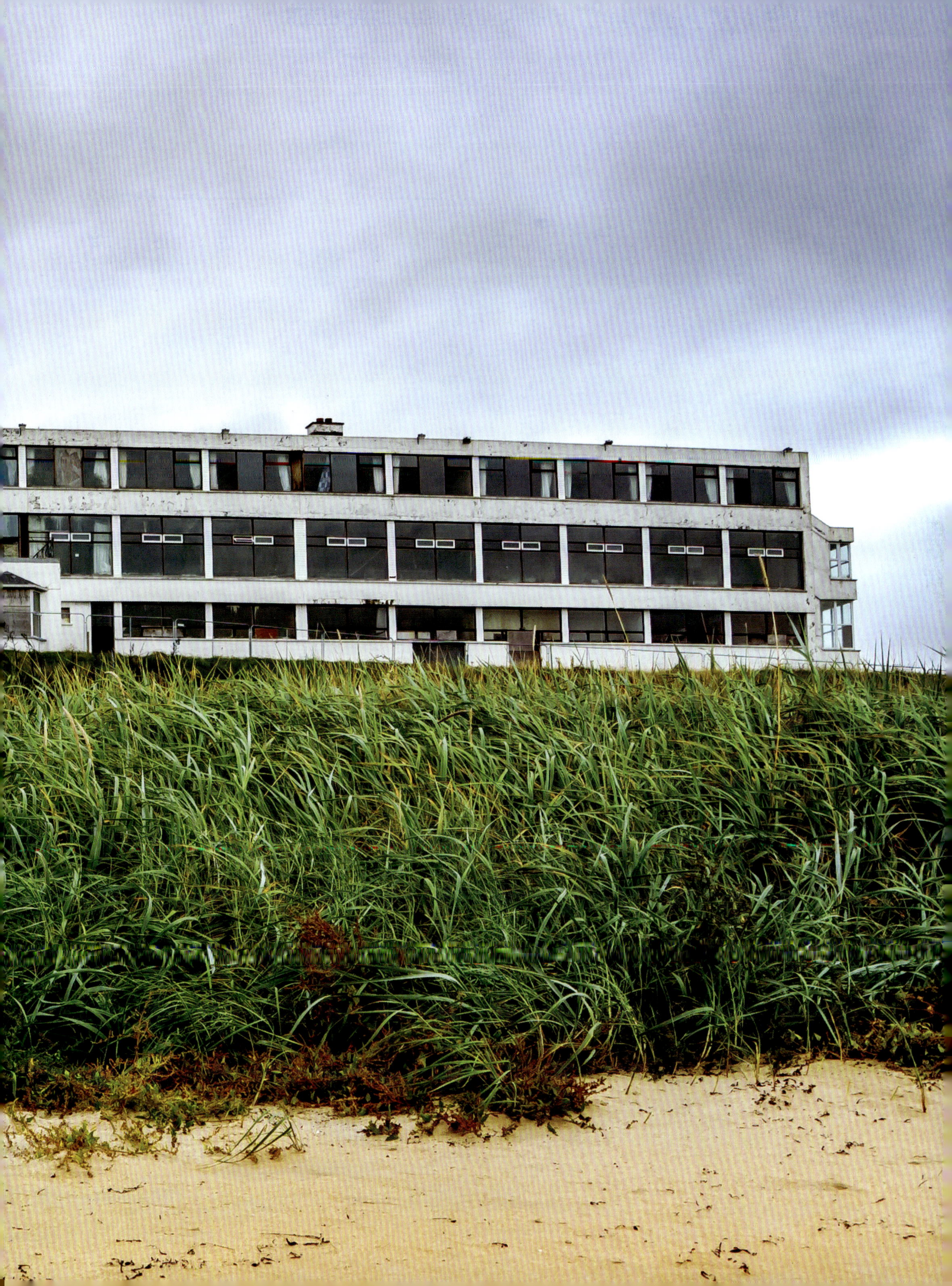

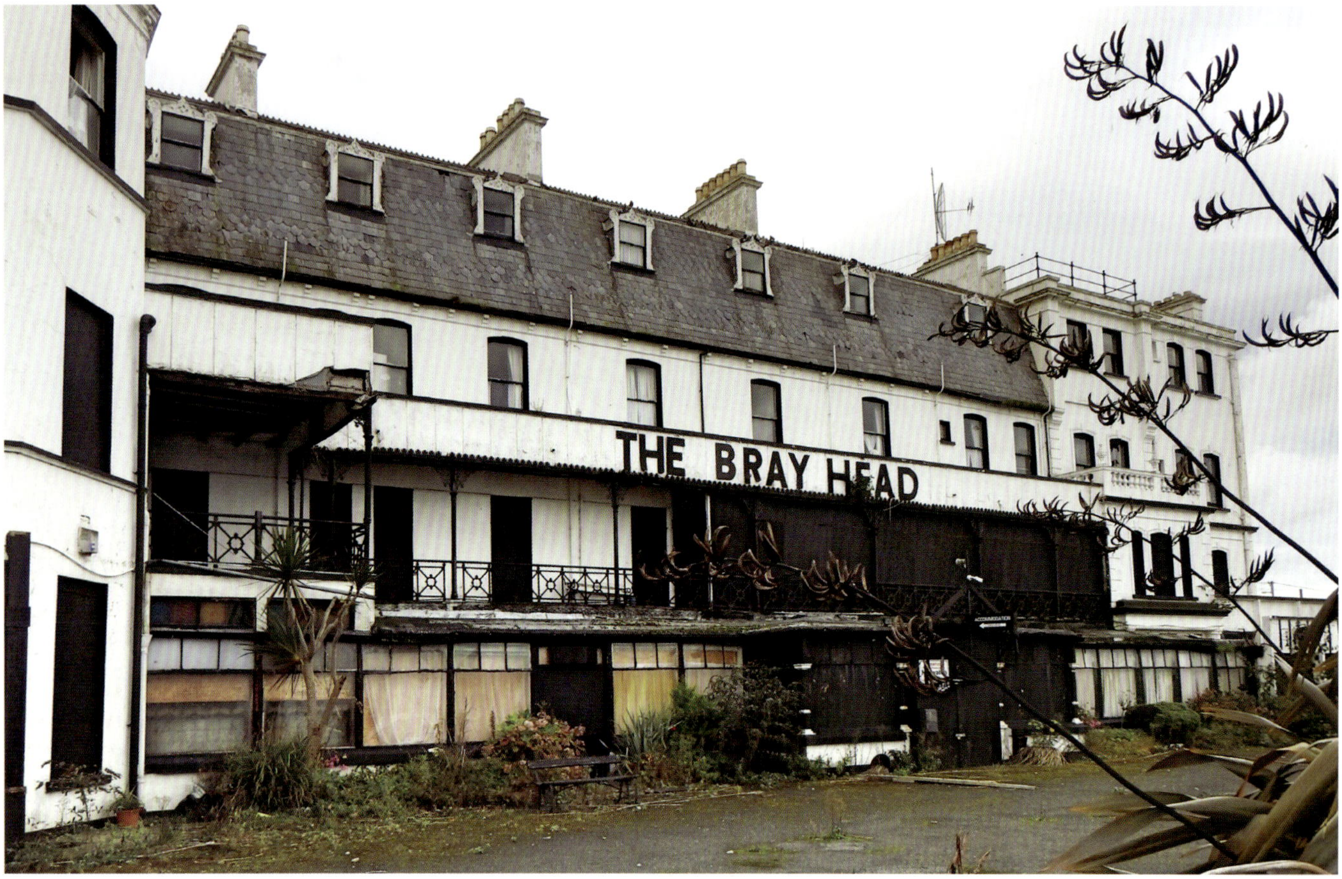

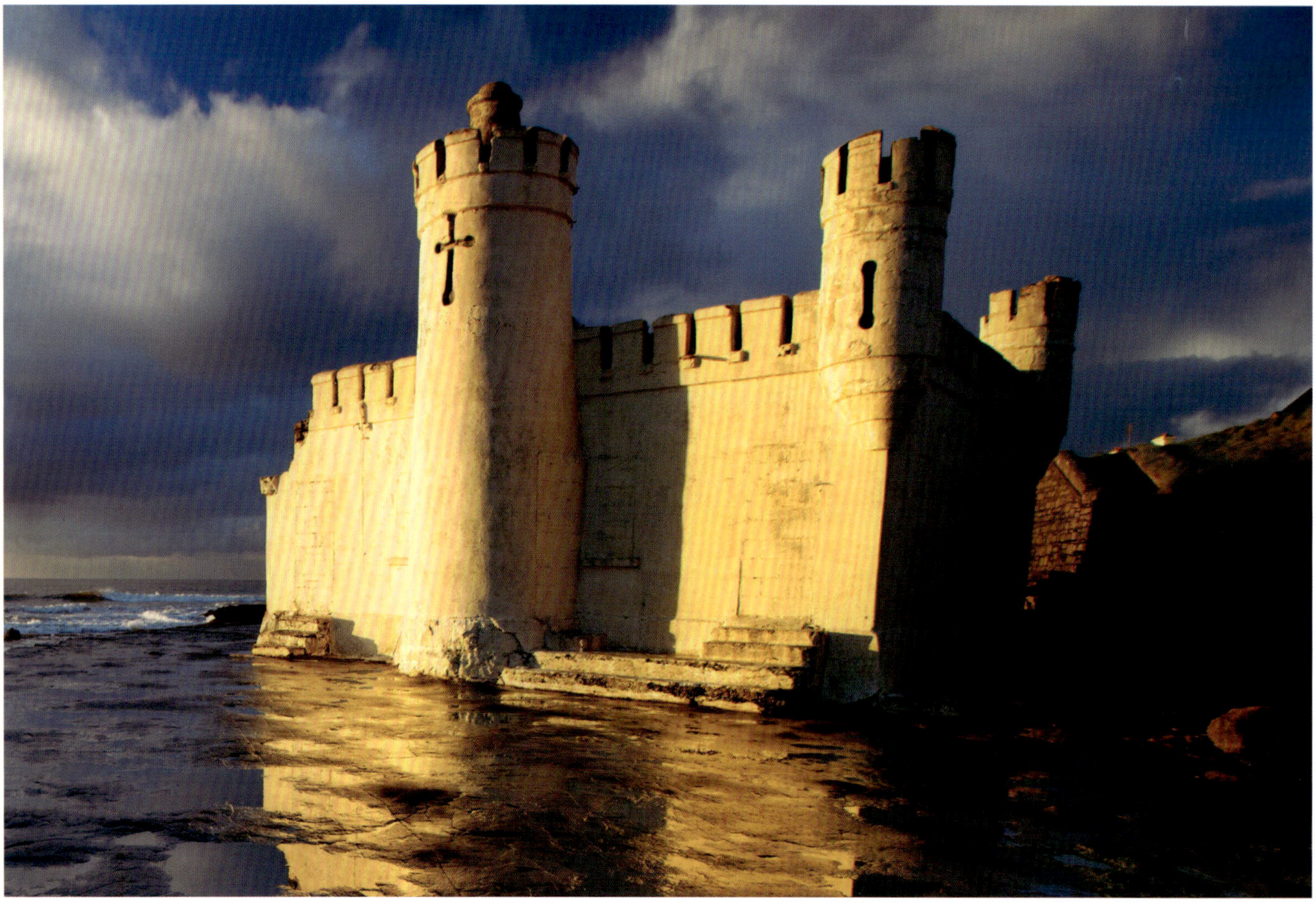

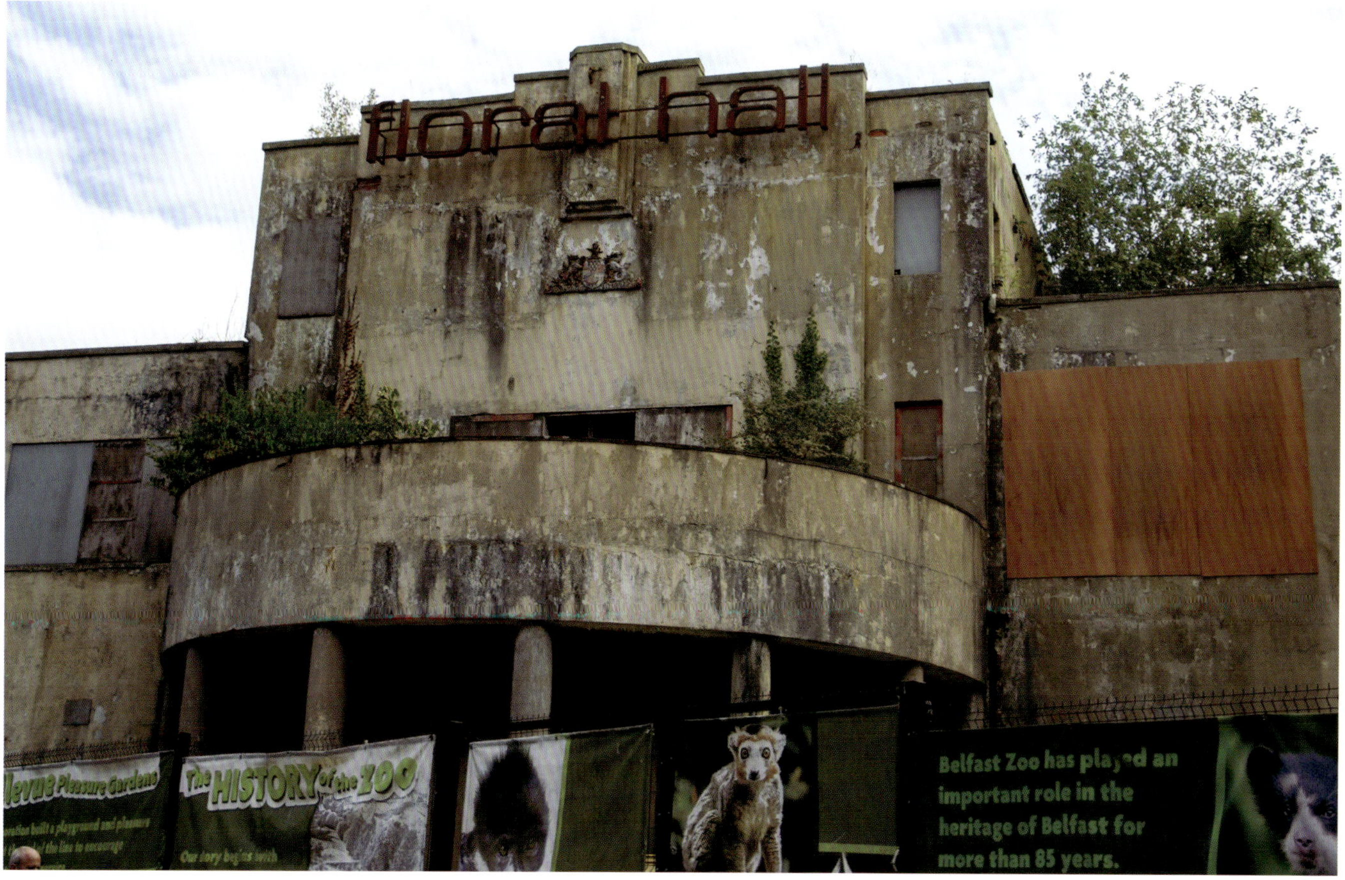

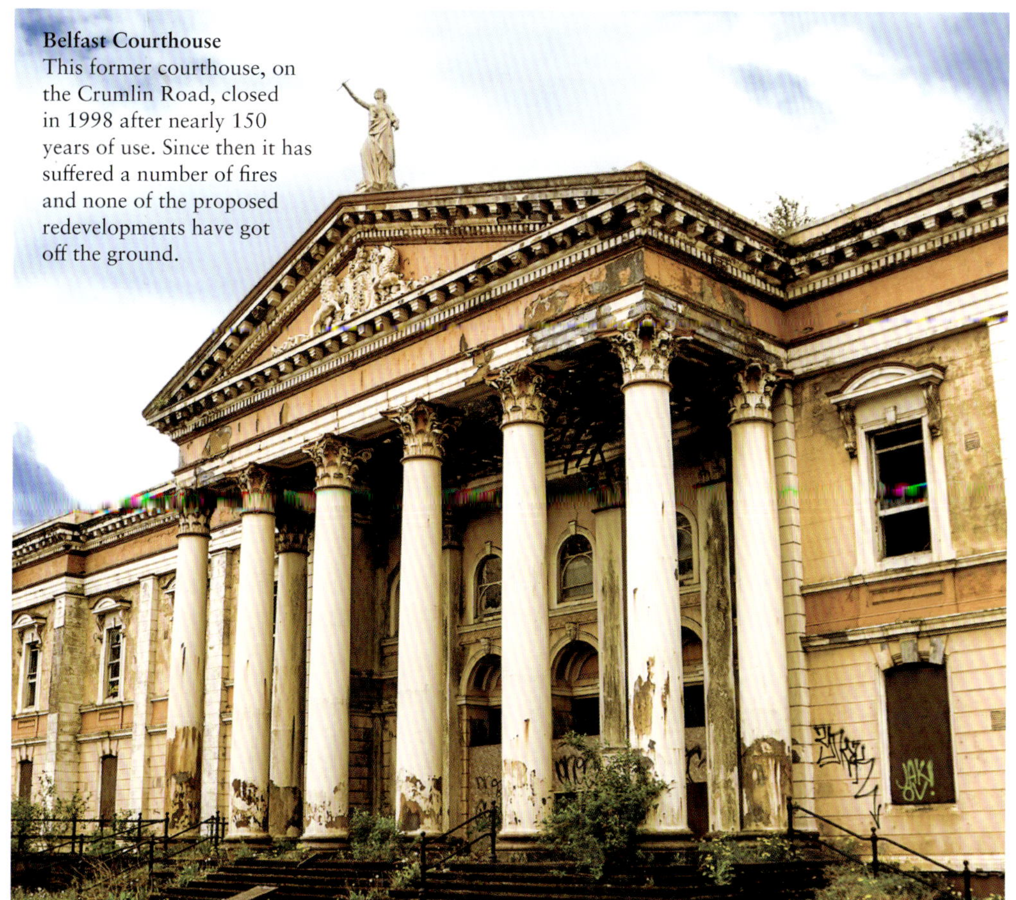

Belfast Courthouse
This former courthouse, on the Crumlin Road, closed in 1998 after nearly 150 years of use. Since then it has suffered a number of fires and none of the proposed redevelopments have got off the ground.

ABOVE:
Floral Hall, Belfast Zoos
Built in the mid-1930s, Floral Hall was a popular dance venue, and, later, performers such as Jimi Hendrix, Pink Floyd and the Small Faces played there. Before it closed in 1972, it had a period as a roller disco.

OPPOSITE ABOVE:
The Bray Head Hotel, Bray, County Wicklow
Dating back to the mid-19th century, the Bray Head Hotel was used as a film location as well as by holidaymakers until it was sold in 2017. In recent years there have been plans to turn it into apartments.

OPPOSITE BELOW:
Cliff Baths, Enniscrone beach, County Sligo
Built in 1850 by the local Orme family – who had high hopes for a resort there – these baths were supplied with fresh seawater from a man-made, rectangular pool that would fill with sea water at high tide.

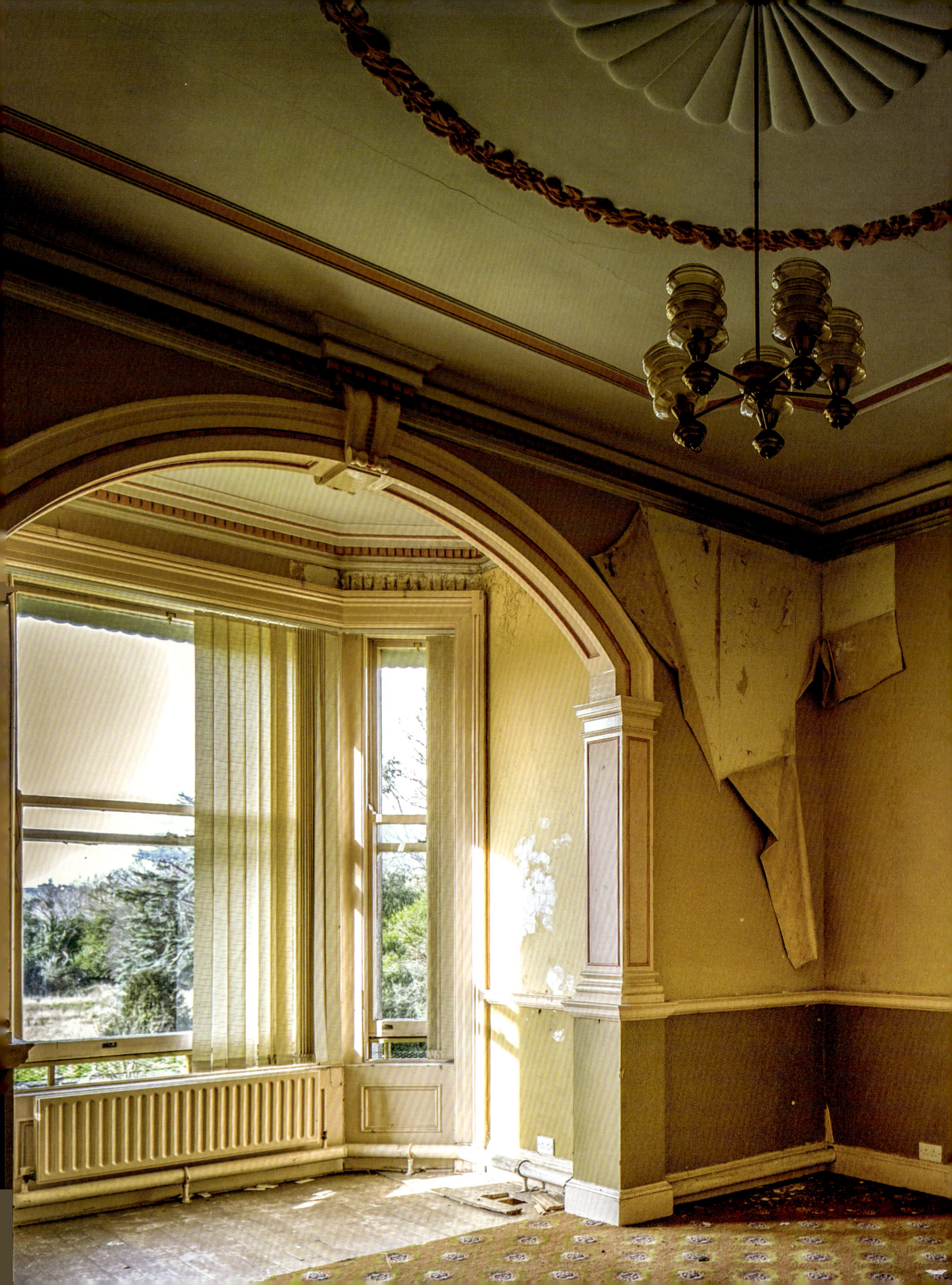

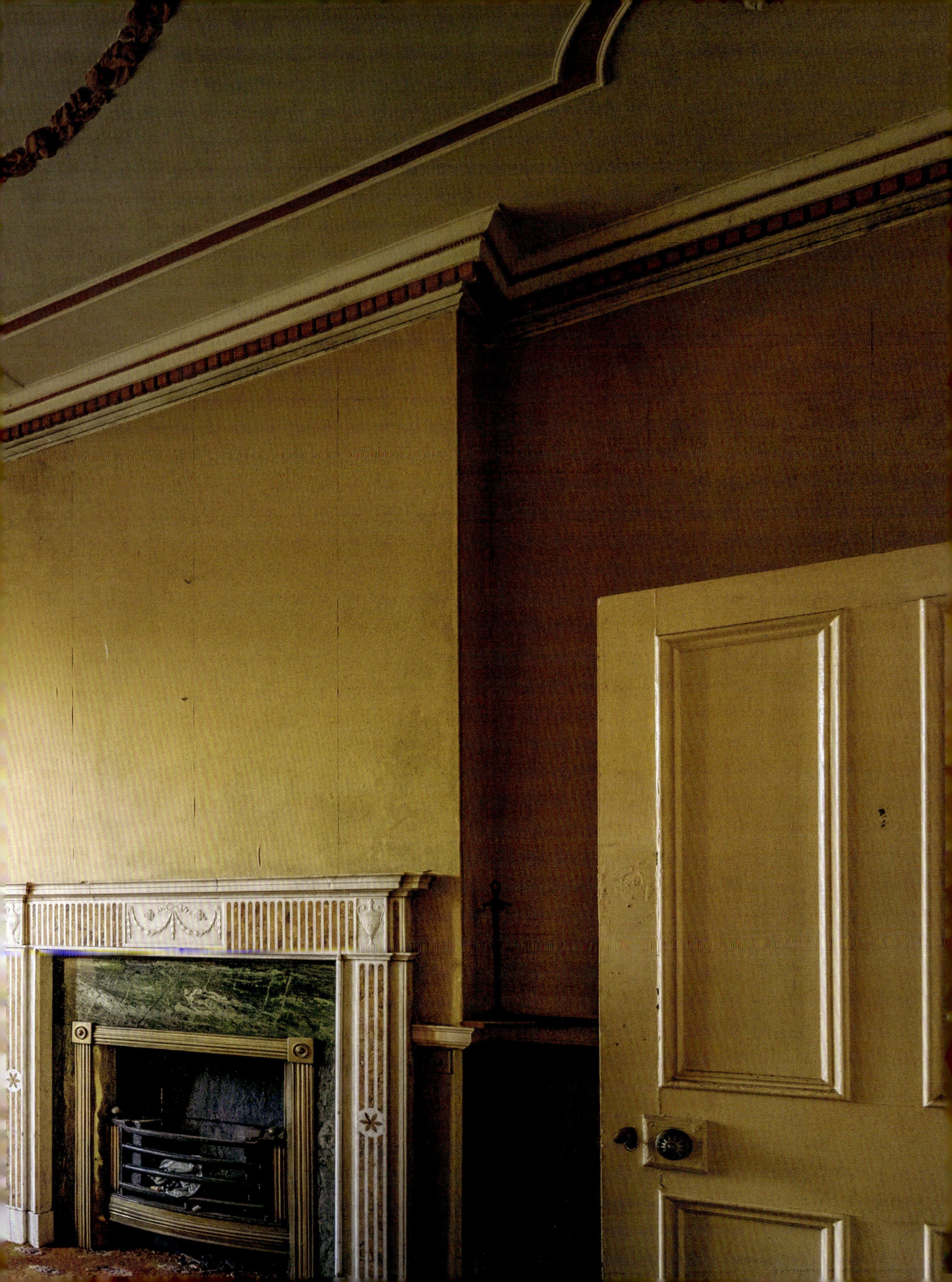

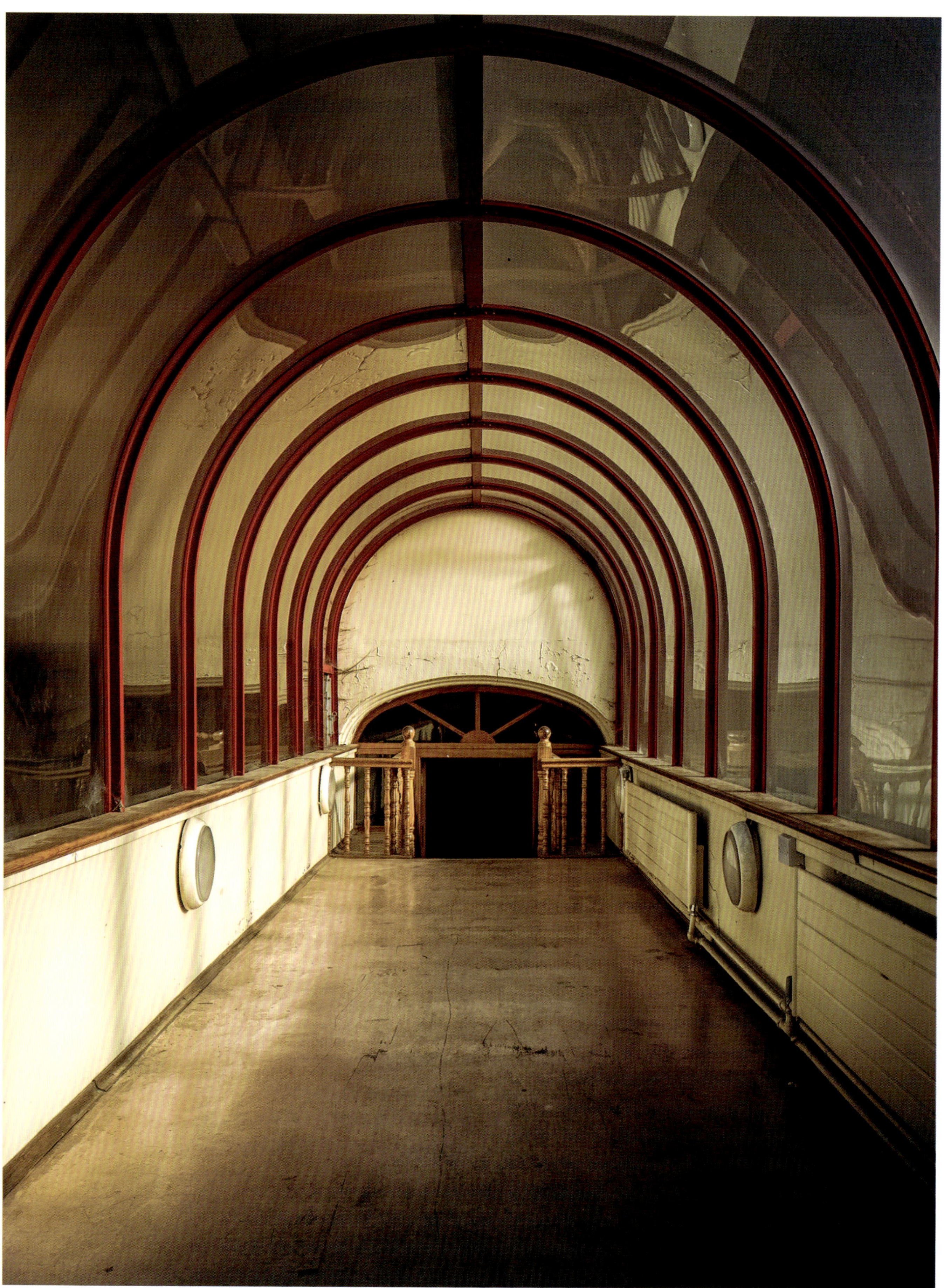

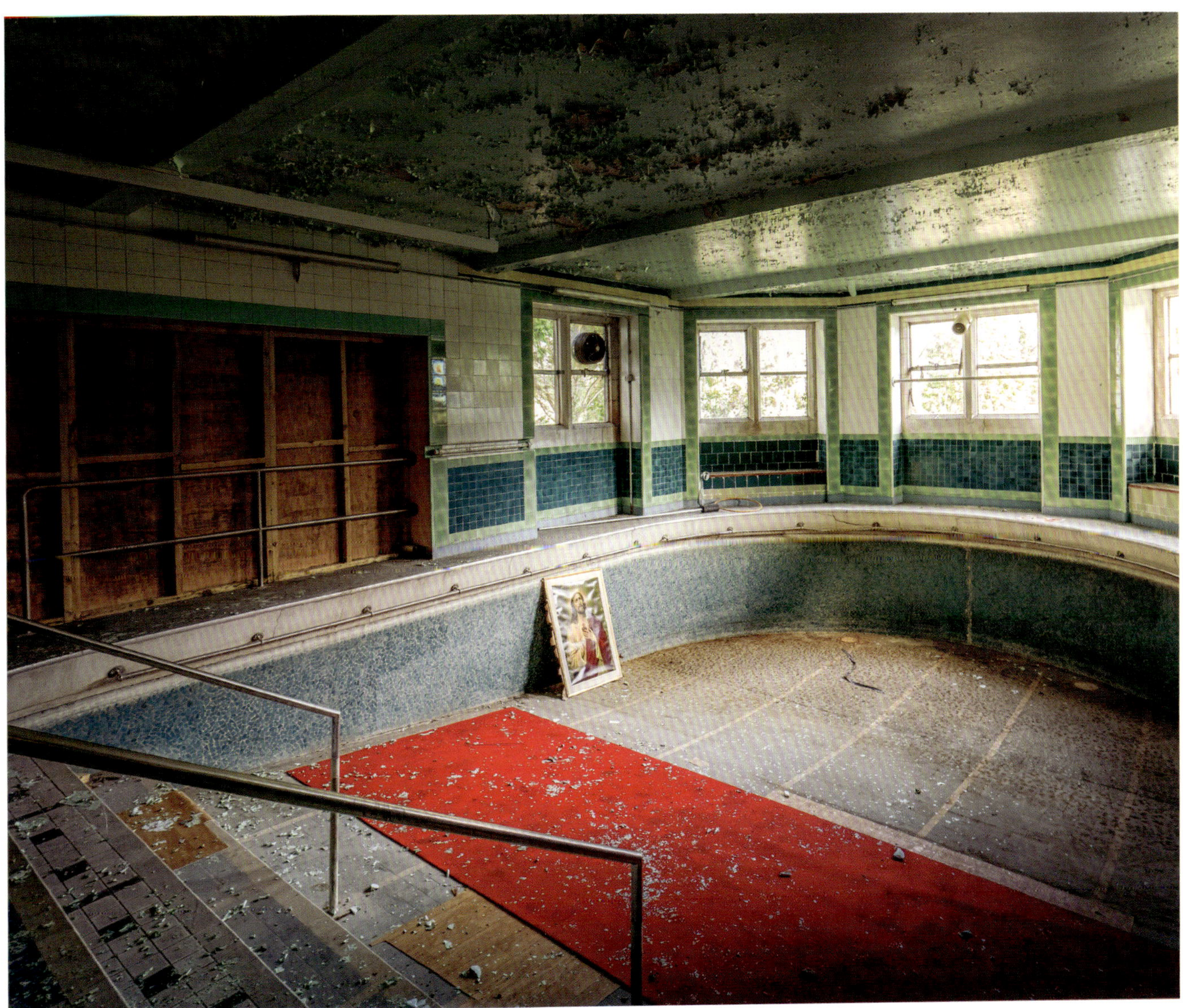

PREVIOUS PAGES & OPPOSITE:
Knockmaroon Lodge, Dublin
This 19th-century lodge was
owned by the Guinness family
in the early 20th century. Arthur
Guinness built a connecting
passageway between it and a new
house he was constructing on the
estate. However, the creation of
the Irish Free State after World
War I left the prominent family
on the wrong side of the political
divide, and Arthur left Dublin for
Britain. When he died, the estate
passed to the Irish state by way
of death duties owed.

ABOVE:
Glenmaroon House, Dublin
An indoor swimming pool was
part of the new development on
the Guinnesses' Knockmaroon
estate, Glenmaroon House,
which was neo-Tudor in style.
After the Guinness era, for a
time the estate was used as a
care home – a dormitory and
a chapel were added to it. The
estate – also including gatehouses
and stables – borders Dublin's
Phoenix Park, which contains
the much-raided 18th-century
Magazine Fort.

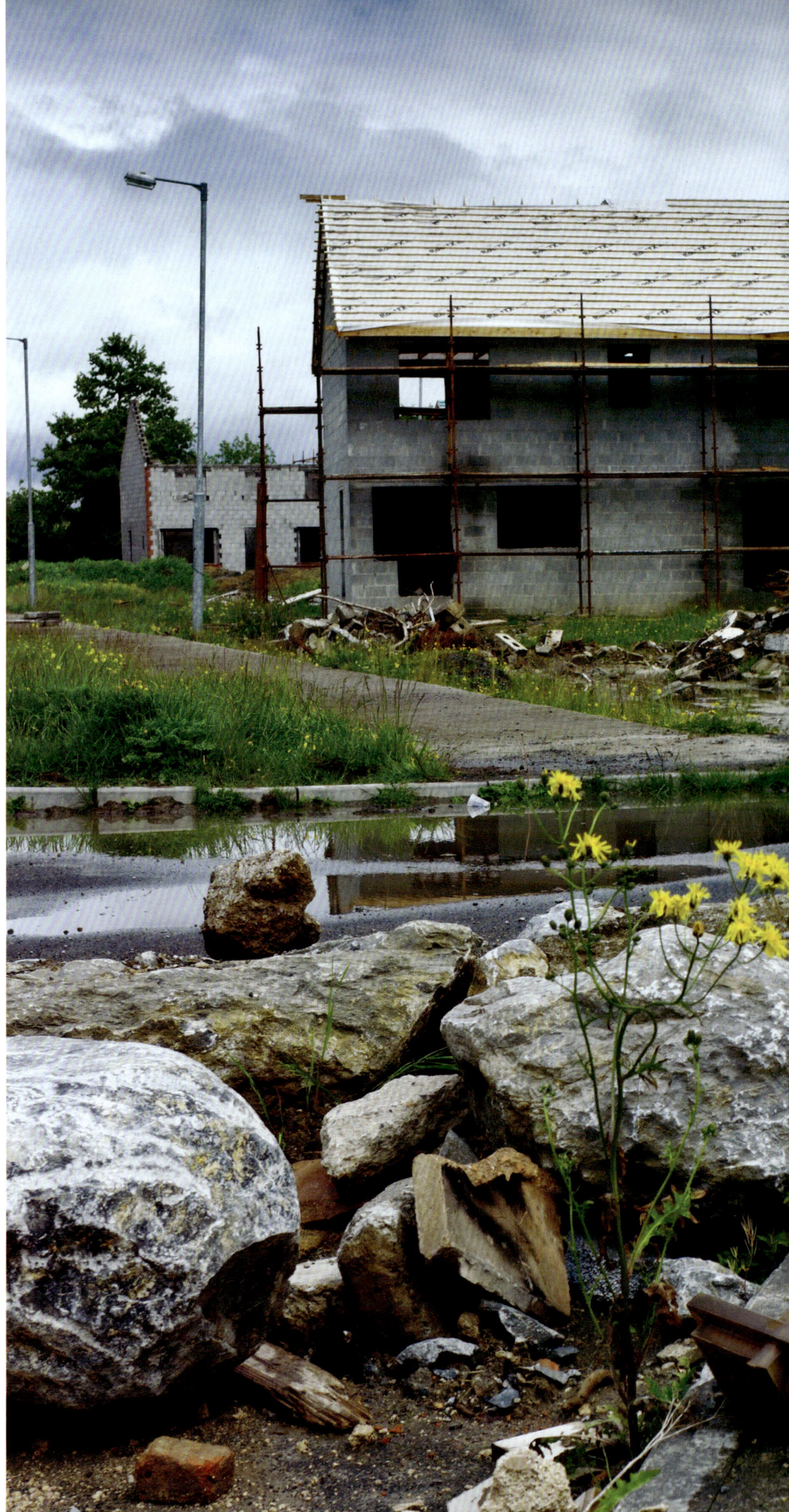

Rathkeale, County Limerick
This half-finished new housing
in the town of Rathkeale is
emblematic of the end of the
Celtic Tiger economic boom.
Across the Irish Republic,
a number of speculative
developments were never
completed. In 2021 it was
reported that there were 123
unfinished estates in the country,
with 58 completely unoccupied.

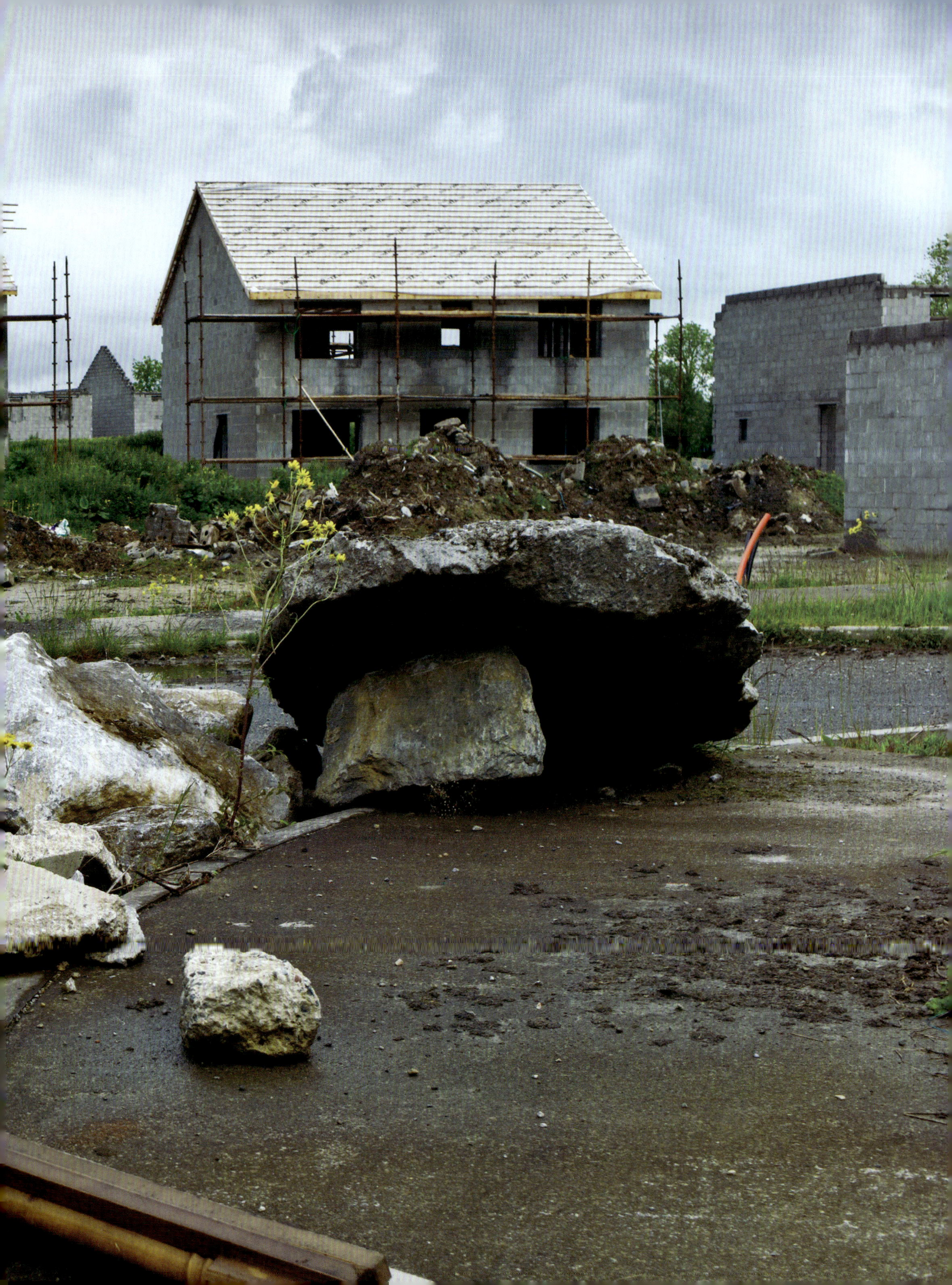

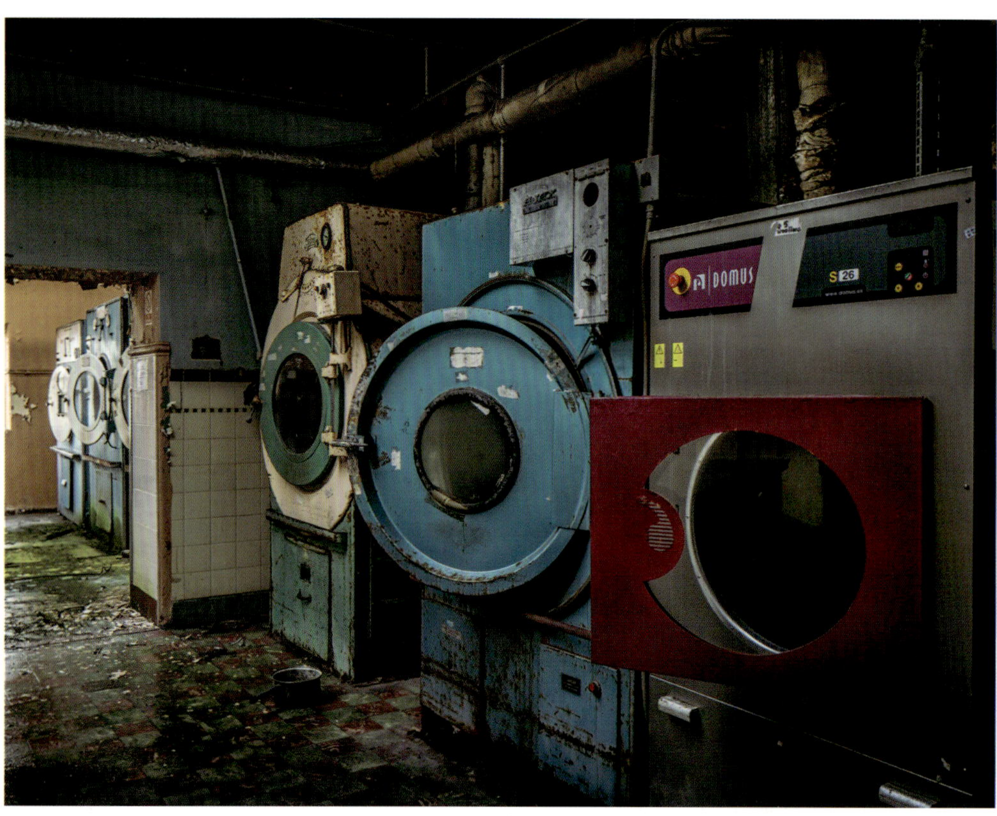

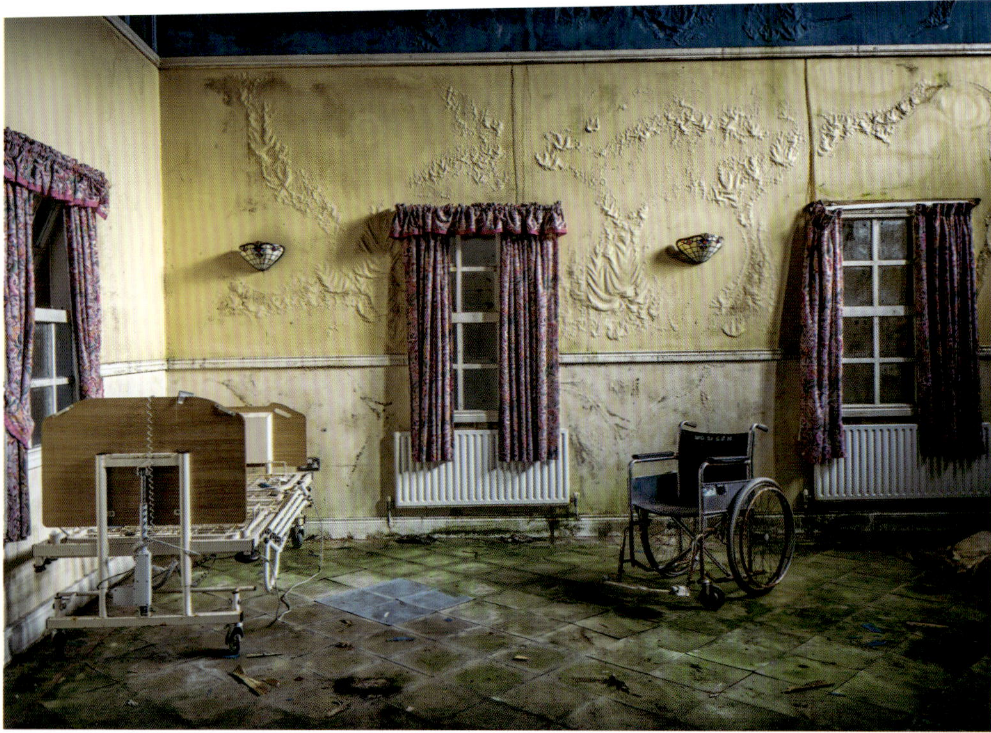

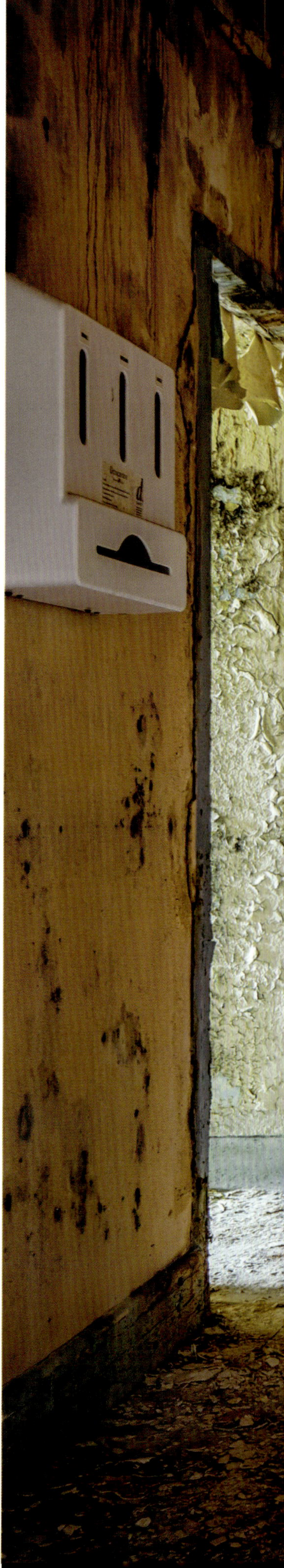

St Brigid's Hospital, Ballinasloe, County Galway

This building was constructed in 1833 and first opened as Connacht Asylum. It was closed in 2013 as the Republic of Ireland moved to caring for the mentally ill 'within the community' or in general hospitals. The asylum was a large part of the town of Ballinasloe – in 1951, there were 5596 people in the town and 2078 'resident patients' at the hospital. It was during this period that it became known as St Brigid's Hospital. Originally, the hospital was designed to accommodate less than 1000 and was intended for 'curable lunatics'. It was one of the earliest 'district asylums' in Ireland.

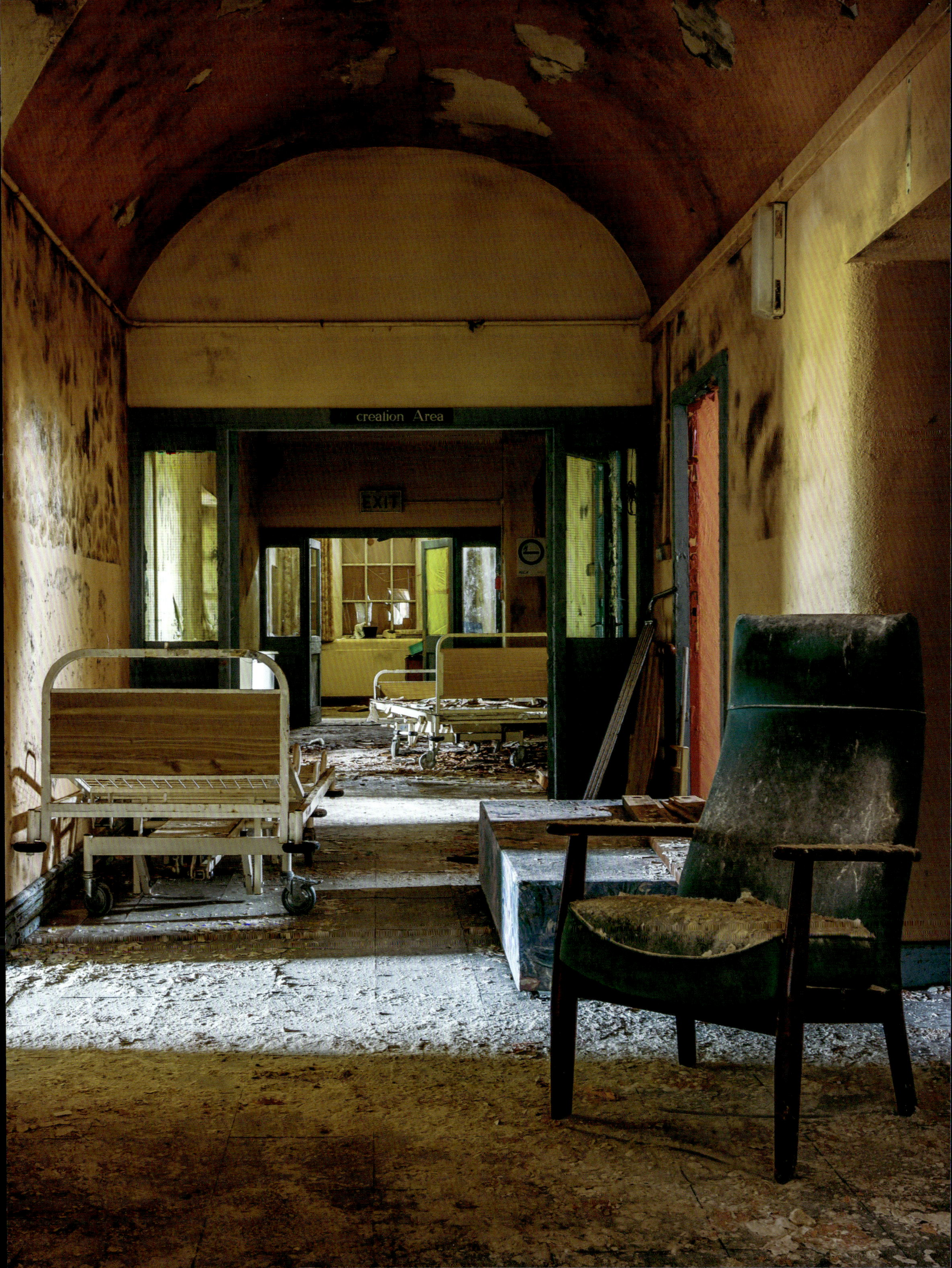
crealion Area
EXIT

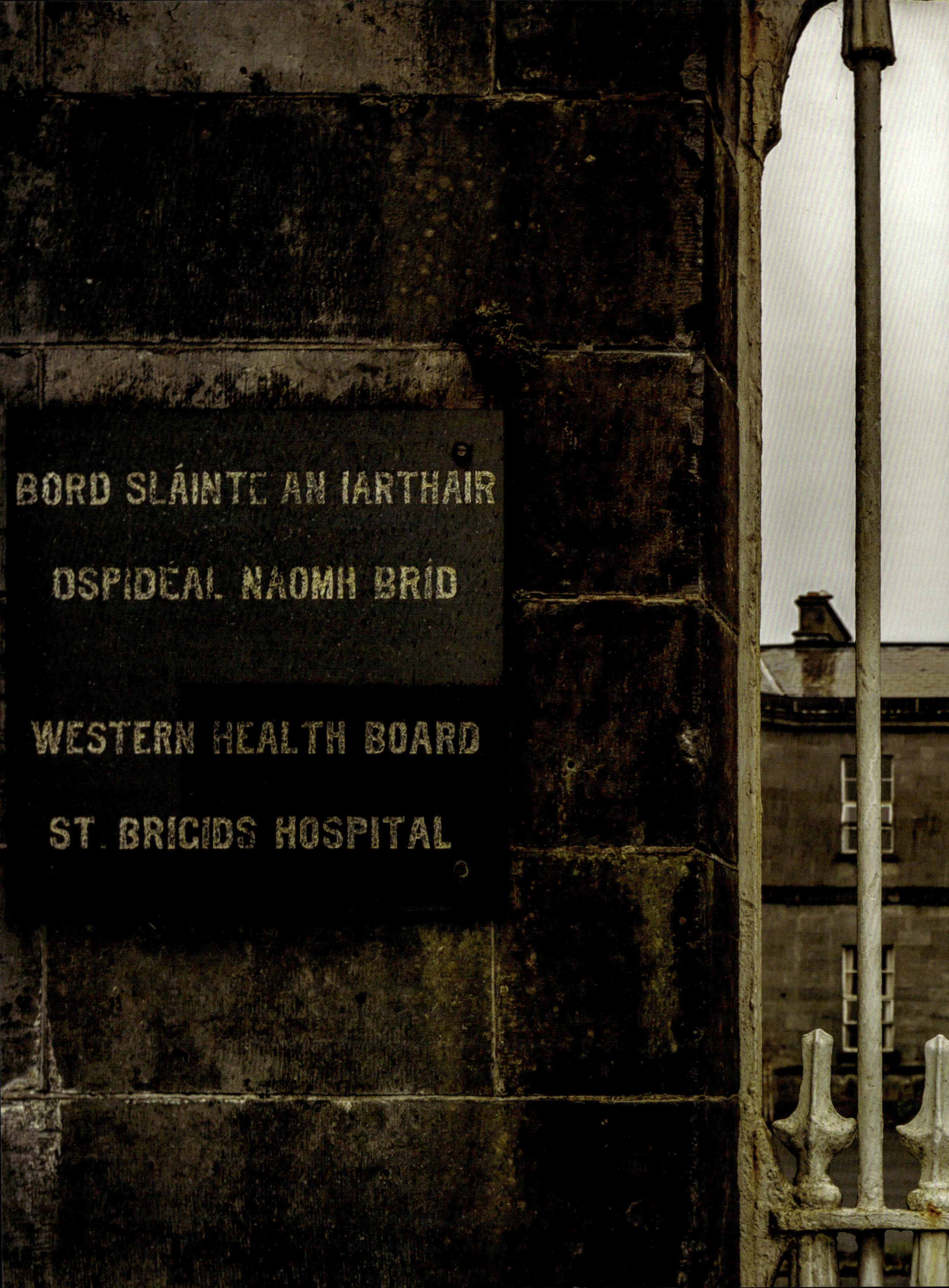

BORD SLÁINTE AN IARTHAIR

OSPIDÉAL NAOMH BRÍD

WESTERN HEALTH BOARD

ST. BRIGIDS HOSPITAL

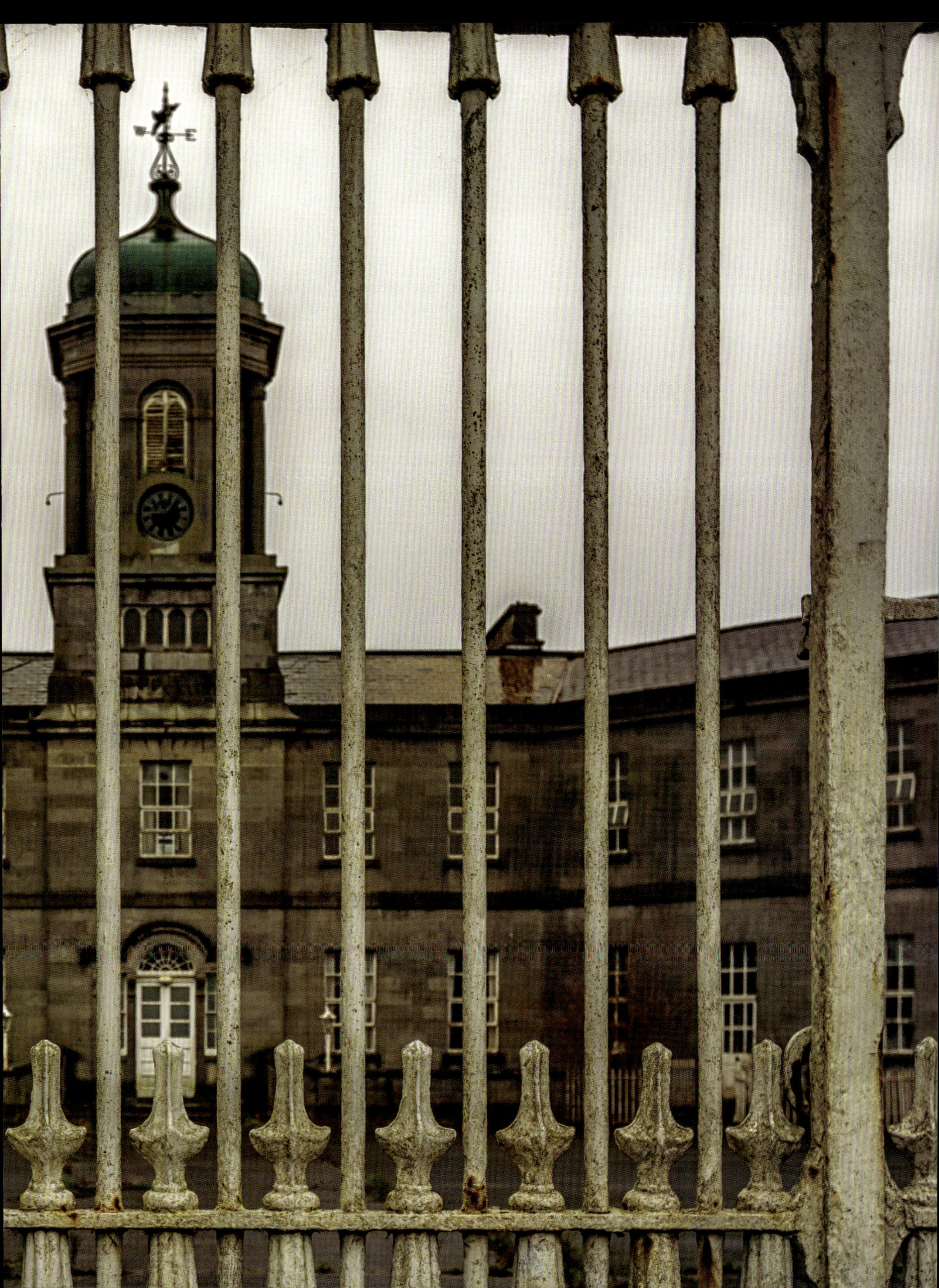

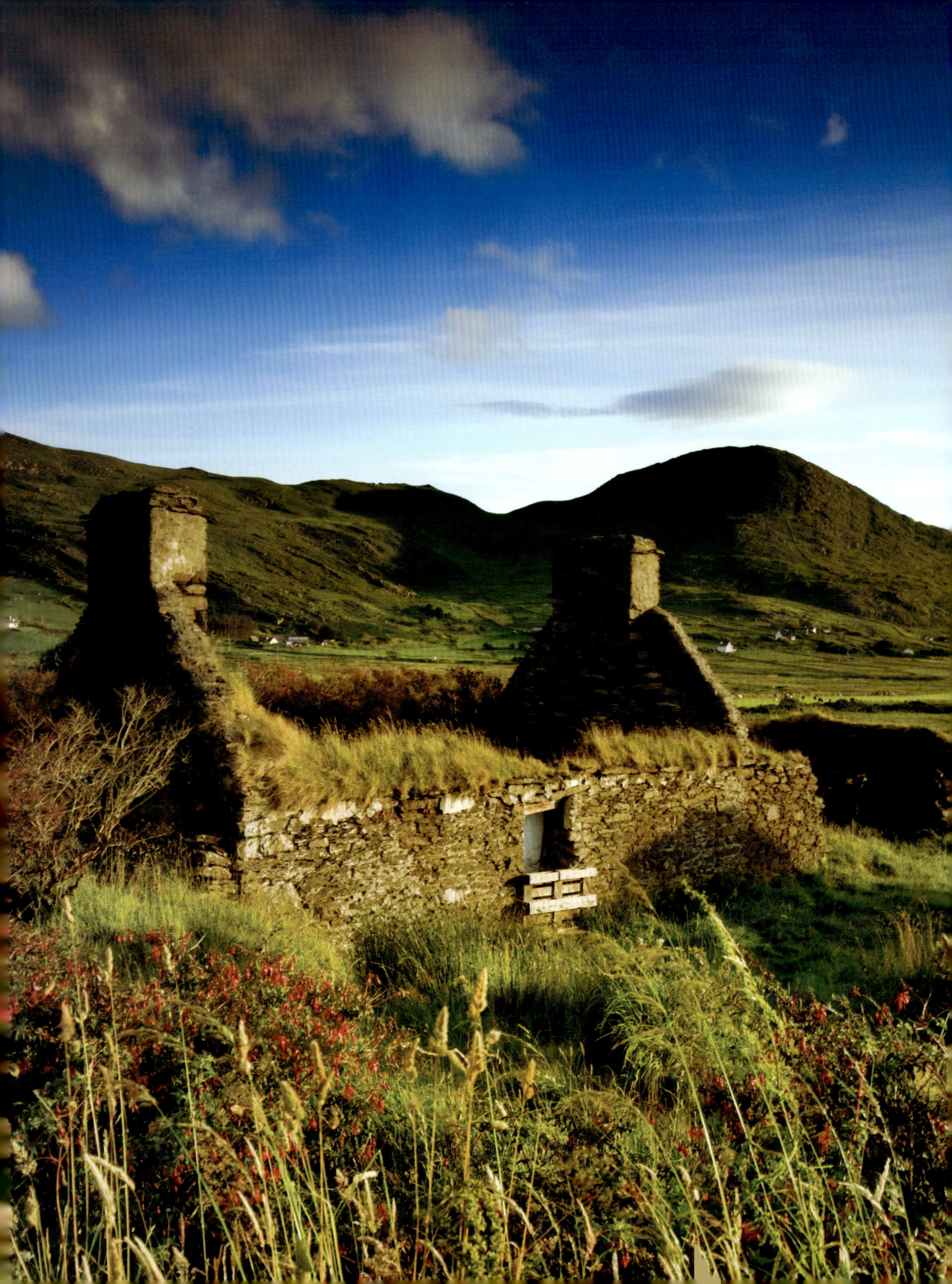

Farms, Cottages & Schools

As the towns and cities of Ireland have grown – and people in rural Irish communities have also sought better lives in North America or even further afield – the villages and fields of the Emerald Isle have gradually been depleted. The result is that there are now many buildings and landscapes across Ireland that have been left to the ravages of nature, with no human intervention. Chief among places suffering rural depopulation are Ireland's many islands, and the challenges of their remoteness and inaccessibility have prompted residents to move to more convenient and prosperous locations. However, as they have gone, they have often left fascinating buildings from previous centuries to be discovered by future generations. They have also allowed animals to reclaim these environments.

The movement of people away from the Irish countryside also sheds light on the efforts that were made duriung the 19th and 20th centuries to bring non-denominational primary education to the rural areas. A raft of small, often one-room, National Schools were built in the smallest of communities. Plenty are now deserted, but the starts they gave to those children will have sustained the former pupils throughout their lives – lives that may well have been lived far away from the green fields of rural Ireland.

Derelict cottage, Waterville, County Kerry
Across Ireland there are many derelict cottages – signs of rural depopulation, as people have been attracted elsewhere by better prospects than living off the land. Ironically, this dwelling is in a village that acted as a focal point for the Irish side of the first transatlantic cables.

Abandoned village, An Port, County Donegal
This is called the 'ghost village' or 'deserted village'. It is thought that the inhabitants left during the Great Famine of the mid-19th century. The former settlement is located in the far west of Donegal, several miles from the nearest still-inhabited village.

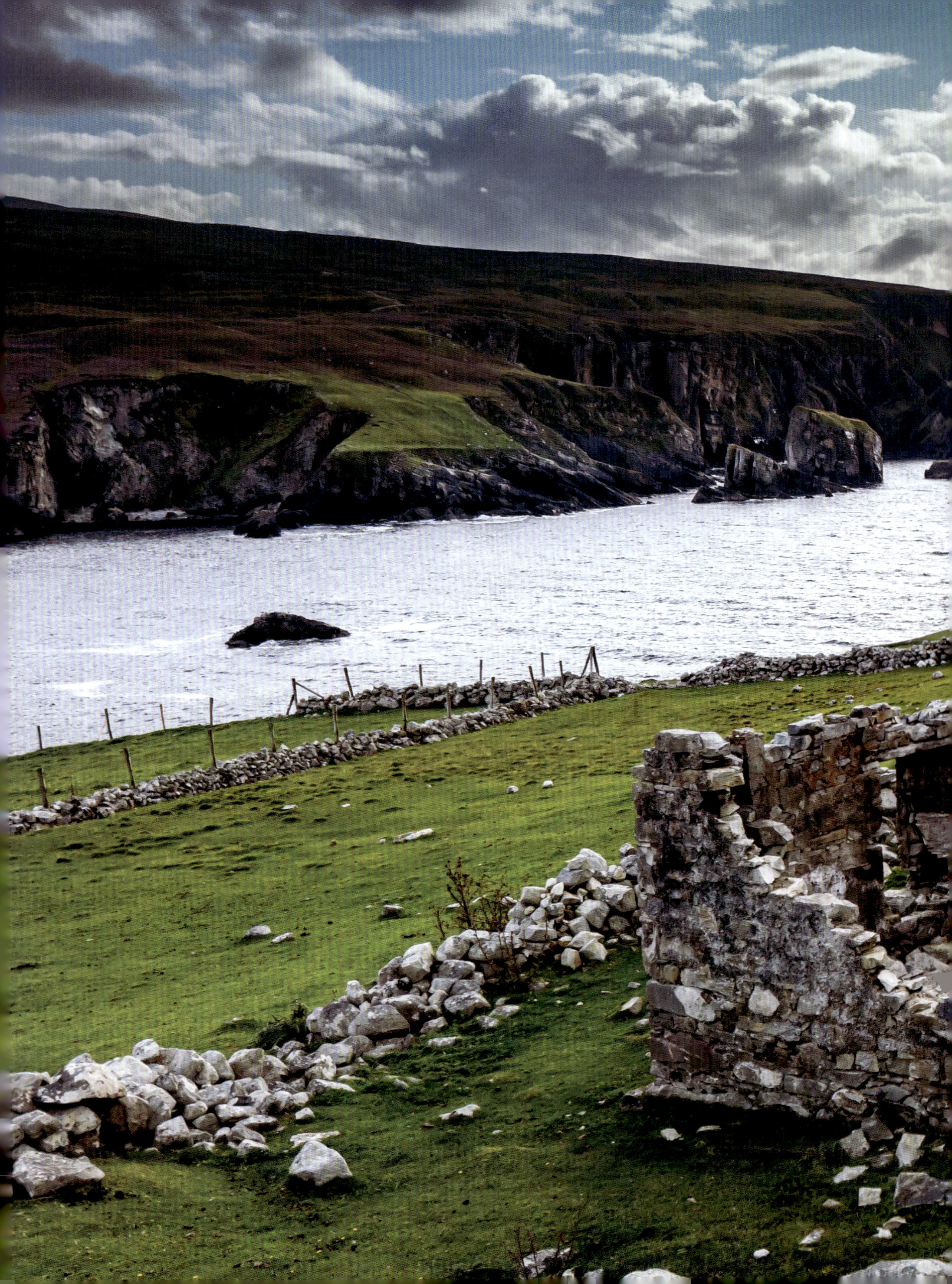

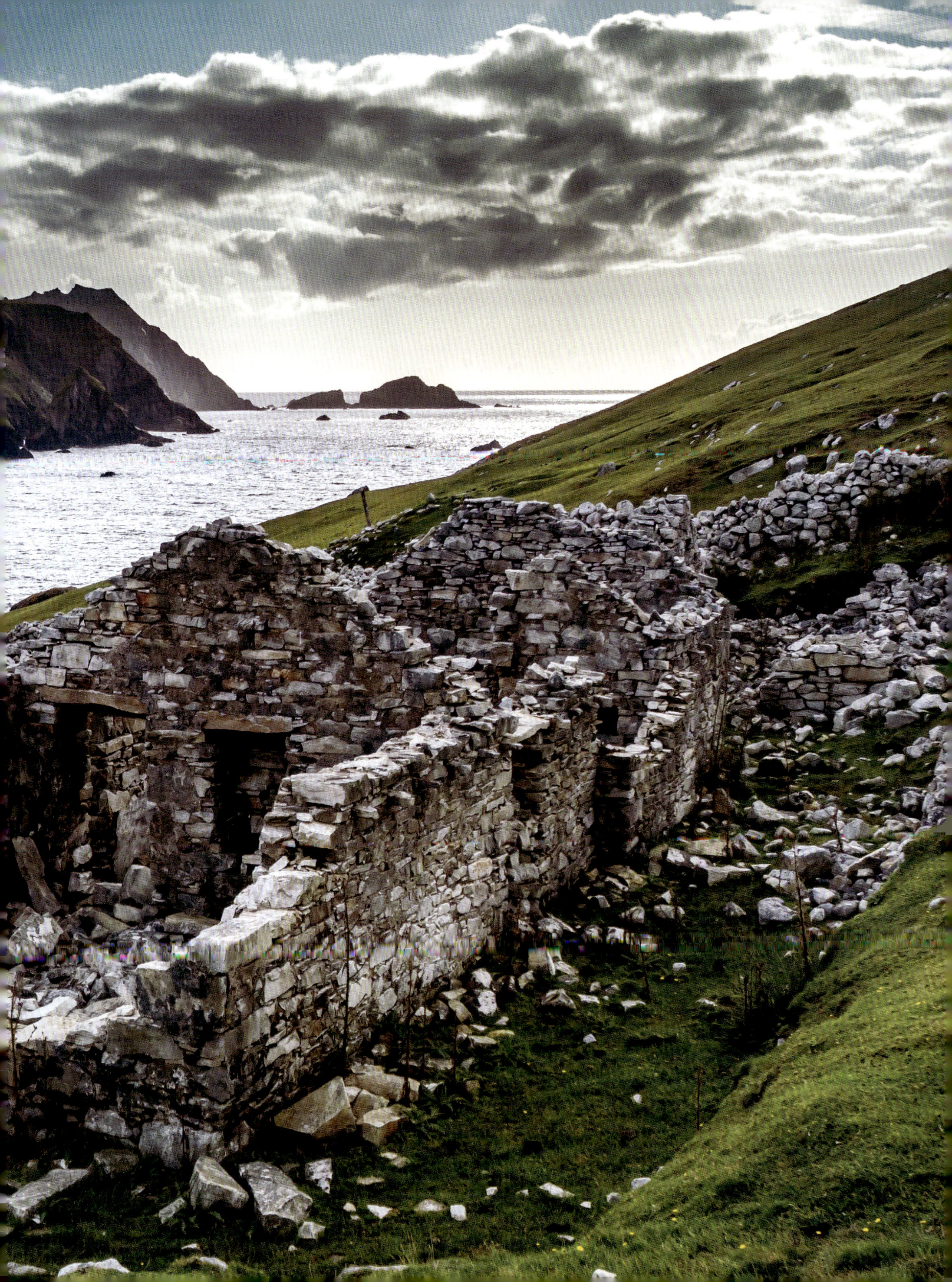

Deserted cottage, Inishmaan, Aran Islands, County Galway
Thatched roofs were commonplace in Irish rural houses into the 19th century, and some still remain. There are a number on the Aran Islands, some of which have been maintained as holiday lets.

Abandoned stone house, Inishmore, Aran Islands, County Galway
Inishmore is the largest of the three Aran Islands, with Inishmaan the next in line. Among the abandoned stone buildings on Inishmore is the prehistoric stone hill fort of Dun Aonghasa, today a popular tourist destination.

Abandoned building, Inishmaan, Aran Islands, County Galway
Inishmaan is geologically linked to the Burren area on the mainland, with the limestone of both areas providing fertile ground conditions where plants can run rampant.

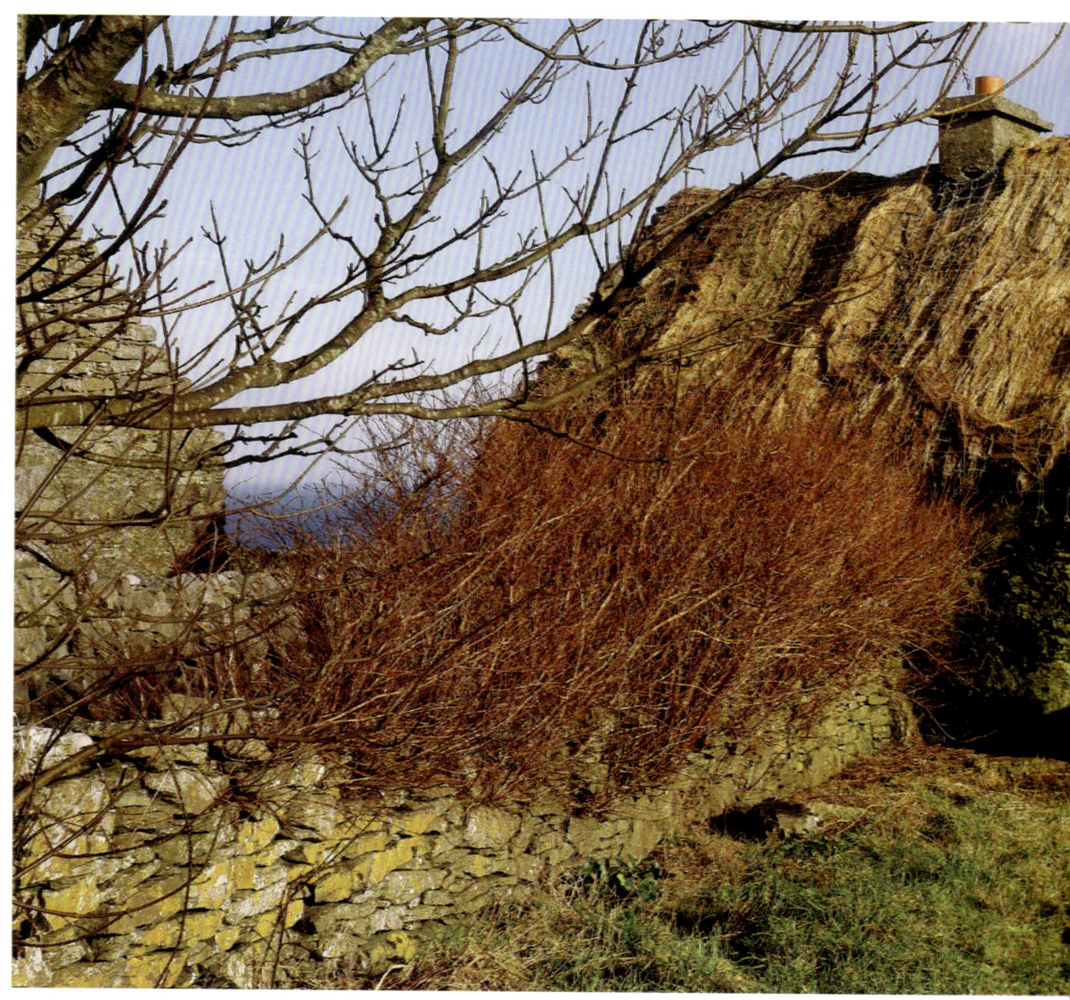

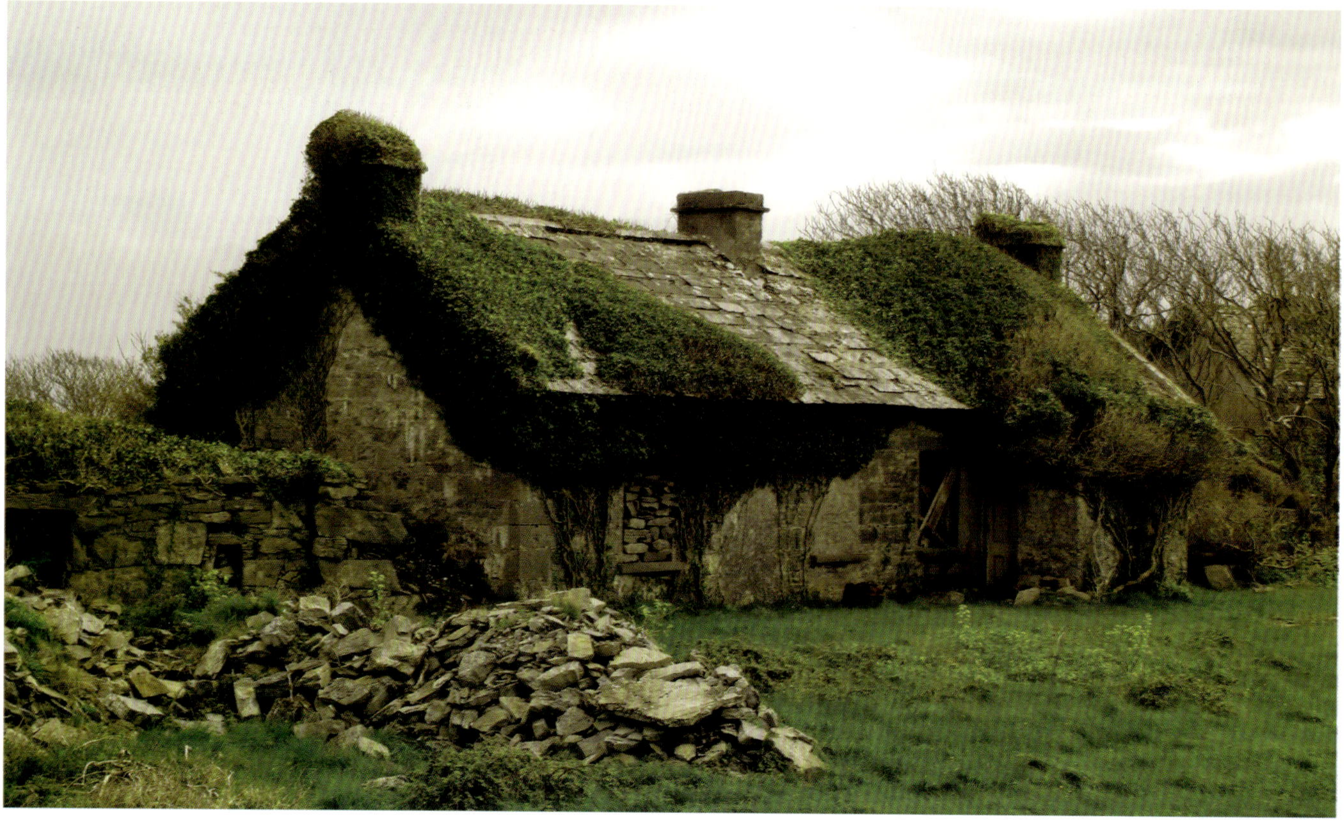

146

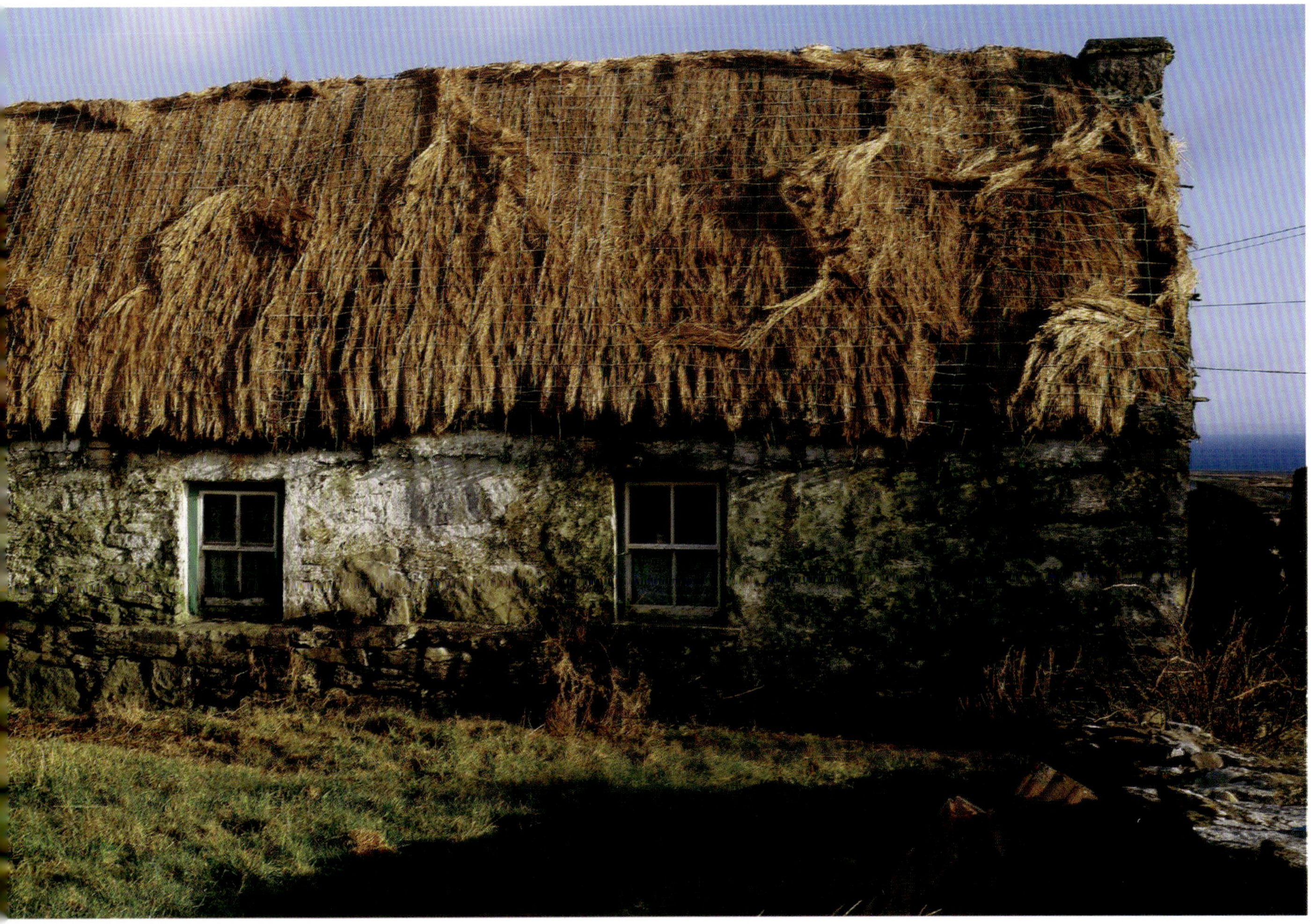

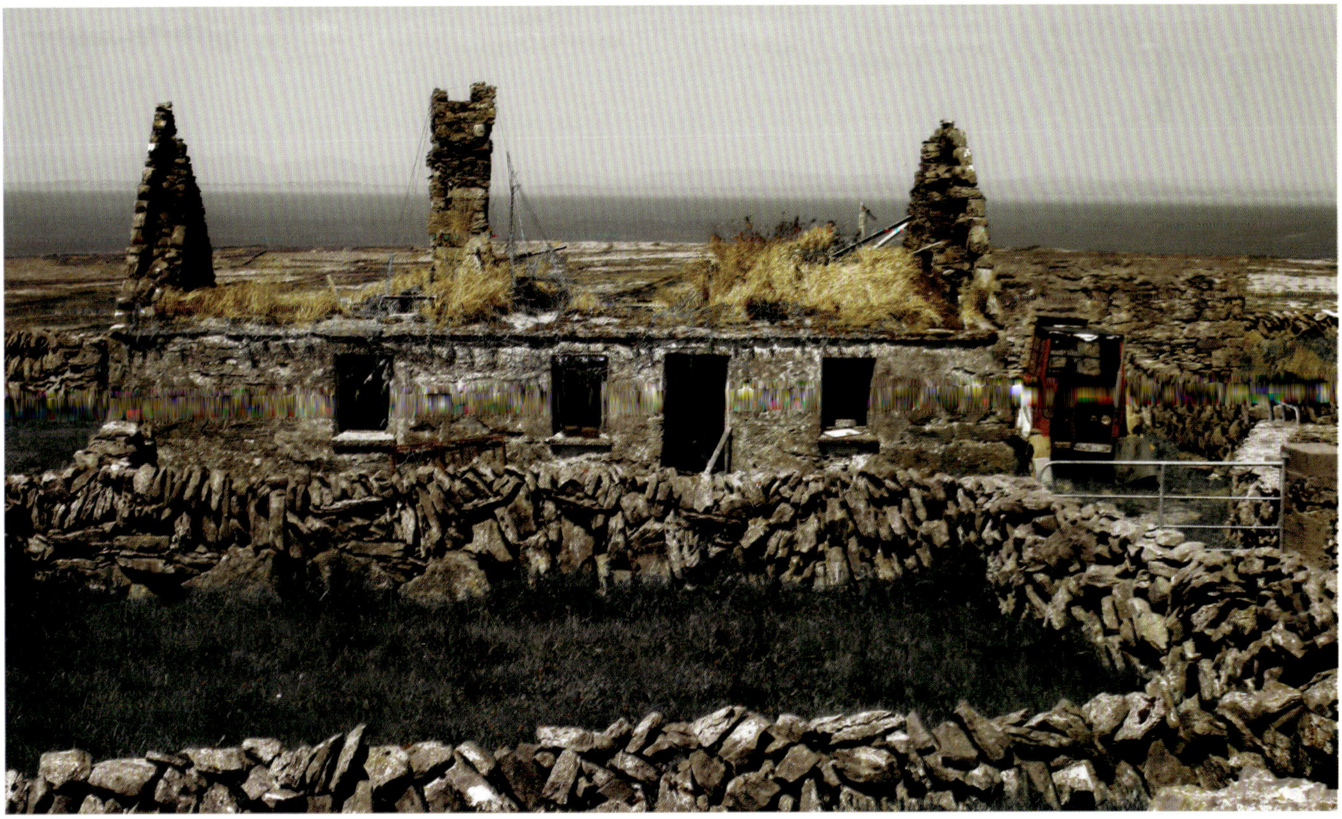

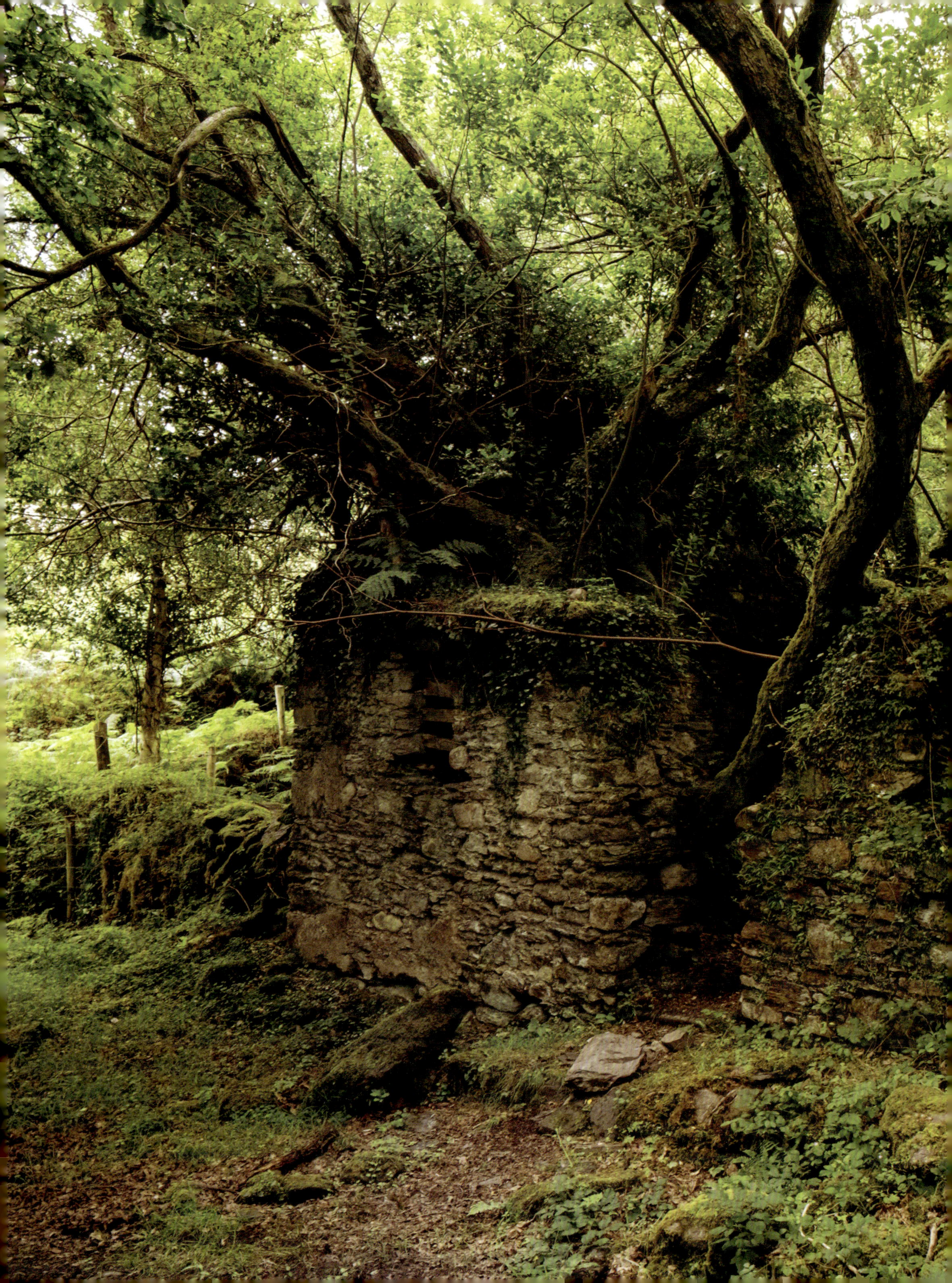

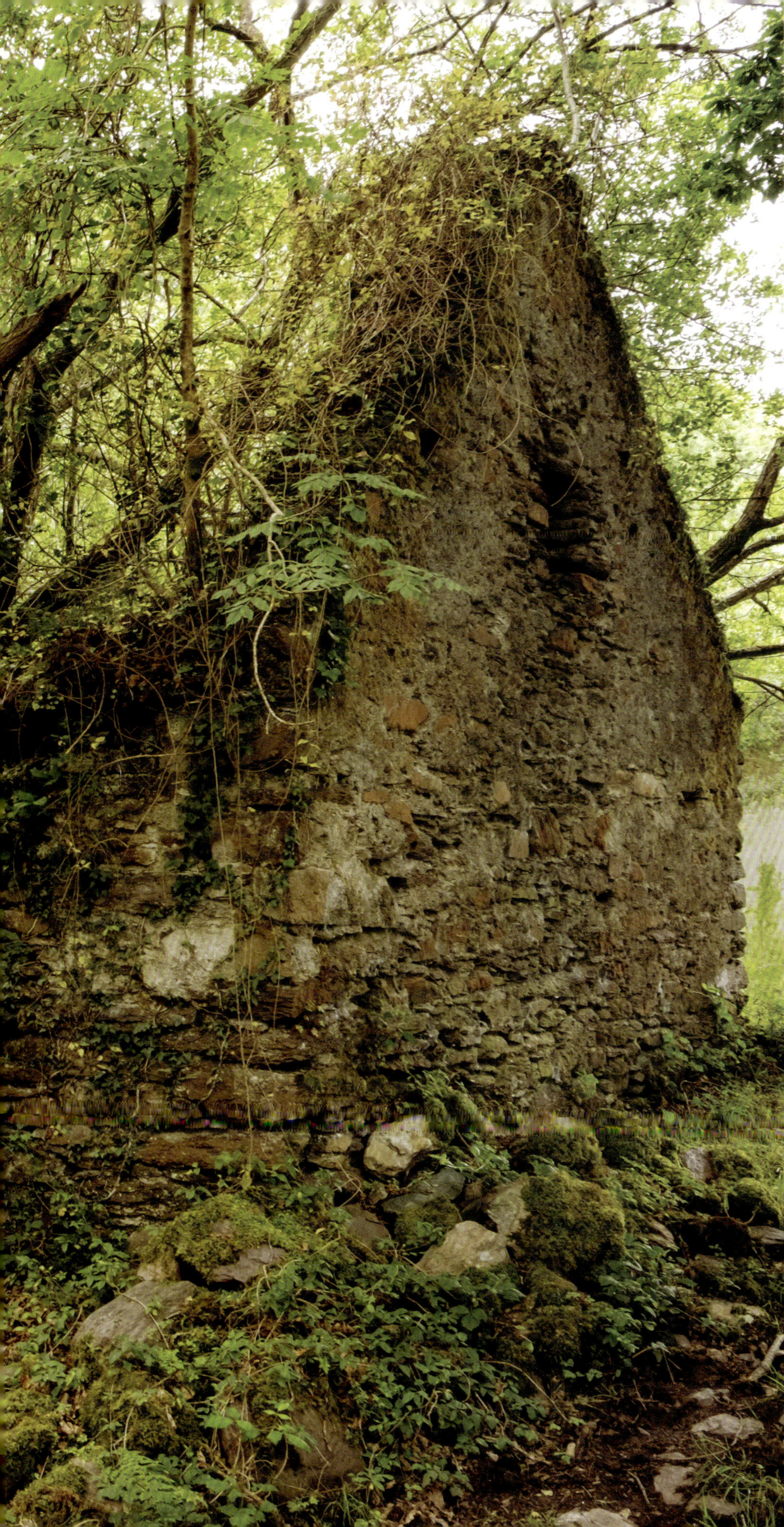

Cottage reclaimed by nature, Kerry Way, County Kerry
This building stands on the Kerry Way hiking trail between the town of Kenmare and the village of Sneem. County Kerry's location facing the Atlantic Ocean, and its mountainous peninsulas, mean that it has some of the highest rainfall in Ireland, which encourages lush vegetation growth.

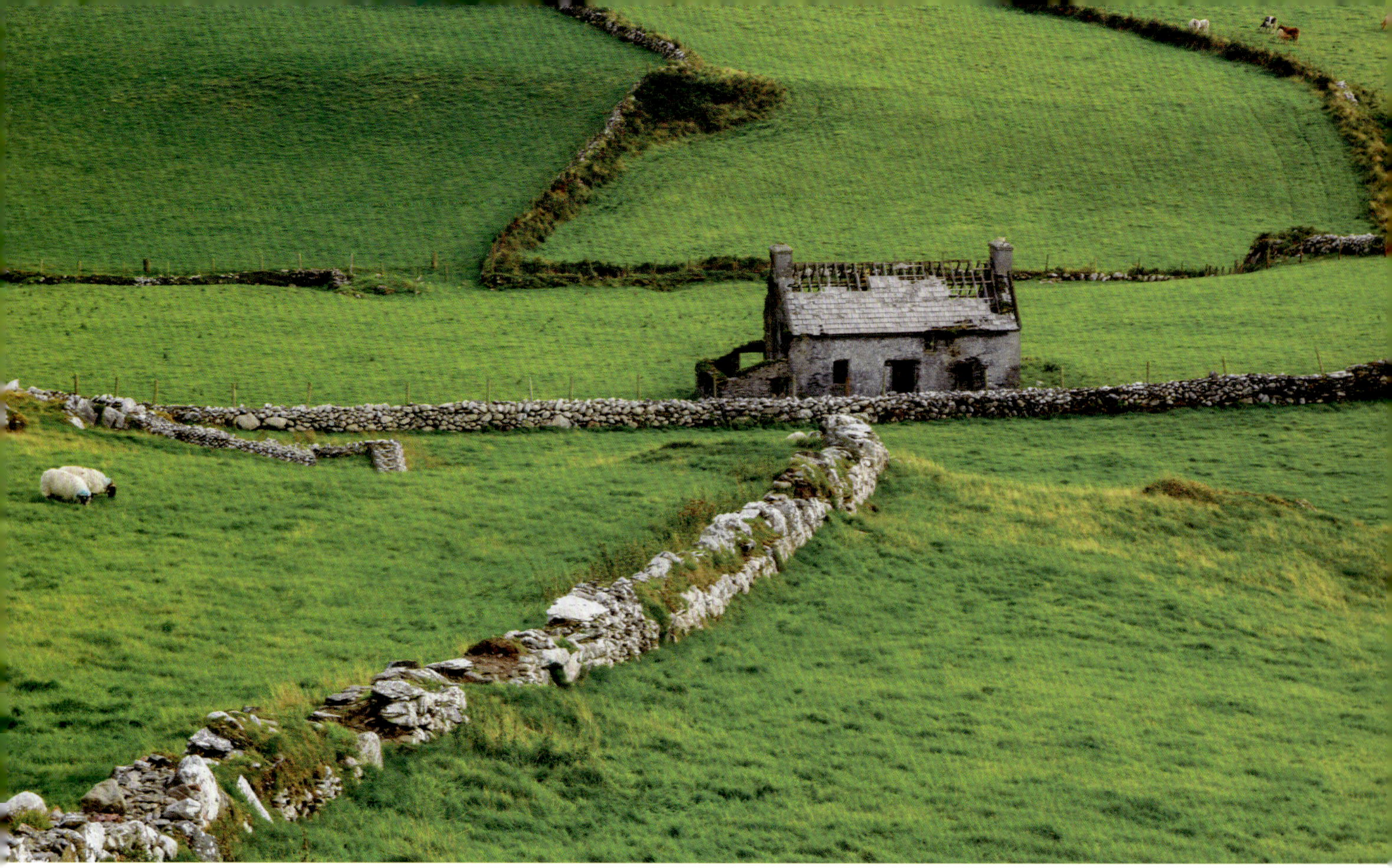

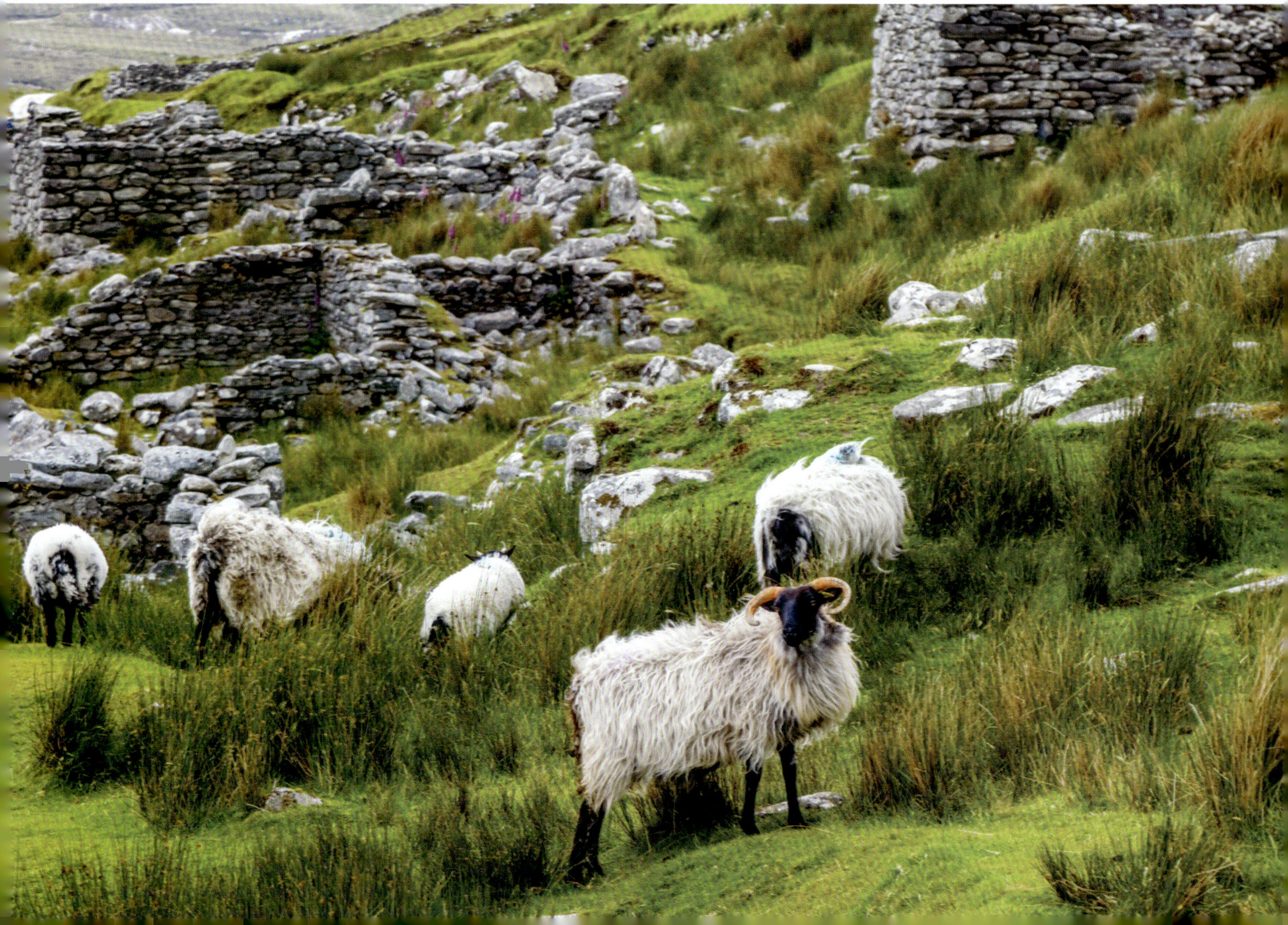

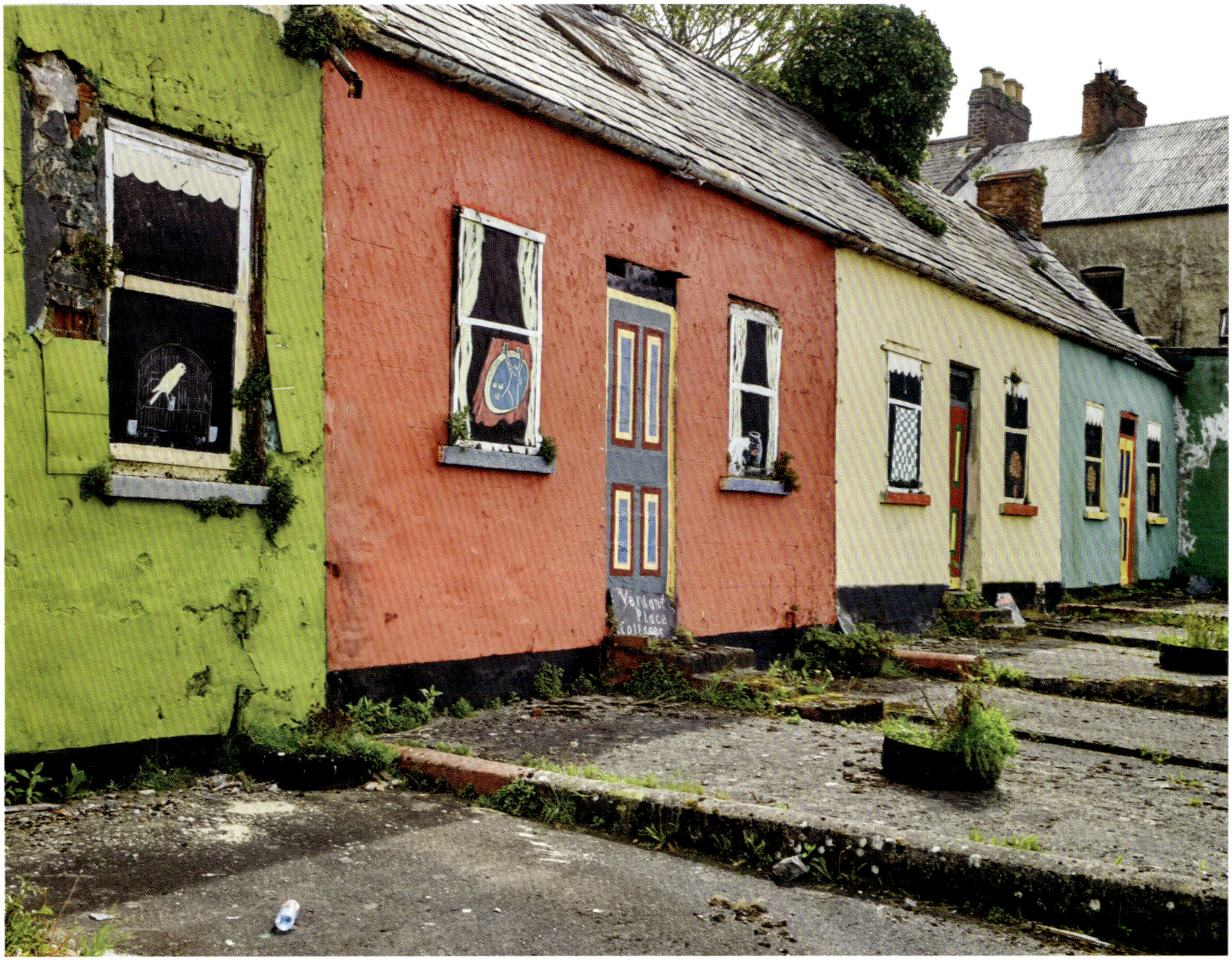

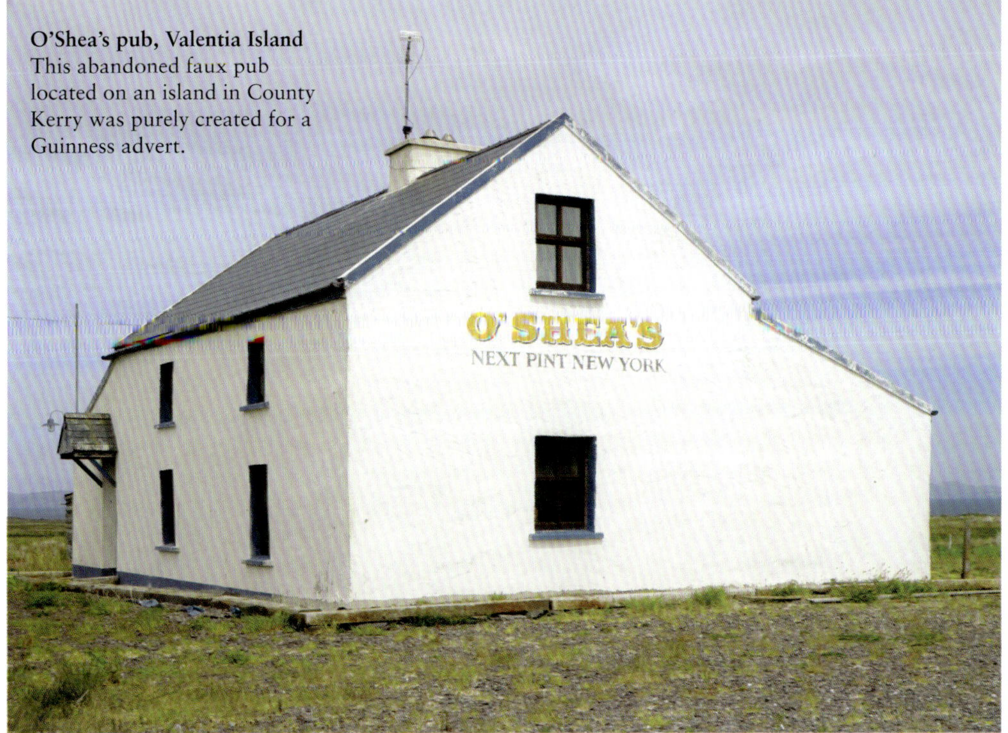

O'Shea's pub, Valentia Island
This abandoned faux pub located on an island in County Kerry was purely created for a Guinness advert.

Abandoned farm, Dursey, County Cork
Dursey is an island off the Beara Peninsula with only a handful of inhabitants. It is connected to the mainland by a cable car, which has been closed in recent years.

Slievemore, Achill Island, County Mayo
This deserted village of nearly 100 buildings now has sheep roaming through it. Slievemore was last inhabited in the early 20th century, when people living in the nearby village of Dooagh stayed in the stone cottages in the summer months to graze animals.

Derelict houses, County Limerick
These colourful long-derelict houses have been painted to give the appearance that they are lived in and have windows.

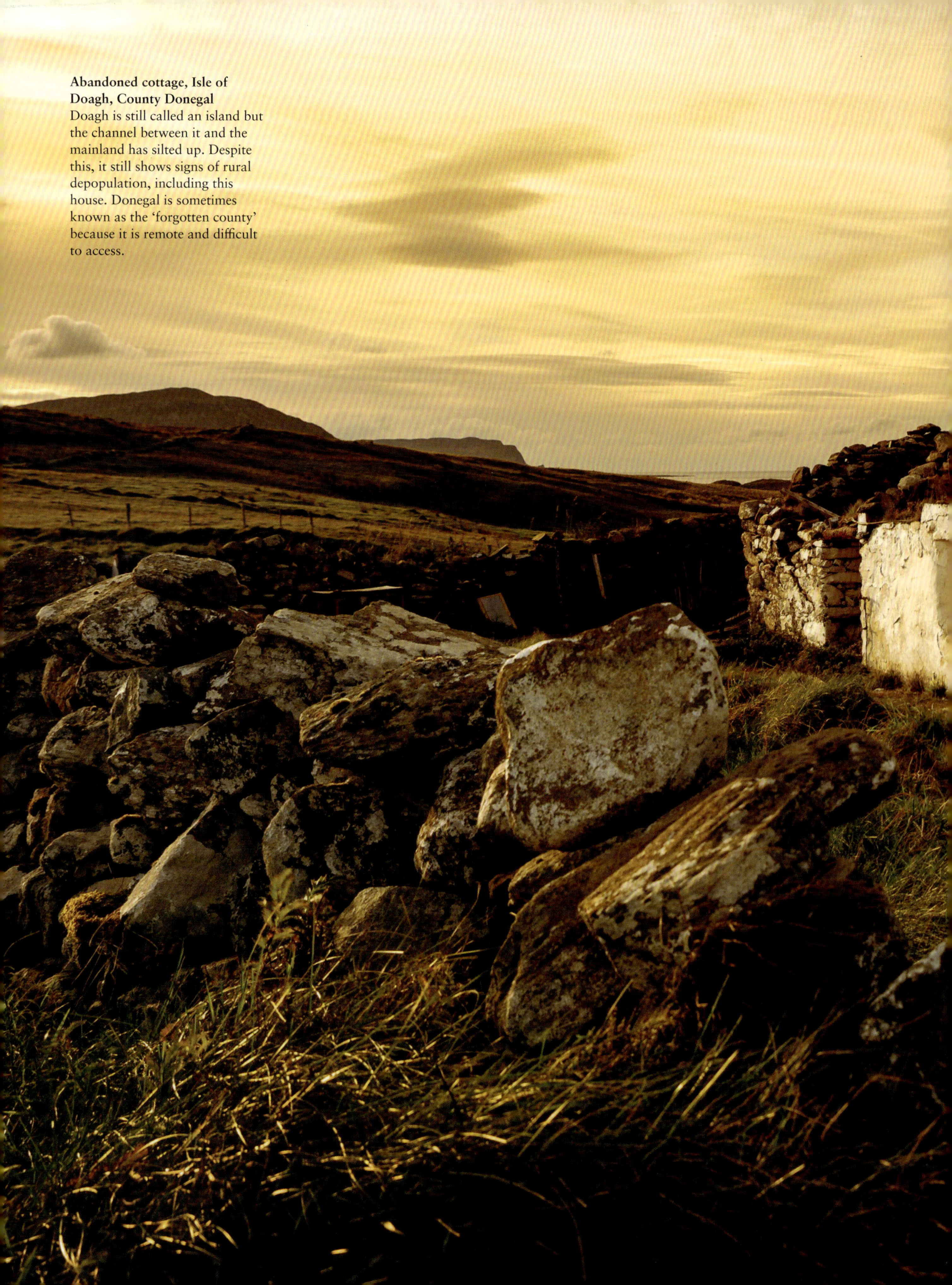

**Abandoned cottage, Isle of
Doagh, County Donegal**
Doagh is still called an island but
the channel between it and the
mainland has silted up. Despite
this, it still shows signs of rural
depopulation, including this
house. Donegal is sometimes
known as the 'forgotten county'
because it is remote and difficult
to access.

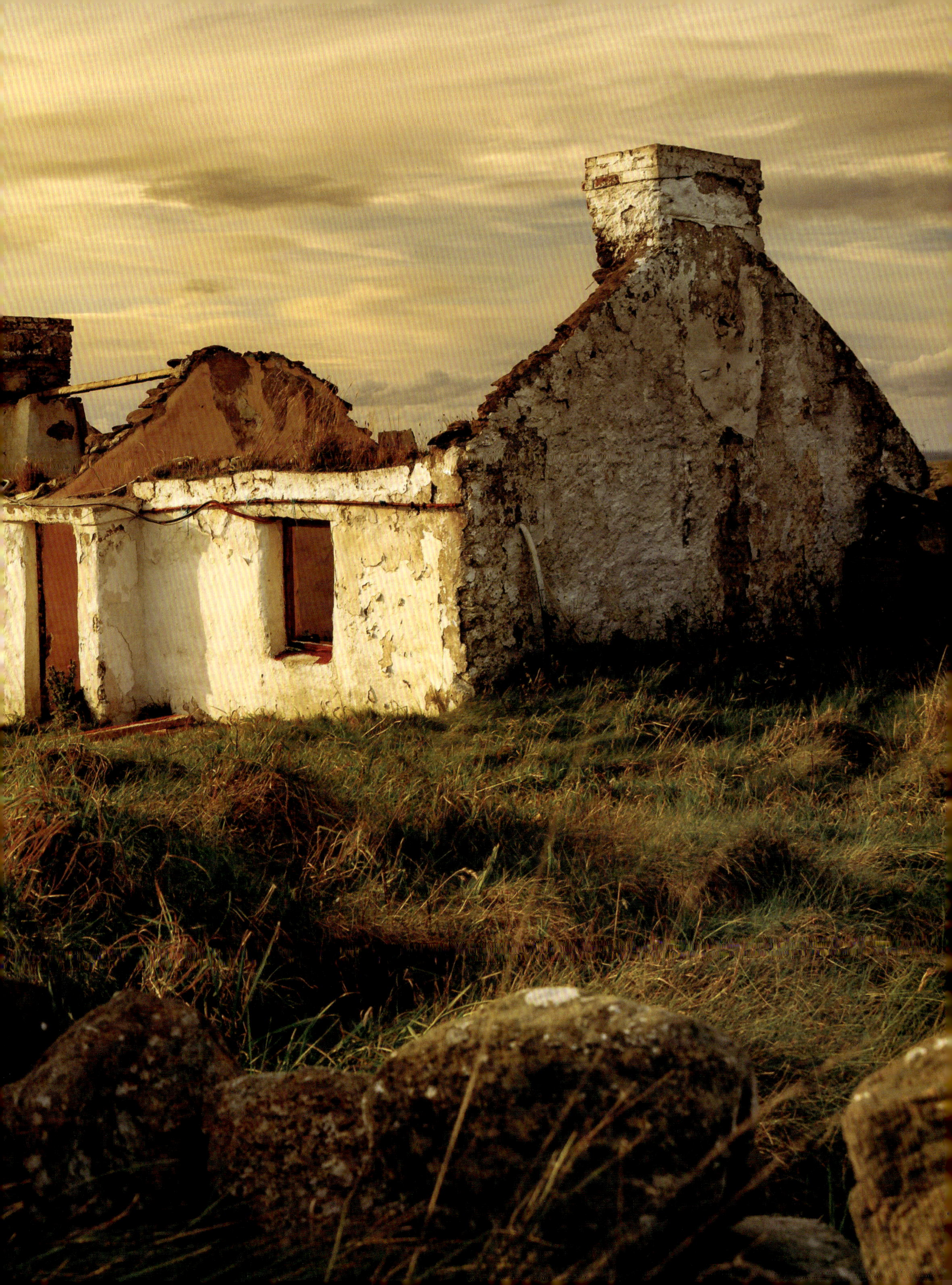

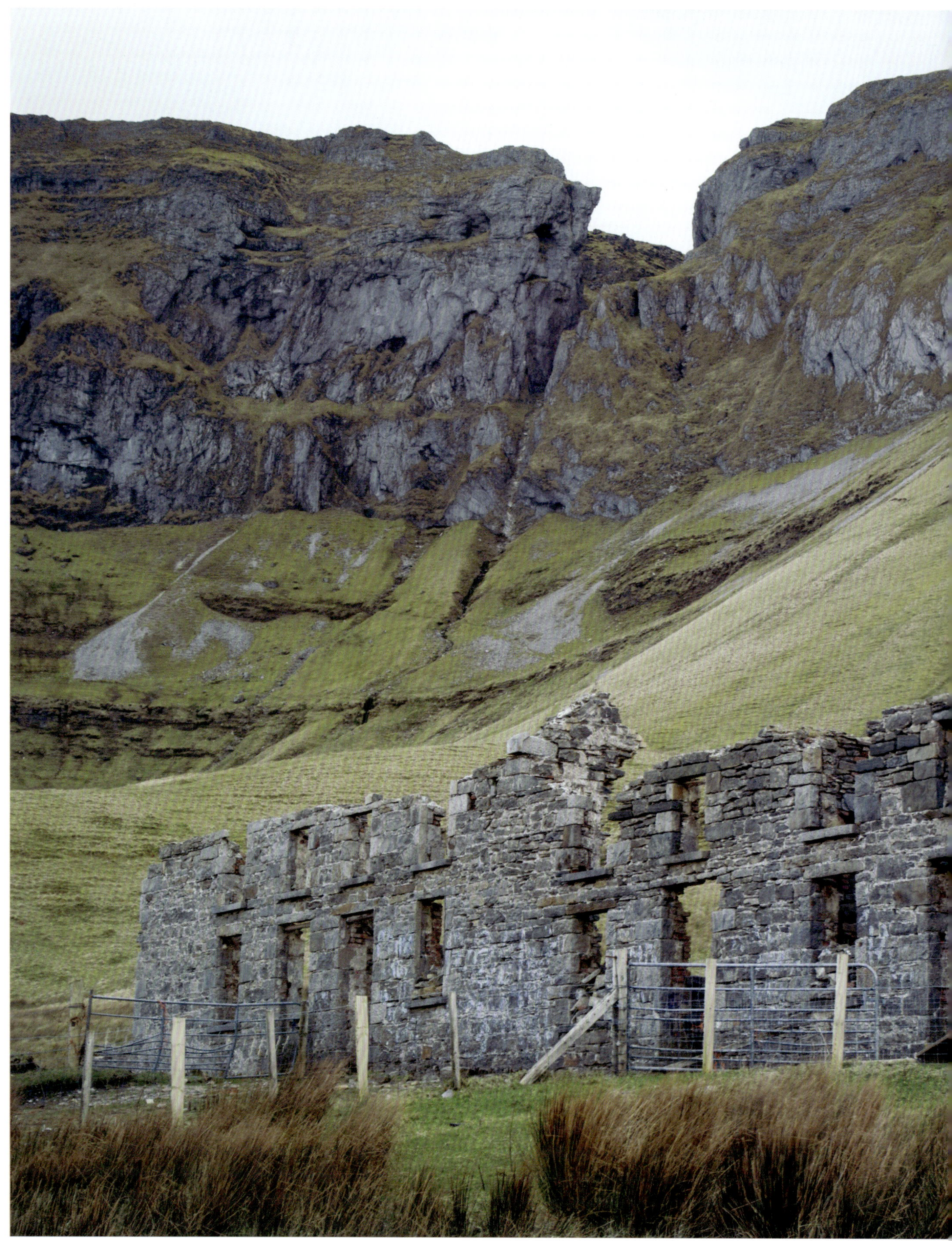

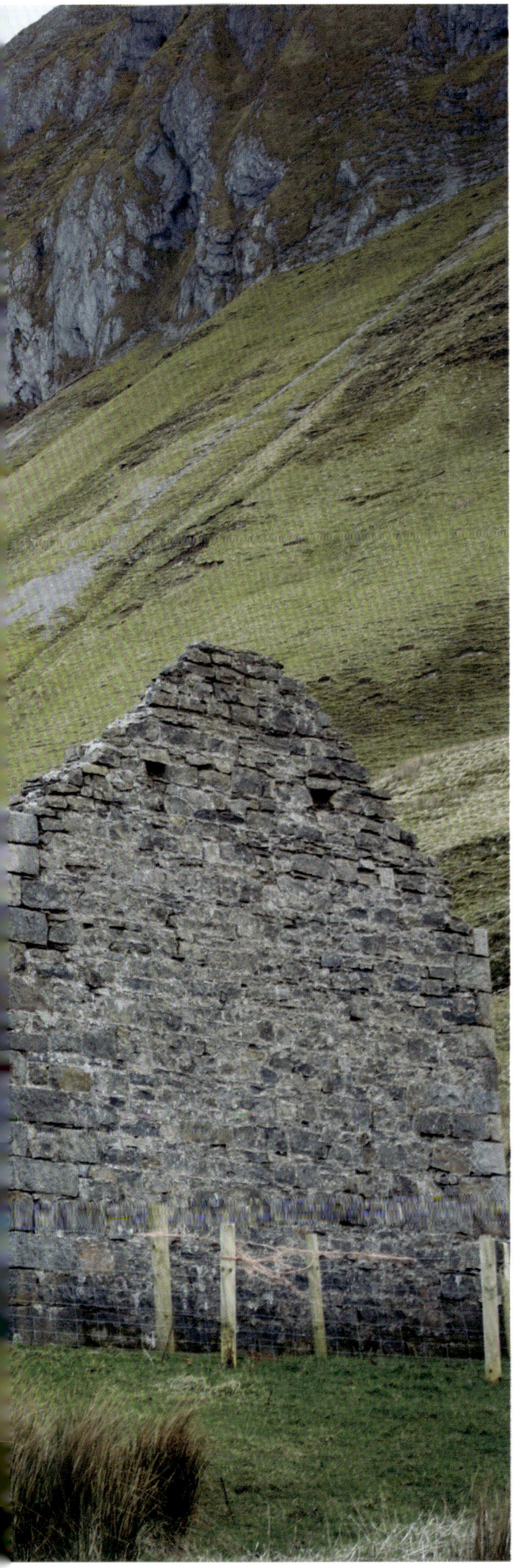

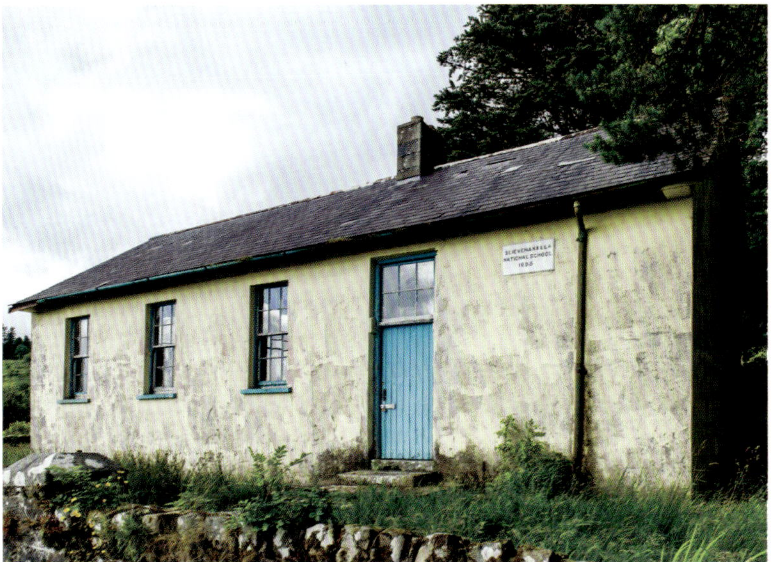

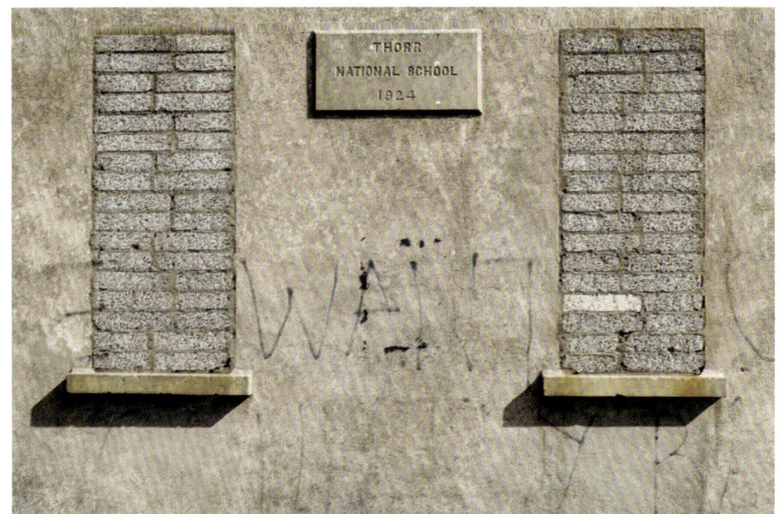

LEFT:

Old school house, Gleniff Horseshoe, County Sligo

The mineral-rich mountains around which the Gleniff Horshoe walk winds its way attracted many miners and this building was a school house for their children. Behind the school is a cave where, according to Irish mythology, the lovers Diarmuid and Grainne hid from the warrior Finn McCool, who is said to have created Giant's Causeway.

ABOVE TOP:

Slievenakilla National School, County Leitrim

The plaque on the outside of this school dates the building to 1895, and it was in the 19th century that National Schools – non-denominational primary schools – were first introduced. Leitrim is the smallest county by population in the Irish Republic and also the least densely populated.

ABOVE BOTTOM:

Thorr National School, County Donegal

This school is in a particularly remote and little-inhabited part of Donegal, characterized by gorse and moorland. The school was opened in 1924 but the area suffered from depopulation as people struggled to make a living. Graffiti on the school reads: 'We want our country back.'

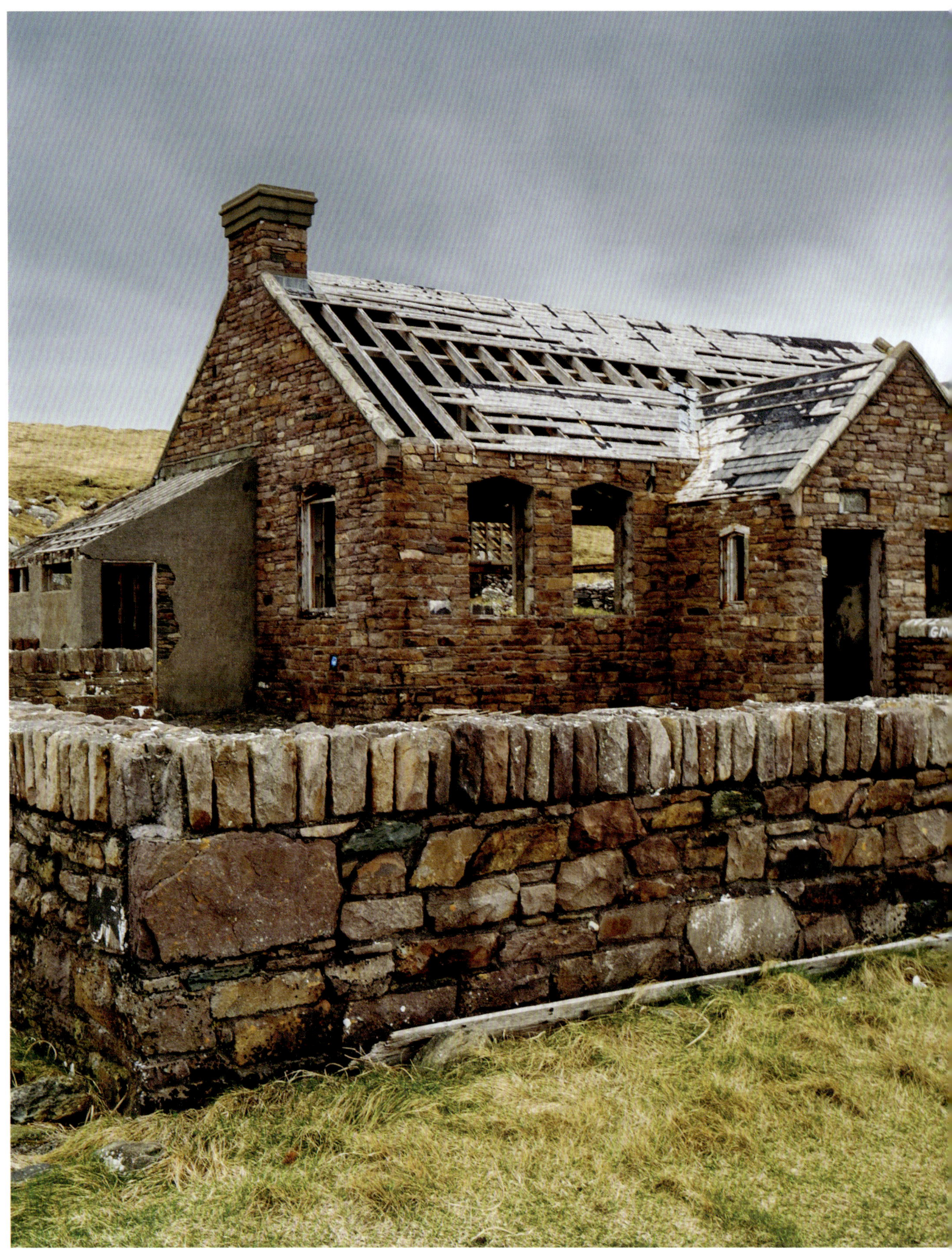

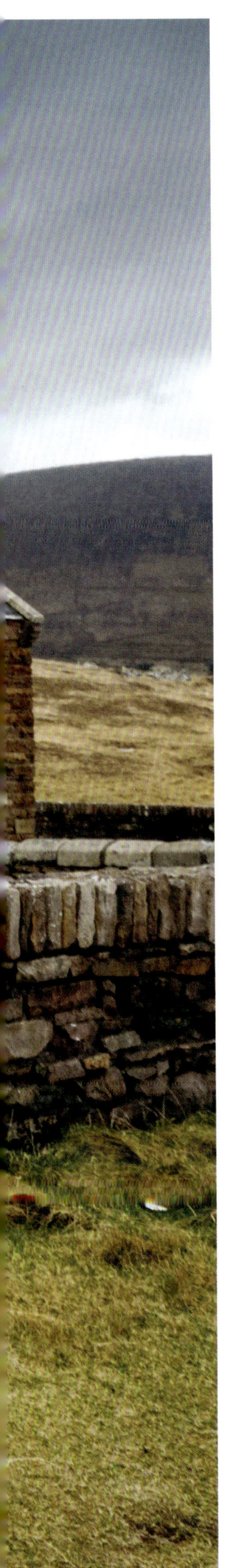

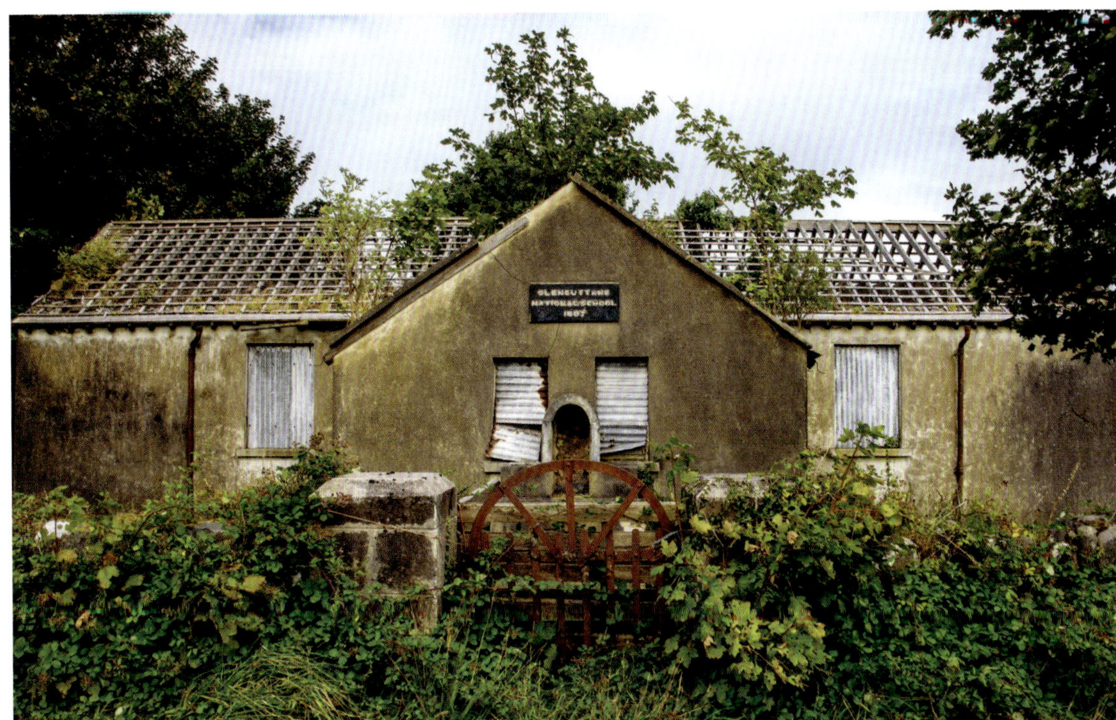

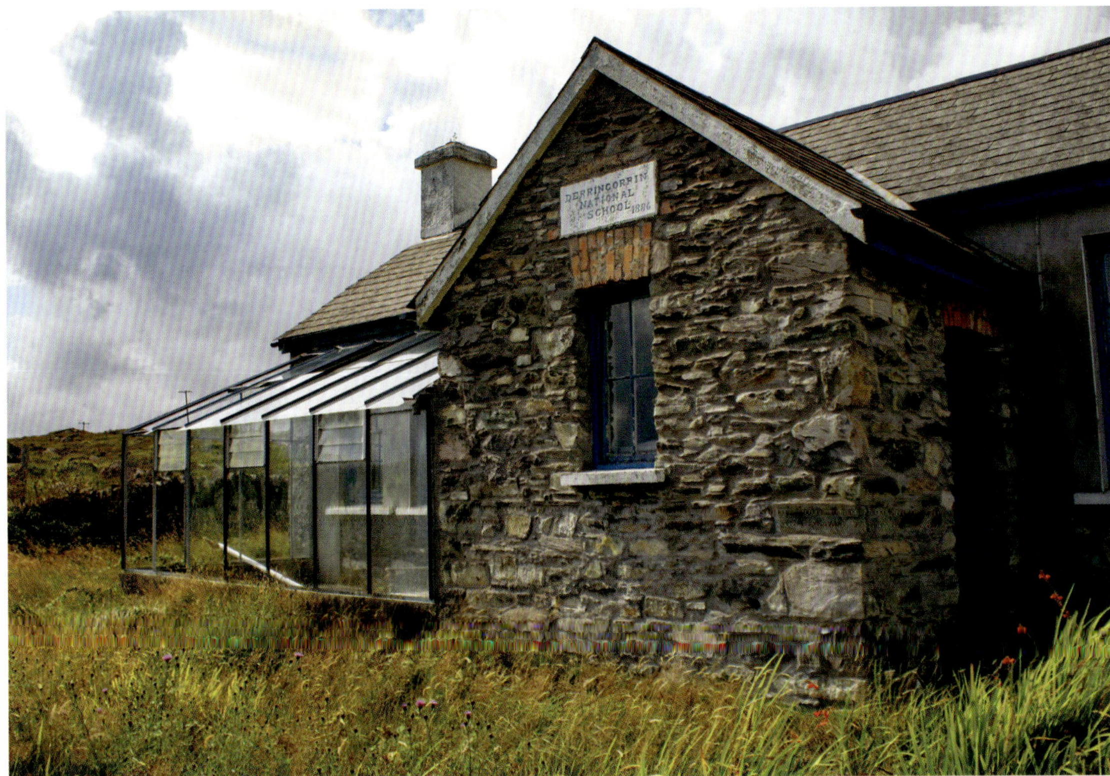

LEFT:
School house, Dunquin, County Kerry
This school house was built for the 1970 David Lean film *Ryan's Daughter*. Other locations on the Dingle Peninsula were used for filming, although bad weather forced the production to relocate – as far away as South Africa.

ABOVE TOP:
Glencuttane National School, County Kerry
This school on the Iveragh Peninsula dates from 1887. Old fields surround it and on higher ground, the land was open for grazing. The school has been relieved of its slate roof, exposing the interior to the elements.

ABOVE BOTTOM:
Derrincorrin National School, County Cork
Dating from 1886, this building on the Beara Peninsula had life beyond the original school house, hence the addition of the conservatory. The nearest village, Adrigole, consists of only 450 people scattered over a large area.

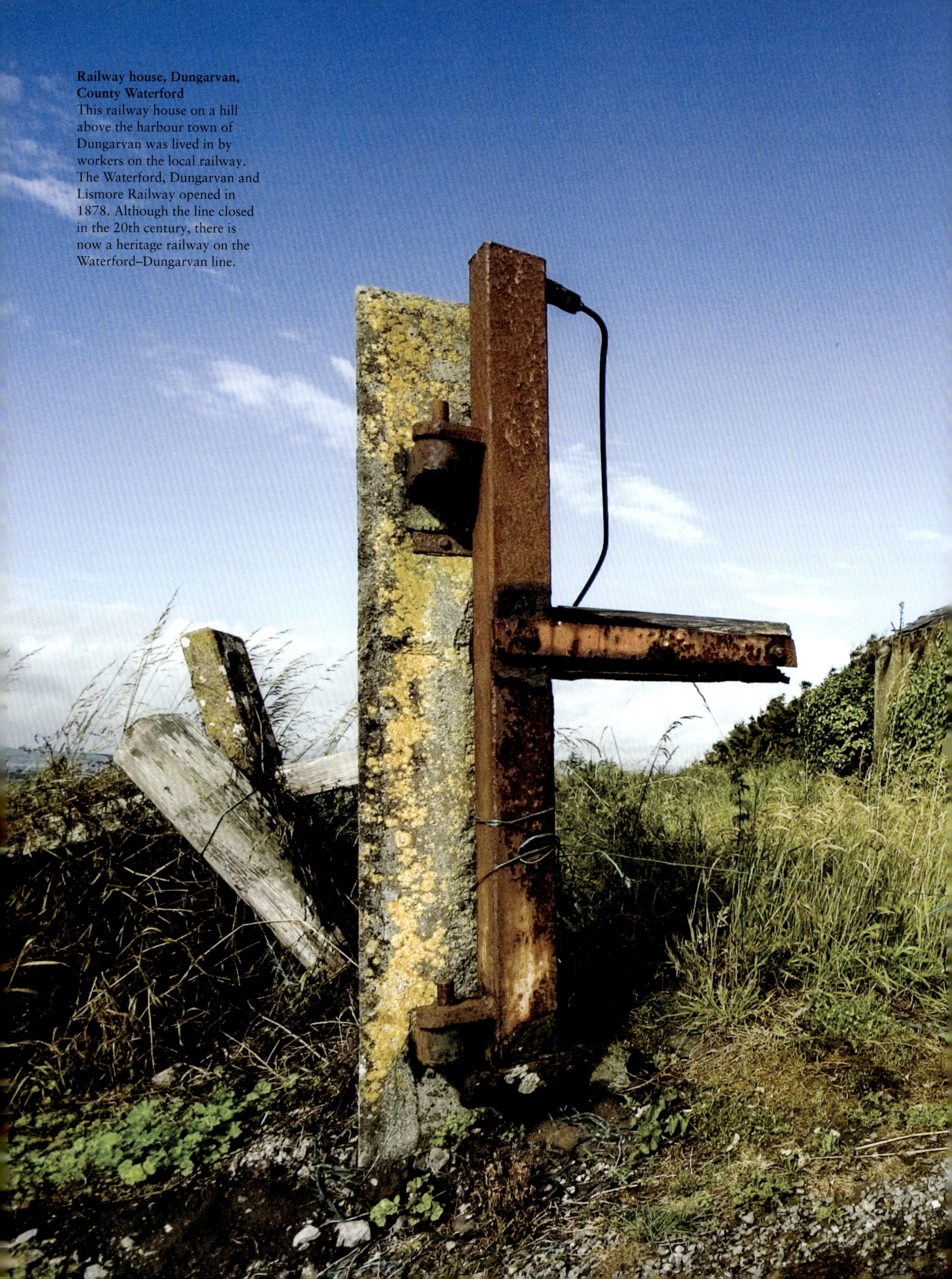

Railway house, Dungarvan,
County Waterford
This railway house on a hill
above the harbour town of
Dungarvan was lived in by
workers on the local railway.
The Waterford, Dungarvan and
Lismore Railway opened in
1878. Although the line closed
in the 20th century, there is
now a heritage railway on the
Waterford–Dungarvan line.

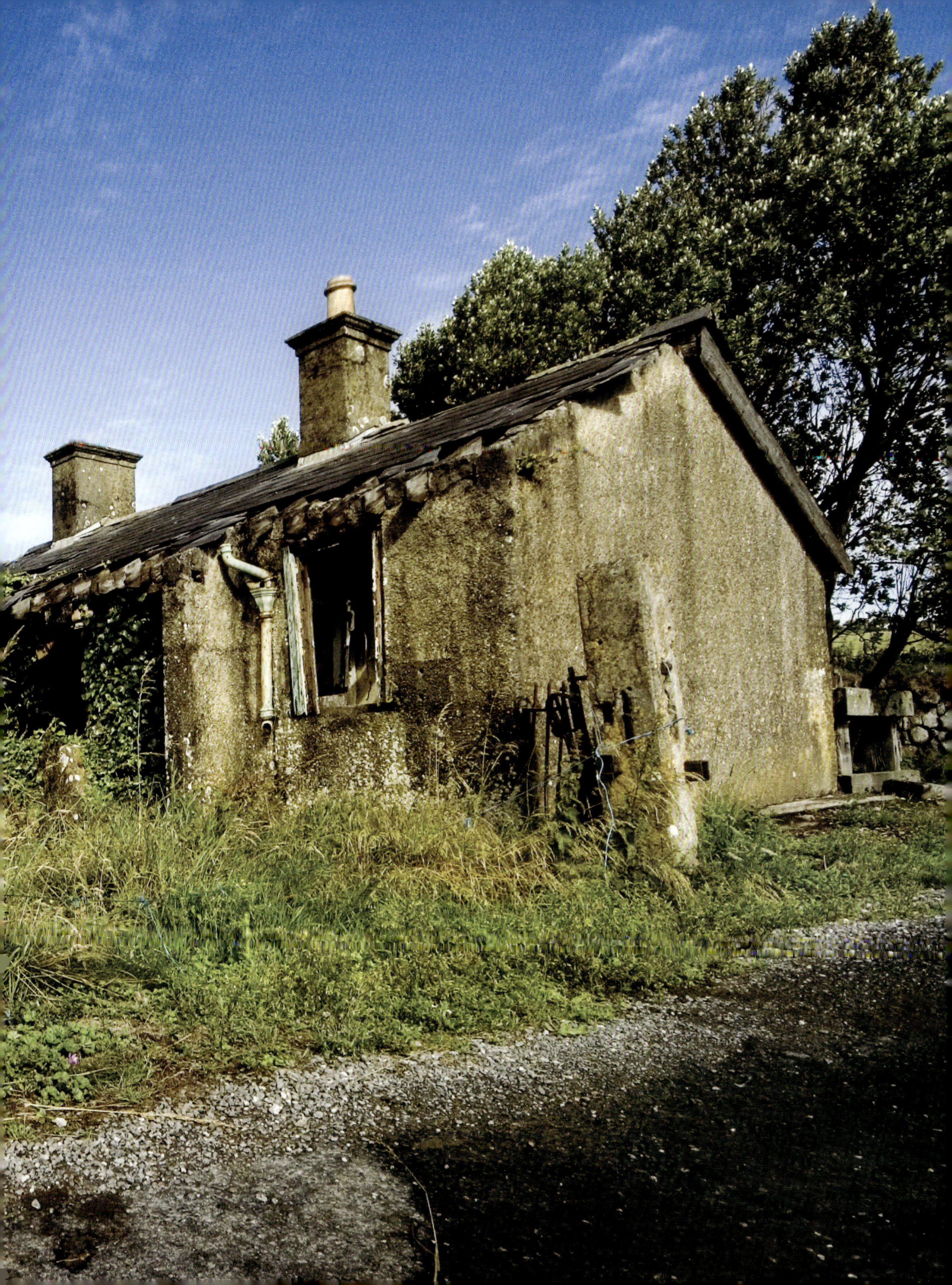

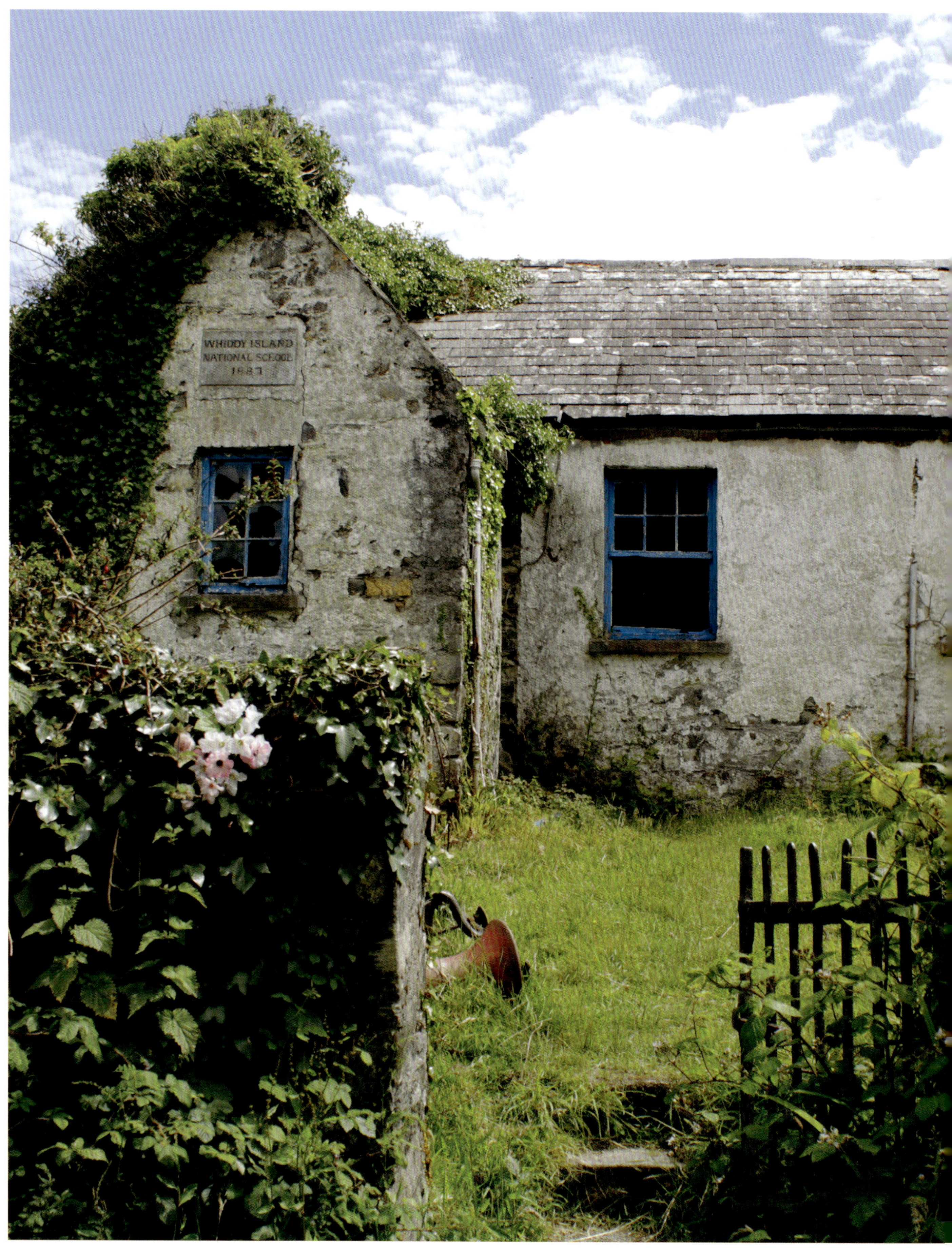

WHIDDY ISLAND
NATIONAL SCHOOL
1887

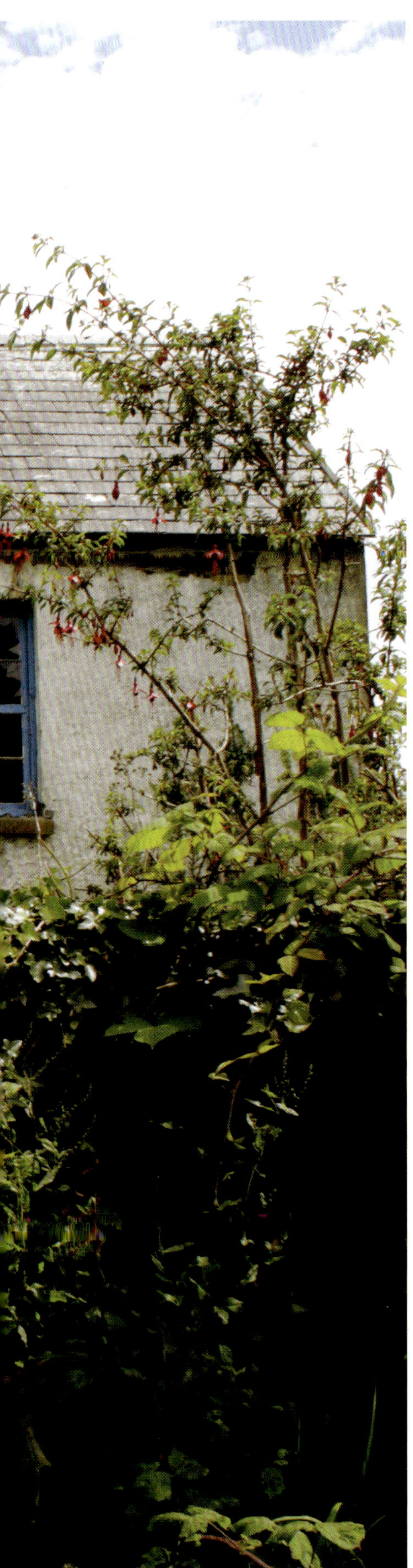

Abandoned school, Whiddy Island, County Cork

This one-room school on an island near Bantry was built in 1887. It ceased classes in December 1947 when there was only a handful of pupils left. After closing, it acted as a museum for a while. Many of the National Schools of this era were painted blue and green, and the blue of Whiddy Island's school has not faded.

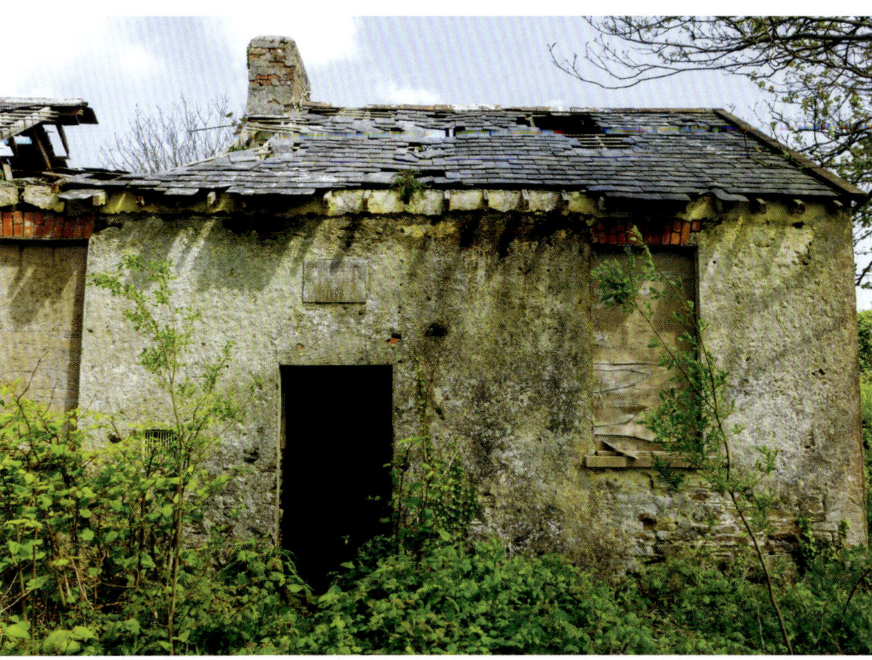

Dunbeacon National School, County Cork

In a village overlooking Dunmanus Bay, Dunbeacon National School consisted of two rooms and was established in 1902. Although disused for many years, its roof survived until 2015. Such schools were often made by locals from materials sourced nearby, but there were also standardized structures, and this one was identical in form to a school in Galway. The two-room design is thought to have been used so that the school could accommodate more senior children in one of the rooms.

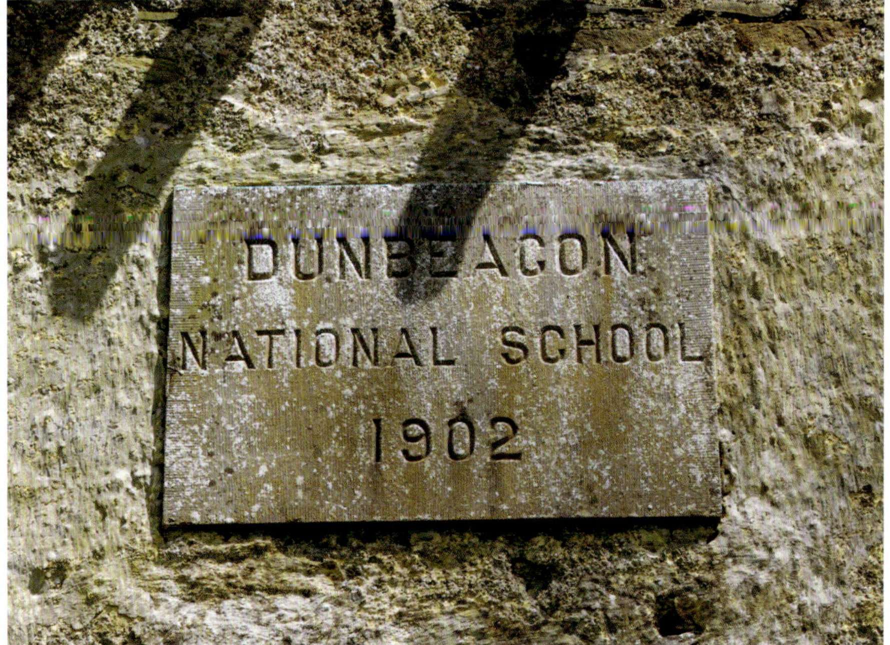

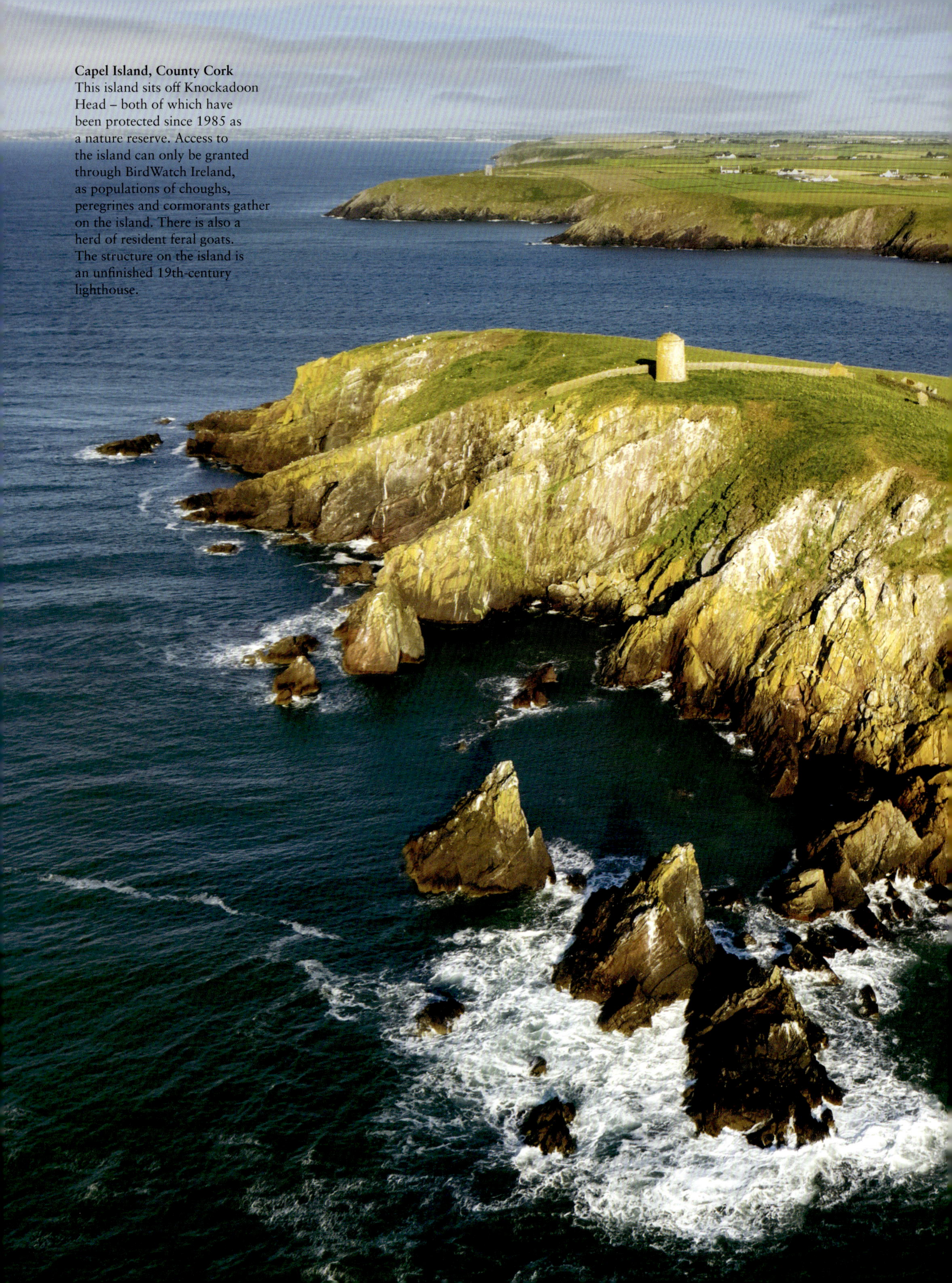

Capel Island, County Cork
This island sits off Knockadoon Head – both of which have been protected since 1985 as a nature reserve. Access to the island can only be granted through BirdWatch Ireland, as populations of choughs, peregrines and cormorants gather on the island. There is also a herd of resident feral goats. The structure on the island is an unfinished 19th-century lighthouse.

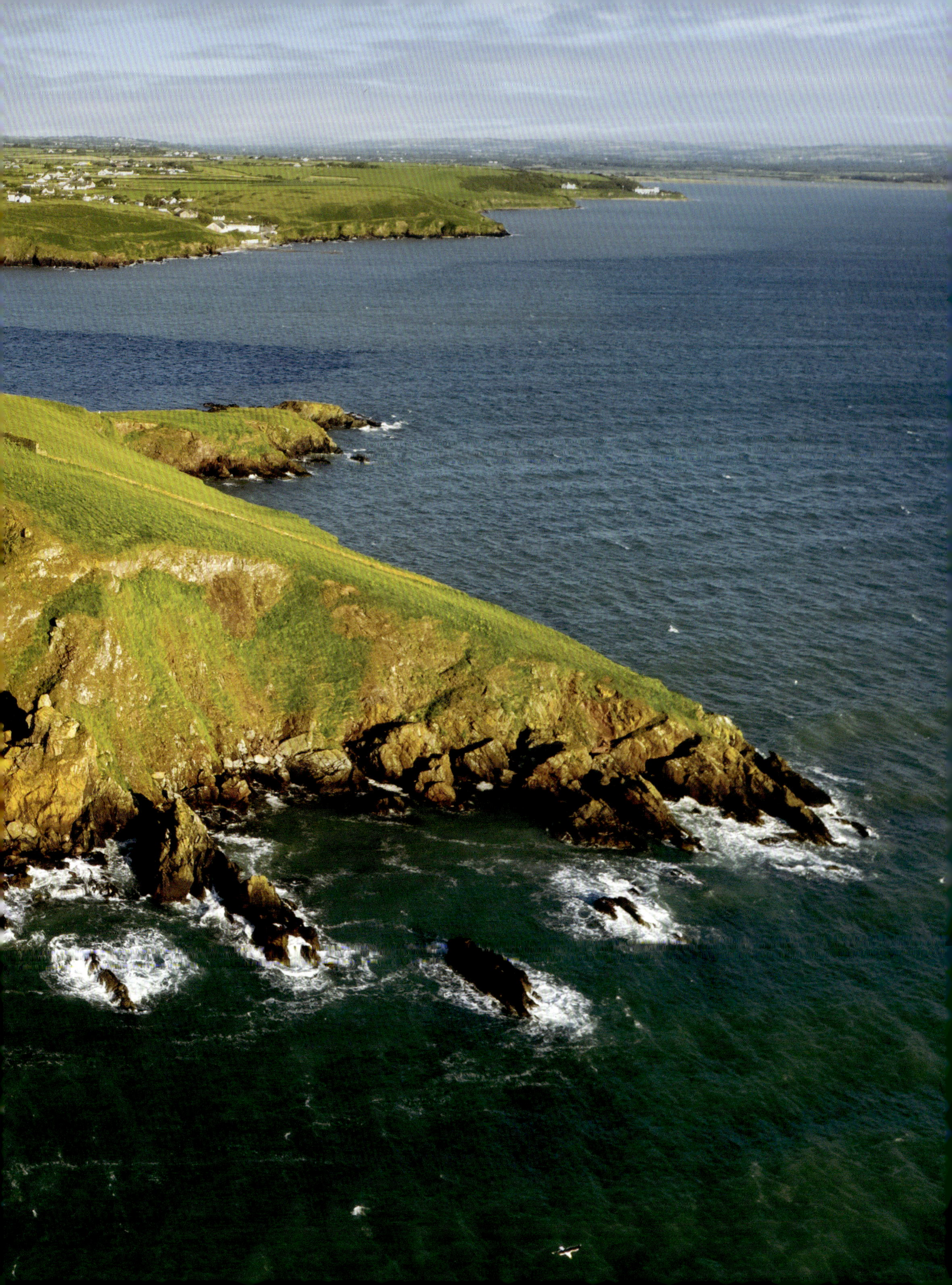

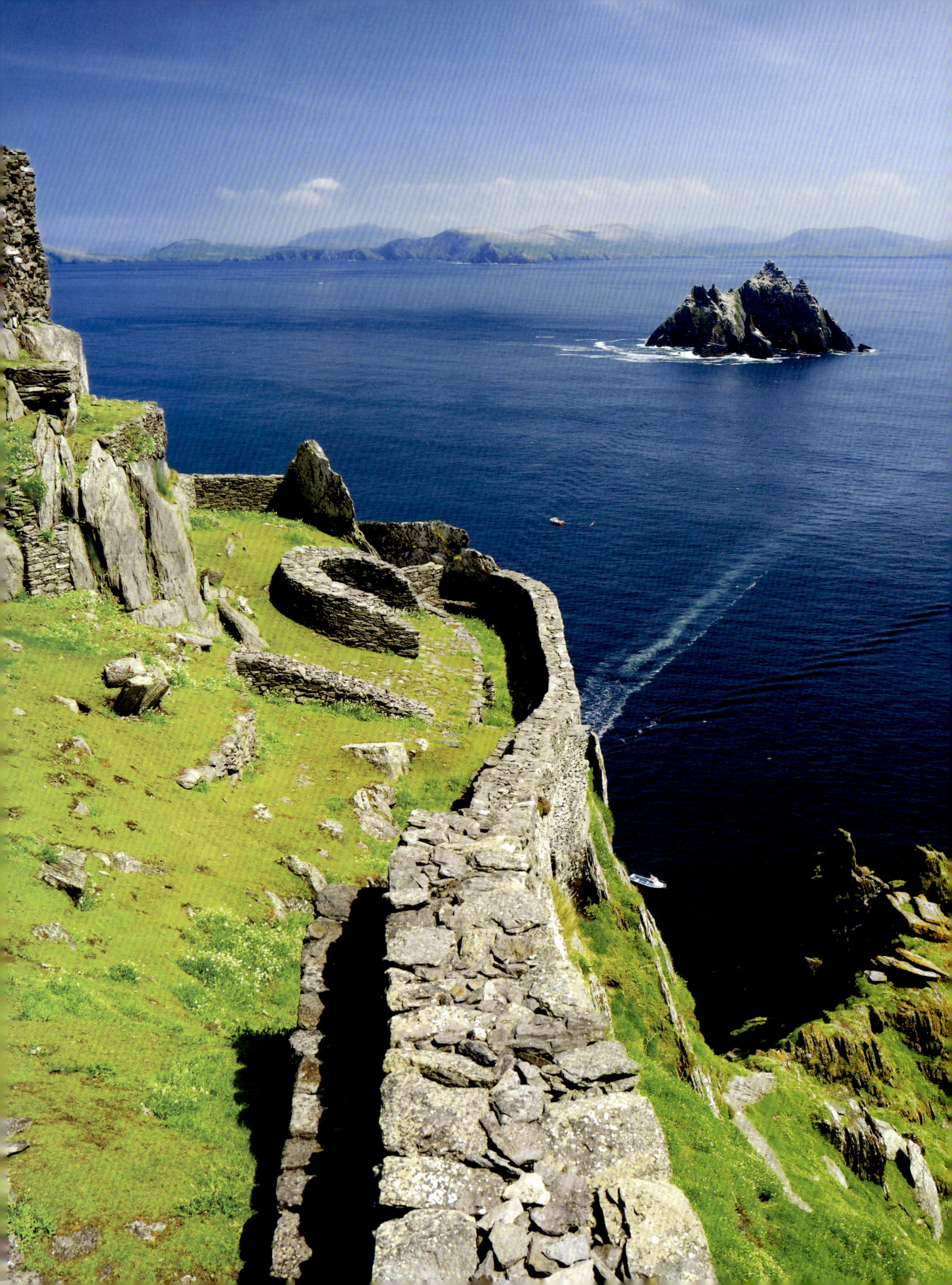

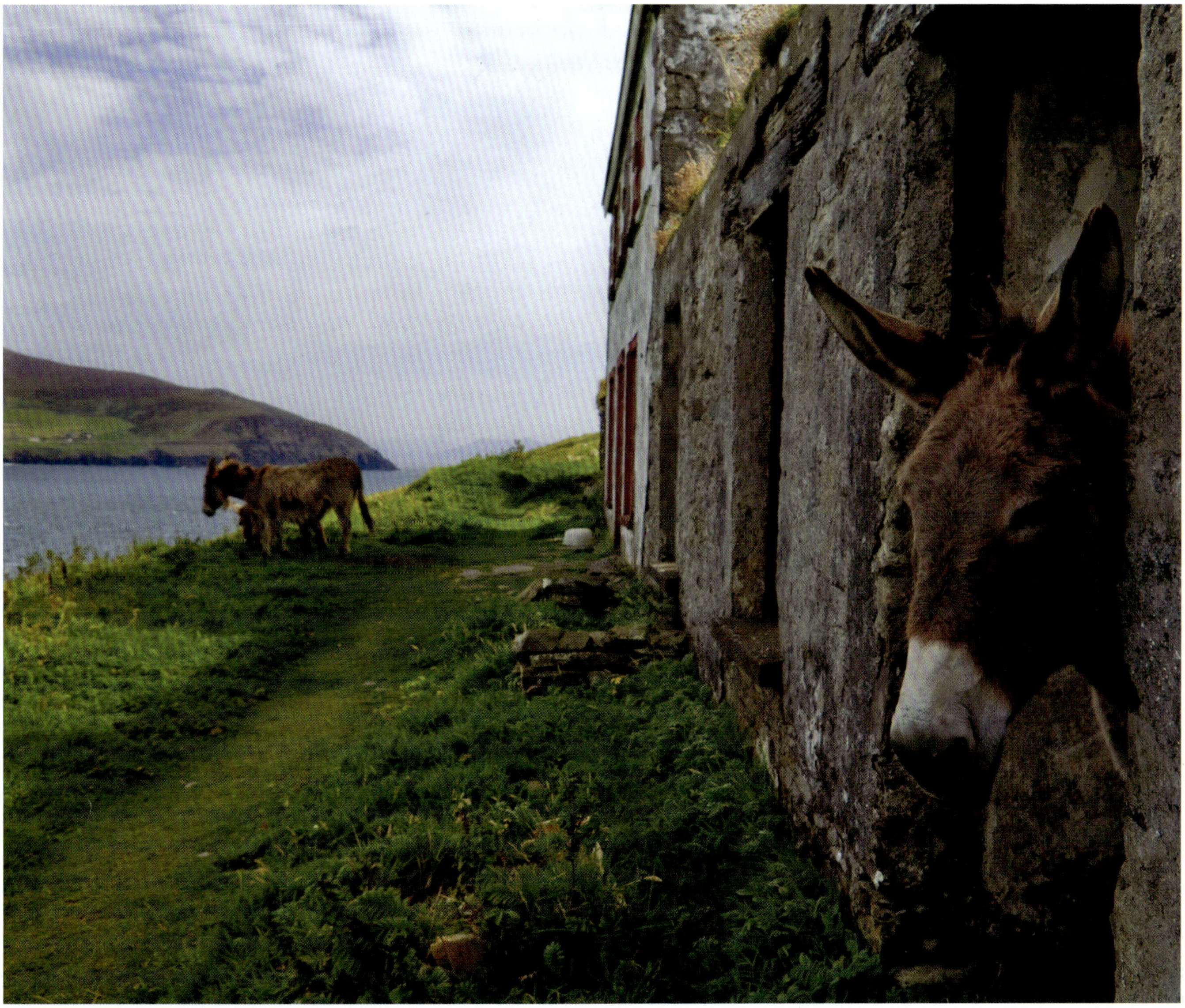

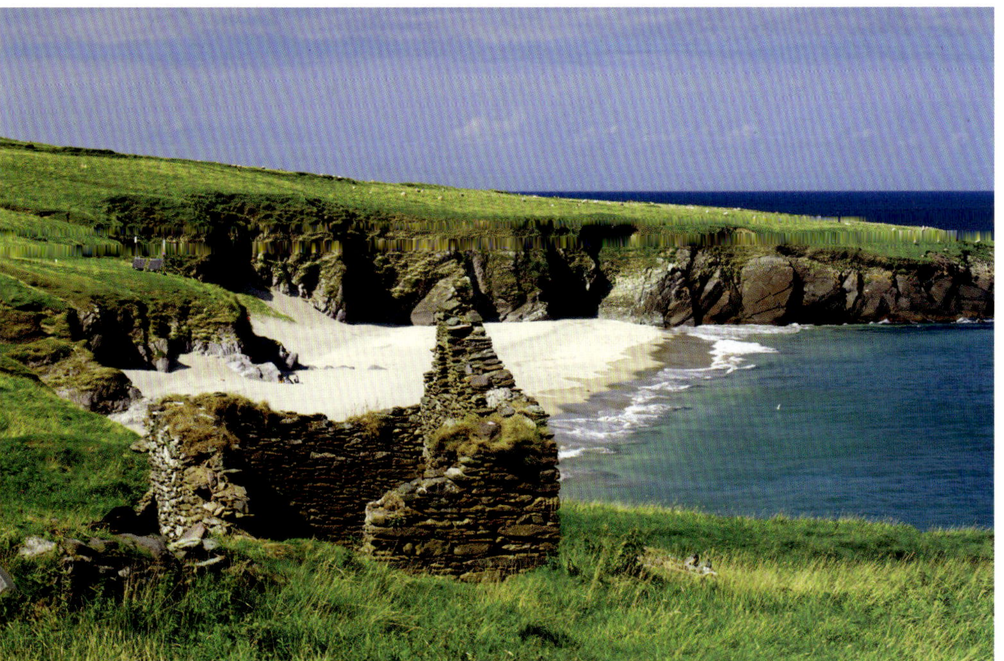

OPPOSITE:
Skellig Michael, County Kerry
A haven for seabirds, Skellig Michael also contains the remains of an early Christian settlement, and is a UNESCO World Heritage Site. In the 21st-century reboot of the *Star Wars* movie franchise, it was used in three of the films to depict the home of Luke Skywalker.

ABOVE & LEFT:
Great Blasket, Blasket Islands, County Kerry
There was once a small fishing community on Great Blasket but harsh living conditions made the inhabitants leave in 1953, many of them emigrating, particularly to Springfield, Massachusetts, USA. The people have gone from the island, but the white sands remain.

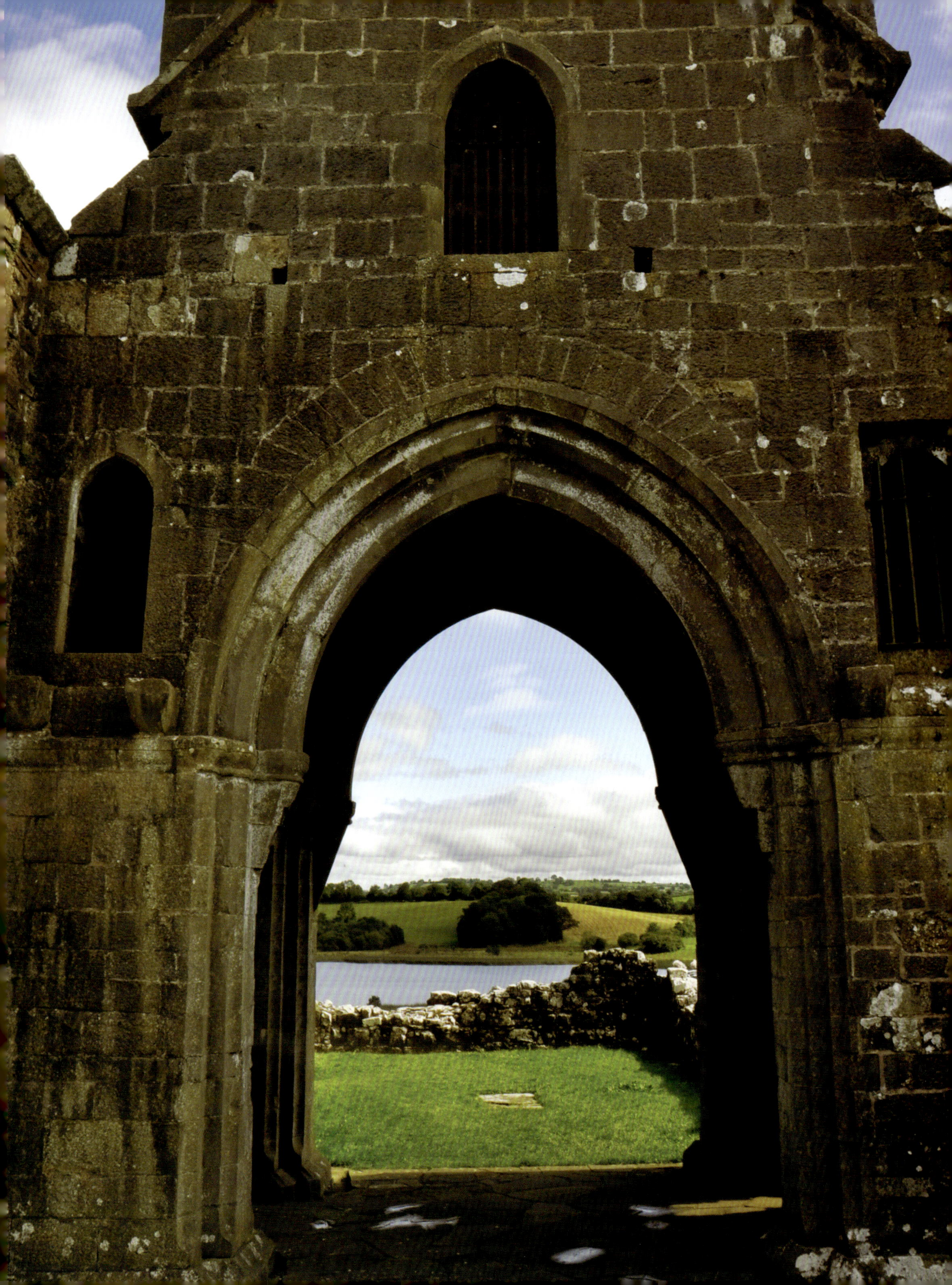

Religious Places

Ireland has a rich and varied religious history. Monasteries were formed far and wide across the country as Christianity spread from the 4th century onwards. An array of saints were involved in founding religious sites, and various orders – including Franciscans, Cistercians, Augustinians and Benedictines – set up ecclesiastical establishments all over the land.

By 1500, dozens of cathedrals, abbeys, monasteries, friaries and churches had been built that still exist today. Some were lone churches serving small populations, whereas others were complexes that came to be referred to as 'cities'. However, many were to very soon have their fortunes overturned, as Henry VIII ordered the monasteries, friaries, convents and priories of England, Wales and Ireland to be disbanded, in his quest to seize the power and assets of the Church. The inhabitants of these religious houses were expelled, their riches plundered and their buildings often ransacked. Further raids by English forces, as well as rivalries between Irish clans, led to more religious buildings being left in ruins, while others were deserted because of ecclesiastic reorganization or changes in population over time. Yet, with all these buildings, their imprint remains on the landscape, and each ruin opens a separate door to the past.

OPPOSITE:
Devenish Island monastic site, County Fermanagh
This former monastery – one of many built on the islands in Lough Erne – was founded in the 6th century by St Molaise. It developed into the focal point of a large parish covering both sides of the lough, but in the 17th century, worship was moved on shore, to the village of Monea.

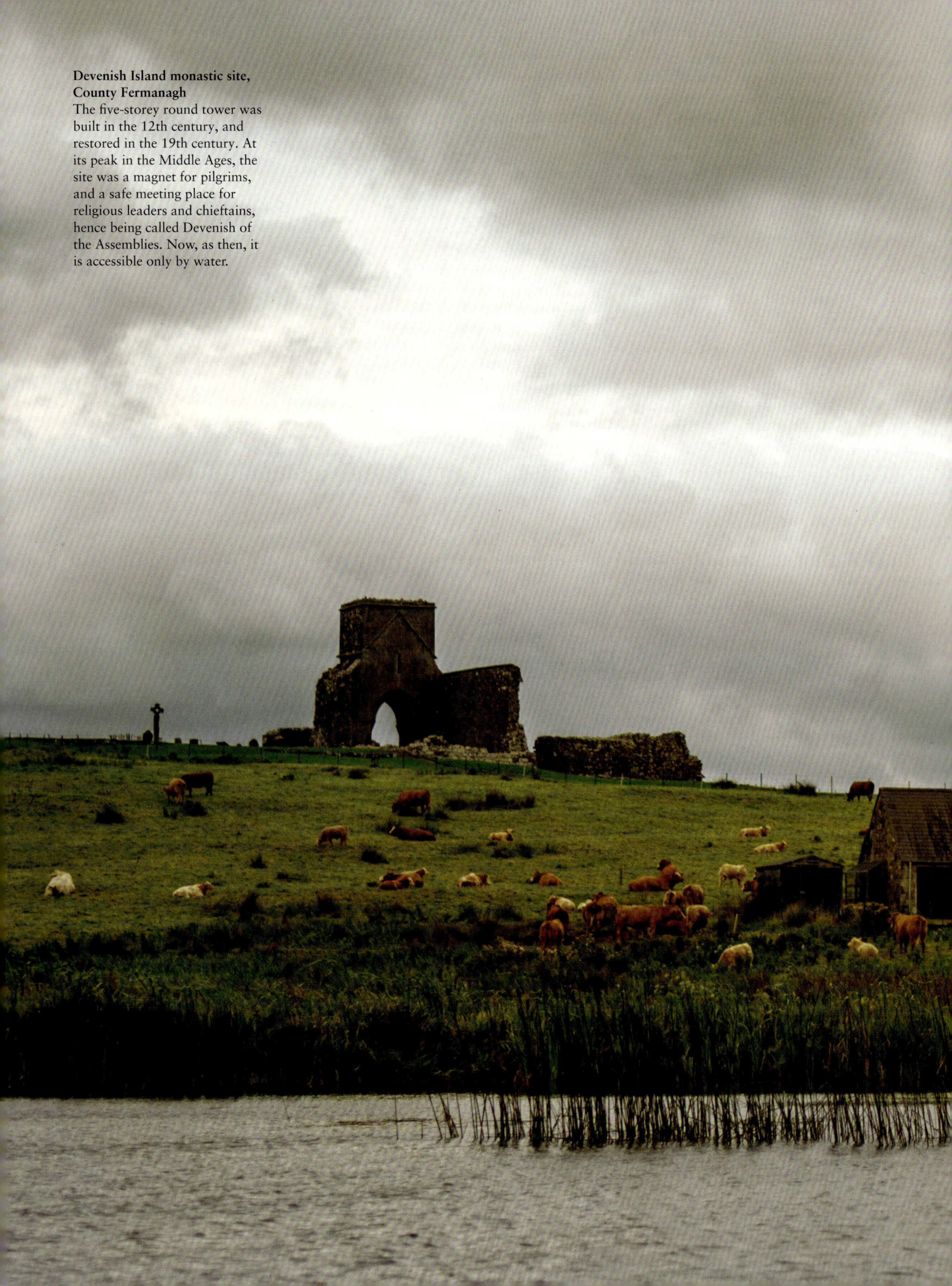

Devenish Island monastic site, County Fermanagh
The five-storey round tower was built in the 12th century, and restored in the 19th century. At its peak in the Middle Ages, the site was a magnet for pilgrims, and a safe meeting place for religious leaders and chieftains, hence being called Devenish of the Assemblies. Now, as then, it is accessible only by water.

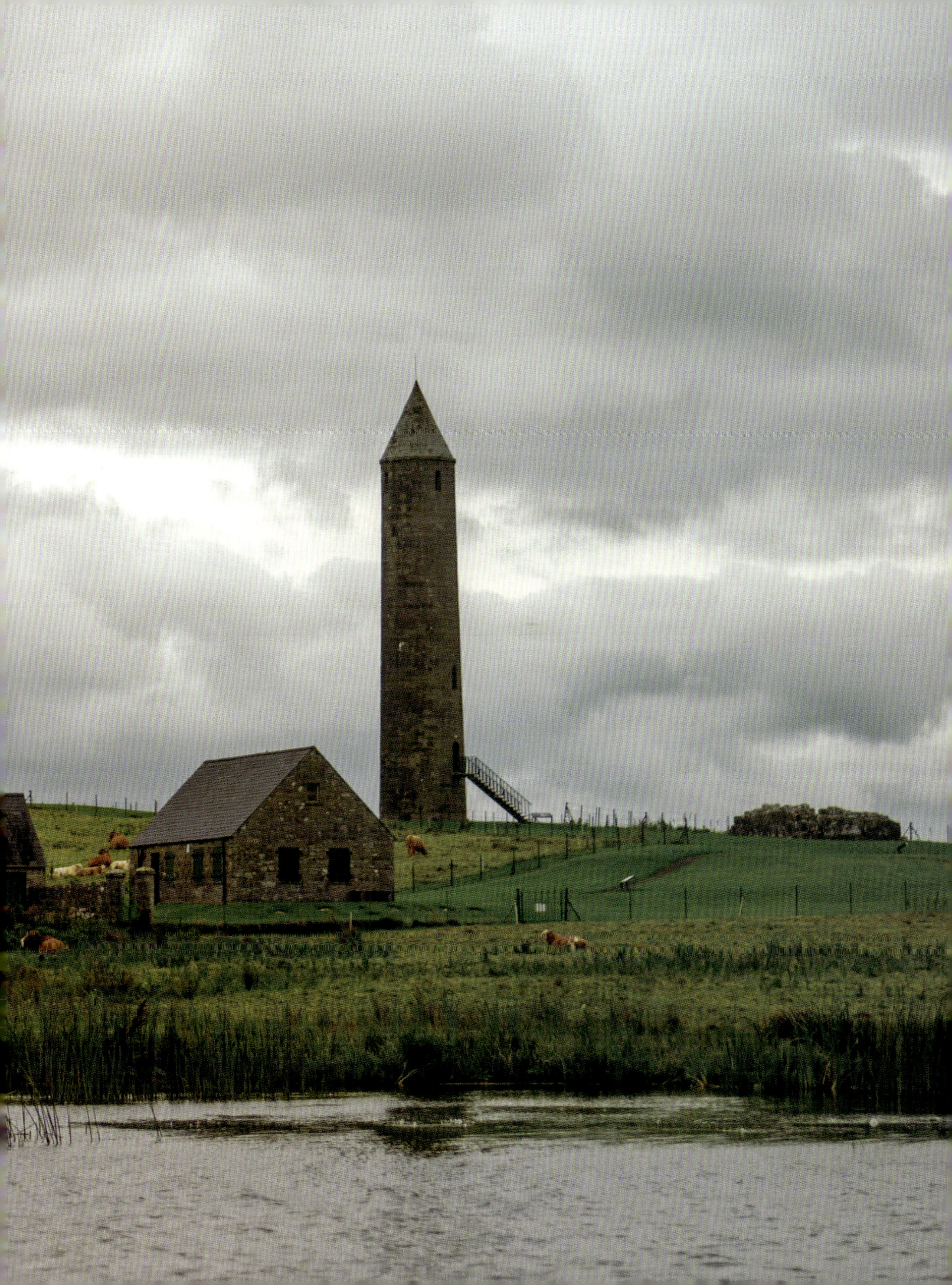

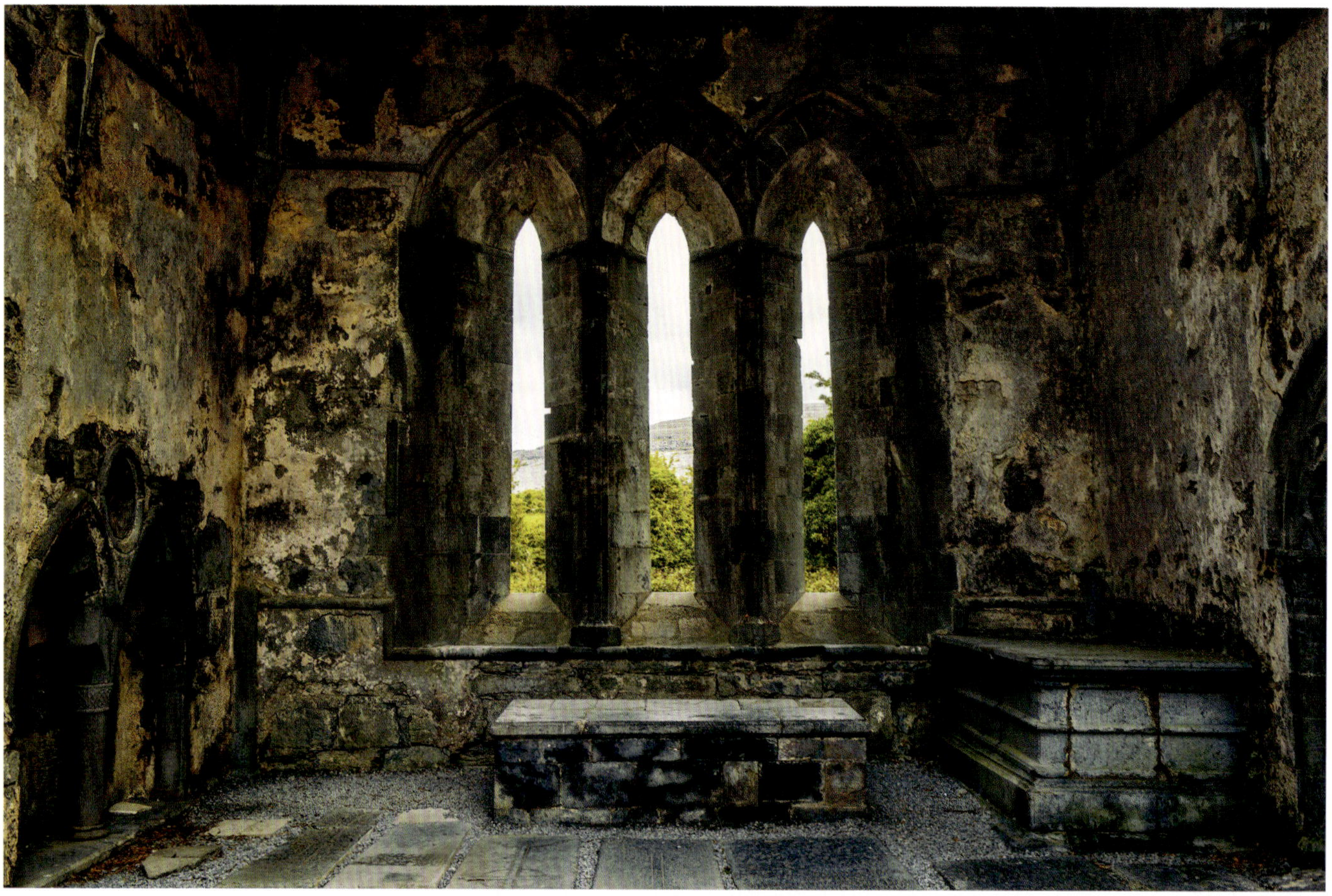

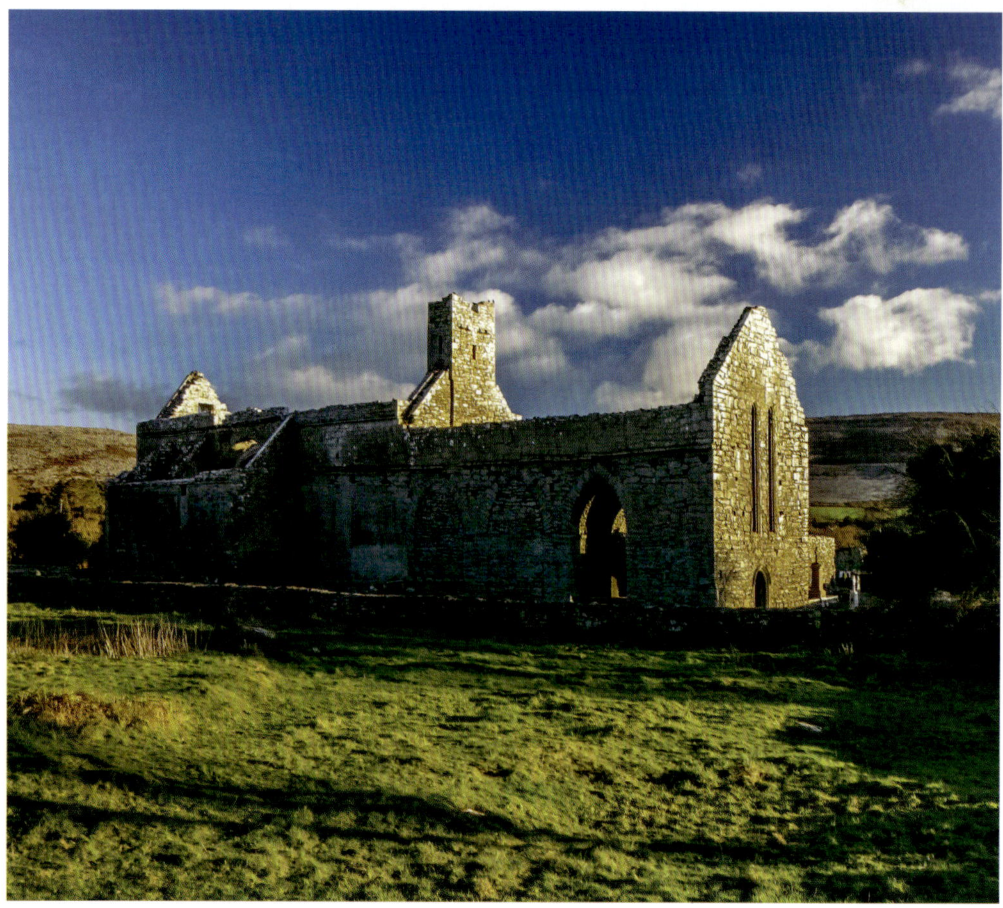

Corcomroe Abbey, County Clare
Built with limestone from the nearby Burren hills, Corcomroe Abbey was founded for Cistercian monks in the 12th century. Henry VIII's dissolution of the monasteries 350 years later resulted in the abbey – with its depictions of plants carved into stone (opposite) – being granted to the local Earl of Thomond.

Corcomroe Abbey is now a ruin, but its graveyard is still in use, a tradition common across Ireland's former religious buildings. The abbey was also known as St Mary of the Fertile Rock, as the Burren has a long growing season and supports a number of exotic plants.

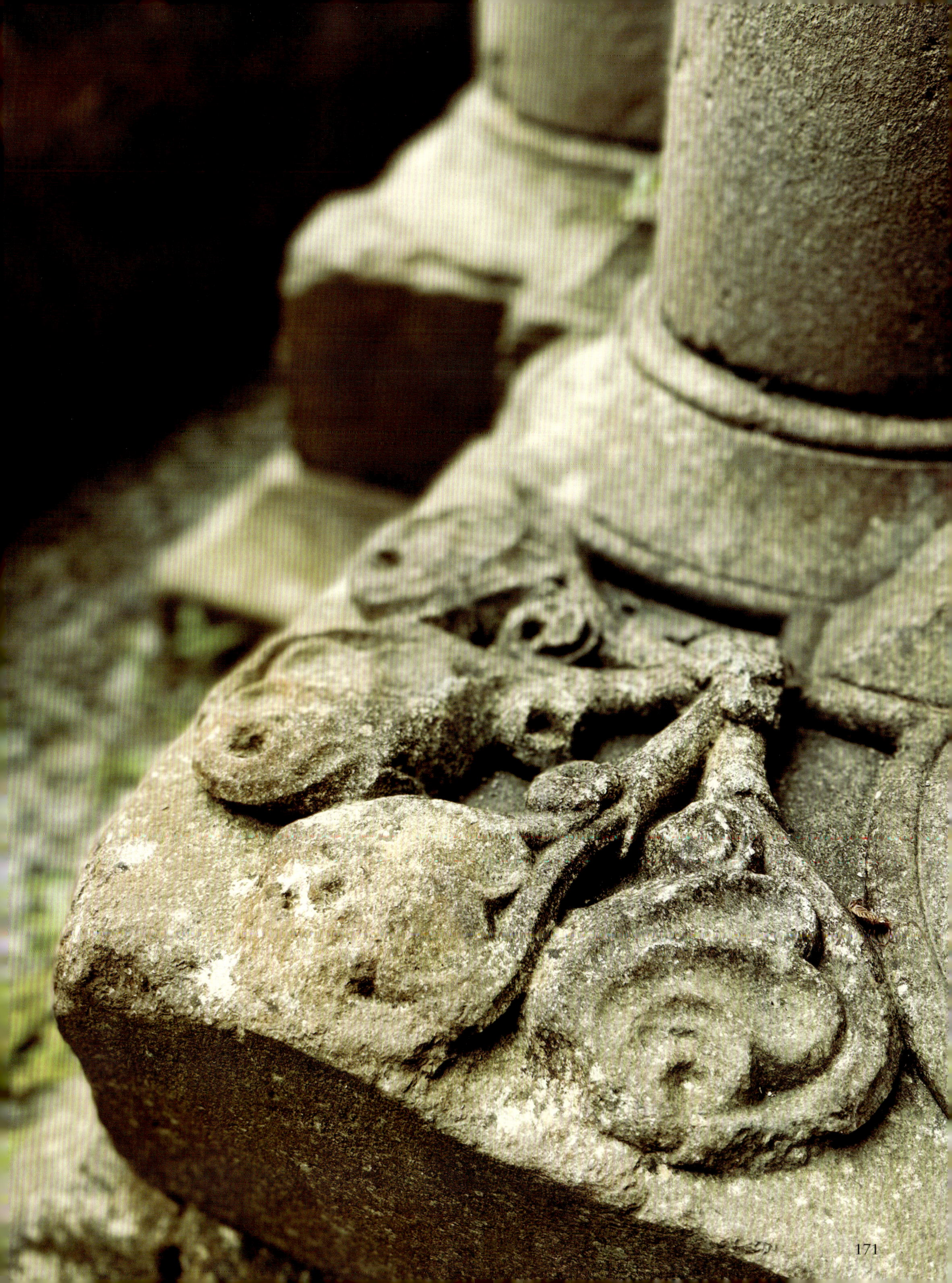

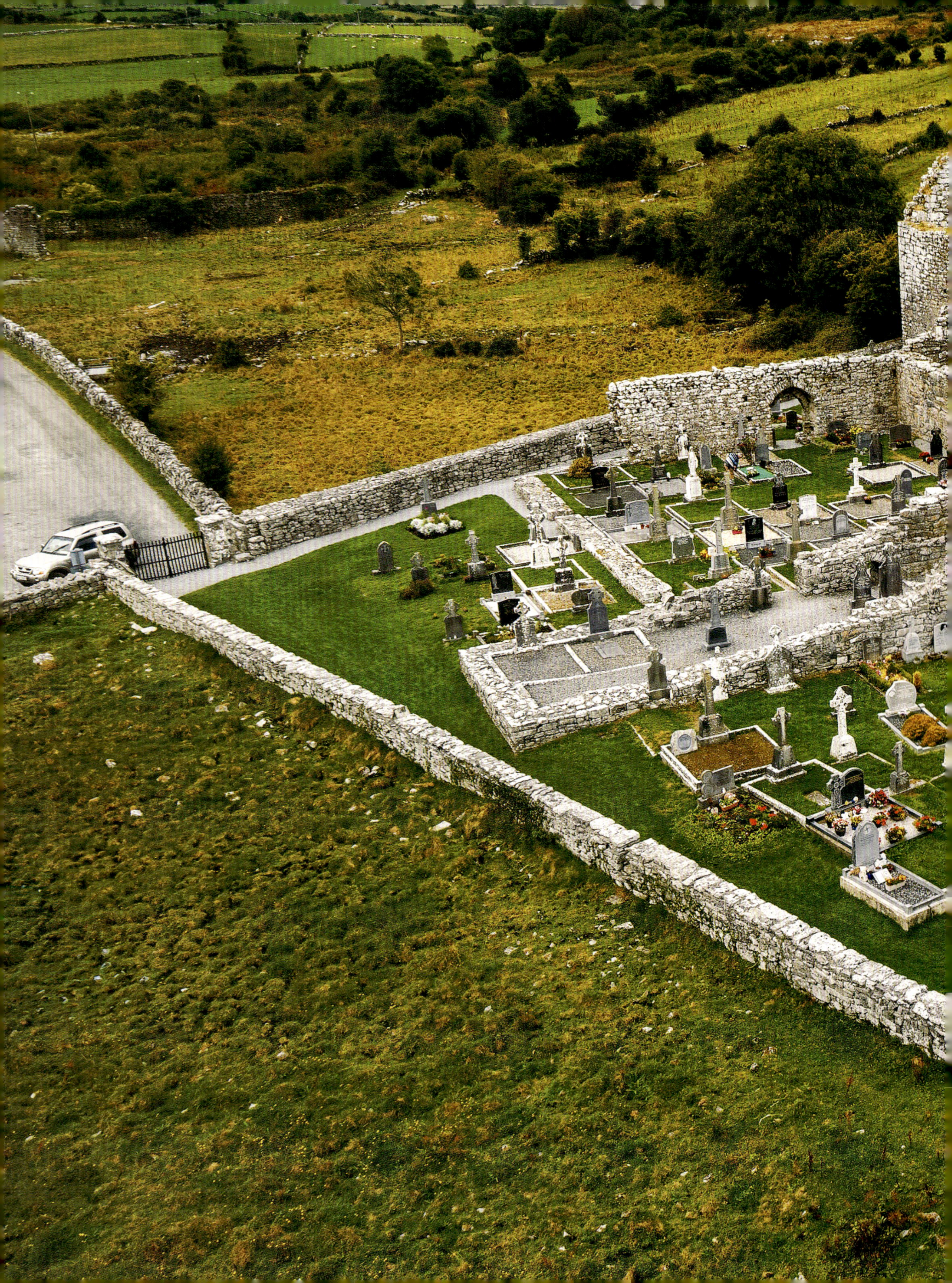

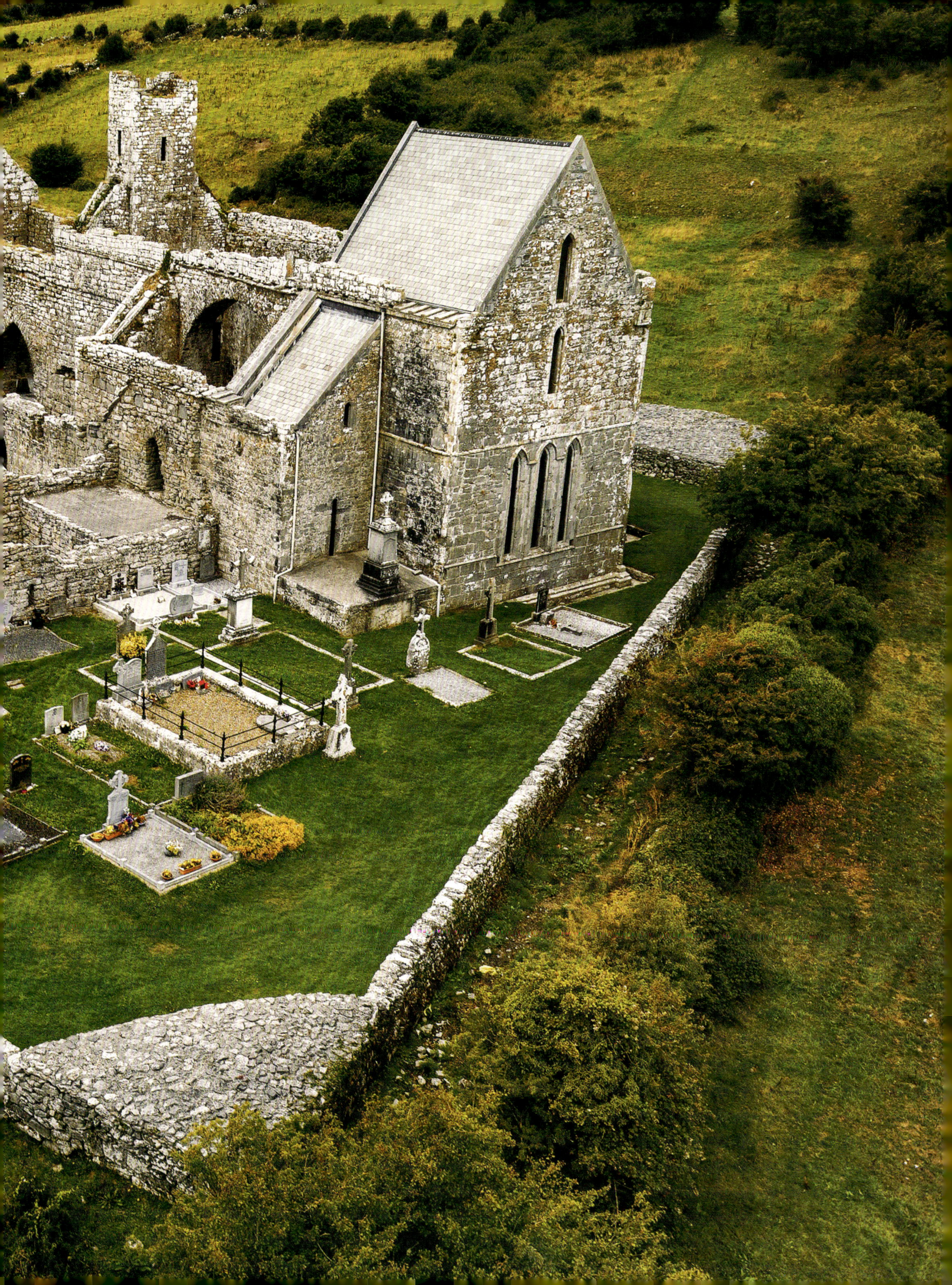

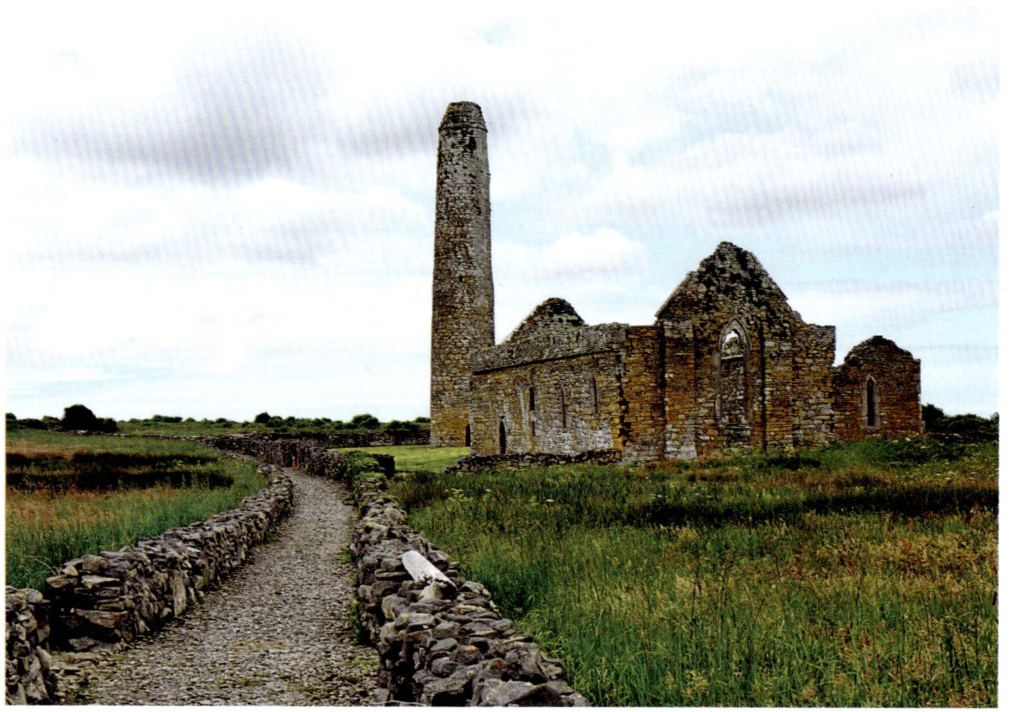

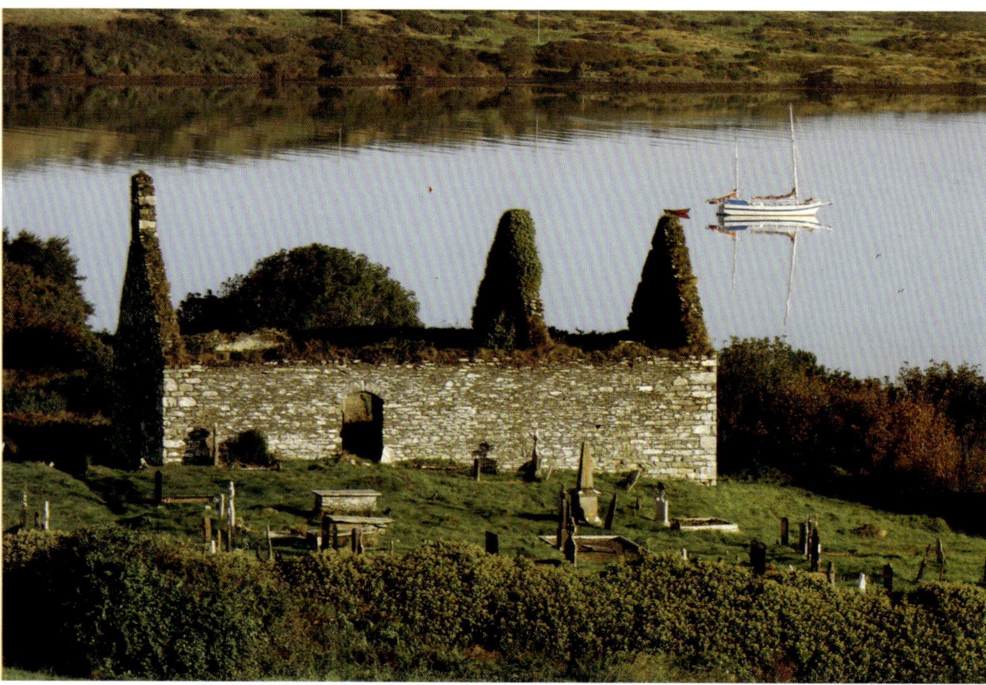

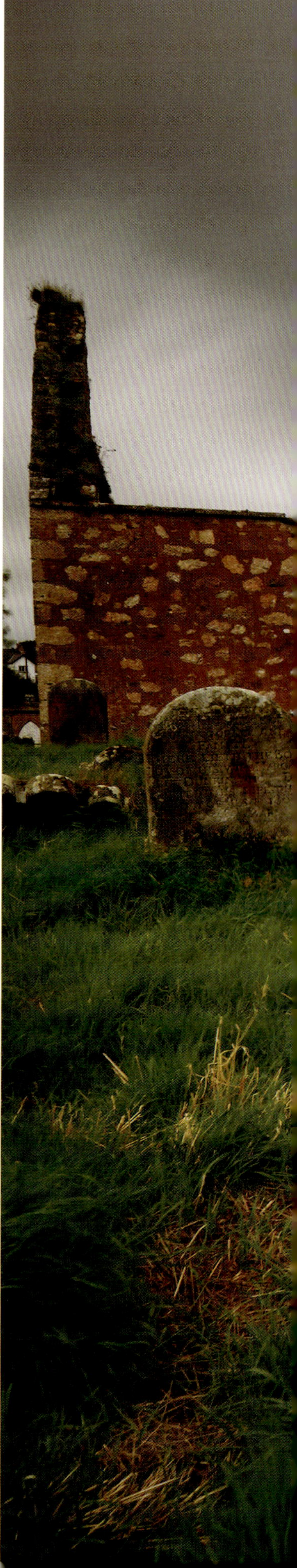

ABOVE TOP:

St Mary's Cathedral, Scattery Island, County Clare

Despite being on a small island off the coast of Clare, this former church administered a diocese in the 12th century, hence why it was called a cathedral. Yet the reorganization of dioceses meant Scattery Island's power was short-lived and the cathedral fell into disrepair. The original monastic settlement was founded in the 6th century by St Senan.

ABOVE BOTTOM:

Tullagh Church, Baltimore, County Cork

When this parish church was originally built in the 1720s, the nearby fishing village of Baltimore had suffered generations of depopulation after it was raided by pirates in 1631. However, in the 19th century, Baltimore started to boom again and St Matthew's, in the village, was built as the new parish church.

RIGHT:

Bonamargy Friary, County Antrim

This friary survived Henry VIII's dissolution of the monasteries only to be destroyed by fire in the 1580s. Built by the McQuillan clan, it was claimed by the rival MacDonnells, and the remains of MacDonnell chieftain Sorley Boy are in its vaults. Just outside the seaside town of Ballycastle, Bonamargy is now surrounded by a golf course.

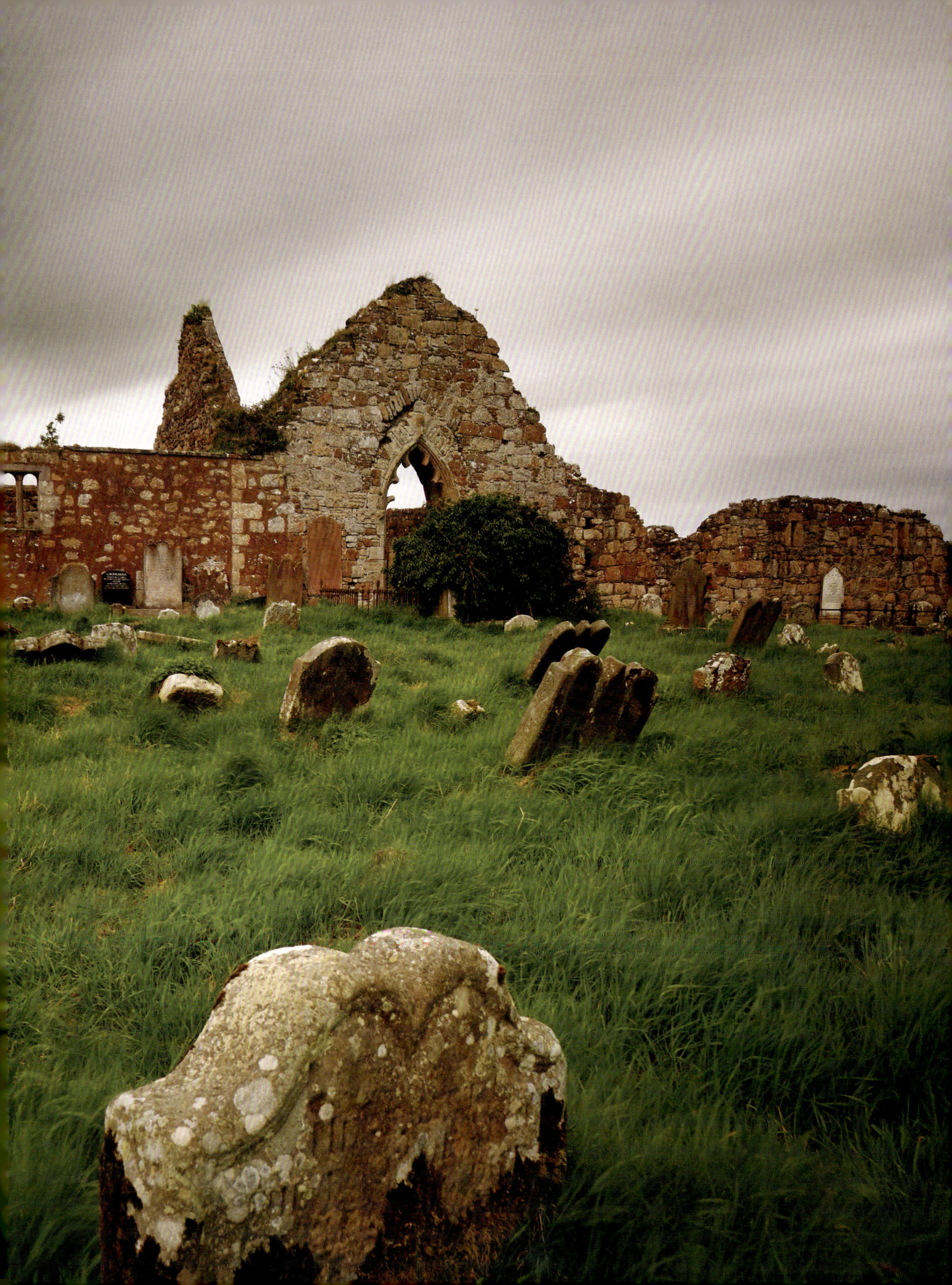

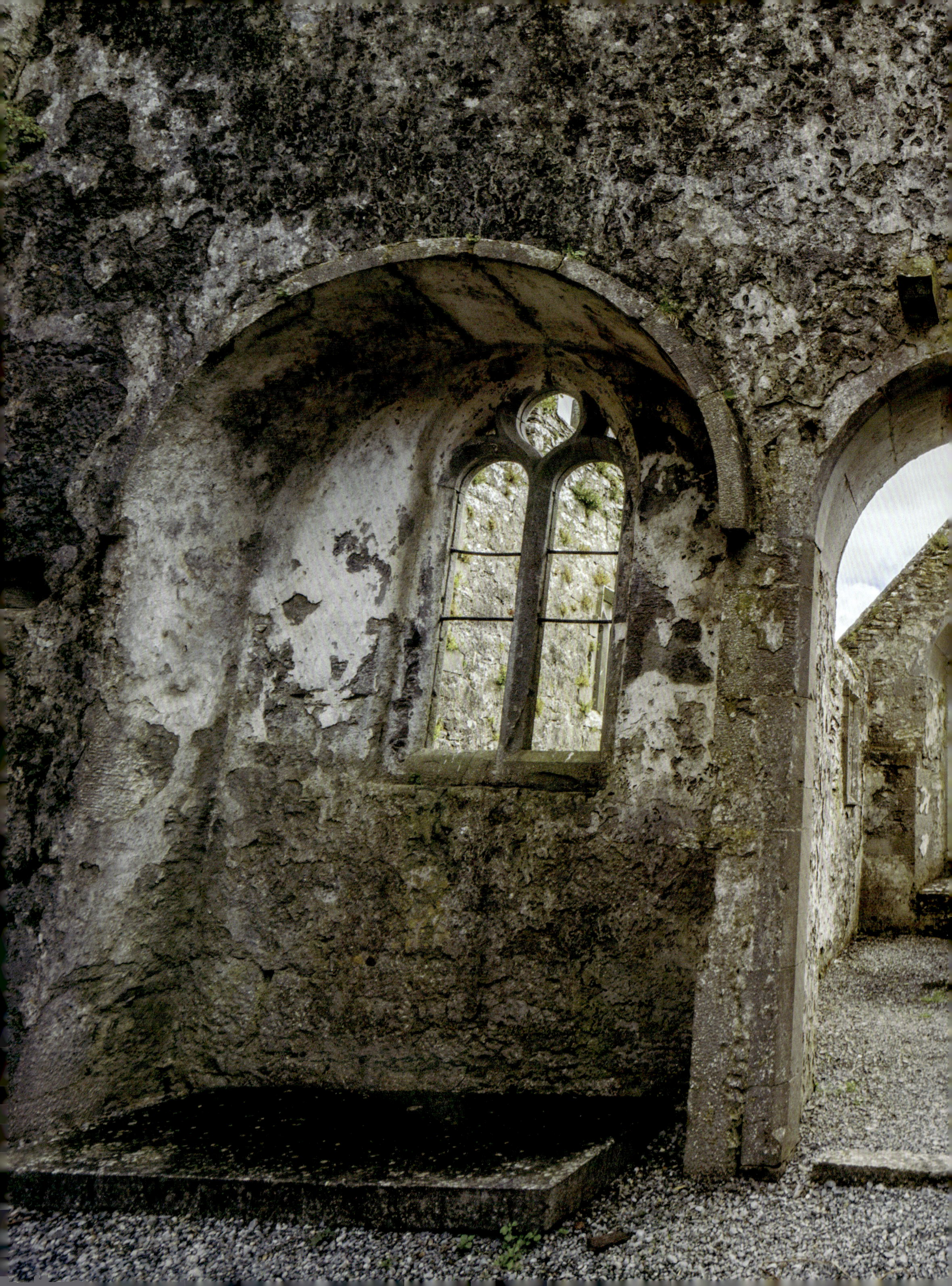

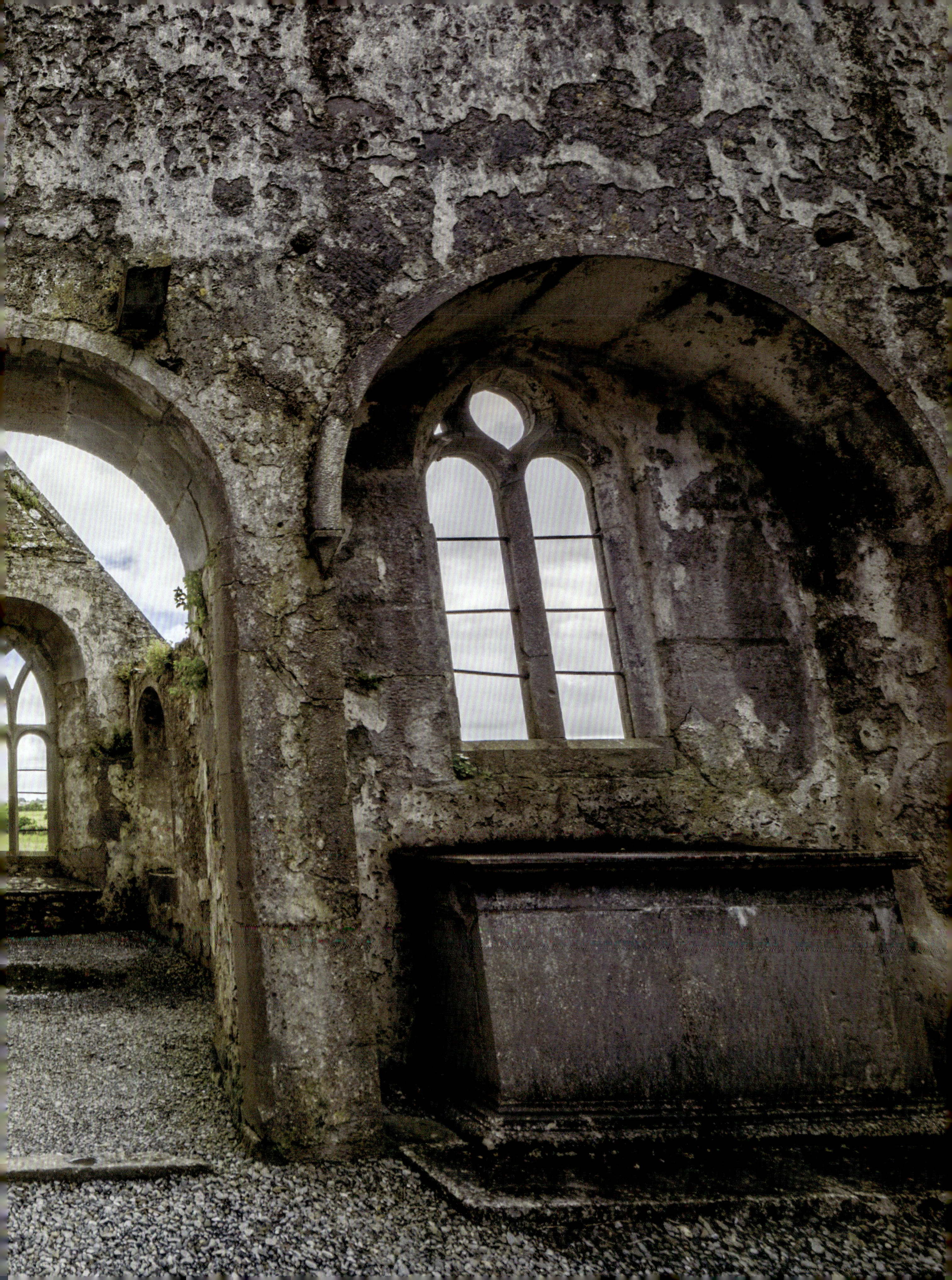

PREVIOUS PAGES:
**Ross Errilly Friary,
County Galway**
Despite the best efforts of the
English, Ross Errilly slipped back
into Franciscans' hands many
times over the centuries – because
control kept being ceded to the
De Burgh family, who had helped
establish it. There are reports that
the medieval friary – the most
complete Franciscan monastic site
in Ireland – was still inhabited
into the 19th century.

RIGHT:
**Jerpoint Abbey,
County Kilkenny**
Stone carvings are well preserved
at this abbey, near Thomastown,
one of the most intact Cistercian
monastic ruins in Ireland.
Founded in the 12th century
on an earlier Benedictine site,
it was closed after Henry VIII's
dissolution of the monasteries.
Today the Dublin–Waterford
railway line runs behind it.

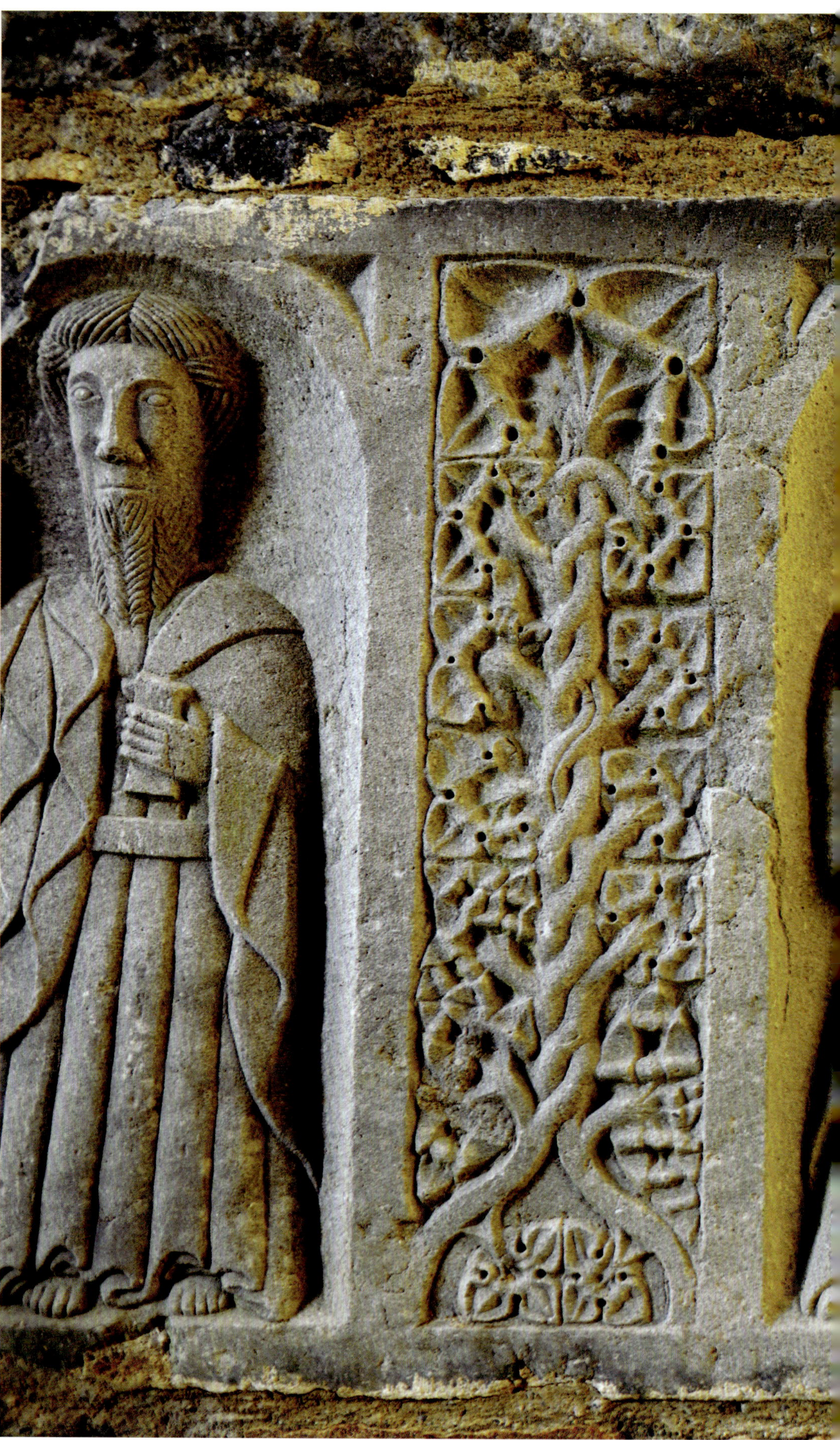

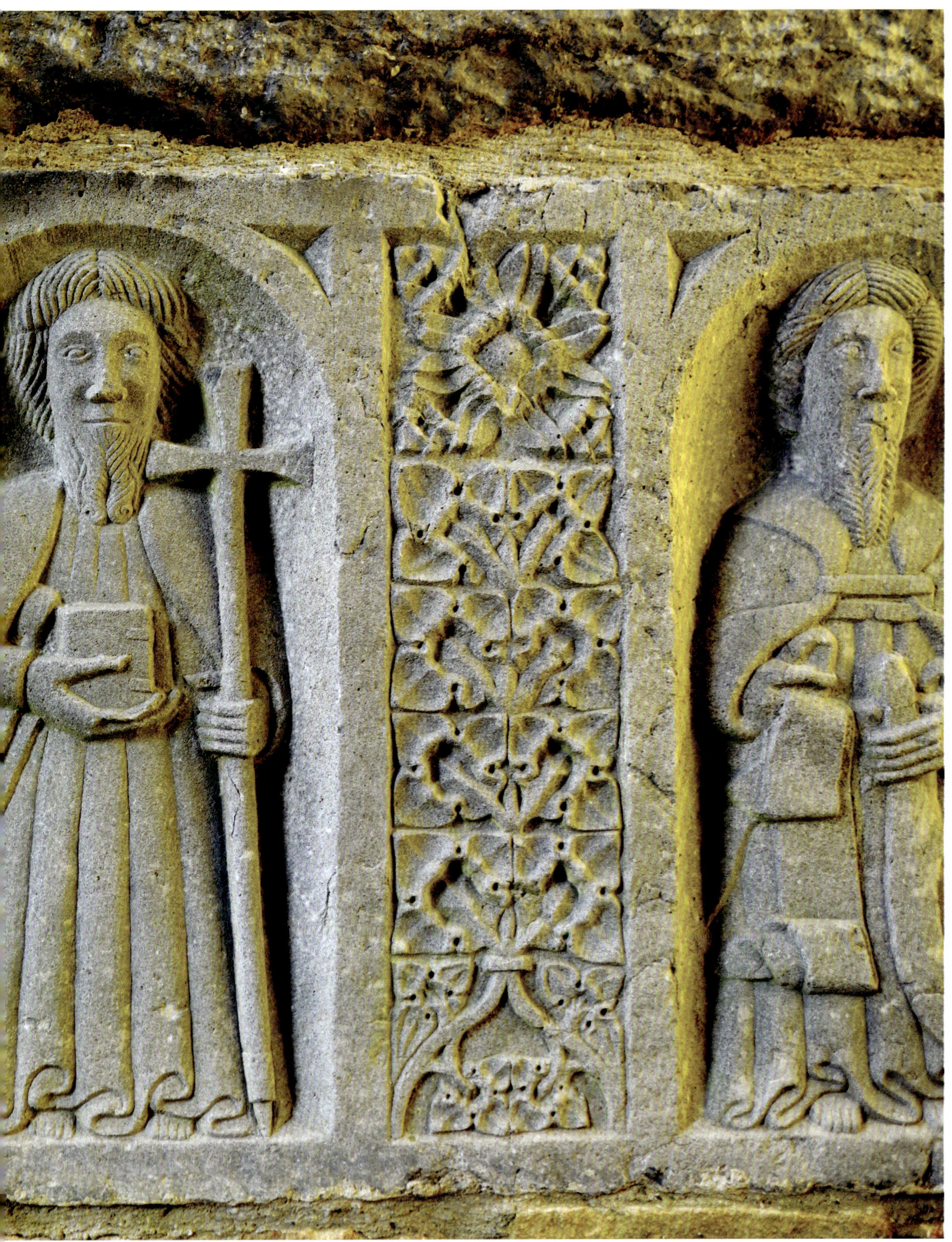

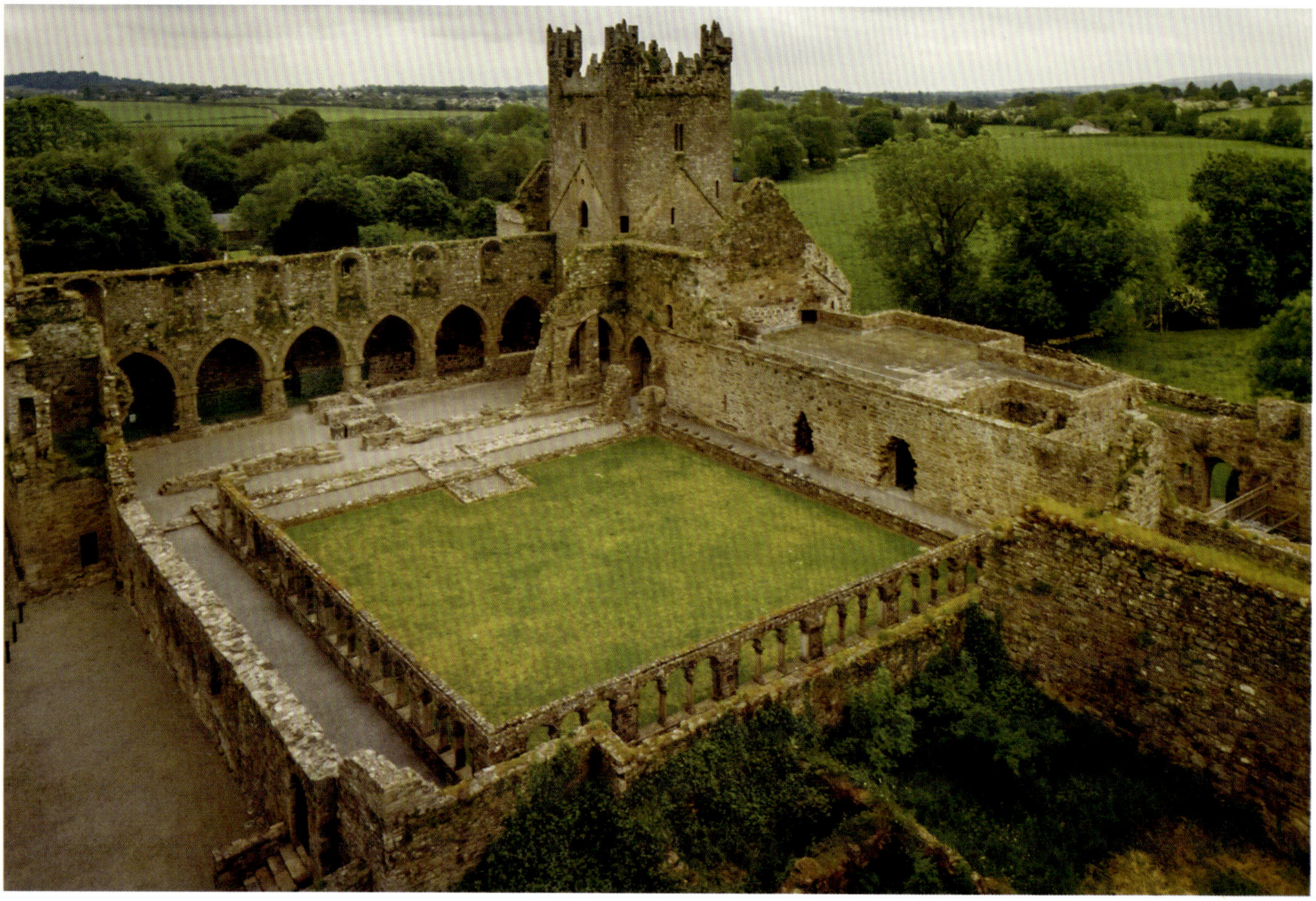

**Jerpoint Abbey,
County Kilkenny**

A stand-out feature of the abbey
ruins is the sculptured cloister,
which dates from the 15th
century and was reconstructed
in 1953. One of the engravings
appears to show a man suffering
from stomach ache. Jerpoint's
tower overlooks the nearby
Tomb of St Nicholas, said to
hold the remains of the saint who
gave us Santa Claus.

**Glendalough Cathedral,
County Wicklow**

This monastic site was founded
by St Kevin in the 6th century
and later destroyed by a Norman
attack in 1214. In its heyday,
Glendalough was part of a
settlement so large it was called
a 'monastic city'. By contrast, St
Kevin was known to have lived
as a hermit in a cave.

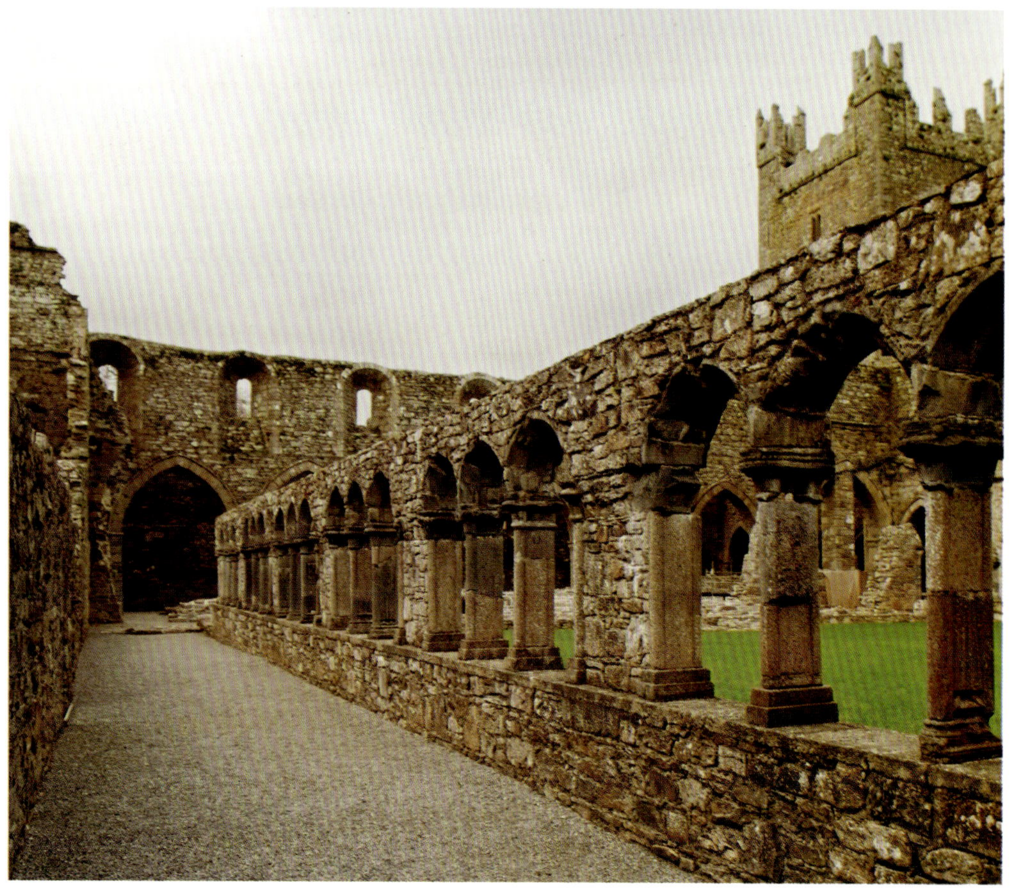

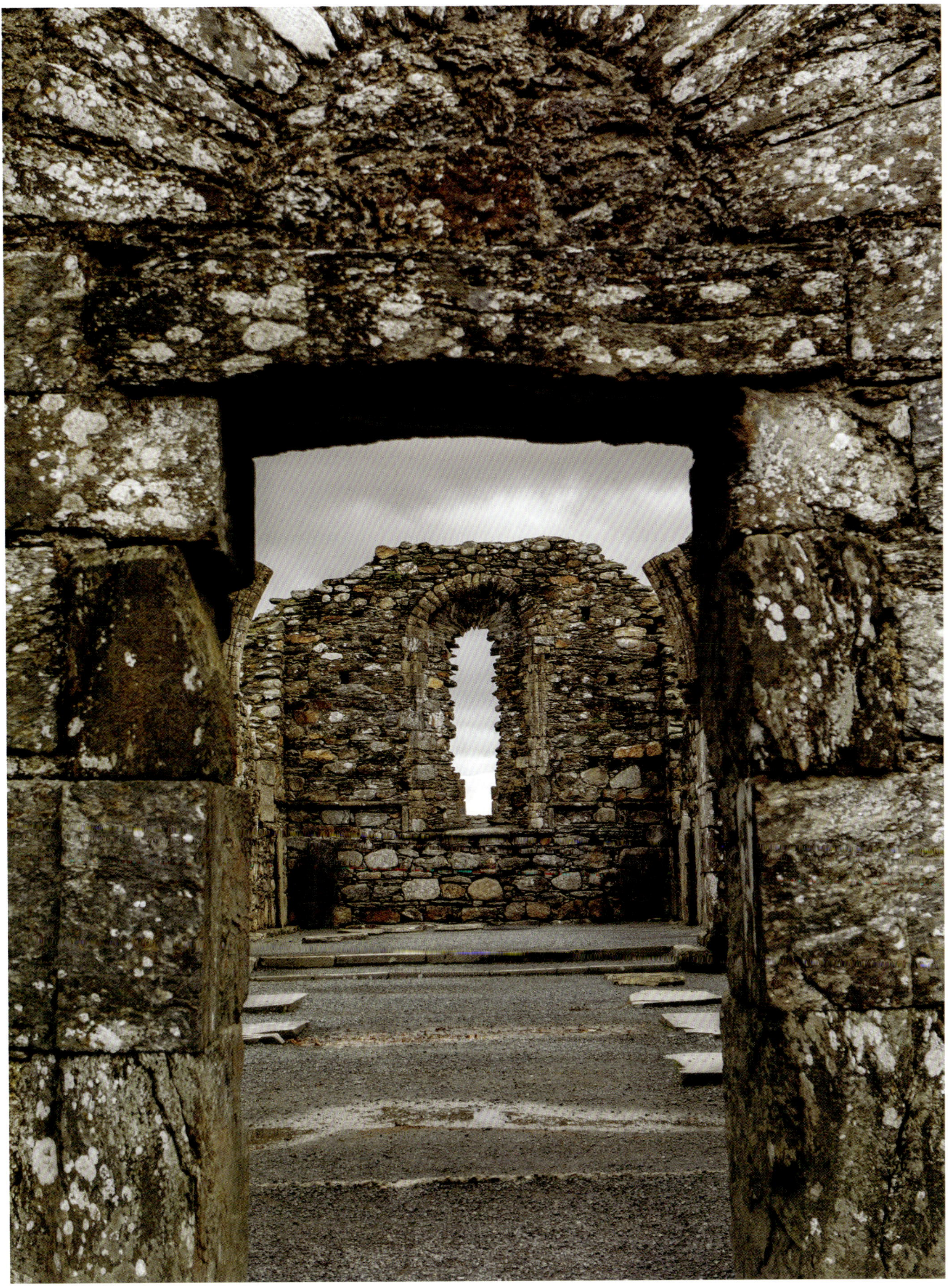

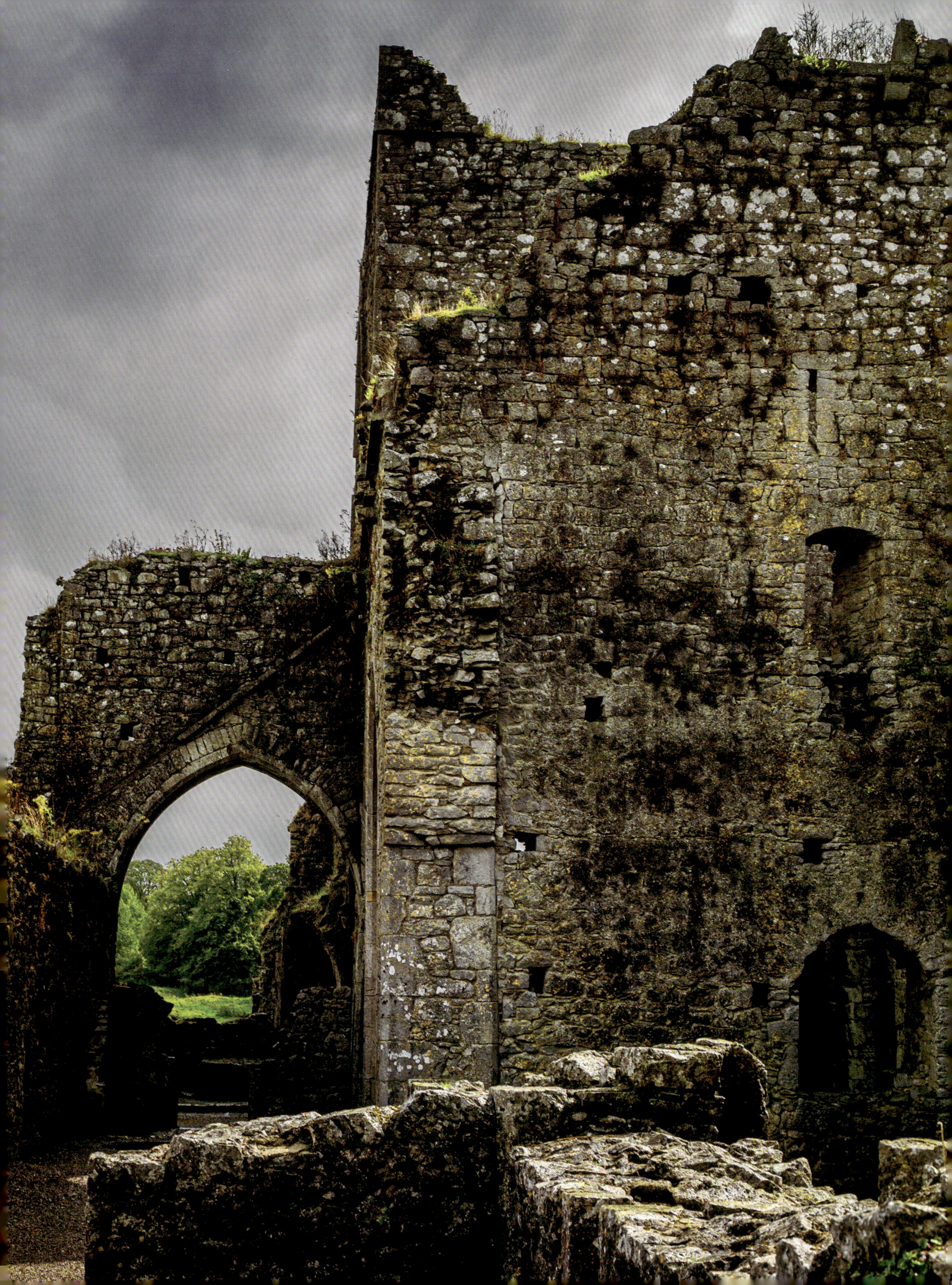

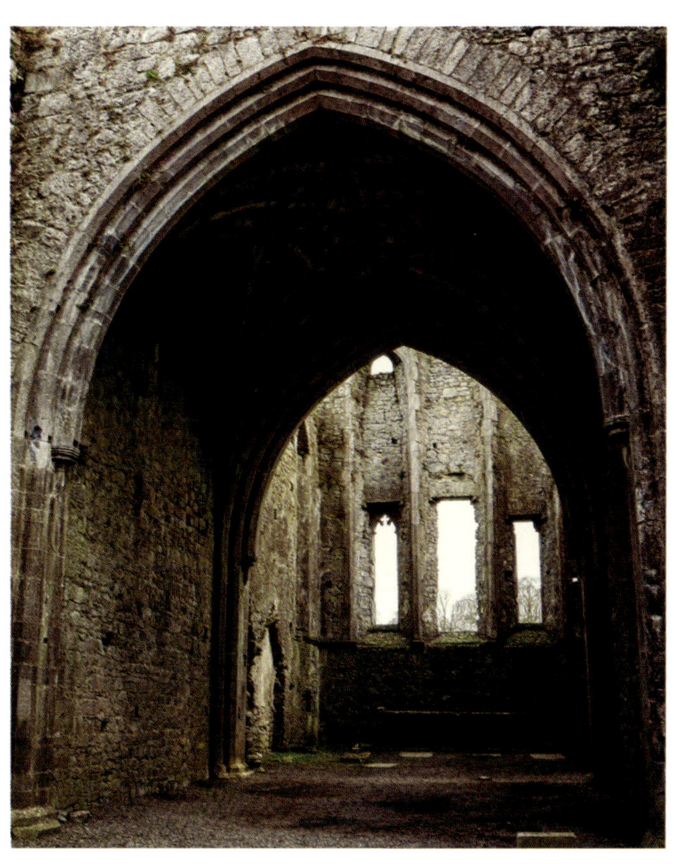

Hore Abbey, County Tipperary
On the site of a Benedictine monastery outside the town of Cashel, Hore Abbey was founded in 1272 by Cistercians. To vacate the site, the Archbishop of Cashel expelled the Benedictines because, it is said, he had a dream they were about to kill him. The abbey was dissolved in 1540 as part of Henry VIII's dissolution of the monasteries.

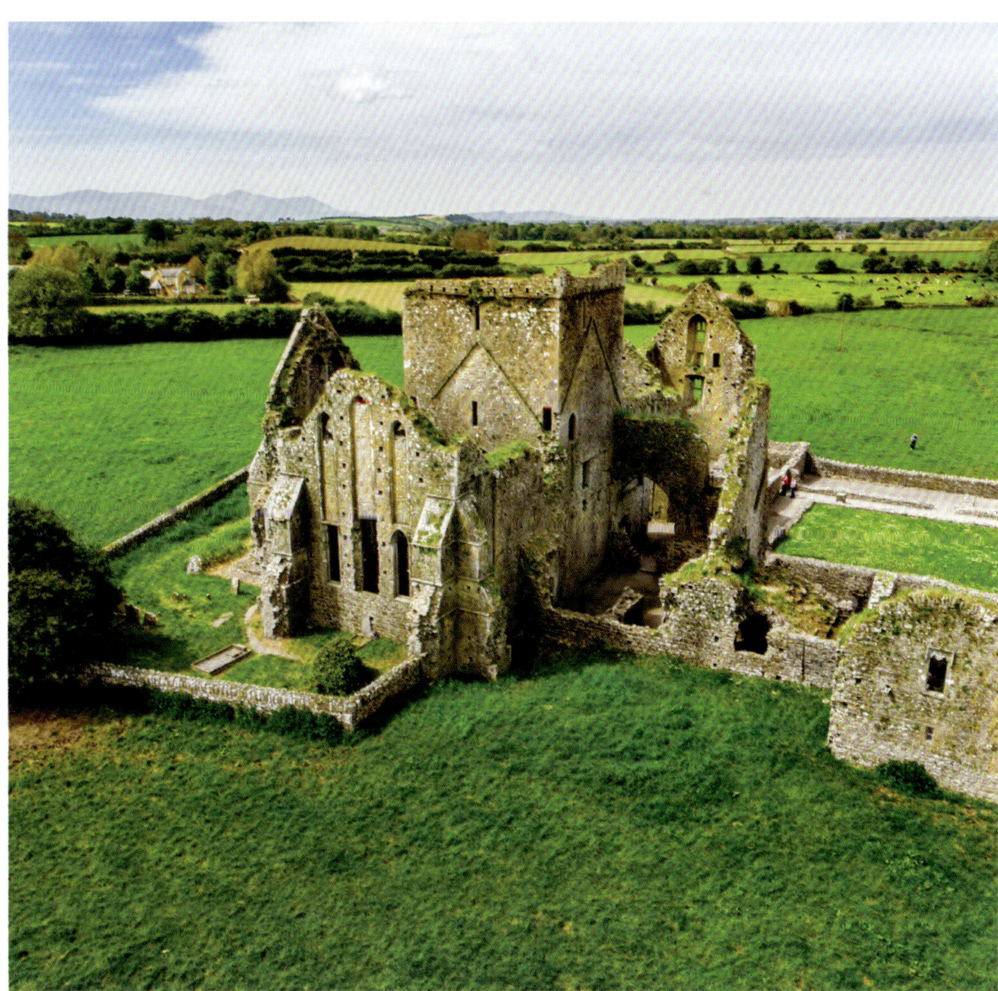

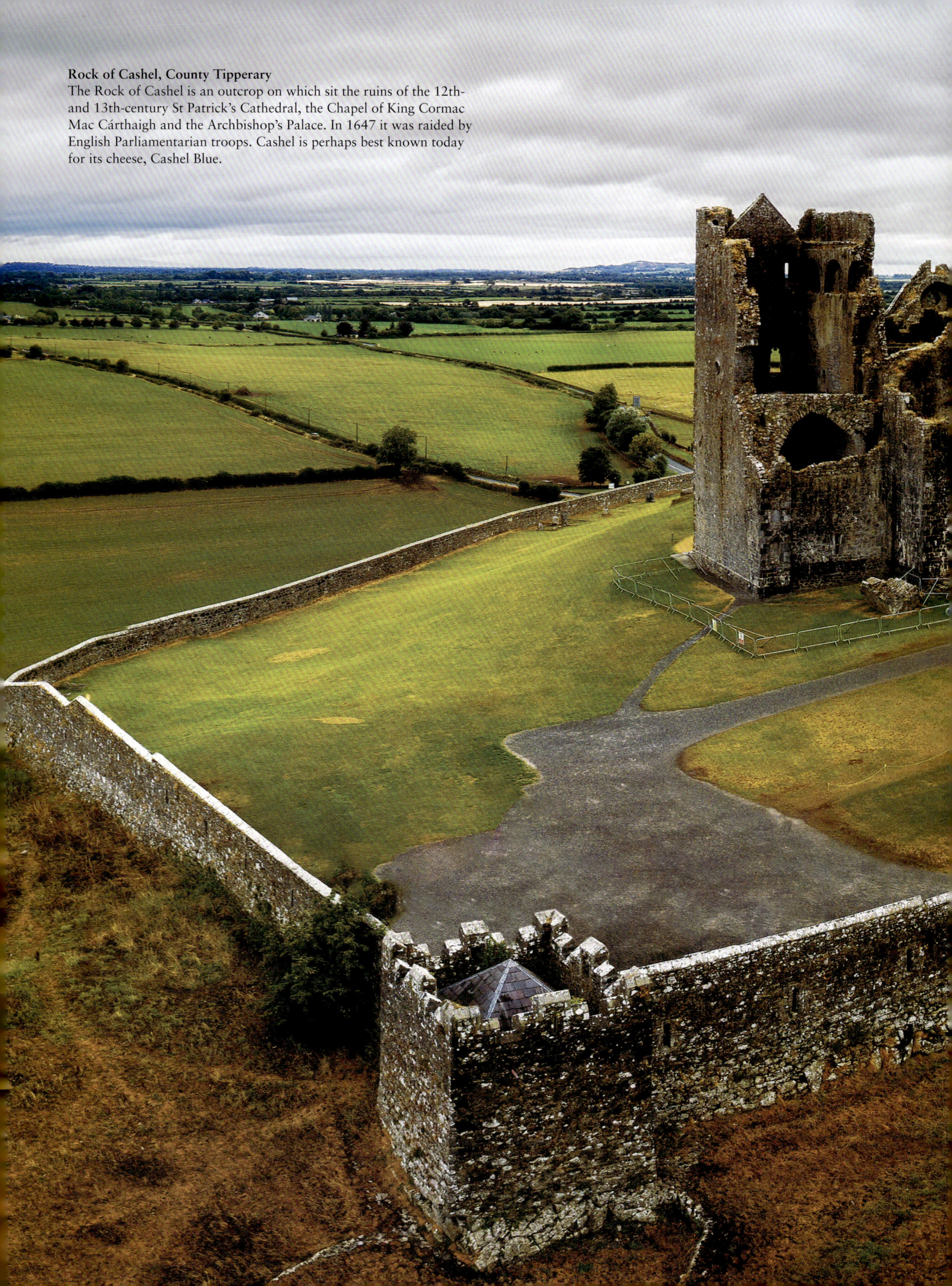

Rock of Cashel, County Tipperary
The Rock of Cashel is an outcrop on which sit the ruins of the 12th-
and 13th-century St Patrick's Cathedral, the Chapel of King Cormac
Mac Cárthaigh and the Archbishop's Palace. In 1647 it was raided by
English Parliamentarian troops. Cashel is perhaps best known today
for its cheese, Cashel Blue.

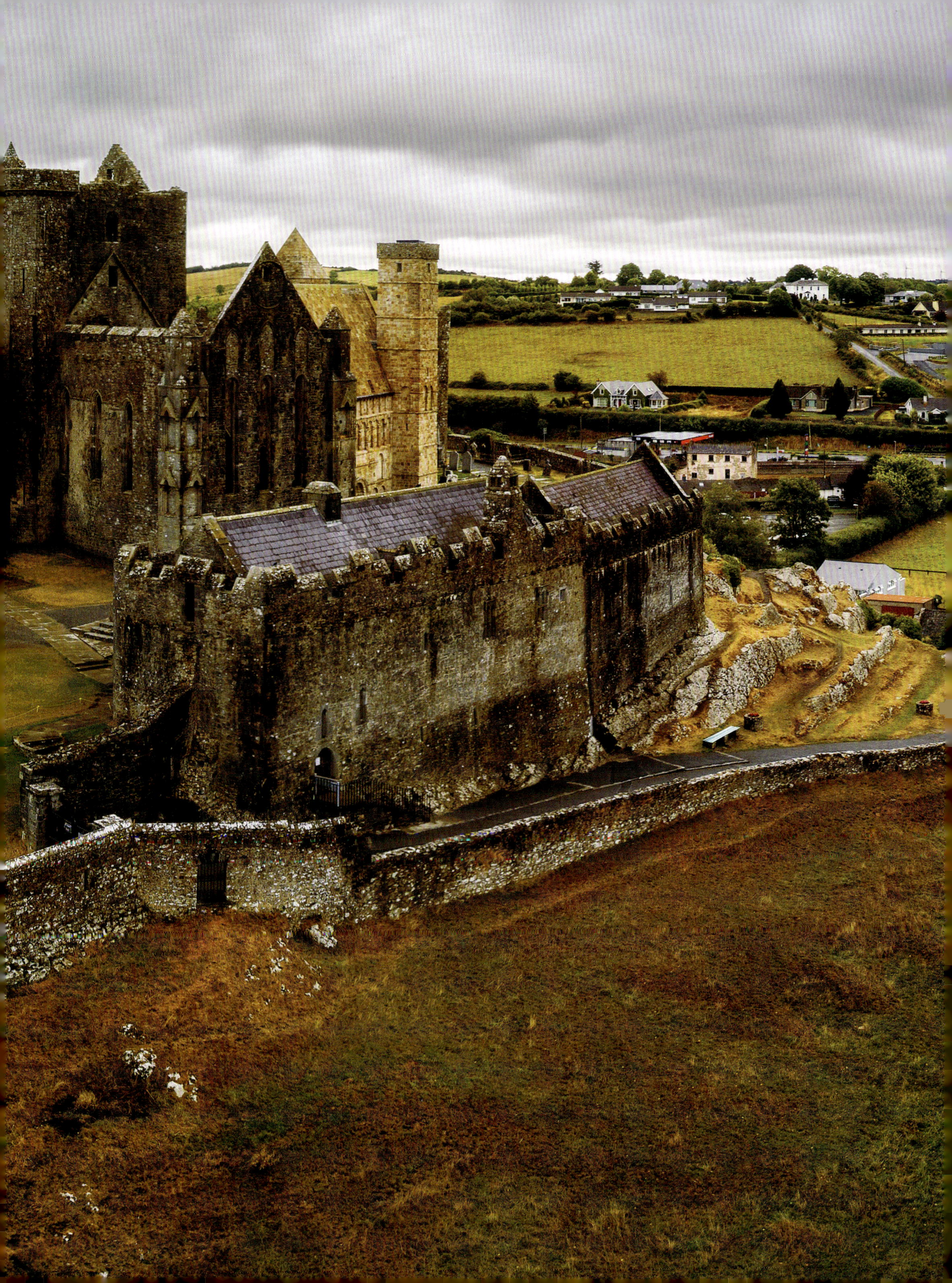

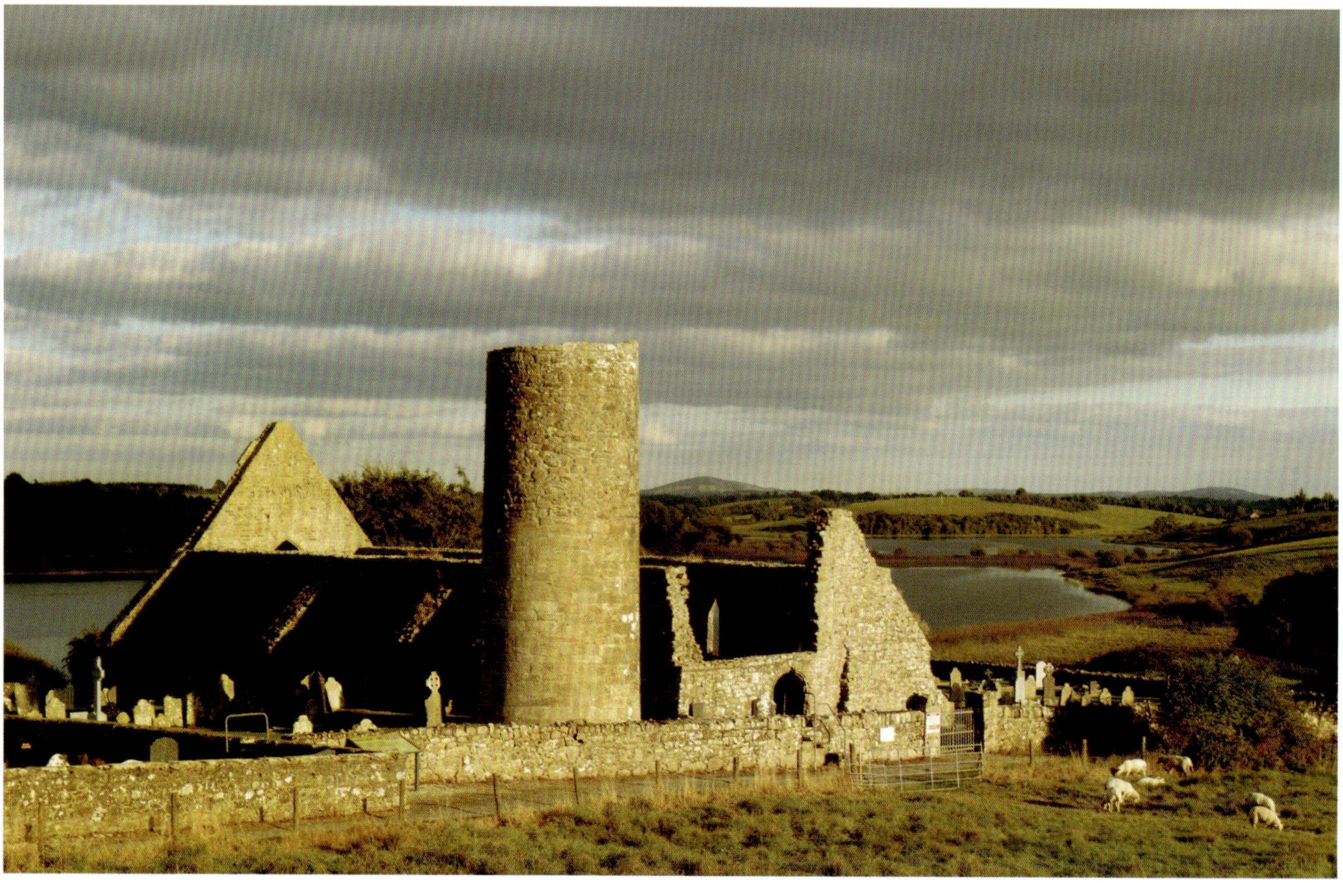

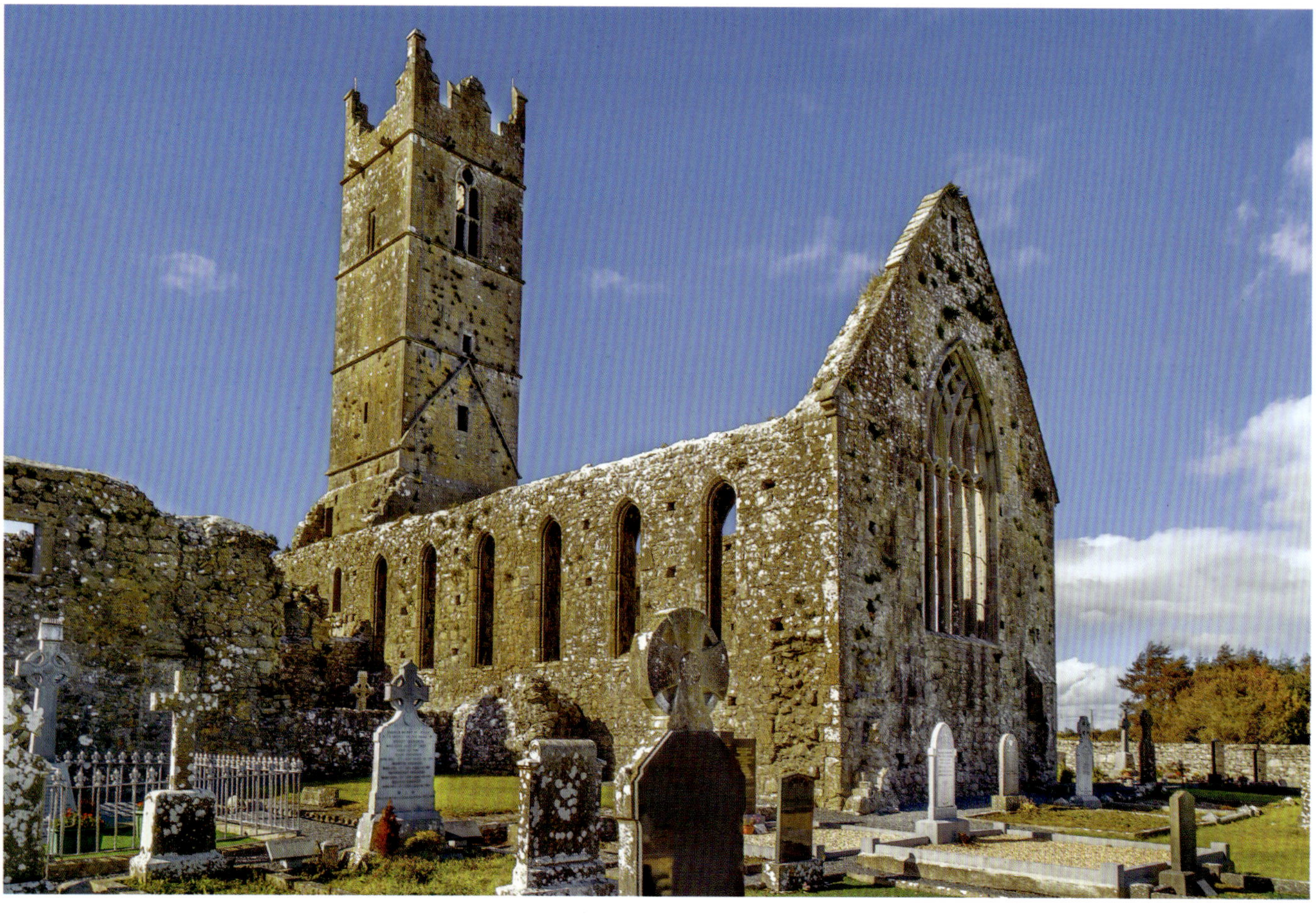

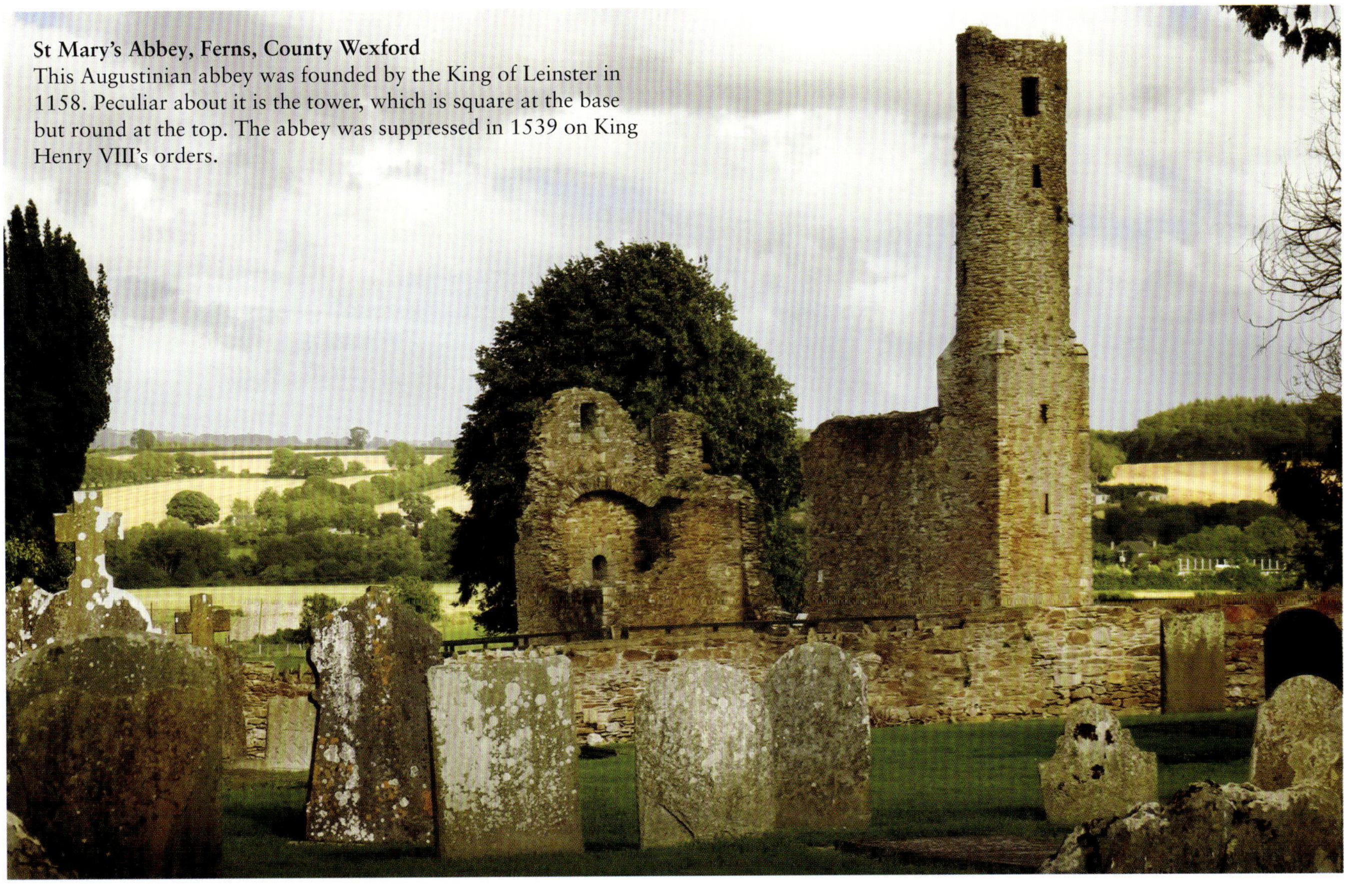

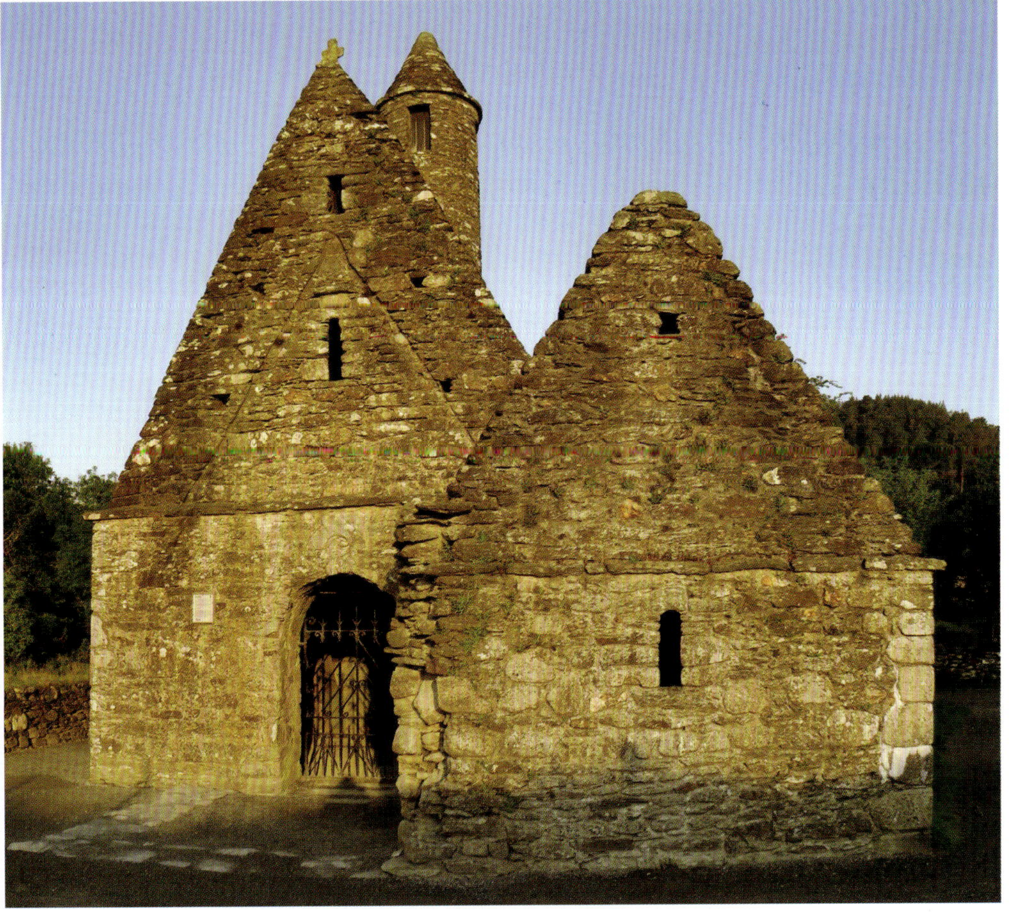

OPPOSITE ABOVE:
**Drumlane Abbey,
County Cavan**
The remarkably intact round
tower at this Augustinian abbey
dates from the 12th century,
replacing the original wood
one. It was attacked and burned
in 1246 in a feud between the
O'Rourke and O'Reilly clans.

OPPOSITE BELOW:
**Claregalway Friary,
County Galway**
Used as barracks by English
forces after the Reformation,
Claregalway Abbey had
previously been a thriving
Franciscan site, under the
protection of the same family
that oversaw Ross Errilly.

LEFT:
**St Kevin's Church, Glendalough,
County Wicklow**
This 12th-century church is
better known as St Kevin's
Kitchen. This is because people
believed the bell tower was a
kitchen's chimney.

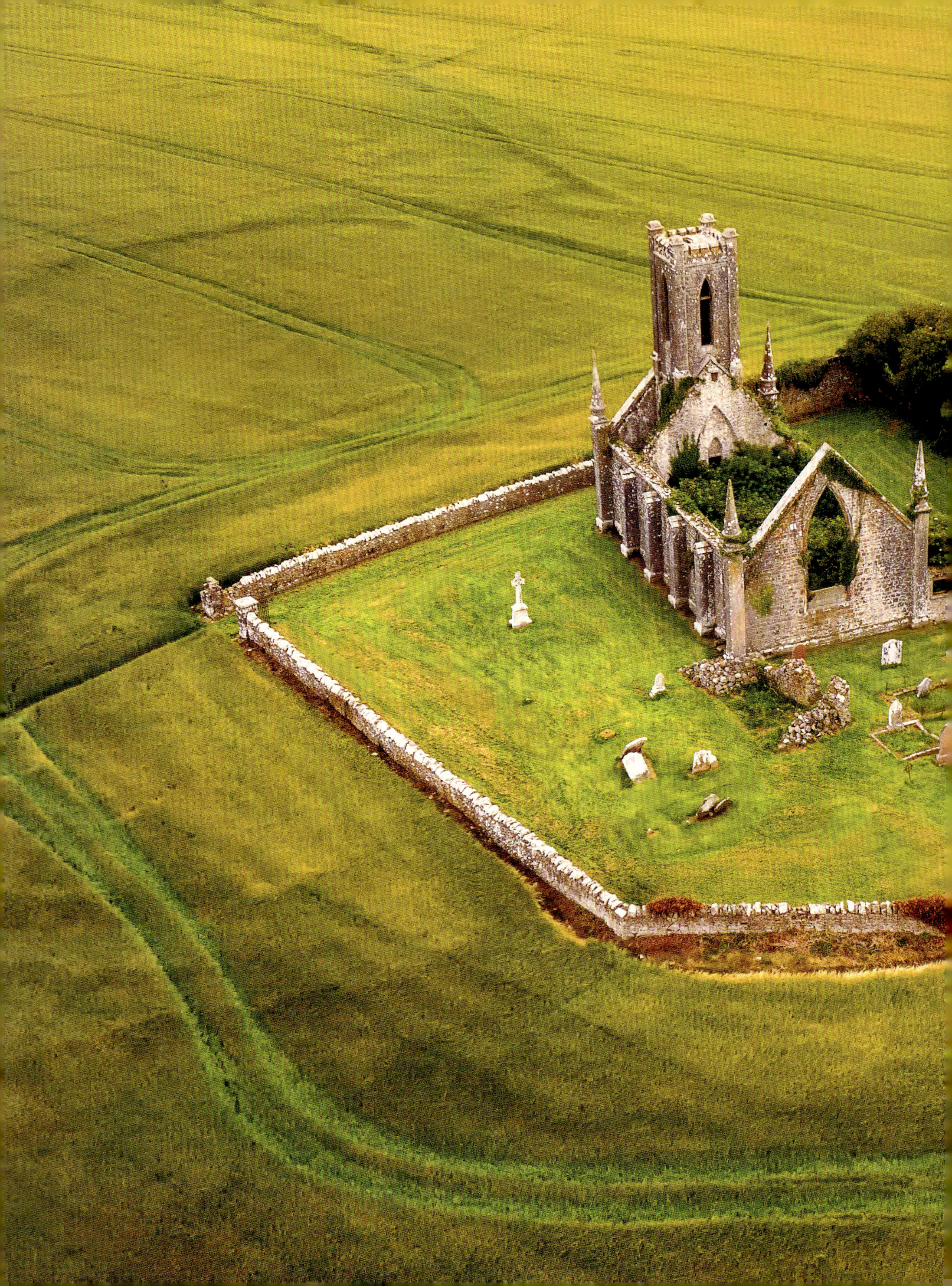

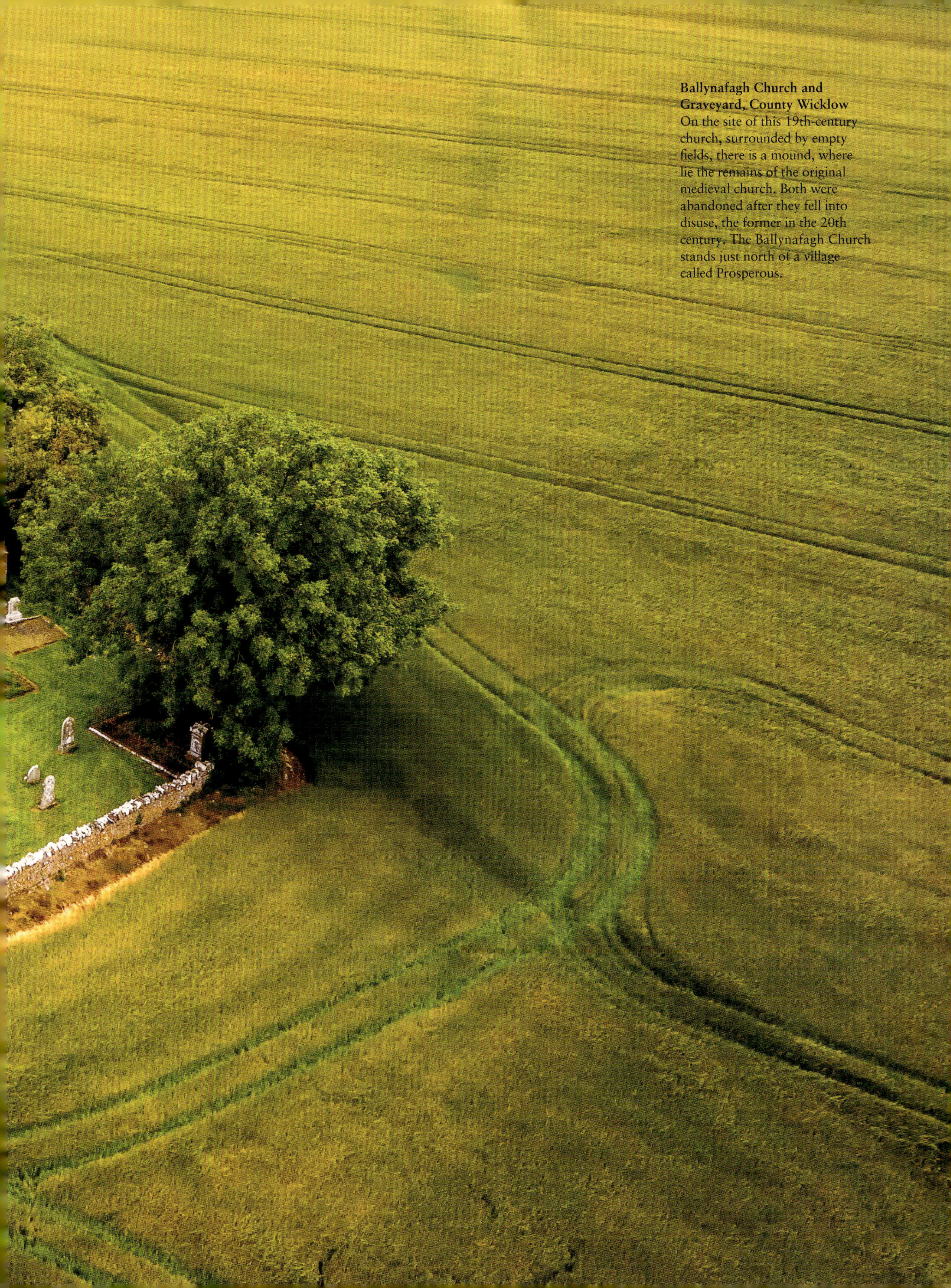

Ballynafagh Church and Graveyard, County Wicklow
On the site of this 19th-century church, surrounded by empty fields, there is a mound, where lie the remains of the original medieval church. Both were abandoned after they fell into disuse, the former in the 20th century. The Ballynafagh Church stands just north of a village called Prosperous.

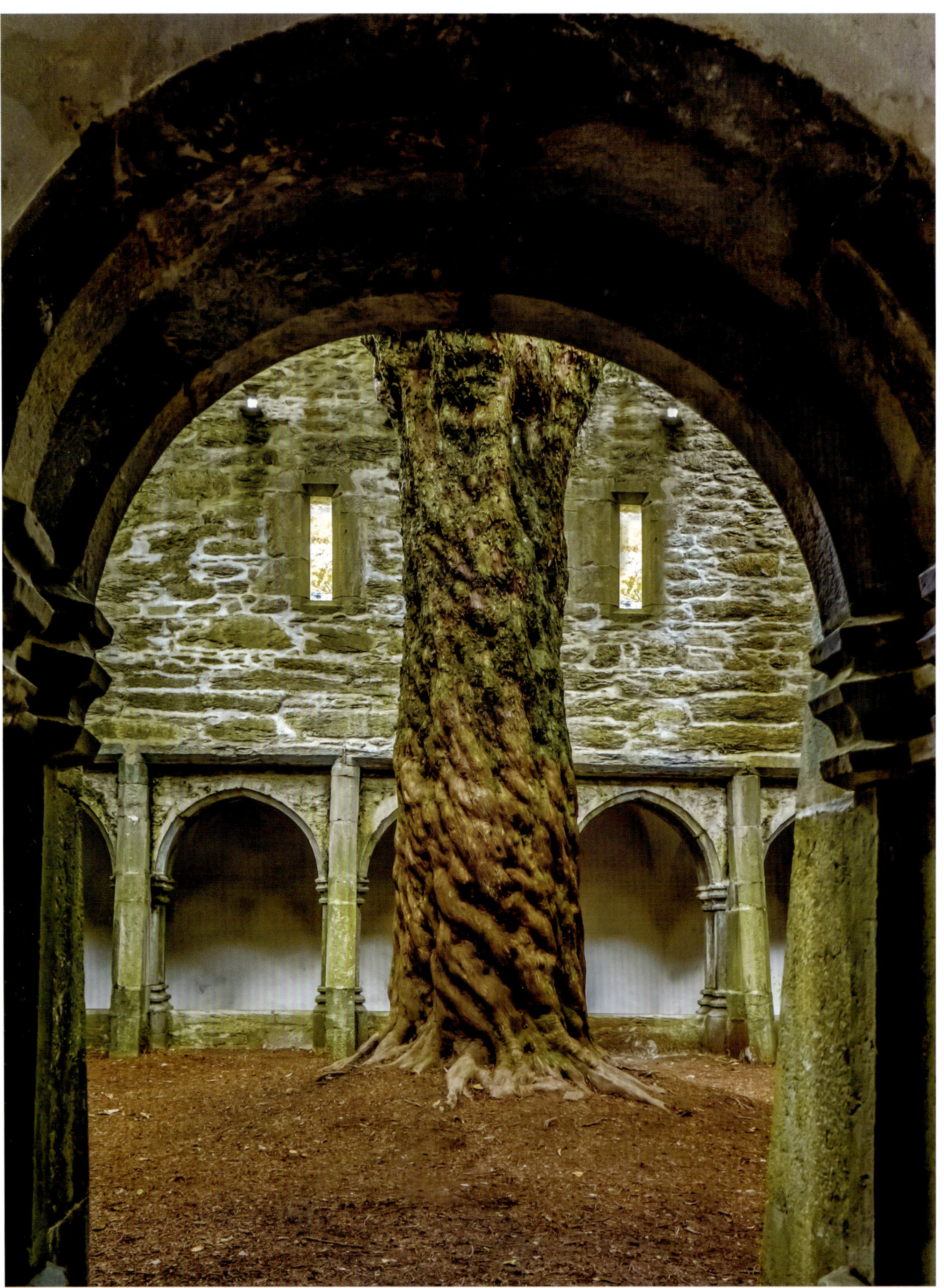

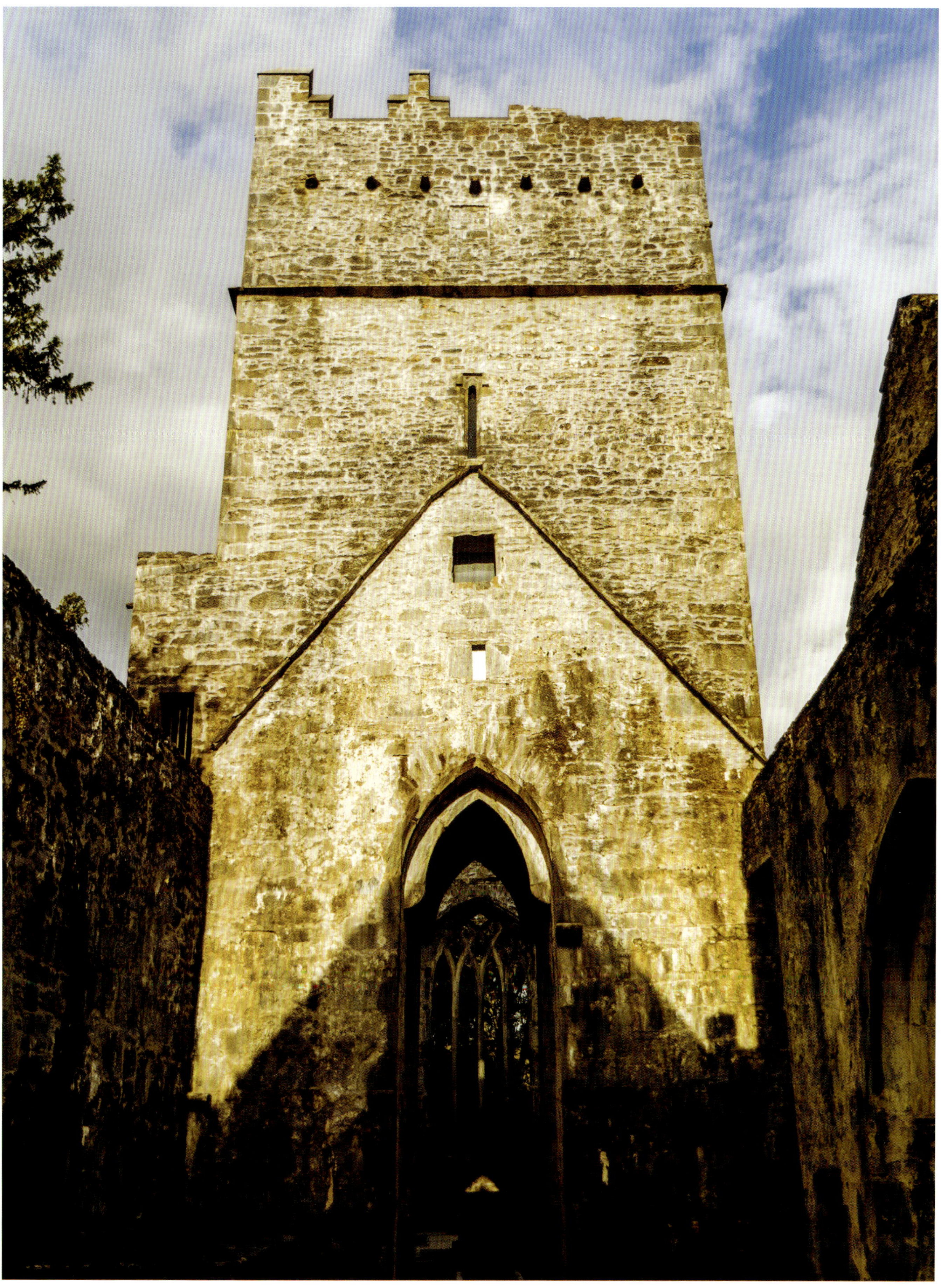

**Muckross Abbey,
County Kerry**
A large yew tree grows in the
middle of the cloister in this
Franciscan abbey, founded in
1448, which was ransacked by
Oliver Cromwell's English forces
in the 17th century. Some say
it is more than 400 years old.
Yew trees were often planted at
ecclesiastical sites because they
were seen as symbols of death
and rebirth.

**Fahy Church, Ballycroy,
County Mayo**
This church looks out on to the
Atlantic Ocean and on a stretch
of coast that was the scene of
a shipwreck in 1588 when 600
sailors from the Spanish Armada
ran aground. There is little
settlement around this ruined
medieval church today, but there
is a thriving church in the nearby
village of Ballycroy.

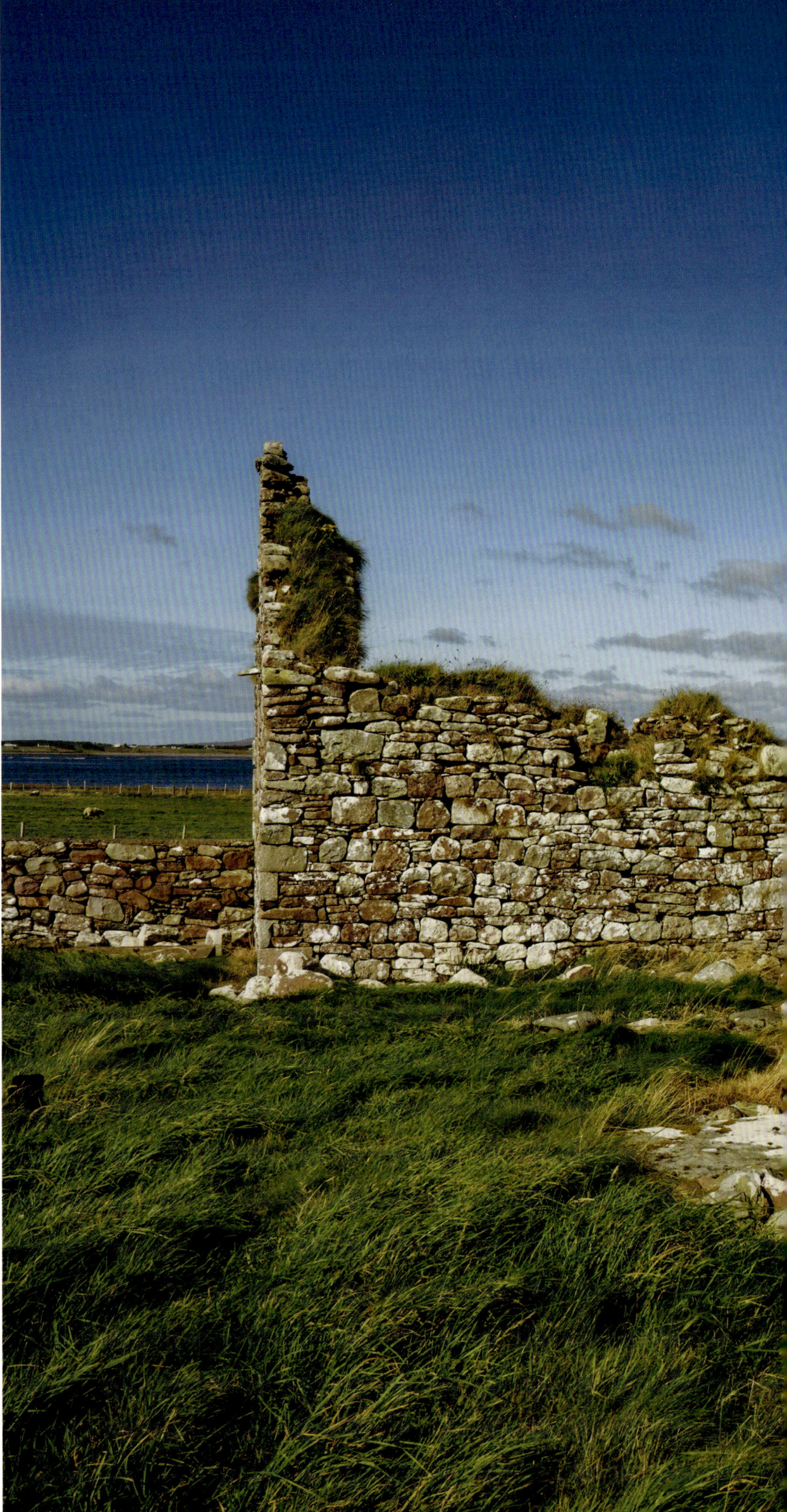

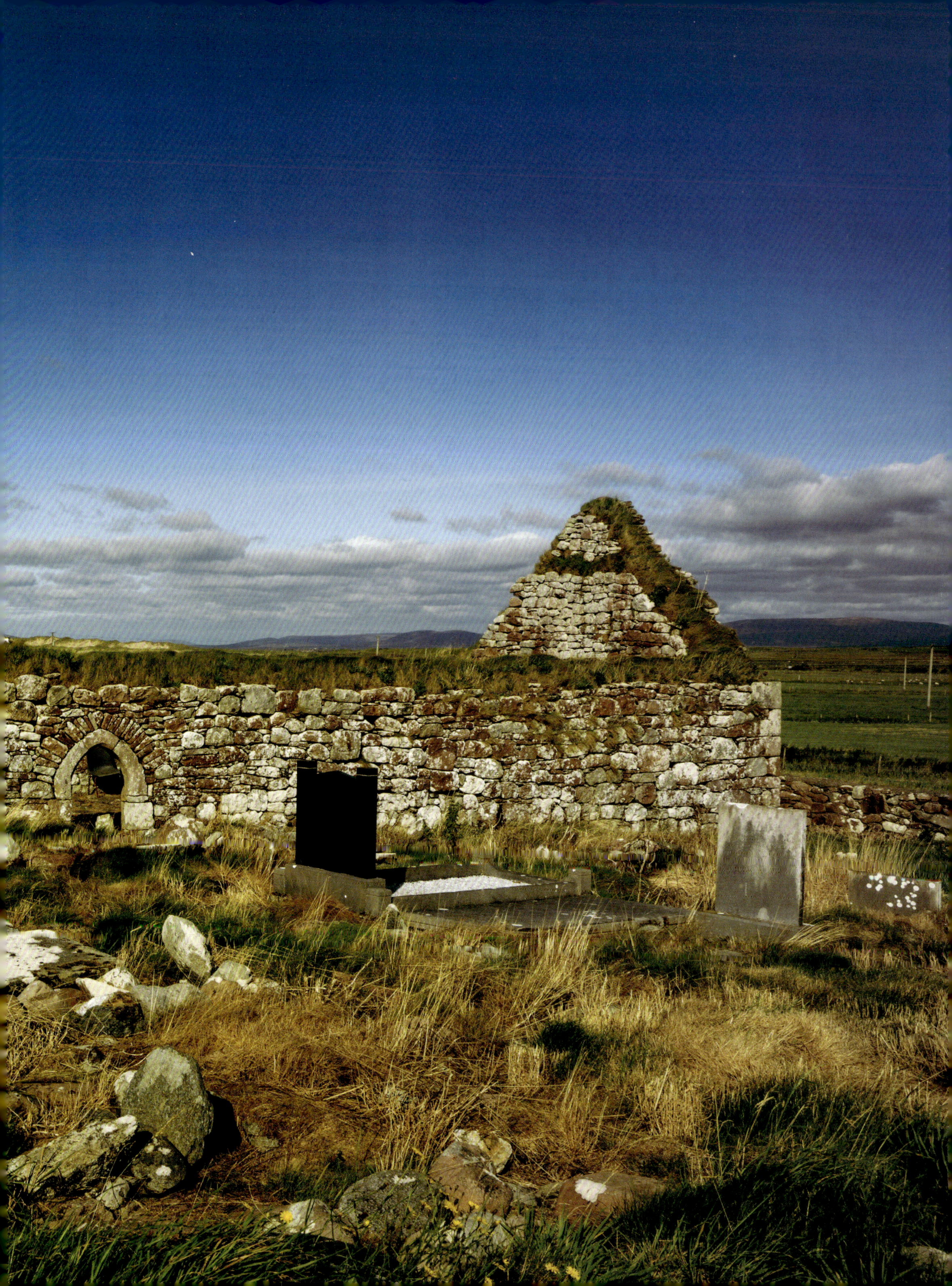

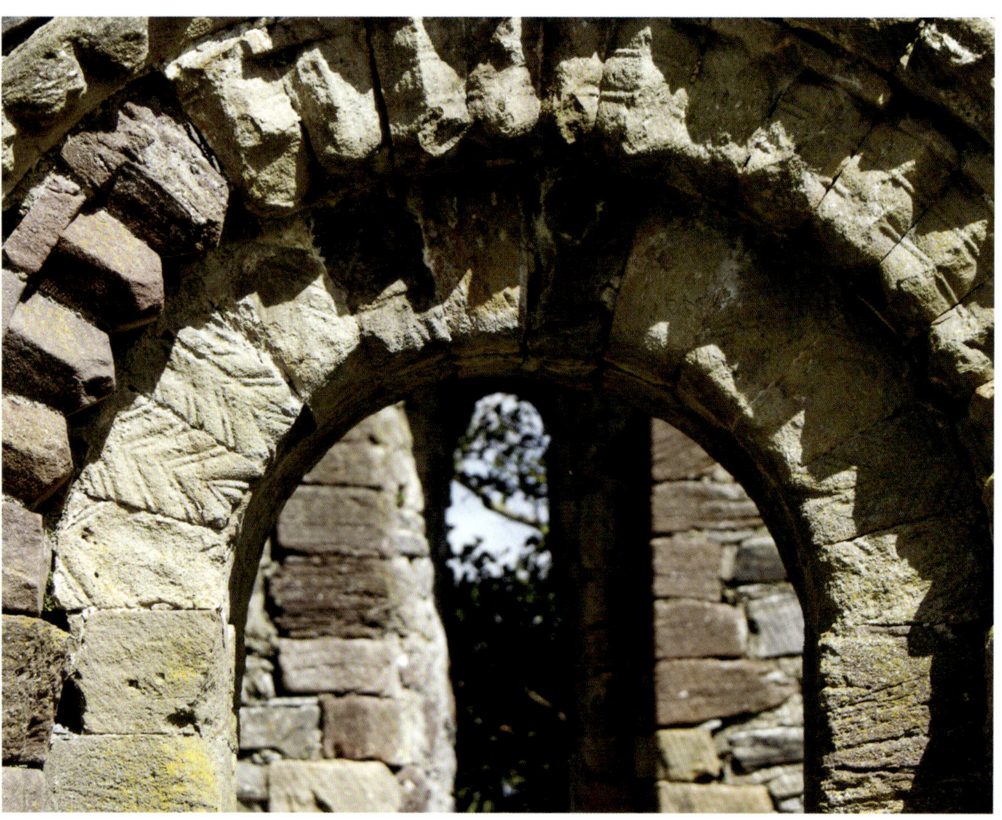

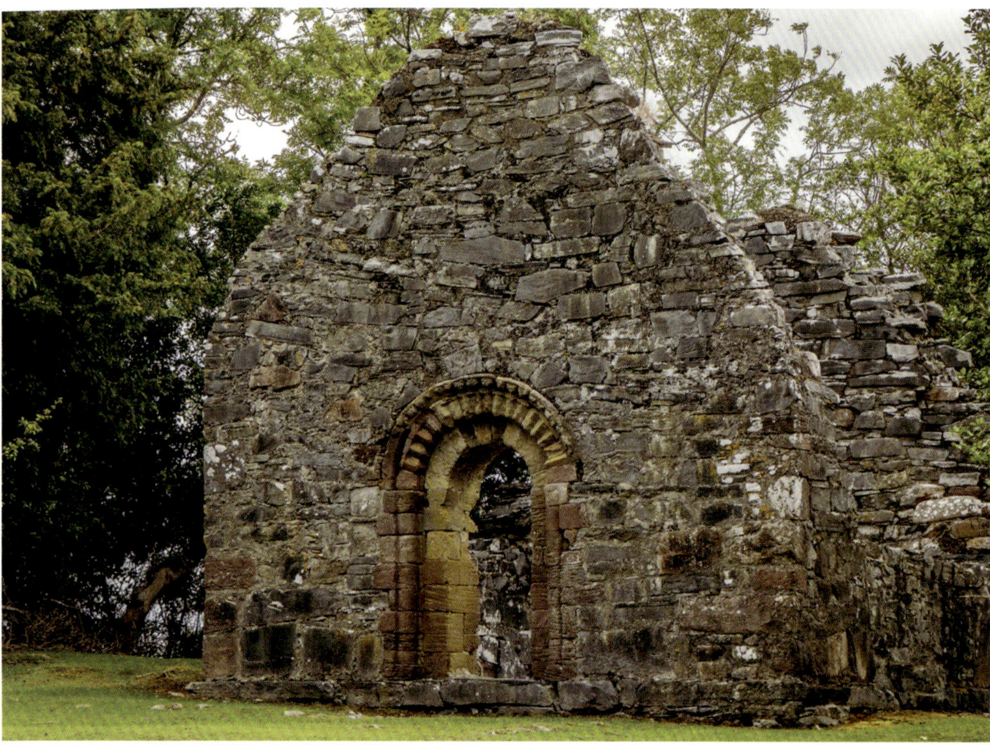

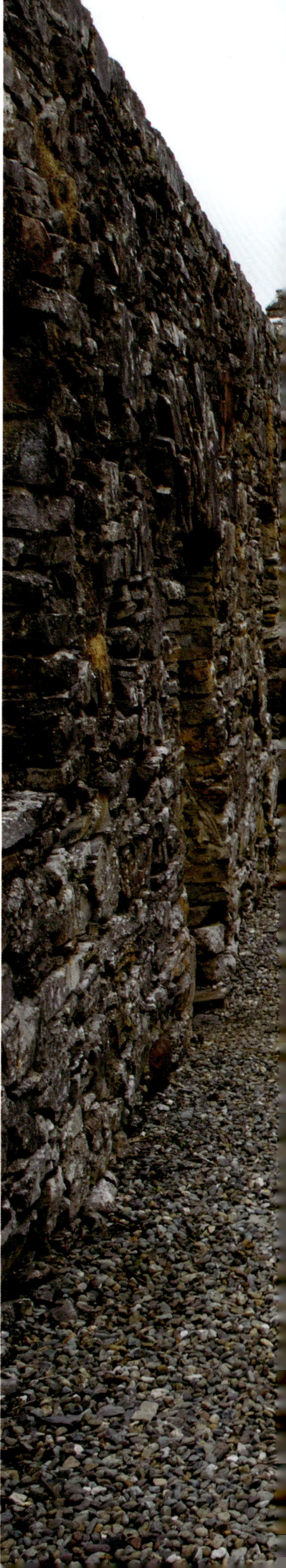

ALL PHOTGRAPHS:
**Innisfallen Abbey,
County Kerry**
The abbey sits on the island of Innisfallen in Lough Leane, where a monastery was founded by St Finian in 640. The religious site was occupied until 1594, when it was shut down during the reign of Elizabeth I. During that time – but over 300 years – the Annals of Innisfallen were written by the monks there, telling the history of Ireland as they saw it. The works are written in Irish and Latin and are housed in the Bodleian Library in Oxford, England.

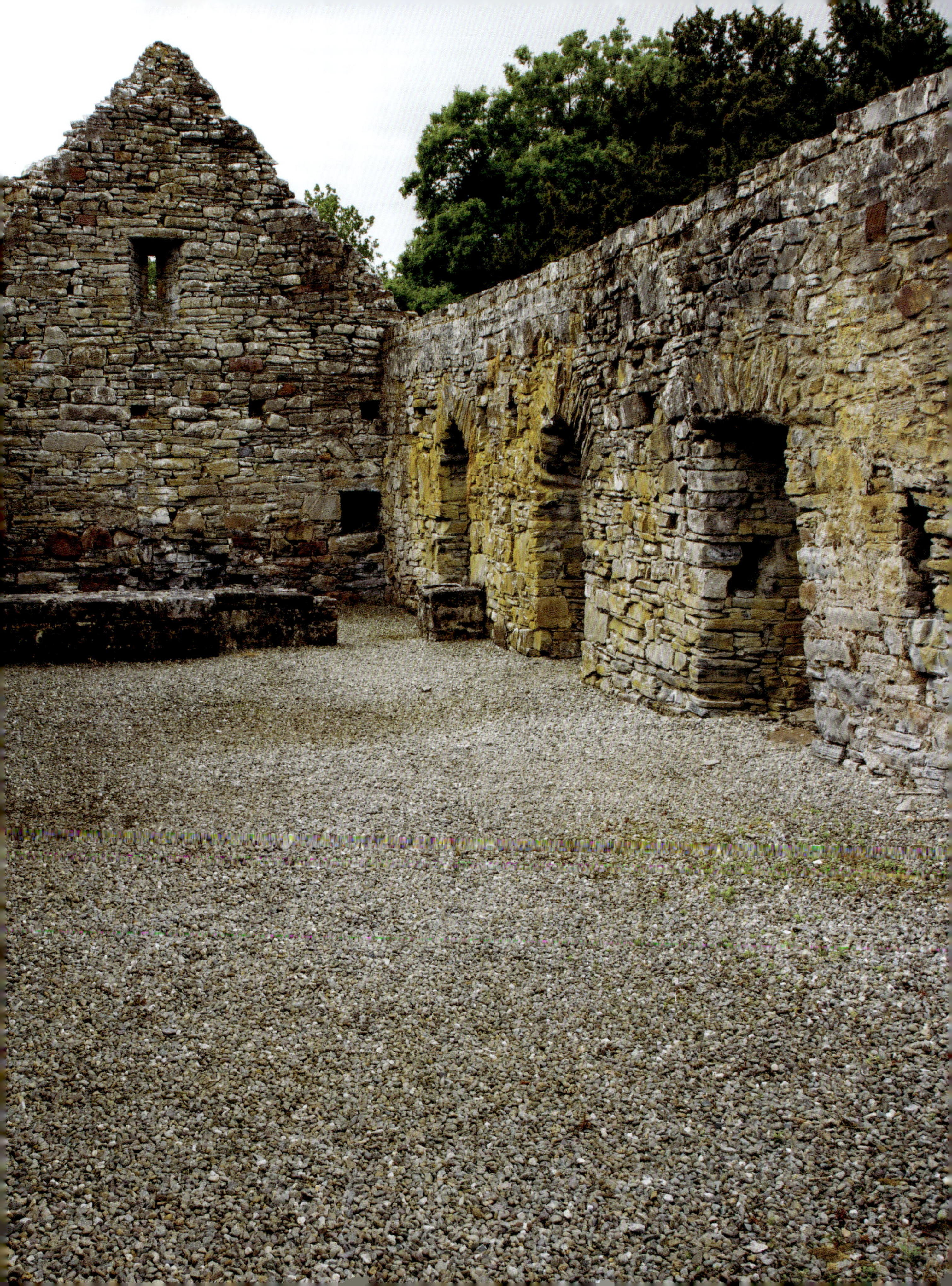

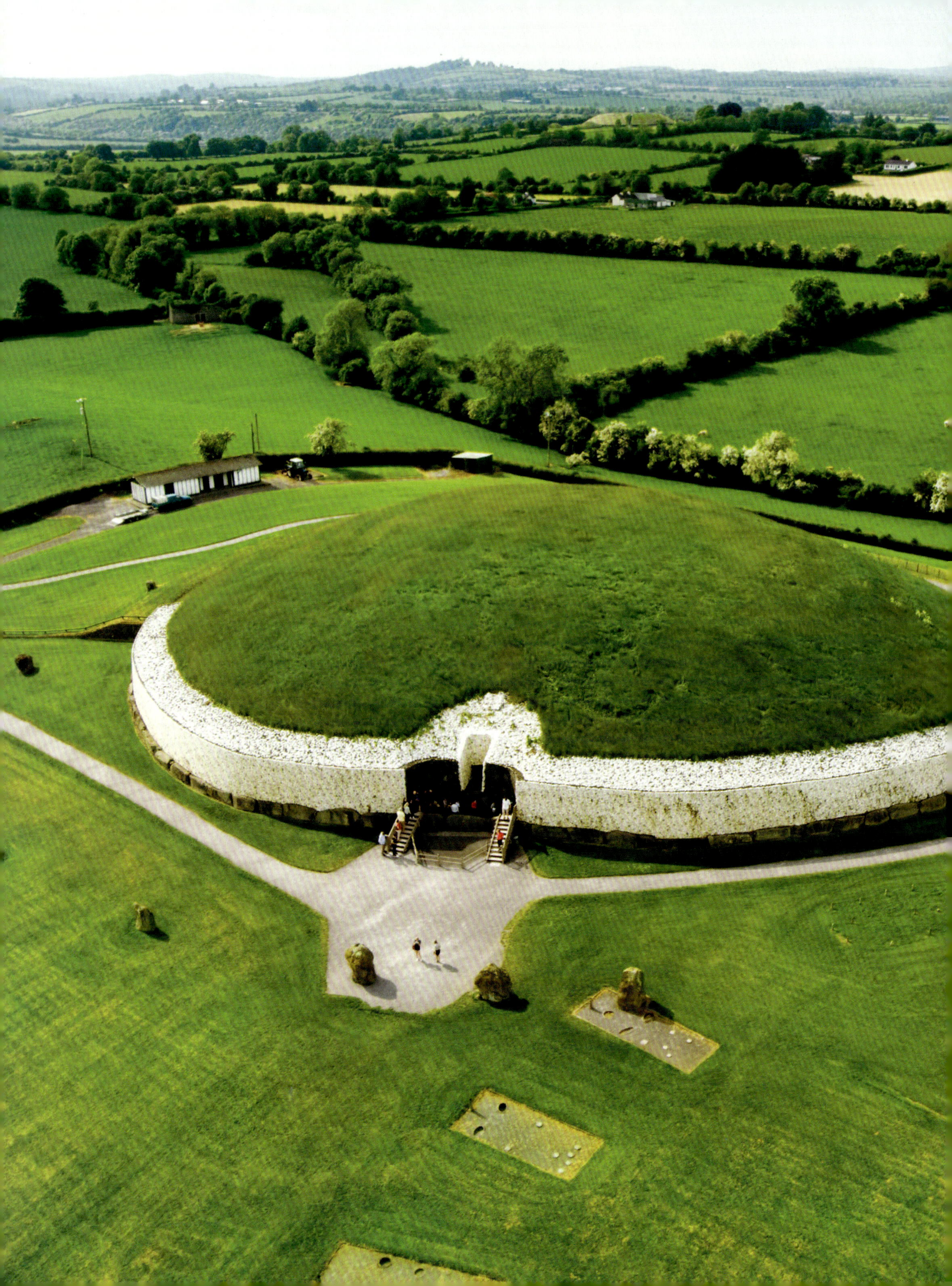

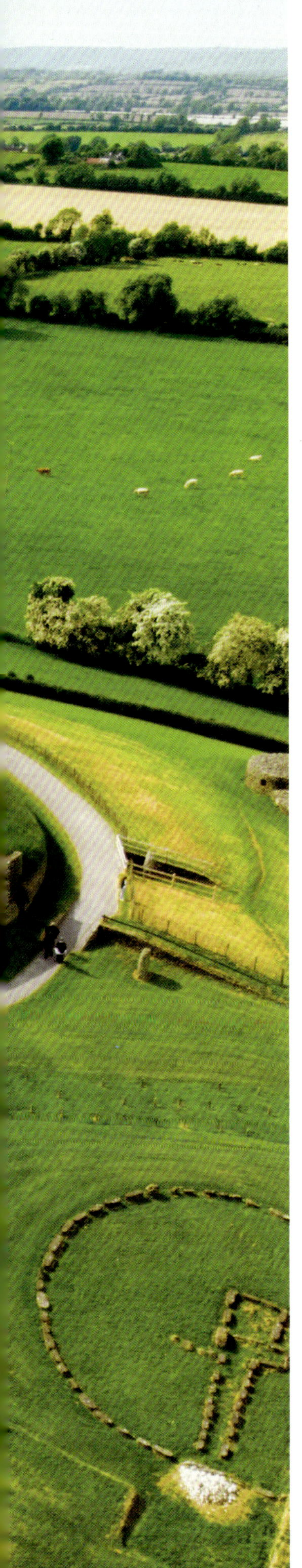

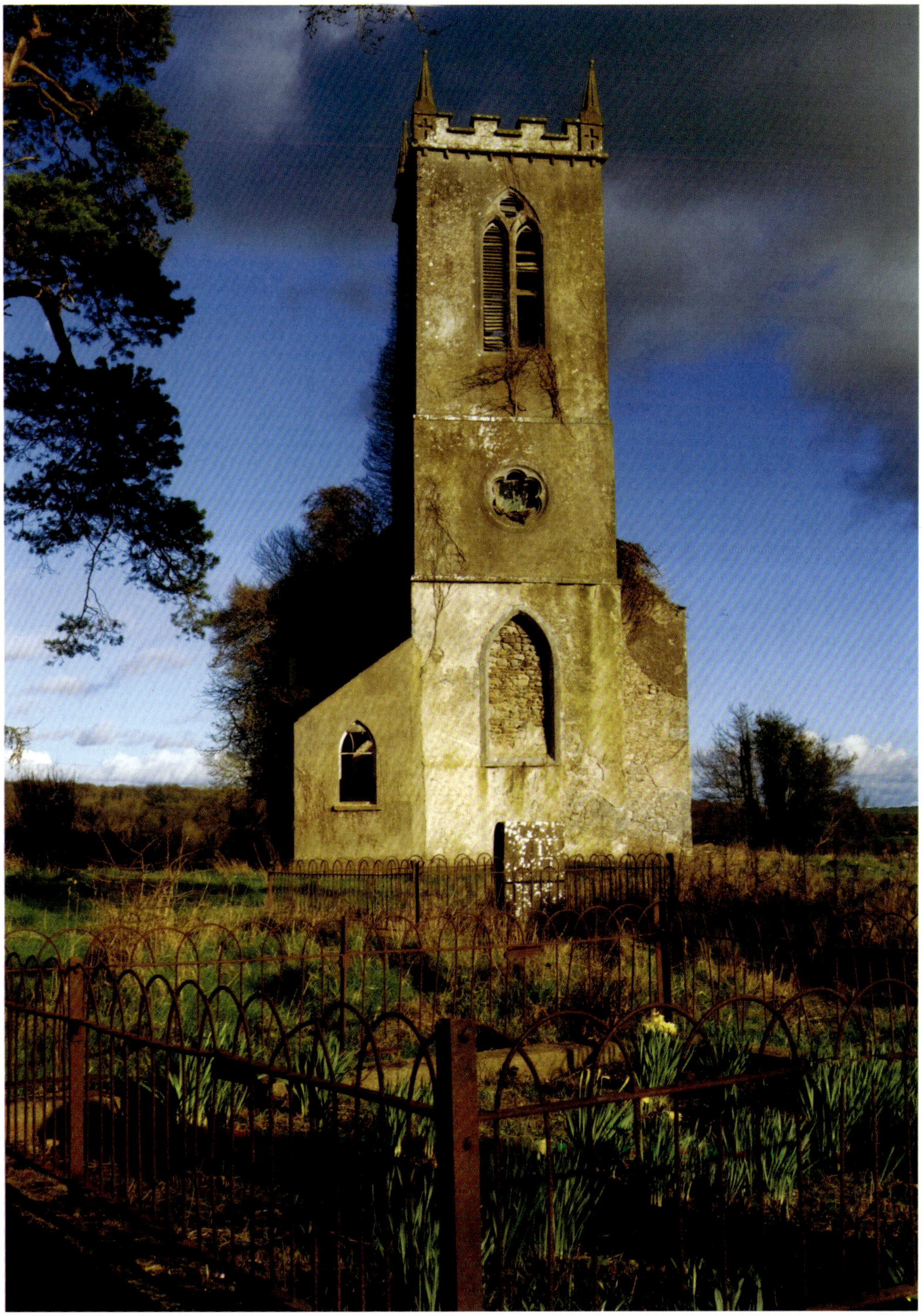

LEFT:

Newgrange, County Meath
Constructed 5200 years ago –
making it older than the Egyptian
Pyramids and Stonehenge –
this tomb was also used as an
astronomical clock. The passage
and chamber within the mound
are aligned with the position of
the rising sun around the winter
solstice, and an aperture allows
sunlight to penetrate those spaces
for 17 minutes on those days.

ABOVE:

**Rathbeagh Church,
County Kilkenny**
This church was desecrated in
the Cromwellian wars of the
17th century. The pond near the
church is called Poll Leabhair
('pond of the book') as, it is said,
the church's liturgical book was
thrown in there by the troops.
Kepple Elias Disney and his wife
Mary – grandparents of Walt
Disney – were from Rathbeagh.

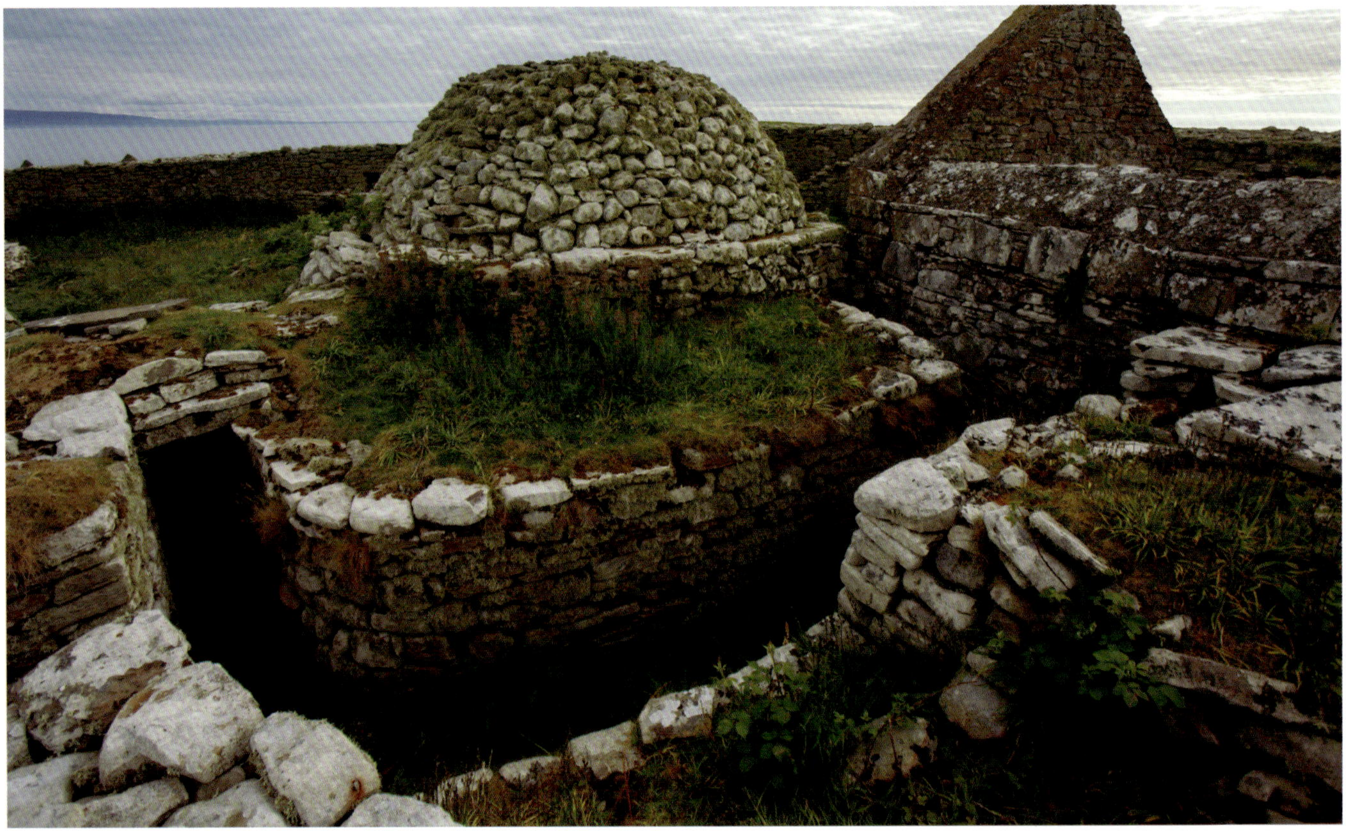

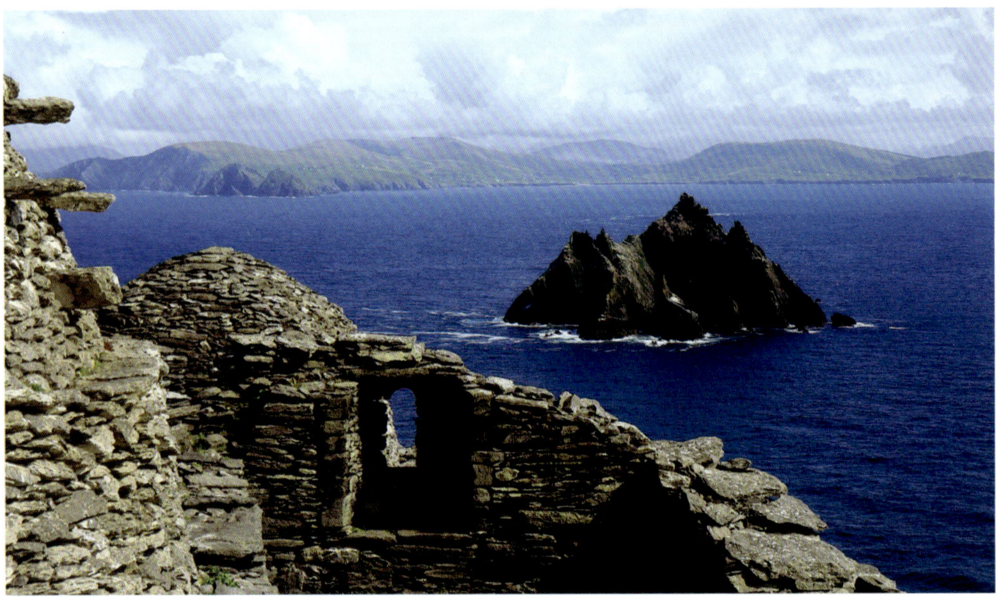

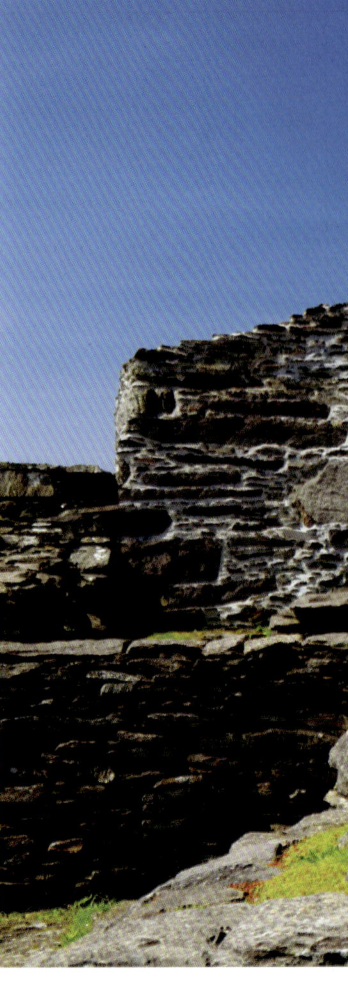

Monastery, Inishmurray Island, County Sligo

Uninhabited it may be today – and a sanctuary only to wildlife – but the remains that exist on Inishmurray show that it was once a thriving community. And very much a sanctuary too for humans, as it was an early Christian settlement. St Molaise founded a monastery there in the 6th century before Vikings raided and the monks left. It then remained uninhabited until it was settled by farmers in around the 12th century. Its population peaked at just over 100 in the 1880s. The last remaining inhabitants left in 1948. Early medieval graves can be seen at the monastic site, as well as the remains of various ecclesiastical buildings and a holy well. There are also dry-stone 'beehive huts', the traditional shelters for early Christian monks.

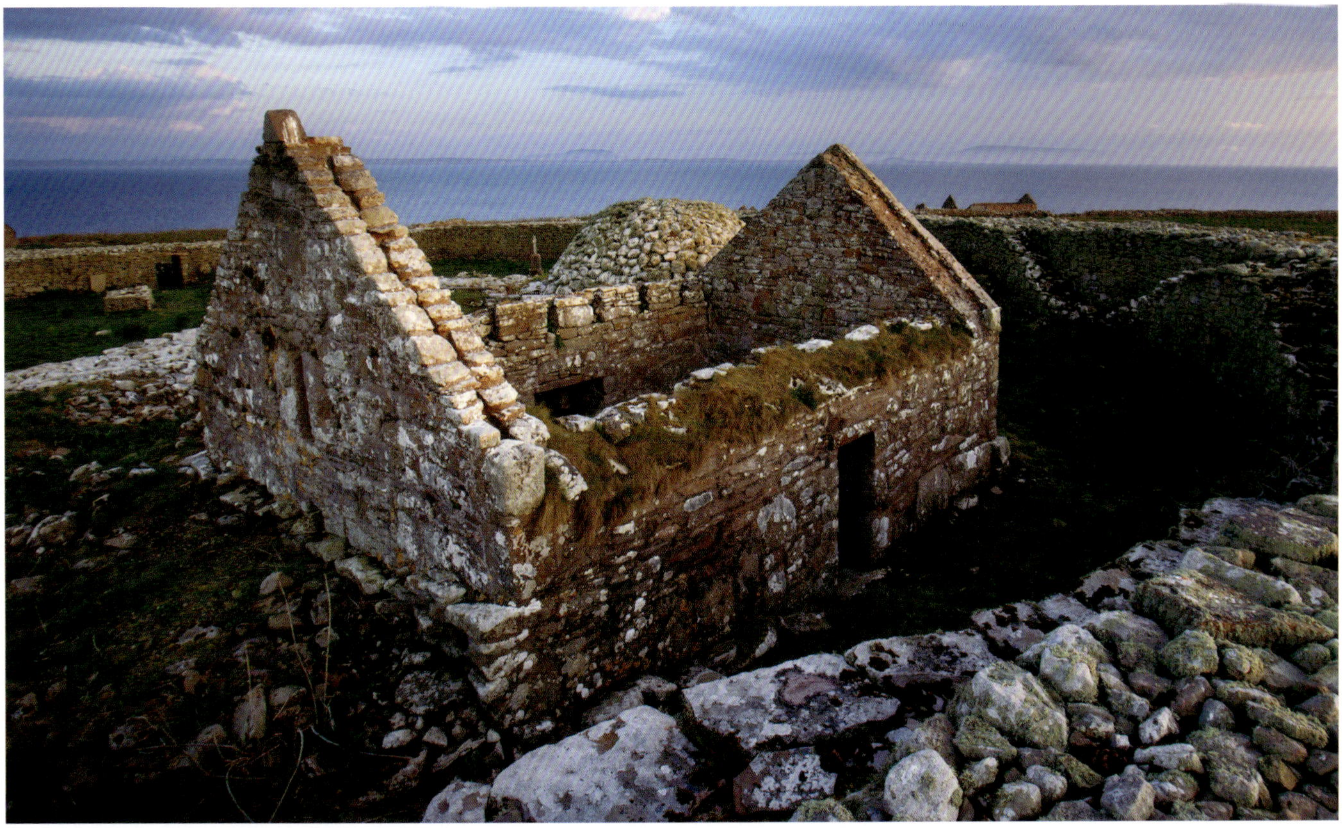

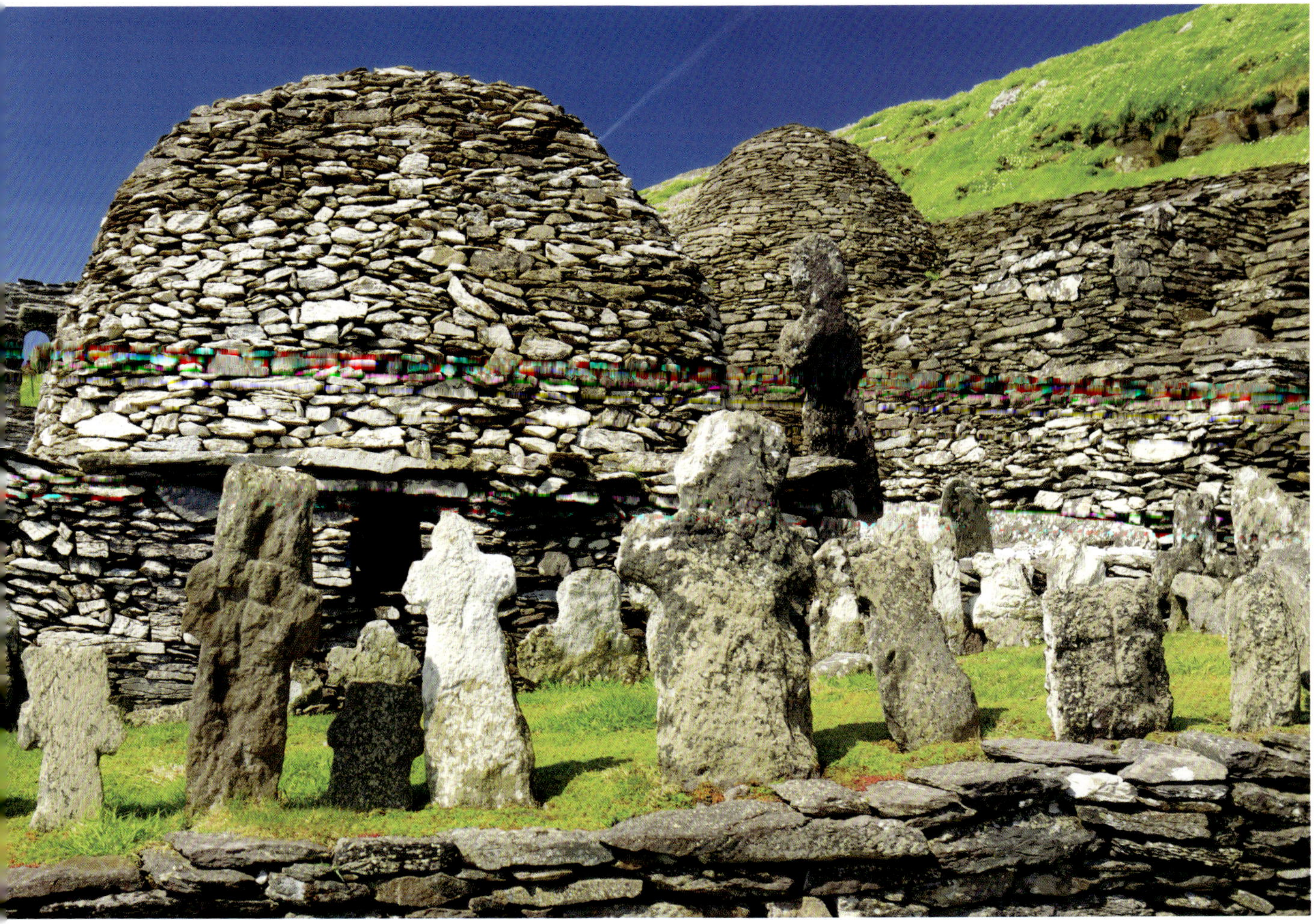

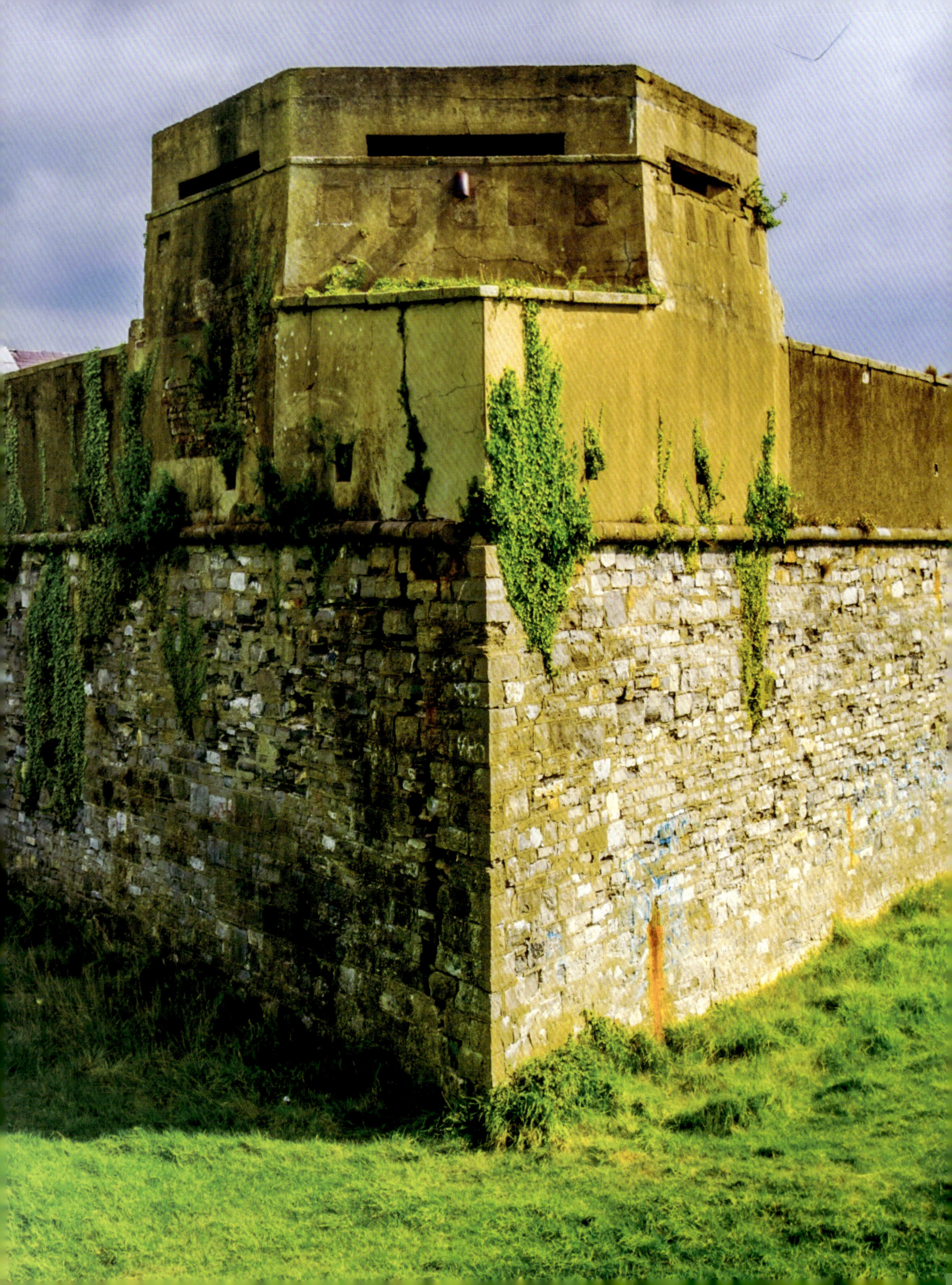

Military Sites

Ireland's historical forts, towers, lookouts and military bases tell a story of various conflicts down the centuries that have taken place on its fields, around its shores, and in its villages, towns and cities. Even off the coasts there are reminders of when Ireland was threatened by attack. However, much of this military infrastructure was built – or ordered – by the British, whose sovereignty over parts of Ireland began as long ago as the 12th century, when the Anglo-Norman invasion assumed control over vast tracts. Later, the British conquest and colonization of Ireland, from the Tudor era onwards, led to the Crown moving to protect its interests with a series of military installations, many of which exist to this day, albeit no longer fulfilling their original purpose. Because of this legacy we have Ireland's distinctive Martello towers and multi-sided forts, and their varying fortunes over the years shed light on the changes over time across Ireland, as the Irish Republic finally gained complete independence from Britain and Northern Ireland remained part of the United Kingdom. Yet, as evidence of people's desire to continually repurpose, some of the startling structures here have remained in use even into the 21st century.

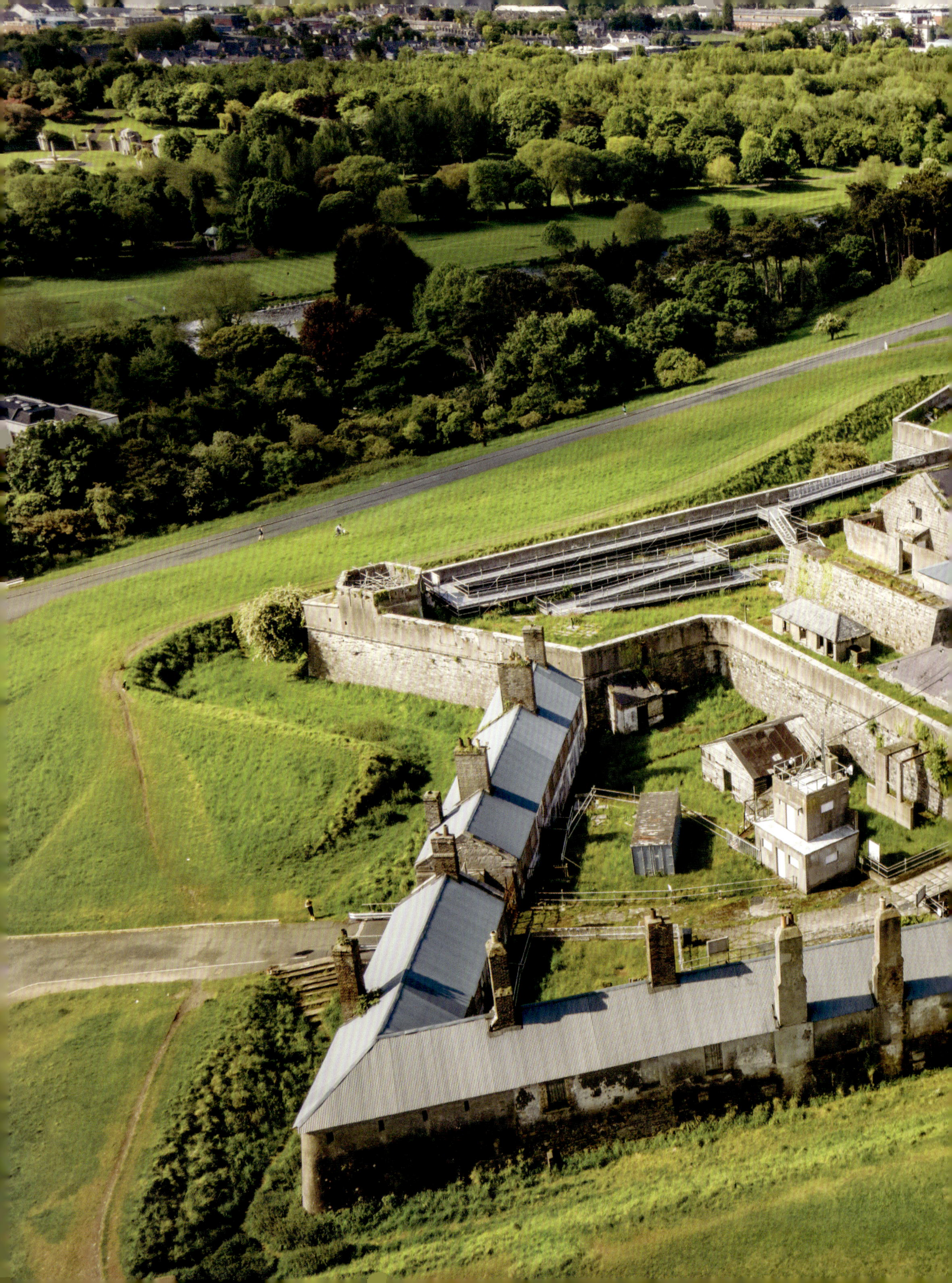

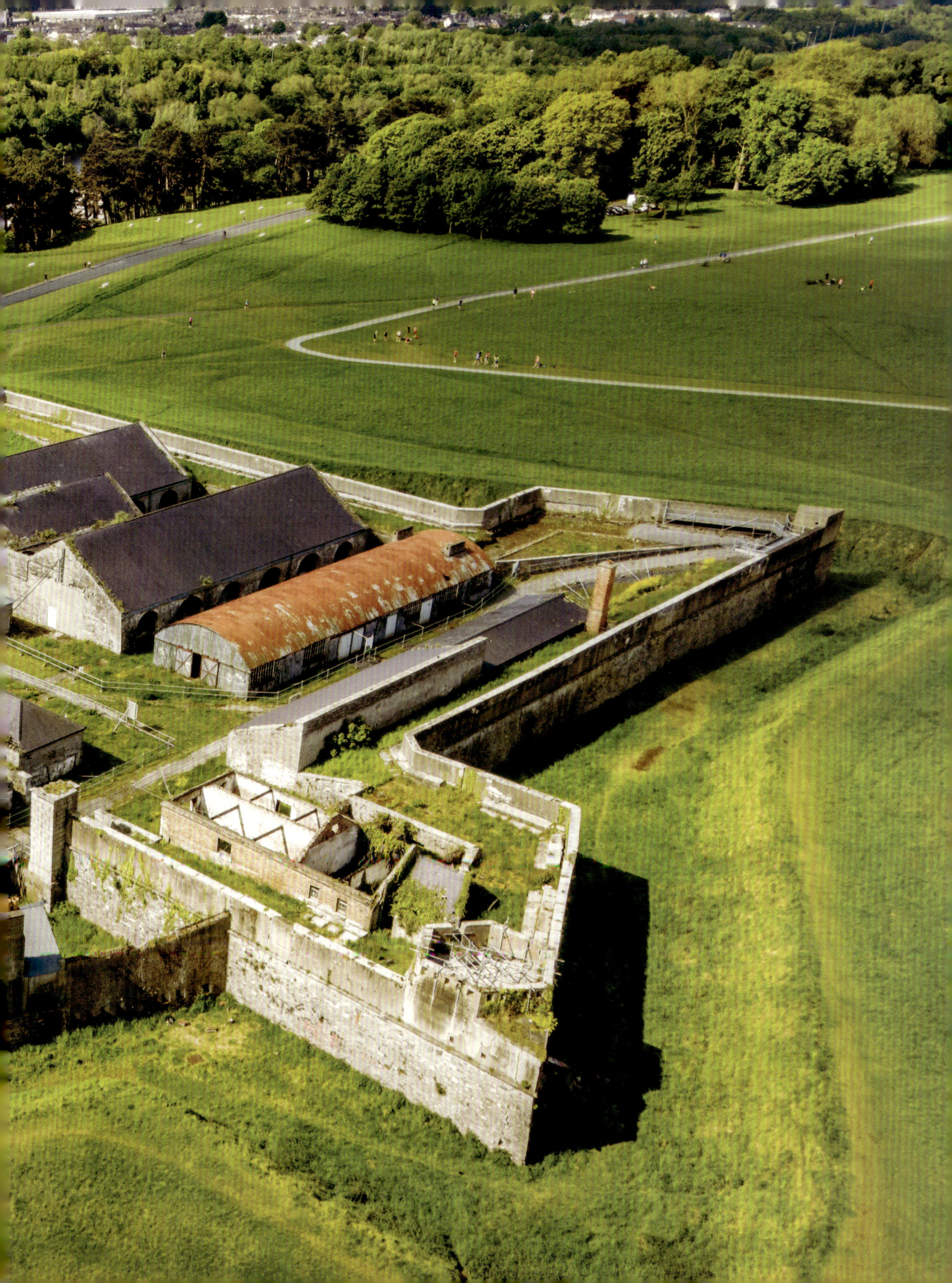

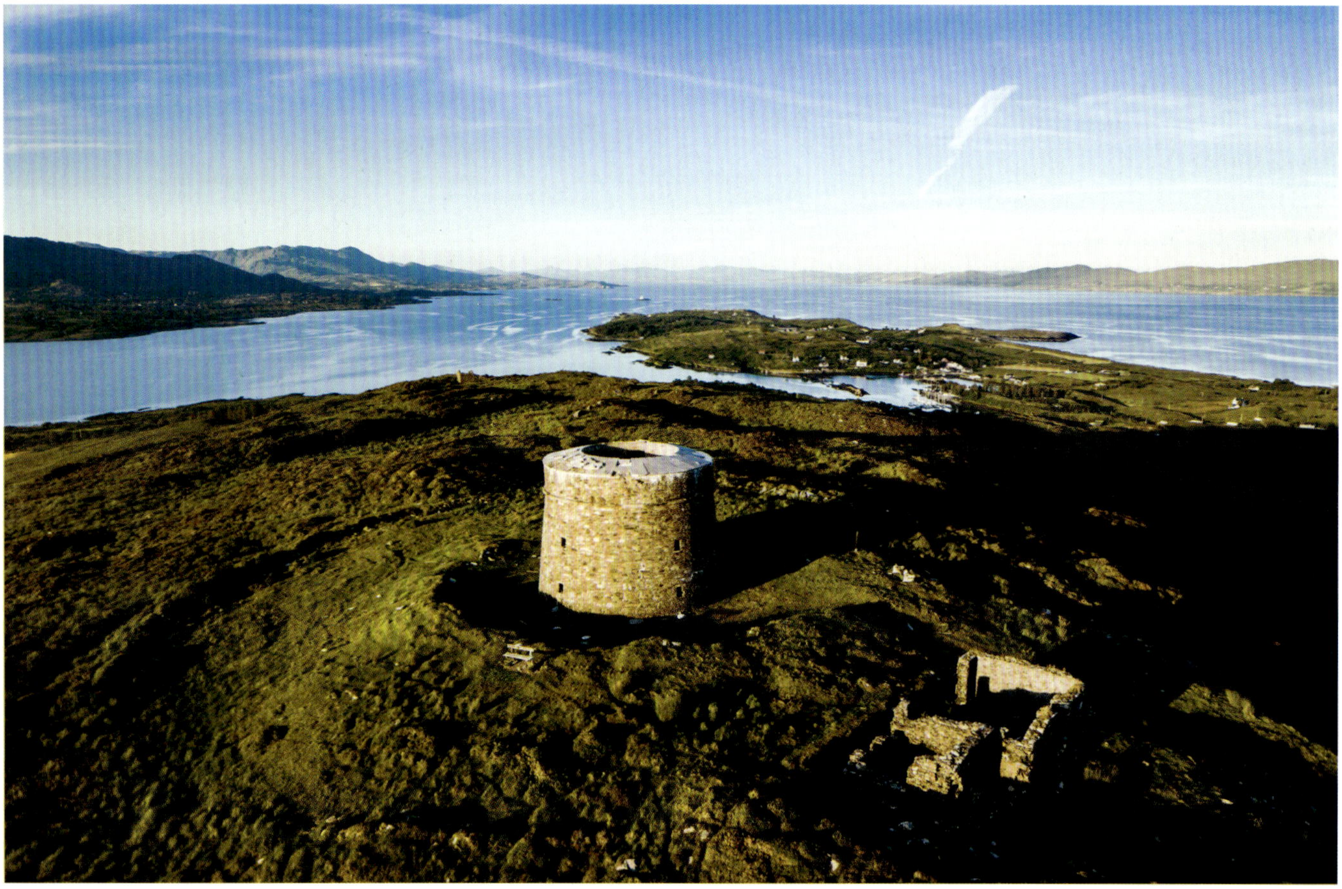

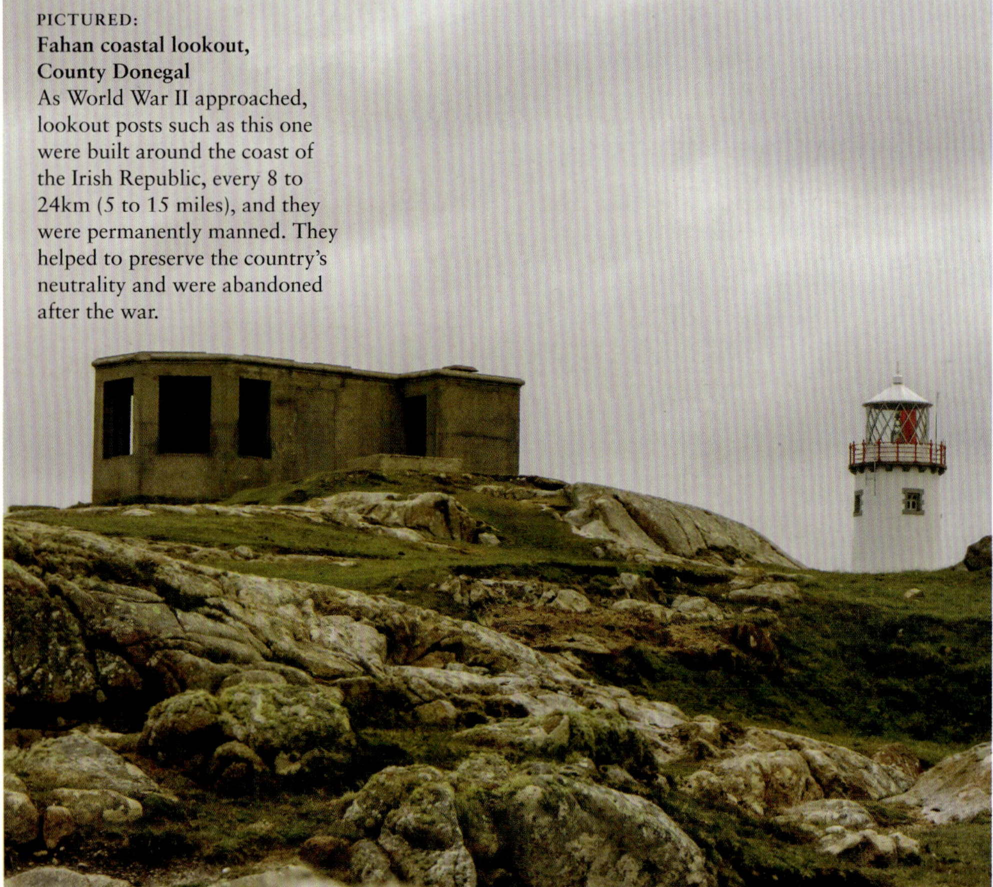

Fahan coastal lookout, County Donegal
As World War II approached, lookout posts such as this one were built around the coast of the Irish Republic, every 8 to 24km (5 to 15 miles), and they were permanently manned. They helped to preserve the country's neutrality and were abandoned after the war.

ABOVE:
Bere Island Fort, County Cork
In the early 19th century, after a French armada had entered Cork's Bantry Bay, the British military built a number of Martello towers on the bay's Bere Island. The forts could accommodate a garrison and withstand cannon fire but also accommodate cannons themselves. The British had first encountered such towers on Corsica in 1794 – in a campaign against the French.

OPPOSITE:
Brow Head Signal Station, County Cork
At the southernmost point of mainland Ireland stands one of the early 19th-century signal towers that the British built around the coast to look out for Napoleonic invaders. The signal towers' distinctive look comes from the weather-proof slates that were used on the exterior.

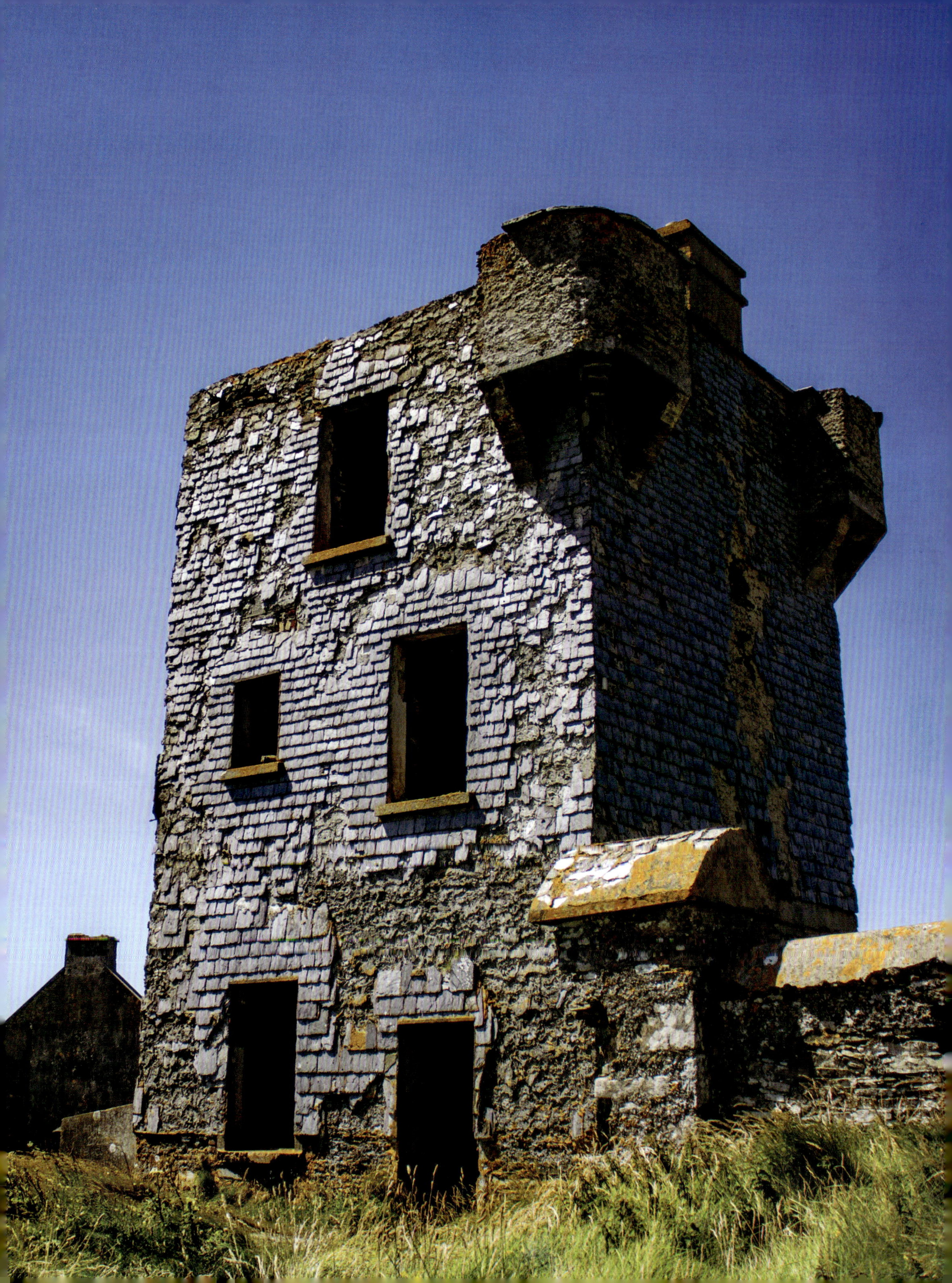

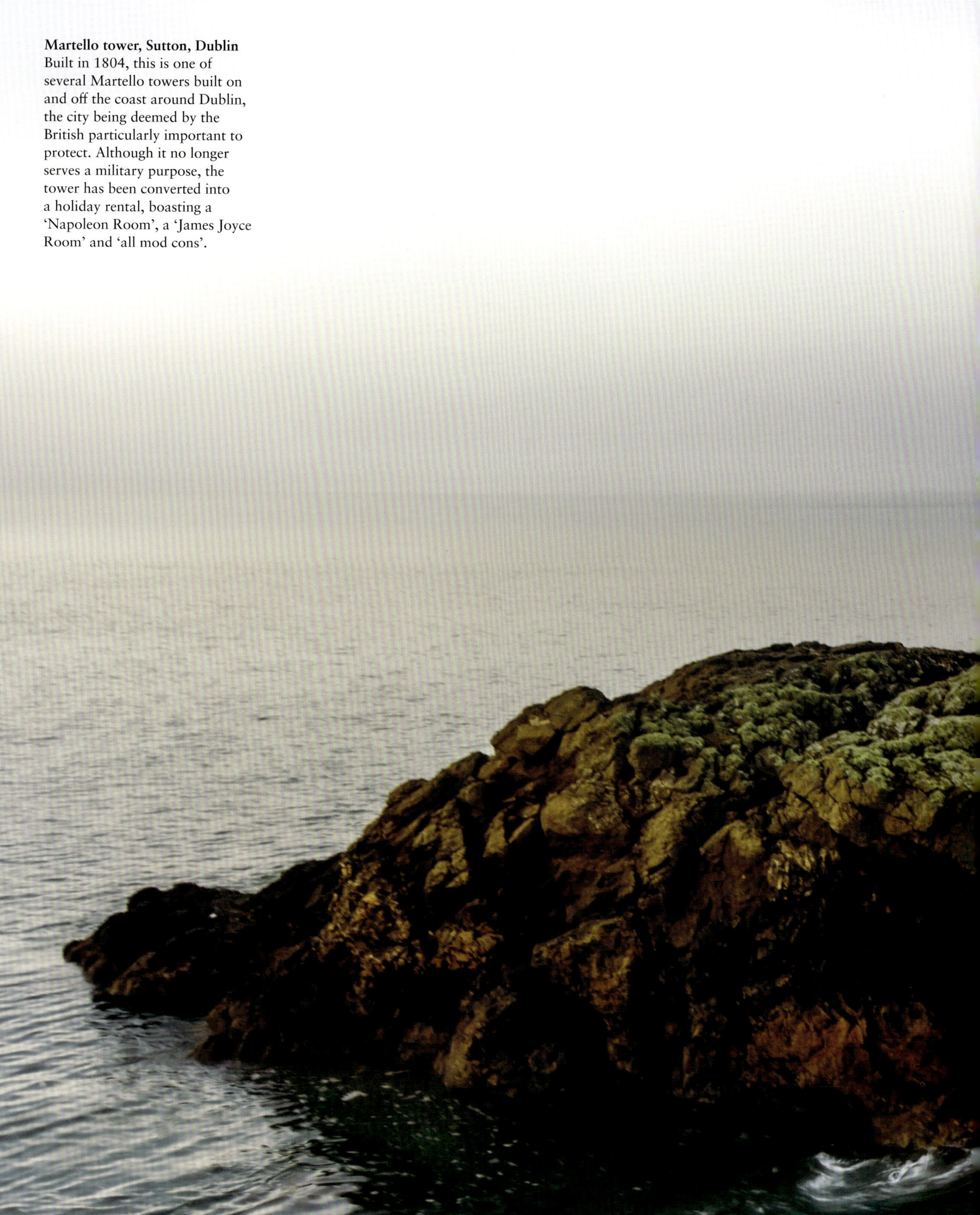

Martello tower, Sutton, Dublin
Built in 1804, this is one of
several Martello towers built on
and off the coast around Dublin,
the city being deemed by the
British particularly important to
protect. Although it no longer
serves a military purpose, the
tower has been converted into
a holiday rental, boasting a
'Napoleon Room', a 'James Joyce
Room' and 'all mod cons'.

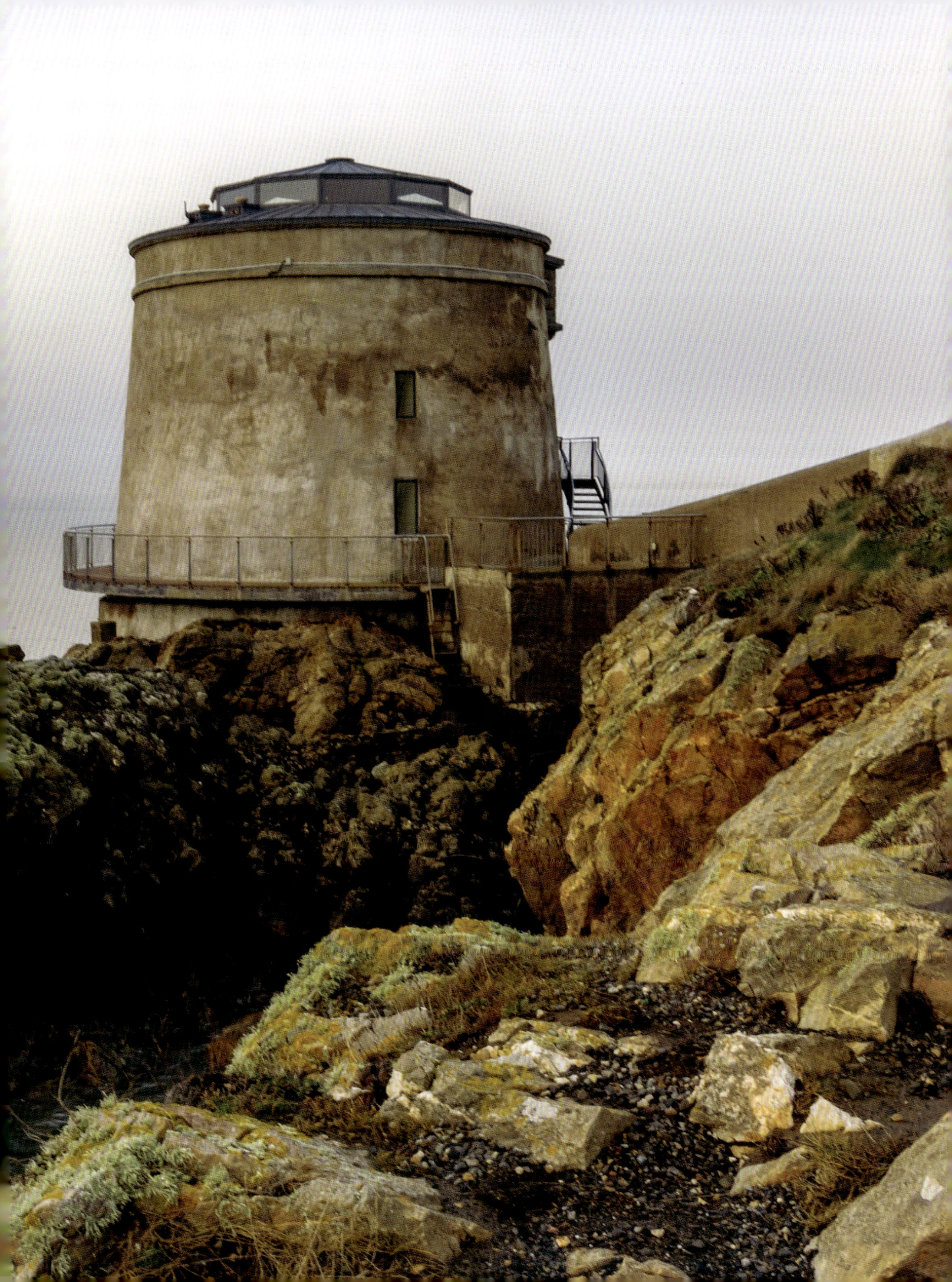

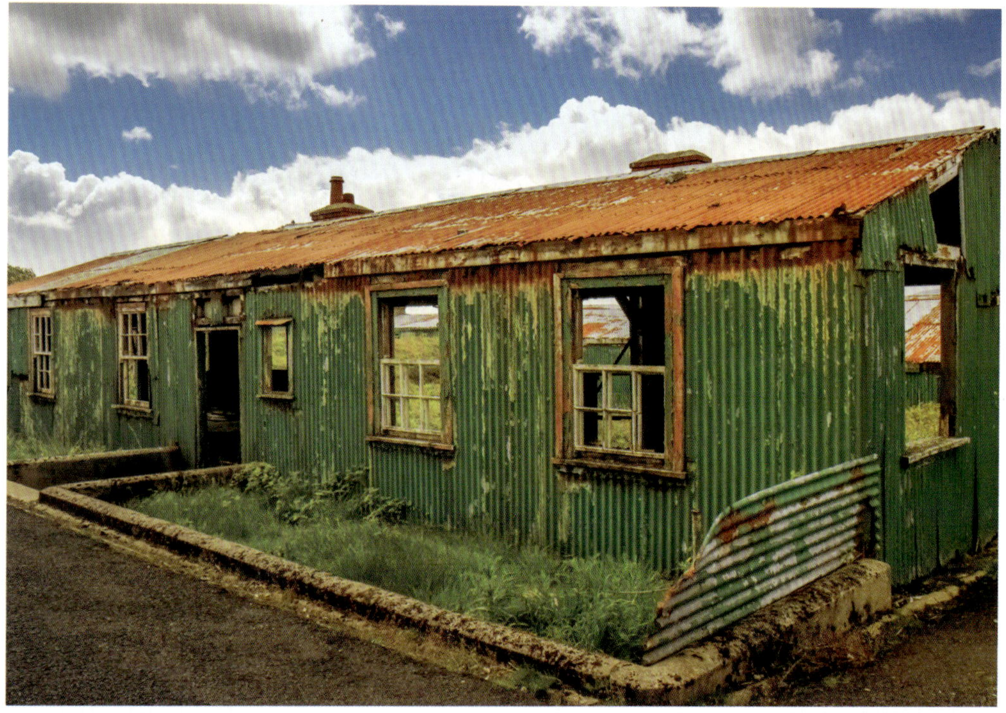

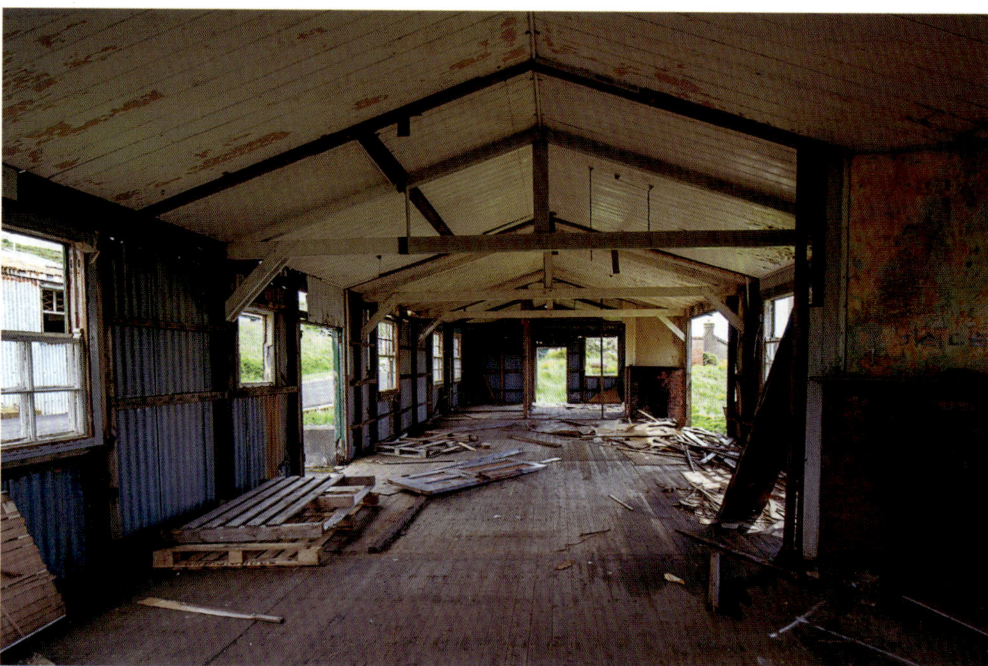

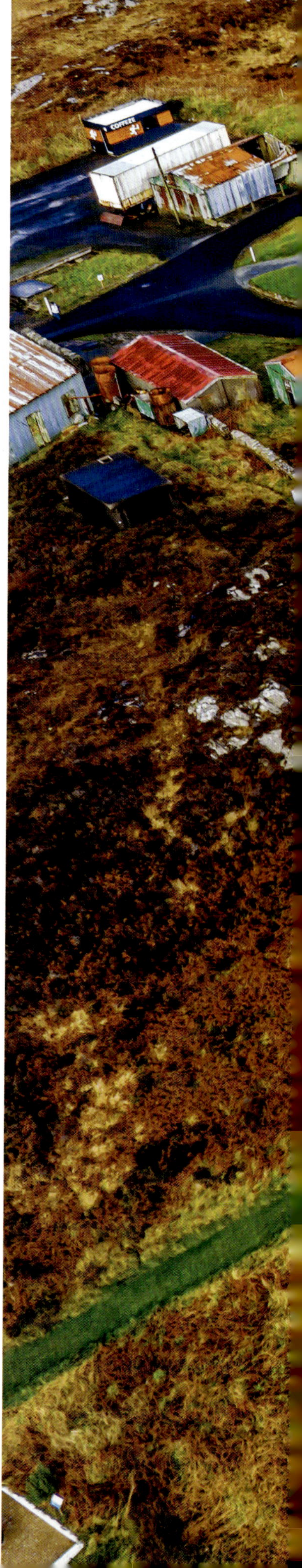

ALL PHOTOGRAPHS:

Fort Dunree, County Donegal

This complex started to be built as the 19th century became the 20th, and the buildings were used as barracks, stores, workshops, messes, a canteen, miliary hospital and even a chapel. The corrugated-iron structures were an addition to the 18th-century Fort Dunree, which was built after Irish revolutionary Wolfe Tone had tried to land with a French fleet at nearby Lough Swilly, in his attempt to end British rule.

Lough Swilly was later used to anchor British ships during World War I. The fort was handed over to the Irish Free State in 1938 and now operates as a museum. Adjoining the site of the derelict buildings is a heritage centre, art gallery and cafe.

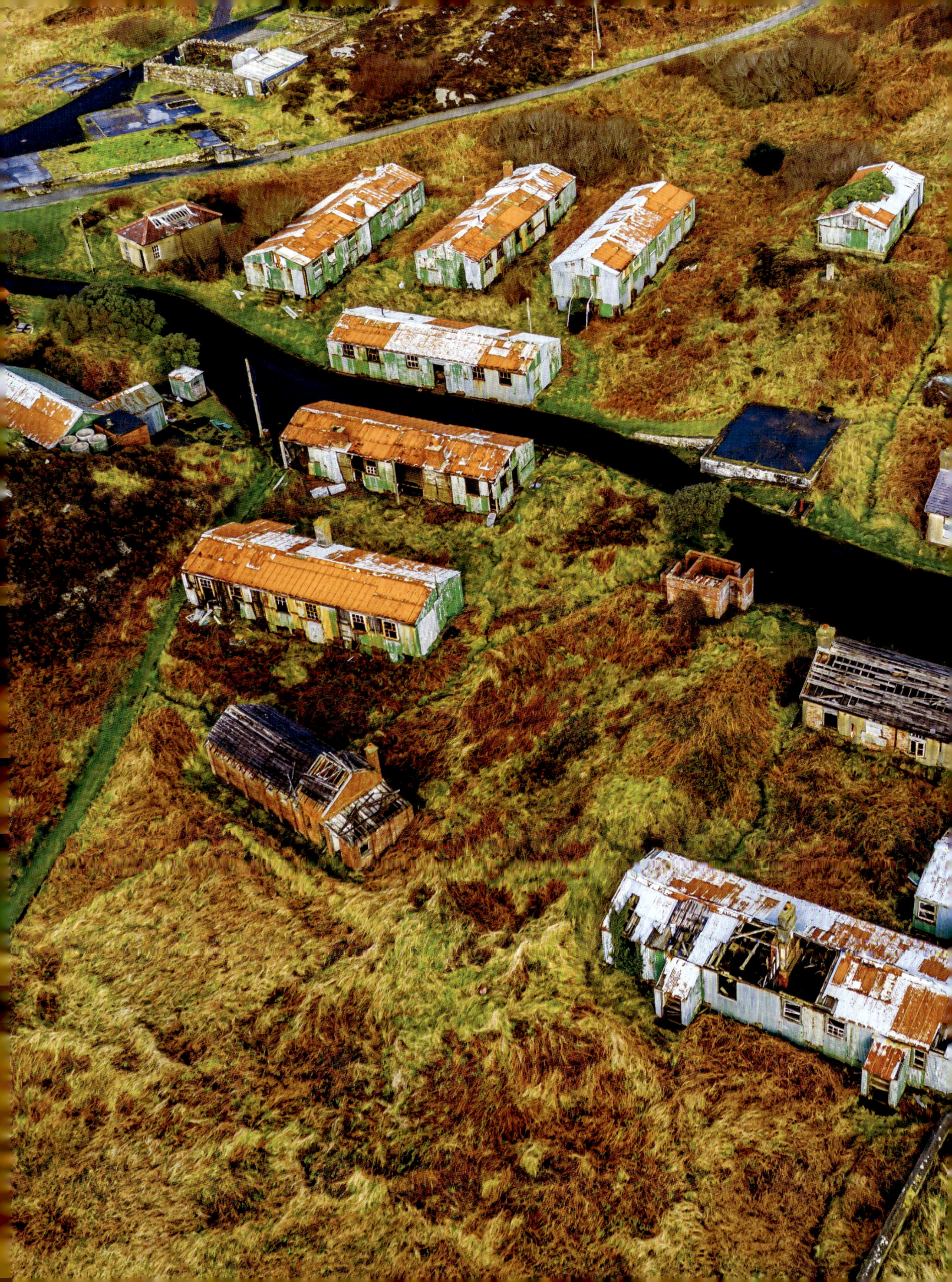

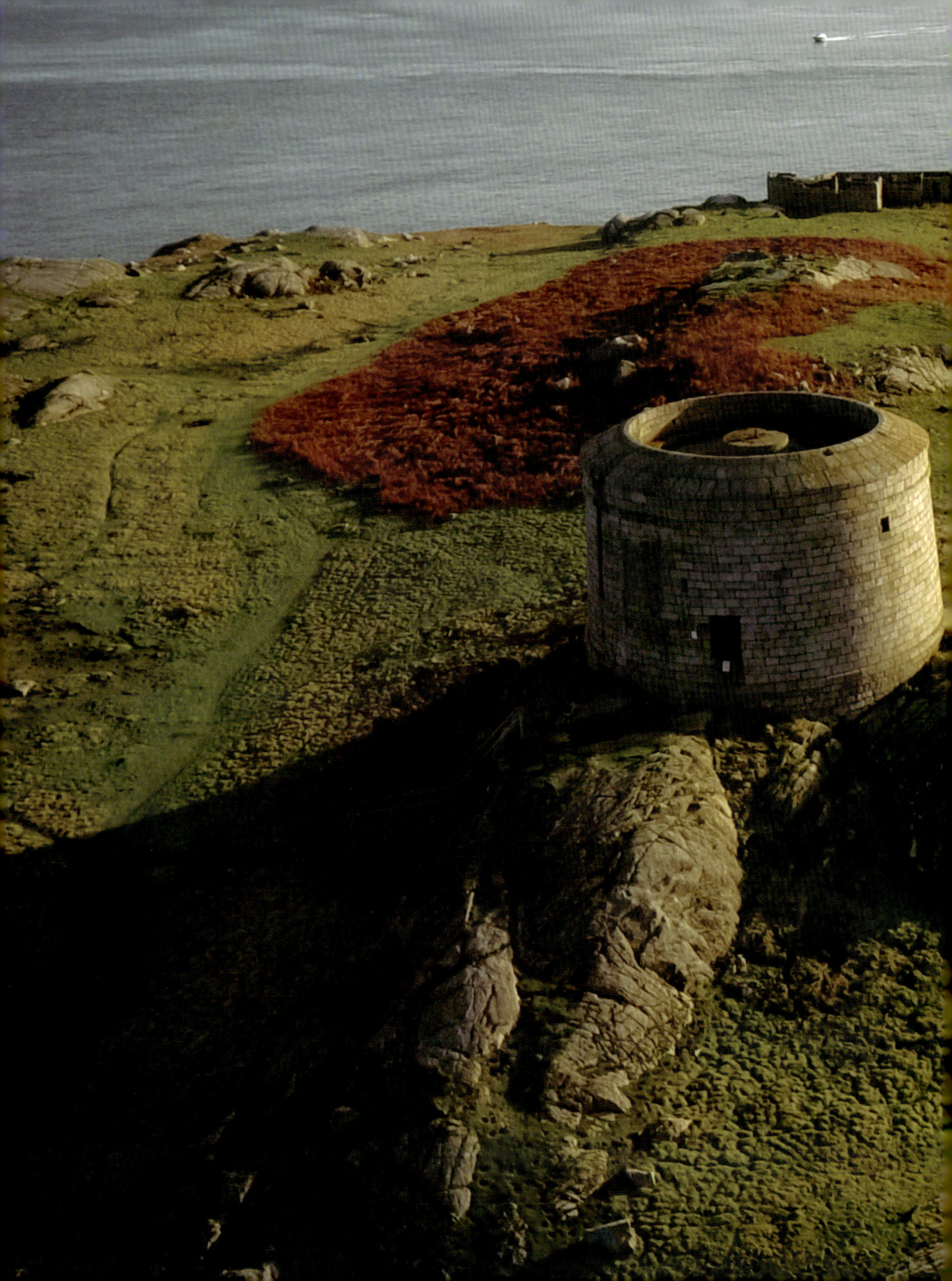

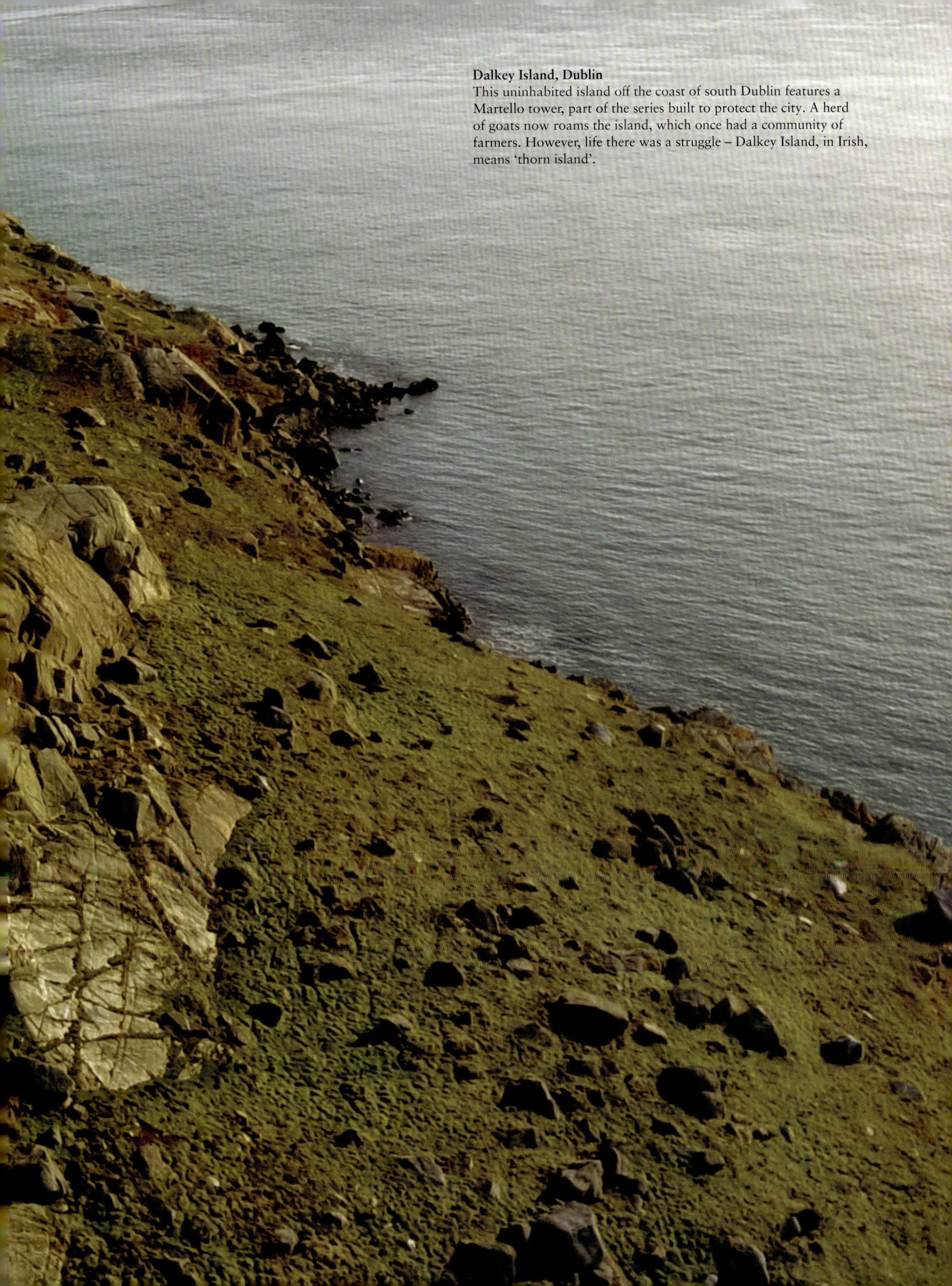

Dalkey Island, Dublin
This uninhabited island off the coast of south Dublin features a
Martello tower, part of the series built to protect the city. A herd
of goats now roams the island, which once had a community of
farmers. However, life there was a struggle – Dalkey Island, in Irish,
means 'thorn island'.

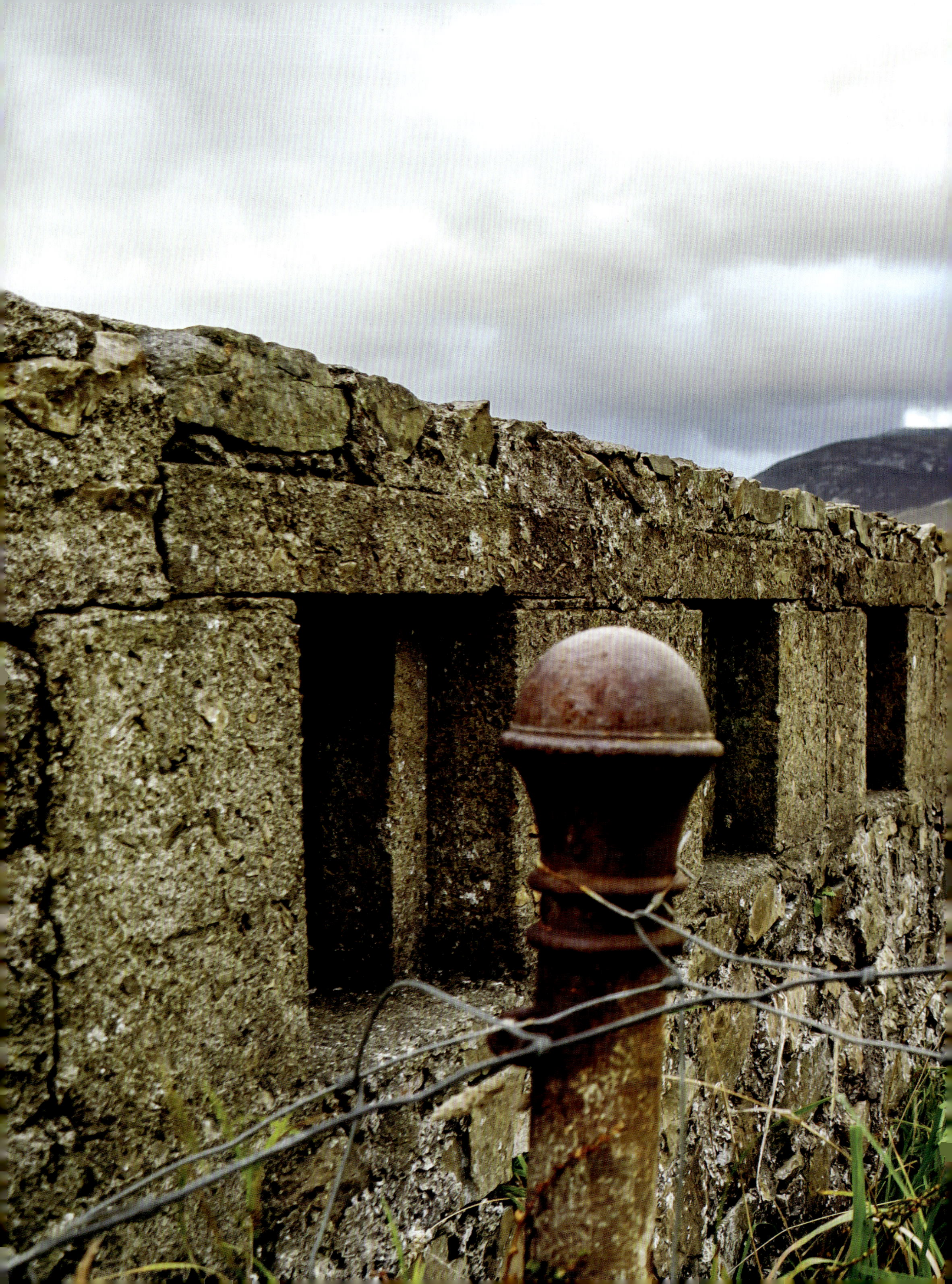

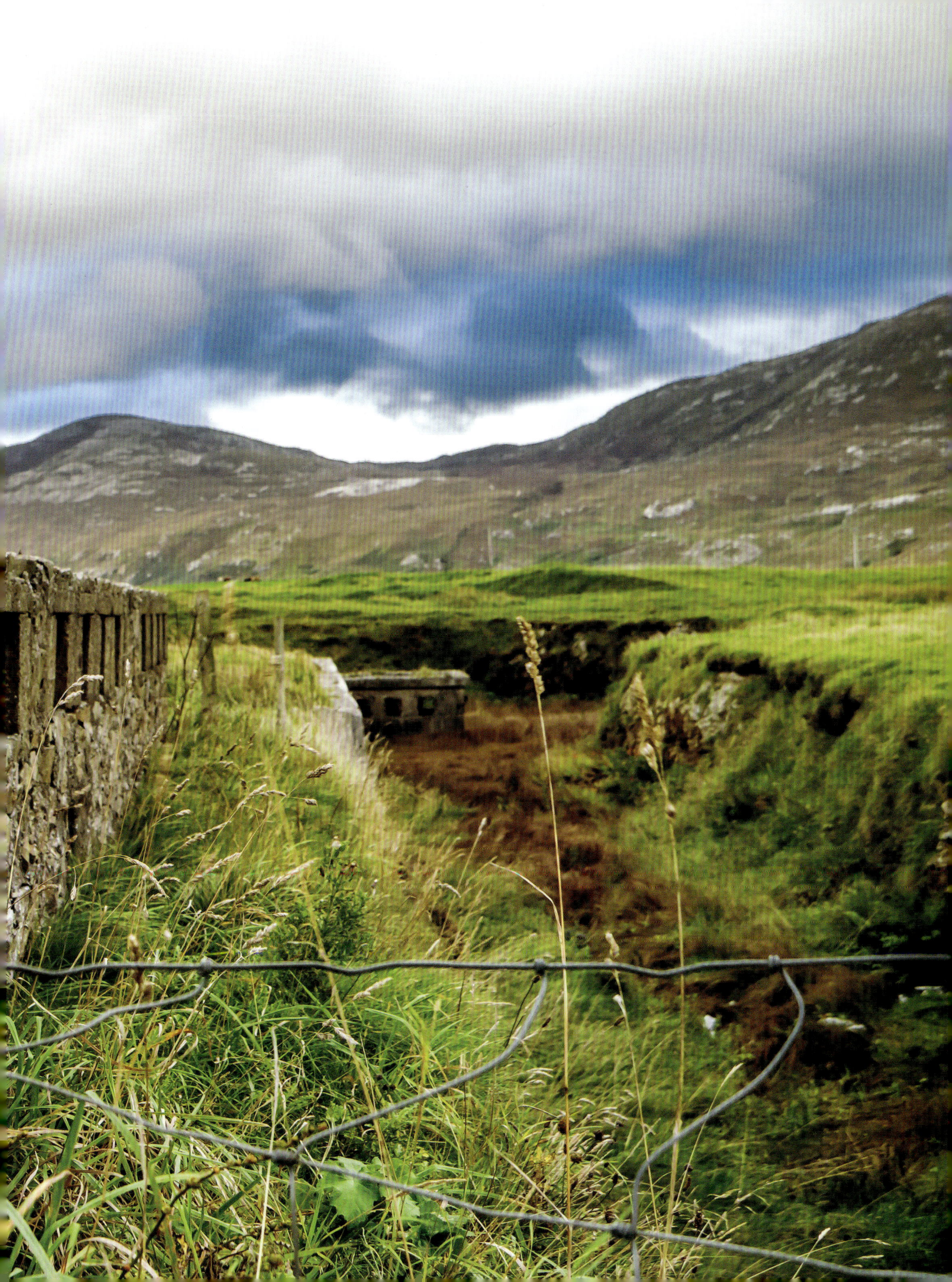

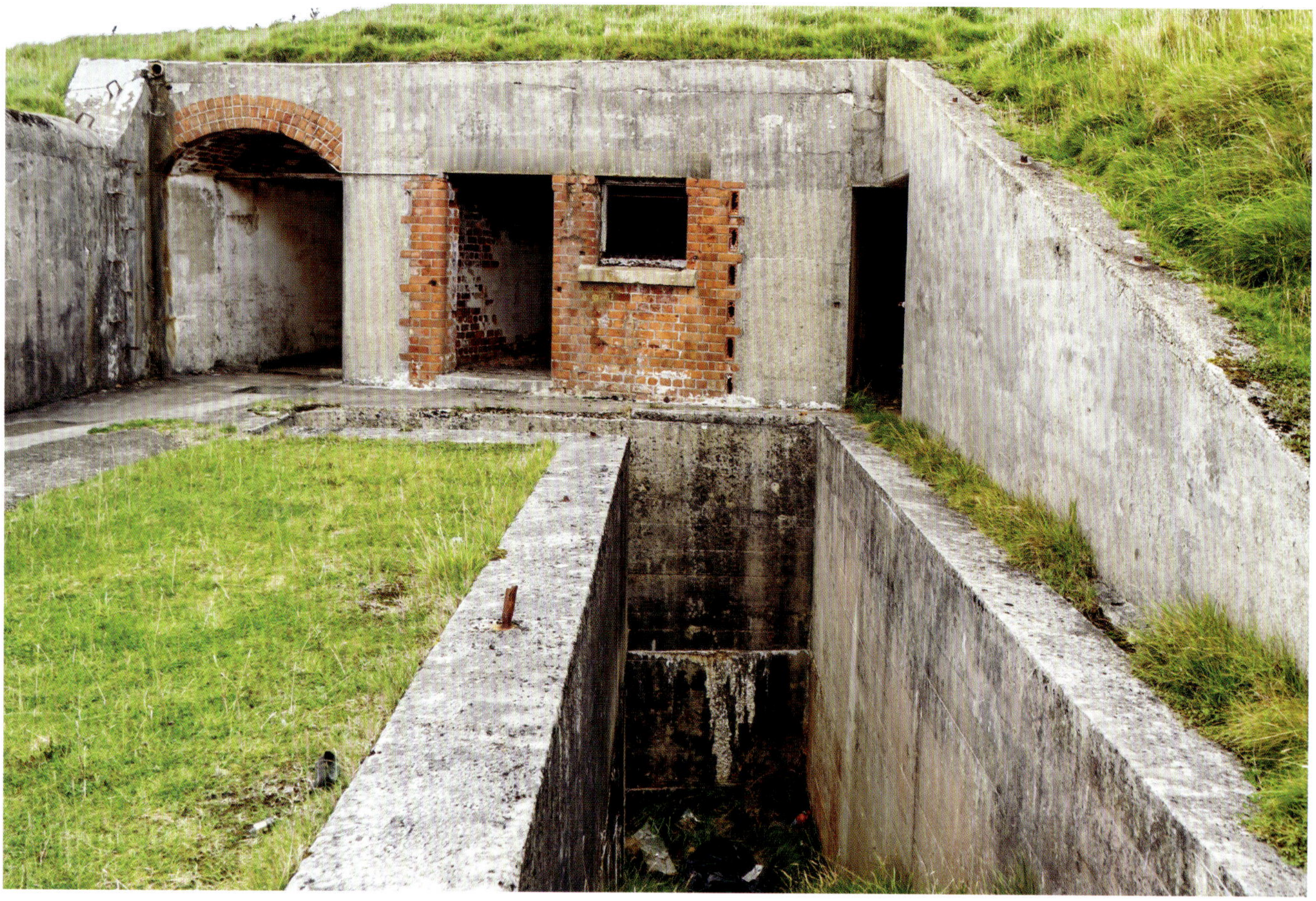

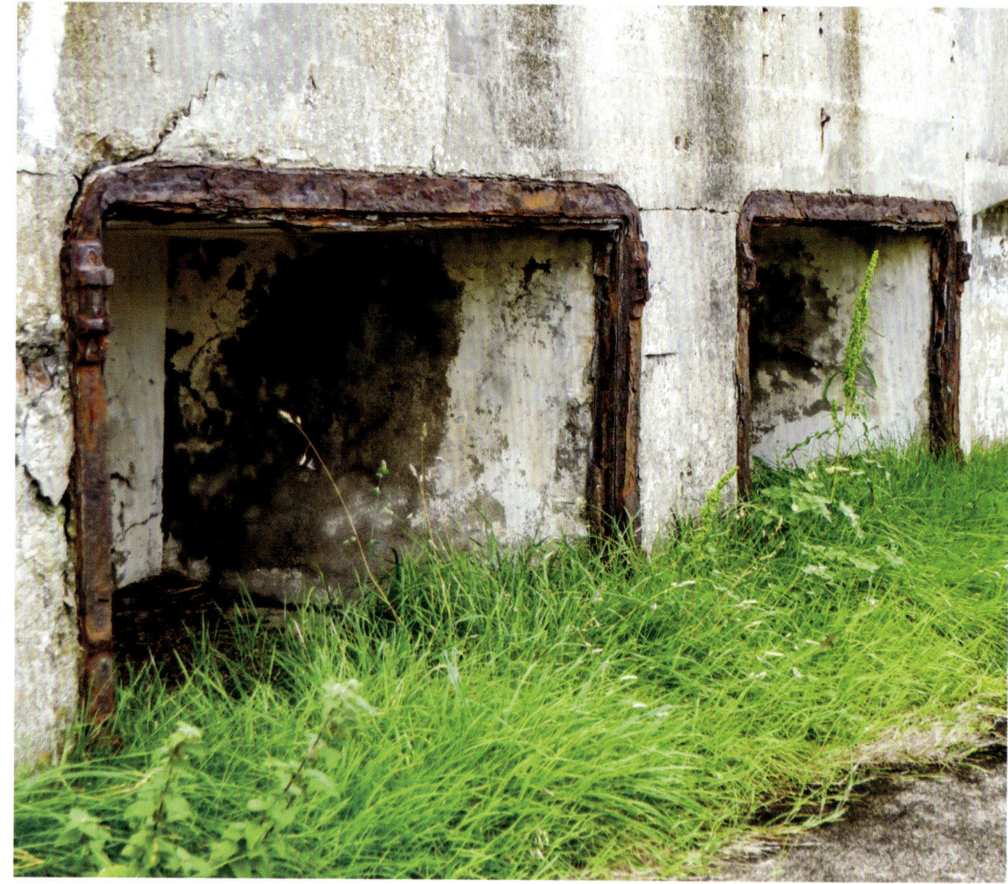

**Lenan Head Fort,
County Donegal**
Built in 1895 to protect Lough
Swilly, Lenan Head Fort – like
Fort Dunree – was handed to
the Irish state in 1938, and
then decommissioned in 1952.
Lough Swilly was one of the
three 'treaty ports' retained by
the United Kingdom in the 1921
Anglo-Irish Treaty – the others
were at Berehaven and Spike
Island off County Cork. Lenan
Head Fort's water tower and
fortifications still remain.

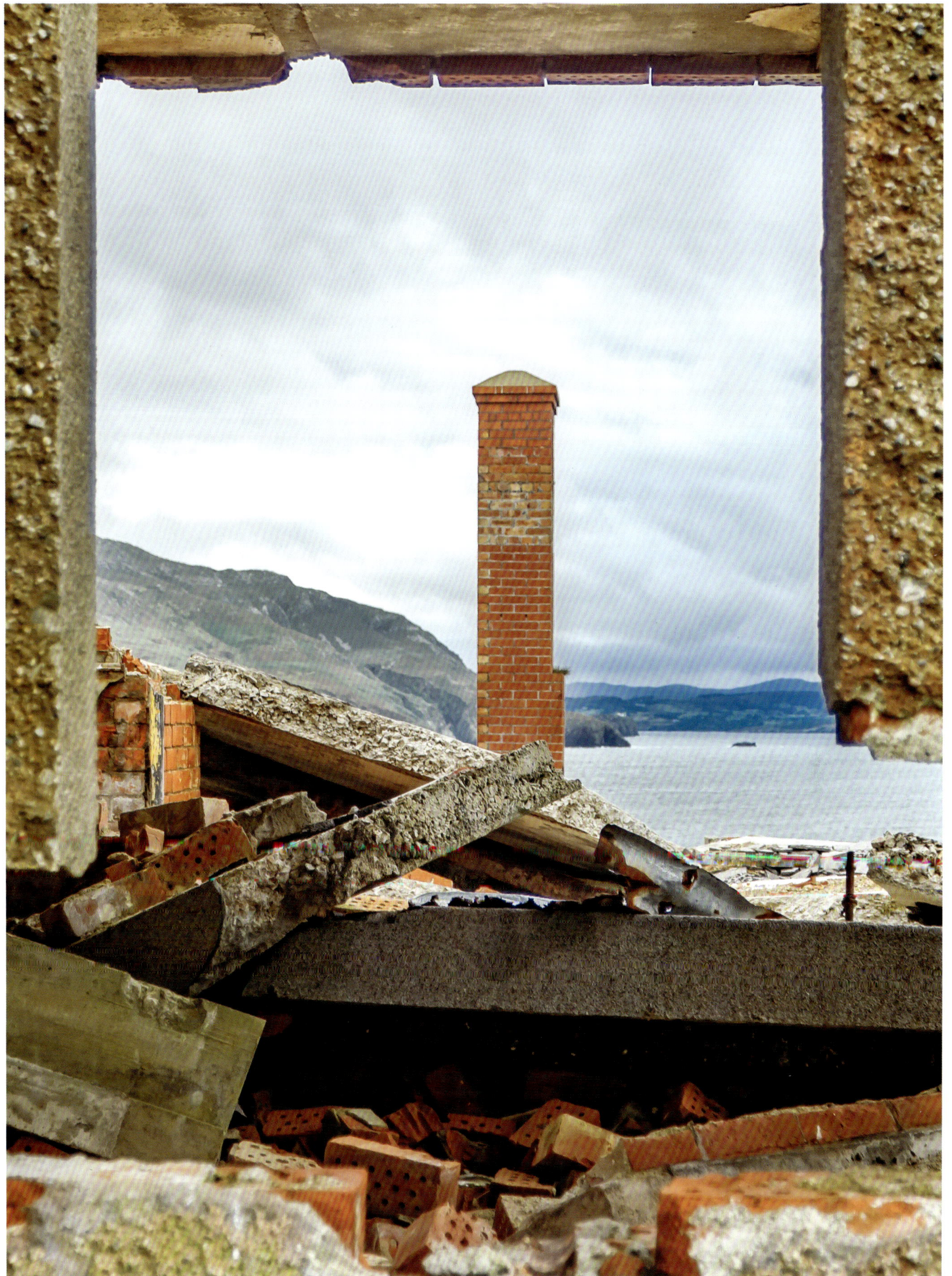

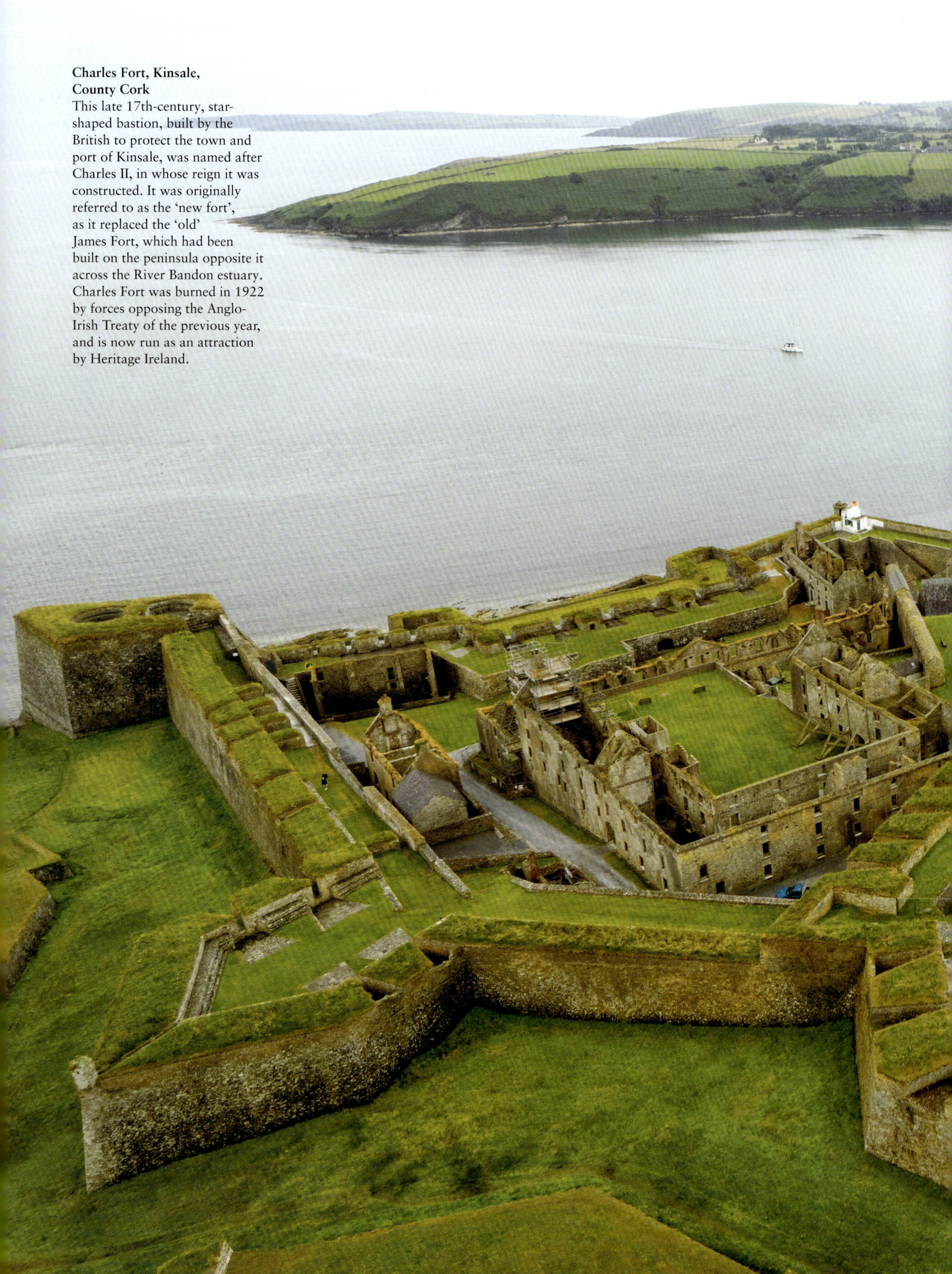

Charles Fort, Kinsale,
County Cork
This late 17th-century, star-shaped bastion, built by the British to protect the town and port of Kinsale, was named after Charles II, in whose reign it was constructed. It was originally referred to as the 'new fort', as it replaced the 'old' James Fort, which had been built on the peninsula opposite it across the River Bandon estuary. Charles Fort was burned in 1922 by forces opposing the Anglo-Irish Treaty of the previous year, and is now run as an attraction by Heritage Ireland.

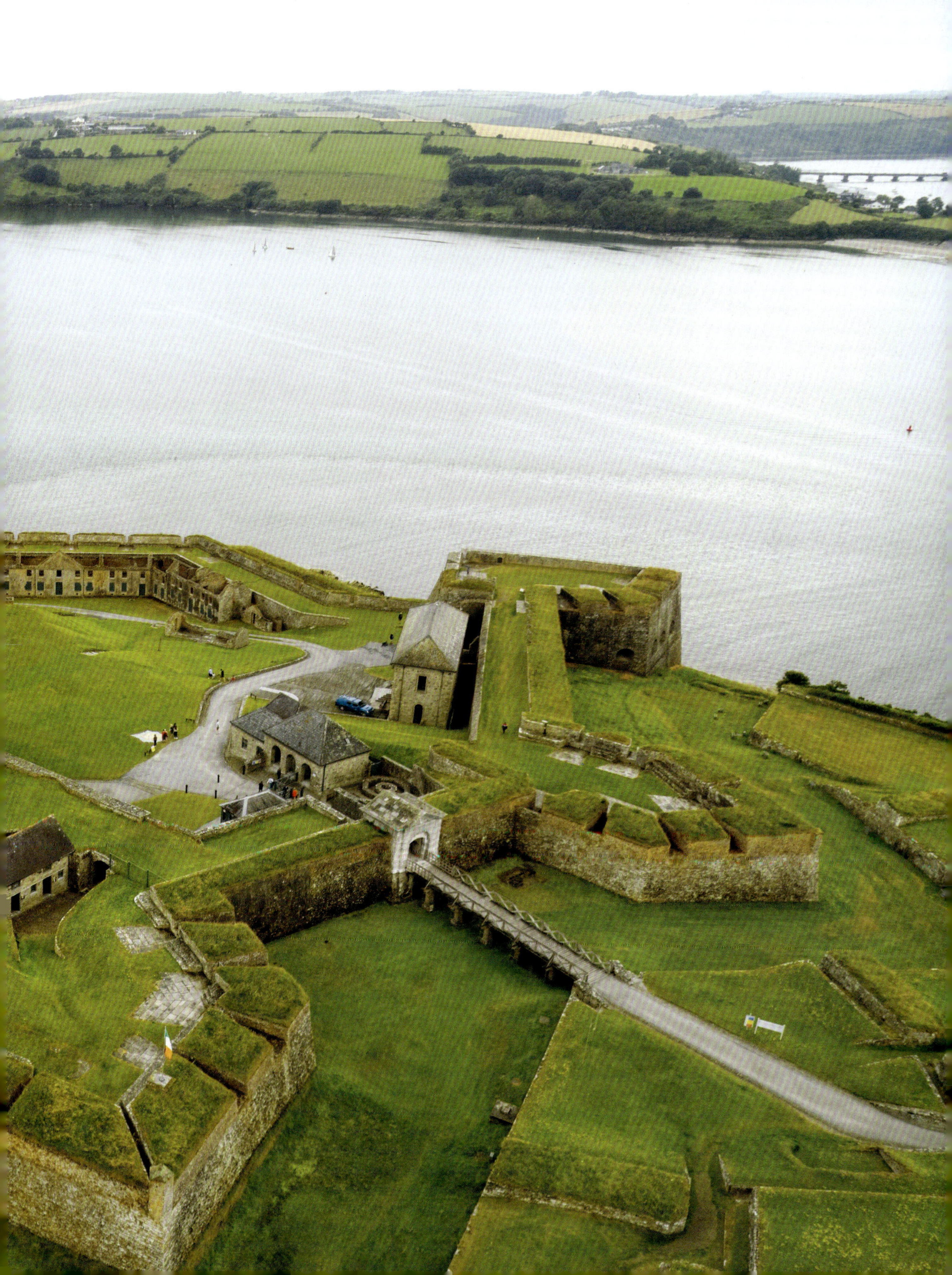

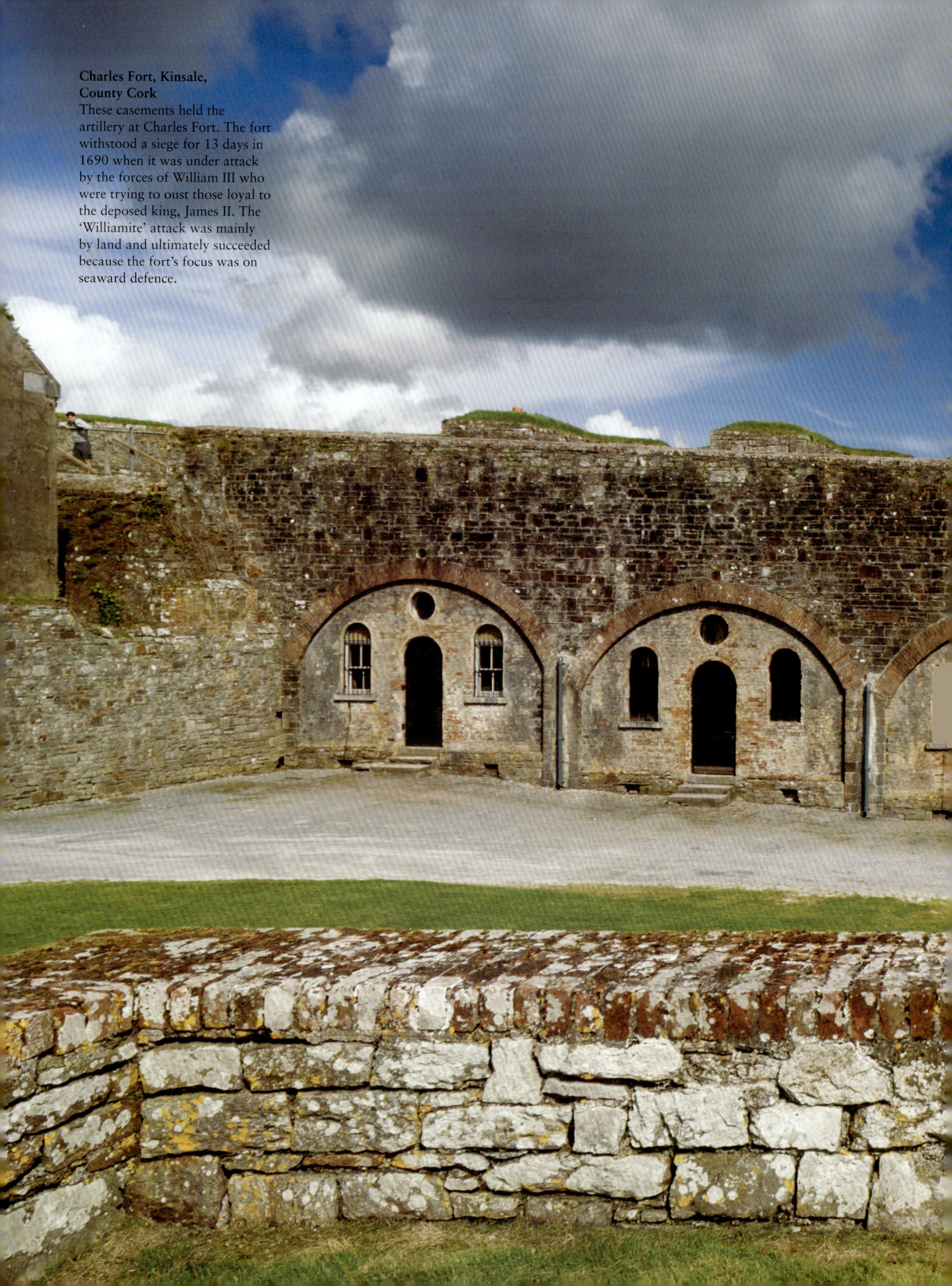

Charles Fort, Kinsale, County Cork
These casements held the artillery at Charles Fort. The fort withstood a siege for 13 days in 1690 when it was under attack by the forces of William III who were trying to oust those loyal to the deposed king, James II. The 'Williamite' attack was mainly by land and ultimately succeeded because the fort's focus was on seaward defence.

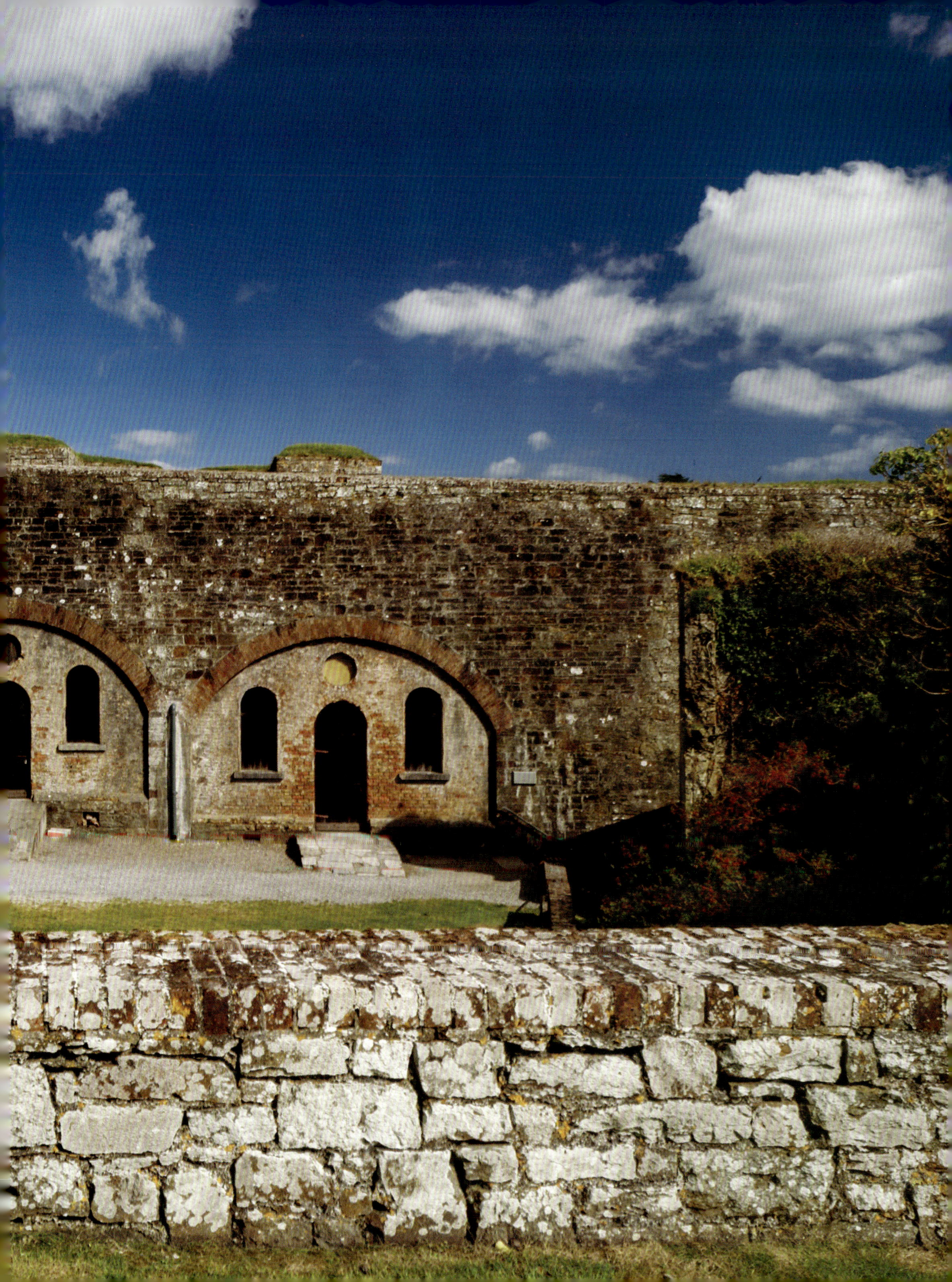

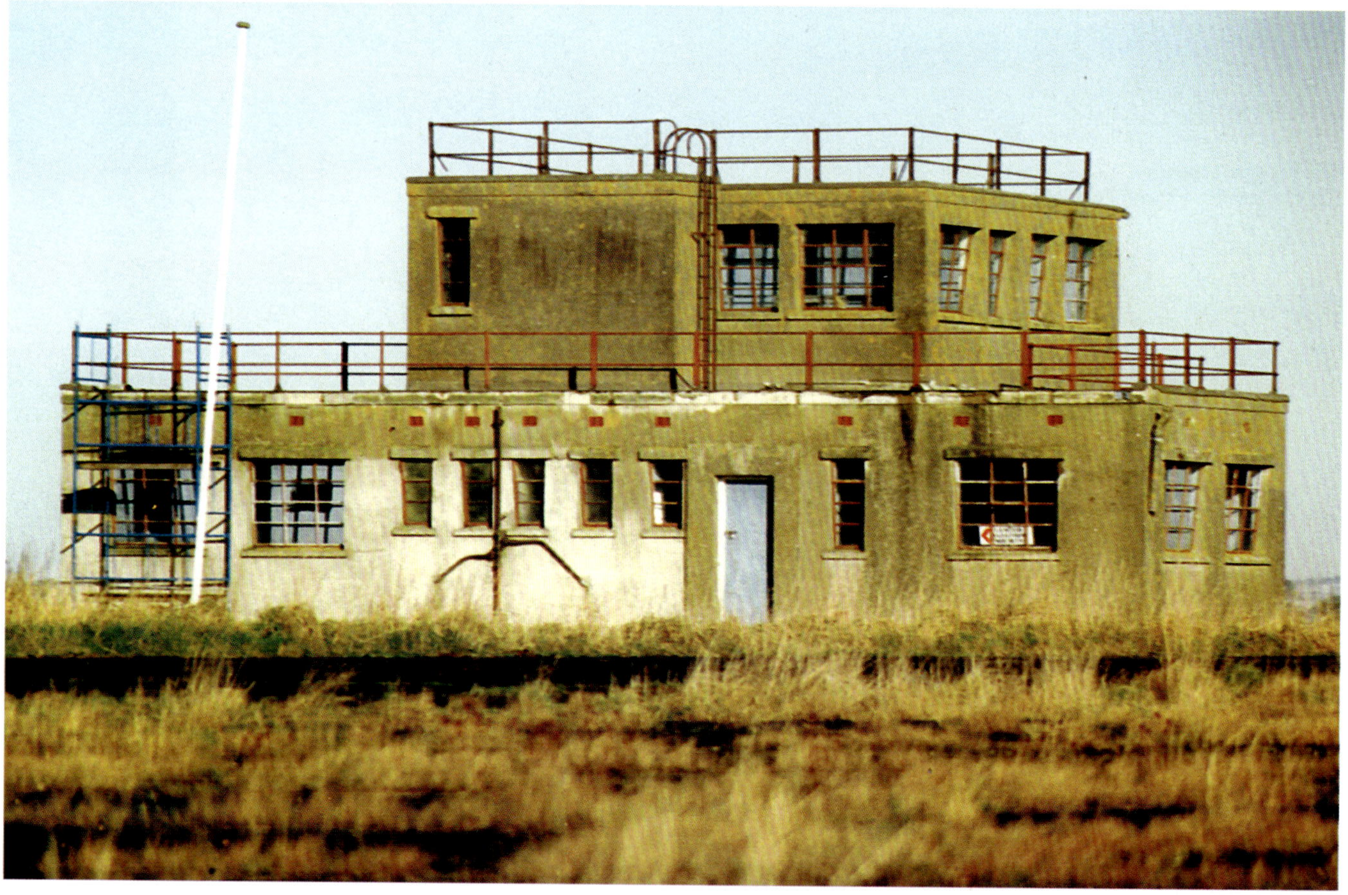

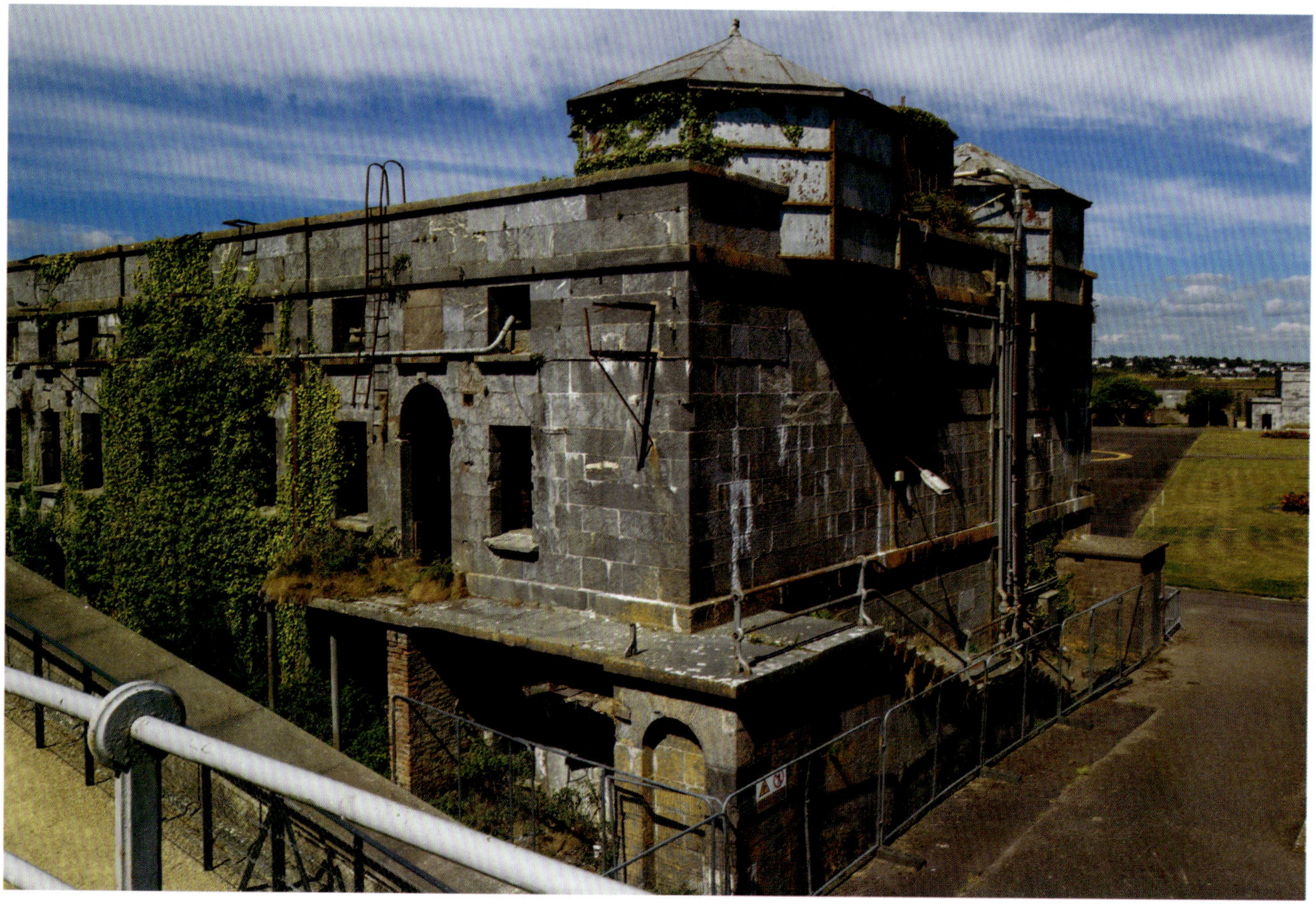

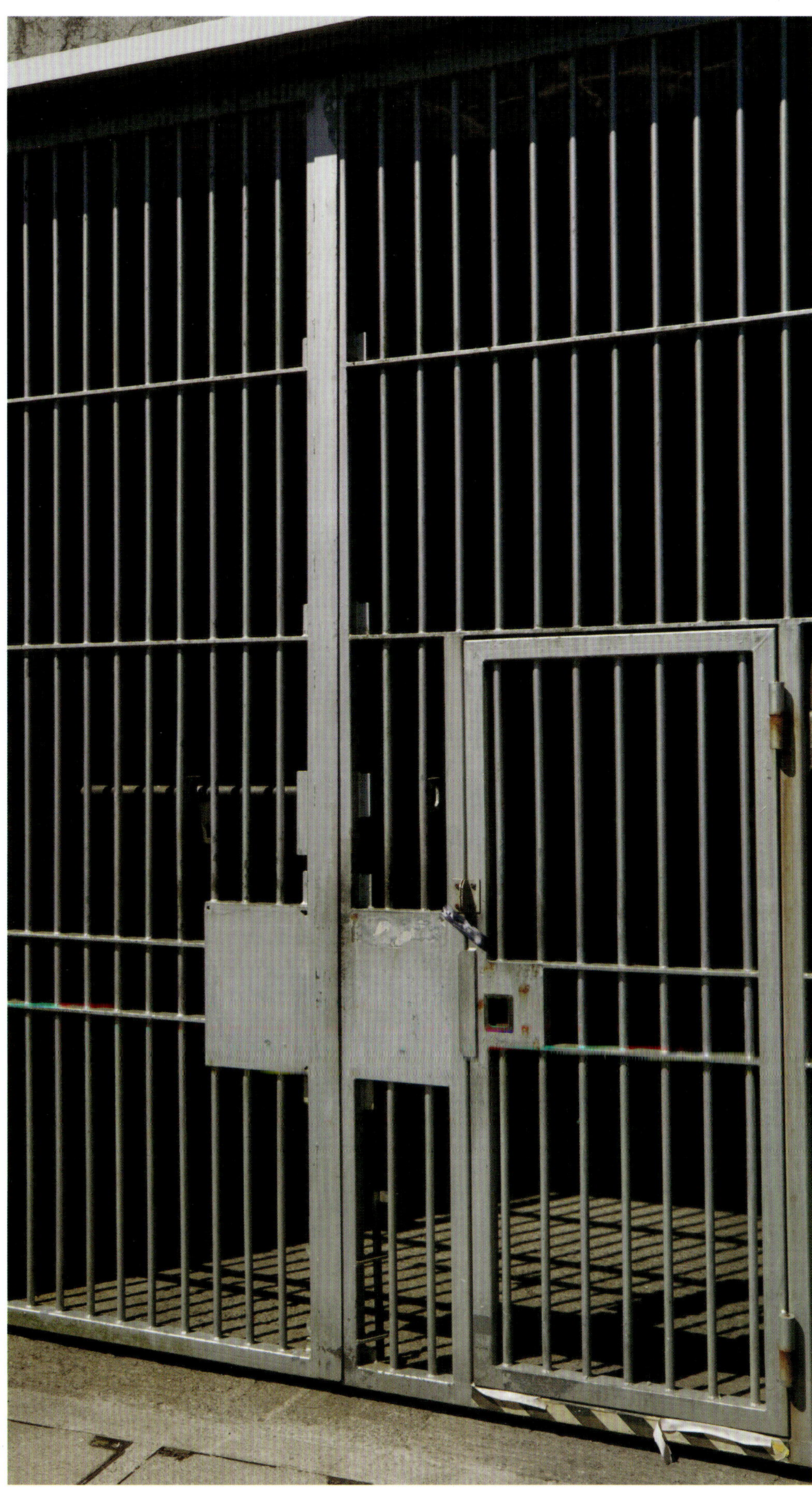

OPPOSITE ABOVE:
USAAF Langford Lodge,
County Antrim
In 1942 the USA Air Force took over this RAF base as a depot for the maintenance and repair of US World War II aircraft. The US site included a bowling alley, a basketball court and ice-cream-making facilities.

LEFT & OPPOSITE BELOW:
Spike Island Prison,
County Cork
Known as 'Ireland's Alcatraz', Spike Island Prison was originally built as a Napoleonic-era fortress but converted into a prison in 1847 when convictions for theft soared during the Irish Famine. Spike Island finally ceased being used as a prison in 2004 and its buildings are now an award-winning tourist destination.

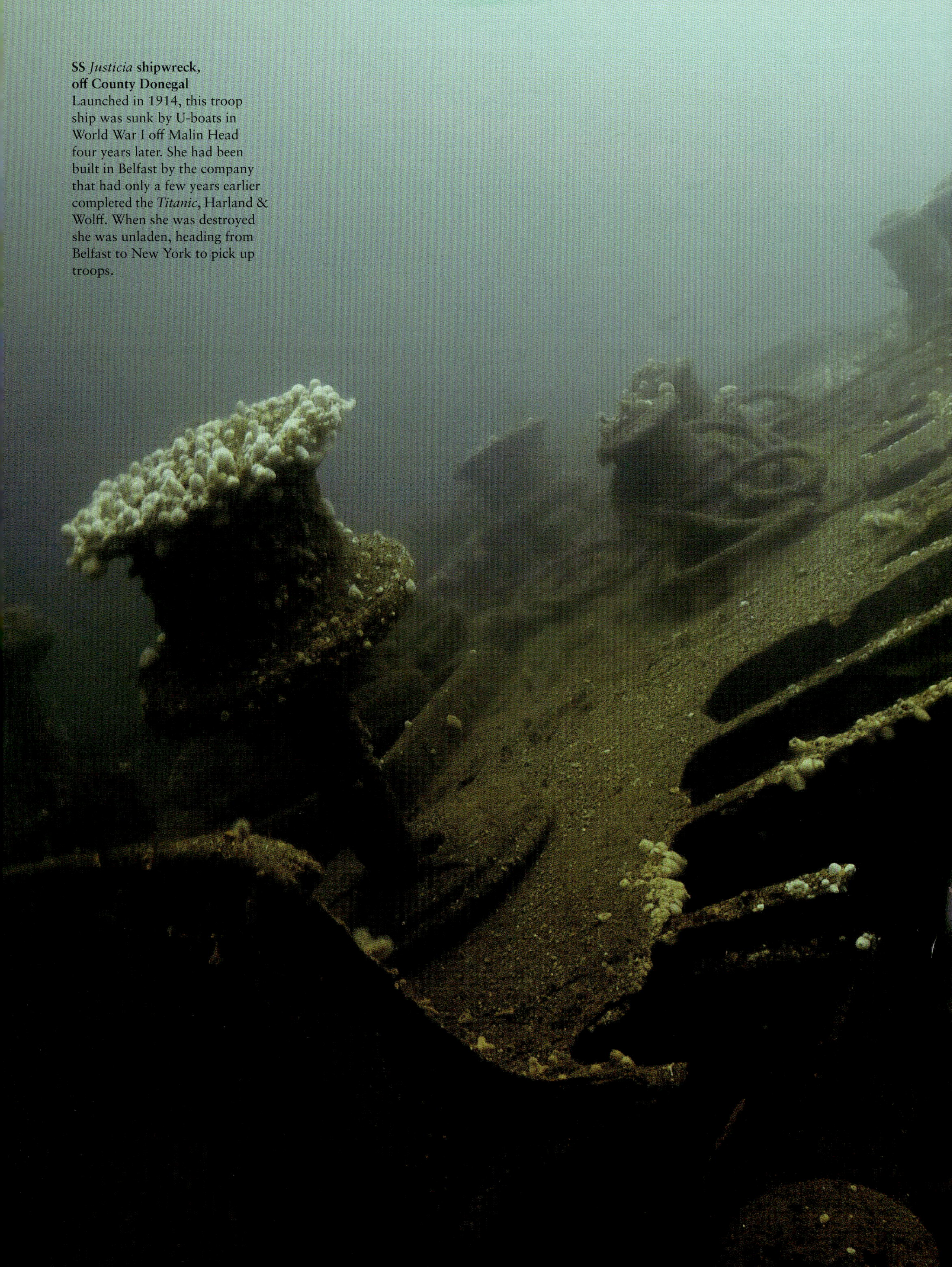

**SS *Justicia* shipwreck,
off County Donegal**
Launched in 1914, this troop
ship was sunk by U-boats in
World War I off Malin Head
four years later. She had been
built in Belfast by the company
that had only a few years earlier
completed the *Titanic*, Harland &
Wolff. When she was destroyed
she was unladen, heading from
Belfast to New York to pick up
troops.

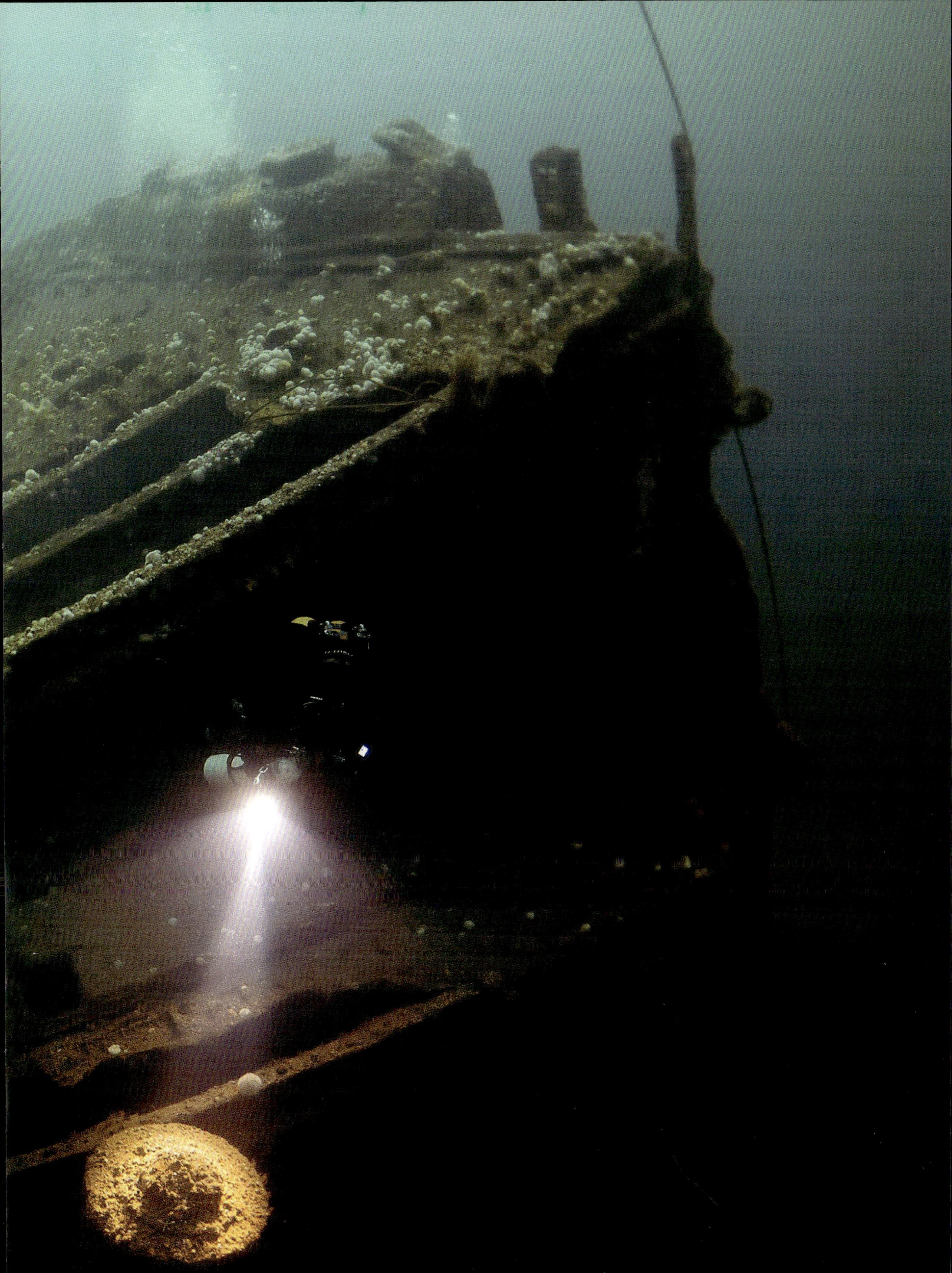

Picture Credits

Alamy: 27 bottom (Arcaid Images), 47 (Joshua Windsor), 56 (Steppenwolf), 57 top (Rafal Rozalski), 62 (Steppenwolf), 66 top (NiallF), 72 & 73 top (Stephen Knox), 84/85 (Stephen Power), 90 top (aphperspective), 92 top (Stephen Power), 94 (Mauritius Images), 95 (Erwan Gardan), 96 top (Radharc Images), 98/99 (PA Images), 102/103 (Richard Cummins), 104/105 (SuperStock), 108 (Ian Dagnall), 110/111 & 112 top (Stephen Barnes/ Construction), 112 bottom (Douglas O'Connor), 113 (Chris Howes/Wild Places Photography), 114/115 (David Creedon), 116 top (Stephen Barnes/Ireland), 116 bottom (Douglas O'Connor), 117 (Stephen Barnes/Business), 122 bottom (Michael Grubka), 123–125 (Stephen Barnes/Northern Ireland), 126/127 (George Sweeney), 130 bottom (Gareth McCormack), 136/137 (Tim Graham), 142 (David Lichtneker), 150 top (Richard Cummins), 150 bottom (James Schwabel), 151 top (Ian Pilbeam), 151 bottom (Imagebroker), 152/153 (Sharon Williams), 154 (AMC), 155 top (Andy Gibson), 155 bottom (Michael David Murphy), 156 (David Soanes), 157 top (Joe Dunckley), 161 both (aphperspective), 165 top (George Munday), 174 top (Sally Mundy), 174 bottom (David Hunter), 186 top (Carl Morrow), 192/193 (Bo Scheeringa), 197 (George Munday), 198 top (Gareth McCormack), 198 bottom (Stefanmissing), 199 top (Gareth McCormack), 204 bottom (David Hunter), 208 bottom (George Sweeney), 216/217 (Michalis Palis), 220 top (world war 2 military airfields), 222/223 (Stocktrek Images)

Dreamstime: 5 (David Morrison), 12 (Kelleherphoto), 26 top (Rubengalvezfoto), 28/29 (Petesteele59), 30/31 (Mirco1), 37 (EMFA16), 46 top (Dcr1979), 46 bottom (Traderbillkraft), 48 (Littleny), 52/53 (Kluwi), 57 bottom (Shawnwilc), 67 (Perboge), 68/69 (Loop Images), 91 (Poiuytzyx), 96 bottom (Kenpicstudio), 100 (Sphotomax), 101 top (Mandy2110), 101 bottom (Klodien), 106 bottom (FotoParaTi), 131 bottom (Adamico), 144/145 (Lukassek), 146 bottom (Lukewschmidt), 164 (MNStudio), 166 (Albertoloyo), 168/169 (Mikeeaton), 180 bottom (krechet), 184/185 (Mirco1), 194 top (Redfishweb), 199 bottom (MNStudio), 209 (Lukassek)

Dreamstime/Danielc1998: 26 bottom, 34/35, 44/45, 54/55, 78/79, 93 top, 180 top, 187 top, 208 top

Getty Images: 64 (Christopher Murray/EyeEm), 86 (James Lissack/EyeEm), 88/89 (2c image), 92 bottom (Ciaran Murphy/500px), 93 bottom (2c image), 146/147 (Gamma-Rapho)

iStock: 66 bottom (Tommy Cahill), 158/159 (Fintex), 175 (Frank Lu), 202/203 (Alan Currie)

Andy Kay, BCD Urbex: 14–17, 38–43, 80–83, 132–135, 138–141

Shutterstock: 7 (matthi), 8 (Remizov), 10/11 (dvlcom), 13 (Raul Ortega), 18/19 (Jan Miko), 20/21 (C Tatiana), 22 (J. Hamilton), 23 (Ballygally View Images), 24/25 (Barbara Barbour), 27 top (Paul Briden), 32/33 (Sean P Kelly), 36 (shawnwil23), 49 top (Foto Para Ti), 49 bottom (Elena Schweitzer), 50/51 (Lukassek), 58/59 (Aleksandr Kalinin), 60 (Mark Gusev), 61 top (E. McA), 61 bottom (Dana R. Lee), 65 (Niall Dunne), 70/71 (Roberto Rizzi), 70 bottom (CarlsPix), 71 bottom (Derick P. Hudson), 73 bottom (GingeSwagTia), 74/75 (shawnwil23), 76 top (SAKhanPhotography), 76 bottom (Mick Harper), 77 (Robert Harding), 87 (Anna Ozimkowska), 90 bottom (Corey Macri), 97 (shawnwil23), 106 top (Perspectiveman), 107 (Mark Gusev), 118/119 (Brendan Howard), 120/121 & 122 top (Derick P. Hudson), 128/129 (Lukassek), 130 top (Dirk Hudson), 131 top (Ross Mahon), 147 bottom (celticpostcards), 148/149 (Wandering views), 157 bottom & 160 (Corey Macri), 162/163 (D. Ribeiro), 165 bottom (Bildagentur Zoonar GmbH), 170 top (Nick Fox), 170 bottom (Pierre Leclerc), 171 (Brad Blake), 172/173 (Nick Fox), 176/177 (Maria Janus), 178/179 (MNStudio), 181 (DPimenta), 182 (Dawid K Photography), 183 top (Madrugada Verde), 183 bottom (MNStudio), 186 bottom (Borisb17), 187 bottom (Standa Riha), 188/189 (Peter Krocka), 190 (LouieLea), 191 (Davaiphotography), 194 bottom & 195 (Isabelle Ohara), 196 (MNStudio), 200 (trabantos), 204 top (Timaldo), 205 (Corey Macri), 206/207 & 210/211 (Thomas Roell), 212–215 (Lukassek), 218/219 (gabriel12), 220 bottom & 221 (Christophe Badouet)